FUZZY SYSTEMS

THEORY AND APPLICATIONS

Other Books By The Same Author:

1. Solved Programming In C
2. Solved Programming In C++
3. Artificial Neural Networks
4. Digital Image Processing
5. Computer Oriented Numerical And Statistical Techniques
6. Introduction To Microprocessors: 8085 And 8086
7. Expert C Programming
8. Expert C++ Programming
9. C++ And Data Structures
10. Data Structures
11. Data Structures: An Algorithmic Approach Using C
12. Data Structures: An Algorithmic Approach Using C++
13. Electronics: Analog And Digital
14. Soft Computing
15. Fuzzy Systems
16. Test Your C Programming Skills
17. Test Your C++ Programming Skills

FUZZY SYSTEMS

THEORY AND APPLICATIONS

Joginder Singh Cheema
Head,
Deptt of Computer Sc. & Applications,
Baba Buddha College, Bir Sahib
Tarntaran

Ikvinderpal Singh
Lecturer,
PG Deptt of Computer Sc. & Applications,
Khalsa College,
Amritsar.

KHANNA BOOK PUBLISHING CO. (P) LTD.

::: *Publisher of Engineering and Computer Books* :::

Head Office : 4C/4344, Ansari Road, Darya Ganj, New Delhi-110002
Phone : 011-23244447/48 Fax : 011-23244447
Regd. Office : 1694-95, Nai Sarak, Delhi-110006
Phone : 011-23283211 Fax : 011-23256658
E-Mail : contact@khannabooks.com
Website : www.khannabooks.com, www.khannapublishers.com

FUZZY SYSTEMS

Joginder Singh Cheema and Ikvinderpal Singh

ISBN: 978-93-80016-49-8

First Edition 2011

Reprint 2015

Published by:

Khanna Book Publishing Co. (P) Ltd.

4C/4344, Ansari Road, Darya Ganj, New Delhi-110 002

Phone: 011-23244448 Telefax: 011-23244447

E-mail: contact@khannabooks.com

Website: www.khannabooks.com

Cover Design & Layout by

Limited Colors, Delhi

Printed in India by:

S.P.S. Printers & Binders, Delhi

Dedicated to God
And
Our Parents

Preface

This Book is meant for a wide range of readers who wish to learn the basic concepts of Fuzzy logic. It can also be helpful for programmers, researchers and management experts who use Fuzzy logic techniques. Fuzzy logic techniques have been clearly dealt with suitable examples. Genetic algorithm operators and the various classifications have been discussed in lucid manner, so that a beginner can understand the concepts with minimal effort.

Chapter 1 covers the introduction to Fuzzy systems, uncertainty, classical logical theory, two valued logic, Multi- valued logic, fuzzy logic theory, advantages and disadvantages of fuzzy logic and the vocabulary of fuzzy logic. It also covers relationship between fuzzy logic and approximate reasoning, Propositional fuzzy logic, Predicate fuzzy logic, higher order fuzzy logic.

Chapter 2 deals with fuzzy logic, objectives of fuzzy logic, linguistic variables, fuzzy reasoning, applications areas of fuzzy logic, fuzzy logic for control, fuzzy sets, design membership function, basic operations in fuzzy sets, possibility theory, fuzzy rules.

Chapter 3 discusses the definition, properties, and operations of classical and fuzzy sets. It contains solved sample problems related to the classical and fuzzy sets. It also covers the concept of fuzzy quantifiers, fuzzy numbers, cardinality of fuzzy set, height of a fuzzy set, types of membership functions and possibility theory.

Chapter 4 deals with Cartesian product of the relation along with the cardinality, operations, properties, and composition of classical and fuzzy relations. It also covers the concept of Fuzzy tolerance and equivalence relation, Fuzzy Graphs and Fuzzy Arithmetic.

Chapter 5 discusses the Fuzzy if then rules, types of fuzzy rules, formation of rules, composition of rules, and aggregation of fuzzy rules. It also covers the properties of fuzzy rules, fuzzy rule based models, defuzzification, fuzzy inference system, sugeno and mamdani method.

Chapter 6 describes various application of fuzzy logic, Fuzzy logic in industrial automation, Fuzzy logic supervisory control for coal power plant, Optimization of a water treatment system, Fuzzy logic in chemical industry, Truck speed limiter control by fuzzy logic, Fuzzy logic and neuro-fuzzy in appliances, Fuzzy logic in adaptive heating system control, Fuzzy logic in data analysis of environmental data for traffic control, Fuzzy technology in sonar system and Fuzzy logic in automotive engineering.

Chapter 7 presents Neuro-Fuzzy Systems, Neural Networks, Network Architectures of ANN, Cooperative fuzzy neural network, hybrid fuzzy neural network, properties of neuro-fuzzy system, Architectures of neuro-fuzzy systems, ANFIS architecture and Examples of neuro-fuzzy modeling.

Chapter 8 is devoted to the most important concept of Genetic Algorithm, Methodology of genetic algorithms, Genetic Operators, Basic steps of the genetic algorithm, Working of Genetic Algorithm, Binary GA implementation and Design issues in GA.

Chapter 9 deals with Fuzzy logic and Probability theory. It covers the concept of vagueness, imprecision, axiomatic structure of probability and fuzzy logic. It also includes concepts like Properties about probability of fuzzy events, Conditional probability of fuzzy events, Independence fuzzy events, Baye's theorem for fuzzy events and fuzzy measures.

Chapter 10 summarizes propositional logic, first order predicate calculus, fuzzy implications, fuzzy inference and fuzzy reasoning (approximate reasoning).

Chapter 11 introduces the concept of fuzzy rule based models and fuzzy system identification in detail.

Chapter 12 is devoted to fuzzy information, fuzzy database systems, fuzzy relational data model, fuzzy object oriented database, fuzzy inheritance, fuzzy SQL and intelligent queries.

Chapter 13 describes the concept of fuzzy logic in artificial intelligence, fuzzy expert system, implementation of fuzzy logic in intelligent agents. It also explains the application of fuzzy logic and neuro fuzzy data analysis in a medical shoe.

Chapter 14 deals with pattern recognition, fuzzy clustering, crisp clustering techniques, K means clustering algorithm, fuzzy c means clustering, feature analysis and application of fuzzy logic used in pattern recognition.

This book can be used by a wide reader audience, ranging from beginners to practicing professionals. It is well suited for advanced or beginning college level students as a complete book for an introductory Fuzzy Systems cause, as a supplementary text, or as an effective independent study guide.

Each and Every chapter contains clear statements of definitions and principles together with illustrative and other descriptive material.

We welcome comments from all readers to improve this textbook as a useful guide for the community of engineers and technologists who will become knowledgeable about the potential of fuzzy system tools for their use in solving the problems that challenge us each day.

Acknowledgements

First we would like to thanks almighty for giving us courage to bring up this book. We duly acknowledge the contribution of our colleagues Prof. Rachhpal Singh(HEAD), Prof. Harbhajan Singh, Prof. Sukhwinder Kaur, Prof. Kawaljit Kaur, Prof. Mani Arora, Mr. Baljinder Singh, Mr. Jagbir Singh, Mr. Sukhwant Singh, Mr. Avtar Singh Sandhu, Mr. Karandeep Singh, Mr. Rajkaran Singh, Mr. Lovedeep Singh, Mr. Kanwarpal Singh, Mr. Navjeet Singh, Mr. Manpreet Singh, Mrs. Mandeep Kaur, Mrs. Jyoti Maini, Ms. Kawaljeet Kaur, Ms. Simranjeet Kaur and Mr. Kawaljeet Singh for their valuable co-operation and guidance. We are grateful to Mr. Puneet Khanna M/s Khanna Book Publishing Co. Pvt. Ltd. for his encouragement and motivation during this project.

Special Thanks

Our special thanks go to Dr. Joginder Singh Kerron, Director Dr. Varyam Singh Bal, Principal, Baba Buddha College, Bir Sahib for their valuable guidance and timely support during the compilation of this book.

Contents

CHAPTER 1

Introduction to Fuzzy System

1.1 INTRODUCTION

The past few years have witnessed a rapid growth in the number and variety of applications of fuzzy logic (FL). FL techniques have been used in image-understanding applications such as detection of edges, feature extraction, classification, and clustering. Fuzzy logic poses the ability to mimic the human mind to effectively employ modes of reasoning that are approximate rather than exact. In traditional hard computing, decisions or actions are based on precision, certainty, and vigor. Precision and certainty carry a cost. In soft computing, tolerance and impression are explored in decision making. The exploration of the tolerance for imprecision and uncertainty underlies the remarkable human ability to understand distorted speech, decipher sloppy handwriting, comprehend nuances of natural language, summarize text, and recognize and classify images. With FL, we can specify mapping rules in terms of words rather than numbers. Computing with the words explores imprecision and tolerance. Another basic concept in FL is the fuzzy if–then rule. Although rule-based systems have a long history of use in artificial intelligence, what is missing in such systems is machinery for dealing with fuzzy consequents or fuzzy antecedents. In most applications, an FL solution is a translation of a human solution. Thirdly, FL can model nonlinear functions of arbitrary complexity to a desired degree of accuracy. FL is a convenient way to map an input space to an output space. FL is one of the tools used to model a multiinput, multioutput system.

Soft computing includes fuzzy logic, neural networks, probabilistic reasoning, and genetic algorithms. Today, techniques or a combination of techniques from all these areas are used to design an intelligence system. Neural networks provide algorithms for learning, classification, and optimization, whereas fuzzy logic deals with issues such as forming impressions and reasoning on a semantic or linguistic level. Probabilistic reasoning deals with uncertainty. Although there are substantial areas of overlap between neural networks, FL, and probabilistic reasoning, in general they are complementary rather than competitive. Recently, many intelligent systems called neuro fuzzy systems have been used. There are many ways to combine neural networks and FL techniques. Before doing so, however, it is necessary to understand basic ideas in the design of FL techniques. In this chapter, we will introduce FL concepts such as fuzzy sets and their properties, FL operators, hedges, fuzzy proposition and rule-based systems, fuzzy maps and inference engine, defuzzification methods, and the design of an FL decision system.

Fuzzy logic is a form of multi-valued logic derived from fuzzy set theory to deal with reasoning that is approximate rather than precise. In contrast with binary sets having binary logic, also known as crisp logic, the fuzzy logic variables may have a membership value of only 0 or 1. Just as in fuzzy set theory with fuzzy logic the set membership values can range (inclusively) between 0 and 1, in fuzzy logic the degree of truth of a statement can range between 0 and 1 and is not constrained to the two truth values {true (1), false (0)} as in classic propositional logic. And when linguistic variables are used, these degrees may be managed by specific functions. Fuzzy logic is an approach to computing based on "degrees of truth" rather than the usual "true or false" (1 or 0) Boolean logic on which the modern computer is based. The idea of fuzzy logic was first advanced by Dr. Lotfi Zadeh of the University of California at Berkeley in the 1960s. Dr. Zadeh was working on the problem of computer understanding of natural language. Natural language (like most other activities in life and indeed the universe) is not easily translated into the absolute terms of 0 and 1. (Whether everything is ultimately describable in binary terms is a philosophical question worth pursuing, but in practice much data we might want to feed a computer is in some state in between and so, frequently, are the results of computing.)

Fuzzy logic includes 0 and 1 as extreme cases of truth (or "the state of matters" or "fact") but also includes the various states of truth in between so that, for example, the result of a comparison between two things could be not "tall" or "short" but ".38 of tallness." Fuzzy logic seems closer to the way our brains work. We aggregate data and form a number of partial truths which we aggregate further into higher truths which in turn, when certain thresholds are exceeded, cause certain further results such as motor reaction. A similar kind of process is used in artificial computer neural network and expert systems.

1.2 THE CASE FOR IMPRECISION

Our understanding of most physical processes is based largely on imprecise human reasoning. This imprecision (when compared to the precise quantities required by computers) is nonetheless a form of information that can be quite useful to humans. The ability to embed such reasoning in hitherto intractable and complex problems is the criterion by which the efficacy of fuzzy logic is judged. Undoubtedly this ability cannot solve problems that require precision – problems such as shooting precision laser beams over tens of kilometers in space; milling machine components to accuracies of parts per billion; or focusing a microscopic electron beam on a specimen the size of a nanometer. The impact of fuzzy logic in these areas might be years away, if ever. But not many human problems require such precision – problems such as parking a car, backing up a trailer, navigating a car among others on a freeway, washing clothes, controlling traffic at intersections, judging beauty contestants, and a preliminary understanding of a complex system. Requiring precision in engineering models and products translates to requiring high cost and long lead times in production and development. For other than simple systems, expense is proportional to precision: more precision entails higher cost. When considering the use of fuzzy logic for a given problem, an engineer or scientist should ponder the need for exploiting the tolerance for imprecision. Not only does high precision dictate high costs but also it entails low tractability in a problem. For example the "traveling sales representative" problem. In this classic optimization problem a sales representative wants to minimize total distance traveled by considering various itineraries and schedules between a series of cities on a particular trip. For a small number of cities, the problem is a trivial exercise in enumerating all the possibilities and choosing the shortest route. As the number of cities continues to grow, the problem quickly approaches a combinatorial explosion impossible to solve through an exhaustive search, even with a computer. For example, for 100 cities there are $100 \times 99 \times 98 \times 97 \times \cdots \times 2 \times 1$, or about 10200, possible routes to consider! No computers exist today that can solve this problem through a brute-force enumeration of all the possible routes. There are real, practical problems analogous to the traveling sales representative problem. For example, such problems arise in the fabrication of circuit boards, where precise lasers drill hundreds of thousands of holes in the board. Deciding in which order to drill the holes (where the board moves under a stationary laser) so as to minimize drilling time is a traveling sales representative problem. Thus, algorithms have been developed to solve the traveling sales representative problem in an optimal sense; that is, the exact answer is not guaranteed but an optimum answer is achievable – the optimality is measured as a percent accuracy, with 0% representing the exact answer and accuracies larger than zero representing answers of lesser accuracy. Suppose we consider a signal routing problem analogous to the traveling sales representative problem where we want to find the optimum path (i.e., minimum travel time) between 100,000 nodes in a network to accuracy within 1% of the exact solution; this requires significant CPU time on a supercomputer. If we take the same problem and increase the precision requirement a modest amount to accuracy of 0.75%, the computing time approaches a few months! Now suppose we can live with an accuracy of 3.5% (quite a bit more accurate than most problems we deal with), and we want to consider an order-of-magnitude more nodes in the network, say 1,000,000; the computing time for this problem is on the order of several minutes. This remarkable reduction in cost (translating time to dollars) is due solely to the acceptance of a lesser degree of precision in the optimum solution. Can humans live with a little less precision? The answer to this question depends on the situation, but for the vast majority of problems we deal with every day the answer is a resounding yes.

1.3 AN HISTORICAL PERSPECTIVE

From an historical point of view the issue of uncertainty has not always been embraced within the scientific community. In the traditional view of science, uncertainty represents an undesirable state, a state that must be avoided at all costs. This was the state of science until the late nineteenth century when physicists realized that Newtonian mechanics did not address problems at the molecular level. Newer methods, associated with statistical mechanics, were developed which recognized that statistical averages could replace the specific manifestations of microscopic entities. These statistical quantities, which summarized the activity of large numbers of microscopic entities, could then be connected in a model with appropriate macroscopic variables. Now, the role of Newtonian mechanics and its underlying calculus which considered no uncertainty was replaced with statistical mechanics which could be described by a probability theory – a theory which could capture a form of uncertainty, the type generally referred to as random uncertainty. After the development of statistical mechanics there has been a gradual trend in science during the past century to consider the influence of uncertainty on problems, and to do so in an attempt to make our models more robust, in the sense that we achieve credible solutions and at the same time quantify the amount of uncertainty. Of course, the leading theory in quantifying uncertainty in scientific models from the late nineteenth century until the late twentieth century had been probability theory. However, the gradual evolution of the expression of uncertainty using probability theory was challenged, first in 1937 by Max Black, with his studies in vagueness, then with the introduction of fuzzy sets by Lotfi Zadeh in 1965.

Zadeh's work [1965] had a profound influence on the thinking about uncertainty because it challenged not only probability theory as the sole representation for uncertainty, but the very foundations upon which probability theory was based: classical binary (two-valued) logic. Probability theory dominated the mathematics of uncertainty for over five centuries. Probability concepts date back to the 1500s, to the time of Cardano when gamblers recognized the rules of probability in games of chance. The concepts were still very much in the limelight in 1685, when the Bishop of Wells wrote a paper that discussed a problem in determining the truth of statements made by two witnesses who were both known to be unreliable to the extent that they only tell the truth with probabilities p1 and p2, respectively.

The Bishop's answer to this was based on his assumption that the two witnesses were independent sources of information [Lindley, 1987]. Probability theory was initially developed in the eighteenth century in such landmark treatises as Jacob Bernoulli's Ars Conjectandi (1713) and Abraham DeMoiver's Doctrine of Chances (1718, 2nd edition 1738). Later in that century a small number of articles appeared in the periodical literature that would have a profound effect on the field. Most notable of these were Thomas Bayes's "An essay towards solving a problem in the doctrine of chances" (1763) and Pierre Simon Laplace's formulation of the axioms relating to games of chance, "Memoire sur la probabilite des causes par les evenemens" (1774). Laplace, only 25 years old at the time he began his work in 1772, wrote the first substantial article in mathematical statistics prior to the nineteenth century. Despite the fact that Laplace, at the same time, was heavily engaged in mathematical astronomy, his memoir was an explosion of ideas that provided the roots for modern decision theory, Bayesian inference with nuisance parameters (historians claim that Laplace did not know of Bayes's earlier work), and the asymptotic approximations of posterior distributions [Stigler, 1986].

By the time of Newton, physicists and mathematicians were formulating different theories of probability. The most popular ones remaining today are the relative frequency theory and the subjectivist or personalistic theory. The later development was initiated by Thomas Bayes (1763), who articulated his very powerful theorem for the assessment of subjective probabilities. The theorem specified that a human's degree of belief could be subjected to an objective, coherent, and measurable mathematical framework within subjective probability theory. In the early days of the twentieth century Researcher developed a formal framework for a conditional probability theory.

The twentieth century saw the first developments of alternatives to probability theory and to classical Aristotelian logic as paradigms to address more kinds of uncertainty than just the random kind. Jan Lukasiewicz developed a multivalued, discrete logic (circa 1930). In the 1960's Arthur Dempster developed a theory of evidence which, for the first time, included an assessment of ignorance, or the absence of information. In 1965 Lotfi Zadeh introduced his seminal idea in a continuous-valued logic that he called fuzzy set theory. In the 1970s Glenn Shafer extended Dempster's work to produce a complete theory of evidence dealing with information from more than one source, and Lotfi Zadeh illustrated a possibility theory resulting from special cases of fuzzy sets. Later in the 1980s other investigators showed a strong relationship between evidence theory, probability theory, and possibility theory with the use of what was called fuzzy measures [Klir and Wierman, 1996], and what is now being termed monotone measures.

Uncertainty can be thought of in an epistemological sense as being the inverse of information. Information about a particular engineering or scientific problem may be incomplete, imprecise, fragmentary, unreliable, vague, contradictory, or deficient in some other way [Klir and Yuan, 1995]. When we acquire more and more information about a problem, we become less and less uncertain about its formulation and solution. Problems that are characterized by very little information are said to be ill-posed, complex, or not sufficiently known. These problems are imbued with a high degree of uncertainty. Uncertainty can be manifested in many forms: it can be fuzzy (not sharp, unclear, imprecise, approximate), it can be vague (not specific, amorphous), it can be ambiguous (too many choices, contradictory), it can be of the form of ignorance (dissonant, not knowing something), or it can be a form due to natural variability (conflicting, random, chaotic, unpredictable). Many other linguistic labels have been applied to these various forms, but for now these shall suffice. Zadeh [2002] posed some simple examples of these forms in terms of a person's statements about when they shall return to a current place in time. The statement "I shall return soon" is vague, whereas the statement "I shall return in a few minutes" is fuzzy; the former is not known to be associated with any unit of time (seconds, hours, days), and the latter is associated with an uncertainty that is at least known to be on the order of minutes. The phrase, "I shall return within 2 minutes of 6pm" involves an uncertainty which has a quantifiable imprecision; probability theory could address this form.

Vagueness can be used to describe certain kinds of uncertainty associated with linguistic information or intuitive information. Examples of vague information are that the data quality is "good," or that the transparency of an optical element is "acceptable." Moreover, in terms of semantics, even the terms vague and fuzzy cannot be generally considered synonyms, as explained by Zadeh [1995]: "usually a vague proposition is fuzzy, but the converse is not generally true."

Discussions about vagueness started with a famous work by the philosopher Max Black. Black [1937] defined a vague proposition as a proposition where the possible states (of the proposition) are not clearly defined with regard to inclusion. For example, consider the proposition that a person is young. Since the term "young" has different interpretations to different individuals, we cannot decisively determine the age(s) at which an individual is young versus the age(s) at which an individual is not considered to be young. Thus, the proposition is vaguely defined. Classical (binary) logic does not hold under these circumstances, therefore we must establish a different method of interpretation. Max Black, in writing his 1937 essay "Vagueness: An exercise in logical analysis" first cites remarks made by the ancient philosopher Plato about uncertainty in geometry, then embellishes on the writings of Bertrand Russell (1923) who emphasized that "all traditional logic habitually assumes that precise symbols are being employed." With these great thoughts as a prelude to his own arguments, he proceeded to produce his own, now-famous quote:

It is a paradox, whose importance familiarity fails to diminish, that the most highly developed and useful scientific theories are ostensibly expressed in terms of objects never encountered in experience. The line traced by a draftsman, no matter how accurate, is seen beneath the microscope as a kind of corrugated trench, far removed from the ideal line of pure geometry. And the "point-planet" of astronomy, the "perfect gas" of thermodynamics, or the "purespecies" of genetics are equally remote from exact realization. Indeed the unintelligibility at the atomic or subatomic level of the notion of a rigidly demarcated boundary shows that such objects not merely are not but could not be encountered. While the mathematician constructs a theory in terms of "perfect" objects, the experimental scientist observes objects of which the properties demanded by theory are and can, in the very nature of measurement, be only approximately true.

More recently, in support of Black's work, Quine [1981] states:

Diminish a table, conceptually, molecule by molecule: when is a table not a table? No stipulations will avail us here, however arbitrary. If the term 'table' is to be reconciled with bivalence, we must posit an exact demarcation, exact to the last molecule, even though we cannot specify it. We must hold that there are physical objects, coincident except for one molecule, such that one is a table and the other is not.

Bruno de Finetti [1974], publishing in his landmark book Theory of Probability, gets his readers' attention quickly by proclaiming, "Probability does not exist; it is a subjective description of a person's uncertainty. We should be normative about uncertainty and not descriptive." He further emphasizes that the frequentist view of probability (objectivist view) "requires individual trials to be equally probable and stochastically independent." In discussing the difference between possibility and probability he states, "The logic of certainty furnishes us with the range of possibility (and the possible has no gradations); probability is an additional notion that one applies within the range of possibility, thus giving rise to graduations ('more or less' probable) that are meaningless in the logic of uncertainty."

In his book, de Finetti gives us warnings:

"The calculus of probability can say absolutely nothing about reality," and in referring to the dangers implicit in attempts to confuse certainty with high probability, he states We have to stress this point because these attempts assume many forms and are always dangerous. In one sentence: to make a mistake of this kind leaves one inevitably faced with all sorts of fallacious arguments and contradictions whenever an attempt is made to state, on the basis of probabilistic considerations, that something must occur, or that its occurrence confirms or disproves some probabilistic assumptions.

In a discussion about the use of such vague terms as "very probable" or "practically certain," or "almost impossible," de Finetti states:

The field of probability and statistics is then transformed into a Tower of Babel, in which only the most naive amateur claims to understand what he says and hears, and this because, in a language devoid of convention, the fundamental distinctions between what is certain and what is not, and between what is impossible and what is not, are abolished. Certainty and impossibility then become confused with high or low degrees of a subjective probability, which is itself denied precisely by this falsification of the language. On the contrary, the preservation of a clear, terse distinction between certainty and uncertainty, impossibility and possibility, is the unique and essential precondition for making meaningful statements (which could be either right or wrong), whereas the alternative transforms every sentence into a nonsense.

1.4 UNCERTAINTY AND INFORMATION

Only a small portion of the knowledge (information) for a typical problem might be regarded as certain, or deterministic. Unfortunately, the vast majority of the material taught in engineering classes is based on the presumption that the knowledge involved is deterministic. Most processes are neatly and surreptitiously reduced to closed-form algorithms – equations and formulas. When students graduate, it seems that their biggest fear upon entering the real world is "forgetting the correct formula." These formulas typically describe a deterministic process, one where there is no uncertainty in the physics of the process (i.e., the right formula) and there is no uncertainty in the parameters of the process (i.e., the coefficients are known with impunity). It is only after we leave the university, it seems, that we realize we were duped in academe, and that the information we have for a particular problem virtually always contains uncertainty. For how many of our problems can we say that the information content is known absolutely, i.e., with no ignorance, no vagueness, no imprecision, no element of chance? Uncertain information can take on many different forms.

There is uncertainty that arises because of complexity; for example, the complexity in the reliability network of a nuclear reactor. There is uncertainty that arises from ignorance, from various classes of randomness, from the inability to perform adequate measurements, from lack of knowledge, or from vagueness, like the fuzziness inherent in our natural language. The nature of uncertainty in a problem is a very important point that engineers should ponder prior to their selection of an appropriate method to express the uncertainty.

Fuzzy sets provide a mathematical way to represent vagueness and fuzziness in humanistic systems. For example, suppose you are teaching your child to bake cookies and you want to give instructions about when to take the cookies out of the oven. You could say to take them out when the temperature inside the cookie dough reaches 375°F, or you could advise your child to take them out when the tops of the cookies turn light brown. Which instruction would you give? Most likely, you would use the second of the two instructions. The first instruction is too precise to implement practically; in this case precision is not useful. The vague term light brown is useful in this context and can be acted upon even by a child. We all use vague terms, imprecise information, and other fuzzy data just as easily as we deal with situations governed by chance, where probability techniques are warranted and very useful. Hence, our sophisticated computational methods should be able to represent and manipulate a variety of uncertainties. Other representations of uncertainties due to ambiguity, nonspecificity, beliefs, and ignorance are introduced in the next chapters.

1.5 FUZZY SYSTEMS

Fuzzy system was first proposed by an American professor, Lotfi A. Zadeh, in 1965 when he presented his seminal paper on "fuzzy sets." Zadeh showed that fuzzy logic unlike classical logic can realize values between false (0) and true (1). Basically, he transformed the crisp set into the continuous set. Fuzzy sets thus have movable boundaries, i.e., the elements of such sets not only represent true or false values but also represent the degree of truth or degree of falseness for each input.

In the literature sources, we can find different kinds of justification for fuzzy systems theory. Human knowledge nowadays becomes increasingly important – we gain it from experiencing the world within which we live and use our ability to reason to create order in the mass of information (i.e., to formulate human knowledge in a systematic manner). Since we are all limited in our ability to perceive the world and to profound reasoning, we find ourselves everywhere confronted by uncertainty which is a result of lack of information (lexical impression, incompleteness), in particular, inaccuracy of measurements. The other limitation factor in our desire for precision is a natural language used for describing/sharing knowledge, communication, etc. We understand core meanings of word and are able to communicate accurately to an acceptable degree, but generally we cannot precisely agree among ourselves on the single word or terms of common sense meaning. In short, natural languages are vague.

Our perception of the real world is pervaded by concepts which do not have sharply defined boundaries – for example, many, tall, much larger than, young, etc. are true only to some degree and they are false to some degree as well. These concepts (facts) can be called fuzzy or gray (vague) concepts – a human brain works with them, while computers may not do it (they reason with strings of 0s and 1s). Natural languages, which are much higher in level than programming languages, are fuzzy whereas programming languages are not. The door to the development of fuzzy computers was opened in 1985 by the design of the first logic chip by Masaki Togai and Hiroyuki Watanabe at Bell Telephone Laboratories. In the years to come fuzzy computers will employ both fuzzy hardware and fuzzy software, and they will be much closer in structure to the human brain than the present-day computers are. The entire real world is complex; it is found that the complexity arises from uncertainty in the form of ambiguity. According to Dr. Lotfi Zadeh, Principle of Compatability, the complexity, and the imprecision are correlated and adds, The closer one looks at a real world problem, the fuzzier becomes its solution (Zadeh 1973) The Fuzzy Logic tool was introduced in 1965, also by Lotfi Zadeh, and is a mathematical tool for dealing with uncertainty. It offers to a soft computing partnership the important concept of computing with words'. It provides a technique to deal with imprecision and information granularity.

The fuzzy theory provides a mechanism for representing linguistic constructs such as "many," "low," "medium," "often," "few." In general, the fuzzy logic provides an inference structure that enables appropriate human reasoning capabilities. On the contrary, the traditional binary set theory describes crisp events, events that either do or do not occur. It uses probability theory to explain if an event will occur, measuring the chance with which a given event is expected to occur. The theory of fuzzy logic is based upon the notion of relative graded membership and so are the functions of mentation and cognitive processes. The utility of fuzzy sets lies in their ability to model uncertain or ambiguous data, Figure 1.1, so often encountered in real life.

It is important to observe that there is an intimate connection between Fuzziness and Complexity. As the complexity of a task (problem), or of a system for performing that task, exceeds a certain threshold, the system must necessarily become fuzzy in nature. Zadeh, originally an engineer and systems scientist, was concerned with the rapid decline in information afforded by traditional mathematical models as the complexity of the target system increased. As he stressed, with the increasing of complexity our ability to make precise and yet significant statements about its behavior diminishes. Realworld problems (situations) are too complex, and the complexity involves the degree of uncertainty – as uncertainty increases, so does the complexity of the problem. Traditional system modeling and analysis techniques are too precise for such problems (systems), and in order to make complexity less daunting we introduce appropriate simplifications, assumptions, etc. (i.e., degree of uncertainty or Fuzziness) to achieve a satisfactory compromise between the information we have and the amount of uncertainty we are willing to accept.In this aspect, fuzzy systems theory is similar to other engineering theories, because almost all of them characterize the real world in an approximate manner.

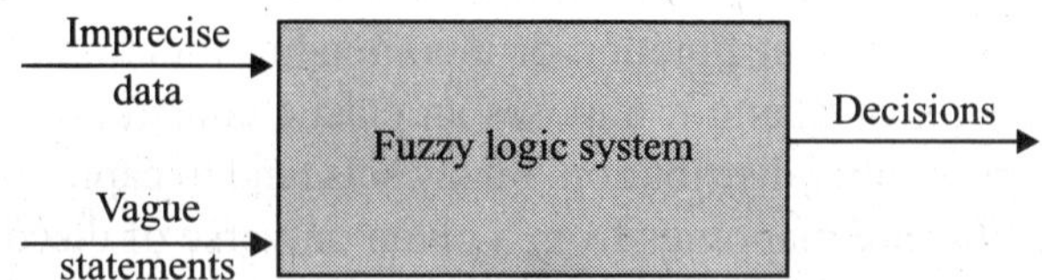

Figure 1.1: A fuzzy logic system which accepts imprecise data and vague statements such as low, medium, high and provides decisions

Fuzzy sets provide means to model the uncertainty associated with vagueness, imprecision, and lack of information regarding a problem or a plant, etc. Consider the meaning of a "short person." For an individual X, the short person may be one whose height is below 4.25. For other individual Y, the short person may be one whose height is below or equal to 3.90. This "short" is called as a linguistic descriptor. The term "short" informs the same meaning to the individuals X and Y, but it is found that they both do not provide a unique definition. The term "short" would be conveyed effectively, only when a computer compares the given height value with the preassigned value of "short." This variable "short" is called as linguistic variable, which represents the imprecision existing in the system.

The uncertainty is found to arise from ignorance, from chance and randomness, due to lack of knowledge, from vagueness (unclear), like the fuzziness existing in our natural language. Lotfi Zadeh proposed the set membership idea to make suitable decisions when uncertainty occurs. Consider the "short" example discussed previously. If we take "short" as a height equal to or less than 4 feet, then 3.90 would easily become the member of the set "short" and 4.25 will not be a member of the set "short." The membership value is "1" if it belongs to the set or "0" if it is not a member of the set. Thus membership in a set is found to be binary i.e., the element is a member of a set or not.

It can be indicated as,

$$x_A(x) = \begin{cases} 1, x \varepsilon A \\ 0, x \notin A' \end{cases}$$

where $\chi A(x)$ is the membership of element x in set A and A is the entire set on the universe.

This membership was extended to possess various "degree of membership" on the real continuous interval [0,1]. Zadeh formed fuzzy sets as the sets on the universe X which can accommodate "degrees of membership." The concept of a fuzzy set contrasts with a classical concept of a bivalent set (crisp set), whose boundary is required to be precise, i.e., a crisp set is a collection of things for which it is known whether any given thing is inside it or not. Zadeh generalized the idea of a crisp set by extending a valuation set { 1, 0} (definitely in/definitely out) to the interval of real values (degrees of membership) between 1 and 0 denoted as [0,1]. We can say that the degree of membership of any particular element of a fuzzy set express the degree of compatibility of the element with a concept represented by fuzzy set. It means that a fuzzy set

A contains an object x to degree a(x), i.e., a(x) = Degree ($x \in A$), and the map a : X → {Membership Degrees} is called a set function or membership function. The fuzzy set A can be expressed as A = {(x, a(x))}, $x \in X$, and it imposes an elastic constrain of the possible values of elements $x \in X$ called the possibility distribution. Fuzzy sets tend to capture vagueness exclusively via membership functions that are mappings from a given universe of discourse

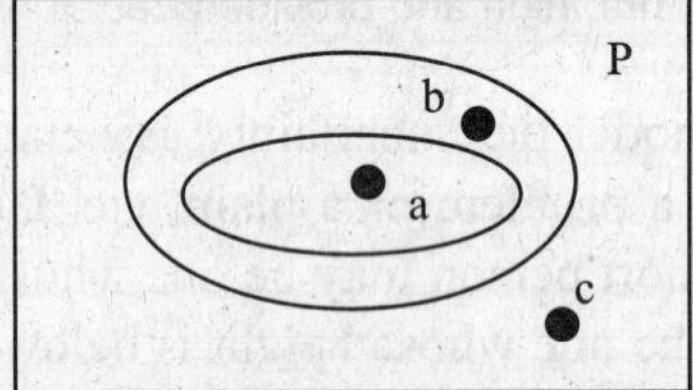

Figure 1.2: Boundary Region of a Fuzzy Set

X to a unit interval containing membership values. It is important to note that membership can take values between 0 and 1. Fuzziness describes the ambiguity of an event and randomness describes the uncertainty in the occurrence of an event. It can be generally seen in classical sets that there is no uncertainty, hence they have crisp boundaries, but in the case of a fuzzy set, since uncertainty occurs, the boundaries may be ambiguously specified. From the Figure 1.2, it can be noted that a is clearly a member of fuzzy set P, c is clearly not a member of fuzzy set P, but the membership of b is found to be vague. Hence a can take membership value 1, c can take membership value 0 and b can take membership value between 0 and 1 [0 to 1], say 0.4, 0.7, etc. This is set to be a partial member ship of fuzzy set P.

The membership function for a set maps each element of the set to a membership value between 0 and 1 and uniquely describes that set. The values 0 and 1 describe "not belonging to" and "belonging to" a conventional set respectively; values in between represent "fuzziness." Determining the membership function is subjective to varying degrees depending on the situation.

It depends on an individual's perception of the data in question and does not depend on randomness. This is important, and distinguishes fuzzy set theory from probability theory (Figure 1.3). In practice fuzzy logic means computation of words. Since computation with words is possible, computerized systems can be built by embedding human expertise articulated in daily language. Also called a fuzzy inference engine or fuzzy rule-base, such a system can perform approximate reasoning somewhat similar to but much more primitive than that of the human brain.

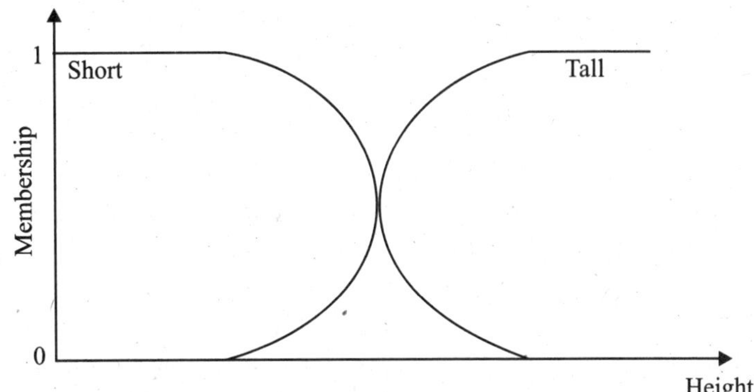

Figure 1.3: The fuzzy sets "tall" and "short".

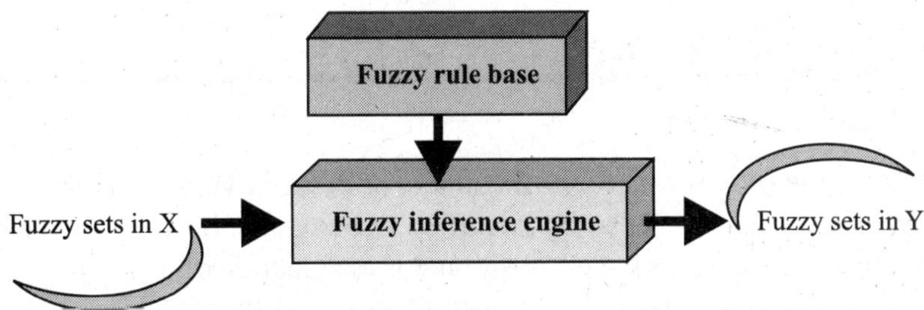

Figure 1.4: Configuration of a Pure Fuzzy Set

Computing with words seems to be a slightly futuristic phrase today since only certain aspects of natural language can be represented by the calculus of fuzzy sets, but still fuzzy logic remains one of the most practical ways to mimic human expertise in a realistic manner. The fuzzy approach uses a premise that humans do not represent classes of objects (e.g. class of bald men, or the class of numbers which are much greater than 50) as fully disjoint but rather as sets in which there may be grades of membership intermediate between full membership and non-membership. Thus, a fuzzy set works as a concept that makes it possible to treat fuzziness in a quantitative manner. Fuzzy sets form the building blocks for fuzzy IF–THEN rules which have the general form "IF X is A THEN Y is B," where A and B are fuzzy sets. The term "fuzzy systems" refers mostly to systems that are governed by fuzzy IF– THEN rules. The IF part of an implication is called the antecedent whereas the second, THEN part is a consequent. A fuzzy system is a set of fuzzy rules that converts inputs to outputs. The basic configuration of a pure fuzzy system is shown in Figure 1.4. The fuzzy inference engine (algorithm) combines fuzzy IF–THEN rules into a mapping from fuzzy sets in the input space X to fuzzy sets in the output space Y based on fuzzy logic principles. From a knowledge representation viewpoint, a fuzzy IF–THEN rule is a scheme for capturing knowledge that involves imprecision. The main feature of reasoning using these rules is its partial matching capability, which enables an inference to be made from a fuzzy rule even when the rule's condition is only partially satisfied.

Fuzzy systems, on one hand, are rule-based systems that are constructed from a collection of linguistic rules; on the other hand, fuzzy systems are nonlinear mappings of inputs (stimuli) to outputs (responses), i.e., certain types of fuzzy systems can be written as compact nonlinear formulas. The inputs and outputs can be numbers or vectors of numbers. These rule-based

systems in theory model represents any system with arbitrary accuracy, i.e., they work as universal approximators. The Achilles' heel of a fuzzy system is its rules; smart rules give smart systems and other rules give smart systems and other rules give less smart or even dumb systems. The number of rules increases exponentially with the dimension of the input space (number of system variables). This rule explosion is called the principle of dimensionality and is a general problem for mathematical models. For the last five years several approaches based on decomposition (cluster) merging and fusing have been proposed to overcome this problem. Hence, Fuzzy models are not replacements for probability models. The fuzzy models sometimes found to work better and sometimes they do not. But mostly fuzzy is evidently proved that it provides better solutions for complex problems.

1.6 CLASSICAL LOGIC THEORY

1.6.1 Fundamental Concepts

In classical logic, a simple proposition P is a linguistic, or declarative, statement contained within a universe of elements, say X, which can be identified as being a collection of elements in X that are strictly true or strictly false. Hence, a proposition P is a collection of elements, i.e., a set, where the truth values for all elements in the set are either all true or all false.

To introduce the basic concepts in the classical logic theory, we consider a typical example of a process (a system, or a plant) that is operated by a console consisting of a lock (with a key) and an ON-OFF switch as shown in Figure 1.5

For this console, we use L to denote the situation of the lock:

$$L = \begin{cases} 1 & \text{if the console is unlocked,} \\ 0 & \text{if the console is locked,} \end{cases}$$

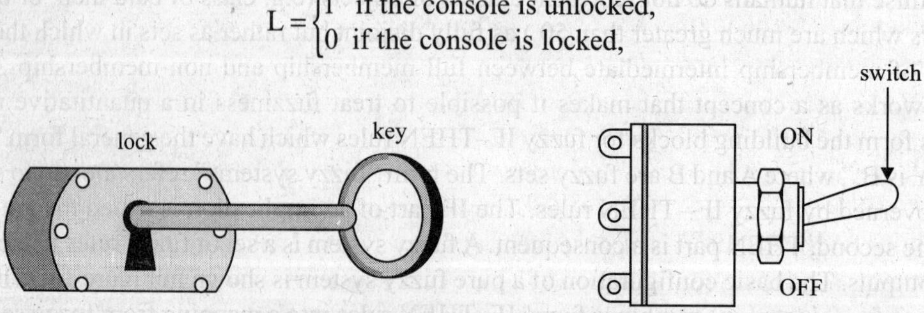

Figure 1.5: A Console Lock with a Switch

Table 1.3: Logic functions of two variables			
x_1 x_2	**1 0 1 0** **1 1 0 0**	**Name of Function**	**Symbol**
y_1	0 0 0 0	Zero function	0
y_2	0 0 0 1	nor(not-or)function	$x_1 \forall x_2$
y_3	0 0 1 0	Proper inequality	$x_1 \leftarrow x_2$
y_4	0 0 1 1	negation	$\bar{x}_2$
y_5	0 1 0 0	proper inequality	$x_1 \rightarrow x_2$
y_6	0 1 0 1	negation	$\bar{x}_1$
y_7	0 1 1 0	nonquivalence	$x_1 \not\Leftrightarrow x_2$
y_8	0 1 1 1	nand(not-and)function	$x_1 \bar{\wedge} x_2$
y_9	1 0 0 0	and function	$x_1 \wedge x_2$
y_{10}	1 0 0 1	equivalence	$x_1 \Leftrightarrow x_2$
y_{11}	1 0 1 0	identity	x_1
y_{12}	1 0 1 1	implication	$x_1 \Leftarrow x_2$
y_{13}	1 1 0 0	identity	x_2
y_{14}	1 1 0 1	implication	$x_1 \Rightarrow x_2$
y_{15}	1 1 1 0	or function	$x_1 \vee x_2$
y_{16}	1 1 1 1	unity	1

which the three inputs (1,1,1) produce an output 1 in Table 1.1 but an output 0 in Table 1.2. The reason is that S = 1 means "ON" in Table 1.1 but it means "OFF" in Table 1.2, due to the nature of the two different switches.

1.6.2 Logical Functions of the Two-Valued Logic

Suppose that we are given n logical variables, $x_1, ..., x_n$. These n variables can have 2^n different combinations of truth values. Hence, there are a total of 2^{2n} possible logical functions defining these variables. For example, for n = 2, there are $2^2 = 4$ combinations of logical variables: (1, 1), (1, 0), (0, 1), and (0, 0). The $2^4 = 16$ logical functions are listed in Table 1.3, where the resulting logical variables are denoted by $y_1, ..., y_{16}$. Logical functions of one or two variables are usually called logical operations.

It can be seen from Table 1.3 that the number of logic functions of n variables grows extremely rapidly with increasing values of n. However, it is known that the logical functions listed in Table 1.3, and those created from them, can be obtained from a set of few primary logical functions. Two sets of primary logical functions are:

(i) negation, and function, and or function;

(ii) negation and the two implications. Using either set of primary logical functions, we can form any other logical functions via appropriate algebraic expressions, called logical formulas. For example, using the first set of primary logical functions, namely, negation – , and function $\wedge$, and or function $\vee$, logical formulas can be defined recursively as follows:

(a) The truth values 0 and 1 are logical formulas.

(b) If x is a logical variable, then both x and $\overline{x}$ are logical formulas.

(c) If x_1 and x_2 are logical formulas, then both $x_1 \wedge x_2$ and $x_1 \vee x_2$ are logical formulas.

(d) The only logical formulas are those defined by (a), (b), and (c). Then, every logical formula of this type defines a logical function by composing it from the three primary logical functions –, ∧, and ∨. To define a unique function, the composition order must be specified, say using parentheses. For example,

$$(x_1 \vee x_2) \wedge (x_1 \vee x_3) \wedge (x_2 \vee x_3)$$

defines a unique logical function of three variables. When two logical formulas a and b are equivalent, we usually write a = b. For instance, one has

$$(x_1 \wedge x_2) \vee (x_1 \wedge x_3) \vee (x_2 \wedge x_3) = (x_2 \wedge x_3) \vee (x_1 \wedge x_3) \vee (x_1 \wedge x_2).$$

This equivalence can be verified by evaluating each of the two formulas for all eight combinations of truth values of the logical variables x_1, x_2, and x_3. The Boolean algebra to be studied in the next section can help simplify such verifications.

1.6.3 Multi-valued Logic

(i) Three-Valued Logic

The classical two-valued logic can be extended to a three-valued logic in various ways, each having its own rationale. In a typical three-valued logic, we denote the truth, falsity, and indeterminacy by values of 1, 0, and 1/2, respectively. The negation $\overline{a}$ of a proposition a is usually defined to be 1-a. Thus, in this three-valued logic, we have $\overline{1} = 0$, $\overline{0} = 1$, and $\overline{(1/2)} = 1/2$

Other primary logical operations, such as ∨, ∧, ⇒, and ⇔ will differ from one logic to another. A commonly used three-valued logic is shown in Table 1.4.

Comparing the three-valued logic shown in Table 1.4 with the twovalued logic, one can see that the only new operations are those involving the new truth value 1/2. It should also be clear that the three-valued logic does not satisfy many basic operation laws of the two-valued logic, such as

$$a \wedge \overline{a} = 0 \text{ and } a \vee \overline{a} = 1.$$

Table 1.4: A Three-Valued Logic

a	b	∧	∨	⇒	⇔
0	0	0	0	1	1
0	1/2	0	1/2	1	1/2
0	1	0	1	1	0
1/2	0	0	1/2	1/2	1/2
1/2	1/2	1/2	1/2	1	1
1/2	1	1/2	1	1	1/2
1	0	0	1	0	0
1	1/2	1/2	1	1/2	1/2
1	1	1	1	1	1

(ii) n-Valued Logic

Once a three-valued logic is accepted as a meaningful and useful tool for applications, it is not difficult to further extend it to an n-valued logic, for $3 < n < n < \infty$ For a given finite positive integer, $n > 3$, an n-valued logic assumes a rational truth value in the range [0,1], defined by the following equally spaced partition:

$$0 = \frac{0}{n-1}, \frac{1}{n-1}, \frac{2}{n-1}, \ldots, \frac{n-2}{n-1}, \frac{n-1}{n-1} = 1.$$

Each of these truth values describes a degree of truth. The commonly used n-valued logic, particularly in fuzzy set and fuzzy systems theories, is the Lukasiewicz-Zadeh n-valued logic. Lukasiewicz developed an n-valued logic in the 1930s, using only the negation and the implication Þ logical operations. Based on that, one can define

$$a \vee b = (a \Rightarrow b) \Rightarrow b,$$

$$a \wedge b = \overline{(\bar{a} \wedge \bar{b})},$$

$$a \Leftrightarrow b = (a \Rightarrow b) \wedge (b \Rightarrow a).$$

The fuzzy set theory was developed by Zadeh in 1960s, which has been thoroughly studied in Chapter 2. To develop an n-valued logic, with $2 \leq n \leq \infty$, such that it is isomorphic to the fuzzy set theory in the same way as the two-valued logic is isomorphic to the classical set theory, Zadeh modified the Lukasiewicz logic and established an infinite-valued logic, by defining the following primary logic operations:

$$\bar{a} = 1 - a$$

$$a \wedge b = \min\{a, b\},$$

$$a \vee b = \max\{a, b\},$$

$$a \Rightarrow b = \min\{1, 1 + b - a\},$$

$$a \Leftrightarrow b = 1 - |a - b|$$

It has been shown, in logic theory, that all these logical operations become the same as those for the two-valued logic when $n = 2$, and the same as those for the three-valued logic shown in Table 1.4 when $n = 3$. More importantly, when $n = \infty$, this logic does not restrict the truth values to be rational: they can be any real numbers in [0,1]. It has also been shown that this infinite-valued logic is isomorphic to the fuzzy set theory that employs the min, max, and 1-a operation for fuzzy set intersection, union, and complement, respectively, in the same way as the classical two-valued logic is isomorphic to the crisp set theory. These verifications are beyond the scope of this text and, hence, are omitted.

1.7 FUZZY LOGIC THEORY

Fuzzy logic is the part of artificial intelligence or machine learning which interprets a human's actions. Computers can interpret only true or false values but a human being can reason the degree of truth or degree of falseness. Fuzzy models interpret the human actions and are also called intelligent systems.

Fuzzy logic is a form of multi-valued logic derived from fuzzy set theory to deal with reasoning that is approximate rather than precise. In contrast with binary sets having binary logic, also known as crisp logic, the fuzzy logic variables may have a membership value of only 0 or 1. Just as in fuzzy set theory with fuzzy logic the set membership values can range (inclusively) between 0 and 1, in fuzzy logic the degree of truth of a statement can range between 0 and 1 and is not constrained to the two truth values {true (1), false (0)} as in classic propositional logic and when linguistic variables are used, these degrees may be managed by specific functions, as discussed below.

The term "fuzzy logic" emerged as a consequence of the development of the theory of fuzzy sets by Lotfi Zadeh[2]. A paper introducing the concept without using the term was published by R.H. Wilkinson in 1963[3] and thus preceded fuzzy set theory. Wilkinson was the first one to redefine and generalize the earlier multivalued logics in terms of set theory. The main purpose of his paper, following his first proposals in his 1961 Electrical Engineering master thesis, was to show how any mathematical function could be simulated using hardwired analog electronic circuits. He did this by first creating various linear voltage ramps which were then selected in a "logic block" using diodes and resistor circuits which implemented the maximum and minimum Fuzzy Logic rules of the INCLUSIVE OR and the AND operations respectively. He called his logic "analog logic".

In 1965 Lotfi Zadeh axiomatized fuzzy set theory, thereby creating the set-theoretical equivalent of the "analog logic" of Wilkinson (without recourse to electrical circuits), not giving Wilkinson any credit.[4] Fuzzy logic has been applied to diverse fields, from control theory to artificial intelligence, yet still remains controversial among most statisticians, who prefer Bayesian logic,[citation needed] and some control engineers, who prefer traditional two-valued logic.

Fuzzy logic provides an inference morphology that enables approximate human reasoning capabilities to be applied to knowledge-based systems. The theory of fuzzy logic provides a mathematical strength to capture the uncertainties associated with human cognitive processes, such as thinking and reasoning. The conventional approaches to knowledge representation lack the means for representing the meaning of fuzzy concepts. As a consequence, the approaches based on first order logic and classical probability theory do not provide an appropriate conceptual framework for dealing with the representation of commonsense knowledge, since such knowledge is by its nature both lexically imprecise and noncategorical. The development of fuzzy logic was motivated in large measure by the need for a conceptual frame-4 work which can address the issue of uncertainty and lexical imprecision.

Some of the essential characteristics of fuzzy logic relate to the following (Zadeh, 1992):

- In fuzzy logic, exact reasoning is viewed as a limiting case of approximate reasoning.
- In fuzzy logic, everything is a matter of degree.
- In fuzzy logic, knowledge is interpreted a collection of elastic or, equivalently, fuzzy constraint on a collection of variables.
- Inference is viewed as a process of propagation of elastic constraints.
- Any logical system can be fuzzified.

There are two main characteristics of fuzzy systems that give them better performance for specific applications.

- Fuzzy systems are suitable for uncertain or approximate reasoning, especially for the system with a mathematical model that is difficult to derive.
- Fuzzy logic allows decision making with estimated values under incomplete or uncertain information.

Fuzzy logic is a logic. Logic refers to the study of methods and principles of human reasoning. Classical logic, as common practice, deals with propositions (e.g., conclusions or decisions) that are either true or false. Each proposition has an opposite. This classical logic, therefore, deals with combinations of variables that represent propositions. As each variable stands for a hypothetical proposition, any combination of them eventually assumes a truth value (either true or false), but never is in between or both (i.e., is not true and false at the same time).

The main content of classical logic is the study of rules that allow new logical variables to be produced as functions of certain existing variables. Suppose that n logical variables, $x_1, ..., x_n$, are given, say

x_1 is true; x_2 is false;

x_n is false.

Then a new logical variable, y, can be defined by a rule as a function of $x_1, ..., x_n$ that has a particular truth value (again, either true or false).

One example of a rule is the following:

Rule: IF x_1 is true AND x_2 is false AND ... AND x_n is false

THEN y is false.

Because one, and only one truth value (either true or false) is assumed by a logical function of a (finite) number of logical variables (hypothetical propositions), the classical logic is also called a two-valued logic.

The fundamental assumption upon which the classical logic is based is that every proposition is either true or false. This principle has been questioned by many philosophers, ever since Aristotle (in his treatise On Interpretation). It is now well understood and well accepted that many propositions are both partially true and partially false. To describe such partial truth values by some new rules, in a way to extend and generalize the two-valued logic, multivalued logics were proposed and developed. As the first attempt, several three-valued logics have now been well established, with their own rationale.

It is common in these logics to introduce a "neither" in between "true" and "false." It has turned out that three-valued logics are successful both logically and mathematically. Motivated by the useful three-valued logics, n-valued logics were developed in the 1930s. In particular, the n-valued logic of Lukasiewicz even allows $n = \infty$.

It has lately been understood that there exists an isomorphism between the two-valued logic and the crisp set theory, and, similarly, there is an isomorphism between the Lukasiewicz logic and the fuzzy set theory. In fact, the isomorphism for the former is the standard characteristic function

$$y = x_A(x) = \begin{cases} 1 & \text{if } x \in A \\ 0 & \text{ifx } \notin A' \end{cases}$$

Where can be interpreted as

$$y = \begin{cases} \text{ture} & \text{if } x \text{ is true,} \\ \text{false} & \text{if } x \text{ is false;} \end{cases}$$

and the next is a fuzzy membership function, which has been thoroughly studied in Chapter 3.

In this chapter, we study in somewhat detail the classical two-valued logic and its operations (the Boolean algebra), a three-valued logic, an n-valued logic (the Zadeh-Lukasiewicz logic with $n = \infty$), and the fuzzy logic. Since the ultimate goal of developing the fuzzy logic is to provide foundations for approximate reasoning, approximate reasoning using fuzzy logic will also be discussed briefly in this chapter. Finally, two important topics, fuzzy relation and fuzzy logic rule base, are studied. In particular, fuzzy logic rule base is the core for fuzzy systems and fuzzy control – the main subjects to be studied in detail in the rest of the book.

1.7.1 Advantages

Following are the advantages of fuzzy logic:

1. Use rules that express the imprecision and approximations of the real world.
2. Easy to understand, test and maintain
3. Easy to be prototyped
4. Robust. They operate even when there is lack of rules or wrong rules.
5. Need less rules
6. Parallel evaluation of rules
7. Accumulate evidences in favour and against

1.7.2 Disadvantages

Following are the disadvantages of fuzzy logic:

1. Need more tests and simulation
2. Do not learn easily
3. Difficult to establish correct rules
4. Lack of precise mathematical model

1.8 THE VOCABULARY OF FUZZY LOGIC

Fuzzy logic suffers from a rich vocabulary of unfamiliar terms and reluctance among its researchers and developers to adhere to a standard vocabulary. It also suffers from an overuse of obscure mathematical symbolism in place of simple and explanatory narrative (but that is another issue). The literature of fuzzy logic and fuzzy systems is filled with a nomenclature derived from its own private world of continuous logic. We find ourselves speaking about fuzzification and defuzzification, hedges, membership functions, and linguistic variables. Before moving on to a more comprehensive and detailed exploration of fuzzy logic, fuzzy systems, and how they work, we need to understand the principal nomenclatures and how they are related to the elements of fuzzy systems.

Although not a complete dictionary of terms associated with fuzzy logic, a preview of the basic vocabulary at the beginning of this chapter will make reading and understanding the material in the chapter 2 much easier. It is not always possible, while maintaining an uncluttered and coherent discussion of fuzzy systems, to ensure that every term is introduced before it is used. Many of these terms, of course, will be discussed in greater depth later in this and subsequent chapters.

1.8.1 Alpha Cut Threshold

An alpha cut threshold truncates the membership function of a fuzzy set or the truth value of a fuzzy rule's predicate at a specific truth value. Any value that falls below the alpha cut threshold is equivalent to zero. Alpha cuts come in two forms: strong (the comparison is less than) and weak (the comparison is less than or equal).

1.8.2 Boolean Logic

Boolean logic is a logic of crisp sets. A crisp set has two truth values: 1 and 0. Propositions in Boolean logic are either true or false, and membership in Boolean sets is either fully inclusive or fully exclusive. Boolean logic was initially formalized by George Boole (1815–1864). In 1854, he published An Investigation into the Laws of Thought, on Which Are Founded the Mathematical Theories of Logic and Probabilities, which unified the mathematical concepts of algebra and logic.

1.8.3 Crisp Set

Boolean sets are often called crisp sets as a way of distinctly differentiating them from fuzzy sets, as well as a way of indicating the sharpness or crispness of their membership function.

1.8.4 Domain

Often confused with the term universe of discourse, the domain of a fuzzy set is the explicit range of values over which the fuzzy set's membership function is defined. For vocabulary fuzzy sets (e.g., the term set of a variable), the domain is generally the same as the support set.

1.8.5 Expectancy

The width of a fuzzy number, usually measured from the center of the fuzzy set, is called the expectancy (a measure of the number's elasticity). The larger the expectancy the more imprecision is built into the fuzzy number. However, we should not confuse imprecision with a lack of accuracy. In many fuzzy models, relaxing the precision of a number increases the model's fault tolerance and reduces its brittleness, thereby making the model more precise over a wider range of values.

1.8.6 Fuzzy Logic

Fuzzy logic is a logic of fuzzy sets. A fuzzy set has, potentially, an infinite range of truth values between one (1) and zero (0). Propositions in fuzzy logic have a degree of truth, and membership in fuzzy sets can be fully inclusive, fully exclusive, or some degree in between. Fuzzy logic was initially formalized by Lotfi Zadeh (1921–) in his seminal 1965 paper "Fuzzy Sets" (see "Further Reading") followed in 1973 with "Outline of a New Approach to the Analysis of Complex Systems and Decision Process" (see "Further Reading").

1.8.7 Fuzzy Number

A bell-shaped, triangular-shaped, or trapezoidal-shaped fuzzy set represents a central value and is, in essence, a fuzzy number. Fuzzy numbers give fuzzy models a great deal of robustness and flexibility. The width of a fuzzy number is a measure of its overall expectancy (the degree to which it corresponds to a crisp number).

1.8.8 Fuzzy Quantifier

Fuzzy sets that are not numbers are fuzzy quantifiers. These sets generally have linear or sigmoid shapes. Concepts such as Tall, Fast, Heavy, and Large are examples of fuzzy quantifiers.

1.8.9 Fuzzy Set

A fuzzy set is distinct from a crisp or Boolean set in that it allows its elements to have a degree of membership. The core of a fuzzy set is its membership function: a surface or line that defines the relationship between a value in the set's domain and its degree of membership. The relationship (Expression 1.1) is functional because it returns a single degree of membership for any value in the domain.

$$t = f(s, x) \tag{1.1}$$

Here, t is a truth membership value (degree of membership in fuzzy set) s is the fuzzy set x is a value from the underlying domain (universe of discourse) Fuzzy sets provide a means of defining a series of overlapping concepts for a model variable, thus permitting rules to address the state of a model in terms of these fuzzy set names. Such names are called linguistic variables. They allow fuzzy sets to represent the underlying semantics of a variable (that is, the concept represented by a variable).

1.8.10 Hedge

Hedges act like adjectives or adverbs in the English language. They modify the shape of the fuzzy set's underlying membership function to or dilute the membership relationships, and they convert scalars (crisp numbers) into fuzzy sets through a process called approximation. They can be used in rules to modify the evaluation of both the premise and the consequent. The following is an example.

if a is very Z,

then b is somewhat Y

Here, very and somewhat are intensifier and dilution hedges.

1.8.11 Linguistic Variable

A fuzzy set that forms part of the term set for a variable and is used in fuzzy rules as part of a fuzzy relation is called a linguistic variable. For example, in the rule **if** height is Tall **then** weight is Heavy both Tall and Heavy are linguistic variables representing one of the possible partitions of height and weight. Fuzzy sets used in this way are called linguistic variables because they are used in place of numbers and allow rules to be cast in form of linguistic statements (such as height is Tall).

1.8.12 Membership Function

The core of a fuzzy set is the membership function. See "Fuzzy Set" for a more complete description.

1.8.13 Overlap

Because fuzzy sets represent degrees of membership, values from the complete universe of discourse for a variable can have memberships in more than one fuzzy set. For example, consider the variable height with a term set of Short, Medium, and Tall. An individual's height can be, to some degree, both Short and Medium. This is because the Short and Medium fuzzy sets overlap (as the values for height increase, they become less Short and more Medium, but the transition is gradual, not abrupt).

1.8.14 Support Set

The region of the membership function in which the truth values are greater than zero is called the support set. The support set plays an important part in the evaluation of a fuzzy model because only within the support set region can a set actually contribute to the outcome of a model.

1.8.15 Term Set

The collection of fuzzy sets that define the semantics of a variable is called the variable's term set. Each variable used in a fuzzy rule must have a term set. The individual fuzzy sets in a term set are the linguistic variables associated with the variable. Thus, Tall in the rule **if** height is Tall **then** weight is Heavy is part of the term set for the variable height and Heavy is part of the term set for the variable weight.

1.8.16 Universe of Discourse

The complete range of values over which a variable can assume values is called the universe of discourse (UoD). Although this term is often applied to the range of values in a fuzzy set, the proper term for the fuzzy set is its domain. The Universe of discourse for a variable is decomposed into a collection of fuzzy sets (the term set), each set of which has a domain that overlays part of the universe of discourse.

1.9 FUZZY LOGIC AND APPROXIMATE REASONING

Fuzzy logic is logic; its ultimate goal is to provide foundations for approximate reasoning using imprecise propositions based on fuzzy set theory, in a way similar to the classical reasoning using precise repositions based on the classical set theory. To introduce this notion, we first recall how the classical reasoning works, using only precise propositions and the two-valued logic. The following syllogism is an example of such reasoning in linguistic terms:

(i) Everyone who is 40 years old or older is old.
(ii) David is 40 years old and Mary is 39 years old.
(iii) David is old but Mary is not.

This is a very precise deductive inference, correct in the sense of the two valued logic.

In this classical (precise) reasoning using the two-valued logic, when the (output) logical variable represented by a logical formula is always true regardless of the truth values of the (input) logical variables, it is called a tautology. If, on the contrary, it is always false, then it is called a contradiction. Various tautologies can be used for making deductive inferences, which are referred to as inference rules. The four frequently used inference rules in classical reasoning are:

modus ponens: $(a \wedge (a \Rightarrow b)) \Rightarrow b;$

modus tollens: $(\bar{b} \wedge (a \Rightarrow b)) \Rightarrow \bar{a};$

syllogism: $(a \Rightarrow b) \wedge (b \Rightarrow c) \Rightarrow (a \Rightarrow c);$

contrapositions: $(a \Rightarrow b) \Rightarrow (\bar{b} \Rightarrow \bar{a}).$

These inference rules are very easily understood and, indeed, have been commonly used in one's daily life. For example, the modus ponens is interpreted as follows:

IF "a is true" AND the statement "IF a is true THEN b is true" is true THEN "b is true."

Using this logic, we see that the deductive inference IF "40 years old or older is old" AND "IF 40 years old or older is old THEN David is old" THEN "David is old" is a modus ponens, and the deductive inference

IF "Mary is not old" AND "IF Mary is 40 years old or older then Mary is old" THEN "Mary is not 40 years old nor older" is a modus tollens.

With the above discussion in mind, we now consider the following example of approximate reasoning in linguistic terms that cannot be handled by the classical (precise) reasoning using two-valued logic:

(i) Everyone who is 40 to 70 years old is old but is very old if he (she) is 71 years old or above; everyone who is 20 to 39 years old is young but is very young if he (she) is 19 years old or below.
(ii) David is 40 years old and Mary is 39 years old.
(iii) David is old but not very old; Mary is young but not very young.

This is of course a meaningful deductive inference, which indeed has been frequently used in one's daily life. This is an example of what is called approximate reasoning. In order to deal with such imprecise inference, fuzzy logic can be employed. Briefly, fuzzy logic allows the imprecise linguistic terms such as:

- fuzzy predicates: old, rare, severe, expensive, high, fast
- fuzzy quantifiers: many, few, usually, almost, little, much
- fuzzy truth values: very true, true, unlikely true, mostly false, false, definitely false

Example 1.1: Let P be the proposition "The structural beam is an 18WF45" and let Q be the proposition "The structural beam is made of steel." Let X be the universe of structural members comprised of girders, beams, and columns; x is an element (beam), A is the set of all wide-flange (WF) beams, and B is the set of all steel beams. Hence,

P: x is in A

Q: x is in B

The five logical connectives already defined can be used to create compound propositions, where a compound proposition is defined as a logical proposition formed by logically connecting two or more simple propositions. Just as we are interested in the truth of a simple proposition, classical logic also involves the assessment of the truth of compound propositions. For the case of two simple propositions, the resulting compound propositions are defined next in terms of their binary truth values.

Given a proposition $P : x \in A, \overline{P} : x \notin A$, we have the following for the logical connectives:

Disjunction

$$P \vee Q : x \in A \text{ or } x \in B$$

Hence, $$T(P \vee Q) = \max\,(T(P), T(Q)) \tag{1.1a}$$

Conjunction

$$P \wedge Q : x \in A \text{ or } x \in B$$

Hence, $$T(P \wedge Q) = \min\,(T(P), T(Q)) \tag{1.1b}$$

Negation

If $$T(P) = 1\ T(\overline{p}) = 0;\ \text{if } T(P) = 0, \text{ then } T(\overline{P}) = 1. \tag{1.1c}$$

Implication

$$(P \rightarrow Q) : x \notin A \text{ or } x \in B$$

Hence, $$T(P \rightarrow Q) = T(\overline{P} \cup Q) \tag{1.1d}$$

Equivalence

$$(P \leftrightarrow Q) : (P \leftrightarrow Q) = \begin{cases} 1 & \text{for } T(P) = T(Q) \\ 0 & \text{for } T(P) \neq T(Q) \end{cases} \tag{1.1e}$$

The logical connective implication, i.e., P ‡Q (P implies Q), presented here is also known as the classical implication, to distinguish it from an alternative form devised in the 1930s by Lukasiewicz, a Polish mathematician, who was first credited with exploring logics other than Aristotelian (classical or binary logic) [Researcher, 1969], and from several other forms (see end of this chapter). In this implication the proposition P is also referred to as the hypothesis or the antecedent, and the proposition Q is also referred to as the conclusion or the consequent. The compound proposition $P \rightarrow Q$ is true in all cases except where a true antecedent P appears with a false consequent, Q, i.e., a true hypothesis cannot imply a false conclusion.

Example 1.2: Consider the following four propositions:

1. If $1 + 1 = 2$, then $4 > 0$.
2. If $1 + 1 = 3$, then $4 > 0$.
3. If $1 + 1 = 3$, then $4 < 0$.
4. If $1 + 1 = 2$, then $4 < 0$.

The first three propositions are all true; the fourth is false. In the first two, the conclusion $4 > 0$ is true regardless of the truth of the hypothesis; in the third case both propositions are false, but this does not disprove the implication; finally, in the fourth case, a true hypothesis cannot produce a false conclusion.

Hence, the classical form of the implication is true for all propositions of P and Q except for those propositions that are in both the truth set of P and the false set of Q, i.e.,

$$T(P \rightarrow Q) = \overline{T(P) \cap T(\overline{Q})} \tag{1.2}$$

This classical form of the implication operation requires some explanation. For a proposition P defined on set A and a proposition Q defined on set B, the implication "P implies Q" is equivalent to taking the union of elements in the complement of set A with the elements in the set B (this result can also be derived by using De Morgan's principles on Eq. (1.2)). That is, the logical implication is analogous to the set-theoretic form

$$(P \rightarrow Q) = (\overline{A} \cup B \text{ is true}) \equiv (\text{either "not in A" or " in B"})$$

so that

$$T\,(P \rightarrow \overline{Q}) = (\overline{P} \vee Q) = (T(\overline{P}), T(Q)) \tag{1.3}$$

This expression is linguistically equivalent to the statement, "$P \rightarrow Q$ is true" when either "not A" or "B" is true (logical or). Graphically, this implication and the analogous set operation are represented by the Venn diagram in Figure 1.7. As noted in the diagram, the region represented by the difference $A \mid B$ is the set region where the implication $P \rightarrow Q$ is false (the implication "fails"). The shaded region in Figure 1.7 represents the collection of elements in the universe where the implication is true; that is, the set

$$\overline{A \mid B} = \overline{A} \cup \overline{\overline{B}} = \overline{A \cap \overline{B}}$$

If x is in A and x is not in B, then

$A \rightarrow B$ fails a $\cdot A \mid B$ (difference)

Now, with two propositions (P and Q) each being able to take on one of two truth values (true or false, 1 or 0), there will be a total of $2^2 = 4$ propositional situations. These situations are illustrated, along with the appropriate truth values, for the propositions P and

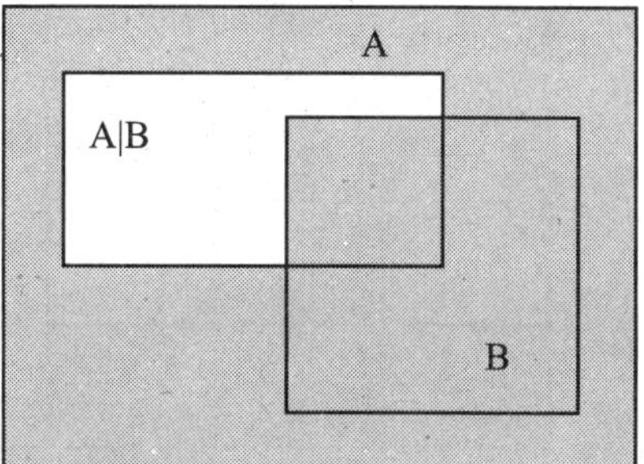

Figure 1.7: Graphical analog of the classical implication operation; gray area is where implication holds.

Table 1.5: Truth table for various compound propositions

P	Q	P '	$P \vee Q$	$P \wedge Q$	$P \rightarrow Q$	$P \leftrightarrow Q$
T(1)	T(1)	F(0)	T(1)	T(1)	T(1)	T(1)
T(1)	F(0)	F(0)	T(1)	F(0)	F(0)	F(0)
F(0)	T(1)	T(1)	T(1)	F(0)	T(1)	F(0)
F(0)	F(0)	T(1)	F(0)	F(0)	T(1)	T(1)

Q and the various logical connectives between them in Table 1.5. The values in the last five columns of the table are calculated using the expressions in Eqs. (1.1) and (1.3). In Table 1.5 T (or 1) denotes true and F (or 0) denotes false. Suppose the implication operation involves two different universes of discourse; P is

a proposition described by set A, which is defined on universe X, and Q is a proposition described by set B, which is defined on universe Y. Then the implication $P \rightarrow Q$ can be represented in set-theoretic terms by the relation R, where R is defined by

$$R = (A \times B) \cup (\overline{A} \times Y) \equiv \text{If A, THEN B}$$

IF $x \in A$ where $x \in X$ and $A \subset X$ (1.4)

THEN $y \in B$ where $y \in Y$ and $B \subset Y$

This implication, Eq. (1.4), is also equivalent to the linguistic rule form, IF A, THEN B. The graphic shown in Figure 1.8 represents the space of the Cartesian product $X \times Y$, showing typical sets A and B; and superposed on this space is the set-theoretic equivalent of the implication. That is,

$P \rightarrow Q$: IF $x \in A$, THEN $y \in B$, or $P \rightarrow Q \equiv \overline{A} \cup B$

The shaded regions of the compound Venn diagram in Figure 1.8 represent the truth domain of the implication, IF A, THEN B ($P \rightarrow Q$). Another compound proposition in linguistic rule form is the expression IF A, THEN B, ELSE C

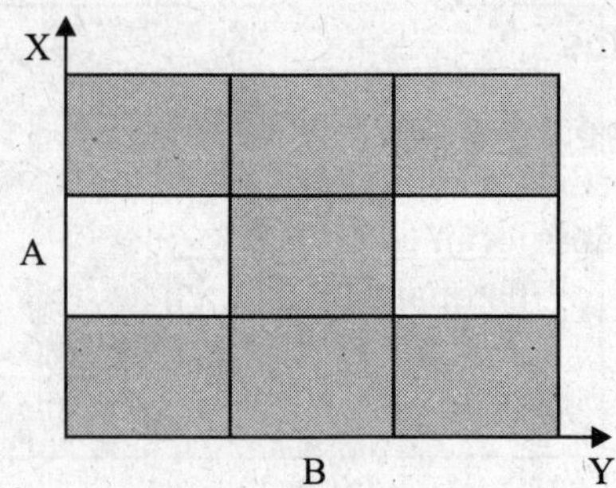

Figure 1.8: The cartesian space showing the implication IF A, THEN B.

1.9.1 Mathematical Fuzzy Logic

In mathematical logic, there are several formal systems of "fuzzy logic"; most of them belong among so-called t-norm fuzzy logics.

1.9.2 Propositional Fuzzy Logics

The most important propositional fuzzy logics are:

Monoidal t-norm-based propositional fuzzy logic MTL is an axiomatization of logic where conjunction is defined by a left continuous t-norm, and implication is defined as the residuum of the t-norm. Its models correspond to MTL-algebras that are prelinear commutative bounded integral residuated lattices.

Basic propositional fuzzy logic BL is an extension of MTL logic where conjunction is defined by a continuous t-norm, and implication is also defined as the residuum of the t-norm. Its models correspond to BL-algebras.

Łukasiewicz fuzzy logic is the extension of basic fuzzy logic BL where standard conjunction is the Łukasiewicz t-norm. It has the axioms of basic fuzzy logic plus an axiom of double negation, and its models correspond to MV-algebras.

Gödel fuzzy logic is the extension of basic fuzzy logic BL where conjunction is Gödel t-norm. t has the axioms of BL plus an axiom of idempotence of conjunction, and its models are called G-algebras.

Product fuzzy logic is the extension of basic fuzzy logic BL where conjunction is product -norm. It has the axioms of BL plus another axiom for cancellativity of conjunction, and its models re called product algebras.

Fuzzy logic with evaluated syntax (sometimes also called Pavelka's logic), denoted by EVŁ, s a further generalization of mathematical fuzzy logic. While the above kinds of fuzzy logic have raditional syntax and many-valued semantics, in EVŁ is evaluated also syntax. This means that ach formula has an evaluation. Axiomatization of EVŁ stems from Łukasziewicz fuzzy logic. A eneralization of classical Gödel completeness theorem is provable in EVŁ.

1.9.3 Predicate Fuzzy Logics

These extend the above-mentioned fuzzy logics by adding universal and existential quantifiers in a manner similar to the way that predicate logic is created from propositional logic. The semantics of the universal resp. existential quantifier in t-norm fuzzy logics is the infimum resp. supremum of the truth degrees of the instances of the quantified subformula.

1.9.4 Higher-order Fuzzy Logics

These logics, called fuzzy type theories, extend predicate fuzzy logics to be able to quantify also predicates and higher order objects. A fuzzy type theory is a generalization of classical simple type theory introduced by B. Russell and mathematically elaborated by A. Church and L. Henkin.

1.9.5 Decidability Issues for Fuzzy Logic

The notions of a "decidable subset" and "recursively enumerable subset" are basic ones for classical mathematics and classical logic. Then, the question of a suitable extension of such concepts to fuzzy set theory arises. A first proposal in such a direction was made by E.S. Santos by the notions of fuzzy Turing machine, Markov normal fuzzy algorithm and fuzzy program. Successively, L. Biacino and G. Gerla showed that such a definition is not adequate and therefore proposed the following one. U denotes the set of rational numbers in [0,1]. A fuzzy subset s : S [0, 1] of a set S is recursively enumerable if a recursive map h : S × N U exists such that, for every x in S, the function h(x, n) is increasing with respect to n and s(x) = lim h(x,n). We say that s is decidable if both s and its complement –s are recursively enumerable. An extension of such a theory to the general case of the L-subsets is proposed in Gerla 2006. The proposed definitions are well related with fuzzy logic. Indeed, the following theorem holds true (provided that the deduction apparatus of the fuzzy logic satisfies some obvious effectiveness property).

Theorem: Any axiomatizable fuzzy theory is recursively enumerable. In particular, the fuzzy set of logically true formulas is recursively enumerable in spite of the fact that the crisp set of valid formulas is not recursively enumerable, in general. Moreover, any axiomatizable and complete theory is decidable.

It is an open question to give supports for a Church thesis for fuzzy logic claiming that the proposed notion of recursive enumerability for fuzzy subsets is the adequate one. To this aim, further investigations on the notions of fuzzy grammar and fuzzy Turing machine should be necessary (see for example Wiedermann's paper). Another open question is to start from this notion to find an extension of Godel's theorems to fuzzy logic.

EXERCISES

1. What do you mean by fuzzy system?
2. Explain the concepts of imprecision?

3. Explain the historical point of view of uncertainty?
4. Explain the concept of uncertainty and information?
5. Why we use fuzzy system?
6. What do you mean by pure fuzzy set?
7. Explain the concept of classical logical theory?
8. Explain the logic function for :
   (i) Two valued logic
   (ii) Multi-valued logic
9. What do you mean by fuzzy logic theory?
10. What are the various characteristic of fuzzy logic?
11. What are the advantages and disadvantages of fuzzy logic?
12. Explain the vocabulary of fuzzy logic?
13. Explain the relationship between fuzzy logic and approximate reasoning?
14. What do you mean by mathematical fuzzy logic?
15. Explain the following:
    (i) Propositional fuzzy logic
    (ii) Predicate fuzzy logic
    (iii) Higher order fuzzy logic

CHAPTER 2

Fuzzy Logic

2.1 INTRODUCTION

Fuzzy logic means inexact reasoning, data granulation, computing with words and so on. Haziness is always present in any realistic process. This vagueness may come up from the analysis of the data inputs and in the directives used to describe the relationships between the informative attributes. Fuzzy logic grants an inference structure that allows the human reasoning capacities to be applied to artificial knowledge-based structures. Fuzzy logic gives a means for adapting linguistic strategy into control actions and thus offers a high-level computation.

A definition of fuzzy logic systems set mathematical determination to the emulation of certain perceptual and lingual attributes related with human cognition, where the science of neural networks provides a new computing tool with learning and adaptation capabilities. The theory of fuzzy logic gives an inference method under cognitive uncertainty, computational neural networks, fuzzy logic offer exciting benefits such as learning, adaptation, fault tolerance, parallelism, and generalization.

In the literary texts sources, we can find different kinds of explanation for fuzzy systems theory. Human knowledge these days becomes more and more important – we increase it from living through the world after only which we live and use our capability to reason to create an order in the mass of information (i.e., to formulate human knowledge in a organized manner). As we are all limited in our ability to perceive the world and to deep reasoning, we find ourselves everywhere faced by uncertainty that is a result of lack of information, in particular, miscalculation of measurements.

The other restriction factor in our request for precision is a natural language used for describing/sharing knowledge, communication, etc. We understand core meanings of word and are able to communicate without error to an adequate degree, but generally we cannot precisely agree among ourselves on the singular word or terms of communal sense meaning. In other words, ordinary languages are unclear.

Our impression of the real world is pervaded by concepts, which do not have severely defined boundaries – for example, many, tall, much larger than, young, etc. are true only to some degree, and they are false to some extent as well. These concepts can be called fuzzy or vague concepts – a human brain works with them, while computers may not do it (they reason with strings of 0s and 1s). Natural languages, which are much higher in level than programming languages, are fuzzy, while programming languages are not. The door to the development of fuzzy computers was opened in 1985 by the design of the first logic chip by Masaki Togai and Hiroyuki Watanabe at Bell Telephone Laboratories. In the years to come fuzzy computers will employ both fuzzy hardware and fuzzy software, and they will be much closer in structure to the human brain than the present-day computers are.

The Fuzzy Logic tool was introduced in 1965 by Lotfi Zadeh. It is a mathematical tool for dealing with uncertainty. It offers to a software computing system the important concept of computing with words'. It grants a technique to deal with vagueness and information granularity. The fuzzy theory provides a mechanism for representing linguistic constructs such as "many," "low," "medium," "often," "few."

Basically, the fuzzy logic provides an inference organization that enables proper human reasoning capabilities that machines do not have. In the other hand, the traditional binary set theory describes crisp events, events that have two options: one or zero. It uses probability theory to explain whether an event is about to happen, measuring the chance with which a given event is expected to come about. The premise of fuzzy logic is based leading the concept of relative graded connection and so are the functions of awareness and cognitive processes.

It is important to keep in mind that there is a close connection between *Fuzziness* and *Complexity*. As the complexity of a task, or of a system for performing that task, exceeds a certain limit, the system must unavoidably become fuzzy in nature. Zadeh, initially an engineer and systems scientist, was concerned with the fast turn down in information afforded by common mathematical models as the complexity of the target system increased.

As he stressed, with the increasing of complexity our skill to make accurate and yet major statements about its behavior diminishes. Real world problems are too complex, and the difficulty involves the degree of vagueness – as uncertainty increases, so does the involvedness of the problem. Habitual system modeling and analysis techniques are too precise for such problems, and in order to make complexity less daunting we set up appropriate simplifications, assumptions, etc. to accomplish a reasonable compromise between the information we have and the amount of uncertainty we are willing to accept. In this aspect, fuzzy systems theory is similar to other engineering theories, because almost all of them describe the real world in an approximate manner.

Engineers define fuzzy logic as a useful tool with diverse applications; especially on solving problems that linear computing is not able to do. A good example of this functionality is the capability for image recognition, since human brain is capable to distinguish an object from an image even if is blur, meanwhile linear computing is able to read just pixels as set of colors. There is an analog factor: vagueness, images may have fuzzy maps.

Fuzzy sets grants means to model the ambiguity associated with vagueness, imprecision, and lack of information concerning a dilemma or a plant, etc. Consider the significance of a "short person." For an entity X, the short person may be one whose height is below 4.20. For another individual Y, the short person may be one whose height is beneath or equal to 3.9. This "short" is called as a linguistic descriptor. The term "short" informs the same meaning to the individuals X and Y, but it is establish that they both do not supply a unique definition. The term "short" would be conveyed successfully, only when a computer compares the given height value with the pre-assigned value of "short." This variable "short" is called as *linguistic variable*, which represents the elusiveness existing in the system.

2.2 FUZZY LOGIC

Fuzzy logic has been used in two different senses. It is important to clarify the distinctions between these two different usages of the term.

1. **In a narrow sense:** Fuzzy logic refers to a logical system that generalizes classical two-valued logic for reasoning under uncertainly.
2. **In a board sense:** fuzzy logic refers to all of the theories and technologies that employ fuzzy sets, which are classes with unsharp boundaries.

Definition:

"Fuzzy logic is used for solving problems with expert systems and real-time systems that must react to an imperfect environment of highly variable, volatile or unpredictable conditions."

For instance, the concept of "warm room temperature" may be expressed as an interval (e.g., [75° F]) in classical set theory. However, the concept does not have a well-defined natural boundary. A representation of the concept closer to human interpretation is to allow a gradual transition from "not warm" to "warm". In order to achieve this, the notion of membership in a set needs to become a matter of degree. This is the essence of fuzzy sets. An example of a classical set and a fuzzy set is shown in Figure 2.1, where the vertical axis represents the degree of membership in a set.

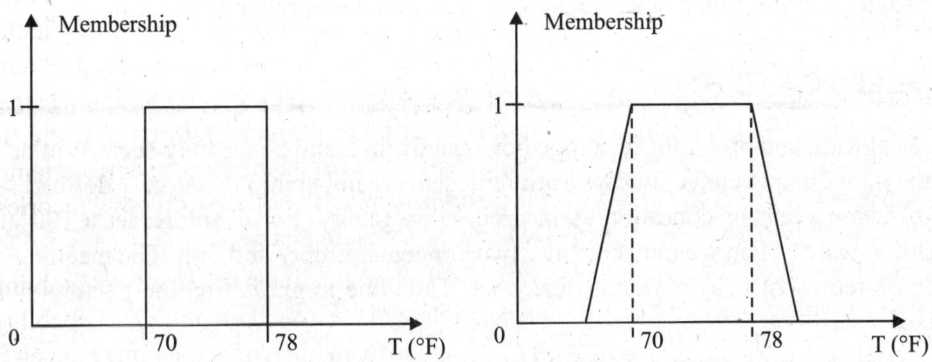

Figure 2.1: Representation of a classical set and a fuzzy set "warm room temperature".

The board sense of fuzzy logic includes the narrow sense of fuzzy logic as a branch. Other areas include fuzzy control, fuzzy pattern recognition, fuzzy arithmetic, fuzzy math, fuzzy probability theory, fuzzy decision analysis, fuzzy neural networks theory, and fuzzy topology, etc. In all these areas, a conventional black-and-white concept is generalized to a matter of degree.

By doing this, one accomplishes two things:

1. Ease of describing human knowledge involving vague concepts
2. Enhanced ability to develop a cost-effective solution to real-world problems.

The term fuzzy logic in this book is most frequently used in the broad sense. Whenever it is used in the narrow sense, we will explicitly state so.

2.3 MOTIVATIONS

Fuzzy logic was motivated by two objectives. First, it aims to alleviate difficulties in developing and analyzing complex systems encountered by conventional mathematics tools. Second, it is motivated by observing that human reasoning can utilize concepts and knowledge that do not have well-defined, sharp boundaries (i.e. vague concepts). The first motivation is directly related to solving **real-world problems**, while the second motivation is related to **artificial intelligence**-the discipline in computer science involved with developing computer systems that exhibit intelligent behaviors similar to those of human beings. The former motivation requires fuzzy logic to work in qualitative and numeric domains, while the latter motivation enables fuzzy logic to have a descriptive and qualitative form because vague concepts are often described qualitatively by words.

These two motivations together not only make fuzzy logic unique and different from other technologies that focus on only one of these goals but also enable fuzzy logic to be a natural bridge between the quantitative world and the qualitative world. As will become clear at a later point, this unique characteristic of fuzzy logic allows this technology to offer an important benefit-it not only provides a cost-effective way to model complex systems involving numeric variables bus also offers a qualitative description of the system that is easy to comprehend.

2.4 DEGREES OF TRUTH

Both degrees of truth and probabilities range between 0 and 1 and hence may seem similar at first. However, they are distinct conceptually; truth represents membership in vaguely defined sets, not likelihood of some event or condition as in probability theory. For example, let a 100-ml glass contain 30 ml of water. Then we may consider two concepts: Empty and Full. The meaning of each of them can be represented by a certain fuzzy set. Then one might define the glass as being 0.7 empty and 0.3 full.

Note that the concept of emptiness would be subjective and thus would depend on the observer or designer. Another designer might equally well design a set membership function where the glass would be considered full for all values down to 50 ml. It is essential to realize that fuzzy logic uses truth degrees as a mathematical model of the vagueness phenomenon while probability is a mathematical model of randomness.

A probabilistic setting would first define a scalar variable for the fullness of the glass, and second, conditional distributions describing the probability that someone would call the glass full given a specific fullness level. This model, however, has no sense without accepting occurrence of some event, e.g. which after a few minutes, the glass will be half empty. Note that the conditioning can be achieved by having a specific observer that randomly selects the label for the glass, a distribution over deterministic observers, or both.

Consequently, probability has nothing in common with fuzziness, these are simply different concepts which superficially seem similar because of using the same interval of real numbers [0, 1]. Still, since theorems such as De Morgan's have dual applicability and properties of random variables are analogous to properties of binary logic states, one can see where the confusion might arise.

2.4.1 Applying Truth Values

A basic application might characterize subranges of a continuous variable. For instance, a temperature measurement for anti-lock brakes might have several separate membership functions defining particular temperature ranges needed to control the brakes properly. Each function maps the same temperature value to a truth value in the 0 to 1 range. These truth values can then be used to determine how the brakes should be controlled.

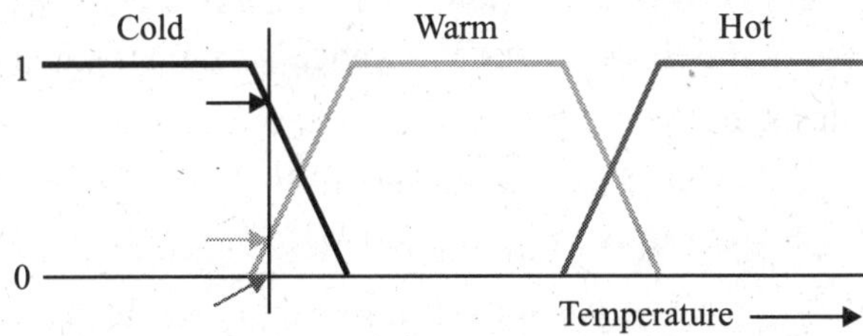

In this image, the meaning of the expressions cold, warm, and hot is represented by functions mapping a temperature scale. A point on that scale has three "truth values" — one for each of the three functions. The vertical line in the image represents a particular temperature that the three arrows (truth values) gauge. Since the red arrow points to zero, this temperature may be interpreted as "not hot". The orange arrow (pointing at 0.2) may describe it as "slightly warm" and the blue arrow (pointing at 0.8) "fairly cold".

2.5 LINGUISTIC VARIABLES

While variables in mathematics usually take numerical values, in fuzzy logic applications, the non-numeric linguistic variables are often used to facilitate the expression of rules and facts.

A linguistic variable such as age may have a value such as young or its antonym old. However, the great utility of linguistic variables is that they can be modified via linguistic hedges applied to primary terms. The linguistic hedges can be associated with certain functions. For example, L. A. Zadeh proposed to take the square of the membership function. This model, however, does not work properly. For more details, see the next sections.

2.6 AN EXAMPLE OF FUZZY REASONING

Fuzzy Set Theory defines Fuzzy Operators on Fuzzy Sets. The problem in applying this is that the appropriate Fuzzy Operator may not be known. For this reason, Fuzzy logic usually uses IF-THEN rules, or constructs that are equivalent, such as fuzzy associative matrices.

Rules are usually expressed in the form:

IF variable IS property THEN action

For example, an extremely simple temperature regulator that uses a fan might look like this:

IF temperature IS very cold THEN stop fan

IF temperature IS cold THEN turn down fan

IF temperature IS normal THEN maintain level

IF temperature IS hot THEN speed up fan

Notice there is no "ELSE". All of the rules are evaluated, because the temperature might be "cold" and "normal" at the same time to different degrees.

The AND, OR, and NOT operators of boolean logic exist in fuzzy logic, usually defined as the minimum, maximum, and complement; when they are defined this way, they are called the Zadeh operators, because they were first defined as such in Zadeh's original papers.

So for the fuzzy variables x and y:

$$\text{NOT } x = (1 - \text{truth}(x))$$

$$x \text{ AND } y = \text{minimum}(\text{truth}(x), \text{truth}(y))$$

$$x \text{ OR } y = \text{maximum}(\text{truth}(x), \text{truth}(y))$$

There are also other operators, more linguistic in nature, called hedges that can be applied. These are generally adverbs such as "very", or "somewhat", which modify the meaning of a set using a mathematical formula.

In application, the programming language Prolog is well geared to implementing fuzzy logic with its facilities to set up a database of "rules" which are queried to deduct logic. This sort of programming is known as logic programming.

Once fuzzy relations are defined, it is possible to develop fuzzy relational databases. The first fuzzy relational database, FRDB, appeared in Maria Zemankova's dissertation. Later, some other models arose like the Buckles-Petry model, the Prade-Testemale Model, the Umano-Fukami model or the GEFRED model by J.M. Medina, M.A. Vila et al. In the context of fuzzy databases, some fuzzy querying languages have been defined, highlighting the SQLf by P. Bosc et al. and the FSQL by J. Galindo et al. These languages define some structures in order to include fuzzy aspects in the SQL statements, like fuzzy conditions, fuzzy comparators, fuzzy constants, fuzzy constraints, fuzzy thresholds, linguistic labels and so on.

Other examples

If a male is 1.8 meters, consider him as tall:

IF male IS true AND height > = 1.8 THEN is_tall IS true; is_short IS false

The fuzzy rules do not make sharp distinction between tall and short:

IF height < = medium male THEN is_short IS agree somewhat

IF height > = medium male THEN is_tall IS agree somewhat

In the fuzzy case, there are no such heights as 1.83 meters, but there are fuzzy values, like the following assignments:

dwarf male = [0, 1.3] m

short male = [1.3, 1.5] m

medium male = [1.5, 1.8] m

tall male = [1.8, 2.0] m

giant male > 2.0 m

For the consequent, there are may also be more than two values:

agree not = 0

agree little = 1

agree somewhat = 2

agree a lot = 3

agree fully = 4

In the binary (or "crisp") case, a person of 1.79 meters is considered of medium height, while another person who is 1.8 meters or 2.25 meters tall is considered tall.

The crisp example differs deliberately from the fuzzy one. The antecedent was not given fuzzy values:

IF male > = agree somewhat AND ... as gender is often considered binary information.

2.7 APPLICATION AREAS OF FUZZY LOGIC

Following are the various application areas of fuzzy logic:

1. Automobile and other vehicle subsystems, such as :automatic transmissions, ABS, cruise control (e.g. Tokyo monorail)
2. Air conditioners
3. Cameras
4. Digital image processing, such as edge detection -
5. Rice cookers
6. Dishwashers
7. Elevators
8. Washing machines and other home appliances

9. Video game artificial intelligence
10. Language filters on message boards and chat rooms for filtering out offensive text
11. Pattern recognition in Remote Sensing
12. Hydrometeor classification algorithms for polarimetric weather radar
13. Fuzzy logic has also been incorporated into some microcontrollers and microprocessors

2.8 WHY USE FUZZY LOGIC FOR CONTROL?

One common answer to this question is that fuzzy logic can be used for controlling a process (i.e., a plant in control engineering terminology) that is too nonlinear or too ill-understood to use conventional control designs. Another answer is that fuzzy logic enables control engineers to easily implement control strategies used by human operators. The first answer echoes the first motivation for fuzzy logic – to deal with complex, systems – while the second answer is related to the second motivation – the ease of describing human knowledge.

We will illustrate these points using a real-world application below. Before we do that, though, we would like to point out that fuzzy logic control broadens the range of applications of control engineering tools and methods. It is not meant to replace but rather to augment existing methodologies for control design.

2.9 FUZZY LOGIC FOR CONTROL

A fuzzy control system is a control system based on fuzzy logic - a mathematical system that analyzes analog input values in terms of logical variables that take on continuous values between 0 and 1, in contrast to classical or digital logic, which operates on discrete values of either 0 and 1 (true and false). Fuzzy logic is widely used in machine control. The term itself inspires a certain skepticism, sounding equivalent to "half-baked logic" or "bogus logic", but the "fuzzy" part does not refer to a lack of rigour in the method, rather to the fact that the logic involved can deal with fuzzy concepts - concepts that cannot be expressed as "true" or "false" but rather as "partially true". Although genetic algorithms and neural networks can perform just as well as fuzzy logic in many cases (in fact, certain neural networks can be shown to be mathematically equivalent to certain fuzzy logic systems), fuzzy logic has the advantage that the solution to the problem can be cast in terms that human operators can understand, so that their experience can be used in the design of the controller. This makes it easier to mechanize tasks that are already successfully performed by humans.

Although an American professor introduced the fuzzy logic theory, it was first implemented in the control of cement kilns in Denmark in 1977. The Japanese were successful in applying fuzzy logic in commercial goods like automobiles and washing machines and their current fuzzy logic market is estimated around 2 billion dollars. America has been left behind in the implementation of fuzzy logic to real world problems.

Fuzzy logic has mostly been applied to control systems. Fuzzy control systems interpret the expert human and replace them for performing certain tasks such as control of a power plant. Fuzzy controllers apply decision rules (if-then rules) by making use of critical variables to interpolate the output between the crisp boundaries.

Some typical examples where fuzzy logic has been implemented are:

1. Railway (Sendai Railways in Japan)
2. Automobile industries (transmission and braking)
3. Heating and cooling systems
4. Copy machines
5. Washing machines

Fuzzy logic has rapidly become one of the most successful of today's technologies for developing sophisticated control systems. The reason for which is very simple. Fuzzy logic addresses such applications perfectly as it resembles human decision making with an ability to generate precise solutions from certain or approximate information. It fills an important gap in engineering design methods left vacant by purely mathematical approaches (e.g. linear control design), and purely logic-based approaches (e.g. expert systems) in system design.

While other approaches require accurate equations to model real-world behaviors, fuzzy design can accommodate the ambiguities of real-world human language and logic. It provides both an intuitive method for describing systems in human terms and automates the conversion of those system specifications into effective models.

2.10 WHAT DOES IT OFFER?

The first applications of fuzzy theory were primaly industrial, such as process control for cement kilns. However, as the technology was further embraced, fuzzy logic was used in more useful applications. In 1987, the first fuzzy logic-controlled subway was opened in Sendai in northern Japan. Here, fuzzy-logic controllers make subway journeys more comfortable with smooth braking and acceleration. Best of all, all the driver has to do is push the start button! Fuzzy logic was also put to work in elevators to reduce waiting time. Since then, the applications of Fuzzy Logic technology have virtually exploded, affecting things we use everyday. Take for example, the fuzzy washing machine . A load of clothes in it and press start, and the machine begins to churn, automatically choosing the best cycle. The fuzzy microwave, Place chili, potatoes, or etc in a fuzzy microwave and push single button, and it cooks for the right time at the proper temperature. The fuzzy car, manuvers itself by following simple verbal instructions from its driver. It can even stop itself when there is an obstacle immedeately ahead using sensors. But, practically the most exciting thing about it, is the simplicity involved in operating it.

2.11 WHAT DO YOU MEAN FUZZY?

Before illustrating the mechanisms which make fuzzy logic machines work, it is important to realize what fuzzy logic actually is. Fuzzy logic is a superset of conventional(Boolean) logic that has been extended to handle the concept of partial truth- truth values between "completely true" and "completely false". As its name suggests, it is the logic underlying modes of reasoning which are approximate rather than exact. The importance of fuzzy logic derives from the fact that most modes of human reasoning and especially common sense reasoning are approximate in nature.

The essential characteristics of fuzzy logic as founded by Zader Lotfi are as follows:

1. In fuzzy logic, exact reasoning is viewed as a limiting case of approximate reasoning.
2. In fuzzy logic everything is a matter of degree.
3. Any logical system can be fuzzified.
4. In fuzzy logic, knowledge is interpreted as a collection of elastic or, equivalently, fuzzy constraint on a collection of variables.
5. Inference is viewed as a process of propagation of elastic constraints.

2.12 INTELLIGENCE, CONTROL AND INFORMATION (ICI)

Fuzzy logic is a technology for developing intelligent control and information systems. We summarize below three facets of fuzzy logic from the viewpoint of machine intelligence, control systems, and information technology.

Fuzzy logic achieves machine intelligence by offering a way for representing and reasoning about human knowledge that is imprecise by nature. Even though representing and reasoning about human knowledge that is imprecise by nature. Even though fuzzy logic is not the only technique for developing AI systems, it is unique in its approach for explicit representation of the impreciseness in human knowledge and problem solving technique s. this facet of fuzzy logic will be revealed throughout the book. In addition to achieving artificial intelligence, fuzzy logic also benefits from machine learning techniques because they can be used to construct fuzzy systems automatically. Neural networks and genetic algorithms are two machine learning techniques that are particularly useful for this purpose.

Fuzzy logic offers a practical way for designing nonlinear control systems. It achieves nonlinearity through piece-wise linear approximation. The basic building block of a fuzzy logic control system is set of fuzzy if-then rules (i.e., fuzzy rule-based models) that approximate a functional mapping. In fact, fuzzy rule-based models are useful not only for control systems, but also for decision making and pattern recognition. The basics of fuzzy rule-based models will be introduced in next Chapters.

Fuzzy logic is becoming increasingly important in advanced <$no page> information systems. In addition to its potential for developing intelligent software agents, it has been used for storing and retrieving imprecise information from databases and information sources, as well as for extracting interesting patterns from a large amount of data. The latter can be applied to medical image analysis, computer vision, and data mining.

Like facets of a diamond, the three facets of fuzzy logic technology shed light on each other and create brilliant and vivid colors. We hope that the remaining Chapters of this book help you to visualize such an exciting image.

2.13 BASIC CONCEPTS OF FUZZY LOGIC

Even though the broad sense of fuzzy logic introduced in the previous chapter covers a wide range of theories and techniques, its core technique is based on four basic concepts:

1. **Fuzzy sets:** Sets having smooth boundaries;
2. **Linguistic variables:** Variables whose values are both qualitatively and quantitatively described by a fuzzy set;
3. **Possibility distribution:** Constraints on the value of a linguistic variable imposed by assigning it a fuzzy set; and
4. **Fuzzy if-then rules:** A knowledge representation scheme for describing a functional mapping or a logic formula that generalizes an implication in two-valued logic.

The first three concepts are fundamental for all sub areas in fuzzy logic. The fourth concept is also important because it is the basis for most industrial applications of fuzzy logic developed to date, including many fuzzy logic control systems.

2.14 TWO PROBLEMS ARE GIVEN RELATED TO FUZZY LOGIC

Problem 1: Rudimentary Air Flows Mixing Control

The first problem is the control of air flow mixing for room temperature control. It is a "rudimentary" control problem because no feedback about the current room temperature is provided. We choose it for its simplicity and its connection no fuzzy logic control. The given task of this problem is to control the amount of hot air flow and cold air flow based on a set target temperature. In this rudimentary version of the problem, we assume that there is no feedback signal about the current room temperature. The amount of hot air flow and cold air flow is controlled by adjusting the voltage to the pump in the mixing stage. The lowest and highest voltage settings are denoted by $\underline{V}$ and $\overline{V}$. If the voltage is set at $\underline{V}$, maximal cold air flow will be allowed. If the voltage is set at $\overline{V}$, maximal hot air flow will be generated. A voltage between $\underline{V}$ and mixes the hot flow and the cold flow proportionally. This problem is depicted in Figure 2.2.

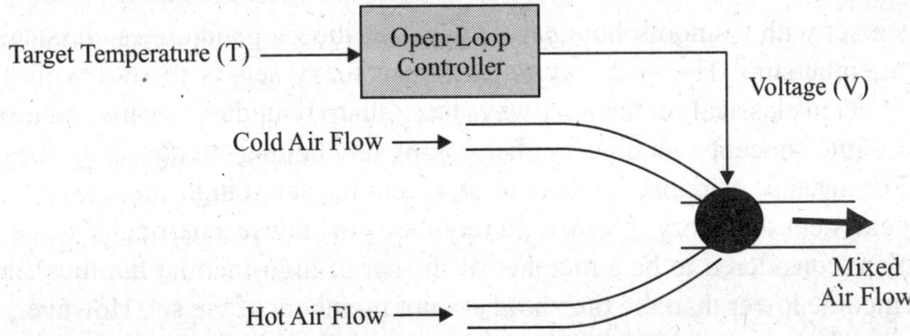

Figure 2.2: Rudimentary Air Flow Mixing Controller.

Problem 2: Automated Washing Machine Control

The second problem is about the automatic selection of cycles and washing time for a washing machine. This problem allows us to illustrate certain fuzzy logic techniques that cannot be demonstrated using the first problem. We chose to use this problem among many candidate applications for two additional reasons. First, the nature of human decision making involved in this problem is easy to understand due to out familiarity with the tasks in our daily lives. Second, a fuzzy logic approach to problem developed by Matsushita Electric Industrial Co. [the automatic washing machine is called "Aisai-go (beloved wife) Day Fuzzy"], as mentioned in previous section, generated a fuzzy vogue in 1990 which triggered the introduction of many other successful consumer products using fuzzy logic. The word "fuzzy" even won the 1990 gold prize for a new word in Japan. This application therefore has an additional historical significance.

The goal of this problem is to simplify the operation of the washing machine while ensuring high-quality results. More specifically, we wish to automate the selection of the wash cycle and wash time based on the quality and the softness of the laundry. To simplify our discussion, we assume that the quantity and the softness of the laundry are provided directly by two sensing techniques. In reality, however, these measures are not measurable directly. They are often inferred from other sensor inputs. Figure 2.3 depicts the problem graphically.

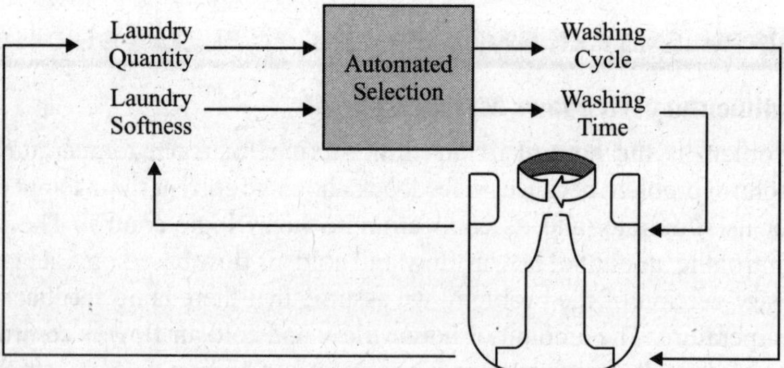

Figure 2.3: Fully automatic washing machine.

2.15 FUZZY SETS

A fuzzy set is a set with a smooth boundary. Fuzzy set theory generalizes classical set theory to allow partial membership. The best way to introduce fuzzy sets is to start with a limitation of classical sets. A set in classical set theory always has a sharp boundary because membership in a set is a black-and-white concept – an object either completely belongs to the set or does not belong to the set at all. For instance, suppose we wish to represent the set of high-income families within the framework of classical set theory. This would require us to choose a particular value as a threshold (say $90,000) are considered to be a member of the set of high-income families, and all families with a yearly income lower than the threshold are not members of the set. However, the fact that a family with a yearly income of $89,999 is not considered high income whereas a family with $1 more yearly income is considered high income is counterintuitive, to say the least. Even through unnatural and sometimes disturbing, such artificially created sharp boundaries have often been used in defining classical sets, primarily due to a lack of a better methodology.

Even through some sets do have sharp boundaries (e.g., the set of married people), many others do not have sharp boundaries (e.g., the set of happily married couples, the set of good graduate schools). Fuzzy set theory directly addresses this limitation by allowing membership in a set to be a matter of degree. The degree of membership in a set is expressed by a number between 0 and 1; 0 means entirely not in the set, 1means completely in the set, and a number in between means partially in the set. This way, a smooth and gradual transition from the regions outside the set can be described. A fuzzy set is thus defined by a function that maps objects in a domain of concern to their membership value in the set. Such a function is called the membership function and is usually denoted by the Greek symbol u for ease of recognition and consistency. For example a more realistic representation of the high-income family can now be expressed by the membership function in Figure 2.4. The membership function of a fuzzy set A is denoted as u_A, and the membership value of x in A is denoted as $u_{A(x)}$. The domain of the membership function, which is the domain of concern from which elements of the set are drawn, is called the universe of discourse. For instance, the universe of discourse of the fuzzy set High Income can be the positive real line [0, ∞).

2.16 DESIGNING MEMBERSHIP FUNCTIONS

A membership function can be designed in three ways:

1. Interview those who are familiar with underlying concept and later adjust it based on a tuning strategy.
2. Construct it automatically from data;
3. Learn it based on feedback from the system performance.

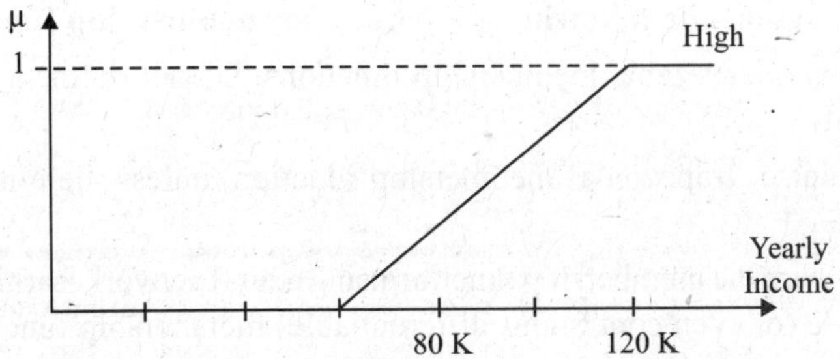

Figure 2.4: Membership function represents the high annual income.

We strongly recommend the use of parameterizable functions that can be defined by a small number of parameters. Using parameterized membership functions cannot only reduce the system design time, it can also facilitate the automated tuning of the system because desired changes to the membership function (e.g., widening vs. narrowing a membership function) can be directly related to corresponding changes in the related parameters.

The parameterizable membership functions most commonly used in practice are the triangular membership function and the trapezoid function. The former has three parameters and the latter has four parameters. An example of these two kinds of membership function and their parameters are shown in Figure 2.5 and 2.6.

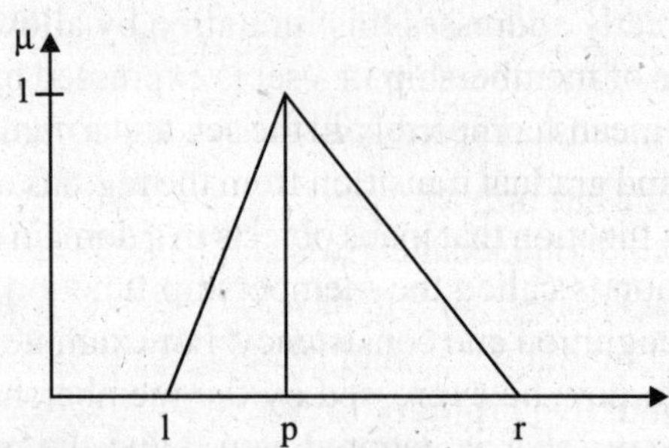

Figure 2.5: A triangular membership function having different parameters.

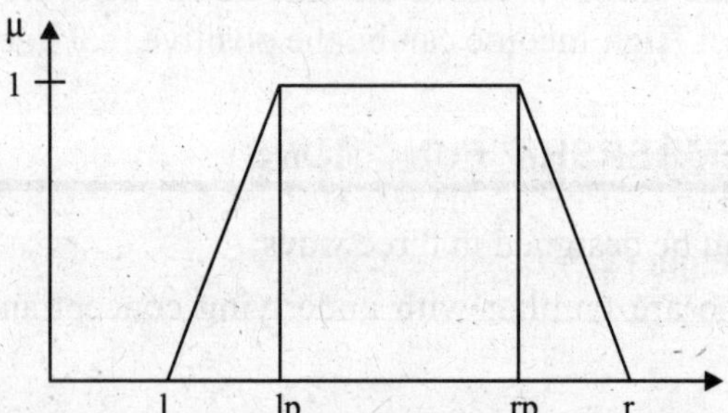

Figure 2.6: A trapezoid membership function having different parameters

To summarize, we present the following guidelines for membership function design:

1. Always use parameterizable membership functions. Do not define a membership function point by point.
2. Use a triangular or trapezoidal membership function, unless there is a good reason to do otherwise.
3. If you want to learn the membership function using neural network learning techniques, choose a differentiable (or even continuous differentiable) membership function (e.g., Gaussian).

2.17 BASIC OPERATIONS IN FUZZY SETS

The three fundamental operations in classical sets are union, intersection, and complement. The union of two sets A and B (denoted $A \cup B$) is the collection of those objects that belong to either A or B. The intersection A and B (denoted $A \cap B$) is the collection of those objects that belong to both A and B. The complement of a set A (denoted as A^c or $\overline{A}$) is the collection of objects not belonging to A. For instance, let A and B be two sets of annual personal income defined as below:

$$A = \{x \mid 100K \le x \le 200K, x \in U\}$$
$$B = \{x \mid 80K \le x \le 140K, x \in U\}$$

where U is the universe of discourse [0, 1000K]. We get

$$A \cap B = \{x \mid 100K \le x \le 140K, x \in U\}$$
$$A \cup B = \{x \mid 80K \le x \le 200K, x \in U\}$$
$$A^C = \{x \mid 0 \le x < 100K \text{ or } 200K \le x \le 1000\text{ K}\}$$

These operations are illustrated in Figure 2.7.

A statement in classical logic has only two possible truth values: T (true) or F (false). Two logic statements can be combined using logic connectives such as AND (conjunction, denoted by $\wedge$), OR (disjunction, denoted by $\vee$), NOT (negation, denoted by $\neg$) and IMPLY (implication, denoted by $\rightarrow$). The truth values of these compound statements are listed in Table 2.1 for all possible cases. We use p and q in the table to denote two arbitrary logic statements (called propositions).

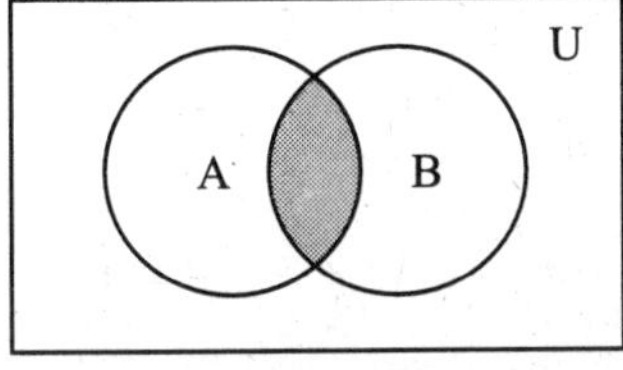

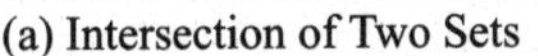

(a) Intersection of Two Sets

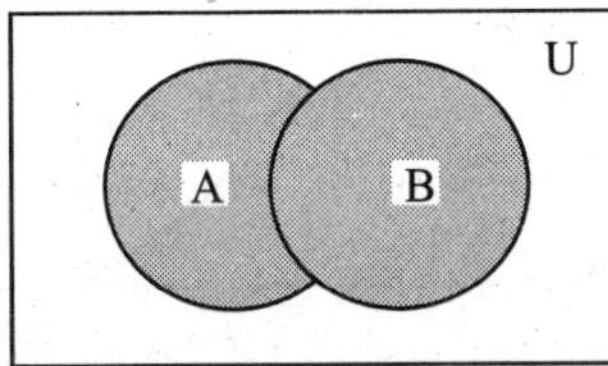

(b) Union of Two Sets

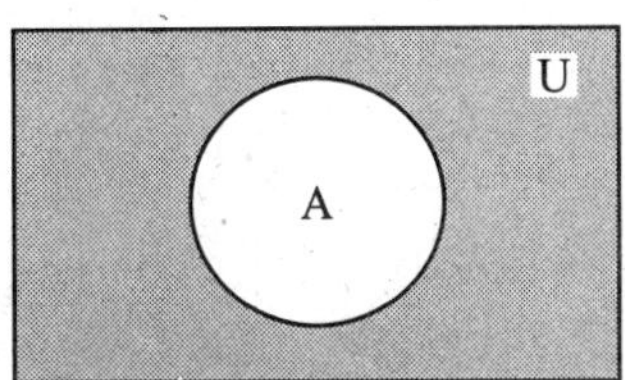

(c) Complement of a Set

Figure 2.7: Basic Set Operations in Fuzzy Logic.

Table 2.1: Truth table of classical logic connectives

p	q	¬p	p∧q	p∨q	p→q
F	F	T	F	F	T
F	T	T	F	T	T
T	F	F	F	T	F
T	T	F	T	T	T

A conjunctive composite statement $p \wedge q$ is true if and only if both p and q are true. A disjunctive composite statement $p \vee q$ is true if and only if either statement is true. A negated statement is true if and only if the original statement is false. We will discuss the implication statement in Section possibility distribution because it is related to fuzzy rules.

Suppose we use the proposition p to represent the sentence "x is in the set A," i.e.,

$$p \text{ is true iff } x \in A$$

and another proposition to represent the sentence "x is in the set B," i.e.,

$$q \text{ is true iff } x \in B$$

where iff stands for "if and only if". It is easy to see that p and q are both true when x is in the intension of A and B, i.e.,

$$(p \wedge q) \text{ is true iff } x \in A \cap B$$

and that p or q is true when x is in the union of A and B, i.e.,

$$(p \vee q) \text{ is true iff } x \in A \cup B$$

Finally, p is false when x is in A's complement, i.e., is true iff

$$\neg p \text{ is true iff } x \in A^C$$

Hence, intersection, union and complement operations in set theory are similar to conjunction, and negation in logic. A common fuzzy disjunction operator is the maximum operator. Hence, fuzzy union is often defined as

$$\mu_{A \cup B}(x) = \max\{\mu_A(x), \mu_B(x)\} \qquad \text{(Eq 2.1)}$$

and is illustrated in Figure 2.8.

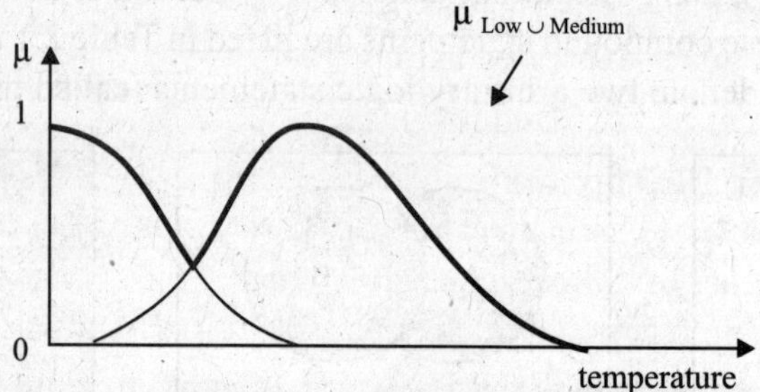

Figure 2.8: Fuzzy Set: Union

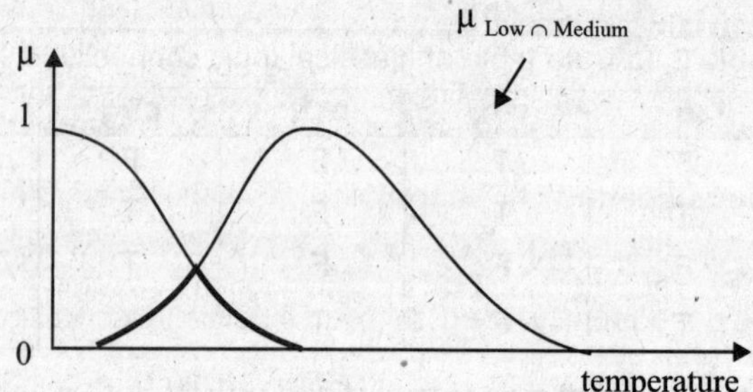

Figure 2.9: Fuzzy Set; Intersection

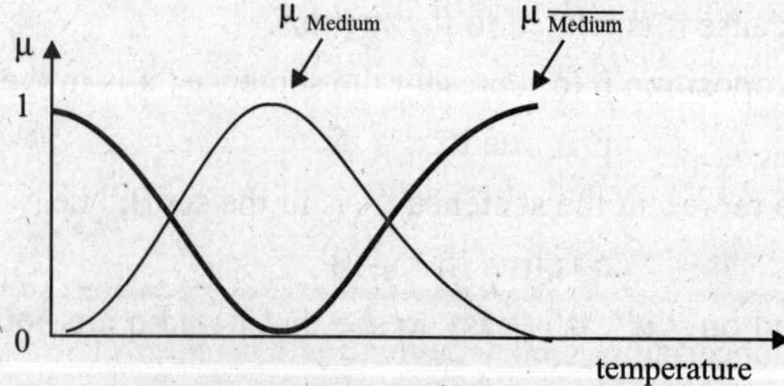

Figure 2.10: Complement of a Fuzzy Set.

A common fuzzy conjunction (AND) operation is the minimum operator. Figure 2.9 shows the result of using min to form the intersection of two fuzzy sets, i.e.,

$$\mu_{A \cap B}(x) = \min \{\mu_A(x), \mu_B(x)\} \qquad \text{(Eq. 2.2)}$$

The complement of a fuzzy set A is defined by the difference between one and the membership degree in A. This is illustrated in Figure 2.10 using the fuzzy set Medium.

$$\mu_{A^c}(x) = 1 - \mu_A(x) \qquad \text{(Eq. 2.3)}$$

2.18 LINGUISTIC VARIABLES

A fuzzy set can be used to describe the value of a variable. For example, the sentence "The amount of trading is heavy" uses a fuzzy set "Heavy" to describe the quantity of the stock market trading in one day. More formally, this is expressed as

Trading Quantity is Heavy

The variable Trading Quantity in this example demonstrates an important concept in fuzzy logic: the linguistic variable. A linguistic variable enables its value to be described both qualitatively by linguistic term (i.e., a symbol serving as the name of a fuzzy set) and quantitatively by a corresponding membership function (which expresses the meaning of the fuzzy set). The linguistic term is used to express concepts and knowledge in human communication, whereas membership function is useful for processing numeric input data.

A linguistic variable is like a composition of a symbolic variable (a variable whose value is a symbol) and a numeric variable (a variable whose value is a number). An example of a symbolic variable is

Shape = Rectangular

where Shape is a variable indicating the shape of an object. An example of numeric variable is

Height = 6'

Numeric variables are frequently used in science, engineering, mathematics, medicine, and many other disciplines.

In our example about stock market trading activities, there are certainly many other linguistic descriptions about the trading quantity such as "light," "moderate," "somewhat heavy," "very heavy," and so on. One of the important concepts in fuzzy logic is that instead of enumerating all these different descriptions, they can be generated from a core set of linguistic terms (called a term set) using modifiers (e.g., "very," "more or less") and connectives (e.g., "and," "or"). In fuzzy logic, we call these modifiers hedges.

2.19 POSSIBILITY THEORY

Possibility theory is an uncertainty theory devoted to the handling of incomplete information. As such, it complements probability theory. It differs from the latter by the use of a pair of dual set-functions (possibility and necessity measures) instead of only one.

A **possibility distribution** is a mapping π from a set of states of affairs S to a totally ordered scale such as the unit interval [0, 1]. The function π represents the knowledge of an agent (about the actual state of affairs) distinguishing what is plausible from what is less plausible, what is the normal course of things from what is not, what is surprising from what is expected. It represents a flexible restriction on what the actual state of affairs is, with the following conventions:

- $\pi(s) = 0$ means that state s is rejected as impossible;
- $\pi(s) = 1$ means that state s is totally possible (= plausible or unsurprizing).

If the state space is exhaustive, at least one of its elements should be the actual world, so that at least one state is totally possible (normalization). Distinct values may simultaneously have a degree of possibility equal to 1.

Assigning a fuzzy set to a linguistic variable contains the value of the variable, just as a crisp set does. The difference between the two, however, is that the notion of possible versus impossible values becomes a matter of degree. We will illustrate this using the following example. Suppose the police report that the suspect of a bombing is a terrorist, between 20 and 30 years old. This can be expressed by assigning the interval [20, 30] to a variable representing the suspect's age:

$$\text{Age(suspect)} = [20, 30].$$

This interval-valued assignment constrains the age of the suspect. More specifically, it states that the suspect's age can be 20, 21,…, 29, or 30. It is, on the other hand, impossible for the suspect to be 19, 31 or any other age not included in the set [20, 30]. Thus, the assignment above introduces a sharp boundary between possible values and impossible values. For situations where such a sharp boundary is undesirable, fuzzy logic offers an appealing alternative – it generalizes the binary distinction between possible vs. impossible to a matter of degree called the possibility. For instance, if we assign the fuzzy set YOUNG, whose membership function is shown in Figure 2.11, to the age of the suspect, we obtain a distribution about the possibility degree of the suspect's age (e.g., the possibility that the suspect is 19 years old is 0.7, while the possibility of 21 through 28 is 1), i.e.,

$$\Pi_{\text{Age(Suspect)}}(x) = \mu_{\text{Young}}(x) \qquad \text{(Eq. 2.4)}$$

where Π denotes a possibility distribution of the suspect's age, and x is a variable representing a person's age. In general, when we assign a fuzzy set A to a variable X, the assignment results in a possibility distribution of X, which is defined by A's membership function:

$$\Pi_x(x) = \mu_A(x) \qquad \text{(Eq. 2.5)}$$

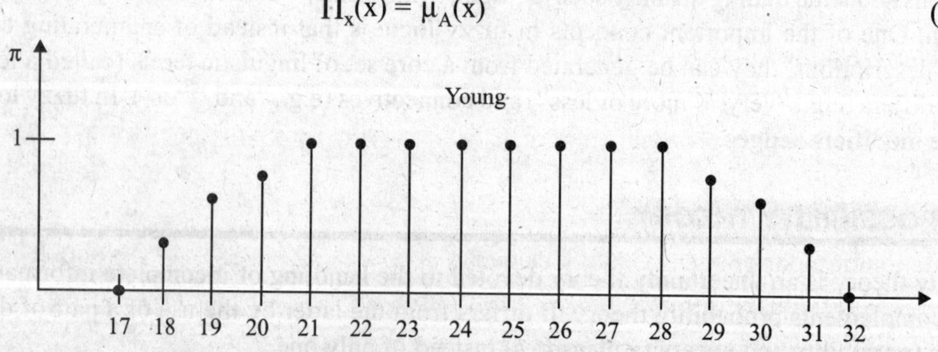

Figure 2.11: Possibility distribution of the fuzzy set (young)

2.20 FUZZY RULES

Fuzzy if-then rules have been applied to many disciplines such as control systems, decision making, pattern recognition, and system modeling. Fuzzy if-then rules also play a critical role in industrial applications ranging from consumer products, robotic, manufacturing, process control, medical imaging, to financial trading.

Let us consider an ancient kingdom in which only seven masters have knowledge about calculating the square root of a real number. Unfortunately, none of them knows a general procedure for calculating the square root of an arbitrary real number. Each one of them, nevertheless, is specialized in solving the problem for a fuzzy region of a real number. For instance, one is an expect for calculating the square root of numbers around 100. One day, the king is challenged to solve a square root square problem by his enemy. He immediately assembles the seven masters in his place. Each master will provide a solution to the king, which is attached with a confidence measure between 0 and 1 (1 means most confident, 0 means no confidence at all). The king will combine all their solutions, each weighted by their confidence measure, into a final solution, which he will present to his enemy. Even though the king and the masters do not know about fuzzy logic, this process turns out to be very close to fuzzy rule-based inference. Each master is like a fuzzy rule; the confidence measure of a master's solution corresponds to the degree a fuzzy rule's condition is satisfied; and the way the masters' recommendations are combined by the king is similar to the way conclusions of multiple fuzzy rules are combined in fuzzy logic.

Mathematically, fuzzy rule-based inference can be viewed as an interpolation scheme because it enables the fusion of multiple fuzzy rules when their conditions are all satisfied to a degree. The degree to which each rule is satisfied determines the weight of the rule's conclusion. Using these weights, fuzzy rule-based inference combines the conclusions of multiple fuzzy rules in a manner similar to linear interpolation. From a logical viewpoint, fuzzy rule-based inference is a generalization of a logical reasoning scheme called modus ponens.

In classical logic, if we know a rule is true and we also know the antecedent of the rule is true, then it can be inferred that the consequent of the rule is true. This is referred to as modus ponens. For example, suppose we know that rule R1 below is true:

R1: IF the annual income of a person of a person is greater that 100,000
THEN the person is rich

we also know that the following statement is true:

Harry annual income is 100,001K

Bases on modus ponens, classical logic can deduce that the following statement is also true;

Harry is rich.

One limitation of modus ponens is that it cannot deal with partial matching. To illustrate this, let us consider rule R1 and a different case:

Robin annual income is $99,999.

People would usually say that Robin is somewhat rich. However modus ponens cannot infer whether Robin is rich or not using rule R1, because Robin annual income does not satisfy the antecedent (i.e., the "IF" part) of R1, even though it is only one dollar short!

The problem has two causes:

1. The antecedent of R1 does not represent a smooth transition into the rich category that is often exhibited in human reasoning.
2. Modus ponens cannot deal with a situation where the antecedent of a rule is partially satisfied.

Viewing such a limitation, fuzzy rule-based inference generalizes modus ponens to allow its inferred conclusion to be modified by the degree to which the antecedent is satisfied. This is the essence of fuzzy rule-based inference.

2.20.1 Structure of Fuzzy Rules

A fuzzy rule is the basic unit for capturing knowledge in many fuzzy systems. A fuzzy rule has two components: an if-part (also referred to as the antecedent) and a then-part (also referred to as the consequent):

IF < antecedent > THEN < consequent >

The antecedent describes a condition, and the consequent describes a conclusion that can be drawn when the condition holds. We introduce the basics of these two components below.

(i) The Antecedent of Fuzzy Rules

For instance, consider the two rules below:

R1: IF the annual income of a person is greater than 120K.

THEN the person is rich.

R2: IF the annual income of a person is high.

THEN the person is Rich.

where High is a fuzzy set defined by the membership function shown in Figure 2.4.

The rule R1 is a conventional one, because its condition is rigid. In contrast, R2 is a fuzzy rule because its condition can be satisfied to a degree for those people whose income lies in the boundary of the fuzzy set High representing high annual income. Like conventional rules, the antecedent of a fuzzy rule may combine multiple simple conditions into a complex one using three logic connectives: AND (conjunction), OR (disjunction), and NOT (negation). For instance, a loan approval system may contain the following fuzzy rule:

IF the annual income of a person is High AND

(the credit report of the person is Fair OR

the person has a Valuable real estate asses) AND

the amount of the loan requested is NOT Jumbo

THEN recommend approving the loan.

(ii) The Consequent of Fuzzy Rules

The consequent of fuzzy rules can be classified into three categories:

1. **Crisp Consequent:** IF....THEN y = a (where a is nonfuzzy numeric value or symbolic value.)
2. **Fuzzy Consequent:** IF.... THEN y is A (where A is a fuzzy set.)
3. **Functional Consequent:** IF x_1 is A_1 AND x_2 is A_2 AND ... x_n is A_n

THEN $$y = a_0 + \sum_{i=1}^{n} a_i \times x_i$$

where $a_0, a_1, \ldots, a_n$ are constants.

Each type of rule consequent has its merit. Generally speaking, fuzzy rules with a crisp consequent can be processed more efficiently. A rule with a fuzzy consequent is easier to understand and more suitable for capturing imprecise human expertise. Finally, rules with a functional consequent can be used to approximate complex nonlinear models using only a small number of rules.

One possible approach to problem 1 in Section 2.14 is to program a rudimentary controlled pump controller to enact the following fuzzy rules:

R1: IF the target temperature T is Low,

THEN set the voltage to $\underline{V}$ (i.e., turn on the cold flow).

R2: IF the target temperature T is High,

THEN set the voltage to $\bar{V}$ (i.e., turn on the hot flow).

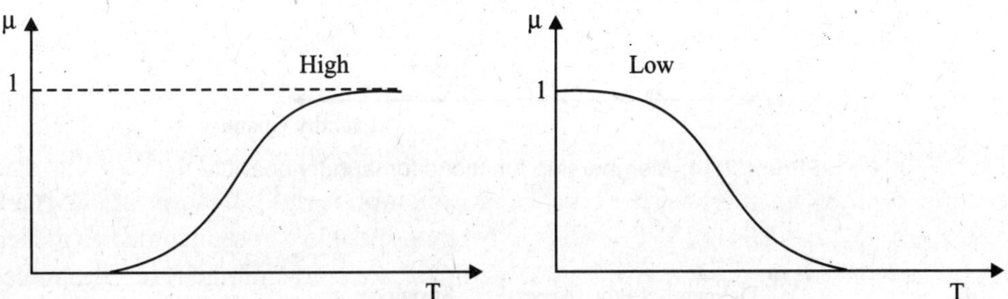

Figure 2.12: Membership functions for target temperature.

For the automatic washing machine problem, rules should combine conditions on laundry quantity and laundry softness using conjunction (AND). Two rules for selecting the wash cycle are listed below:

R1: IF Laundry Quantity is Normal AND

Laundry Softness is Hard

THEN Washing Cycle is Strong

R2: IF Laundry Quantity is Large AND
Laundry Softness is Normal Hard
THEN Washing Cycle is Normal

The membership functions for fuzzy conditions about laundry softness and laundry quantity are depicted in Figure 2.13 and 2.14 respectively. The membership function for fuzzy decisions regarding the wash cycle are shown in Figure 2.15. A complete set of fuzzy rules for the selection of a cycle is shown in Table 2.2.

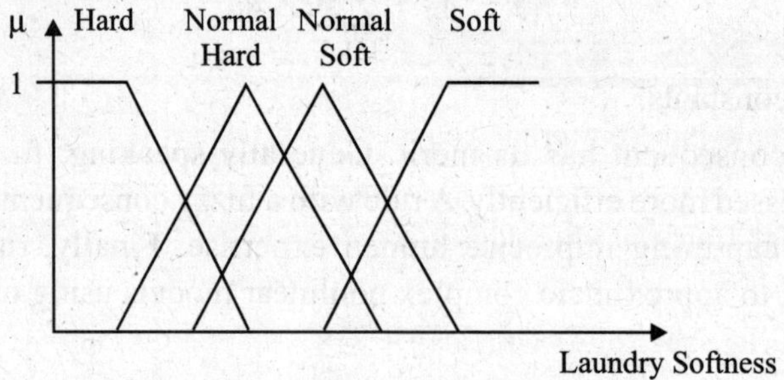

Figure 2.13: Membership functions represents for softness

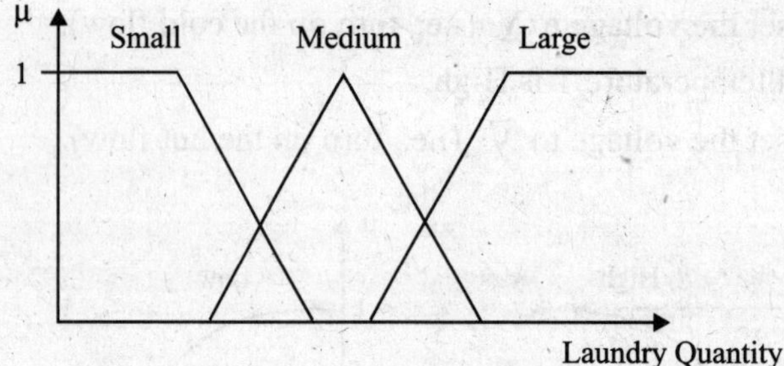

Figure 2.14: Membership functions for laundry quantity

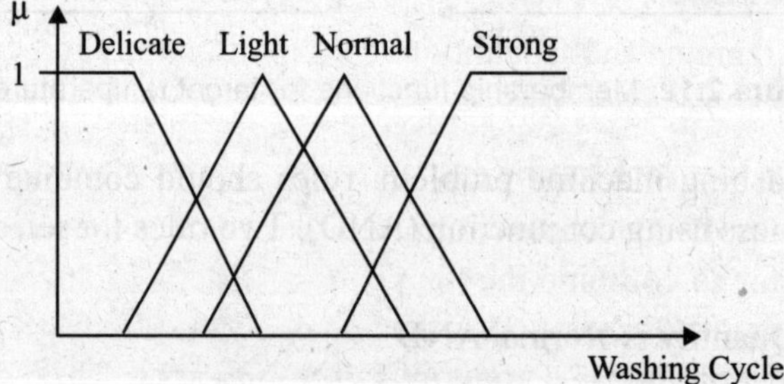

Figure 2.15: Membership functions for washing cycles

Table 2.2: Fuzzy rules for washing cycle			
Laundry Quantity → **Laundry Softness ↓**	**Small**	**Medium**	**Large**
Soft	Delicate	Light	Normal
Normal Soft	Light	Normal	Normal
Normal Hard	Light	Normal	Strong
Hard	Light	Normal	Strong

2.21 FUZZY RULE-BASED INFERENCE

The algorithm of fuzzy rule-based inference consists of three basic steps and an additional optional step.

1. **Fuzzy Matching:** Calculate the degree to which the input data match the condition of the fuzzy rules.
2. **Inference:** Calculate the rule's conclusion based on its matching degree.
3. **Combination:** Combine the conclusion inferred by all fuzzy rules into a final conclusion.
4. **Defuzzification (optional):** For applications that need a crisp output (e.g., in control systems), an additional step is used to convert a fuzzy conclusion into a crisp one.

We will illustrate the basics of these four steps using the flow mixing problem and the automatic washing machine problem.

2.21.1 Fuzzy Matching

Let us first consider fuzzy matching for the flow mixing control rules. The rudimentary flow mixing control is described in Section 2.20.1. The degree to which the input target temperature satisfies the condition of rule R3 "target temperature is Low" is the same as the degree to which the input target temperature T belongs to the fuzzy set Low. For the convenience of our discussion, we denote the degree of matching between input data d and rule r as Matching Degree (d, r). Thus, we summarize the discussion above as

$$\text{Matching Degree(T, R3)} = \mu_{\text{Low}}\ (\text{T})$$

where "=" represents assignment (not equality test). Similarly, we have

$$\text{Matching Degree(T, R4)} = \mu_{\text{High}}\ (\text{T})$$

Figure 2.16 illustrates this step for the case of input target temperature T = 80° F.

When a rule has multiple conditions combined using AND (conjunction), we simply use a fuzzy conjunction operator to combine the matching degree of each condition. One of the most commonly used fuzzy conjunction operators is the min operator. Another fuzzy conjunction operator used for this purpose is the product (i.e., multiplication) operator.

In Figure 2.17, the use of min operator for combining the degree of matching of conjunction conditions for washing cycle selection rules.

For the first rule in the figure the condition "Laundry Quantity is Heavy" matches the sensor input 0.5 degree; and the condition "Laundry Softness" matches the sensor input 0.2 degree. Combining the two matching degrees using min, we obtain 0.2 as the degree to which the input data match the antecedent of the following rule:

IF Laundry Quantity is Heavy AND

Laundry Softness is Hard

THEN ....

Similarly, we can find that the degree the input data match the second rule in figure 2.17 is 0.5.

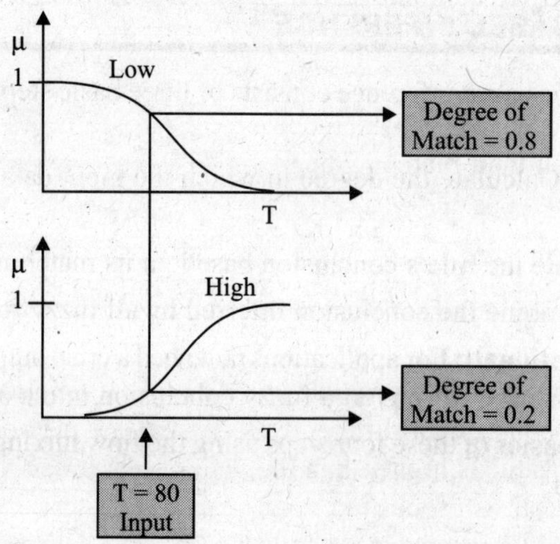

Figure 2.16: Fuzzy Matching for Simple Conditions

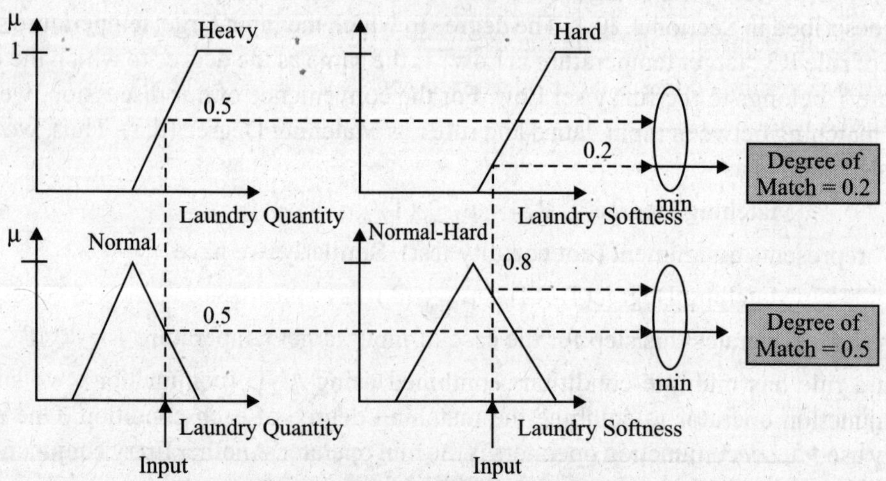

Figure 2.17: Fuzzy Matching for Conjunctive Conditions

In general, the degree to which a rule in the form of

IF X_1 is $A^1_{i_1}$ AND X_2 is $A^2_{i_2}$ AND .... X_n is A^1_{in} THEN.......

matches the input data

$$X_1 = x^0_1, X_2 = x^0_2, \ldots. X_n = x^0_n$$

is computed by the following formula:

$$\text{Matching Degree} = \min\ \{\mu A^1_{i_1}(x^0_1), \mu\ A^2_{i_2}(x^0_2), \ldots.. \mu x^1_{i_n}(x^0_n)\} \qquad \text{(Eq 2.6)}$$

If the antecedent of a rule includes conditions connected by OR (disjunction), we use a fuzzy disjunction operator (e.g., max) to combine matching degree accordingly.

2.21.2 Inference

After the fuzzy matching step, a fuzzy inference step is invoked for each of the relevant rules to produce a conclusion based on their matching degree. How should the conclusion be produced?

There are two methods:

1. The clipping method
2. The scaling method

Both methods generate an inferred conclusion by suppressing the membership function of the consequent.

The clipping and scaling methods produce their inferred conclusion by suppressing the membership function of the consequent differently. The clipping method cuts off the top of the membership function whose value is higher than the matching degree. The scaling method scales down the membership function in proportion to the matching degree. These two methods are illustrated in Figure 2.18 and 2.19 using a hypothetical fuzzy consequent "Y is A." It is easy to see that both methods are consistent with modus ponens in classical logic:

- When the matching degree is (i.e., the antecedent is completely satisfied), the inferred conclusion is identical to the rule's consequent.
- When the matching degree is 0 (i.e., the antecedent is not satisfied at all), no conclusion can be inferred from the rule.

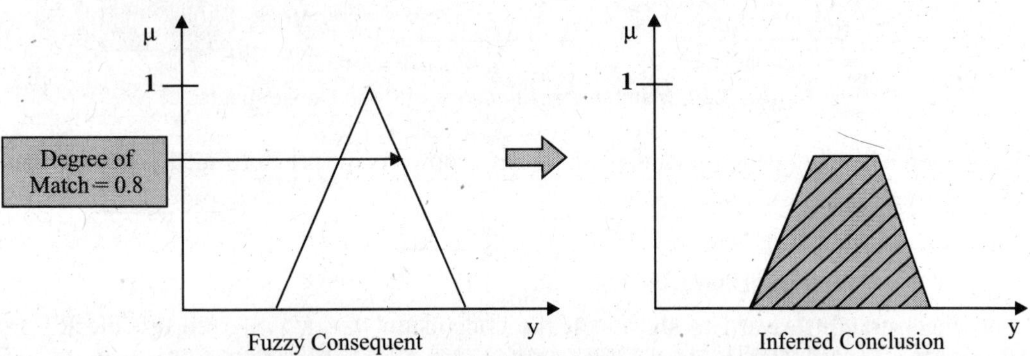

Figure 2.18: Clipping Method for the Fuzzy Inference

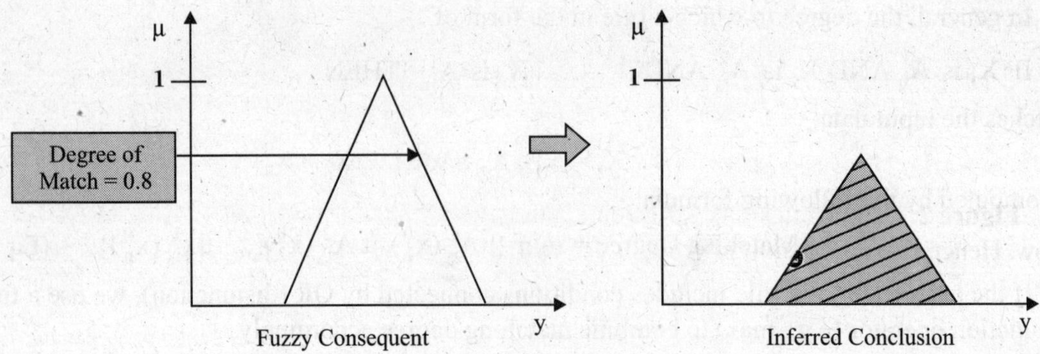

Figure 2.19: Scaling Method for the Fuzzy Inference

In the case of a crisp consequent, the two methods degenerate into an identical one. We will use the air flow mixing control problem to illustrate this. Recall that the rules for this problem are

R3: If T is Low THEN $V = \underline{V}$.

R4: If T is High THEN $V = \overline{V}$.

To apply fuzzy inference to these rules with crisp consequents, we need to first convert them into an equivalent fuzzy set representation. For instance, the crisp value $\underline{V}$ is equivalent to a membership function that assigns value 1 to $\underline{V}$, and 0 to all other values as shown in Figure 2.20(a). Similarly, we can construct the membership function of crisp value $\overline{V}$ as shown in Figure 2.20(b).

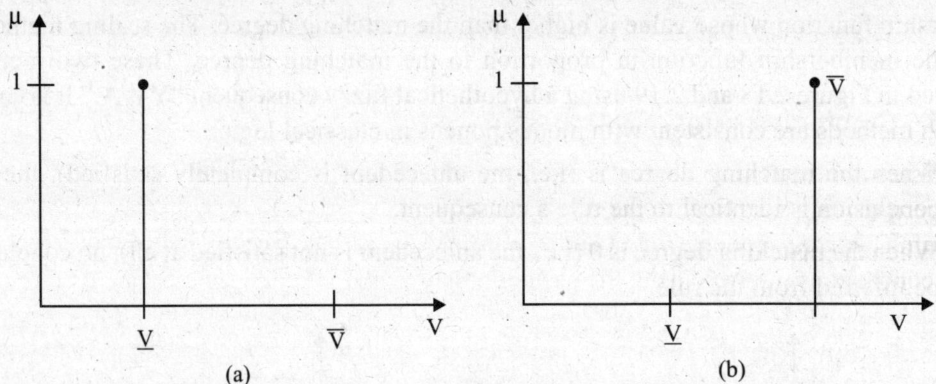

Figure 2.20: Membership Functions of Crisp Consequents

Suppose the input target temperature is T we have shown in the previous section that the matching degrees between T and the two rules are

$$\text{Matching Degree}(T, R3) = \mu_{Low}(T)$$

$$\text{Matching Degree}(T, R4) = \mu_{High}(T)$$

It is then straightforward to show that the conclusion V = V' inferred by rule R3 and the conclusion V = V" inferred by R4 have the following membership function for both the clipping method and the scaling method:

$$\mu_{V'}(V) = \begin{cases} \mu_{Low}(T) & V = \underline{V} \\ 0 & V = \overline{V} \end{cases} \quad \text{(Eq. 2.7)}$$

$$\mu_{V'}(V) = \begin{cases} 0 & V = \underline{V} \\ \mu_{Low}(T) & V = \overline{V} \end{cases} \quad \text{(Eq. 2.8)}$$

Figure 2.21 illustrates this for R3 and a target temperature that is 0.8 degree in the fuzzy set Low. Hence, the conclusion inferred by R3 in this case is

$$\mu_{V'}(V) = \begin{cases} 0.8 & V = \underline{V} \\ 0 & V = \overline{V} \end{cases} \quad \text{(Eq. 2.9)}$$

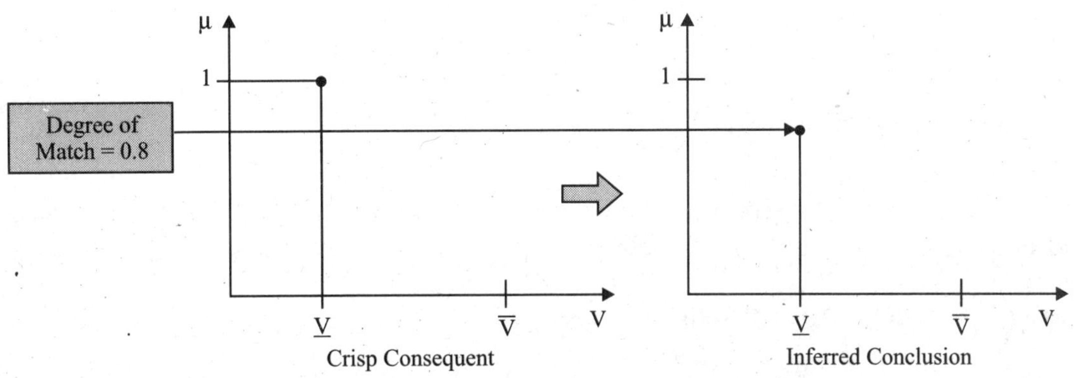

Figure 2.21: A Fuzzy Inference for a Crisp Consequent

2.21.3 Combining Fuzzy Conclusions

A third step is needed to combine the inference results of these rules. This is accomplished typically by superimposing all fuzzy conclusions about a variable. This is illustrated in Figure 2.22 for combining two fuzzy conclusions obtained using the scaling method, and in Figure 2.23 for combining fuzzy conclusions inferred using the clipping method.

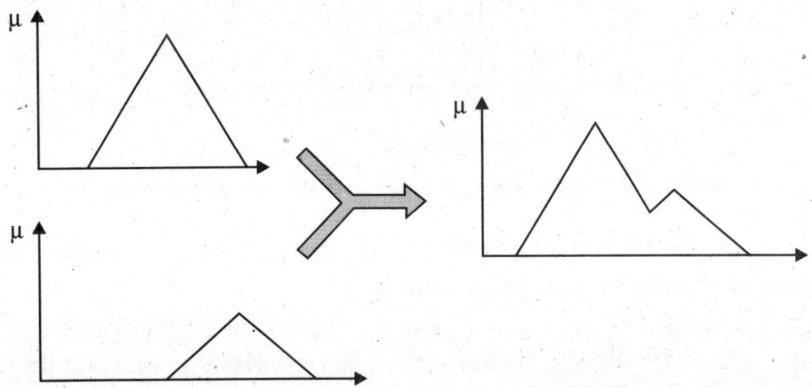

Figure 2.22: Combining Fuzzy Conclusions Inferred by the Scaling Method

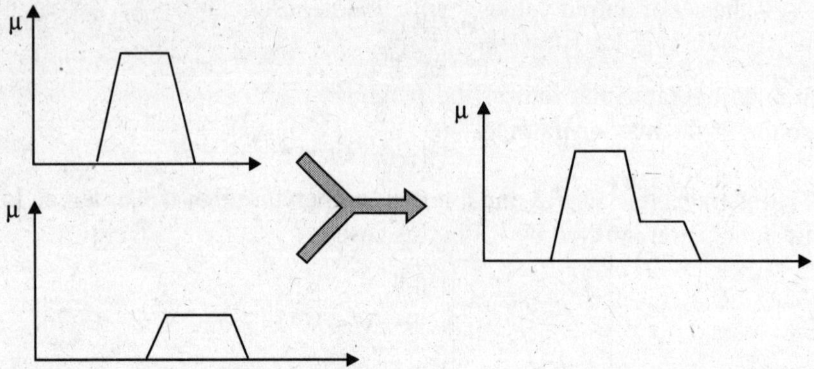

Figure 2.23: Combining Fuzzy Conclusions Inferred by the Clipping Method

2.21.4 Defuzzification

For a fuzzy system whose final output needs to be in a crisp (nonfuzzy) form, a fourth step is needed to convert the final combined fuzzy conclusion into a crisp one. This step is called the defuzzification. A fuzzy rule-based controller, for instance, uses such a step to generate a crisp control command.

There are two major defuzzification techniques:

1. The Mean of Maximum (MOM) method
2. The Center of Area (COA) or the centroid method

The mean of maximum defuzzification calculates the average of all variable values with maximum membership degrees. Figure 2.24 shows the result of applying MOM defuzzification to a combined fuzzy conclusion.

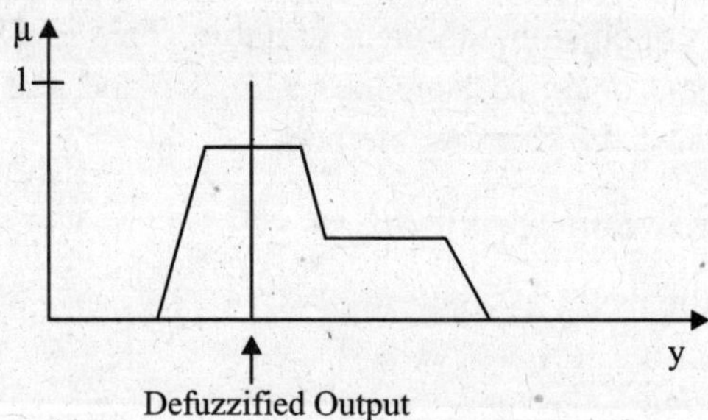

Figure 2.24: An example of mean of maximum defuzzification

Suppose "y is A" is a fuzzy conclusion to be deffuzzified. We can express the MOM defuzzification method using the following formula:

$$\text{MOM}(A) = \frac{\sum_{y^* \varepsilon p} y^*}{|P|} \quad \text{(Eq 2.10)}$$

where P(A) is the set of output values y with the highest membership degree in A, i.e.,

$$P = \{y^* \mid \mu_A(y^*)\ \sup_y \mu_A(y)\} \qquad \text{(Eq 2.11)}$$

where sup is an operator that returns the maximum value of a continuous function (i.e., the continuous version of the max operator).

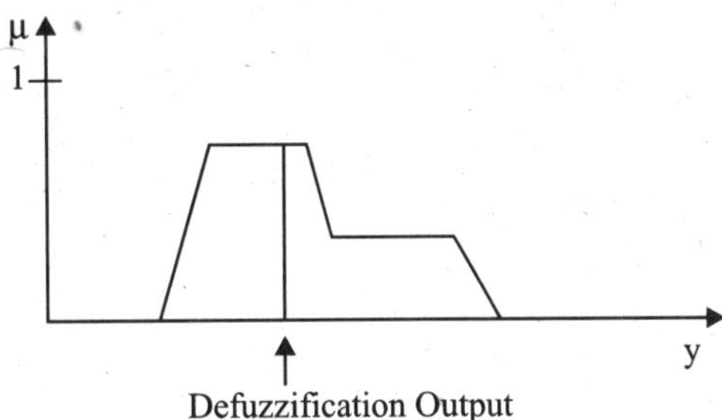

Figure 2.25: An Example of Center of Area Defuzzification

The centroid (or COA) defuzzification method calculates the weighted average of a fuzzy set. The result of applying COA defuzzification to a fuzzy conclusion "Y is A" can be expressed by the formula

$$y = \frac{\sum_i \mu_A(y_i) \times y_i}{\sum_i \mu_A(y_i)} \qquad \text{(Eq 2.12)}$$

if y discrete, and by the formula

$$y = \frac{\int \mu_A(y_i) \times y_i dy}{\int \mu_A(y_i) dy} \qquad \text{(Eq. 2.13)}$$

if y is continuous.

2.21.5 Putting All Four Steps Together

Figure 2.26 and 2.27 show the result of combining all four steps for the flow mixing controller and the automatic washing machine, respectively. The clipping inference method and the centroid defuzzification technique are used in these two examples.

The defuzzified output for the flow mixing controller can be expressed as a function of the input target temperature using the formula below:

$$V = \frac{\mu_{LOW}(T) \text{ x } \underline{V} + \mu_{HIGH}(T) \text{ x } \overline{V}}{\mu_{LOW}(T) + \mu_{HIGH}(T)} \qquad \text{(Eq. 2.14)}$$

This formula clearly shows that fuzzy rule-based inference indeed performs a kind of interpolation, as we explain in earlier sections.

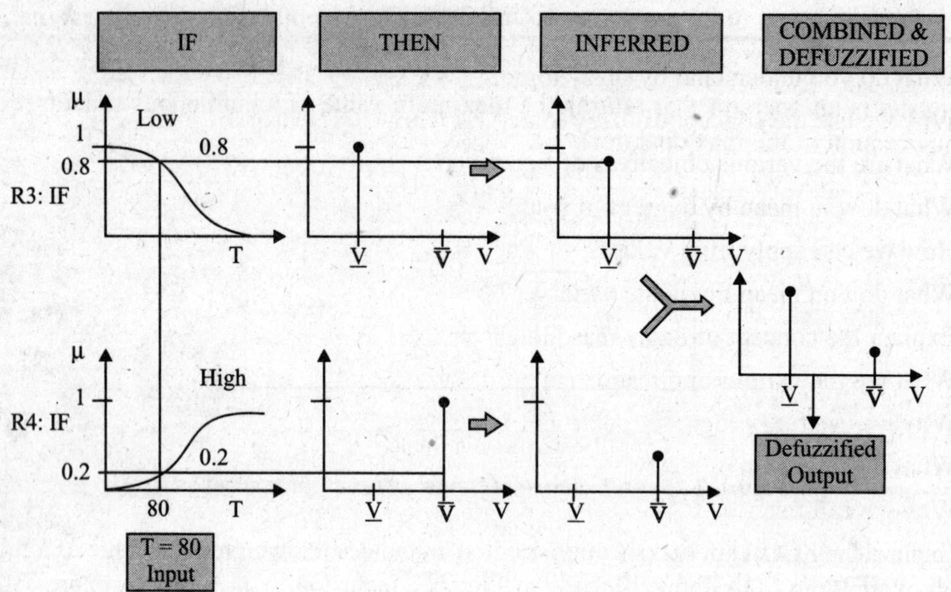

Figure 2.26: Fuzzy Rule-based Inference Rudimentary Flow Mixing Controller

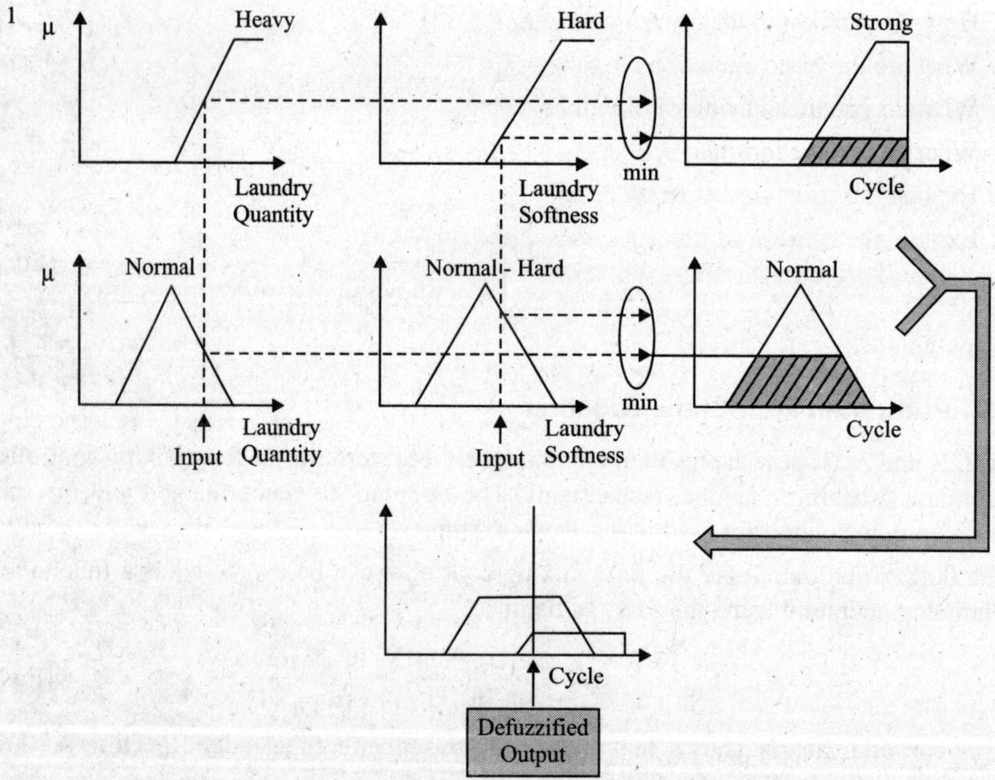

Figure 2.27: Fuzzy Inference of Fuzzy Logic Automatic Washing Machine

EXERCISES

1. What do you understand by fuzzy logic?
2. Why we use the concept of fuzzy logic? Explain with the help of example?
3. What are the various objectives of fuzzy logic?
4. What do you mean by degrees of truth?
5. How we can apply truth values?
6. What do you mean linguistic variables?
7. Explain the concept of fuzzy reasoning?
8. What are the various applications areas of fuzzy logic?
9. Why we use fuzzy logic for control?
10. What do you mean by fuzzy?
11. Why we call fuzzy as ICI?
12. Explain the basic concepts of fuzzy logic with the help of examples?
13. What do you mean by fuzzy sets?
14. Difference between sharp boundaries and smooth boundaries?
15. How we can design membership function?
16. What are the basic operations in fuzzy sets?
17. What do you mean by possibility theory?
18. What do you mean by fuzzy rules?
19. Explain the structures of fuzzy rules?
20. Explain the concept of fuzzy rule based inference?

CHAPTER 3

Classical Sets and Fuzzy Sets

3.1 INTRODUCTION

The theory on classical sets and the basic ideas of the fuzzy sets are discussed in detail in this chapter. The various operations, laws and properties of fuzzy sets are introduced along with that of the classical sets. The classical set we are going to deal is defined by means of the definite or crisp boundaries. This means that there is no uncertainty involved in the location of the boundaries for these sets. But whereas the fuzzy set, on the other hand is defined by its vague and ambiguous properties, hence the boundaries are specified ambiguously. The crisp sets are sets without ambiguity in their membership. The fuzzy set theory is a very efficient theory in dealing with the concepts of ambiguity. The fuzzy sets are dealt after reviewing the concepts of the classical or crisp sets.

The universe of discourse is the universe of all available information on a given problem. Once this universe is defined we are able to define certain events on this information space. We will describe sets as mathematical abstractions of these events and of the universe itself. Figure 3.1 a shows an abstraction of a universe of discourse, say X, and a crisp (classical) set A somewhere in this universe. A classical set is defined by crisp boundaries, i.e., there is no uncertainty in the prescription or location of the boundaries of the set, as shown in Figure 3.1a where the boundary of crisp set A is an unambiguous line. A fuzzy set, on the other hand, is prescribed by vague or ambiguous properties; hence its boundaries are ambiguously specified, as shown by the fuzzy boundary for set $\underset{\sim}{A}$ in Figure 3.1b.

We introduced the notion of set membership, from a one-dimensional viewpoint. Figure 3.1 again helps to explain this idea, but from a two-dimensional perspective. Point a in Figure 3.1a is clearly a member of crisp set A; point b is unambiguously not a member of set A. Figure 3.1b shows the vague, ambiguous boundary of a fuzzy set on the same universe X: the shaded boundary represents the boundary region of $\underset{\sim}{A}$. In the central (unshaded) region of the fuzzy set, point a is clearly a full member of the set.

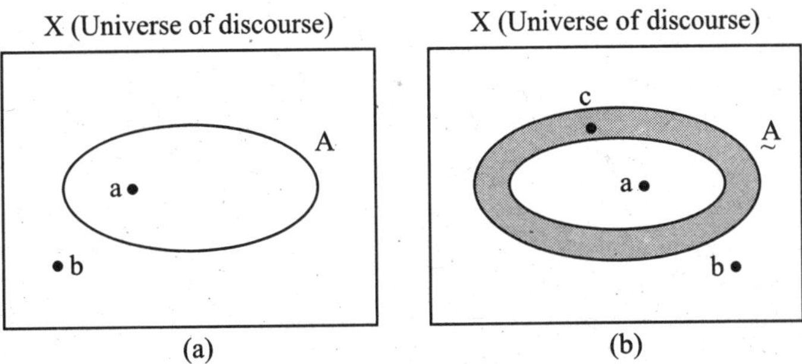

Figure: 3.1 Diagrams for (a) crisp set boundary and (b) fuzzy set boundary.

Outside the boundary region of the fuzzy set, point b is clearly not a member of the fuzzy set. However, the membership of point c, which is on the boundary region, is ambiguous. If complete membership in a set (such as point a in Figure 3.1b) is represented by the number 1, and no-membership in a set (such as point b in Figure 3.1b) is represented by 0, then point c in Figure 3.1b must have some intermediate value of membership (partial membership in fuzzy set $\underset{\sim}{A}$) on the interval [0, 1]. Presumably the membership of point c in $\underset{\sim}{A}$ approaches a value of 1 as it moves closer to the central (unshaded) region in Figure 3.1b of $\underset{\sim}{A}$, and the membership of point c in $\underset{\sim}{A}$ approaches a value of 0 as it moves closer to leaving the boundary region of $\underset{\sim}{A}$.

It will be shown that fuzzy set theory is a mathematically rigorous and comprehensive set theory useful in characterizing concepts (sets) with natural ambiguity. It is instructive to introduce fuzzy sets by first reviewing the elements of classical (crisp) set theory.

3.2 SET THEORY

The problem of capturing the vagueness present in the real world is difficult to overcome using classical set theory alone. As a result several extensions to set theory have been proposed that deal with different aspects of uncertainty. Some of the most popular methods for this are fuzzy set theory, rough set theory, and their hybridization, fuzzy-rough set theory. This chapter starts with a quick introduction to classical set theory, using a simple example to illustrate the concept. Then an introduction to fuzzy sets is given, covering the essentials required for a basic understanding of their use. There are many useful introductory resources regarding fuzzy set theory, for example. Following this, rough set theory is introduced with an example dataset to illustrate the fundamental concepts. Finally, fuzzy-rough set theory is detailed.

3.3 CLASSICAL SETS

A classical set is a collection of objects in a given domain. An object either belongs to the set or does not belong to the set. Therefore, these is a sharp boundary between members of the set and those not in the set. The difficulty in expressing sets with smooth boundaries motivated the development of fuzzy sets.

A set may defined in two ways: (1) by enumerating its elements, or (2) by describing the common properties of its elements. The former is called an extensional definition and the latter, an intentional definition. An intentional definition is usually preferred to an extensional definition for three major reasons. First, an intentional. Definition of a set is usually more concise than the set's extensional definition. In fact, enumerating all elements of a set is sometimes impossible (e.g., the set of real numbers between 1 and 10 has an infinite number of elements). Second, an intentional definition explicitly expresses the meaning of a set, Third, an in tensional definition can be used to recognize new elements of a set when the properties of the element change or when the definition properties change.

Suppose we wish to represent the set of universities in Texas whose total student population is greater than 40,000. Let the universe of discourse U be the set of universities in the United States. The extensional definition would list to such universities: Universities of Texas at Austin (UTA), and Texas A&M Universities (TAMU).

$$A = (UTA, TAMU)$$

An intensional definition of the set is given below for comparison.

$$A = \{u \mid \text{total-student-population}(u) > 40{,}000 \text{ AND state}(u) = \text{Texas}\}$$

Membership of an element in a set is denoted by the symbol $\in$. For instance, the fact that Texas A&M Universities is a member of set a can be expressed as

$$TAMU \in A$$

In contrast, the nonmembership relation is denoted by $\notin$. For instance, Rice $\notin$ A because the student population of Rice University is less than 40,000.

A set S_1, is a subset of set is a subset of set S_2, denoted as $S_1 \subset S_2$ if every element of S_1 is also an element S_2. For instance, let us define a set B to be the set of public universities in Texas. Since both UTA and TAMU are public universities in Texas, set A is a subset of B, i.e., $A \subset B$. The inverse of the subset relation is a superset, also referred to as inclusion. The set B defined earlier includes (is a superset of) the set A, denoted as $B \supset A$. A set without any elements is an empty set, denoted by the symbol ϕ. The empty set is a subset of any set.

The cardinality of a set, denoted as [S], is the number of elements in the set. For instance, the set of Texas universities having at least 40,000 students has exactly two elements. Therefore, its cardinality is 2, i.e., $|A| = 2$.

3.3.1 Classical Set Theory

In classical set theory, elements can belong to a set or not at all. For example, in the set of old people, defined here as {Rod, Jane, Freddy}, the element Rod belongs to this set whereas the element George does not. No distinction is made within a set between elements; all set members belong fully. This may be considered to be a source of information loss for certain applications. Returning to the example, Rod may be older than Freddy, but by this formulation both are considered to be equally old. The order of elements within a set is not considered. More formally, let U be a space of objects, referred to as the universe of discourse, and x an element of U. A classical (crisp) set A, $A \subseteq U$, is defined as a collection of elements $x \in U$, such that each element x can belong to the set or not belong. A classical set A can be represented by a set of ordered pairs (x, 0) or (x, 1) for each element, indicating $x \notin A$ or $x \in A$, respectively. Two sets A and B are said to be equal if they contain exactly the same elements; every element of A is an element of B and every element of B is an element of A. The cardinality of a set A is a measure of the number of elements of the set, and is often denoted |A|. For example, the set {Rod, Jane, Freddy} has a cardinality of 3 (|{Rod, Jane, Freddy}| = 3). A set with no members is called the empty set, usually denoted " and has a cardinality of zero.

Define a universe of discourse, X, as a collection of objects all having the same characteristics. The individual elements in the universe X will be denoted as x. The features of the elements in X can be discrete, countable integers or continuous valued quantities on the real line.

Examples of elements of various universes might be as follows:

The clock speeds of computer CPUs

The operating currents of an electronic motor

The operating temperature of a heat pump (in degrees Celsius)

The Richter magnitudes of an earthquake

The integers 1 to 10

Most real-world engineering processes contain elements that are real and non-negative. The first four items just named are examples of such elements. However, for purposes of modeling, most engineering problems are simplified to consider only integer values of the elements in a universe of discourse. So, for example, computer clock speeds might be measured in integer values of megahertz and heat pump temperatures might be measured in integer values of degrees Celsius. Further, most engineering processes are simplified to consider only finite-sized universes. Although Richter magnitudes may not have a theoretical limit, we have not historically measured earthquake magnitudes much above 9; this value might be the upper bound in a structural engineering design problem. As another example, suppose you are interested in the stress under one leg of the chair in which you are sitting. You might argue that it is possible to get an infinite stress on one leg of the chair by sitting in the chair in such a manner that only one leg is supporting you and by letting the area of the tip of that leg approach zero.

Although this is theoretically possible, in reality the chair leg will either buckle elastically as the tip area becomes very small or yield plastically and fail because materials that have infinite strength have not yet been developed. Hence, choosing a universe that is discrete and finite or one that is continuous and infinite is a modeling choice; the choice does not alter the characterization of sets defined on the universe. If elements of a universe are continuous, then sets defined on the universe will be composed of continuous elements. For example, if the universe of discourse is defined as all Richter magnitudes up to a value of 9, then we can define a set of "destructive magnitudes," which might be composed (1) of all magnitudes greater than or equal to a value of 6 in the crisp case or (2) of all magnitudes "approximately 6 and higher" in the fuzzy case.

A useful attribute of sets and the universes on which they are defined is a metric known as the cardinality, or the cardinal number. The total number of elements in a universe X is called its cardinal number, denoted n_x, where x again is a label for individual elements in the universe. Discrete universes that are composed of a countably finite collection of elements will have a finite cardinal number; continuous universes comprised of an infinite collection of elements will have an infinite cardinality. Collections of elements within a universe are called sets, and collections of elements within sets are called subsets. Sets and subsets are terms that are often used synonymously, since any set is also a subset of the universal set X. The collection of all possible sets in the universe is called the whole set. For crisp sets A and B consisting of collections of some elements in X, the following notation is defined:

$X \in X \Rightarrow$ x belongs to X
$X \in A \Rightarrow$ x belongs to A
$X \notin A \Rightarrow$ x does not belong to the A

For sets A and B on X, we also have

$A \subset B \Rightarrow$ A is fully contained in B(if $x \in A$, then $x \in B$)
$A \subseteq B \Rightarrow$ A is contained in or is equivalent to B
$A \leftrightarrow B \Rightarrow A \subseteq B$ and $B \subseteq A$ (A is equivalent to B)

We define the null set, ∅, as the set containing no elements, and the whole set, X, as the set of all elements in the universe. The null set is analogous to an impossible event, and the whole set is analogous to a certain event. All possible sets of X constitute a special set called the power set, P(X). For a specific universe X, the power set P(X) is enumerated in the following example.

Example 3.1: We have a universe comprised of three elements, X = {a, b, c}, so the cardinal number is $n_x = 3$. The power set is

$$P(X) = \{\varnothing, \{a\}, \{b\}, \{c\}, \{a, b\}, \{a, c\}, \{b, c\}, \{a, b, c\}\}$$

The cardinality of the power set, denoted $n_{P(x)}$, is found as $n_{P(x)} = 2^n x = 2^3 = 8$

Note that if the cardinality of the universe is infinite, then the cardinality of the power set is also infinity, i.e., $n_X = \infty \Rightarrow n_{P(X)} = \infty$

Example 3.2: Let universe comprised of four elements X = {1, 2, 3, 4} find cardinal number, power set, and cardinality of the power set.

Solution: The cardinal number is the number of elements in the defined set.

The defined set X consists of four elements 1, 2, 3, and 4. Therefore, the Cardinal number = $\eta_x = 4$. The power set consists of all possible sets of X. It is given by,

Power set P(x) = {∅, {1}, {2}, {3}, {4}, {1, 2}, {1, 3}, {1, 4}, {2, 3}, {2, 4}, {3, 4}, {1, 2, 3}, {2, 3, 4}, {1, 3, 4}, {1, 2, 4}, {1, 2, 3, 4}} Cardinality of the power set is given by, $n_{P(x)} = 2^n x = 2^4 = 16$

3.4 OPERATIONS ON CLASSICAL SETS

There are various operations that can be performed in the classical or crisp sets. The results of the operation performed on the classical sets will be definite. The operations that can be performed on the classical sets are dealt in detail below:

Let A and B be two sets on the universe X. The union between the two sets, denoted A U B, represents all those elements in the universe that reside in (or belong to) the set A, the set B, or both sets A and B. (This operation is also called the logical or; another form of the union is the exclusive or operation. The exclusive or will be described in the next sections.) The intersection of the two sets, denoted $A \cap B$, represents all those elements in the universe X that simultaneously reside in (or belong to) both sets A and B. The complement of a set A, denoted $\bar{A}$, is defined as the collection of all elements in the universe that do not reside in the set A. The difference of a set A with respect to B, denoted A | B, is defined as the collection of all elements in the universe that reside in A and that do not reside in B simultaneously. These operations are shown below in set-theoretic terms.

Union $A \cup B = \{x |\ x \in \text{ or } x \in B\}$

Intersection $A \cap B = \{x |\ x \in A \text{ and } x \in B\}$

Complement $\bar{A} = \{x |\ x \notin A, x \in X\}$

Difference $A | B = \{x |\ x \in A \text{ and } x \notin B\}$

These four operations are shown in terms of Venn diagrams in Figures 3.2–3.5.

3.4.1 UNION

The Union of two classical sets A and B is denoted by AUB. It represents all the elements in the universe that reside in either the set A, the set B or both sets A and B. This operation is called the logical OR. In set theoretic form it is represented as

$$A \cup B = \{x/x \in A \text{ or } x \in B\}.$$

In Venn diagram form it can be represented as shown in Figure 3.2.

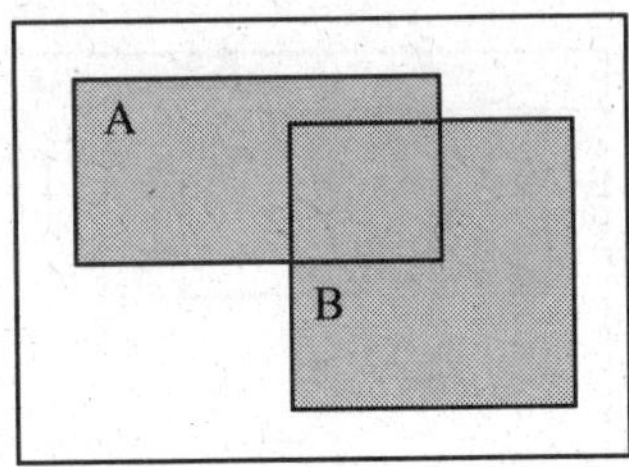

Figure 3.2: Union of Sets A and B (logical or).

3.4.2 Intersection

The intersection of two sets A and B is denoted $A \cap B$. It represents all those elements in the universe X that simultaneously reside in (or belongs to) both sets A and B. In set theoretic form it is represented as $A \cap B = \{x/x \in A \text{ and } x \in B\}$.

In Venn diagram form it can be represented as shown in Figure 3.13.

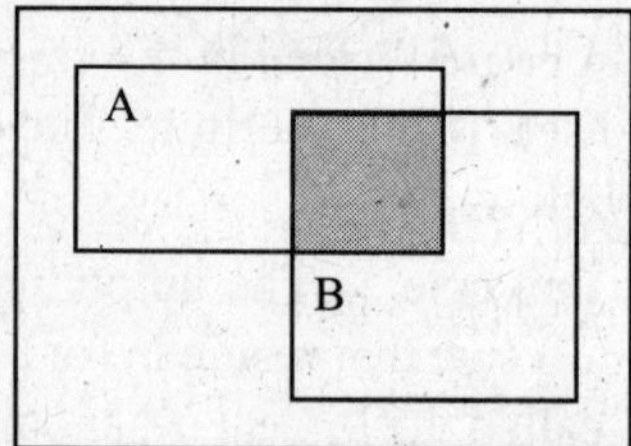

Figure 3.3: Intersection of Sets A and B.

3.4.3 Complement

The complement of set A denoted $\bar{A}$, is defined as the collection of all elements in the universe that do not reside in the set A. In set theoretic form it is represented as $\bar{A} = \{x/x / \in A, x \in X\}$ .In Venn diagram form it is represented as shown in Figure 3.4.

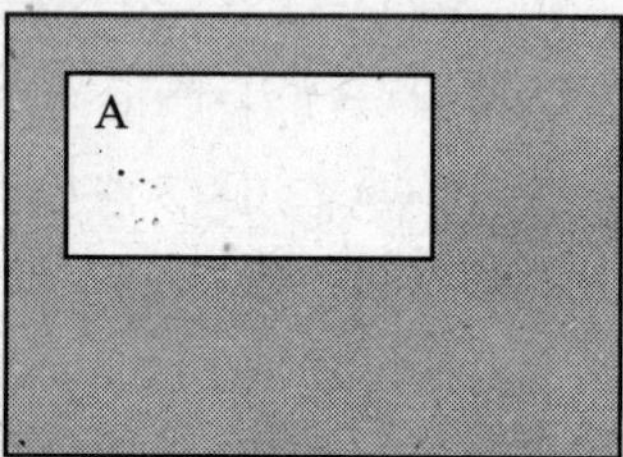

Figure 3.4: Complement of Set A.

3.4.4 Difference

The difference of a set A with respect to B, denoted A|B is defined as collection of all elements in the universe that reside in A and that do not reside in B simultaneously. In set theoretic form it is represented as $A|B = \{x/x \in A \text{ and } x \in B\}$.

In Venn diagram form it is represented as shown in Figure 3.5.

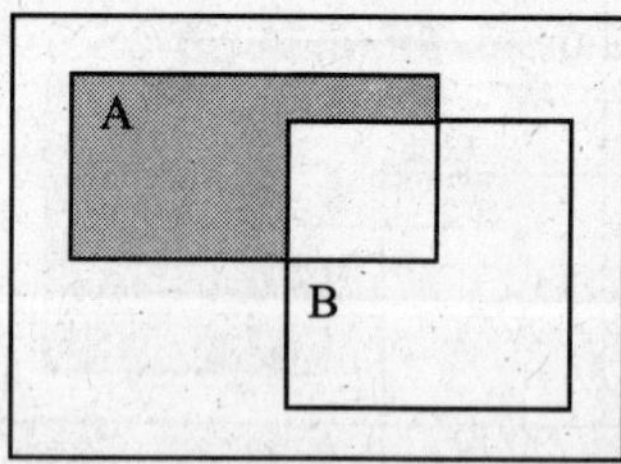

Figure 3.5: Difference operation A | B.

3.4.5 Properties of Classical (Crisp) Sets

In any mathematical operations the properties plays a major role. Based upon the properties, the solution can be obtained for the problems. The following are the important properties of classical sets:

Commutativity	$A \cup B = B \cup A$
	$A \cap B = B \cap A$
Associativity	$A \cup (B \cup C) = (A \cup B) \cup C$
	$A \cap (B \cap C) = (A \cap B) \cap C$
Distributivity	$A \cup (B \cap C) = (A \cup B) \cap (A \cup C)$
	$A \cap (B \cup C) = (A \cap B) \cup (A \cap C)$
Idempotency	$A \cup A = A$
	$A \cap A = A$
	$A \cup \phi = A$
	$A \cap X = A$
	$A \cap \phi = \phi$
	$A \cup X = X$
Transitivity	If $A \subseteq B$ and $B \subseteq C$, then $A \subseteq C$
Involution	$\overline{\overline{A}} = A$

The double-cross-hatched area in Figure 3.6 is a Venn diagram example of the associativity property for intersection, and the double-cross-hatched areas in Figures 3.7 and 3.8

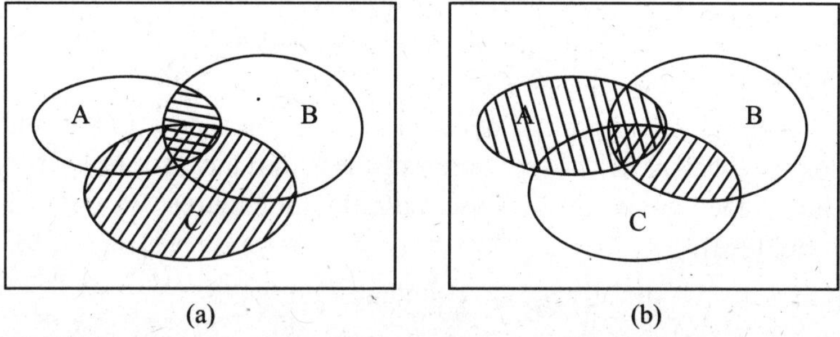

Figure 3.6: Venn Diagrams for (a) (A ∩B) ∩ C and (b) A ∩ (B ∩C).

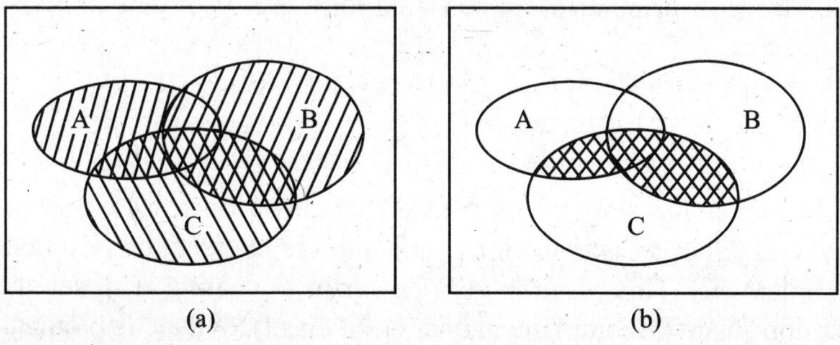

Figure 3.7: Venn diagrams for (a) (A ∪ B)) ∩C and (b) (A ∩C) ∪ (B ∩C).

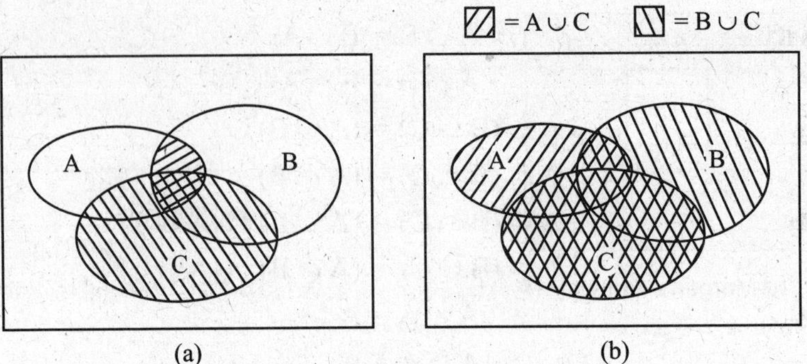

Figure 3.8: Venn Diagrams for (a) $(A \cap B) \cup C$ and (b) $(A \cup C) \cap (B \cup C)$.

are Venn diagram examples of the distributivity property for various combinations of the intersection and union properties. Two special properties of set operations are known as the excluded middle axioms and De Morgan's principles. These properties are enumerated here for two sets A and B. The excluded middle axioms are very important because these are the only set operations described here that is not valid for both classical sets and fuzzy sets. There are two excluded middle axioms (given in Eqs. (3.1)). The first, called the axiom of the excluded middle, deals with the union of a set A and its complement; the second, called the axiom of contradiction, represents the intersection of a set A and its complement.

Axiom of the excluded middle $\quad A \cup \bar{A} = X \quad$ (3.1a)

Axiom of the contradiction $\quad A \cap \bar{A} = \phi \quad$ (3.1b)

De Morgan's principles are important because of their usefulness in proving tautologies and contradictions in logic, as well as in a host of other set operations and proofs. De Morgan's principles are displayed in the shaded areas of the Venn diagrams in Figures 3.9 and 3.10 and described mathematically in Eq. (3.2).

$$\overline{A \cap B} = \bar{A} \cup \bar{B} \tag{3.2a}$$

$$\overline{A \cup B} = \bar{A} \cap \bar{B} \tag{3.2b}$$

In general, De Morgan's principles can be stated for n sets, as provided here for events, E_i:

$$\overline{E_1 \cup E_2 \cup \ldots\ldots \cup E_n} = \bar{E}_1 \cap \bar{E}_2 \cap \ldots\ldots \cap \bar{E}_n \tag{3.3a}$$

$$\overline{E_1 \cap E_2 \cap \ldots\ldots \cap E_n} = \bar{E}_1 \cup \bar{E}_2 \cup \ldots\ldots \cup \bar{E}_n \tag{3.3b}$$

From the general equations, Eqs. (3.3), for De Morgan's principles we get a duality relation: the complement of a union or an intersection is equal to the intersection or union, respectively, of the respective complements. This result is very powerful in dealing with set structures since we often have information about the complement of a set (or event), or the complement of combinations of sets (or events), rather than information about the sets themselves.

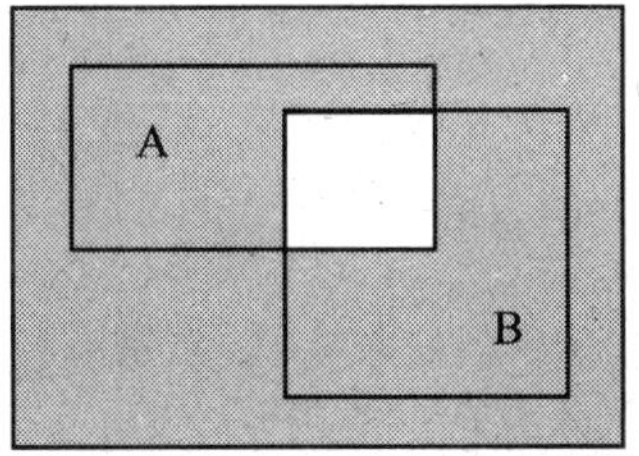

Figure 3.9: De Morgan's Principle $(\overline{A \cap B})$.

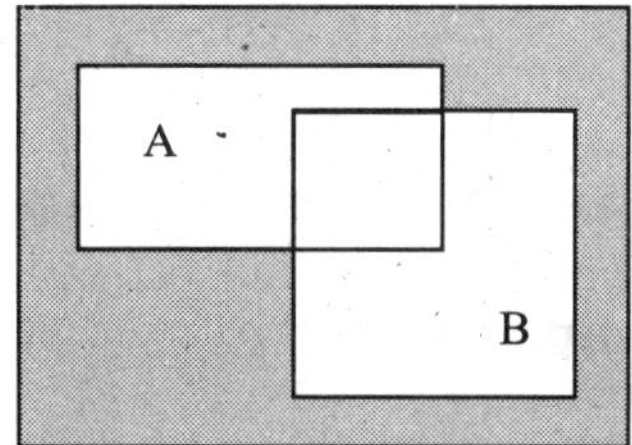

Figure 3.10: De Morgan's Principle $(\overline{A \cup B})$.

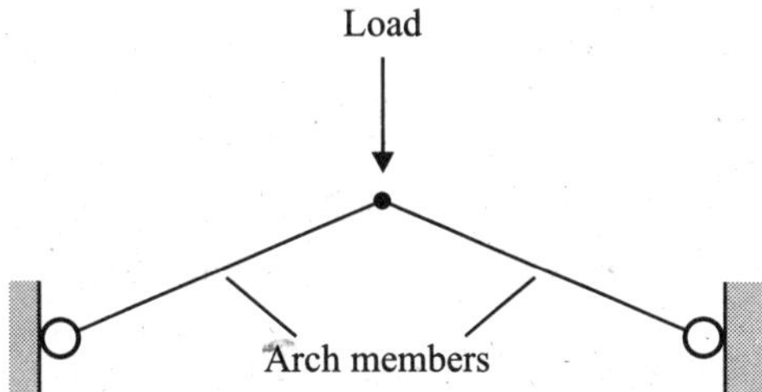

Figure 3.11: A Two-member Arch.

3.5 MAPPING OF CLASSICAL SETS TO A FUNCTION

Mapping of set theoretic forms to function theoretic forms is an important concept. In general it can be used to map elements or subsets on one universe of discourse to elements or sets in another universe. Suppose X and Y are two different universe of discourse. If an element x is contained in X and corresponds to an element y contained in Y, it is generally represented as $f: X \rightarrow Y$, which is said as the mapping from X to Y. The characteristic function χ_A is defined by

$$\chi_A(x) = \begin{cases} 1 & x \in A, \\ 0 & x \notin A, \end{cases}$$

where χ_A represents the membership in set a for the elements x in the universe. The membership mapping for the crisp set A is shown in Figure 3.6. Let us define two sets A and B on the Universe X.

3.5.1 Union

The union of these two sets in terms of function theoretic form is given as follows:

$$A \cup B \rightarrow \chi_{A \cup B}(x) = \chi_A(x) V \chi_B(x)$$
$$= \max (\chi_A(x), \chi_B(x)).$$

Here V indicates the maximum operator.

3.5.2 Intersection

The intersection of two sets in function theoretic form is given as

$$A \cap B \rightarrow \chi_{A \cap B}(x) = \chi_A(x) \Lambda \chi_B(x)$$
$$= \max(\chi_A(x), \chi_B(x)).$$

Here Λ indicates the minimum operator.

3.5.3 Complement

The complement of single set on universe X, say A is given by

$$\bar{A} \rightarrow \chi_{\bar{A}}(x) = 1 - \chi_A(x).$$

3.5.4 Containment

The two sets A and B in universe, if one set (A) is contained in another set B, then

$$A \subseteq B \rightarrow \chi_A(x) \leq \chi_B(x).$$

Thus, the mapping of classical sets to functions is mentioned here.

Example 3.3: Given the classical sets, A = {9, 5, 6, 8, 10} B = {1, 2, 3, 7, 9} C = {1, 0} defined on universe X = { Set of all 'n' natural no} Prove the classical set properties associativity and distributivity.

Solution: The associative property is given by

1. A U (B U C) = (A U B) U C.

   LHS

   A U (B U C)

   (a) U C = {2, 3, 7, 9, 1, 0}.

   (b) A U (B U C) = {5, 6, 8, 10, 2, 3, 7, 9, 1, 0}. (3.4)

   RHS

   (A U B) U C

   (a) (A U B) = {9, 5, 6, 8, 10, 1, 2, 3, 7}.

   (b) (A U B) U C = {9, 5, 6, 10, 8, 1, 2, 3, 7, 0}. (3.5)

   From (3.4) and (3.5)

   LHS = RHS

   A U (B U C) = (A U B) U C.

2. $(A \cap (B \cap C) = (A \cap B) \cap C$

   LHS

   (a) $(B \cap C) = \{1\}$.

   (b) $A \cap (B \cap C) = \{\varphi\}$. (3.6)

   RHS

   $(A \cap B) \cap C$

(a) $(A \cap B) = \{9\}$.

(b) $(A \cap B) \cap C = \{\varphi\}$. (3.7)

From (3.6) and (3.7)

LHS = RHS

$A \cap (B \cap C) = (A \cap B) \cap C$.

Thus associative property is proved.

The distributive property is given by,

1. $A \cup (B \cap C) = (A \cup B) \cap (A \cup C)$

   LHS

   (a) $B \cap C = \{1\}$.

   (b) $A \cup (B \cap C) = \{9, 5, 6, 8, 10, 1\}$ (3.8)

   RHS

   $(A \cup B) \cap (A \cup C)$

   (a) $(A \cup B) = \{9, 5, 6, 8, 10, 1, 2, 3, 7\}$.

   (b) $(A \cup C) = \{9, 5, 6, 8, 10, 1, 0\}$.

   (c) $(A \cup B) \cap (A \cup C) = \{9, 5, 6, 8, 10, 1\}$. (3.9)

   From (3.8) and (3.9)

   LHS = RHS

   $A \cup (B \cap C) = (A \cup B) \cap (A \cup C)$.

2. $A \cap (B \cup C) = (A \cap B) \cup (A \cap C)$

   LHS

   (a) $(B \cup C) = \{1, 2, 3, 7, 9, 0\}$.

   (b) $A \cap (B \cup C) = \{9\}$. (3.10)

   RHS

   (a) $A \cap B = \{9\}$.

   (b) $A \cap C = \{\varphi\}$.

   (c) $(A \cap B) \cup (A \cap C) = \{9\}$. (3.11)

   From (3.10) and (3.11),

   LHS = RHS

   $A \cap (B \cup C) = (A \cap B) \cup (A \cap B)$.

Hence distributive property is proved.

3.6 FUZZY SETS

A fuzzy set is a set with a smooth (unsharp) boundary. It generalizes the notion of membership from a black and white binary categorization in classical set theory into one that allows partial membership. The notion of membership in fuzzy sets thus becomes a matter of degree, which is a number between 0 and 1. A membership degree of 0 represents complete non-membership, while a membership degree of 1 represents a complete membership. Mathematically speaking, a fuzzy set is characterized by a mapping from its universe of discourse into the interval, [0, 1]. This mapping is the membership function of the set. Usually, the membership or characteristic function is denoted by the Greek lower-case latter m.(For instance, we may define the fuzzy set High Temperature using the membership function shown in Figure 3.12).

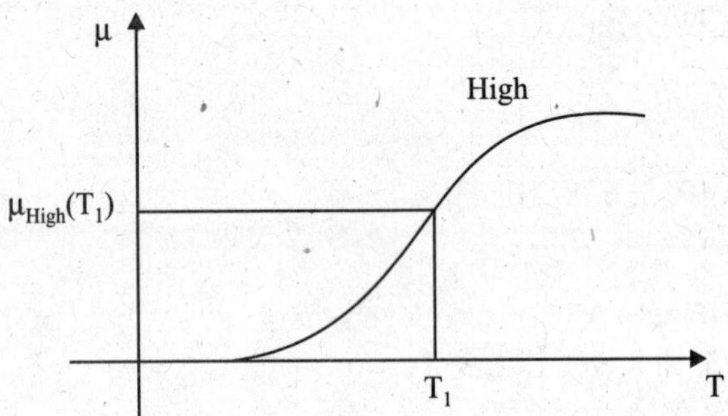

Figure 3.12: Membership Function of High Temperature

A set of core fuzzy sets about a variable forms a term set, which is the basis for generating composite fuzzy sets using hedges. For instance, Low, Medium, and High whose membership functions are shown in Figure 3.13 form a complete term set for the temperature T process. We say that a term set is complete if, for any element in the given universe of discourse, there is at least one term in the term set that covers the given element.

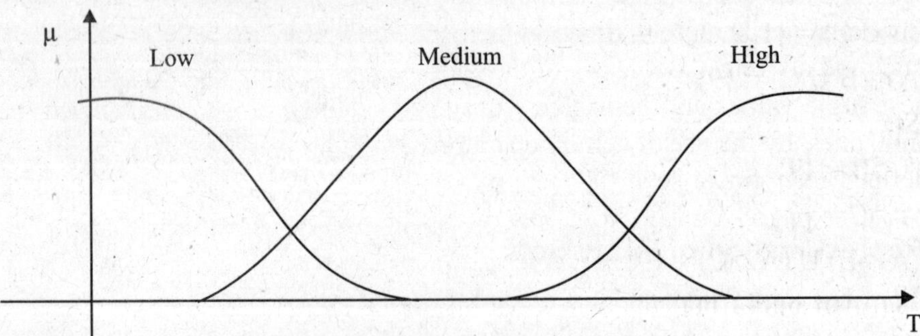

Figure 3.13: A complete Term Set for Temperature.

3.6.1 Definition

A fuzzy set can be defined as a set of ordered pairs A = {x, μA(x)|x ∈ U}. The function μA(x) is called the membership function for A, mapping each element of the universe U to a membership degree in the range [0, 1]. The universe may be discrete or continuous. Any fuzzy set containing at least one element with a membership degree of 1 is called normal. It may be better to represent the set of old people as a fuzzy set, Old. The membership function for this set is given in Figure 3.14, defined over a range of ages (the universe). Given that the age of Rod is 74, it can be determined that this element belongs to the set Old with a membership degree of 0.95. Similarly, if the age of Freddy is 38, the resulting

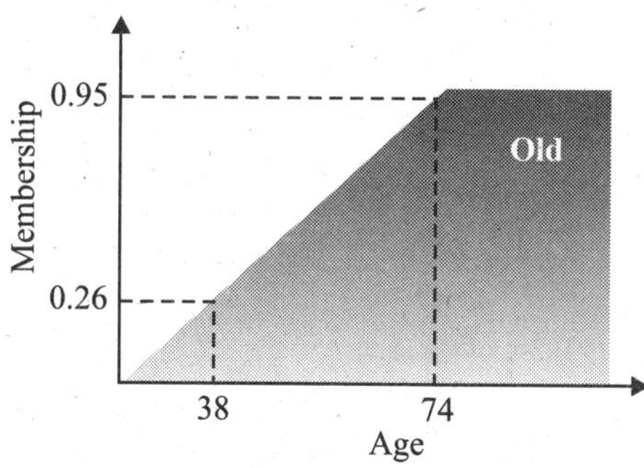

Figure 3.14: Fuzzy Set Representing the Concept Old.

degree of membership is 0.26. Here, both Rod and Freddy belong to the (fuzzy) set of old people, but Rod has a higher degree of membership to this set. The specification of membership functions is typically subjective, as can be seen in this example. There are many justifiable definitions of the concept Old. Indeed people of different ages may define this concept quite differently. One way of constructing the membership function is by using a voting model, and this way the generated fuzzy sets can be rooted in reality with clear semantics. An alternative to this is the integration of the probability distribution of variables. For example, integrating the probability distribution of height gives a possible version of the tall fuzzy set. This does not help with hedges and sets such as very tall, and so although the integration of the distribution gives a voting model, it needs more to arrive at the hedges. In fuzzy logic the truth value of a statement is linguistic (and no longer Boolean), of the form very true, true, more or less true, not very false, false. These logic values are themselves fuzzy sets; some may be compounded fuzzy sets from other atomic ones, by the use of certain operators. As with ordinary crisp sets, different operations can be defined over fuzzy sets.

3.6.2 Representation of Fuzzy Sets

A fuzzy set can be defined in two ways: (1) by enumerating membership values of those elements in the set (completely or partially), or (2) by defining the membership function mathematically.

Obviously, the first approach is possible only if the set is discrete, because a continuous fuzzy set has an infinite number of elements. Generally speaking, a fuzzy set A can be defined through enumeration using the expression

$$A = \sum_i \mu_A(x_i)/x_i \qquad (3.12)$$

where the summation and addition operators refer to the union(disjunction) operation and the notation $\mu_A(x_i) / x_i$ refers to a fuzzy set containing exactly one(partial) element x with a membership degree $\mu_A(x_i)$. For brevity, we do not list those elements x_i whose membership degree in set A is zero.

Example 3.4: Given the discrete universe of discourse, U = {1, 2,…., 20}, Small and Medium are fuzzy subsets of U characterized by the following membership functions:

Small = 1/1+ 1/2 + 0.9/3 + 0.6/4 + 0.3/5 + (0.1/6),

Medium = 0.1/2 + 0.3/3 + 0.7/4 + 1/5 + 1/6 + 0.7/7 + 0.5/8 + 0.2/9

The two fuzzy sets are also depicted graphically in Figure 3.15.

Let us return to the example about Texas universities. Suppose we wish to represent the set of Texas universities with a large student population. This can be defined using the two approaches described above.

1. By enumeration: We can define the set by the listing those Texas universities considered to have, to an extent, large student populations as well as their membership degrees.

   LargeTexasUniv = 1/UT + 1/TAMU + 0.5/UH + 0.3/Rice

2. Alternatively, we can define the set by explicitly describing its characteristics: Texas Universities with Large total student population:

$$\mu_{\text{LargeTexasUniv}}(x) = \mu_{\text{Large}}(\text{TotalStudentPopulation}(x))$$

$$= \begin{cases} 0 & P < 20000 \\ \dfrac{(P - 20000)}{20000} & 20000 \le P \le 40000 \\ 1 & P > 40000 \end{cases}$$

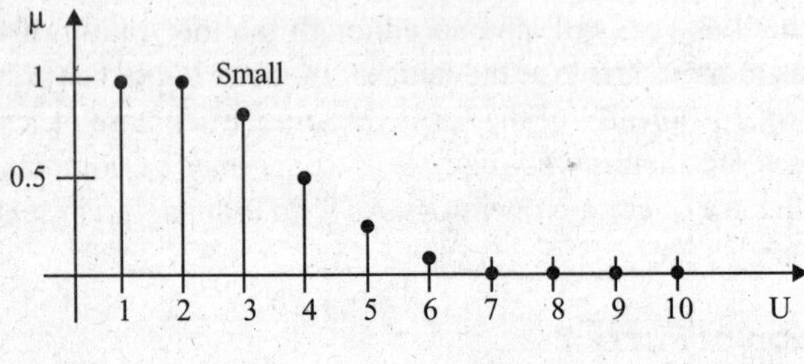

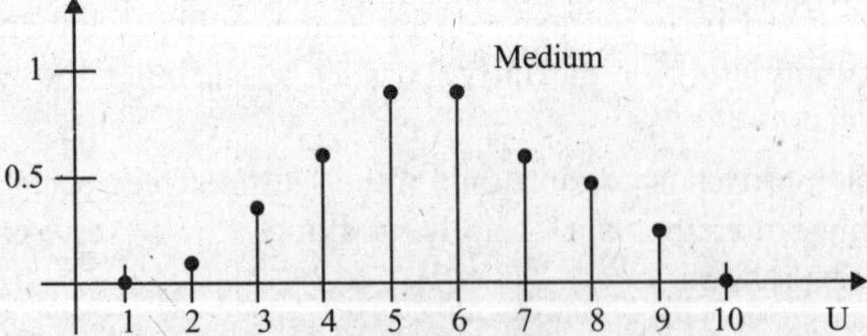

Figure 3.15: Definitions of the Terms Small and Medium

In the example above, the first approach is an extensional definition of the set, while the second approach is an intensional definition of the set.

3.6.3 Simple Example of Fuzzy Sets

An example should help with the understanding of the basic concepts and operators introduced above. Suppose that the universe of discourse, X, is a class of students and that a group, A, of students within this class are said to be tall in height. Thus A is a fuzzy subset of X (but X itself is not fuzzy), since the boundary between tall and not tall cannot be naturally defined with a fixed real number. Rather, describing this vague concept using a gradual membership function as characterized in Figure 3.16. is much more appealing. Similarly the fuzzy term very tall can be represented by another fuzzy (sub-) set as also shown in this figure. Given such a definition of the fuzzy set A = tall, a proposition like "student x is tall" can be denoted by $\mu_{A(x)}$. Assume that Andy is a student in the class and that he has a 80% possibility of being considered as a tall student. This means that

μ_A(andy) = 0.8. Also

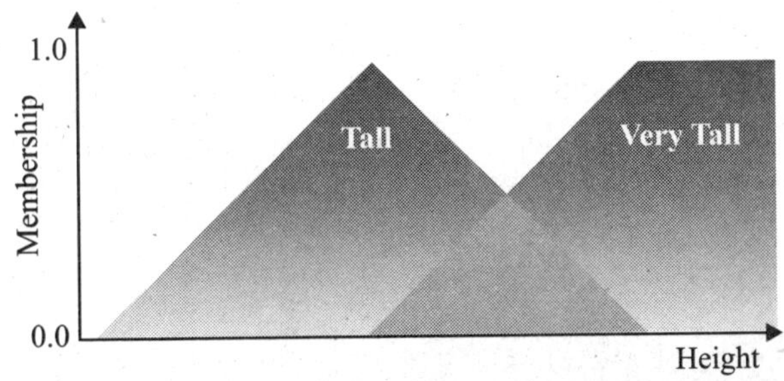

Figure 3.16: Representation of Fuzzy Sets "Tall" and "Very Tall"

suppose that another fuzzy set B is defined on the same universe X, whose members are said to be young in age, and that μ_B(andy) = 0.7, meaning that Andy is thought to be young with a possibility of 70%. From this, using the operations defined above, the following can be derived that is justifiable with respect to common-sense intuitions:

- $\mu_{\neg A}$(Andy) = 1 – 0.8 = 0.2, indicating the possibility of Andy being not
- $\mu_{A \cup B}$(Andy) = max(μ_A(Andy), μ_B(Andy)) = max (0.8, 0.7) = 0.8, including the possibility of Andy being tall of young
- $\mu_{A \cap B}$(Andy) = min(μ_A(Andy), μ_B(Andy)) = min (0.8, 0.7) = 0.7, including the possibility being both tall and young

Not only having an intuitive justification, these operations are also computationally very simple. However, care should be taken not to explain the results from the conventional Boolean logic point of view. The laws of excluded-middle and contradiction do not hold in fuzzy logic anymore. To make this point clearer, let us attempt to compare the results of $A \cup \neg A$ and $A \cap \neg A$ obtained by fuzzy logic with those by Boolean probabilistic logic (although such a comparison is itself a common source for debate in the literature). Applying fuzzy logic to the case above of Andy gives that

- $\mu_{A \cup \neg A}$(Andy) = max(μ_A(Andy), $\mu_{\neg A}$ (Andy)) = max (0.8, 0.2) = 0.8
- $\mu_{A \cap \neg A}$(Andy) = min(μ_A(Andy), $\mu_{\neg A}$ (Andy)) = min (0.8, 0.2) = 0.8

However, using the theory of probability, different results would be expected such that

- p("Andy is tall" or "Andy is not tall") = 1
- p("Andy is tall" and "Andy is not tall") = 0

This important difference is caused by the deliberate avoidance of the excluded-middle and contradiction laws in fuzzy logic. This avoidance enables fuzzy logic to represent vague concepts that are difficult to capture otherwise. If the memberships of x belonging to A and ¬A are neither 0 nor 1, then it should not be surprising that x is also of a nonzero membership belonging to A and ¬A at the same time.

3.7 HISTORY OF FUZZY SETS

In 1965, professor Lotfi Zadeh (Electrical Engineering and Electronics Research Laboratory, University of California, Berkeley) published his seminal paper on the idea of fuzzy sets, thus establishing the foundation of a comprehensive and mathematically sound logic of imprecisely or ambiguously defined sets. This has come to be known as fuzzy logic, first given full treatment in Zadeh's 1973 paper "Outline of a New Approach to the Analysis of Complex Systems and Decision Process".

3.8 THE ANATOMY OF A FUZZY SET

The core idea of fuzzy logic rests with the concept of a fuzzy set. These sets are not fuzzy in the conventional English-language sense of the word: blurred, hazy, out of focus, or indistinct. Rather, they are fuzzy in the way they treat their set boundaries. Fuzzy sets have a semipermeable membrane. In a fuzzy set, an element can be in three states: not a member of the set, a full member of the set, or a partial member of the set. Set membership is thus represented as a continuous range of values in the interval [0, 1] with [0] indicating no set membership, [1] indicating complete set membership, and values in the range [> 0, < 1] indicating a partial degree of membership.

Fuzzy logic is a superset of Boolean logic. Consequently, fuzzy sets are, in many respects, supersets of Boolean sets. A fuzzy set incorporates as part of its structure the intrinsic degrees of membership associated with each element. Figure 3.17 illustrates schematically the general components of a fuzzy set.

A fuzzy set has three principal components: a degree of membership measure along the vertical (Y) axis, the possible domain values for the set along the horizontal (X) axis, and the set membership function (a continuous curve that connects a domain value to its degree of membership in the set). The connecting curve is the crucial part of the fuzzy set. It defines the set membership relations. In addition to an underlying domain or universe of discourse, a fuzzy set also has a support set. This is the region of the domain at which the membership values are greater than zero.

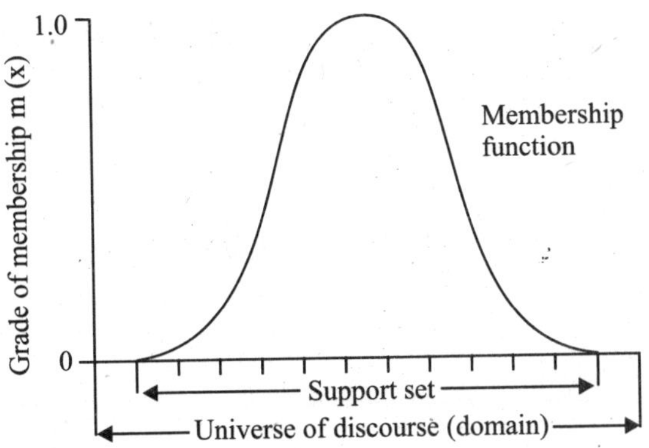

Figure 3.17: General Components of a Fuzzy Set.

3.9 THE TAXONOMY OF FUZZY SETS

Comparing the crisp set Tall (see Figure 3.18) with its fuzzy counterpart will illustrate these differences and expose the structure of a basic fuzzy set. Figure 3.19 shows one possible fuzzy set representation for the concept Tall.

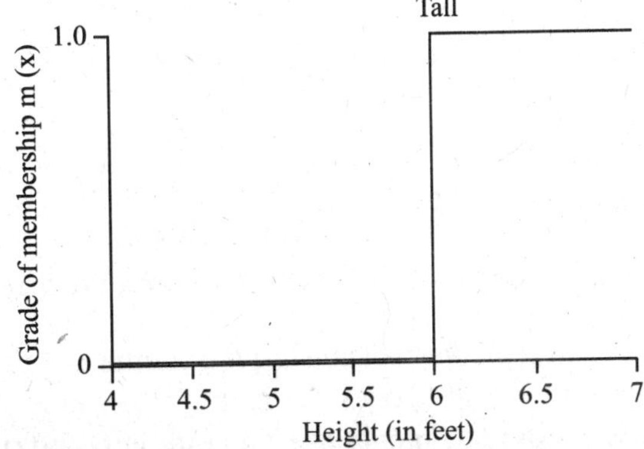

Figure 3.18: The Boolean Tall Set.

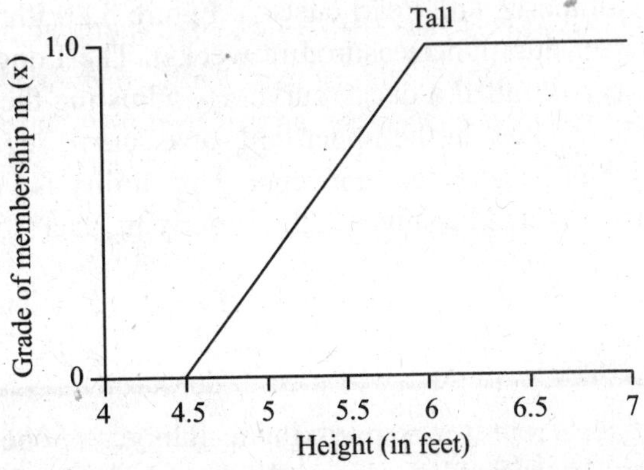

Figure 3.19: The Fuzzy Set Tall (for Men).

The Tall fuzzy set defines how heights are related to the concept of Tall. All heights below 4.5 feet have zero membership values (and are outside the support set). From 4.5 to 6 feet, the degree of membership in the fuzzy set Tall gradually increases. At 6 feet it reaches [1.0] (all heights above 6 feet are fully members of the set). Alternatively, we can view the membership value as the degree of compatibility between the value of height and the concept Tall. As heights increase they become more and more compatible with the idea of Tall. At 6 feet and above all values of Height are completely compatible with the idea of Tall.

3.10 FUZZY QUANTIFIERS

The fuzzy set Tall represents a class of fuzzy sets known as quantifiers. These are sets whose structure is not built around a central value (see the next section "Fuzzy Numbers").

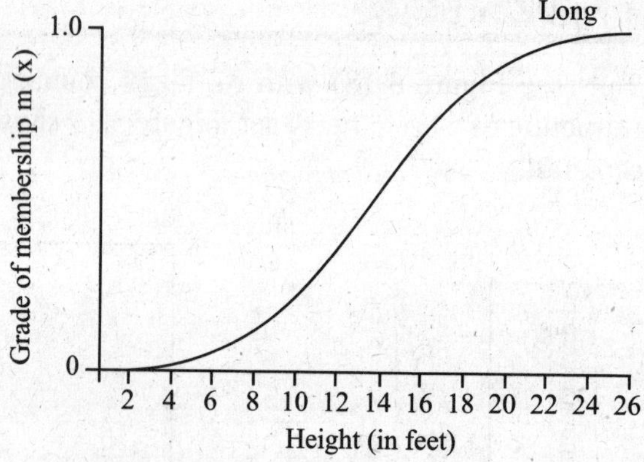

Figure 3.20: Fuzzy Set for a Long Project.

A quantifier represents an open concept and is quite common in fuzzy expert systems. Although the membership function for the Tall fuzzy set (Figure 3.20) was a straight line, implying a linear relationship, quantifier sets more commonly use sigmoid (left- and right-facing S-shaped) curves. Sigmoid curves, with inflection points and attenuated surfaces, can model a wide variety of growth curves (such as logistics, Gompertz, and Pearl curves). Figure 3.20 illustrates the fuzzy set for a Long project (with the project duration measured in weeks). The Long fuzzy set uses a growth curve. The left-facing S-curve is called a decay curve. By adjusting the inflection point on an S-curve, as well as the degree of skew in the upper and lower curve segments, decay and growth curves can represent many highly nonlinear concepts. This ability is very important in types of fuzzy models that are sensitive to small changes in the underlying data (such as risk assessment and sustainability models).

3.11 FUZZY NUMBERS

A much larger class of fuzzy sets represents approximate numbers of one type or another. Some of these fuzzy sets are explicitly "fuzzified" numbers, whereas others simply represent fuzzy numeric intervals over the domain of a particular variable (see the section "Fuzzy Term Sets"). Fuzzy numbers can take many shapes: bell curves, triangles, and trapezoids. Within each of these shapes the actual meaning of the fuzzy set depends on the width or spread of the set itself. Figure 3.21 illustrates a typical bell-shaped fuzzy number. This is a numeric quantity, About 20.

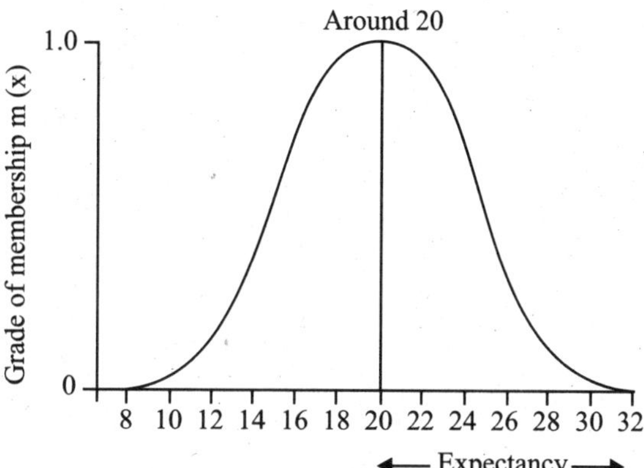

Figure 3.21: The Fuzzy Number about 20.

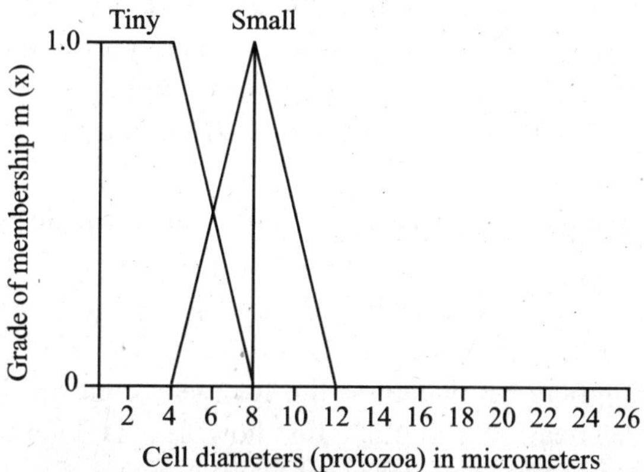

Figure 3.22: The Fuzzy Number Small.

The fuzzy set About 20 shows two principal attributes of fuzzy numbers: a central value and a degree of spread2 around the value. This degree of spread is called the expectancy (e) of the fuzzy number and is an important property. When e = 0, the fuzzy number is a single point and corresponds to a normal scalar value (called a singleton). As the expectancy increases, the number becomes fuzzier. This fuzziness is directly connected to the robustness or brittleness of a fuzzy model as well as to the separation of related concepts in the model. And, because expectancy increases confusion over the exact value of a fuzzy number, a wide expectancy also increases information entropy. Another very common fuzzy number shape is the triangle. Due primarily to the low computational cost of creating and interrogating triangular fuzzy sets they are used extensively in control applications. In general, a triangular fuzzy number is more brittle and therefore less robust than a bell-shaped fuzzy number. Figure 3.22 illustrates a triangular fuzzy set for the concept Small and shows that fuzzy numbers are often used to represent the underlying numbers in terms of a particular concept. In this instance, the cell diameter of a protozoa is taken to be Small (to some degree) when it lies between 4 and 12 micrometers.

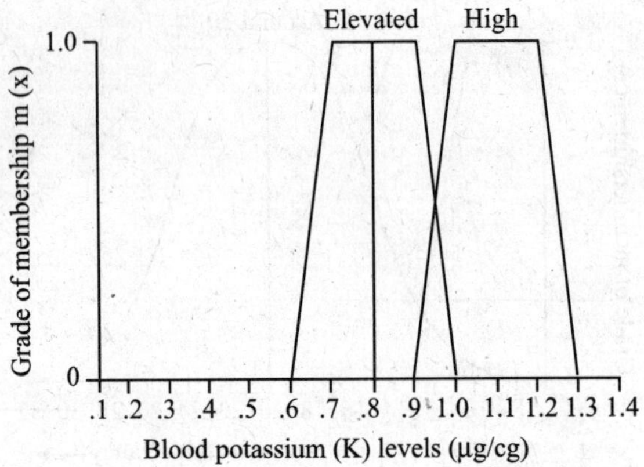

Figure 3.23: The Fuzzy Numbers for Elevated and High.

The fuzzy number Small in Figure 3.22 is also bounded by another fuzzy number, Tiny. Although this might appear to be a linear fuzzy quantifier, it is actually a representative of the third type of fuzzy number, the trapezoid. A trapezoidal representation is slightly but crucially different from the bell and triangle numbers. Figure 3.23 shows two overlapping fuzzy numbers represented as trapezoids.

The semantics of a trapezoidal number are slightly different from the bell and triangular numbers because the set does not pivot, so to speak around a single, central number. Although we can continue to treat a trapezoid as a special case of the triangular fuzzy set (with a plateau width of zero), some model builders consider the trapezoid as a categorical or class fuzzy set—interpreting the plateau as a class of numbers equivalent to the fuzzy set concept. In this case, for example, Elevated is a class of values near {0.6 to 1.0}. Just how near is determined by the width of the trapezoid's expectancy spread (which is measured from the edge, not the center, of the plateau). The existence of a plateau means that a set of values in the fuzzy set has maximum membership values in the set. In both the bell and the triangular sets only a single value is completely compatible with the set concept. On either side of this single number, the fuzzy membership values can (and usually do) drop off rather rapidly. By introducing plateaus into the fuzzy number, we establish a class of values that in a fuzzy model tends to create local areas of concentration.

3.11.1 A Symmetric Fuzzy Numbers

Unlike crisp numbers that have a precise value, fuzzy numbers have a certain amount of ambiguity or spread around them. This spread or expectancy is actually measured in two directions, to the left and the right of the central value (or, for a trapezoid, the edges of the plateau of values). Having two measures of fuzziness allows fuzzy numbers to have asymmetric shapes. A fuzzy number can have both a kurtosis and a skew (although these are not computed or measured as the equivalent concepts in statistics). Figure 3.24 illustrates several asymmetric fuzzy numbers in a robotic arm controller.

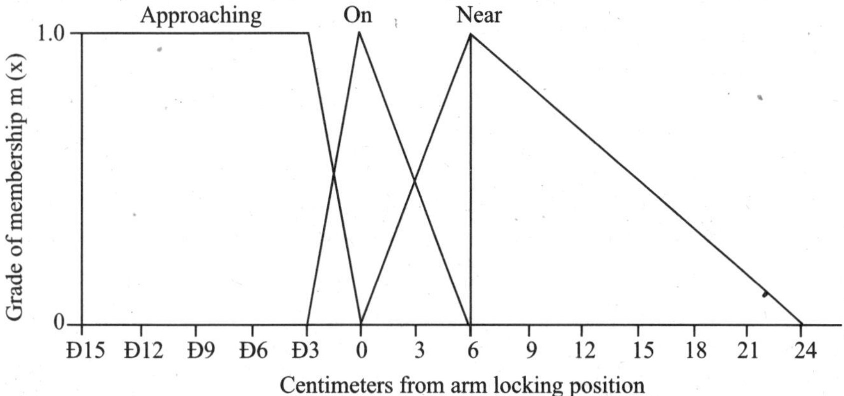

Figure 3.24: Asymmetric fuzzy numbers.

Nonsymmetric fuzzy sets are frequently encountered in control systems (such as the robotic arm controller) but they also play important roles in both the development of complex nonlinear expert systems as well as in the automatic, genetic tuning of rule-based fuzzy systems.

3.12 PSYCHOMETRIC FUZZY SETS

In the previous fuzzy set examples the underlying domains were drawn from a measurement associated with the property of data. Tall is a concept overlaid on the measured values of Height. Long is a concept overlaid on the measured values of project duration. Many models, however, use or produce fuzzy sets that correspond to concepts unsupported by any measured data. Such fuzzy sets often represent subjective mappings between a concept and its intensity or degree of realization. Hence, these fuzzy sets use a psychometric scaling for their domain. Psychometric (or nonmeasured) fuzzy sets include a broad range of concepts, such as Risk, Aptitude, Aggression, Sustainability, Indicated, Acceptable, and Compatible. Figure 3.25 shows a fuzzy set representation for Risk.

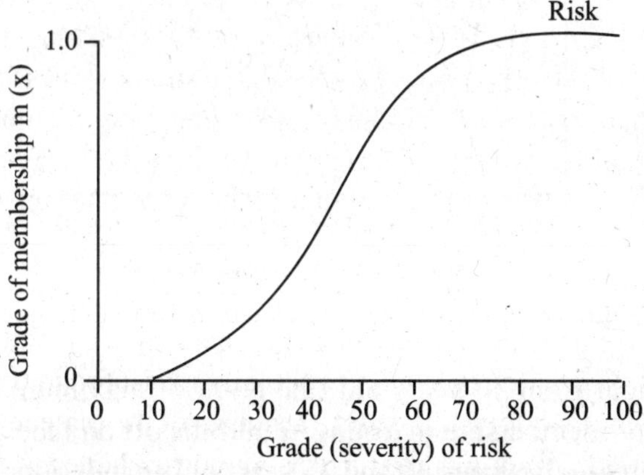

Figure 3.25: The Psychometric Risk Fuzzy Set.

The underlying domain must correspond to the granularity of the model. The wider the domain, the larger the degree of evident separation (a matter of resolution or discrimination) between the relative domain points. In the Risk example (Figure 3.24), a small movement along the membership function around the slope at them[.5] region would be difficult to detect if the domain were [0, 10], would be moderately easy to see with range [0, 100], and would produce a large displacement with range [0, 1000]. At the same time, the range of the psychometric scale must be associated with the model's objectives in resolving small or large changes along the horizontal axis.

3.13 COLLECTIONS OF FUZZY SETS (TERM SETS)

In fuzzy systems, the underlying numeric (and often categorical and enumeration) variables are broken down into a collection of fuzzy sets. These fuzzy sets ordinarily define the underlying semantics of the variable and are the names by which fuzzy rule-based systems refer to the variable itself. Because it is through the underlying fuzzy sets that fuzzy models reference their variables, these sets are often called linguistic variables. As an example, Figure 3.26 shows the variable Client_Age with its set of underlying fuzzy sets. Each underlying fuzzy set defines a portion of the variable's domain. But this portion is not uniquely defined. Fuzzy sets overlap as a natural consequence of their elastic boundaries. Such an overlap not only implements a realistic and functional semantic mechanism for defining the nature of a variable when it assumes various data values but provides a smooth and coherent transition from one state to another. This transition from one semantic state to another can be seen, for example, for the YoungAdult and MiddleAged fuzzy sets (Figure 3.26).

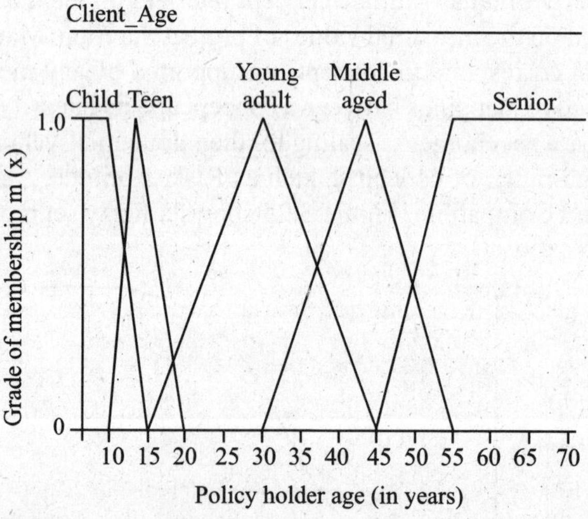

Figure 3.26: The Linguistic Variables for Client Age

As we move to the right from 30 years old (the point of maximum grade of membership in YoungAdult), the degree of membership in YoungAdult falls off and the degree of membership in MiddleAged begins to increase. Between 30 and 45 years old an individual is, to some degree, both a young adult and middle aged. When they are close to 30, their membership in the middle-aged concept is very small, and when then they are close to 45 their membership in the young adult concept is very small (and goes to zero at both of these end points). As we move further to the right, the individual's compatibility with the idea of middle aged begins to fall off and they become more and more representative of a senior citizen.

3.14 FUZZY SET OPERATIONS

Define three fuzzy sets $\underset{\sim}{A}$, $\underset{\sim}{B}$ and $\underset{\sim}{C}$ on the universe X. For a given element x of the universe, the following function-theoretic operations for the set-theoretic operations of union, intersection, and complement are defined for $\underset{\sim}{A}$, $\underset{\sim}{B}$ and $\underset{\sim}{C}$ on X:

Union $$\mu_{\underset{\sim}{A}\cup\underset{\sim}{B}}(x) = \mu_{\underset{\sim}{A}}(x)\vee\mu_{\underset{\sim}{B}}(x) \tag{3.13}$$

Intersection $$\mu_{\underset{\sim}{A}\cap\underset{\sim}{B}}(x) = \mu_{\underset{\sim}{A}}(x)\wedge\mu_{\underset{\sim}{B}}(x) \tag{3.14}$$

Complement $$\mu_{\overline{\underset{\sim}{A}}}(x) = 1-\mu_{\underset{\sim}{A}}(x) \tag{3.15}$$

Venn diagrams for these operations, extended to consider fuzzy sets, are shown in Figures 3.27–3.29. The operations given in Eqs. (3.13) – (3.15) are known as the standard fuzzy operations. There are many other fuzzy operations, and a discussion of these is given later in this chapter. Any fuzzy set $\underset{\sim}{A}$ defined on a universe X is a subset of that universe. Also by definition, just as with classical sets, the membership value of any element x in the null set ∅ is 0, and the membership value of any element x in the whole set X is 1. Note that the null set and the whole set are not fuzzy sets in this context (no tilde understrike).

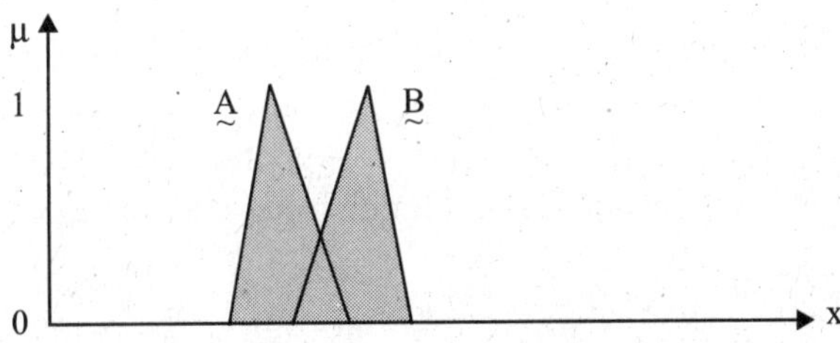

Figure 3.27: Union of Fuzzy Sets $\underset{\sim}{A}$ and $\underset{\sim}{B}$.

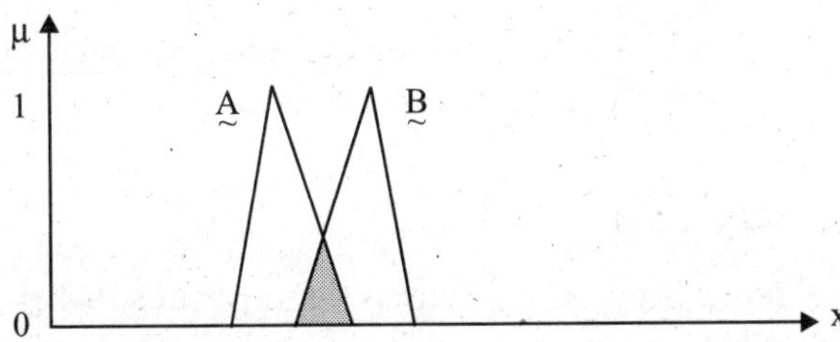

Figure 3.28: Intersection of Fuzzy Sets $\underset{\sim}{A}$ or $\underset{\sim}{B}$.

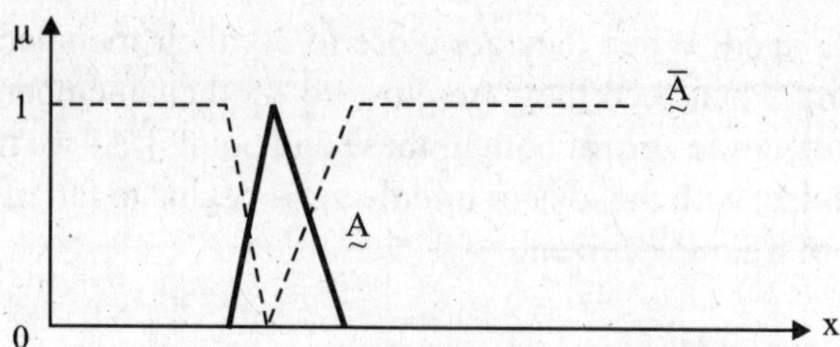

Figure 3.29: Complement of Fuzzy Set $\underset{\sim}{A}$.

The appropriate notation for these ideas is as follows:

$$\underset{\sim}{A} \subseteq X \Rightarrow \mu_{\underset{\sim}{A}}(x) \leq \mu_X(x) \quad (3.16a)$$

For all $x \in X, \mu_\phi(x) = 0$ (3.16b)

For all $x \in X, \mu_x(x) = 1$ (3.17c)

The collection of all fuzzy sets and fuzzy subsets on X is denoted as the fuzzy power set $P(\underset{\sim}{X})$.

It should be obvious, based on the fact that all fuzzy sets can overlap, that the cardinality, $n_{p(x)}$, of the fuzzy power set is infinite; that is, $n_{p(x)} = \infty$. De Morgan's principles for classical sets also hold for fuzzy sets, as denoted by these expressions:

$$\overline{\underset{\sim}{A} \cap \underset{\sim}{B}} = \bar{\underset{\sim}{A}} \cup \bar{\underset{\sim}{B}} \quad (3.17a)$$

$$\overline{\underset{\sim}{A} \cup \underset{\sim}{B}} = \bar{\underset{\sim}{A}} \cap \bar{\underset{\sim}{B}} \quad (3.17b)$$

As enumerated before, all other operations on classical sets also hold for fuzzy sets, except for the excluded middle axioms. These two axioms do not hold for fuzzy sets since they do not form part of the basic axiomatic structure of fuzzy sets (see Appendix A); since fuzzy sets can overlap, a set and its complement can also overlap. The excluded middle axioms, extended for fuzzy sets, are expressed by

$$\bar{\underset{\sim}{A}} \cup \bar{\underset{\sim}{A}} \neq X \quad (3.18a)$$

$$\bar{\underset{\sim}{A}} \cap \bar{\underset{\sim}{A}} \neq \phi \quad (3.19b)$$

Extended Venn diagrams comparing the excluded middle axioms for classical (crisp) sets and fuzzy sets are shown in Figures 3.30 and 3.31, respectively.

3.14.1 Properties of Fuzzy Sets

Fuzzy sets follow the same properties as crisp sets. Because of this fact and because the membership values of a crisp set are a subset of the interval [0,1], classical sets can be

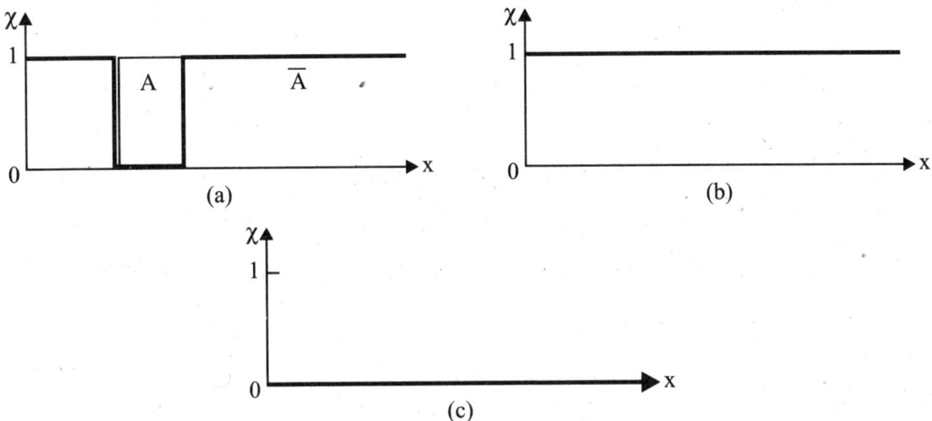

Figure 3.30: Excluded middle axioms for crisp sets. (a) Crisp set A and its complement; (b) crisp $A \cup \overline{A} = X$ (axiom of excluded middle); (c) crisp $A \cap \overline{A} = \phi$ (axiom of contradiction).

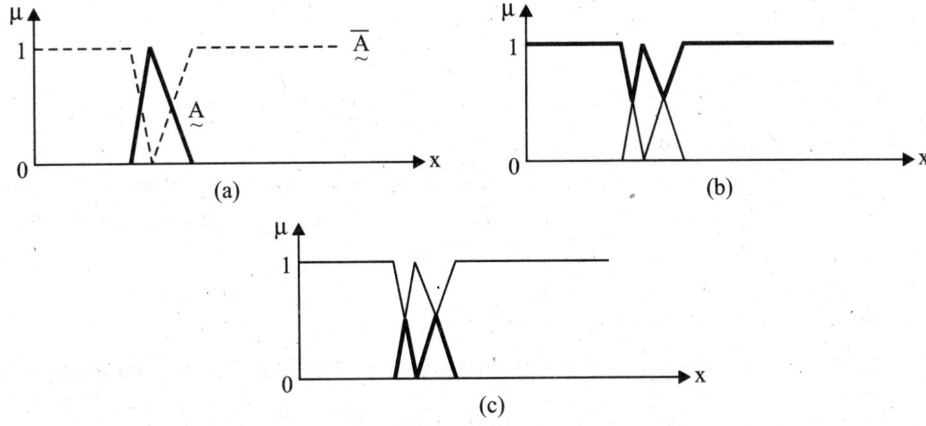

Figure 3.31: Excluded middle axioms for fuzzy sets. (a) Fuzzy set $\underset{\sim}{A}$ and its complement; (b) fuzzy $\underset{\sim}{A} \cup \overline{\underset{\sim}{A}} \neq X$ (axiom of excluded middle); (c) fuzzy $\underset{\sim}{A} \cap \overline{\underset{\sim}{A}} \neq \phi$ (axiom of contradiction). thought of as a special case of fuzzy sets. Frequently used properties of fuzzy sets are listed below.

Commutativity $\underset{\sim}{A} \cup \underset{\sim}{B} = \underset{\sim}{B} \cup \underset{\sim}{A}$

$\underset{\sim}{A} \cap \underset{\sim}{B} = \underset{\sim}{B} \cap \underset{\sim}{A}$

Associativity $\underset{\sim}{A} \cup (\underset{\sim}{B} \cup \underset{\sim}{C}) = (\underset{\sim}{A} \cup \underset{\sim}{B}) \cup \underset{\sim}{C}$

$\underset{\sim}{A} \cap (\underset{\sim}{B} \cap \underset{\sim}{C}) = (\underset{\sim}{A} \cap \underset{\sim}{B}) \cap \underset{\sim}{C}$

Distributivity $\underset{\sim}{A} \cup (\underset{\sim}{B} \cap \underset{\sim}{C}) = (\underset{\sim}{A} \cup \underset{\sim}{B}) \cap (\underset{\sim}{A} \cup \underset{\sim}{C})$

$\underset{\sim}{A} \cap (\underset{\sim}{B} \cup \underset{\sim}{C}) = (\underset{\sim}{A} \cap \underset{\sim}{B}) \cup (\underset{\sim}{A} \cap \underset{\sim}{C}))$

Idempotency $\underset{\sim}{A} \cup \underset{\sim}{A} = \underset{\sim}{A}$

and $\underset{\sim}{A} \cap \underset{\sim}{A} = \underset{\sim}{A}$

$$\underset{\sim}{A} \cup \phi = \underset{\sim}{A}$$

and $$\underset{\sim}{A} \cap X = \underset{\sim}{A}$$

$$\underset{\sim}{A} \cap \phi = \phi$$

and $$A \cup X = X$$

Transitivity If $\underset{\sim}{A} \subseteq \underset{\sim}{B}$ and $\underset{\sim}{B} \subseteq \underset{\sim}{C}$, then $\underset{\sim}{A} \subseteq \underset{\sim}{C}$

Involution $$\overline{\overline{\underset{\sim}{A}}} = \underset{\sim}{A}$$

3.14.2 The Cardinality of Fuzzy Sets

The cardinality of a set is the total number of elements in the set. Since an element can partially belong to a fuzzy set, a natural generalization of the classical notion of cardinality is to weigh each element by its membership degree, which gives us the following formula for calculating the cardinality of a fuzzy set:

$$\text{Card (A)} = \sum_{x_i} \mu_A(x_i) \tag{3.20}$$

For instance, the cardinality of the fuzzy set Large Texas University is

Card (Large Texas University) = 1 + 1 + 0.5 + 0.3 = 2:8

The cardinality of fuzzy sets is useful for answering questions such as "How many large universities are there in Texas?" Therefore, it plays an important role in fuzzy databases and information systems.

3.14.3 Height: Normal Versus Subnormal

The height of a fuzzy set is the highest membership value of its membership function:

$$\text{Height (A)} = \max_{x_i} \mu_A(x_i) \tag{3.21}$$

For example, the height of the fuzzy set in Figure 3.32 is 0.5. A fuzzy set with height 1 is called a normal fuzzy set. In contrast, a fuzzy set whose height is less than 1 is called a subnormal fuzzy set. The fuzzy in figure 3.32, for example, is subnormal.

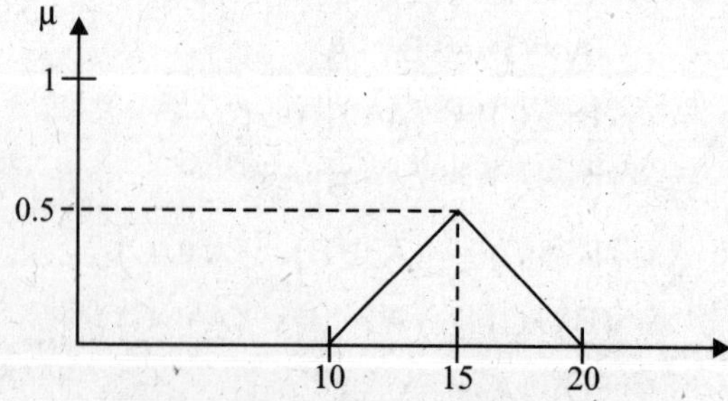

Figure 3.32: A Subnormal Fuzzy Set

3.14.4 Support and Alpha-level Cuts

The support of a fuzzy set A is the set of element whose degree of membership in A is greater than 0. For instance, the support of the fuzzy set in Figure 3.32 is the open interval (10, 20). Let A be a fuzzy set in the universe of discourse U. We can formally define support as follows:

$$\text{Spt} = \{x \in U \mid \mu_A(x) < 0\} \tag{3.22}$$

It should be pointed out that the support of a fuzzy set is a crisp (classical) set.

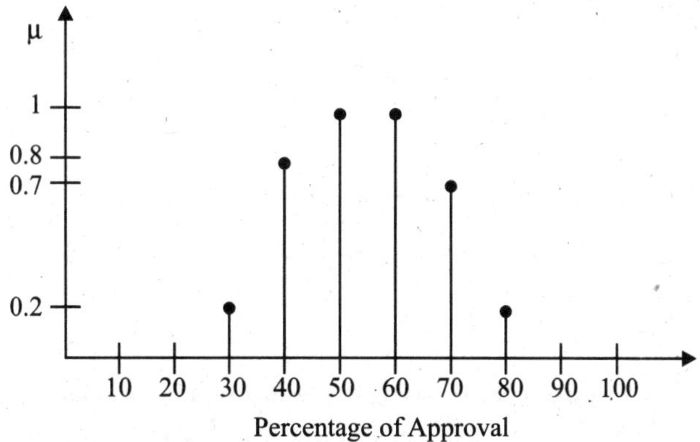

Figure 3.33: The Membership Function of Moderately Approved Presidential Candidate

The notion of α-cut (also called a-level) is more general than that of support. Let α_0 be a number between 0 and 1. The α-cut of a fuzzy set A at α_0, denoted as $A_{\alpha 0}$, is the set of elements whose degree of membership in A is no less than α_0. Mathematically, the a-cut of a fuzzy set A in U is defined as

$$A_{\alpha 0} = \{x \in U \mid \mu_A(x) \geq \alpha_0\} \tag{3.23}$$

For example, let us consider the concept "moderately approved" regarding the public's opinion of a presidential candidate. The universe of discourse is the percentage of those people supporting the candidate in a national poll. To simplify out discussion, we use a discrete universe of discourse: U = {0%, 10%, 20%,…., 100%}. The membership function of the fuzzy set moderately approved is shown in figure 3.33. We can construct the a-cut of the fuzzy set at 0.7 as

Moderately $\text{Approved}_{0.7}$ = {40%, 50%, 60%, 70%}

Similarly, we can construct the following a-cuts:

Moderately $\text{Approved}_{0.2}$ = {30%, 40%, 50%, 60%, 70%, 80%}

Moderately $\text{Approved}_{0.8}$ = {40%, 50%, 60%}

Obviously, as the alpha value increases, the set generated by a-cutting a fuzzy set becomes smaller. It can be shown that if $\alpha_1 < \alpha_2$, we have $A_{\alpha 1} \supseteq A_{\alpha 2}$. Where Êdenotes a crisp superset (i.e. suppositions) relation.

3.14.5 Resolution Identity

Based on the notion of a-cuts, fuzzy set can be decomposed into multiple crisp sets (i.e., a-level sets) using different a values. Intuitively, each a-level specifies a slice of the membership function. Therefore, it is conceivable that the original membership function can be reconstructed by "pilling up" these slices in order.

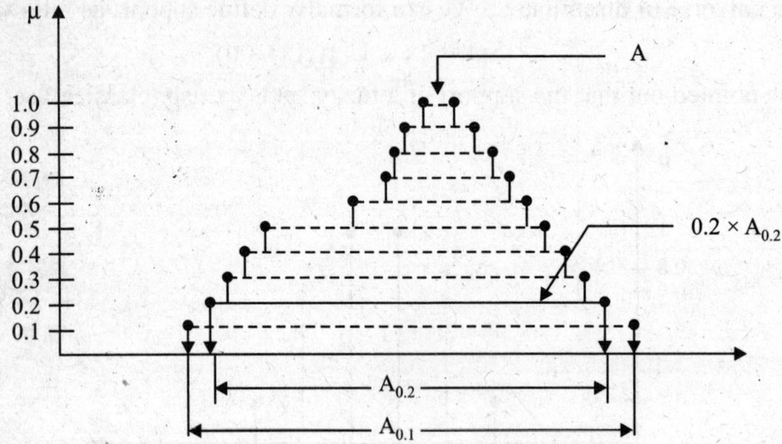

Figure 3.34: Resolution Identify of a Fuzzy Set

The foundation for reconstructing a membership function from its a-cuts is the resolution identity in fuzzy set theory. Let A be a discrete fuzzy set. We can order the Nonzero membership values of the elements in the support set into a list in increasing order (without duplicates): $(\alpha_0, \alpha_1, \ldots, \alpha_n)$. The resolution identity principle in fuzzy set theory states that

$$A = \alpha_0 \, X \, A_{\alpha 0} + \alpha_1 \, X \, A_{\alpha 1} + \ldots\ldots + \alpha_n \, X \, A_{\alpha n} \qquad (3.24)$$

where $\alpha_i \, X \, A_{\alpha i}$ represents a fuzzy set such as the one below:

$$\mu_{\alpha_i X A_{\alpha_i}} = \begin{cases} \alpha_i & \text{if } \mu A \geq \alpha_i \\ 0 & \text{otherwise} \end{cases} \qquad (3.25)$$

and + represents the disjunction operator. In other words, the original fuzzy set A can be viewed as the union of all those fuzzy sets constructed from an a_i in the list $(\alpha_0, \alpha_1, \ldots, \alpha_n)$ such that (1) their support is the a_i level cut of A, and (2) their membership function is flat at the alpha value a_i. The shape of the membership function $\alpha_i \, X \, A_{\alpha i}$ is hence a rectangle with a height of α_i as illustrated in Figure 3.34. Figure 3.35 shows the result of superimposing $0.1 \, X \, A_{0.1}$ and $0.2 \, X \, A_{0.2}$ and so on.

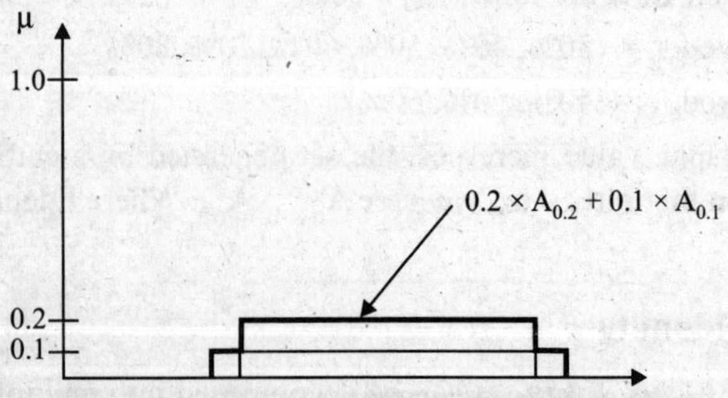

Figure 3.35: Combining Two Scaled α-Cuts.

It should be noted that the a-values in the resolution identity of a discrete fuzzy set may not be equally separated. They are determined by the membership function of the set. For instance, the resolution identity of the fuzzy set in Figure 3.33 consists of four a-cuts with a-values 0.2, 0.7, 0., and 1, respectively, as shown in Figure 3.36.

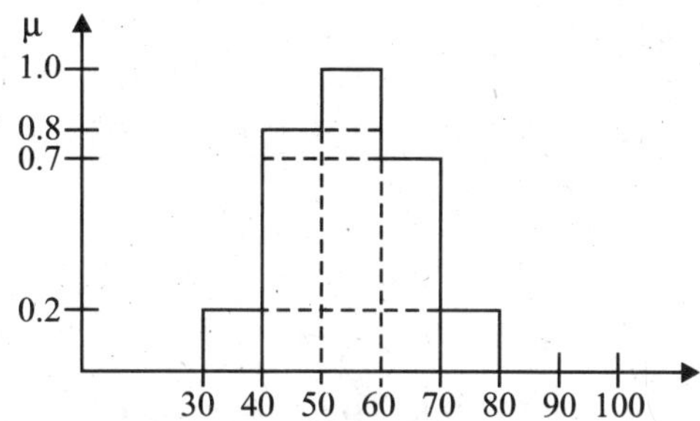

Figure 3.36: Resolution Identity of the Fuzzy Set Moderately Approved.

Example 3.5: Consider two fuzzy sets A and B find Complement, Union, Intersection, Difference, and De Morgan's law.

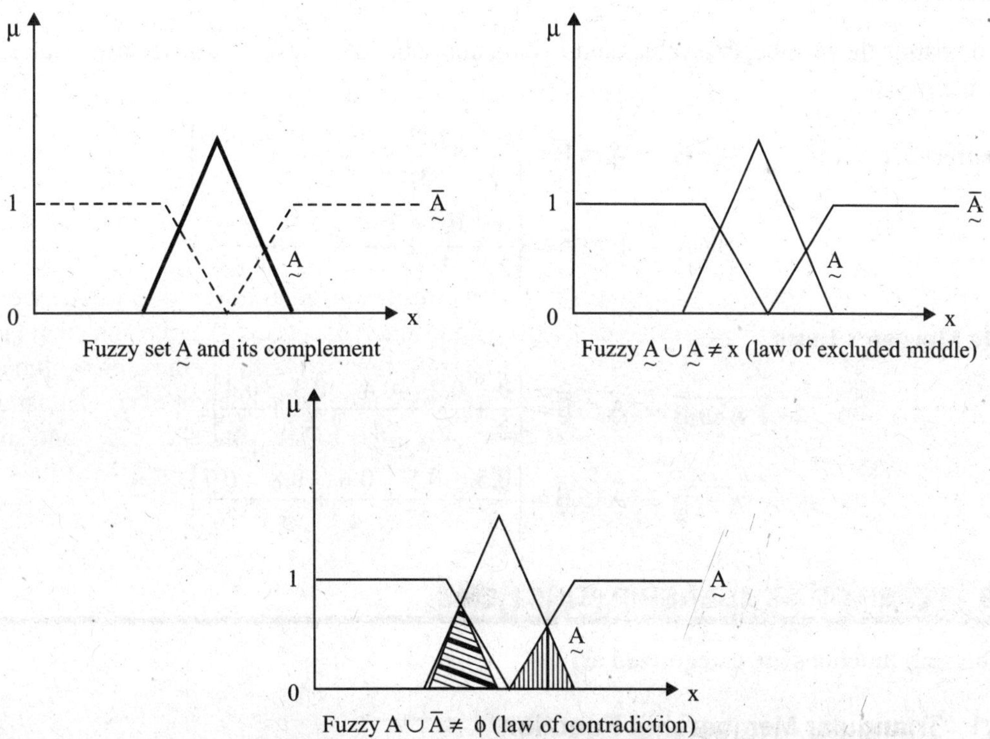

Figure 3.37: Excluded Middle Law for Fuzzy Set

$$\bar{\underset{\sim}{A}} = \left\{\frac{1}{2} + \frac{0.5}{3} + \frac{0.6}{4} + \frac{0.2}{5} + \frac{0.6}{6}\right\},$$

$$\bar{\underset{\sim}{B}} = \left\{\frac{0.5}{2} + \frac{0.8}{3} + \frac{0.4}{4} + \frac{0.7}{5} + \frac{0.3}{6}\right\},$$

Solution:

$$\bar{\underset{\sim}{A}} = \left\{\frac{0}{2} + \frac{0.5}{3} + \frac{0.4}{4} + \frac{0.8}{5} + \frac{0.4}{6}\right\}.$$

Complement $$\bar{\underset{\sim}{B}} = \left\{\frac{0.5}{2} + \frac{0.2}{3} + \frac{0.6}{4} + \frac{0.3}{5} + \frac{0.7}{6}\right\}.$$

Union $$\underset{\sim}{A} \cup \underset{\sim}{B} = \left\{\frac{1}{2} + \frac{0.8}{3} + \frac{0.6}{4} + \frac{0.7}{5} + \frac{0.6}{6}\right\}$$

Comparing the membership values and writing maximum of the two values determine Union of the fuzzy set.

Intersection $$\underset{\sim}{A} \cap \underset{\sim}{B} = \left\{\frac{0.5}{2} + \frac{0.5}{3} + \frac{0.4}{4} + \frac{0.2}{5} + \frac{0.3}{6}\right\}$$

Comparing the membership values and writing minimum of the two values determine intersection of the fuzzy set.

Difference $$\underset{\sim}{A} / \underset{\sim}{B} = \underset{\sim}{A} \cap \bar{\underset{\sim}{B}} = \left\{\frac{0.5}{2} + \frac{0.2}{3} + \frac{0.6}{4} + \frac{0.2}{5} + \frac{0.6}{6}\right\}.$$

$$\underset{\sim}{B} / \underset{\sim}{A} = \underset{\sim}{B} \cap \bar{\underset{\sim}{A}} = \left\{\frac{0}{2} + \frac{0.5}{3} + \frac{0.4}{4} + \frac{0.7}{5} + \frac{0.3}{6}\right\}.$$

De Morgan's Laws

$$\overline{\underset{\sim}{A} \cup \underset{\sim}{B}} = \bar{\underset{\sim}{A}} \cap \bar{\underset{\sim}{B}} = \left\{\frac{0}{2} + \frac{0.2}{3} + \frac{0.4}{4} + \frac{0.3}{5} + \frac{0.4}{6}\right\},$$

$$\overline{\underset{\sim}{A} \cap \underset{\sim}{B}} = \bar{\underset{\sim}{A}} \cup \bar{\underset{\sim}{B}} = \left\{\frac{0.5}{2} + \frac{0.5}{3} + \frac{0.6}{4} + \frac{0.8}{5} + \frac{0.7}{6}\right\}.$$

3.15 TYPES OF MEMBERSHIP FUNCTIONS

Membership functions are categorized as:

3.15.1 Triangular Membership Function

A triangular membership function is specified by three parameters {a, b, c} as follows:

$$\text{triangle}(x\text{: a, b, c}) = \begin{cases} 0 & x < a \\ (x - a)/(b - a) & a \le x \le b \\ (c - x)/(c - b) & b \le x \le c \\ 0 & x > c \end{cases} \tag{3.26}$$

The precise appearance of the function is determined by the choice of parameters a, b and c. Figure 3.38(a) illustrates an example of a triangular membership function defined triangle (x; 20, 60, 80).

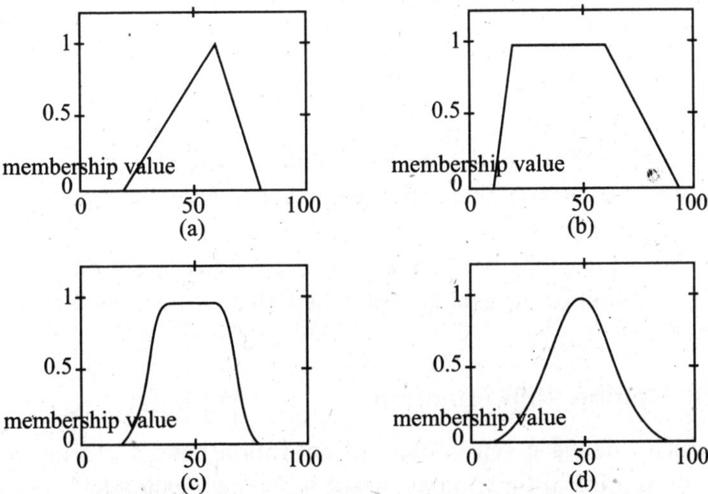

Figure 3.38: Examples of Four types of membership functions: (a) triangle(x; 20, 60, 80); (b) trapezoid(x; 10, 20, 60, 95); (c) Bell(x; 20, 4, 50); (d) gaussian(x; 50, 20)

3.15.2 Trapezoidal Membership Function

A trapezoidal membership function is specified by four parameters {a, b, c, d} as follows:

$$\text{trapezoid}(x\text{: a, b, c, d}) = \begin{cases} 0 & x < a \\ (x - a)/(b - a) & a \le x \le b \\ 1 & b \le x < c \\ (c - x)/(c - b) & c \le x \le c \\ 0 & x > d \end{cases} \tag{3.27}$$

Figure 3.38(b) illustrates an example of a trapezoidal membership function defined by trapezoid(x; 10, 20, 60, 95). Obviously, the triangular membership function is a special case of the trapezoidal membership function.

3.15.3 Gaussian Membership Functions

A Gaussian membership function is specified by two parameters {m, s} as follows:

$$\text{Gaussian}(x: m, \sigma) = \exp\left(\frac{(x-m)^2}{\sigma^2}\right) \quad (3.28)$$

where m and σ denote the center and width of the function, respectively. We can control the shape of the function by adjusting the parameter σ. A small σ will generate a "thin" membership function, while a big σ will lead to a "flat" membership function.

3.15.4 Bell-shaped Membership Function

A bell-shaped membership function is specified by three parameters {a, b, c} as follows:

$$\text{bell}\ (x: a, b, c) = \frac{1}{1+\left(\frac{x-c}{a}\right)^{2b}} \quad (3.29)$$

where the parameter b is usually positive. Note that this membership function is a direct generalization of the Cauchy distribution used in probability theory. A desired bell-shaped membership function can be obtained by a proper selection of the parameters a, b and c. Specifically, we can adjust c and a to vary the center and width of the function and then use b to control the slopes at the crossover points. Figure 3.38(c) illustrates an example of a bell-shaped membership function defined by bell(x; 20, 4, 50).

3.15.5 Sigmoidal Membership Functions

Terms on the boundaries of the given domain of definition have a profile that is most readily described in terms of a sigmoidal function as shown in the next example.

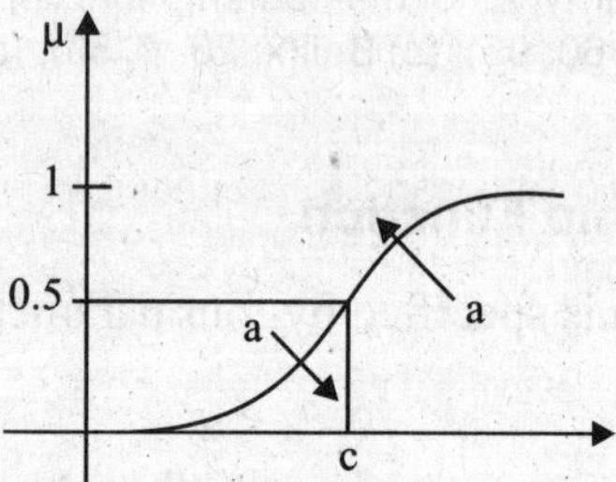

Figure 3.39: Sigmoidal Membership Function

As parameter increases, the transition from 0 to 1 becomes sharper. The function thus approximates the step function as approaches positive infinity. Finally, note that μ(c) = 0.5 for all sigmoidal membership functions, indicating the break-even point of the definition where transition from membership to nonmembership occurs.

3.15.6 S Membership Functions

The S membership function is a smooth membership function with two parameters: a and b. The shape of the function is shown in Figure 3.40. The membership value is 0 for points below a, 1 for points above b, and 0.5 for the midpoint between a and b. The name of this type of membership function, as you may guessed, comes from the "S" shape of the function.

$$S(x: a, b) = \begin{cases} 0 & x < a \\ 2\left(\frac{x-a}{b-a}\right)^2 & a \le x \le \frac{a+b}{2} \\ 1-2\left(\frac{x-a}{b-a}\right)^2 & \frac{a+b}{2} \le x < b \\ 1 & x \ge b \end{cases} \tag{3.30}$$

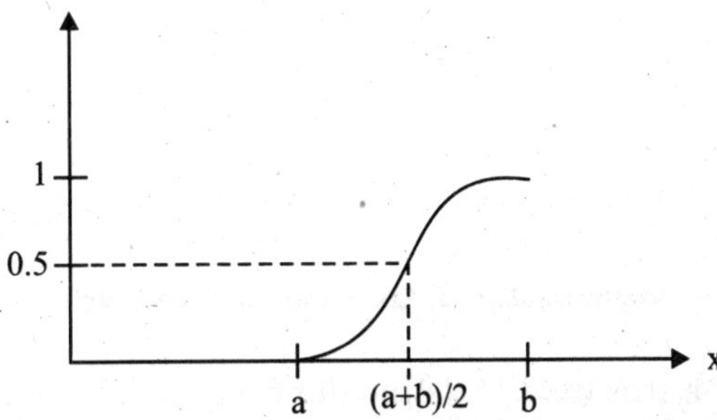

Figure 3.40: S Membership Function

3.15.7 Π Membership Function

There are two Π membership functions. The first Π membership function is defined with two parameters: a and b. The function has a membership value 1 at point a, membership value 0.5 at a – b and a + b, respectively. Unlike the S function, the Õ function decreases toward zero asymptotically as we move away from point a, as shown in Figure 3.41

$$\Pi_1 (x: a, b) = \frac{1}{1+\left(\frac{x-a}{2}\right)^2} \tag{3.31}$$

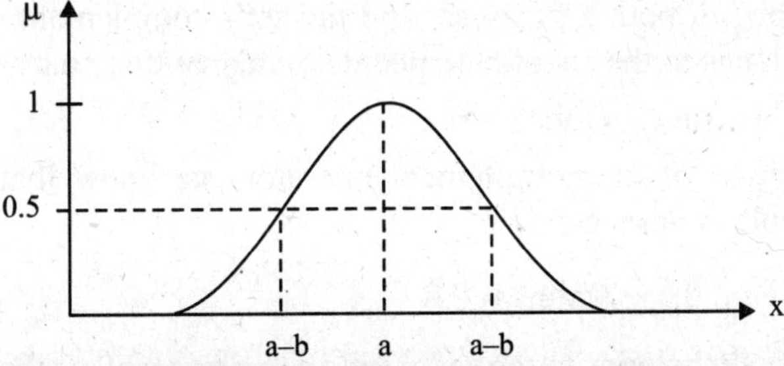

Figure 3.41: Π_1 Membership Function

The other membership function that has the "Π" shape is given in Eq. 3.32 and shown in Figure 3.42. This membership function has four parameters.

$$\Pi_2(x: lw, lp, rp, rw) = \begin{cases} \dfrac{lw}{lp + lw - x} & x < lp \\ 1 & lp \le x \le rp \\ \dfrac{rw}{x - rp + r} & x > rp \end{cases} \tag{3.32}$$

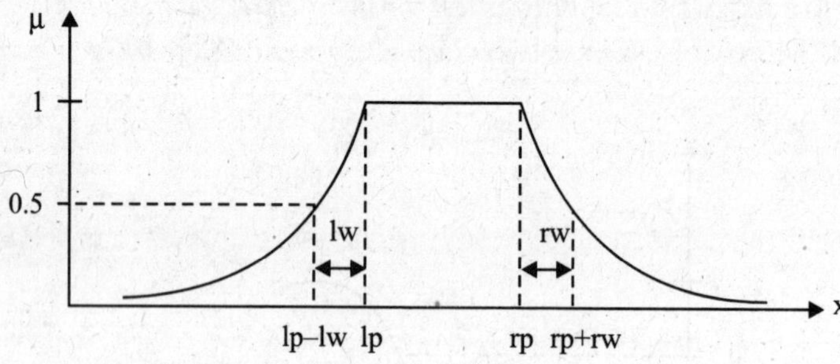

Figure 3.42: Π_2 Membership Function

This membership function was used to define the fuzzy set "Good Stopping Accuracy" in the Sendai Subway Train Control System:

$$\mu_{GoodStoppingAccuracy}(x) = \Pi_2(x; 20, 20, 30, 30)$$

where x is the distance (in cm) between stopping position and target position is considered 100 percent good stopping accuracy, while a train stopped at 50 cm away is considered to satisfy good stopping accuracy up to 50 percent.

3.16 FALLING OF THE LAW OF EXCLUDED MIDDLE AND THE LAW OF CONTRADICTION

Because fuzzy set theory generalizes the black-and-white situations of set membership to allow various "grey areas," it has to violate two fundamental laws of set theory – the law of excluded middle. $A \cup \overline{A} = U$, and the law of contradiction, $A \cap \overline{A} = \phi$. In other words, it is possible for an element to partially belong to both a fuzzy set and the set's complement. For instance, suppose John is a person who belongs to the set of bald people to degree 0.2, i.e.,

$$\mu_{Bald}\,(John) = 0.2$$

Based on the definition of the complement operator, we know that John belongs to the complement of bald people to degree 0.8, i.e.,

$$\mu_{\overline{Bald}}\,(John) = 0.8$$

Therefore, John partially belongs to the set of bald people as well as the set of people who are not bald.

Generally speaking, any element partially belonging to a fuzzy set is also a partial member of its complement. Knowing this difference between classical sets and fuzzy sets is important because it helps us to formally compare and analyze the two theories. Due to the fact that the law of excluded middle and the law of contradiction are not axioms of fuzzy set theory, formula equivalents in classical set theory are not necessarily equivalent in fuzzy set theory.

3.17 HEDGES

A hedge is a modifier to a fuzzy set. It modifies the meaning of the original set to create a compound fuzzy set. "Very" and "More or Less" are two commonly used hedges. Their definitions are listed below.

Very:

$$\mu_{\text{Very A}}(x) = [\mu_A(x)]^2 \qquad (3.33)$$

More or Less:

$$\mu_{\text{MoreOrLess A}}(x) = \sqrt{\mu_A(x)} \qquad (3.34)$$

We illustrate these hedges in Figure 3.43 through their application to the concept High temperature. As shown by the figure, "Very" has the effect of narrowing the membership function, while "More or Less" widens the membership function. This is intuitively appealing because the criteria for "Very High" should be more stringent than those for "High", while the criteria for "More or Less high" should be relaxed. In general, we should have

$$\mu_{\text{Very A}}(x) \leq \mu_A(x) \leq \mu_{\text{MoreOrLess A}}(x)$$

In principle, a hedge can be applied to any fuzzy sets.

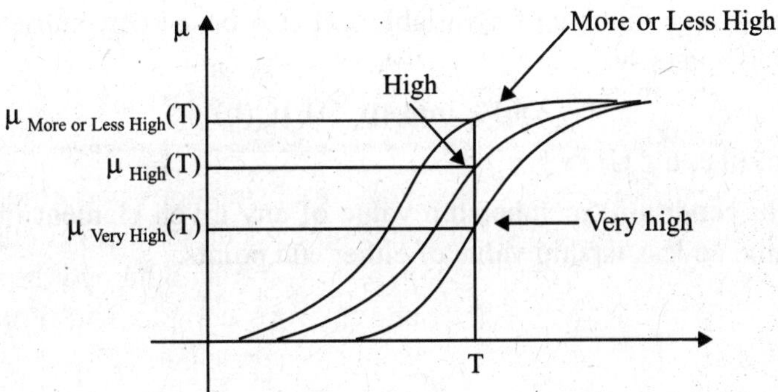

Figure 3.43 Definition of Very High

3.18 COMPLEMENT OF A FUZZY SET

The idea of complement reflects negation. We may define the complement of a fuzzy set in terms of the algebraic complement of its membership function, μ.

Let A be a fuzzy seA be a fuzzyer U. Then its complement, ¬A, is defined, in terms of $\mu_A(u)$, as

$$\mu_{ØA}(u) = 1 - \mu_A(u)$$

Figure 3.44 showre 3.44 shdement of the membership function High. Note that the above definition overlaps wbn overlaps iition of the term High. In fact, there exists some T_0 such that $\mu_{NotHigh}(T_0)$, which we T_0), which ie break-even point of the membership function. It is easy to see that the break-even pobreak-evenzy set A always has 0.5 membership degree in A.

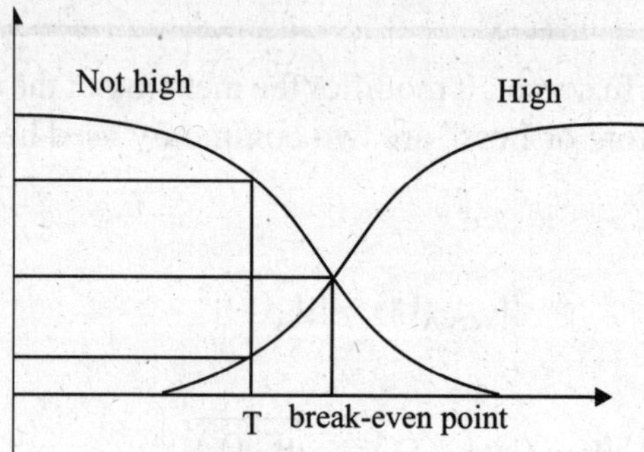

Figure 3.44 Definition of Not High

3.19 CONVEX FUCONVEX S

Another useful concej useful conset theory is the notion of convexity. Intuitively, a fuzzy set is convex if its memberif its membn does not have a "valley". The fuzzy set in Figure 3.45, for example, is not conve, is not coit has a valley around a. Formally, a convex fuzzy set can be described as follows. d as follow

Let U be a univerU be a uniurse of a variable x. Let A be a fuzzy subset of U. The set A is convex if and only if if and only

$$1 - \lambda)b) \geq \min\{\mu_A(a), \mu_A(b)\} \quad (3.35)$$

For all a, b ε U anall a, b ε U l ∩ 1.

This condition sta condition membership value of any given element in the interval [a, b] should be no less thanbe no less thrship value of either end points.

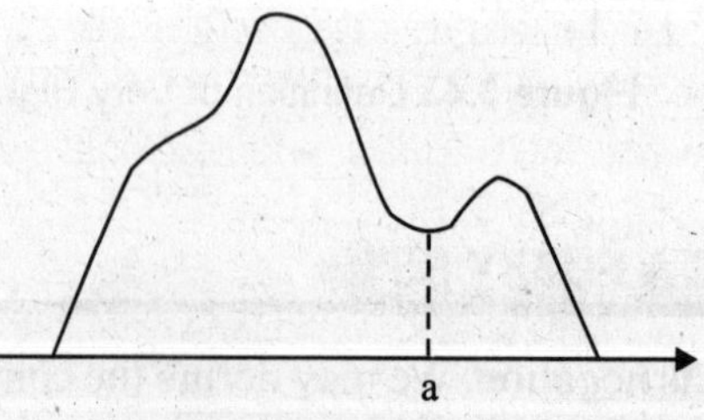

gure 3.45: A Non-convex Fuzzy Set

3.20 POSSIBILITY THEORY

Possibility distribution states the possible value of the variable or the possibility that the variable takes a certain value. A possibility distribution, π, maps a given domain of definition into the interval [0, 1]. We can view a possibility distribution, as a mechanism for interpreting factual statements involving fuzzy sets. The statement, "Temperature is High," where High is defined as μ_{High}: T → [0, 1], translates into a possibility distribution, $\pi(T) = \mu_{High}(T)$. Complex statements involving more than one fuzzy set translate into possibility distribution as well. In fact this is precisely how we interpret linguistic statements, given a priori or defined through an inference process.

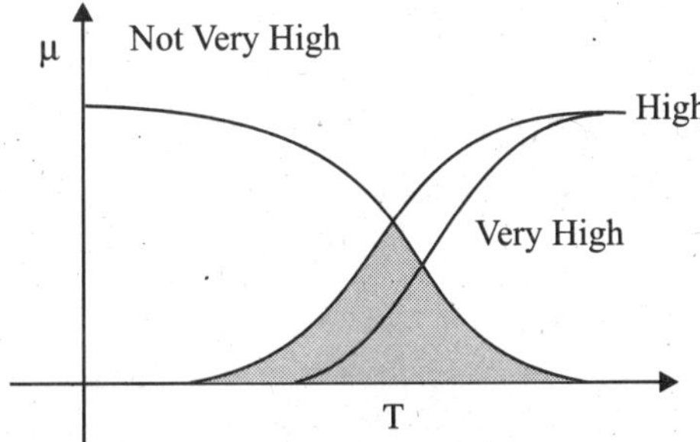

Figure 3.46: A Possibility Distribution of High AND NOT VERY HIGH

The statement, "Temperature is High but not too High," translates into a possibility distribution in terms of conjunction of the terms High and NOT VERY High:

$$\pi(T) = \mu n(\mu_{High}(T), m_{NOT\ VERY\ High}(T)).$$
$$= \min[\mu_{High}(T), 1 - (\mu_{High}(T))^2]$$

EXERCISES

1. Explain the difference between crisp set boundary and fuzzy set boundary?
2. What do you mean by set theory?
3. What do you mean by classical sets?
4. Explain the various operations on classical set?
5. Explain the properties of classical set?
6. How we can map classical sets to a function?
7. What do you mean by fuzzy set? Explain with the help of example.
8. Explain the representation of the fuzzy set?
9. What do you mean by fuzzy quantifiers?
10. What do you mean by fuzzy numbers?

11. Explain the various operations of fuzzy sets?
12. Explain the various properties of fuzzy sets?
13. What do you mean by cardinality of fuzzy set?
14. What do you mean by height of a fuzzy set?
15. Explain the concept of support and alpha level cuts in fuzzy sets?
16. Explain the resolution identify of a fuzzy set?
17. What are the various types of membership functions?
18. Explain the law of excluded middle and law of contradiction?
19. What do you mean by hedges?
20. Explain the complement of fuzzy set?
21. What do you mean by convex fuzzy set?
22. What do you mean by possibility theory?

CHAPTER 4

Fuzzy Relations, Fuzzy Graphs, and Fuzzy Arithmetic

4.1 INTRODUCTION

This chapter introduces the notion of a relation as the basic idea behind operations on sets such as Cartesian products, composition of relations, and equivalence properties. Like a set, a relation is of fundamental importance in all engineering, science, and mathematically based fields Relations can be also be used to represent similarity. Relations are intimately involved in logic, approximate reasoning, rule based systems, nonlinear simulation, synthetic evaluation, classification, pattern recognition, and control. Relations will be referred to repeatedly in this text in many different applications areas. Relations represent mappings for sets just as mathematical functions do; relations are also very useful in representing connectives in logic. This chapter begins by describing Cartesian products as a means of producing ordered relationships among sets. Following this is an introduction to classical (crisp) relations – structures that represent the presence or absence of correlation, interaction, or propinquity between the elements of two or more crisp sets; in this case, a set could also be the universe. There are only two degrees of relationship between elements of the sets in a crisp relation: the relationships "completely related" and "not related," in a binary sense.

Basic operations, properties, and the cardinality of relations are explained and illustrated. Two composition methods to relate elements of three or more universes are illustrated. Fuzzy relations are then developed by allowing the relationship between elements of two or more sets to take on an infinite number of degrees of relationship between the extremes of "completely related" and "not related." In this sense, fuzzy relations are to crisp relations as fuzzy sets are to crisp sets; crisp sets and relations are constrained realizations of fuzzy sets and relations. Both tolerance and equivalence relations are illustrated with some examples. Finally, the chapter concludes with a section on value assignments, which discusses various methods to develop the elements of relations, and a list of additional composition operators.

4.2 CARTESIAN PRODUCT

An ordered sequence of r elements, written in the form $(a_1, a_2, a_3, \ldots, a_r)$, is called an ordered r-tuple; an unordered r-tuple is simply a collection of r elements without restrictions on order. In a ubiquitous special case where r = 2, the r-tuple is referred to as an ordered pair. For crisp sets $A_1, A_2, \ldots, A_r$, the set of all r-tuples $(a_1, a_2, a_3, \ldots, a_r)$, where $a_1 \in A_1$, $a_2 \in A_2$, and $a_r \in A_r$, is called the Cartesian product of $A_1, A_2, \ldots, A_r$, and is denoted by $A_1 \times A_2 \times \ldots \times A_r$. The Cartesian product of two or more sets is not the same thing as the arithmetic product of two or more sets. When the extension principle is introduced. When all the A_r are identical and equal to A, the Cartesian product $A_1 \times A_2 \times \ldots \times A_r$ can be denoted as A_r.

Example 4.1: The elements in two sets A and B are given as A = {0, 1} and B = {e, f, g} find the Cartesian product A × B, B × A, A × A, B × B.

Solution: The Cartesian product for the given sets is as follows:

$$A \times B = \{(0, e), (0, f), (0, g), (1, e), (1, f), (1, g)\},$$

$$B \times A = \{(e, 0), (e, 1), (e, 1), (f, 1), (g, 1)\},$$

$$A \times A = A^2 = \{(0, 0), (0, 1), (1, 0), (1, 1)\},$$

$$B \times B = B^2 = \{(e, e), (e, f), (e, g), (f, e), (f, f), (f, g), (g, e), (g, f), (g, g)\}.$$

4.3 CRISP RELATIONS

A subset of the Cartesian product $A_1 \times A_2 \times \ldots \times A_r$ is called an r-ary relation over $A_1, A_2, \ldots, A_r$. Again, the most common case is for r = 2; in this situation the relation is a subset of the Cartesian product $A_1 \times A_2$ (i.e., a set of pairs, the first coordinate of which is from A_1 and the second from A_2). This subset of the full Cartesian product is called a binary relation from A_1 into A_2. If three, four, or five sets are involved in a subset of the full Cartesian product, the relations are called ternary, quaternary, and quinary, respectively. In this text, whenever the term relation is used without qualification, it is taken to mean a binary relation. The Cartesian product of two universes X and Y is determined as

$$X \times Y = \{x, y) \mid x \in X, y \in Y\} \tag{4.1}$$

which forms an ordered pair of every $x \in X$ with every $y \in Y$, forming unconstrained matches between X and Y. That is, every element in universe X is related completely to every element in universe Y. The strength of this relationship between ordered pairs of elements in each universe is measured by the characteristic function, denoted χ, where a value of unity is associated with complete relationship and a value of zero is associated with no relationship, i.e.,

$$\chi_{X \times Y}(x, y) = \begin{cases} 1, & (x, y) \in X \times Y \\ 0, & (x, y) \notin X \ Y \end{cases} \tag{4.2}$$

One can think of this strength of relation as a mapping from ordered pairs of the universe, or ordered pairs of sets defined on the universes, to the characteristic function. When the universes, or sets, are finite the relation can be conveniently represented by a matrix, called a relation matrix. An r-ary relation can be represented by an r-dimensional relation matrix. Hence, binary relations can be represented by two-dimensional matrices (used throughout this text).

An example of the strength of relation for the unconstrained case is given in the Sagittal diagram shown in Figure 4.1. Lines in the Sagittal diagram and values of unity in the relation matrix

$$R = \begin{array}{c} \\ 1 \\ 2 \\ 3 \end{array} \begin{array}{c} \begin{array}{ccc} a & b & c \end{array} \\ \begin{bmatrix} 1 & 1 & 1 \\ 1 & 1 & 1 \\ 1 & 1 & 1 \end{bmatrix} \end{array}$$

correspond to the ordered pairs of mappings in the relatiolements in e elements in the two universes are defined as X = {1, 2, 3} and Y = {a, b, c}.

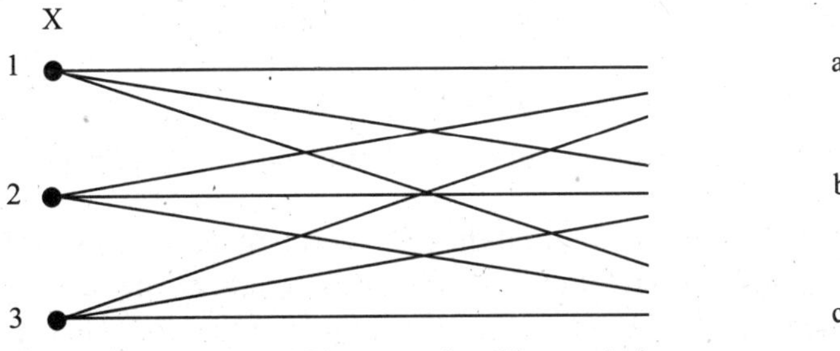

Figure 4.1: Sagittal Diagram of an Unconstrai

A more general crisp relation, R, exists when matches betwn two univets in two universes are constrained. Again, the characteristic function is used to assign vaship in the rionship in the mapping of the Cartesian space X × Y to the binary values of (0, 1):

$$X_R(x,y) = \begin{cases} 1, & (x,y) \in R \\ 0, & (x,y) \notin R \end{cases} \tag{4.3}$$

Example 4.2: Let R be a relation among the three sets

X= {Hindi, English}, Y = {Doxllar, Euro, Pound, Rupees}, andepal, Unite Nepal, United States, Canada} R (x, y, z) = {Hindi, Rupees, India}

{Hindi, Rupees, Nepal}

{English, Dollar, Canada}

{English, Dollar, United States}.

Solution: The relation can be represented as follows:

Hindi

	India	Nepal	US
Dollar	0	0	0
Euro	0	0	0
Pound	0	0	0
Rupees	1	1	0

English

	India	Nepal	US
Dollar	0	0	1
Euro	0	0	0
Pound	0	0	0
Rupees	0	0	0

Example 4.3: In many biological models, members of certain species can reproduce only with certain members of another species. Hence, only some elements in two or more universes have a relationship (nonzero) in the Cartesian product. An example is shown in Figure 4.2 for two two-member species, i.e., for X = {1, 2} and for Y = {a, b}. In this case the locations of zeros in the relation matrix

$$R = \{(1, a), (2, b)\} \; R \subset X \times Y$$

X Y
1 a
2 b

Figure 4.2: Relation Matrix and Sagittal Diagram for a Constrained Relation.

and the absence of lines in t he Sagittal diagram correspond to pairs of elements between the two universes where there is "no relation"; that is, the strength of the relationship is zero. Special cases of the constrained and the unconstrained Cartesian product for sets where r = 2 (i.e., for A^2) are called the identity relation and the universal relation, respectively.

For example, for A = {0, 1, 2} the universal relation, denoted U_A, and the identity relation, denoted I_A, are found to be

$$U_A = \{(0, 0), (0, 1), (0, 2), (1, 0), (1, 1), (1, 2), (2, 0), (2, 1), (2, 2)\}$$
$$I_A = \{(0, 0), (1, 1), (2, 2)\}$$

Example 4.4: Relations can also be defined for continuous universes. Consider, for example, the continuous relation defined by the following expression:

$$R = \{(x, y) \mid y \geq 2x, x \in X, y \in Y\}$$

which is also given in function-theoretic form using the characteristic function as

$$\chi R(X, Y) = \begin{cases} 1, & y \geq 2x \\ 0, & y < 2x \end{cases}$$

Graphically, this relation is equivalent to the shaded region shown in Figure 4.3.

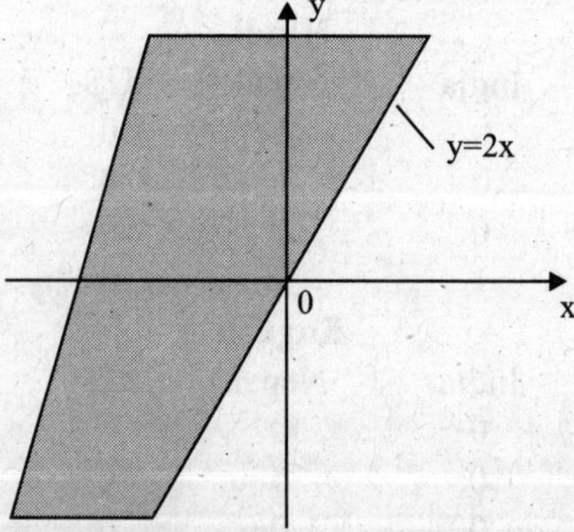

Figure 4.3: Relation Corresponding to the Expression y > 2x.

4.3.1 Cardinality of Crisp Relations

Suppose n elements of the universe X are related (paired) to m elements of the universe Y. If the cardinality of X is n_X and the cardinality of Y is n_Y then the cardinality of the relation, R, between these two universes is $n_{X\times Y}$ $n_X{*}n_Y$. The cardinality of the power set describing this relation, $P(X \times Y)$, is then $n_{P(X\times Y)} = 2^{(n_X n_Y)}$.

4.3.2 Operations on Crisp Relations

Define R and S as two separate relations on the Cartesian universe X × Y, and define the null relation and the complete relation as the relation matrices $\underset{\sim}{O}$ and $\underset{\sim}{E}$, respectively. An example of a 4 × 4 form of the $\underset{\sim}{O}$ and $\underset{\sim}{E}$ matrices are given here:

$$O = \begin{bmatrix} 0 & 0 & 0 & 0 \\ 0 & 0 & 0 & 0 \\ 0 & 0 & 0 & 0 \\ 0 & 0 & 0 & 0 \end{bmatrix}$$

$$F = \begin{bmatrix} 1 & 1 & 1 & 1 \\ 1 & 1 & 1 & 1 \\ 1 & 1 & 1 & 1 \\ 1 & 1 & 1 & 1 \end{bmatrix}$$

The following function-theoretic operations for the two crisp relations (R, S) can now be defined.

Union	$R \cup S \to \chi_{R\cup S}(x, y) : \chi_{R\cup S}(x, y) = \max[\chi_R(x, y), \chi_S(x, y)]$
Intersection	$R \cap S \to \chi_{R\cap S}(x, y) : \chi_{R\cap S}(x, y) = \min[\chi_R(x, y), \chi_S(x, y)]$
Complement	$\bar{R} \to \chi_{\bar{R}}(x, y) : \chi_{\bar{R}}(x, y) = 1 - \chi_R(x, y)$
Containment	$R \subset S \to \chi_R(x, y) : \chi_R(x, y) \le \chi_S(x, y)$
Identity	$\phi \to O$ and $X \to E$

4.3.3 Properties of Crisp Relations

The properties of commutativity, associativity, distributivity, involution, and idempotency all hold for crisp relations just as they do for classical set operations. Moreover, De Morgan's principles and the excluded middle axioms also hold for crisp (classical) relations just as they do for crisp (classical) sets. The null relation, **O**, and the complete relation, **E**, are analogous to the null set, ∅, and the whole set, X, respectively, in the set-theoretic case (see Chapter 3).

4.3.4 Composition

Let R be a relation that relates, or maps, elements from universe X to universe Y, and let S be a relation that relates, or maps, elements from universe Y to universe Z. A useful question we seek to answer is whether we can find a relation, T, that relates the same elements in universe X that R contains to the same elements in universe Z that S contains. It turns out we can find such a relation using an operation known as composition. For the Sagittal diagram in Figure 4.4, we see that the only "path" between relation R and relation S is the two routes that start at x_1 and end at z_2 (i.e., $x_1 - y_1 - z_2$ and $x_1 - y_3 - z_2$). Hence, we wish to find a relation T that relates the ordered pair (x_1, z_2), i.e., $(x_1, z_2) \in$ T. In this example,

$$R = \{(x_1, y_1), (x_1, y_3), (x_2, y_4)\}$$
$$S = \{(y_1, z_2), (y_3, z_2)\}$$

There are two common forms of the composition operation; one is called the max–min composition and the other the max–product composition. (Five other forms of the composition operator are available for certain logic issues; these are described at the end of this chapter.) The ax–min composition is defined by the set-theoretic and membership function-theoretic expressions

$$T = R \circ S$$
$$\chi_T(x, z) = \bigvee_{y \in Y} (\chi_R(x, y) \wedge \chi_S(y, z)) \tag{4.4}$$

and the max–product (sometimes called max–dot) composition is defined by the set theoretic and membership function-theoretic expressions

$$T = R \circ S$$
$$\chi_T(x, z) = \bigvee_{y \in Y} (\chi_R(x, y) \wedge \chi_S(y, z)) \tag{4.5}$$

X Y Z
x_1 y_1
x_2 y_2 z_1
x_3 y_3 z_2
y_4

Figure 4.4: Sagittal Diagram Relating Elements of Three Universes.

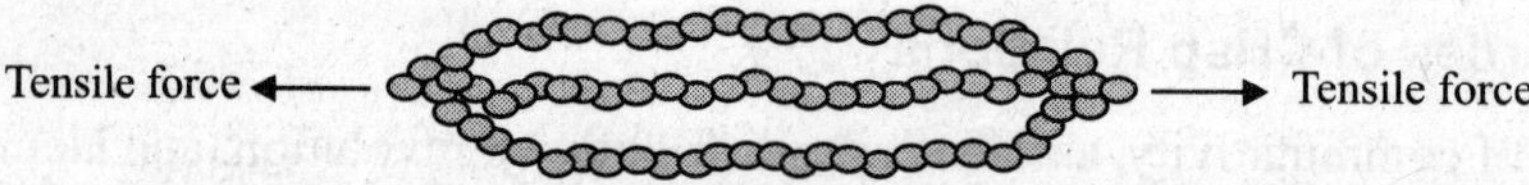

Figure 4.5: Chain Strength Analogy for Max–Min Composition.

There is a very interesting physical analogy for the max–min composition operator. Figure 4.5 illustrates a system comprising several chains placed together in a parallel fashion. In the system, each chain comprises a number of chain links. If we were to take one of the chains out of the system, place it in a tensile test machine, and exert a large tensile force on the chain, we would find that the chain would break at its weakest link. Hence, the strength of one chain is equal to the strength of its weakest link; in other words, the minimum (∧) strength of all the links in the chain governs the strength of the overall chain.

Now, if we were to place the entire chain system in a tensile device and exert a tensile force on the chain system, we would find that the chain system would continue to carry increasing loads until the last chain in the system broke. That is, weaker chains would break with an increasing load until the strongest chain was left alone, and eventually it would break; in other words, the maximum ($\vee$) strength of all the chains in the chain system would govern the overall strength of the chain system. Each chain in the system is analogous to the min operation in the max–min composition, and the overall chain system strength is analogous to the max operation in the max–min composition.

Example 4.5: The matrix expression for the crisp relations shown in Figure 4.4 can be found using the max–min composition operation. Relation matrices for R and S would be expressed as

$$R = \begin{array}{c} \\ x_1 \\ x_2 \\ x_3 \end{array} \begin{array}{c} \begin{array}{cccc} y_1 & y_2 & y_3 & y_4 \end{array} \\ \begin{bmatrix} 1 & 0 & 1 & 0 \\ 0 & 0 & 0 & 1 \\ 0 & 0 & 0 & 0 \end{bmatrix} \end{array}$$

and

$$S = \begin{array}{c} \\ y_1 \\ y_2 \\ y_3 \\ y_4 \end{array} \begin{array}{c} \begin{array}{cc} z_1 & z_2 \end{array} \\ \begin{bmatrix} 0 & 1 \\ 0 & 0 \\ 0 & 1 \\ 0 & 0 \end{bmatrix} \end{array}$$

The resulting relation T would then be determined by max–min composition, Eq. (4.4), or max–product composition, Eq. (4.5). (In the crisp case these forms of the composition operators produce identical results; other forms of this operator, such as those listed at the end of this chapter, will not produce identical results.) For example,

$$\text{ì}_T(x_1, z_1) = \max[\min(1, 0), \min(0, 0), \min(1, 0), \min(0, 0)] = 0$$

$$\text{ì}_T(x_1, z_2) = \max[\min(1, 1), \min(0, 0), \min(1, 1), \min(0, 0)] = 1$$

and for the rest,

$$T = \begin{array}{c} \\ x_1 \\ x_2 \\ x_3 \end{array} \begin{array}{c} \begin{array}{cc} z_1 & z_2 \end{array} \\ \begin{bmatrix} 0 & 1 \\ 0 & 0 \\ 0 & 0 \end{bmatrix} \end{array}$$

4.4 FUZZY RELATIONS

A fuzzy relation generalizes the notion of a classical black-and-white relation into one that allows partial membership. For example, a binary relation "friend" will classify all human relationships into either being friend or not being friend. A fuzzy relation "Friend," in contrast, can describe the degree of friendship between tow persons.

The classical notation of relation describes a relationship that holds between two or more objects. A relationship between two objects is represented by a binary relation, a relation with two arguments. For example, the parent relationship between a parent and his/her child can be represented as a binary relation. More generally, we can use an n-ary relation, a relation with n arguments, to describe a relationship between n objects. For instance, we can use an n-ary relation to describe that student X took course Y during semester Z in year W. This relation has four arguments such as took_course (student, course, semester, year). An n-ary relation can be formally defined as set of ordered lists of n objects. Each list describes a case in which the relation holds.

A binary relation on variables x and y, whose domains are X and Y respectively, can be defined as a set of ordered pairs in $X \times Y$. For instance, the binary relation "less than" between two real numbers can be formally defined as

$$R = \{(x, y) \mid x < y, x, y \in R\}$$

It is easy to see that the relation is a subset of X x Y. In general, an n-ary relation on $x_1, x_2, \ldots, x_n$ whose domains are $X_1, X_2, \ldots, X_n$ is a subset of $X_1 \times X_2 \times \ldots \times X_n$.

Since a relation can be viewed as a set, we can easily generalize the classical notion of a relation using fuzzy sets. We will show how to generalize binary relations. First, we can represent a binary relation R on x, y with domains X, Y as a function that maps an ordered pair (x, y) in $X \times Y$ to 0 (i.e., the relation does not hold between x and y) or 1 (i.e., the relation holds between x and y), i.e.,

$$R = X \times Y \rightarrow \{0, 1\}$$

A fuzzy relation generalizes the classical notion of relation into a matter of degree. As we mentioned earlier, the fuzzy relation Friend describes the degree of friendship between two persons.

Fuzzy relations also map elements of one universe, say X, to those of another universe, say Y, through the Cartesian product of the two universes. However, the "strength" of the relation between ordered pairs of the two universes is not measured with the characteristic function, but rather with a membership function expressing various "degrees" of strength of the relation on the unit interval [0,1]. Hence, a fuzzy relation $\underset{\sim}{R}$ is a mapping from the Cartesian space $X \times Y$ to the interval [0,1], where the strength of the mapping is expressed by the membership function of the relation for ordered pairs from the two universes, or $\mu\underset{\sim}{R}(x, y)$.

Similarly, a fuzzy relation Petite between height and weight of a person describes the degree by which a person with a specific height and weight is considered petite. Formally, fuzzy relation R between variables x and y, whose domains are X and Y, respectively, is defined by a function that maps ordered pairs in $X \times Y$ to their degree in the relation, which is a number between 0 and 1, i.e., $R: X \times Y \rightarrow [0, 1]$.

More generally, a fuzzy n-ary relation R in $x_1, x_{2,\ldots,} x_n$ whose domains are $X_1, X_2, \ldots, X_n$, respectively, is defined by a function that maps an n-tuple $< x_1, x_{2,\ldots,} x_n >$ in $X_1 \times, X_2 \times \ldots, \times X_n$, to a number in the interval, i.e., $R: X_1 \times X_2 \times \ldots \times X_n \rightarrow [0, 1]$. Just as a classical relation can be viewed as a set, a fuzzy relation can be viewed as a fuzzy subset. From this perspective, the mapping above is equivalent to the membership function of a multidimensional fuzzy set.

If the possible values of x and y are discrete, we can express a fuzzy relation in a matrix form. For example, suppose we wish to express a fuzzy relation Petite in terms of the height and the weight of a female. Suppose the range of the height and the weight of interest to us are {5' 5'1", 5'2", 5'3", 5'4", 5'5",5'6"}, denoted h,, and {90, 95, 100, 105, 110, 115, 120, 125} (in lb.) denoted w, respectively. We can express the fuzzy relation in a matrix form as shown below:

Each entry in the matrix indicates the degree a female with the corresponding height (i.e., the row

	90	95	100	105	110	115	120	125
5	1	1	1	1	1	1	0.5	0.2
5'1"	1	1	1	1	1	0.9	0.3	0.1
5'2"	1	1	1	1	1	0.7	0.1	0
5'3"	1	1	1	1	0.5	0.3	0	0
5'4"	0.8	0.6	0.4	0.2	0	0	0	0
5'5"	0.6	0.4	0.2	0	0	0	0	0
5'6"	0	0	0	0	0	0	0	0

heading) and weight (i.e., the column heading) is considered to be petite. For instance, the entry corresponding to a height of 5'3" and a weight of 115 lb. has a value 0.3, which is the degree to which such a female person will be considered a petite person; i.e., Petite(5'3", 115 lb) = 0.3.Once we define the Petite fuzzy relation, we can answer two kinds of questions:

- What is the degree that a female with a specific height and a specific weight is considered to be petite?
- What is the possibility that a petite person has a specific pair of height and weight measures?

4.4.1 Composition of Fuzzy Relations

We have shown that once we have a fuzzy relation, we can directly answer two kinds of interesting questions. We can view these question-answer capabilities as inferences (e.g., inferring the possible weight-height combinations knowing that a person is petite). An even more useful king of inference is the following:

- Given a two-dimensional fuzzy relation and the possible values of one variable, infer the possible values of the other variable.

For instance, we may wish to know the possible weight of a petite female called Michelle who is about 5'4" tall where "about" indicates impression. The answer to this question can be obtained through the composition of fuzzy relations, which is also referred to as the compositional rule of inference. To find out the answer, we will then consider whether it is possible for such a person to weigh 90 lb, 95 lb, ..., 120 lb. Because we are interested in finding all possible weights of the person, we may get multiple positive answers. Furthermore, the answer should indicate the degree of possibility for each weight.

How do we find out whether it is possible for Michelle to have a specific weight, say 110 lb?, If we think about this for a moment, it is not difficult to realize that we need to consider all possible heights of a the person and see if petite person with such a height can weigh 110 lb. For example, we may start with 5 feet and check if the following two conditions are both rule:

- What is the possibility that Michelle's height is 5 feet given that she is about 5'4" tall?
- What is the possibility that a petite person is 5 feet tall and weighs 110 lb?

If the answers to both questions are positive, wee infer that 110 lb is a possible weight of Michelle. We can ask two similar questions for the next height, which is 5 feet 2 inches.

- What is the possibility that Michelle's height is 5 feet 2 inches given that she is about 5'4" tall?
- What is the possibility that a petite person is 5 feet 2 inches tall and weighs 110 lb?

The procedure can be repeated for all the remaining height measures (i.e., 5'4", 5'6",..., 6'). We can represent such a procedure in predicate logic. Predicate logic is a logic system that uses "predicate," as building blocks for constructing logic formulae. A predicate is like a function that maps its arguments to either true or false. The arguments of a predicate are usually variables or constants. Predicates are often connected into a logic formula using and (denoted $\wedge$), or (denoted $\vee$), and imply (denoted $\rightarrow$). A bidirectional implication is denoted by $\leftrightarrow$. Variables are quantified by a "for all" quantifier ($\forall$) or a "there exists" quantifier ($\exists$). These notations are summarized in Table 4.1. To help you get familiar with these notations, we will use them in the discussion below.

Table 4.1: Predicate Logic Notations

Symbol	Meaning
$\wedge$	and
$\vee$	or
$\forall$	for all
$\exists$	there exists
$\leftrightarrow$	if and only if
$\rightarrow$	imply

We use three predicates to describes the reasoning process above in logic:

Possible-height(h_i): The predicate is true if h_i is a possible height of a person.

Possible-height(w_j): The predicate is true if w_j is a possible height of a person.

Petite (h_i, w_j): the predicate is true if a person with height h_i and w_j weight is petite.

Notice that the first two predicates represent crisp (i.e., nonfuzzy) constraints on possible heights and weights, whereas the last predicate represents a crisp binary relation. Therefore, they cannot truly represent the possibility distribution of About 5'4", or the fuzzy relation Petite. However, we will use these predicates to show how the inference procedure above can be expressed in classical logic. We will then generalize such a logic expression to obtain the compositional rule of inference in fuzzy logic. We first represent the inference procedure described earlier in logic as follows:

[(Possible-height (5') ∧ Petite (5', 90)) ∨
(Possible-height (5'2") ∧ Petite (5', 90)) ∨
⋮
(Possible-height(6') ∧ Petite (6', 90))] ↔ Possible-weight(90)

Since the same procedure can be used to determine whether it is possible for a person to weigh 95, 100, 105, ..., 125 pounds, we can use a more general expression in logic as follows:

$\forall w_j$ [(Possible-height (5') ∧Petite (5', w_j)) ∨
(Possible-height (5'2") ∧Petite (5'2", w_j)) ∨
⋮
(Possible-height(6') ∧ Petite (6', w_j))] ↔ Possible-weight(w_j)

This can be rewritten into a more compact form:

$$\forall w_j \text{ Possible-weig}\left(\text{ht}(w_j) \leftrightarrow \bigvee_{h_i} \text{Possible-height}(h_i) \wedge \text{Petite}(h_i, w_j)\right) \quad (4.6)$$

In fact, this is a special case (i.e., the binary case) of the composition of a fuzzy relation. In fuzzy logic, as we already know, both the notion of possibility and the notion of relation become matters of degree. Let us return to our original question, "what are the possible weights of a petite female called Michelle who is about 5' 4" tall?" Suppose the meaning of petite is expressed by the fuzzy relation Petite in the previous section. We introduce the following notations to represent about related possibility distributions:

- $\Pi_{height(x)}$ (h_i): The possibility degree for a person's height to be h_i.
- Π_{petite}(h_i, w_j): The possibility degree for a petite person to have a height of h_i, and a weight of w_j.

Furthermore, the conjunctions (∧) and disjunctions (∨) in Equation 4.6 in binary logic need to be generalized to a fuzzy conjunction (⊗) and a fuzzy disjunction (⊗) operator. Therefore, we can infer Michelle's possible weight form her possible height and also the fact that she is petite using a generalized version of Equation 4.6, which is given below:

$$\Pi_{weight(x)}(w_j) = \bigotimes_{h_i} (\Pi_{Height(x)}(h_i) \otimes \Pi_{Petite}(h_i, w_j)) \quad (4.7)$$

This is an application of the compositional rule of inference to our example. We define the compositional rule of inference more formally below.

Let X and Y be the universe of discourse for variables x and y, respectively and x_i and y_j be elements of X and Y. Let R be a fuzzy relation that maps X × Y to [0, 1] and the possibility distribution of X is known to be Π_x (x_i). The compositional rule of inference infers the possibility distribution of Y as follows:

$$\Pi_Y(y_j) = \bigotimes_{x_i} (\Pi_x(x_i) \otimes \Pi_R(x_i, y_j)) \quad (4.8)$$

The computation steps for the compositional rule of inference are similar to those of matrix multiplication. The fuzzy conjunction and disjunction operations in Equation 4.8 correspond respectively to the multiplication and summation steps in matrix multiplication.

The compositional rule of inference is not uniquely defined. By choosing different fuzzy conjunction and fuzzy disjunction operators, we get different compositional rules of inference. We list two that are commonly used in practice:

1. max-min composition:

$$\Pi_Y(y_j) = \max_{x_i} (\min(\Pi_x(x_i), \Pi_R(x_i, y_j))) \tag{4.9}$$

2. max-product composition:

$$\Pi_Y(y_j) = \max_{x_i} (\Pi_x(x_i), \Pi_R(x_i, y_j))) \tag{4.10}$$

Returning to our example, let us assume About-5'4" is defined as

About-5'4" = {0/5, 0/5'", 0.4/5'2", 0.8/5'3", 1/5'4", 0.8/5'5", 0.4/5'6"} (4.11)

Using the max-min compositional rule of inference, we can compute the weight possibility distribution of a petite person about 5'4" tall:

$$\Pi_{weight}(90) = (0 \wedge 1) \vee (0 \wedge 1) \vee (0.4 \wedge 1) \vee (0.8 \wedge 1) \vee (1 \wedge 0.8) \vee (0.8 \wedge 0.6) \vee (0.4 \wedge 0) = 0.8 \tag{4.12}$$

Similarly, we can compute the possibility degree for other weights. The final result is

$$\Pi_{weight} = \{0.8/90, 0.8/95, 0.8/100, 0.8/105, 0.5/110, 0.4/115, 0.1/120, 0/125\}$$

Mathematically, the composition of fuzzy relations can be defined using three basic operations: projection, cylindrical extension, and intersection. We introduce the first two concepts before we give a formal definition of the composition of fuzzy relations.

Cylindrical Extension

Cylindrical extension and projection are dual operations. The former extends the dimension of a fuzzy relation while the latter reduces the dimension of a fuzzy relation.

Typically, we apply cylindrical extension to two fuzzy relations so that they have the same dimensionality in order to apply set operations (i.e. intersections and union) to them. For example, we can apply cylindrical extension to the fuzzy set About 5'4" to H × W. The result is

$$\text{About-5'4''} = \begin{array}{c} \\ 5 \\ 5'1'' \\ 5'2'' \\ 5'3'' \\ 5'4'' \\ 5'5'' \\ 5'6'' \end{array} \begin{array}{c} \begin{array}{cccccccc} 90 & 95 & 100 & 105 & 110 & 115 & 120 & 125 \end{array} \\ \begin{pmatrix} 0 & 0 & 0 & 0 & 0 & 0 & 0 & 0 \\ 0 & 0 & 0 & 0 & 0 & 0 & 0 & 0 \\ 0.4 & 0.4 & 0.4 & 0.4 & 0.4 & 0.4 & 0.4 & 0.4 \\ 0.8 & 0.8 & 0.8 & 0.8 & 0.8 & 0.8 & 0.8 & 0.8 \\ 1 & 1 & 1 & 1 & 1 & 1 & 1 & 1 \\ 0.8 & 0.8 & 0.8 & 0.8 & 0.8 & 0.8 & 0.8 & 0.8 \\ 0.4 & 0.4 & 0.4 & 0.4 & 0.4 & 0.4 & 0.4 & 0.4 \end{pmatrix} \end{array} \tag{4.13}$$

Figure 4.6 shows graphically the effect of applying cylindrical extension to a fuzzy subset A of U to the extended dimension U × V. As shown in the figure, the membership function of the extended fuzzy set has a cylinder shape from which the operation gets its name.

Definition Let R be a fuzzy subset of $U_{i1} \times U_{i2} \times \ldots \times U_{ik}$, where $(i_1, i_2, \ldots, i_k)$, is a subsequence of $(1, 2, \ldots, n)$. The cylindrical extension of R in $U_1 \times U_2 \times \ldots \times U_n$ is a fuzzy subset of $U_1 \times U_2 \times \ldots \times U_n$, denoted as R, whose membership function is defined as

$$\mu_R(U_1, U_2, \ldots, U_n) = \mu_R(U_{i1}, U_{i2}, \ldots, U_{ik}) \tag{4.14}$$

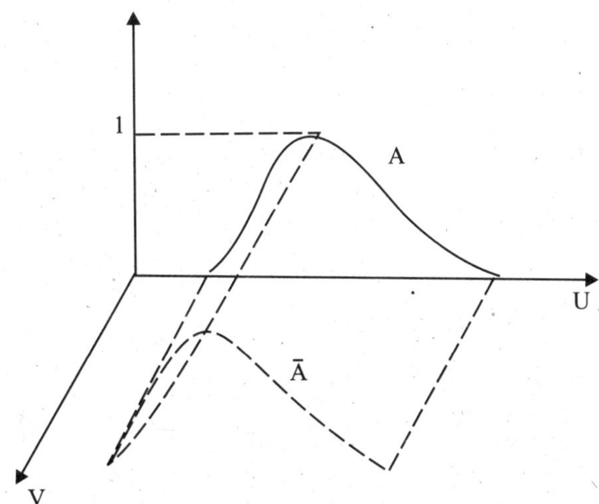

Figure 4.6: An Example of Cylindrical Extension

Projection

The projection operation, as the name suggest projects a fuzzy relation to a subset of selected dimensions. This operation is often used to extract the possibility distribution of a few selected variables from a given fuzzy relation. For instance, the projection of the Petite fuzzy relation to the universe of weight gives us a possibility distribution of a petite female person's weight. Projection to a fuzzy relation is analogous to computing the marginal probability on a joint probability distribution, we perform fuzzy disjunction across a row or a column of a fuzzy relation. Hence, the result of projecting the Petite relation to weight is

$$\mu_{Proj_w \text{ Petite}} = \{1/90, 1/95, 1/100, 1/105, 1/110, 1/115, 0.5/120, 0.2/125\} \tag{4.15}$$

4.4.2 Cardinality of Fuzzy Relations

Since the cardinality of fuzzy sets on any universe is infinity, the cardinality of a fuzzy relation between two or more universes is also infinity.

4.4.3 Operations on Fuzzy Relations

Let $\underset{\sim}{R}$ and $\underset{\sim}{S}$ be fuzzy relations on the Cartesian space $X \times Y$. Then the following operations apply for the membership values for various set operations:

Union $\mu_{\underset{\sim}{R} \cup \underset{\sim}{S}}(x, y) = \max(\mu_{\underset{\sim}{R}}(x, y), |\mu_{\underset{\sim}{S}}(x, y))$

Intersection $\mu_{\underset{\sim}{R} \cap \underset{\sim}{S}}(x, y) = \min(\mu_{\underset{\sim}{R}}(x, y), \mu_{\underset{\sim}{S}}(x, y))$

Complement $\mu\bar{\underset{\sim}{R}}(x, y) = 1 - \mu_{\underset{\sim}{R}}(x, y)$

Containment $\underset{\sim}{R} \subset \underset{\sim}{S} \Rightarrow \mu_{\underset{\sim}{R}}(x, y), \leq \mu_{\underset{\sim}{S}}(x, y)$

4.4.4 Properties of Fuzzy Relations

Just as for crisp relations, the properties of commutativity, associativity, distributivity, involution, and idempotency all hold for fuzzy relations. Moreover, De Morgan's principles hold for fuzzy relations just as they do for crisp (classical) relations, and the null relation, **O**, and the complete relation, **E**, are analogous to the null set and the whole set in set-theoretic form, respectively.

Commutativity $\mu_{\underset{\sim}{R} \cup \underset{\sim}{S}}(x, y) = \mu_{\underset{\sim}{S} \cap \underset{\sim}{R}}(x, y)$.

Associativity $\mu_{(\underset{\sim}{R} \cup \underset{\sim}{S}) \cup \underset{\sim}{T}}(x, y) = \mu_{\underset{\sim}{R} \cup (\underset{\sim}{S} \cup \underset{\sim}{T}}(x, y)$.

Distributivity $\mu_{(\underset{\sim}{R} \cup \underset{\sim}{S}) \cap \underset{\sim}{T}}(x, y) = \mu_{\underset{\sim}{R} \cup (\underset{\sim}{S} \cap \underset{\sim}{T}}(x, y)$.

Idempotency $\mu_{\underset{\sim}{R} \cup \underset{\sim}{R}}(x, y) = \mu_{\underset{\sim}{R}}$.

Involtution $\mu_{\bar{\bar{\underset{\sim}{R}}}}(x, y) = \mu_{\underset{\sim}{R}}(x, y)$.

Fuzzy relations are not constrained, as is the case for fuzzy sets in general, by the excluded middle axioms. Since a fuzzy relation $\underset{\sim}{R}$ is also a fuzzy set, there is overlap between a relation and its complement; hence,

$$\underset{\sim}{R} \cup \bar{\underset{\sim}{R}} \neq \mathbf{E}$$

$$\underset{\sim}{R} \cap \bar{\underset{\sim}{R}} \neq \mathbf{O}$$

As seen in the foregoing expressions, the excluded middle axioms for relations do not result, in general, in the null relation, **O**, or the complete relation, **E**.

4.4.5 Fuzzy Cartesian Product and Composition

Because fuzzy relations in general are fuzzy sets, we can define the Cartesian product to be a relation between two or more fuzzy sets. Let $\underset{\sim}{A}$ be a fuzzy set on universe X and $\underset{\sim}{B}$ be a fuzzy set on universe Y; then the Cartesian product between fuzzy sets $\underset{\sim}{A}$ and $\underset{\sim}{B}$ will result in a fuzzy relation $\underset{\sim}{R}$, which is contained within the full Cartesian product space, or

$$\underset{\sim}{A} \times \underset{\sim}{B} = \underset{\sim}{R} \subset X \times Y \quad (4.16)$$

where the fuzzy relation $\underset{\sim}{R}$ has membership function

$$\mu_{\underset{\sim}{R}}(x, y) = \mu_{\underset{\sim}{A} \times \underset{\sim}{B}}(x, y) = \min(\mu_{\underset{\sim}{A}}(x), \mu_{\underset{\sim}{B}}(y)) \quad (4.17)$$

The Cartesian product defined $\underset{\sim}{A} \times \underset{\sim}{B} = \underset{\sim}{R}$ by, Eq. (4.16), is implemented in the same fashion as is the cross product of two vectors. Again, the Cartesian product is not the same operation as the arithmetic product. In the case of two-dimensional relations (r = 2), the former employs the idea of pairing of elements among sets, whereas the latter uses actual arithmetic products between elements of sets. Each of the fuzzy sets could be thought of as a vector of membership values; each value is associated with a particular element in each set. For example, for a fuzzy set (vector) $\underset{\sim}{A}$ that has four elements, hence column vector of size 4 × 1, and for a fuzzy set (vector) $\underset{\sim}{B}$ that has five elements, hence a row vector size of 1 × 5, the resulting fuzzy relation, ,will be represented by a matrix of size 4 × 5, i.e., $\underset{\sim}{R}$, will have four rows and five columns. This result is illustrated in the following example.

Example 4.6: Suppose we have two fuzzy sets, $\underset{\sim}{A}$ defined on a universe of three discrete temperatures, $X = \{x_1, x_2, x_3\}$, and $\underset{\sim}{B}$ defined on a universe of two discrete pressures, $Y = \{y_1, y_2\}$, and we want to find the fuzzy Cartesian product between them. Fuzzy set $\underset{\sim}{A}$ could represent the "ambient" temperature and fuzzy set $\underset{\sim}{B}$ the "near optimum" pressure for a certain heat exchanger, and the Cartesian product might represent the conditions (temperature–pressure pairs) of the exchanger that are associated with "efficient" operations. For example, let

$$\underset{\sim}{A} = \frac{0.2}{x_1} + \frac{0.5}{x_2} + \frac{1}{x_3} \text{ and } \underset{\sim}{B} = \frac{0.3}{y_1} + \frac{0.9}{y_2}$$

Note that can be represented as a column vector of size 3 × 1 and $\underset{\sim}{B}$ can be represented by a row vector of 1 × 2. Then the fuzzy Cartesian product, using Eq. (4.17), results in a fuzzy relation $\underset{\sim}{R}$, (of size 3 × 2) representing "efficient" conditions, or

$$\underset{\sim}{A} \times \underset{\sim}{B} = \underset{\sim}{R} = \begin{matrix} & y_1 & y_2 \\ x_1 & 0.2 & 0.2 \\ x_2 & 0.3 & 0.5 \\ x_3 & 0.3 & 0.9 \end{matrix}$$

4.5 FUZZY COMPOSITION

Fuzzy composition can be defined just as it is for crisp (binary) relations. Suppose $\underset{\sim}{R}$, is a fuzzy relation on the Cartesian space X × Y, $\underset{\sim}{S}$ is a fuzzy relation on Y × Z, and $\underset{\sim}{T}$ is a fuzzy relation on X × Z, then fuzzy max–min composition is defined in terms of the set-theoretic notation and membership function-theoretic notation in the following manner:

$$\underset{\sim}{T} = \underset{\sim}{R} \circ \underset{\sim}{S}$$

$$\mu_{\underset{\sim}{T}}(x, z) = \bigvee_{y \in Y} (\mu_{\underset{\sim}{R}}(x, y) \wedge \mu_{\underset{\sim}{S}}(y, z)) \tag{4.18a}$$

and fuzzy max–product composition is defined in terms of the membership function theoretic notation as

$$\mu_{\underset{\sim}{T}}(x, z) = \bigvee_{y \in Y} (\mu_{\underset{\sim}{R}}(x, y) \cdot \mu_{\underset{\sim}{S}}(y, z)) \tag{4.18b}$$

It should be pointed out that neither crisp nor fuzzy compositions are commutative in general; that is,

$$\underset{\sim}{R} \circ \underset{\sim}{S} \neq \underset{\sim}{S} \circ \underset{\sim}{R} \tag{4.19}$$

Equation (4.19) is general for any matrix operation, fuzzy or otherwise, that must satisfy consistency between the cardinal counts of elements in respective universes. Even for the case of square matrices, the composition converse, represented by Eq. (4.19), is not guaranteed.

Example 4.7: Let us extend the information contained in the Sagittal diagram shown in Figure 4.4 to include fuzzy relationships for $X \times Y$ (denoted by the fuzzy relation $\underset{\sim}{R}$) and $Y \times Z$ (denoted by the fuzzy relation $\underset{\sim}{S}$). In this case we change the elements of the universes to, $X = \{x_1, x_2\}$, $Y = \{y_1, y_2\}$, and $Z = \{z_1, z_2, z_3\}$

Consider the following fuzzy relations:

$$\underset{\sim}{R} = \begin{array}{c} \\ x_1 \\ x_2 \end{array} \begin{array}{c} \begin{array}{cc} y_1 & y_2 \end{array} \\ \begin{bmatrix} 0.7 & 0.5 \\ 0.8 & 0.4 \end{bmatrix} \end{array}$$

and

$$\underset{\sim}{S} = \begin{array}{c} \\ x_1 \\ x_2 \end{array} \begin{array}{c} \begin{array}{ccc} z_1 & z_2 & z_3 \end{array} \\ \begin{bmatrix} 0.9 & 0.6 & 0.2 \\ 0.1 & 0.7 & 0.5 \end{bmatrix} \end{array}$$

Then the resulting relation, $\underset{\sim}{T}$, which relates elements of universe X to elements of universe Z, i.e., defined on Cartesian space $X \times Z$, can be found by max–min composition, Eq. (4.18a), to be, for example, $\mu_T(x_1, z_1) = \max [\min (0.7, 0.9), \min(0.5, 0.1)] = 0.7$ and the rest,

$$\underset{\sim}{T} = \begin{array}{c} \\ x_1 \\ x_2 \end{array} \begin{array}{c} \begin{array}{ccc} z_1 & z_2 & z_3 \end{array} \\ \begin{bmatrix} 0.7 & 0.6 & 0.5 \\ 0.8 & 0.6 & 0.4 \end{bmatrix} \end{array}$$

and by max–product composition, Eq. (4.18b), to be, for example, $\mu_T(x_2, z_2) = \max [\min (0.8, 0.6), \min(0.4, 0.7)] = 0.48$ and the rest,

$$\underset{\sim}{T} = \begin{matrix} & z_1 & z_2 & z_3 \\ x_1 & 0.63 & 0.42 & 0.25 \\ x_2 & 0.72 & 0.48 & 0.20 \end{matrix}$$

4.6 FUZZY TOLERANCE AND EQUIVALENCE RELATIONS

Relations exhibit various other properties apart from that discussed in previous sections. It is already said that the relation can be used in graph theory. The various other properties that are dealt here include reflexivity, symmetry, and transitivity. These are discussed in detail for the crisp and fuzzy relations and are called as equivalence relation. Apart from these, tolerance relations of both fuzzy and crisp relations are also described.

4.6.1 Crisp Relation: Crisp Equivalence Relation

A relation R is called as an equivalence relation if it satisfies the following properties. They are (1) reflexivity, (2) symmetry, and (3) transitivity.

1. **Reflexivity** When a relation satisfies the reflexive property then every vertex in the graph originates a single loop. This is shown below. For matrix relation reflexivity is given by,

   $(x_i, x_j) \in R$ or $\div_R(x_i, x_j) = 1.$

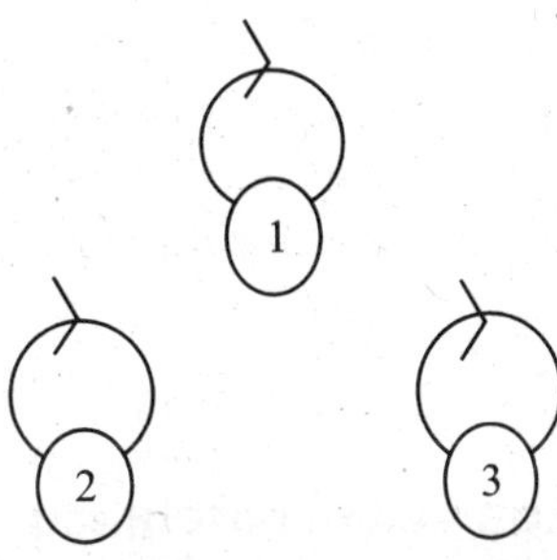

2. **Symmetry** When a relation satisfies symmetric property then in the graph for every edge pointing from vertex i to vertex j there is a edge pointing in the opposite direction, i.e., from vertex j to vertex i. This is shown below. For matrix relation symmetry is given by

   $(x_i, x_j) \in R \rightarrow (x_i, x_j) \in R$ or $\div_R(x_i, x_j) = \div_R(x_j, x_i).$

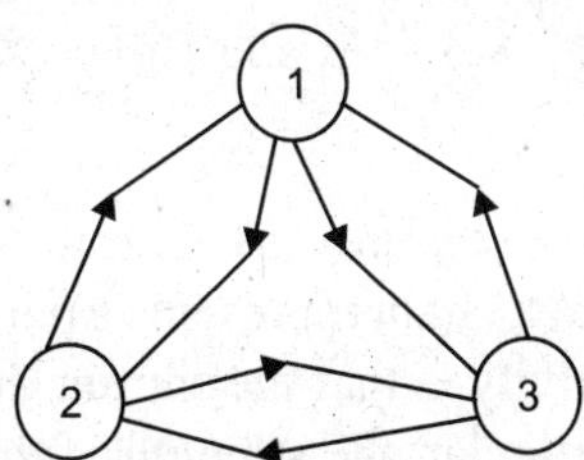

3. **Transitivity** When a relation satisfies transitivity property then every pair of edges in the graph, one pointing from vertex i to vertex j and the other from vertex j to vertex k(i, j, k = 1, 2, 3) there is an edge pointing from vertex i directly to vertex k. This is shown below.

   For matrix relation transitivity is given by

$$(x_i, x_j) \in R \text{ and } (x_j, x_k) \in R \rightarrow (x_i, x_k) \in R$$

or

$$\div_R(x_i, x_j) \text{ and } \div_R(x_j, x_k) = 1 \rightarrow \div_R(x_i, x_k) = 1.$$

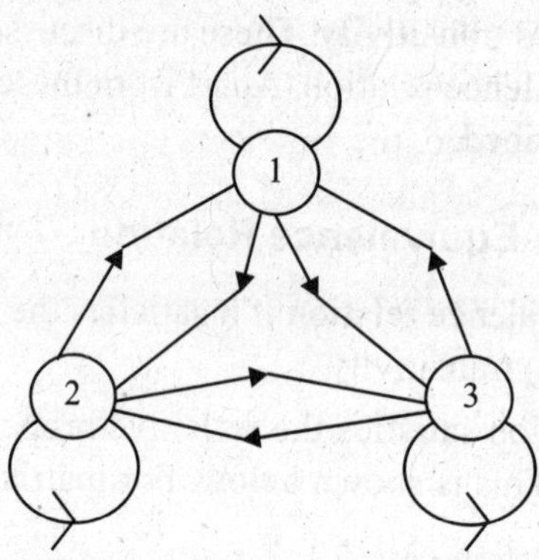

4. **Crisp Tolerance Relation** A binary relation R on a universe X that is reflexive and symmetric is called as compatibility relation or a tolerance relation. When a relation is a reflexive and symmetric it is called as proximity relation. A tolerance relation R can be reformed into an equivalence relation by at most (n–1) composition with itself, where n is the cardinal number of the set defining R, in the case X, i.e.,

$$R^{n-1} = R_1 \circ R_1 \circ \cdots \circ R_1 = R.$$

4.6.2 Fuzzy Relation: Fuzzy Equivalence Relation

A fuzzy relation, $\underset{\sim}{R}$, on a single universe X is also a relation from X to X. It is a fuzzy equivalence relation if all three of the following properties for matrix relations define it:

Reflexivity $\mu_{\underset{\sim}{R}}(x_i, x_i) = 1$ (4.20a)

Symmetry $\mu_{\underset{\sim}{R}}(x_i, x_j) = \mu_{\underset{\sim}{R}}(x_j, x_i)$ (4.20b)

Transitivity $\mu_{\underset{\sim}{R}}(x_i, x_j) = \lambda_1 \text{ and } \mu_{\underset{\sim}{R}}(x_j, x_k) = \lambda_2 \rightarrow \mu_{\underset{\sim}{R}}(x_i, x_k) = \lambda$ (4.20c)

Where $\lambda \geq \min[\lambda_1, \lambda_2]$.

Looking at the physical analog (see Figure 4.5) of a composition operation, we see it comprises a parallel system of chains, where each chain represents a particular path through the chain system. The physical analogy behind transitivity is that the shorter the chain, the stronger the relation (the stronger is the chain system). In particular, the strength of the link between two elements must be greater than or equal to the strength of any indirect chain involving other elements, i.e., Eq. (4.20c).

It can be shown that any fuzzy tolerance relation, $\underset{\sim}{R}_1$, that has properties of reflexivity and symmetry can be reformed into a fuzzy equivalence relation by at most (n – 1) compositions, just as a crisp tolerance relation can be reformed into a crisp equivalence relation. That is,

$$\underset{\sim}{R}_1^{n-1} = \underset{\sim}{R} \circ \underset{\sim}{R} \circ \ldots \circ \underset{\sim}{R}_1 = \underset{\sim}{R} \tag{4.21}$$

Example 4.8: Suppose, in a biotechnology experiment, five potentially new strains of bacteria have been detected in the area around an anaerobic corrosion pit on a new aluminum–lithium alloy used in the fuel tanks of a new experimental aircraft. In order to propose methods to eliminate the biocorrosion caused by these bacteria, the five strains must first be categorized. One way to categorize them is to compare them to one another. In a pairwise comparison, the following "similarity" relation, $\underset{\sim}{R}_1$, is developed. For example, the first strain (column 1) has a strength of similarity to the second strain of 0.8, to the third strain a strength of 0 (i.e., no relation), to the fourth strain a strength of 0.1, and so on. Because the relation is for pairwise similarity it will be reflexive and symmetric. Hence, is reflexive and symmetric. However, it is not transitive, e.g.,

$$\underset{\sim}{R}_1 = \begin{bmatrix} 1 & 0.8 & 0.1 & 0.1 & 0.2 \\ 0.8 & 1 & 0.4 & 0 & 0.9 \\ 0 & 0.4 & 1 & 0 & 0 \\ 0.1 & 0 & 0 & 1 & 0.5 \\ 0.2 & 0.9 & 0 & 0.5 & 1 \end{bmatrix}$$

is reflexive and symmetric. However, it is not transitive. e.g.,

$$\mu_{\underset{\sim}{R}}(x_1, x_2) = 0.8, \quad \mu_{\underset{\sim}{R}}(x_2, x_5) = 0.9 \geq 0.8$$

But

$$\mu_{\underset{\sim}{R}}(x_1, x_5) = 0.2 \leq \min(0.8, 0.9)$$

One composition results in the following relation:

$$\underset{\sim}{R}_1^2 = \underset{\sim}{R} \circ \underset{\sim}{R}_1 = \begin{bmatrix} 1 & 0.8 & 0.4 & 0.2 & 0.8 \\ 0.8 & 1 & 0.4 & 0.5 & 0.9 \\ 0.4 & 0.4 & 1 & 0 & 0.4 \\ 0.2 & 0.5 & 0 & 1 & 0.5 \\ 0.8 & 0.9 & 0.4 & 0.5 & 1 \end{bmatrix}$$

where transitivity still does not result; for example,

$$\mu_{\underset{\sim}{R}^2}(x_1, x_2) = 0.8 \geq 0.5, \quad \text{and} \quad \mu_{\underset{\sim}{R}^2}(x_2, x_4) = 0.5$$

Finally, after one or two more compositions, transitivity results:

$$\underset{\sim}{R}_1^3 = \underset{\sim}{R}_1^4 = \underset{\sim}{R} = \begin{bmatrix} 1 & 0.8 & 0.4 & 0.5 & 0.8 \\ 0.8 & 1 & 0.4 & 0.5 & 0.9 \\ 0.4 & 0.4 & 1 & 0.4 & 0.4 \\ 0.5 & 0.5 & 0.4 & 1 & 0.5 \\ 0.8 & 0.9 & 0.4 & 0.5 & 1 \end{bmatrix}$$

$$R_{\underset{\sim}{1}}^{3}(x_1, x_2) = 0.8 \geq 0.5$$
$$R_{\underset{\sim}{1}}^{3}(x_2, x_4) = 0.5 \geq 0.5$$
$$R_{\underset{\sim}{1}}^{3}(x_1, x_4) = 0.5 \geq 0.5$$

Graphs can be drawn for fuzzy equivalence relations, but the arrows in the graphs between vertices will have various "strengths," i.e., values on the interval [0, 1]. Once the fuzzy relation $\underset{\sim}{R}$ in Example 4.8 is an equivalence relation, it can be used in categorizing the various bacteria according to preestablished levels of confidence. There is an interesting graphical analog for fuzzy equivalence relations. An inspection of a three-dimensional plot of the preceding equivalence relation, $R_{\underset{\sim}{1}}^{3}$, is shown in Figure 4.7. In this graph, which is a plot of the membership values of the equivalence relation, we can see that, if it were a watershed, there would be no location where water would pool, or be trapped. In fact, every equivalence relation will produce a surface on which water cannot be trapped; the converse is not true in general, however. That is, there can be relations that are not equivalence relations but whose three-dimensional surface representations will not trap water. An example of the latter is given in the original tolerance relation, $R_{\underset{\sim}{1}}$, of Example 4.8.

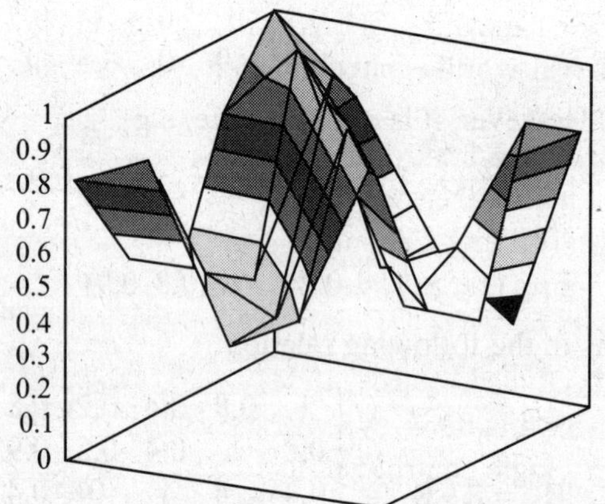

Figure 4.7: Three-dimensional Representation of an Equivalence Relation.

Another way to show this same information is to construct a two-dimensional contour of the relation using various contour levels; these correspond to different degrees of membership. The graphic in Figure 4.8 shows contour plots for the tolerance relation, $R_{\underset{\sim}{1}}^{2}$ and the equivalence level, . The contours in Figure 4.8a would trap water (the lightest areas are inside other darker areas), $R_{\underset{\sim}{1}}^{3}$ whereas water would not be trapped in the contour diagram of Figure 4.8b.

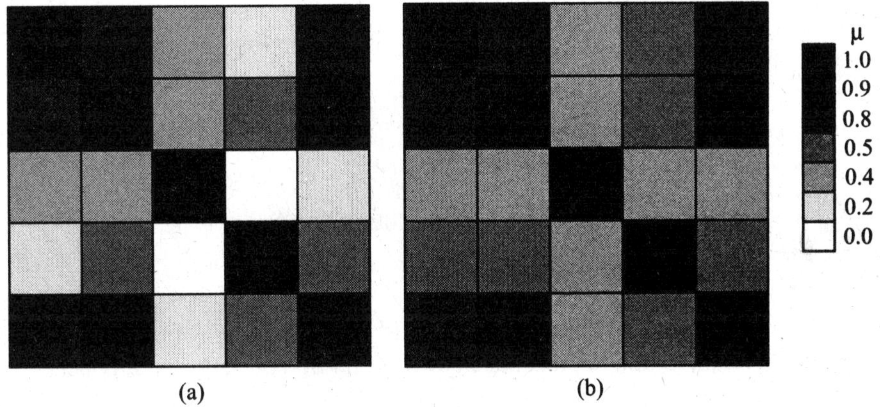

Figure 4.8: Two-dimensional Contours of (a) Tolerance Relation R_1^2 and (b) Equivalence Relation R_1^3.

4.7 FUZZY GRAPHS

A fuzzy relation may not have a meaningful linguistic label such as the petite relation does. In fact, most fuzzy relations used in real-world applications do not represent a concept; rather they represent a functional mapping from a set of input variables to one or more output variables. Often, a set of fuzzy rules used in a fuzzy logic controller describes a fuzzy relation from the observed state variables to a control decision. In other words, a fuzzy relation underlying a fuzzy logic controller can be constructed by a set of if-then fuzzy rules. How is this achieved? To answer this question, we need to introduce fuzzy graphs.

The term "fuzzy graph" has been used for two different concepts in the literature, one introduced by Zadeh, and the other introduced by Rosenfeld. Rosenfeld's fuzzy graph is a generalization of conventional graph theory. In this book, we will discuss only Zadeh's fuzzy graph because it is much more relevant to fuzzy logic control and its industrial applications.

A fuzzy graph describes a functional mapping between a set of input linguistic variables and an output linguistic variable. Assume that a function $f: U \rightarrow V$, $X \in U$, $Y \in V$, is approximated by the following fuzzy IF-THEN rules:

f: IF X is small THEN Y is small.
IF X is medium THEN Y is large.
IF X is large THEN Y is small.

which form a fuzzy graph f* (Figure 4.9), where

$$f^* = \text{small} \times \text{small} + \text{medium} \times \text{large} + \text{large} \times \text{small}$$

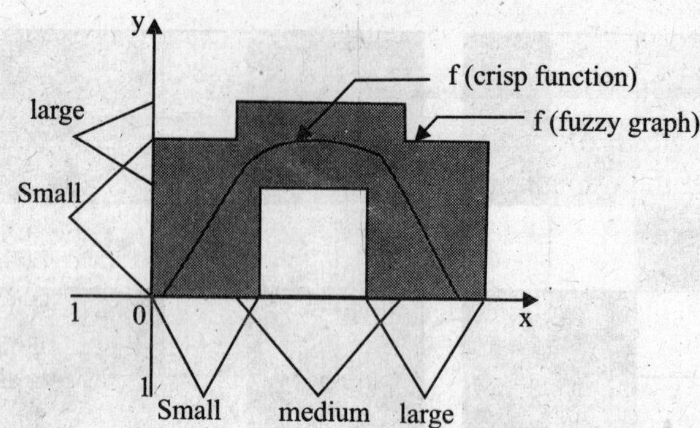

Figure 4.9: Fuzzy Graph Approximation by a Disjunction of Cartesian Products

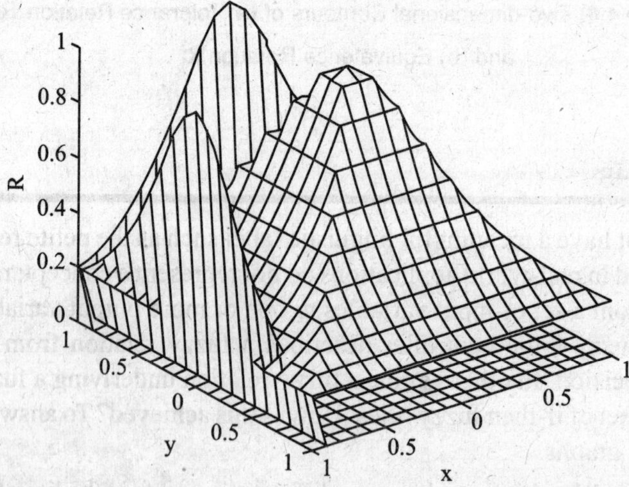

Figure 4.10: A Fuzzy Relation Formed by a Cartesian Product

In f*, + and x denote, respectively, the disjunction and Cartesian product. An expression of the form $A \times B$ where A and B are words (fuzzy sets) is referred as a Cartesian granule.

Suppose that x and y are two variables with universes of discourse X and Y respectively, and A and B are two fuzzy subsets of X and Y. The Cartesian product of A and B denoted by $A \times B$, is defined as

$$\mu_{A \times B}(u, v) = \mu_A(u) \otimes \mu_B(v) \tag{4.22}$$

Figure 4.10 shows a fuzzy relation formed by a Cartesian product using min as the fuzzy conjunction operator. A fuzzy graph f * from X to Y is union of Cartesian products involving linguistic input-output associations (i.e., pairs of "x is A_i" and "y is B_i") i.e.,

$$f^* = \bigcup_i A_i \times B_i$$

The resulting fuzzy graph is basically a fuzzy relation.

4.8 FUZZY NUMBERS

A fuzzy number is a fuzzy subset of the universe of a numeric number. For instance, a fuzzy real number is a fuzzy subset of the domain of real numbers. A fuzzy integer is a fuzzy subset of the domain of integers. An example of a fuzzy real number, About-10, is shown in Figure 4.11.

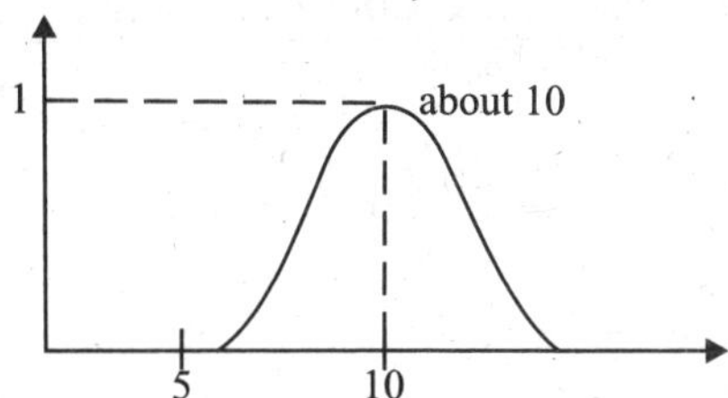

Figure 4.11: A Fuzzy Number

4.9 FUZZY ARITHMETIC

In this chapter we wish to use the extension principle to perform algebraic operations on fuzzy numbers (as illustrated in previous examples in this chapter). We define a normal, convex fuzzy set on the real line to be a fuzzy number, and denote it $\underset{\sim}{I}$.

Let $\underset{\sim}{I}$ and $\underset{\sim}{J}$ be two fuzzy numbers, with $\underset{\sim}{I}$ defined on the real line in universe X and $\underset{\sim}{J}$ defined on the real line in universe Y, and let the symbol "denote a general arithmetic operation, i.e., $* \equiv \{+,-,\times,\div\}$. An arithmetic operation (mapping) between these two number, denoted $\underset{\sim}{I} * \underset{\sim}{J}$, will be defined on universe Z, and can be accomplished using the extension principle, by

$$\mu \underset{\sim}{I} * \underset{\sim}{J}(z) = \underset{x * y = z}{\vee} (\mu_{\underset{\sim}{I}}(x) \wedge \mu_{\underset{\sim}{J}}(y)) \tag{4.23}$$

Equation (4.23) results in another fuzzy set, the fuzzy number resulting from the arithmetic operation on fuzzy numbers $\underset{\sim}{I}$ and $\underset{\sim}{J}$.

Example 4.9: We want to perform a simple addition ($* \equiv +$) of two fuzzy numbers. Define a fuzzy one by the normal, convex membership function defined on the integers,

$$\underset{\sim}{1} = \left\{\frac{0.2}{0} + \frac{1}{1} + \frac{0.2}{2}\right\}$$

Now, we want to add "fuzzy one" plus "fuzzy one," using the extension principle, Eq. (4.23), to get

$$\underset{\sim}{1} + \underset{\sim}{1} = \underset{\sim}{2} = \left(\frac{0.2}{0} + \frac{1}{1} + \frac{0.2}{2}\right) + \left(\frac{0.2}{0} + \frac{1}{1} + \frac{0.2}{2}\right)$$

$$= \left\{ \frac{\min(0.2, 0.2)}{0} + \frac{\max[\min(0.2, 1) \min(1, 0.2)]}{1} \right.$$

$$+ \frac{\max[\min(0.2, 0.2), \min(1, 1), \min(0.2, 0.2]}{2}$$

$$\left. + \frac{\max[\min(1, 0.2), \min(0.2, 1]}{3} + \frac{\min(0.2, 0.2)}{4} \right\}$$

$$= \left\{ \frac{0.2}{2} + \frac{0.2}{1} + \frac{1}{2} + \frac{0.2}{3} + \frac{0.2}{4} \right\}$$

Note that there are two ways to get the resulting membership value for a 1 (0 + 1 and 1 + 0), three ways to get a 2 (0 + 2, 1 + 1, 2 + 0), and two ways to get a 3 (1 + 2 and 2 + 1). These are accounted for in the implementation of the extension principle.

The support for a fuzzy number, say , is given by

$$\text{supp } \underset{\sim}{I} \; \{x \mid \mu_{\underset{\sim}{I}} \; X > 0\} = I \tag{4.24}$$

which is an interval on the real line, denoted symbolically as I. Since applying Eq. (4.23) to arithmetic operations on fuzzy numbers results in a quantity that is also a fuzzy number, we can find the support of the fuzzy number resulting from the arithmetic operation $\underset{\sim}{I} * \underset{\sim}{J}$ i.e.,.

$$\underset{I*J}{\text{sup p}}(z) = I * J \tag{4.25}$$

which is seen to be the arithmetic operation on the two individual supports (crisp intervals), I and J, for fuzzy numbers $\underset{\sim}{I}$ and $\underset{\sim}{J}$, respectively.

The support of a fuzzy set is equal to its ë-cut value at ë = 0^+. In general, we can perform ë-cut operations on fuzzy numbers for any value of ë. General arithmetic operations:

$$(\underset{\sim}{I} * \underset{\sim}{J})_1 = I_\lambda * J_\lambda \tag{4.26}$$

Equation 4.26 shows that the ë-cut on a general arithmetic operation ($* \equiv \{+, -, \times, \div\}$) on two fuzzy numbers is equivalent to the arithmetic operation on the respective ë-cuts of the two fuzzy numbers. Both $(\underset{\sim}{I} * \underset{\sim}{J})_\lambda$ and $I_\lambda * J_\lambda$ are interval quantities; and manipulations of these quantities can make use of classical interval analysis.

Example 4.10: We have two fuzzy sets $\underset{\sim}{A}$ and $\underset{\sim}{B}$, each defined on its own universe as follows:

$$\underset{\sim}{A} = \left\{ \frac{0.2}{1} + \frac{1}{2} + \frac{0.7}{4} \right\} \text{ and } \underset{\sim}{B} = \left\{ \frac{0.5}{1} + \frac{1}{2} \right\}$$

We wish to determine the membership values for the algebraic product mapping

$$f(\underset{\sim}{A}, \underset{\sim}{B}) = \underset{\sim}{A} \times \underset{\sim}{B} \text{ (arithmetic product)}$$

$$= \left\{\frac{\min(0.2, 0.5)}{1} + \frac{\max[\min(0.2, 1), \min(0.5, 1)]}{2} + \frac{\max[\min(0.7, 0.5), \min(1,1)]}{4} + \frac{\min(0.7, 1)}{8}\right\}$$

$$= \left\{\frac{0.2}{1} + \frac{0.5}{2} + \frac{1}{4} + \frac{0.7}{8}\right\}$$

In this case, the mapping involves two ways to produce a 2 (1×2 and 2×1) and two ways to produce a 4(4×1 and 2×2); hence the maximum operation expressed in Eq.

$$\mu_{\underset{\sim}{B}}(y) = \max_{y = f(x_1, .. x_2 ... x_n)} \{\min[\mu \underset{\sim}{A}_1(x_1), \mu \underset{\sim}{A}_2(x_2), ... \mu \underset{\sim}{A}_n(x_n)]\} \tag{4.27}$$

is necessary.

The extension principle can also be useful in propagating fuzziness through generalized relations that are discrete mappings of ordered pairs of elements from input universes to ordered pairs of elements in an output universe.

Example 4.11: Suppose we have the integers 1 to 10 as the elements of two identical but different universes; let

$$U_1 = U_2 = \{1, 2, 3, \ldots, 10\}$$

Then define two fuzzy numbers $\underset{\sim}{A}$ and $\underset{\sim}{B}$ on universe U_1 and U_2, respectively:

$$\text{Define } \underset{\sim}{A} = \underset{\sim}{2} = \text{"approximately 2"} = \left\{\frac{0.6}{1} + \frac{1}{2} + \frac{0.8}{3}\right\}$$

$$\text{Define } \underset{\sim}{B} = \underset{\sim}{6} = \text{"approximately 6"} = \left\{\frac{0.8}{5} + \frac{1}{6} + \frac{0.7}{7}\right\}$$

The product of ("approximately 2") × ("approximately 6") should map to a fuzzy number "approximately 12," which is a fuzzy set defined on a universe, say V, of integers, V = {5, 6, . . . , 18, 21}, as determined by the extension principle, Eq. (4.27), or

$$\underset{\sim}{2} \times \underset{\sim}{6} = \left(\frac{0.6}{1} + \frac{1}{2} + \frac{0.8}{3}\right) \times \left(\frac{0.8}{3} + \frac{1}{6} + \frac{0.7}{7}\right)$$

$$= \left\{\frac{\min(0.6, 0.8)}{5} + \frac{\min(0.6, 1)}{6} + \ldots + \frac{\min(0.8, 1)}{18} + \frac{\min(0.8, 0.7)}{21}\right\}$$

$$= \left\{\frac{0.6}{5} + \frac{0.6}{6} + \frac{0.6}{7} + \frac{0.8}{10} + \frac{1}{12} + \frac{0.7}{14} + \frac{0.8}{15} + \frac{2.8}{18} + \frac{0.7}{21}\right\}$$

In this example each of the elements in the universe, V, is determined by a unique mapping of the input variables. For example, $1 \times 5 = 5$, $2 \times 6 = 12$, etc. Hence, the maximum operation expressed in Eq. (4.27) is not necessary. It should also be noted that the result of this arithmetic product is not convex, and hence does not appear to be a fuzzy number (i.e., normal and convex). However, the nonconvexity arises from numerical aberrations from the discretization of the two fuzzy numbers, $\underset{\sim}{2}$ and $\underset{\sim}{6}$, and not from any inherent problems in the extension principle.

4.10 INTERVAL ANALYSIS IN ARITHMETIC

Let I_1 and I_2 be two interval numbers defined by ordered pairs of real numbers with lower and upper bounds:

$$I_1 = [a, b], \text{ where } a \le b$$
$$I_2 = [c, d], \text{ where } c \le d$$

When a = b and c = d, these interval numbers degenerate to a scalar real number. We again define a general arithmetic property with the symbol *, where $* \equiv \{+,-,\times,\div\}$. Symbolically, the operation

$$I_1 * I_2 = [a, b] * [c, d]$$

represents another interval. This interval calculation depends on the magnitudes and signs of the elements a, b, c, and d. Table 4.2 shows the various combinations of set-theoretic intersection (∩)") and set-theoretic union (∪) for the six possible combinations of these elements (a < b and c < d still hold). Based on the information in Table 4.2, the four arithmetic interval operations associated with above Equation are given as follows:

$$[a, b] + [c, d] = [a + c, + b + d] \quad (4.28)$$
$$[a, b] - [c, d] = [a - d, + b - c] \quad (4.29)$$
$$[a, b] \times [c, d] = [\min(ac, ad, bc, bd), \max(ac, ad, bc, bd)] \quad (4.30)$$
$$[a, b] \div [c, d] = [a,b] \times \left[\frac{1}{d}, \frac{1}{c}\right] \text{provided that } 0 \notin [c, d] \quad (4.31)$$
$$\alpha[a, b] = \begin{cases} [\alpha a, \alpha b] & \text{for } \alpha > 0 \\ [\alpha b, \alpha a] & \text{for } \alpha > 0 \end{cases} \quad (4.32)$$

where ac, ad, bc, and bd are arithmetic products and 1/d and 1/c are quotients.

The caveat applied to Eq. (4.31) is that the equivalence stated is not valid for the case when $c \le 0$ and $d \ge 0$ (obviously the constraint c < d still holds), i.e., zero cannot be contained within the interval [c, d]. Interval arithmetic follows properties of associativity and commutativity for both summations and products, but it does not follow the property of distributivity.

Table 4.2: Set operations on intervals

Cases	Intersection	Union
a > d	φ	[c, d] ∪ [a, b]
c > b	φ	[a, b] ∪ [c, d]
a > c, b < d	[a, b]	[c, d]
c > a, d < b	[c, d]	[a, b]
a < c < b < d	[c, b]	[a, d]
c < a < d < b	[a, d]	[c, b]

Rather, intervals do follow a special subclass of distributivity known as subdistributivity, i.e., for three intervals, I, J, and K,

$$I \cdot (J + K) \subset I \cdot J + I \cdot K \tag{4.33}$$

The failure of distributivity to hold for intervals is due to the treatment of two occurrences of identical interval numbers (i.e., I) as two independent interval numbers.

Example 4.12:

$$-3 \cdot [1, 2] = [-6, -3]$$

$$[0, 1] - [0, 1] = [-1, 1]$$

$$[1, 3] \cdot [2, 4] = [\min(2, 4, 6, 12), \max(2, 4, 6, 12)] = [2, 12]$$

$$[1, 2] \div [1, 2] = [1, 2] \cdot [1/2, 1] = [1/2, 2]$$

Consider the following example of subdistributivity.

For $I = [1, 2], J = [2, 3], K = [1, 4]$, then

$$I \cdot (J - K) = [1, 2] \cdot ([2, 3] - [1, 4]) = [1, 2] \cdot [-2, 2] = [-4, 4]$$

$$I \cdot J - I \cdot K = [1, 2] \cdot [2, 3] - [1, 2] \cdot [1, 4] = [2, 6] - [1, 8] = [-6, 5]$$

Now, $[-4, 4] \neq [-6, 5]$, but $[-4, 4] \subset [-6, 5]$.

Interval arithmetic can be thought of in the following way. When we add or multiply two crisp numbers, the result is a crisp singleton. When we add or multiply two intervals we are essentially performing these operations on the infinite number of combinations of pairs of crisp singletons from each of the two intervals; hence, in this sense, an interval is expected as the result. In the simplest case, when we multiply two intervals containing only positive real numbers, it is easy conceptually to see that the interval comprising the solution is found by taking the product of the two lowest values from each of the intervals to form the solution's lower bound, and by taking the product of the two highest values from each of the intervals to form the solution's upper bound. Even though we can see conceptually that an infinite number of combinations of products between these two intervals exist, we need only the endpoints of the intervals to find the endpoints of the solution.

EXERCISES

1. What do you mean by Cartesian product?
2. What do you mean by crisp relation?
3. Explain the cardinality of crisp relation?
4. Explain the operations performed on crisp relation?
5. Explain the properties of crisp relation?
6. What do you mean by composition operations?
7. What do you mean by fuzzy relations?
8. Explain the composition of fuzzy relation?
9. What do you mean by cardinality of fuzzy relations?

10. What are the basic operations performed on fuzzy relation?
11. What are the properties of fuzzy relation?
12. Explain the concept of fuzzy Cartesian product and composition?
13. Explain the concept of fuzzy tolerance and equivalence relation?
14. What do you mean by fuzzy graph?
15. What do you mean by fuzzy number?
16. What do you mean by fuzzy arithmetic? Explain the various arithmetic operations performed on fuzzy numbers?
17. Explain the interval analysis in fuzzy arithmetic?

CHAPTER 5

Fuzzy If-then Rules

5.1 INTRODUCTION

Rules form the basis for the fuzzy logic to obtain the fuzzy output. The rulebased system is different from the expert system in the manner that the rule comprising the rule-based system originates from sources other than that of human experts and hence is different from expert systems. The rule-based form uses linguistic variables as its antecedents and consequents. The antecedents express an inference or the inequality, which should be satisfied. The consequents are those, which we can infer, and is the output if the antecedent inequality is satisfied. Among all the techniques developed using fuzzy sets fuzzy if-then rules are by far the most visible due to their wide range of successful applications fuzzy if –then rules have been applied to many disciplines. Such as control system, decision making, pattern recognition, and system modeling. Fuzzy if- then rules also play a critical role in industrial applications ranging from consumer products, manufacturing, process control, medical imaging, to financial trading.

A fuzzy if-then rule associates a condition described using linguistic variables and fuzzy sets to a conclusion. From a knowledge representation viewpoint, a fuzzy if-then rule is a scheme for capturing knowledge that involves imprecision. The main feature of reasoning using these rules (i.e., fuzzy rule –based reasoning) is its partial matching capability, which enables an inference to be made from a fuzzy rule even when the rule;s condition is only partially satisfied.

Learning fuzzy if-then rules is both easy and challenging. It is easy to understand the basics of fuzzy if-then and to start building your own application using a commercially available fuzzy logic development tool such as the Matlab Fuzzy Logic Tool Box. It is challenging, however, to master fuzzy if-then rules for two reasons. First, there are two different kinds of fuzzy rules: fuzzy mapping rules and fuzzy implication rules. Understanding the fundamental differences between these two is important for developing their successful application. Second, there are several fuzzy rule-based inference techniques. Understanding the theoretical foundation of these techniques and their relationship to suitable applications can be challenging.

The fuzzy rule-based system uses IF–THEN rule-based system, given by, IF antecedent, THEN consequent. The formation of the fuzzy rules is discussed in this chapter.

5.2 BASICS OF FUZZY RULES

A fuzzy if-then rule is a knowledge representation scheme use for capturing knowledge (typically human knowledge) that is imprecise and inexact by nature. This is achieved by using linguistic variables to describe elastic conditions (i.e. conditions that can be satisfied to a degree) in the "if-part" of fuzzy rules.

The main feature of fuzzy rule-based inference is its capability to perform inference under partial matching. That is, it computes the degree the input data matches the condition of a rule. Figure 5.1 illustrates one way to calculate the matching degree between a fuzzy input A' and a fuzzy condition A that was introduced in Chapter 2.

$$\text{matchingdegree}(A, A') = \sup_{x} \min(\mu_A(x), \mu_{A'}(x)) \quad (5.1)$$

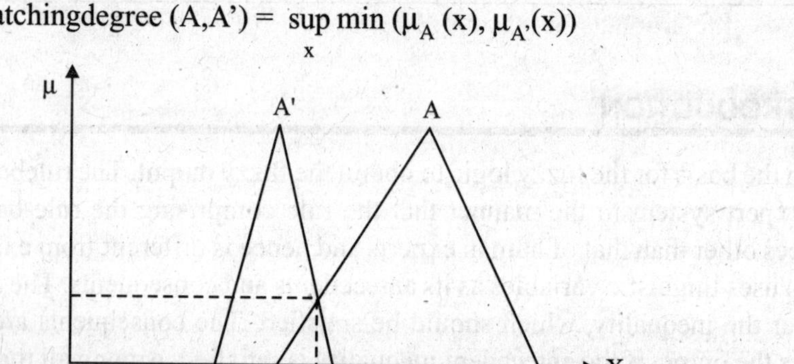

Figure 5.1: Matching Fuzzy Input A' with a Fuzzy Condition A

This matching degree is combined with the consequent (i.e., "then" part) of the rule to form a conclusion inferred by the fuzzy rule. The higher the matching degree, the closer the inferred conclusion to the rule's consequent.

5.3 TWO TYPES OF FUZZY RULES

There are two types of fuzzy rules:

1. **Fuzzy Mapping Rules-** A fuzzy mapping rule describes a functional mapping relationship between inputs and an output using linguistic terms,
2. **Fuzzy Implication Rules-** while a fuzzy implication rule describes a generalized logic implication relationship between two logic formulas involving linguistic variables and imprecise linguistic terms.

5.3.1 Fuzzy Mapping Rules

In many real-world problems, we are interested in finding the functional relationship between a set of observable parameters and one or multiple parameters whose values we do not know. For example, a financial trading broker is interested in the relationship between the history of various financial indices and future stock values. A control engineer is interested in finding an appropriate control law, which can also be viewed as a functional relationship between observable state variables and controllable parameters. Indeed, fuzzy logic controllers use rules of this type to approximate a mapping (typically nonlinear) from the observed state to a desired control action. In fact, most industrial applications of fuzzy logic use fuzzy mapping rules.

The need to approximate a function of interest is often due to one or more of the following reasons.

First, the mathematical structure of the function is not precisely known. Were the structure known, one could use various parameter identification techniques to find the parameters.

Second, the function is so complex that finding its precise mathematical form is either impossible or practically unfeasible due to its high cost.

Third, even if finding the function is not impractical, implementing the function in its precise mathematical form in a product or service may be too costly. This is particularly important for low-cost high volume products. (e.g., automobiles, cameras, and other consumer products.)

5.3.2 Fuzzy Implication Rules

Fuzzy implication rules are a generalization of "implication" in two-valued logic. Their aim is to mimic human reasoning in its ability to reason with ideas or statements that are imprecise by nature. Even though it is obvious that human beings perform certain kinds of approximate reasoning, it is unclear how one can characterize such a reasoning process due to our present limited understanding of the human reasoning process to date. Consequently, there has not been posited a unique set of desired properties for fuzzy implication rules. Rather, several sets of desired properties have been developed, as we shall see later in the next chapter. Even though the set of desired properties is not unique, they are useful for comparing different reasoning schemes using fuzzy implication rules. We want to point out this "nonuniqueness" aspect of fuzzy implication, because it is in sharp contrast with many other techniques in science and engineering that were built on a set of well-defined axioms, properties or principles.

The inference of fuzzy implications generalizes two kinds of logic inference using the implications in classical logic: modus ponens and modus tollens. While we will describe these inferences in detail in the next chapter, we can briefly illustrate here these logic inferences using the following implication:

IF a person's IQ is high THEN the person is smart

Given the implication and the fact that "William's IQ is high", modus ponens enables us to infer that "William is smart," On the other hand, if we are given the implication and the fact that "William is no smart," modus tollens enables us to infer that "William's IQ is not high."

Even though classical logic can perform these two kinds of inferences, they are limited in two ways. First, these inferences insist on perfect matching. If William's IQ is more or less high, for instance, no modus ponens inference can be made from the implication above because "more or less smart" is not identical to "smart". However, our "common-sense reasoning" usually suggests that we can infer that "William is more or less smart." Second these inferences cannot handle uncertainty. For instance, if William told us his IQ is high but cannot provide documents supporting the claim, we may be somewhat uncertain about the claim. Under such a circumstance, however, logic cannot reason about the uncertainty.

These limitations motivated L.A. Zadeh to develop a reasoning scheme that generalizes classical logic so that (1) it can conduct "common-sense" reasoning under partial matching, and (2) it can reason about the certainty degree of a statement. In particular, logic implications are generalized to allow partial matching. In our example, this means that we can infer "William is somewhat smart" from "William's IQ is somewhat high" and the fuzzy implication "If William's IQ is High, then William is smart." as shown below.

Given: William's IQ is High → William is Smart.
William's IQ is somewhat High.

Infer: William is somewhat Smart.

The second limitation of logic (i.e. inability to deal with uncertainty) has motivated another extension to classical logic: multivalues logic. Multivalued logic extends the truth values in logic from binary (i.e., true and false) to multiple (i.e., more than two) so that different degrees of certainty are expressed by different truth values. Since fuzzy logic also generalizes the truth values in classical logic beyond true and false, it is related to multi-multivalued logic in that it also addresses the first limitation of logic (i.e., restricted to a perfect match). The reason that a fuzzy implication can address the first problem is that it uses linguistic variables in its antecedent (i.e., if parts). Consequently, the statement in the antecedent describes an elastic condition that can be partially satisfied. In our example "A person's IQ" is a linguistic variable in the antecedent, and "A person's IQ is high" describes an elastic condition about a person's IQ. This enables a person with a somewhat high IQ to partially match the condition.

The distinctions between fuzzy implication rules and fuzzy mapping rules are subtle, yet important. Prof. Zadeh mentioned in this book's Forward that fuzzy logic has four principle facets:

1. Logical Facet
2. Set-Theoretic Facet
3. Relational Facet
4. Epistemic Facet

Fuzzy implication rules are primarily in the logic facet, whereas fuzzy mapping rules are in the relational facet because functional mapping is a kind of relation. We summarize several major differences between these two types of fuzzy rules in Table 5.1.

Table 5.1: A comparison of two types of fuzzy rules

	Fuzzy Implication Rules	Fuzzy Mapping Rules
Purpose	Generalize implications for handling impression	Approximate functional
Desired Inference	generalized modus ponens and modus tollens	Forward only
Application	Diagnostics, high-level decision making	Control, system modeling, and signal processing
Related Disciplines	classical logic, multivalued logic (other extended logic systems)	System ID, piecewise linear interpolation, neural networks
Typical Design Approach	designed individually	Designed as a rule set
Suitable Problem Domains	domains with continuous and discrete variable	Continuous nonlinear domains

The remainder of this chapter will focus on fuzzy mapping rules, because they are central to fuzzy logic control and most industrial applications.

5.4 FORMATION OF RULES

The formation of rules is in general the canonical rule formation. For any linguistic variable, there are three general forms in which the canonical rules can be formed. They are:

1. Assignment statements
2. Conditional statements
3. Unconditional statements

5.4.1 Assignment Statements

These statements are those in which the variable is assignment with the value. The variable and the value assigned are combined by the assignment operator "=." The assignment statements are necessary in forming fuzzy rules. The value to be assigned may be a linguistic term.

The examples of this type of statements are:

y = low,

Sky color = blue,

Climate = hot

a = 5

p = q + r

Temperature = high

The assignment statement is found to restrict the value of a variable to a specific equality.

5.4.2 Conditional Statements

In this statements, some specific conditions are mentioned, if the conditions are satisfied then it enters the following statements, called as restrictions.

If x = y Then both are equal,

If Mark > 50 Then pass,

If Speed > 1, 500 Then stop.

These statements can be said as fuzzy conditional statements, such as If condition C' Then restriction F'

5.4.3 Unconditional Statements

There is no specific condition that has to be satisfied in this form of statements. Some of the unconditional statements are:

Go to F/o

Push the value

Stop

The control may be transferred without any appropriate conditions. The unconditional restrictions in the fuzzy form can be:

R^1 : Output is B^1

AND

R^2 : Output is B^2

AND

. . . , etc.

where B^1 and B^2 are Fuzzy consequents.

Both conditional and unconditional statements place restrictions on the consequent of the rule-based process because of certain conditions. The fuzzy sets and relations model the restrictions.

Table 5.2: Canonical form – fuzzy rule-based system

Rule 1:	If condition C^1 THEN restriction R^1
Rule 2:	If condition C^2 THEN restriction R^2
Rule 3:	If condition C^n THEN restriction R^n

The linguistic connections like "and," "or," "else" connects the conditional, unconditional, and restriction statements. The consequent of rules or output is denoted by the restrictions R^1, R^2, ... , R^n. The rule-based system with a set of conditional rules (canonical form of rules) is shown in Table 5.2.

5.5 DECOMPOSITION OF RULES

There might be a compound rule structure involved in many applications. An example for a compound rule structure is

IF x = y THEN both are equal

ELSE

IF x ≠ y

THEN

IF x > y THEN X is highest

ELSE

IF y > x THEN Y is highest

ELSE

IF x and y are equal to zero THEN no output is obtained.

By he properties and operations defined on fuzzy sets in Chap. 3, any compound rule structure can be decomposed and reduced to number of simple canonical rules. There are various methods for decomposition of rules. They are:

5.5.1 Multiple Conjunction Antecedents

This uses fuzzy intersection operation. Since it involves linguistic "AND" connective

IF x is $\underset{\sim}{P}^1$ AND $\underset{\sim}{P}^2$ ... AND $\underset{\sim}{P}^n$ THEN y is Q^T,

Where

$$\underset{\sim}{P}^T = \underset{\sim}{P}^1 \text{ AND } \underset{\sim}{P}^2 \ldots \text{ OR } \underset{\sim}{P}^n$$

The membership for this can be

$$\mu\underset{\sim}{P}^r(x) = \min\left[\mu\underset{\sim}{P}^1(x), \mu\underset{\sim}{P}^2(x), \ldots, \mu\underset{\sim}{P}^n(x)\right].$$

Hence the rule can be

IF x is $\underset{\sim}{P}^r$ THEN $\underset{\sim}{Q}^r$

5.5.2 Multiple Disjunctive Antecedents

This uses fuzzy union operations. It involves linguistic "OR" connections

IF x is $\underset{\sim}{P}^1$ OR $\underset{\sim}{P}^2$ OR $\underset{\sim}{P}^n$ THEN y is Q^T,

Where

$$\underset{\sim}{P}^r = \underset{\sim}{P}^1 \text{ OR } \underset{\sim}{P}^2 \ldots \text{ OR } \underset{\sim}{P}^n$$

$$= \underset{\sim}{P}^1 \cup \underset{\sim}{P}^2 \ldots \cup \underset{\sim}{P}^n.$$

The membership for this can be

$$\mu\underset{\sim}{P}^r(x) = \max\left[\mu\underset{\sim}{P}^1(x), \mu\underset{\sim}{P}^2(x), \ldots, \mu\underset{\sim}{P}^n(x)\right].$$

Hence the rule can be

IF x is $\underset{\sim}{P}^r$ THEN y is $\underset{\sim}{Q}^r$

5.5.3 Conditional Statements with Else

(a) If $\underset{\sim}{P}^1$ THEN ($\underset{\sim}{Q}^1$ ELSE $\underset{\sim}{Q}^2$).

Considering this as one compound statement, splitting this into two canonical form rules, we get

IF $\underset{\sim}{P}^1$ THEN Q^1 OR IF NOT $\underset{\sim}{P}^1$ THEN Q^2.

(b) IF $\underset{\sim}{P}^1$ THEN (Q^1 ELSE $\underset{\sim}{P}^2$ THEN ($\underset{\sim}{Q}^2$)).

The decomposition for this can be of the form

IF $\underset{\sim}{P}^1$ THEN Q^1 OR

IF NOT $\underset{\sim}{P}^1$ THEN $\underset{\sim}{P}^2$ THEN Q^2.

5.5.4 Nested If–Then Rules

IF $\underset{\sim}{P}^1$ THEN (IF $\underset{\sim}{P}^2$ THEN ($\underset{\sim}{Q}^2$)).

This can be decomposed into

IF $\underset{\sim}{P}^1$ AND $\underset{\sim}{P}^2$ THEN Q^1.

Thus the compound rules are decomposed into single canonical rules. Then this rule may be reduced to a series of relations.

5.6 AGGREGATION OF FUZZY RULES

The fuzzy rule-based system may involve more than one rule. The process of obtaining the overall conclusion from the individually mentioned consequents contributed by each rule in the fuzzy rule this is known as aggregation of rule.

There are two methods for determining the aggregation of rules:

5.6.1 Conjunctive System of Rules

The rules that are connected by "AND" connectives satisfy the connective system of rules. In this case, the aggregated output may be found by the fuzzy intersection of all individual rule consequents,

$$Y = y^1 \text{ AND } y^2 \text{ and } \ldots \text{ AND } y^r$$

(or)

$$y = y^1 \wedge y^2 \wedge \ldots. \wedge y^r$$

Then the membership friction is defined as

$$\mu_y(y) = \min \mu_{y^1}(y), \mu_{y^2}(y), \ldots., \mu_{y^n}(y),) \text{ for } y \in y.$$

5.6.2 Disjunctive System of Rules

The rules that are connected by "OR" connectives satisfies the disjunctive system of rules. In this case, the aggregated output may be found by the fuzzy union of all individual rule consequents

$$y = y^1 \text{ OR } y^2 \text{ OR} \ldots \text{ OR } y^r$$

(or)

$$y = y^1 \cup y^2 \cup \ldots \cup y^r$$

Then the membership function is defined as

$$\mu_{y(y)} = \min \mu_{y^1}(y), \mu_{y^2}(y), \ldots., \mu_{y^n}(y),) \text{ for } y \in y.$$

5.7 PROPERTIES OF SET OF RULES

The properties for the sets of rules are:

(a) Completeness

(b) Consistency

(c) Continuity

(d) Interaction

(a) Completeness A set of IF–THEN rules is complete if any combination of input values result in an appropriate output value.

(b) Consistency A set of IF–THEN rules is inconsistent if there are two rules with the same rules-antecedent but different rule-consequents.

(c) Continuity A set of IF–THEN rules is continuous if it does not have neighboring rules with output fuzzy sets that have empty intersection.

(d) Interaction In the interaction property, suppose that is a rule, "IF x is A THEN y is B," this meaning is represented by a fuzzy relation R2, then the composition of A and R does not deliver B

$$\underset{\sim}{A} \circ \underset{\sim}{R} = \underset{\sim}{B}$$

These are the properties of the fuzzy set of rules

5.8 FUZZY RULE-BASED MODELS FOR FUNCTION APPROXIMATION

There are four major concepts in fuzzy rule-based models thus are:

1. Fuzzy Partition
2. Mapping of Fuzzy Subregions To Local Models
3. Fusion of Multiple Local Models
4. Defuzzification.

These four concepts together enable the construction of a complex global using a set of simpler local models.

5.8.1 Fuzzy Partition

A classical partition of a space is a collection of disjoint subspaces whose union is the entire space. For example, Figure 5.2 shows an example of classical partition for an input space involving two variables: X_1 and X_2. The partition is constructed by first partitioning the range of X_1 into four intervals (i.e., I_1, I_2, I_3 and I_4) and the range of X_2 into three intervals (I.e., J_1, J_2 and J_3). Each pair of intervals I_k and J_{l} specifies a subspace A_{kl} that can be described as

$$zX_1 \in I_k \text{ and } X_2 \in J_1$$

A total of 12 subspaces partition the entire input space in this example.

Figure 5.3 shows a fuzzy partition for a system that controls the contrast of a TV based on two inputs:

1. The distance between the viewer and the TV
2. The brightness of the room.

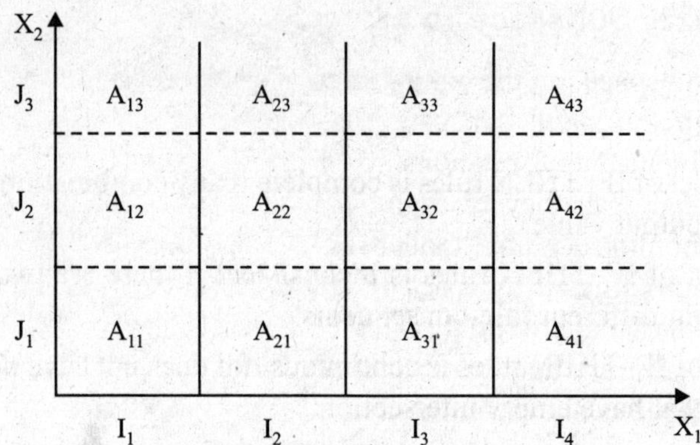

Figure 5.2: An EXample of Classical Partition

In this example, the distance between the viewer and the TV, denoted d, is classified into three fuzzy sets: Near, Medium, and Far. Similarly, the brightness of the room, denoted by b, is classified into two fuzzy sets: Bright and Dark. A fuzzy partition of the entire input space is thus formed by six fuzzy subregions specified by pairs of fuzzy sets (i.e., one for each variable). Fig 5.3 shows two of the six fuzzy subregions:

d is Medium AND b is Dark.

d is Far AND b is Dark.

As shown in the figure, the to fuzzy subregions partially overlap with each other because fuzzy sets Medium and Far partially overlap. Obviously, the same observation can be made for other neighboring fuzzy regions.

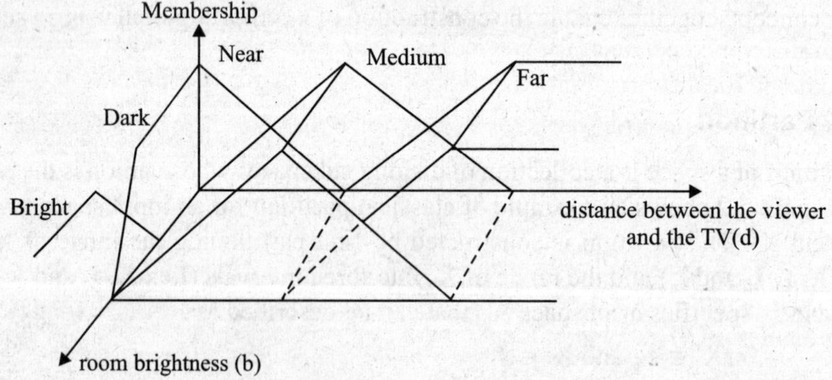

Figure 5.3: An Example of Fuzzy Partition

In a general sense, a fuzzy partition of a space is a collection of fuzzy subspaces whose boundaries partially overlap and whose union is the entire space. Even though there are different operators to choose from for the union operation in fuzzy sets.

5.8.2 Mapping a Fuzzy Subspace To a Local Model

A local model for a subspace of the entire input space describes the system's input-output mapping relationship in the small subspace. In contrast a global model for an input space describes the system's input-output relationship for the entire input space. Because the scope of the local model is smaller than they of a global model, it is usually easier to develop a local model. In particular, a nonlinear global model (i.e., whose input-output mapping function is not linear) can often be approximated by a set of linear local models. This can be understood by remembering the well-known approximation technique called "piecewise linear approximation," which approximates an arbitrary nonlinear function using segments of lines. An example of such an approximation technique is shown in Figure 5.4, where the dotted line indicates the function being approximated.

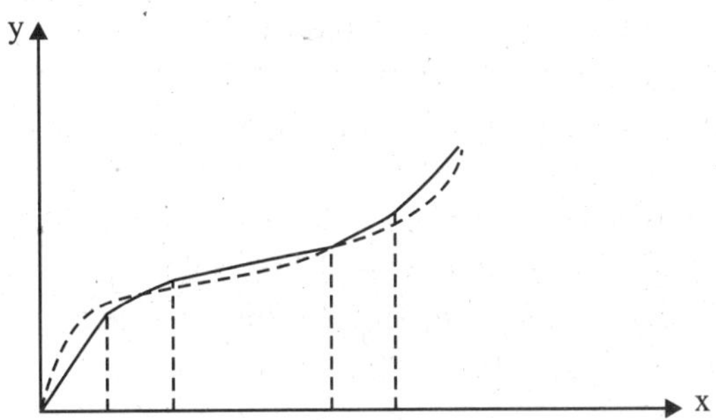

Figure 5.4: Piecewise Linear Approximation

Piecewise linear approximation has two major components:

1. Partitioning the input space to crisp regions.
2. Mapping each partitioned region to a linear local model.

The main difference between fuzzy modeling and piecewise linear approximation is that the transition from one local subregion to a neighboring one is gradual rather than abrupt.

The local model associated with each fuzzy subspace can be of four different types:

1. Crisp constant
2. Fuzzy constant
3. Linear model
4. Nonlinear model

The one that is most frequently used among fuzzy logic applications is the second type: fuzzy constant. We discuss each type of local model below.

1. **Crisp Constant:** This type of local model is simply a crisp (nonvisual) constant (e.g., 4.5), e.g.,

$$\text{IF } x_2 \text{ is Small THEN } y = 4.5$$

2. **Fuzzy Constant:** A local model that is a fuzzy constant (e.g., SMALL) belong to this type. An example is given below:

IF x is Small THEN y is Medium.

3. **Linear Model:** This kind of local model describes the output as a linear function of the input variables, such as in the rule below:

$$\text{IF x is small AND } x_2 \text{ is Large THEN } y = 2x_1 + 5x_2 + 3.$$

4. **Nonlinear Model:** Theoretically speaking, a local model can be more complex than a linear model. In practice, however, there is rarely such a need. A fuzzy model that fuses local models of the first three types is often sufficient to approximate an unknown complex plant or system. Nonlinear local models have been introduced in a hybrid neuro-fuzzy system that uses neural networks to represent nonlinear local models associated with the rule.

5.8.3 Fusion of Local Models Through Interpolative Reasoning

Fuzzy models use interpolative reasoning to fuse multiple local models into a global model. The basic behind interpolative reasoning is analogous to drawing a conclusion from a panel of experts, each of whom is specialized in a subarea of the entire problem. Each expert's opinion is associated with a weight, which reflects the degree to which the current situation is in the expert's specialized subarea. These weighted opinions are then combined to form an overall opinion. In this analogy, an expert corresponds to a fuzzy if-then rule, the specialized subarea of the expert corresponds to the fuzzy subspace associated with the if-part of the rule. The weight of an expert's opinion is determined by the degree to which the current situation belongs to the subspace.

5.8.4 Defuzzification

We may interpret a possibility distribution either through linguistic approximation, or through defuzzification.

There are two major defuzzification techniques:

1. The Mean of Maximum (MOM) method
2. The Center of Area (COA) or the centroid method

1. **The Mean of Maximum (MOM) method-** The mean of maximum defuzzification calculates the average of all variable values with maximum membership degrees. Figure 5.5 shows the result of applying MOM defuzzification to a combined fuzzy conclusion.

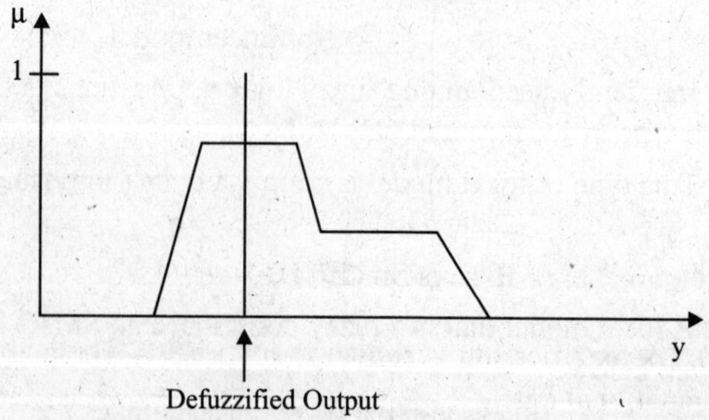

Figure 5.5: An Example of Mean of Maximum Defuzzification

Suppose "y is A" is a fuzzy conclusion to be deffuzzified. We can express the MOM defuzzification method using the following formula:

$$\text{MOM}(A) = \frac{\sum_{y^* \varepsilon p} y^*}{|P|} \tag{5.2}$$

where P(A) is the set of output values y with the highest membership degree in A, i.e.,

$$P = \{y^* \,|\, \mu_A(y^*) \sup_y \mu_A(y)\} \tag{5.3}$$

where sup is an operator that returns the maximum value of a continuous function (i.e., the continuous version of the max operator).

(2) The Center of Area (COA) or the centroid method- The centroid (or COA) defuzzification method calculates the weighted average of a fuzzy set. The result of applying COA defuzzification to a fuzzy conclusion "Y is A" can be expressed by the formula

$$y = \frac{\sum_i \mu_A(y_i) \times y_i}{\sum_i \mu_A(y_i)} \tag{5.4}$$

if y discrete, and by the formula]

$$y = \frac{\int \mu_A(y_i) \times y_i dy}{\int \mu_A(y_i) dy} \tag{5.5}$$

if y is continuous.

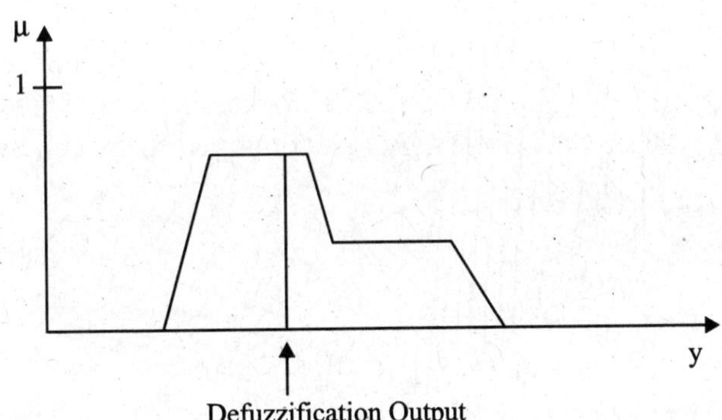

Figure 5.6: An Example of Center of Area Defuzzification

An example of COA defuzzification is shown in Figure 5.6. The main disadvantage of COA method is its high computational cost.

5.9 THE HEIGHT METHOD

The third defuzzification technique is the height method, which can be viewed as a two-step procedure. First, we convert the consequent membership function C_i into crisp consequent $y = c_i$ where C_i is the center of gravity of C_i. The centroid defuzzification is then applied to the rules with crisp consequents, which gives us the following formula:

$$y = \frac{\sum_{i=1}^{M} W_i C_i}{\sum_{i=1}^{M} W_i} \tag{5.6}$$

where w_i is the degree to which the ith rule matches the input data. The main benefit of the height method is its simplicity. The calculation of C_i can be performed during compilation.

5.10 A THEORETICAL FOUNDATION OF FUZZY MAPPING RULES

5.10.1 A Mathematical Representation of Fuzzy Mapping Rules

A fuzzy mapping rule imposes an elastic constraint on possible associations between input and output variables. The constraint is elastic because a fuzzy rule can describe input-output associations that are somewhat possible (i.e., the gray area between totally possible and totally impossible). The degree of possibility of an input-output association imposed by a rule R can be expressed as a possibility distribution, denoted by Π_R.

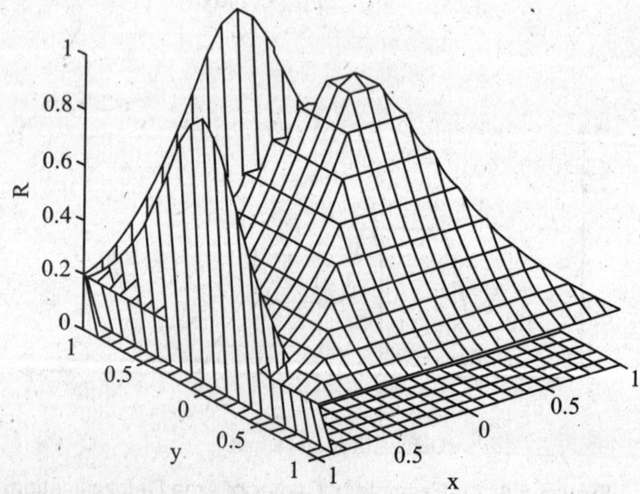

Figure 5.7: A Fuzzy Relation Formed by a Fuzzy Mapping Rule

Since a fuzzy relation is a general way for describing a possibility distribution, it is natural to use it to represent the possibility distribution imposed by a fuzzy rule.

A fuzzy mapping rule is represented mathematically as fuzzy relations formed by the Cartesian product of the variables referred to in the rule's if-part and-then part. For example, the mapping rule

IF x is A, THEN y is B

is mathematically represented as a fuzzy relation R defined as $\mu_R(x, y) = \mu_{A\times B}(x, y)$. If is mathematically represented for the Cartesian product, the fuzzy relation R becomes $\mu_R(x, y) = \min\{\mu_A(x), \mu_B(y)\}$. The two-dimensional membership function of a fuzzy relation constructed this way is depicted in Figure 5.7.

5.11 FUZZY INFERENCE SYSTEM

Fuzzy inference systems (FISs) are also known as fuzzy rule-based systems, fuzzy model, fuzzy expert system, and fuzzy associative memory. This is a major unit of a fuzzy logic system. The decision-making is an important part in the entire system. The FIS formulates suitable rules and based upon the rules the decision is made. This is mainly based on the concepts of the fuzzy set theory, fuzzy IF–THEN rules, and fuzzy reasoning. FIS uses "IF. . . THEN. . . " statements, and the connectors present in the rule statement are "OR" or "AND" to make the necessary decision rules. The basic FIS can take either fuzzy inputs or crisp inputs, but the outputs it produces are almost always fuzzy sets. When the FIS is used as a controller, it is necessary to have a crisp output. Therefore in this case defuzzification method is adopted to best extract a crisp value that best represents a fuzzy set. The whole FIS is discussed in detail in the following subsections.

5.11.1 Construction and Working of Inference System

Fuzzy inference system consists of a fuzzification interface, a rule base, a database, a decision-making unit, and finally a defuzzification interface. A FIS with five functional block described in Figure 5.8. The function of each block is as follows:

- a rule base containing a number of fuzzy IF–THEN rules;
- a database which defines the membership functions of the fuzzy sets used in the fuzzy rules;
- a decision-making unit which performs the inference operations on the rules;

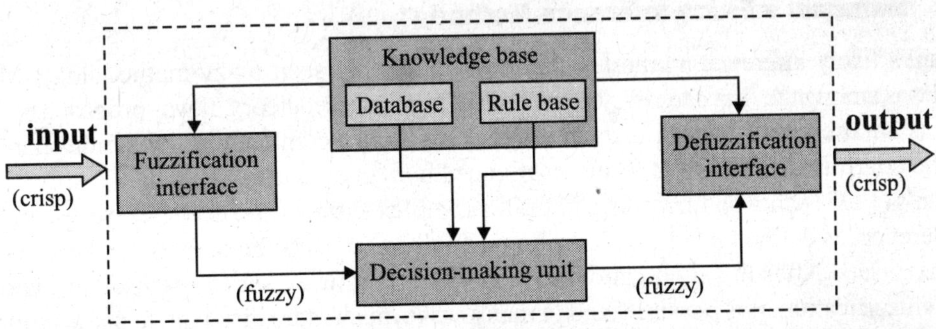

Figure 5.8: Fuzzy Inference System

- a fuzzification interface which transforms the crisp inputs into degrees of match with linguistic values; and
- a defuzzification interface which transforms the fuzzy results of the inference into a crisp output.

The working of FIS is as follows. The crisp input is converted in to fuzzy by using fuzzification method. After fuzzification the rule base is formed. The rule base and the database are jointly referred to as the knowledge base. Defuzzification is used to convert fuzzy value to the real world value which is the output. The steps of fuzzy reasoning (inference operations upon fuzzy IF–THEN rules) performed by FISs are:

1. Compare the input variables with the membership functions on the antecedent part to obtain the membership values of each linguistic label. (this step is often called fuzzification.)
2. Combine (through a specific t-norm operator, usually multiplication or min) the membership values on the premise part to get firing strength (weight) of each rule.
3. Generate the qualified consequents (either fuzzy or crisp) or each rule depending on the firing strength.
4. Aggregate the qualified consequents to produce a crisp output. (This step is called defuzzification.)

5.11.2 Fuzzy Inference Methods

The most important two types of fuzzy inference method are Mamdani's fuzzy inference method, which is the most commonly seen inference method. This method was introduced by Mamdani and Assilian (1975). Another well-known inference method is the so-called Sugeno or Takagi–Sugeno–Kang method of fuzzy inference process. This method was introduced by Sugeno (1985).

This method is also called as TS method. The main difference between the two methods lies in the consequent of fuzzy rules. Mamdani fuzzy systems use fuzzy sets as rule consequent whereas TS fuzzy systems employ linear functions of input variables as rule consequent. All the existing results on fuzzy systems as universal approximators deal with Mamdani fuzzy systems only and no result is available for TS fuzzy systems with linear rule consequent.

5.11.3 Mamdani's Fuzzy Inference Method

Mamdani's fuzzy inference method is the most commonly seen fuzzy methodology. Mamdani's method was among the first control systems built using fuzzy set theory. It was proposed by Mamdani (1975) as an attempt to control a steam engine and boiler combination by synthesizing a set of linguistic control rules obtained from experienced human operators. Mamdani's effort was based on Zadeh's (1973) paper on fuzzy algorithms for complex systems and decision processes. Mamdani type inference, as defined it for the Fuzzy Logic Toolbox, expects the output membership functions to be fuzzy sets. After the aggregation process, there is a fuzzy set for each output variable that needs defuzzification. It is possible, and in many cases much more efficient, to use a single spike as the output membership functions rather than a distributed fuzzy set. This is sometimes known as a singleton output membership function, and it can be thought of as a pre-defuzzified fuzzy set. It enhances the efficiency of the defuzzification process because it greatly simplifies the computation required by the more general Mamdani method, which finds the centroid of a two-dimensional function. Rather than integrating across the two-dimensional function to find the centroid, the weighted average of a few data points. Sugeno type systems support this type of model. In general, Sugeno type systems can be used to model any inference system in which the output membership functions are either linear or constant. An example of a Mamdani inference system is shown in Figure 5.9. To compute the output of this FIS given the inputs, six steps has to be followed:

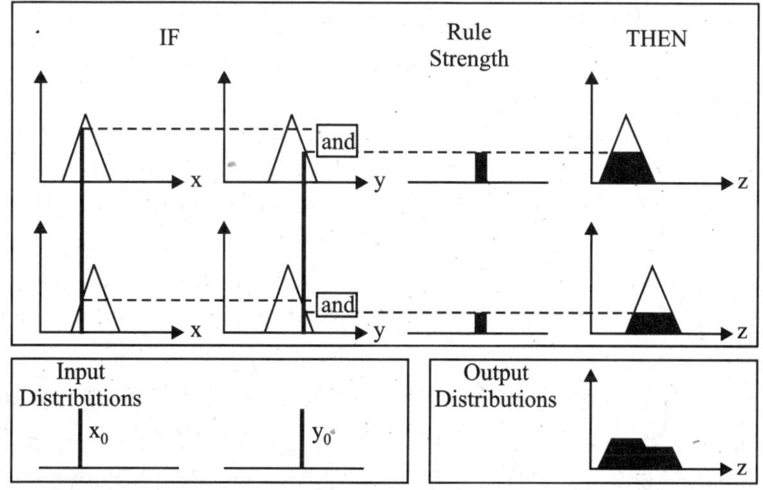

Figure 5.9: A Two Input, Two Rule Mamdani Fis with Crisp Inputs

1. Determining a set of fuzzy rules
2. Fuzzifying the inputs using the input membership functions
3. Combining the fuzzified inputs according to the fuzzy rules to establish a rule strength
4. Finding the consequence of the rule by combining the rule strength and the output membership function
5. Combining the consequences to get an output distribution
6. Defuzzifying the output distribution (this step is only if a crisp output (class) is needed).

The following is a more detailed description of this process

1. **Creating Fuzzy Rules:** Fuzzy rules are a collection of linguistic statements that describe how the FIS should make a decision regarding classifying an input or controling an output. Fuzzy rules are always written in the following form:

   if (input 1 is membership function 1) **and/or** (input 2 is membership function 2) **and/or**. . . **then** (outputn is output membership functionn).

   For example:

   if temperature is high **and** humidity is high **then** room is hot.

There would have to be membership functions that define high temperature (input 1), high humidity (input 2), and a hot room (output 1). This process of taking an input such as temperature and processing it through a membership function to determine "high" temperature is called fuzzification and is discussed in section, "Fuzzification." Also, "AND"/"OR" in the fuzzy rule should be defined. This is called fuzzy combination and is discussed in following section.

2. **Fuzzification:** The purpose of fuzzification is to map the inputs from a set of sensors (or features of those sensors such as amplitude or spectrum) to values from 0 to 1 using a set of input membership functions. In the example shown in Figure 5.9, there are two inputs, x0 and y0 shown at the lower left corner. These inputs are mapped into fuzzy numbers by drawing a line up from the inputs to the input membership functions above and marking the intersection point. These input membership functions, as discussed previously, can represent fuzzy concepts such as "large" or "small," "old" or "young," "hot" or "cold," etc. For example, x0 could be the EMG energy coming from the front of the forearm and y0 could be the EMG energy coming from the back of the forearm. The membership functions could then represent large amounts of tension coming from a muscle or small amounts of tension. When choosing the input membership functions, the definition of large and small may be different for each input.
3. **Consequence:** The consequence of a fuzzy rule is computed using two steps:
   (i) Computing the rule strength by combining the fuzzified inputs using the fuzzy combination process discussed in previous section. This is shown in Figure 5.9. In this example, the fuzzy "AND" is used to combine the membership functions to compute the rule strength.
   (ii) Clipping the output membership function at the rule strength.
4. **Combining Outputs Into an Output Distribution:** The outputs of all of the fuzzy rules must now be combined to obtain one fuzzy output distribution. This is usually, but not always, done by using the fuzzy "OR." Figure 5.9 shows an example of this. The output membership functions on the right-hand side of the figure are combined using the fuzzy OR to obtain the output distribution shown on the lower right corner of the Figure 5.9.
5. **Defuzzification of Output Distribution:** In many instances, it is desired to come up with a single crisp output from an FIS. For example, if one was trying to classify a letter drawn by hand on a drawing tablet, ultimately the FIS would have to come up with a crisp number to tell the computer which letter was drawn. This crisp number is obtained in a process known as defuzzification. There are two common techniques for defuzzifying:
   (i) Center of Mass: This technique takes the output distribution and finds its center of mass to come up with one crisp number. This is computed as follows:

$$z = \frac{\sum_{j=1}^{q} Z_j u_c(Z_j)}{\sum_{j=1}^{q} u_c(Z_j)}$$

where z is the center of mass and u_c is the membership in class c at value z_j . An example outcome of this computation is shown in Figure 5.10.

(ii) Mean of Maximum: This technique takes the output distribution and finds its mean of maxima to come up with one crisp number. This is computed as follows:

$$z = \sum_{j=1}^{l} \frac{Z_j}{l}$$

where z is the mean of maximum, z_j is the point at which the membership function is maximum, and L is the number of times the output distribution reaches the maximum level. An example outcome of this computation is shown in Figure 5.11.

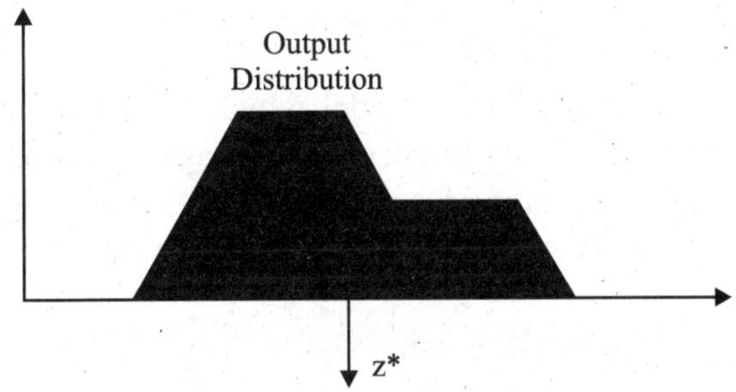

Figure 5.10: Defuzzification Using the Center of Mass

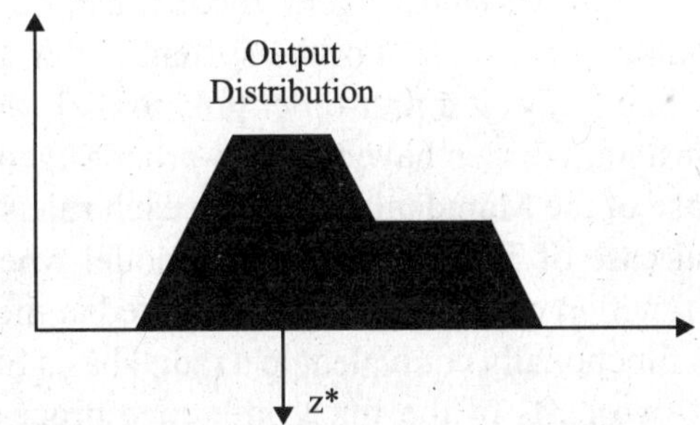

Figure 5.11: Defuzzification Using the Mean of Maximum

6. **Fuzzy Inputs:** In summary, Figure 5.12 shows a two input Mamdani FIS with two rules. It fuzzifies the two inputs by finding the intersection of the crisp input value with the input membership function. It uses the minimum operator to compute the fuzzy AND for combining the two fuzzified inputs to obtain a rule strength. It clips the output membership function at the rule strength. Finally, it uses the maximum operator to compute the fuzzy OR for combining the outputs of the two rules.

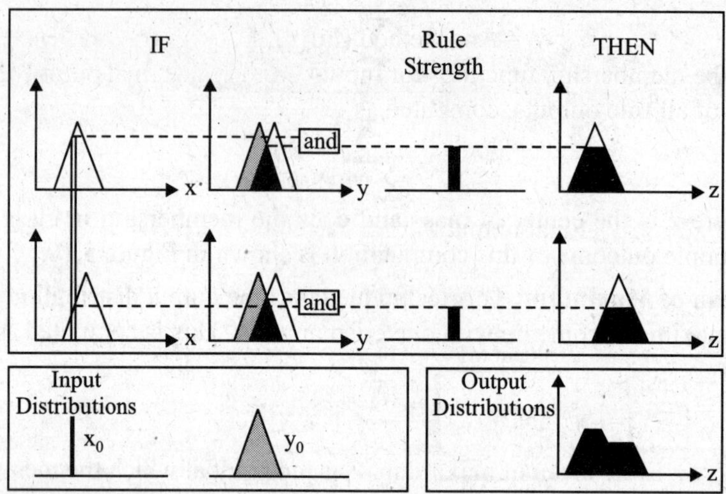

Figure 5.12: A Two Input, Two Rule Mamdani Fis with a Fuzzy Input

5.11.4 Takagi–Sugeno Fuzzy Method (TS Method)

In this section, the basic of Sugeno fuzzy model which is implemented into the neural-fuzzy system. The Sugeno fuzzy model was proposed by Takagi, Sugeno, and Kang in an effort to formalize a system approach to generating fuzzy rules from an input–output data set. Sugeno fuzzy model is also know as Sugeno–Takagi model. A typical fuzzy rule in a Sugeno fuzzy model has the format

IF x is A and y is B THEN z = f(x, y),

where AB are fuzzy sets in the antecedent; Z = f(x, y) is a crisp function in the consequent. Usually f(x, y) is a polynomial in the input variables x and y, but it can be any other functions that can appropriately describe the output of the output of the system within the fuzzy region specified by the antecedent of the rule. When f(x, y) is a first-order polynomial, we have the first-order Sugeno fuzzy model. When f is a constant, we then have the zero-order Sugeno fuzzy model, which can be viewed either as a special case of the Mamdani FIS where each rule's consequent is specified by a fuzzy singleton, or a special case of Tsukamoto's fuzzy model where each rule's consequent is specified by a membership function of a step function centered at the constant. Moreover, a zero-order Sugeno fuzzy model is functionally equivalent to a radial basis function network under certain minor constraints. The first two parts of the fuzzy inference process, fuzzifying the inputs and applying the fuzzy operator, are exactly the same. The main difference between Mamdani and Sugeno is that the Sugeno output membership functions are either linear or constant. A typical rule in a Sugeno fuzzy model has the form

IF Input 1 = x AND Input 2 = y, THEN Output is z = ax + by + c.

For a zero-order Sugeno model, the output level zis a constant (a = b = 0).The output level z_i of each rule is weighted by the firing strength w_i of the rule. For example, for an AND rule with Input 1 = x and Input 2 = y, the firing strength is

$$w_i = \text{AndMethod}\,(F_1\,(x), F_2\,(y)),$$

where F1,2(·) are the membership functions for Inputs 1 and 2. The final output of the system is the weighted average of all rule outputs, computed as

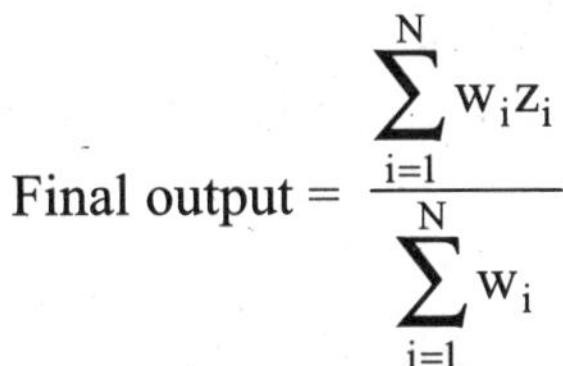

$$\text{Final output} = \frac{\sum_{i=1}^{N} w_i z_i}{\sum_{i=1}^{N} w_i}$$

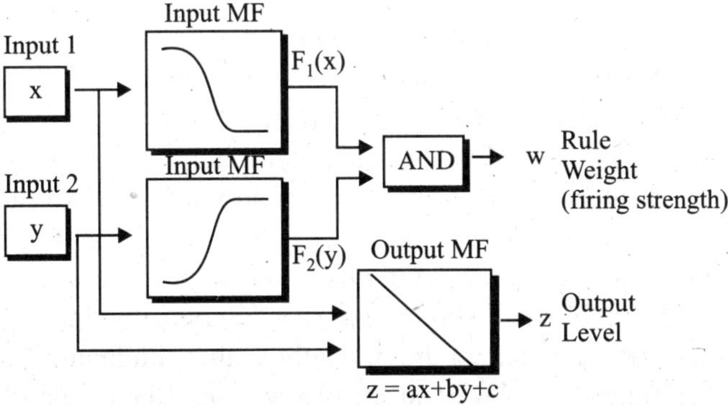

Figure 5.13: Sugeno Rule

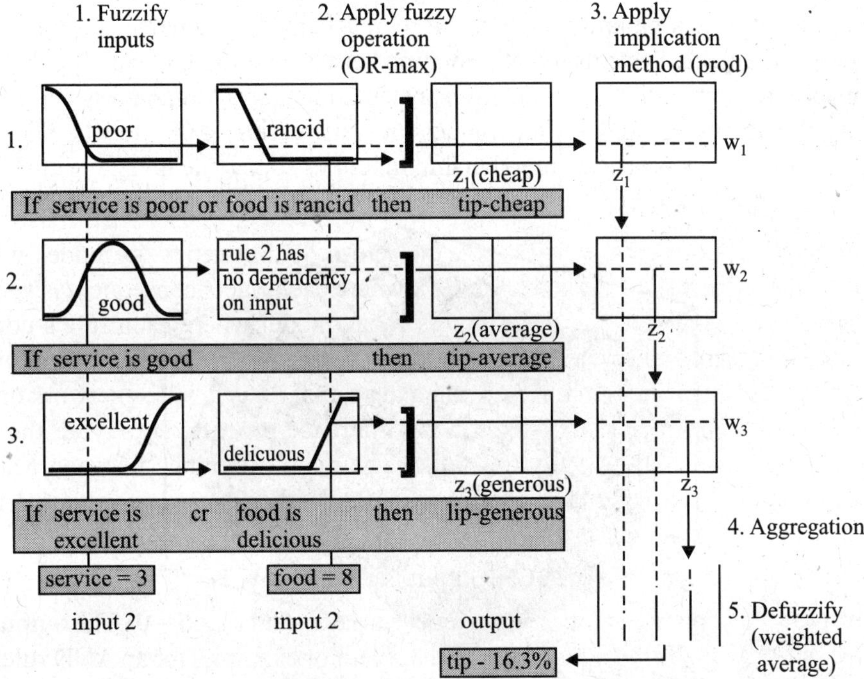

Figure 5.14: Fuzzy Tipping Model

A Sugeno rule operates as shown in Figure 5.13.

Figure 5.14 shows the fuzzy tipping model developed in previous sections of this manual adapted for use as a Sugeno system. Fortunately, it is frequently the case that singleton output functions are completely sufficient for the needs of a given problem. As an example, the system tippersg.fis is the Sugeno type representation of the now-familiar tipping model (Figure 5.14).

- a = readfis('tippersg');

  gensurf(a)

The above command gives the surface view of fuzzy tipping model as shown in Figure 5.15. The easiest way to visualize first-order Sugeno systems is to think of each rule as defining the location of a "moving singleton." That is, the singleton output spikes can move around in a linear fashion in the output space, depending on what the input is. This also tends to make the system notation very compact and efficient. Higher-order Sugeno fuzzy models are possible, but they introduce significant complexity with little obvious merit. Sugeno fuzzy models whose output membership functions are greater than first-order are not supported by the Fuzzy Logic Toolbox. Because of the linear dependence of each rule on the input variables of a system, the Sugeno method is ideal for acting as an interpolating supervisor of multiple linear controllers that are to be applied, respectively, to different operating conditions of a dynamic nonlinear system. For example, the performance of an aircraft may change dramatically with altitude and Mach number. Linear controllers, though easy to compute and well suited to any given flight condition, must be updated regularly and smoothly to keep up with the changing state of the flight vehicle. A Sugeno FIS is extremely well suited to the task of smoothly interpolating the linear gains that would be applied across the input space; it is a natural and efficient gain scheduler. Similarly, a Sugeno system is suited for modeling nonlinear systems by interpolating between multiple linear models. Because it is a more compact and computationally efficient representation than a Mamdani system, the Sugeno system lends itself to the use of adaptive techniques for constructing fuzzy models. These adaptive techniques can be used to customize the membership functions so that the fuzzy system best models the data.

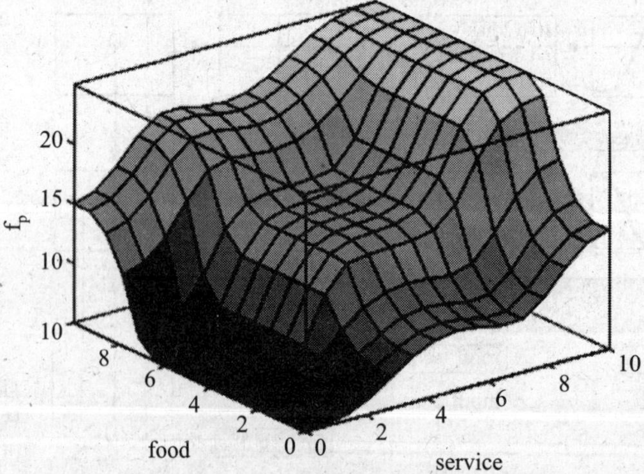

Figure 5.15: Surface View

5.11.5 Comparison Between Sugeno and Mamdani Method

The main difference between Mamdani and Sugeno is that the Sugeno output membership functions are either linear or constant. Also the difference lies in the consequents of their fuzzy rules, and thus their aggregation and defuzzification procedures differ suitably. The number of the input fuzzy sets and fuzzy rules needed by the Sugeno fuzzy systems depend on the number and locations of the extrema of the function to be approximated. In Sugeno method a large number of fuzzy rules must be employed to approximate periodic or highly oscillatory functions. The minimal configuration of the TS fuzzy systems can be reduced and becomes smaller than that of the Mamdani fuzzy systems if nontrapezoidal or nontriangular input fuzzy sets are used.

Sugeno controllers usually have far more adjustable parameters in the rule consequent and the number of the parameters grows exponentially with the increase of the number of input variables. Far fewer mathematical results exist for TS fuzzy controllers than do for Mamdani fuzzy controllers, notably those on TS fuzzy control system stability. Mamdani is easy to form compared to Sugeno method.

5.11.6 Advantages of Sugeno and Mamdani Method

Following are the advantages of sugeno and mamdani methods:

Advantages of the sugeno method

Follow'ing are the advantages of the sugeno method:

1. It is computationally efficient.
2. It works well with linear techniques (e.g., PID control).
3. It works well with optimization and adaptive techniques.
4. It has guaranteed continuity of the output surface.
5. It is well suited to mathematical analysis.

Advantages of the mamdani method

Following are the advantages of the mamdani method:

1. It is intuitive.
2. It has widespread acceptance.
3. It is well suited to human input.

Fuzzy inference system is the most important modeling tool based on fuzzy set theory. The FISs are built by domain experts and are used in automatic control, decision analysis, and various other expert systems.

EXERCISES

1. What do you mean by Fuzzy if then rules?
2. Explain the various types of fuzzy rules?

3. What do you mean by fuzzy mapping rules?
4. What do you mean by fuzzy implication rules?
5. Explain the comparison of two types of fuzzy rules?
6. Explain the formation of rules?
7. Explain the de composition of rules?
8. What do you mean by aggregation of fuzzy rules?
9. Explain the properties of fuzzy rules?
10. Explain the various fuzzy rule based models?
11. What do you mean by defuzzification?
12. What are the two major defuzzification techniques?
13. What do you mean by height method?
14. Explain the mathematical representation of fuzzy mapping rules?
15. What do you mean by fuzzy inference system?
16. Explain the construction and working of fuzzy inference system?
17. Explain the two most important methods of fuzzy inference system?
18. Explain the comparison between sugeno and mamdani method?
19. What are the various advantages of sugeno and mamdani method?
20. Explain in detail mamdani's fuzzy inference method?

CHAPTER 6

Applications of Fuzzy Logic

6.1 INTRODUCTION

This chapter introduces some engineering applications of fuzzy logic and fuzzy control systems. The purpose of this introduction is mainly to illustrate workability and applicability of fuzzy logic and fuzzy control in reaFuzzy If-then Rulesl-life situations, based on the fuzzy systems theories developed in the previous chapters of the book.

Main applications are introduced in the following order: Fuzzy logic in industrial automation, Fuzzy logic supervisory control for coal power plant, Optimization of a water treatment system, Truck speed limiter control by fuzzy logic, Fuzzy logic and neuro-fuzzy in appliances etc. For each application, a description of the functionality of the system is given, followed by the fuzzy logic rules and computer simulation results.

6.2 FUZZY LOGIC IN INDUSTRIAL AUTOMATION

In recent years, fuzzy logic has proven well its broad potential in industrial automation applications. In this application area, engineers primarily rely on proven concepts. For discrete event control, they mostly use ladder logic, a programming language resembling electrical wiring schemes and running on so called programmable logic controllers (PLC). For continuous control, either bang-bang type or PID type controllers are mostly employed.

While PID type controllers do work fine when the process under control is in a stable condition, they do not cope well in other cases:

- The presence of strong disturbances (non-linearity)
- Time-varying parameters of the process (non-linearity)
- Presence of dead times

The reason for this is that a PID controller assumes the process to behave in a strictly linear fashion. While this simplification can be made in a stable condition, strong disturbances can push the process operation point far away from the set operating point. Here, the linear assumption usually does not work any more. The same happens if a process changes its parameters over time.

In these cases, the extension or replacement of PID controllers with fuzzy controllers has been shown to be more feasible more often than using conventional but sophisticated state controllers or adaptive approaches. However, this is not the only area where there is potential for fuzzy logic based solutions.

6.2.1 Multi-variable Control

The real potential of fuzzy logic in industrial automation lies in the straightforward way fuzzy logic renders possible the design of multi-variable controllers. In many applications, keeping a single process variable constant can be done well using a PID or bang-bang type controller. However, set values for all these individual control loops are often still set manually by operators. The operators analyze the process condition, and tune the set values of the PID controllers to optimize the operation. This is called "supervisory control" and mostly involves multiple variables.

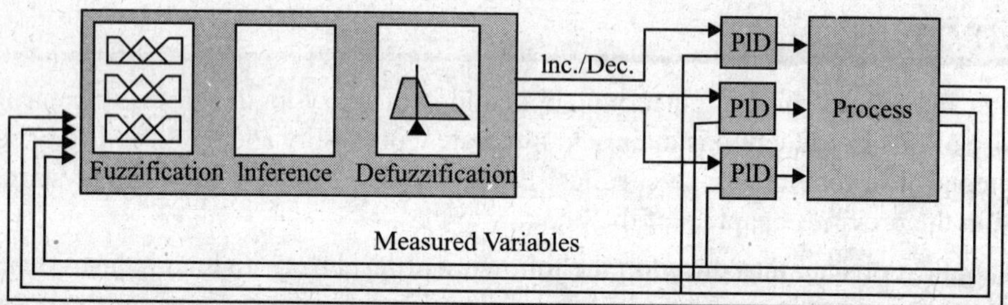

Figure 6.1: Using a Fuzzy Logic Controller to Determine the Set Values for Underlying PID Control Loops

Alas, both PID and bang-bang type controllers can only cope with one variable. This usually results in several independently operating control loops. These loops are not able to "talk to each other". In cases where it is desirable or necessary to exploit interdependencies of physical variables, one is forced to set up a complete mathematical model of the process and to derive differential equations from it that are necessary for the implementation of a solution. In the world of industrial automation, this is rarely feasible:

- Creating a mathematical model for a real-word problem can involve years of work.
- Most mathematical models involve extensive simplifications and linearizations that require "fudge" factors to optimize the resulting controller later on.
- Tuning the fudge factors of a controller derived from a mathematical model is "fishing in the dark", because optimizing the system at one operating point using global factors usually degrades the performance at other operating points.

Also, many practitioners do not have the background required for rigorous mathematical modeling. Thus, the general observation in industry is that single process variables are controlled by simple control models such as PID or bang-bang, while supervisory control is done by human operators.

This is where fuzzy logic provides an elegant and highly efficient solution to the problem. Fuzzy logic lets engineers design supervisory multi-variable controllers from operator experience and experimental results rather than from mathematical models. A possible structure of a fuzzy logic based control system in industrial automation applications is exemplified by Figure 6.1. Each single process variable is kept constant by a PID controller, while the set values for the PID controller stem from the fuzzy logic system. This arrangement is typical for cases like control of several temperature zones of an oven or control of oxygen concentrations in different zones of a wastewater basin. In other cases, it could be reasonable to develop the complete closed loop control solution in a fuzzy system.

This illustrates why it is very desirable to integrate conventional control engineering techniques, such as ladder logic or instruction list language for digital logic and PID control blocks tightly together with fuzzy logic functionality.

6.2.2 Merging Fuzzy Logic and PICs

In 1990, when more and more successful applications proved the potential of fuzzy logic in industrial automation, the German company Moeller GmbH and the U.S./German company Inform Software created the *fuzzy*PLC based on the observation that fuzzy logic needs tight integration with conventional industrial automation techniques.

The *fuzzy*PLC Hardware and Firmware

Figure 6.2: The fuzzyPLC contains fuzzy and conventional logic processing capabilities, field bus connections, and interfaces.

To make it available at a low cost, the core of the *fuzzy*PLC uses a highly integrated two-chip solution. An analog ASIC handles the analog/digital interfaces at industry standard 12 bit resolution. Snap-On modules can extend the periphery for large applications of up to about 100 signals. An integrated field bus connection, based on RS485, provides further expansion by networking. The conventional and the fuzzy logic computation is handled by a 16/32 bit RISC microcontroller. The operating system and communication routines, developed by Moeller, are based on a commercial real time multitasking kernel. The fuzzy inference engine, developed by Inform Software, is implemented and integrated into the operating system in a highly efficient manner, so that scan times of less than one millisecond are possible. The internal RAM of 256 KB can be expanded by memory cards using flash technology. Thus, the *fuzzy*PLC is capable of solving quite complex and fast industrial automation problems in spite of its compact and low price design.

The FuzzyPLC Engineering Software

The *fuzzy*PLC is programmed by an enhanced version of the standard fuzzy logic system development software *fuzzy*TECH from Inform Software. *fuzzy*TECH is an all-graphical, design, simulation, and optimization environment with implementation modules for most microcontrollers and industrial computers. To support the complete functionality of the *fuzzy*PLC, *fuzzy*TECH has been enhanced with editors and functions to support the conventional programming of the PLC. Thus, a user only needs one tool to program both conventional and fuzzy logic parts of the solution.

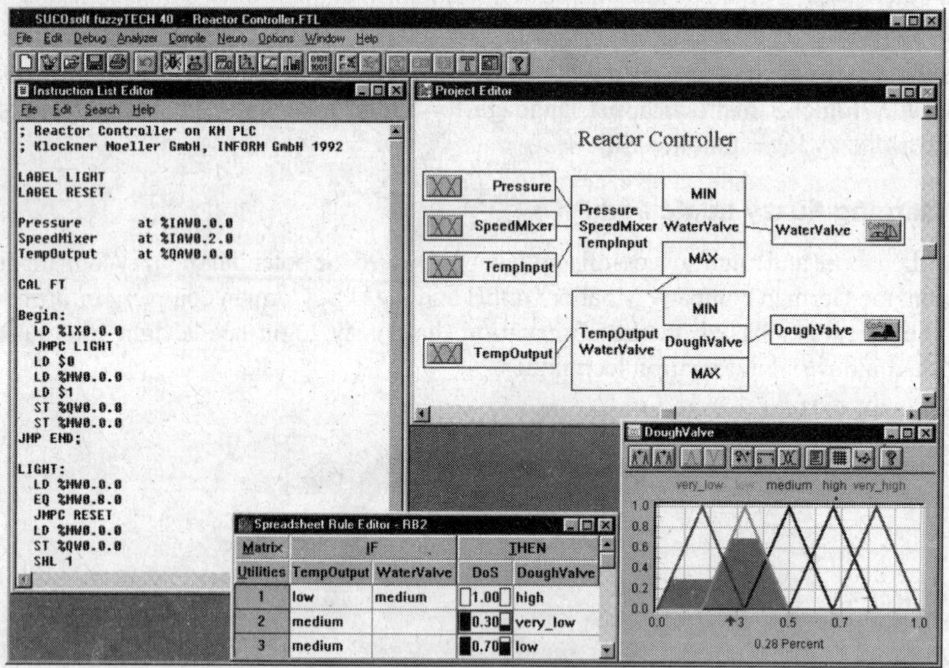

Figure 6.3: Both the Traditional Logic and the Fuzzy Logic System is Programmed by FuzzyTECH 4.0.

The *fuzzy*TECH software combines all necessary editors for membership functions, linguistic variables, rule tables, and system structure with analyzer functions and optimization features. The software runs on a PC and is linked to the *fuzzy*PLC by a standard serial cable (RS232) or the field bus (RS485). Through this link, the developer downloads the designed system to the *fuzzy*PLC. Because fuzzy logic systems often require optimization "on-the-fly", *fuzzy*TECH and the *fuzzy*PLC feature "online-debugging" where the system running on the *fuzzy*PLC is completely visualized by the graphical editors and analyzers of *fuzzy*TECH. Plus, in online-debugging modes, any modification of the fuzzy logic system is instantly translated to the *fuzzy*PLC without halting operation.

6.2.3 Application Case Studies

In this section, we review eight (8) recent highly successful applications of fuzzy logic in industrial automation using the *fuzzy*PLC:

1. Anti-Sway Control of Cranes
2. Fire Zone Control in Waste Incineration Plants
3. Dosing Control in Waste Water Treatment Plants
4. Control of Tunnel Inspection Robots
5. Positioning in Presses
6. Temperature Control in Plastic Molding Machines
7. Climate Control and Building Automation
8. Wind Energy Converter Control

1. Anti-Sway Control of Cranes: In crane control, the objective is to position a load over a target point. While the load connected to the crane head by flexible cables may well sway within certain limits during transportation, the sway must be reduced to almost zero for load release when the target position is reached. Hence, a controller must use at least two input variables, for example position and sway angle. Thus, a simple PID controller cannot be used as it is restricted to one input. Conventional solutions of the problem require highly elaborate approaches, like model based control or state variable controllers that need intensive engineering and hardware resources. These technologies tend to push system costs into regions that make anti-sway systems economically unaffordable. For these reasons, most cranes are still operated manually.

Figure 6.4: The 64 ton crane of Hochtief Corp. uses fuzzyPLC based anti-sway positioning control

In spite of the difficulties involved with automated control, human operators can control cranes quite well in most cases. Because fuzzy logic is a technology that facilitates control system design based directly on such human experiences, it has been used for crane automation for almost a decade. The types of cranes include container cranes in harbors, steel pan cranes, and cranes in a manufacturing environment. Recently, a 64 ton crane that transports concrete modules for bridges and tunnels over a distance of 500 yards has been automated with a *fuzzy*PLC in Germany.

The benefit was a capacity gain of about 20% due to the faster transportation and an increase in safety. Accidents were frequent, because the crane operators walk parallel to the crane during operation with a remote controller. Before, when they had to watch the load to concentrate on the sway angle, they frequently stumbled over parts lying on the ground. The crane was commissioned in Spring 1995 and the fuzzy logic anti-sway controller has been continuously enabled by the crane operator, showing the high degree of acceptance by the operators. This fact is of special importance since not only technological feasibility but also psychological aspects are important for the success of an industrial automation solution.

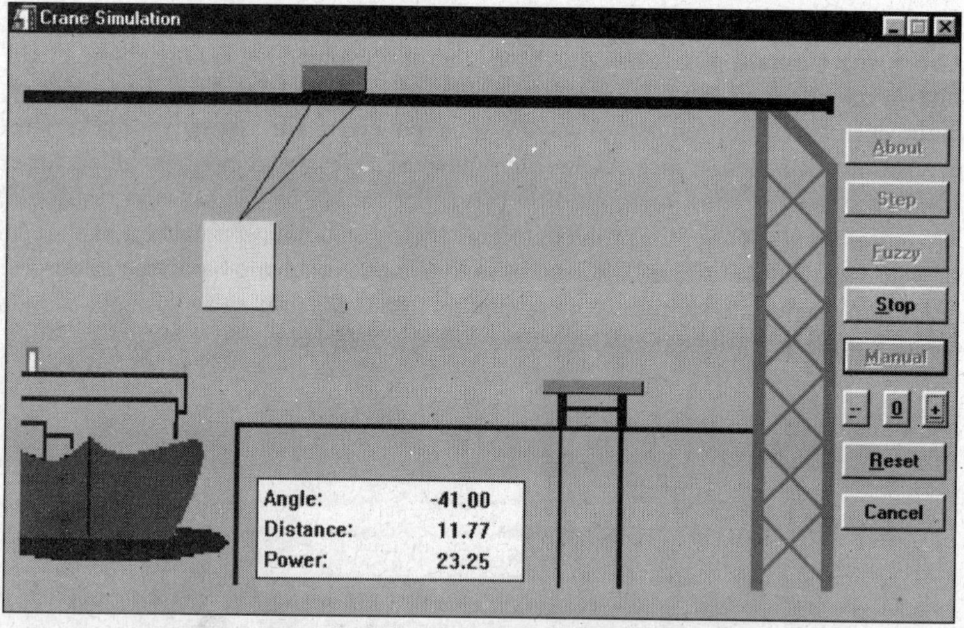

Figure 6.5: A software simulation of the crane controller is contained in [6.4]

A software simulation and a simple example of an anti-sway crane controller for didactic purposes can be found in [6.4]. The real solution uses about 10 inputs, 2 outputs, and 4 rule blocks with a total of 75 rules.

2. Fire Zone Control in Waste Incineration Plants: Maintaining a stable burning temperature in waste incineration plants is important to minimize the generation of toxic gases, such as dioxin and furan, as well as to avoid corrosion in the burning chambers. There are two primary difficulties of this temperature control process:

- The caloric value of the waste fluctuates strongly.
- The fire position and shape cannot be measured directly.

Because the heat generated from the burning process is used to produce electrical energy, a stable incineration process is also of high commercial interest.

Figure 6.6: In a waste incineration plant, a crane continuously delivers waste from the bunker to the belt running through the burning zone. The exhaust gases are cooled and cleaned.

In recent applications at waste incineration plants in the cities of Hamburg and Mannheim in Germany, fuzzy logic has been successfully applied. In Mannheim, where two *fuzzy*PLCs were used to control the burning process, the steam generation capacity of one furnace is 28 Mg/h. Using the industry standard conventional controller, steam generation fluctuated by as much as 10 Mg/h in just one hour. The fuzzy logic controller was capable of reducing this fluctuation to less than ±1 Mg/h. This dramatically improved robustness and also caused the NOx and SO2 emission to drop slightly, and the CO emission to drop to half.

3. Dosing Control in Waste Water Treatment Plants: Waste water treatment processes are a combination of biological, chemical, and mechanical processes. This makes the creation of a complete mathematical model for their control intractable. However, there is a large amount of human experience that can be exploited for automated controller design. As such operator experience can be efficiently put to work by fuzzy logic, many plants already use this technique.

In a recent application in Bonn, dosing of liquid FeCl3 for phosphate precipitation has been successfully automated using the *fuzzy*PLC. Recently changes in legislation require water treatment plants in Germany to limit the total amount of phosphate in the released water to 1 milligram per liter. To extract the phosphate from the water, FeCl3 is added, which converts the phosphate into FePO4 that is sedimented with the sludge. Because a violation of the legal phosphate limit results in severe penalties, the operators tend to overdose the FeCl3.

Figure 6.7: By injecting FeCl3 into the sludge, dissolved phosphate precipitates from the waste water

To optimize the FeCl3 dosing, a fuzzy logic controller that uses the input variables phosphate concentration, its derivative, water flow, its derivative, and dry substance contents was designed. The output of the fuzzy logic controller is the change of the set variable for the injected FeCl3. An underlying conventional PI type controller stabilizes the FeCl3 flow to this set point. The PI type controller is implemented as a function block in the *fuzzy***PLC** as well. This is an example of the combination of fuzzy logic and conventional control engineering techniques.

The total fuzzy logic controller uses 207 rules to express the control strategy based on the five (5) input variables of the fuzzy logic control block. The total implementation time was three (3) staff months and resulted in savings of about 50% of the FeCl3 compared to the manual control before. Taking implementation time and hardware/software costs into consideration with the savings on FeCl3 results a return in investment time of half a year.

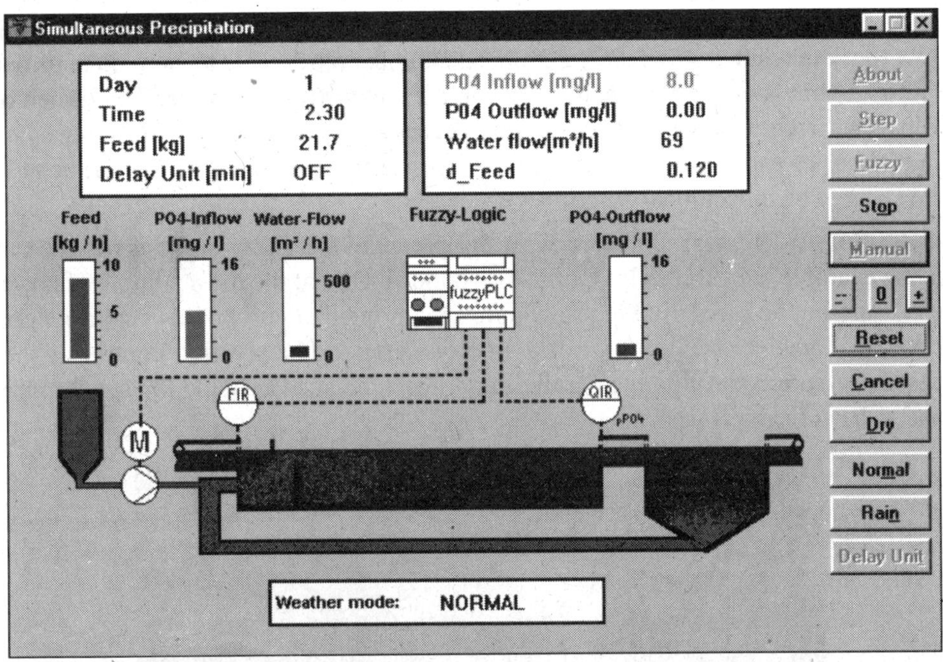

Figure 6.8: A software simulation of a simplified precipitation controller is contained in [4]

4. Control of Tunnel Inspection Robots: The German Aerospace corporation DASA has developed a sewage pipe inspection system using two robot units and a support truck. The objective of the robots is to detect leakage in segments of the pipe by applying air pressure to the sealed space between the two robots. Because the vertical access shafts can be quite far away from each other, the robots have to operate up to 400 yards away from the truck. The robots are connected to each other and the truck by cables that provide air pressure, electrical energy, and control signals to the robots.

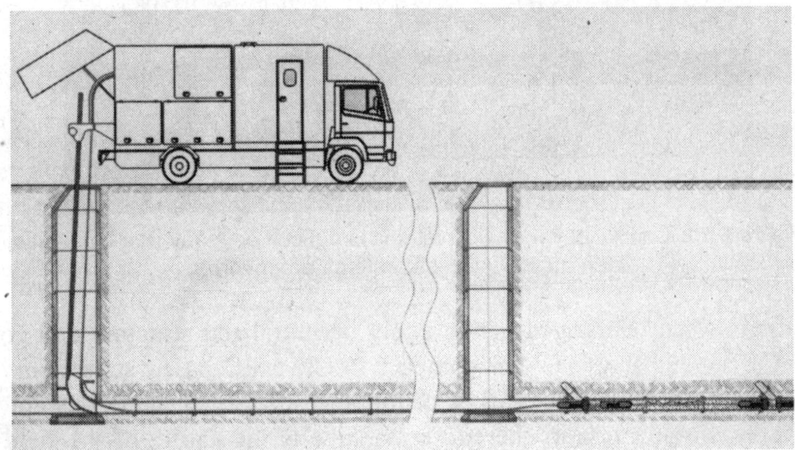

Figure 6.9: The two robot units in the sewage pipe (right) are supplied from a specialized truck by cables

When DASA developed the system, a severe control problem came up. To avoid entanglement of the cables that can result in the robots getting stuck in the pipe, cable tension must be controlled very carefully. A conventional approach using complex state variable controllers turned out to be too costly in terms of both money and design time. A control system implemented on two *fuzzy*PLCs using about 200 rules each showed very good results in a very short engineering time at less than 10% of the costs of a conventional solution.

5. Positioning of Presses: One area with big potential for fuzzy solutions is the control of drives. In this example, we discuss hydraulic axis control. One of the most complex fuzzy projects was done for a hydraulic press used to press laminates, printed circuit boards, and floor coverings. The task was the synchronized control of a 14-axis system. The position control of the axis, a superimposed pressure controller, the parallel running of the steel belt and the synchronization of all axes had to be solved.

Figure 6.10: Control of hydraulic systems is difficult as many non-linearities, Such as the "stick-slip" effect, are involved

The automation system employed has a highly decentralized structure and consists of two large master PLCs, a number of smaller compact PLCs, a PC based supervisory system, and seven *fuzzy*PLCs. All units are networked using the integrated field bus interfaces. Very important for the synchronization of the entire machine is the ability of the field bus network to satisfy the real time requirements. One typical problem involved in the control of hydraulic systems is the so-called "stick slip effect". The transition of an axis from standstill to motion is highly non-linear because of the transition from stick friction to slip friction. This makes designing a good controller for hydraulic systems difficult. In the cited application, fuzzy logic rendered a good solution technique, freeing system design from the burden of the theory of non linear systems synthesis. The overall design time using fuzzy logic was only a third of what a conventional approach had required in past applications of conventional control for similar presses.

6. Temperature Control in Plastic Molding Machines: In plastic molding machines, temperature control is crucial to achieve high and consistent product quality. This requires laborious tuning of the involved control algorithms, because the dead times involved in an extrusion machine are significant and there is significant coupling between the different temperature zones.

Figure 6.11: To achieve high product quality, keeping the temperature constant is critical in molding plastic

To cut down the commission time for these machines, KM corporation has developed a self-tuning controller using the *fuzzy*PLC. At start up time, some parameters are estimated that are used to scale the non linear fuzzy controller. In contrast to conventional tuning algorithms, this controller does not require a cooling down of the machine to room temperature before self tuning can work. Even very difficult temperature zones with big dead times can be handled by this algorithm and the result is a very robust controller. This is important because the temperature properties of an empty machine and one filled with plastic material are extremely different. Compared to conventional systems, the fuzzy logic enhanced temperature controller performs with a faster response time and a significantly smaller overshoot combined with extreme robustness.

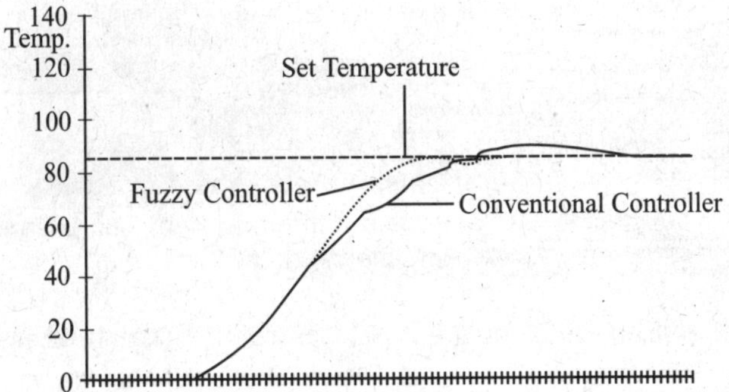

Figure 6.12: The fuzzy logic controller in the molding machine reaches the set point faster and avoids overshoot

7. Climate Control Using Fuzzy Logic: Climate control systems reveal a high potential for energy savings. In a recent application at a major hospital in Europe, the integration of fuzzy logic saves about 25% on electrical energy, equivalent to the amount of 50,000 per year.

Figure 16.13: An application of fuzzy logic in the a/c system of a large hospital in germany saved more than 25% on energy costs

The fuzzy logic controller outputs the set values for the coolant valve, the water heater valve, and the humidifier water valve. The fuzzy logic control strategy uses different temperature and humidity sensors to determine how to operate the air conditioning process in a way that conserves energy. Again, the capability of processing interdependent variables results in significant advantages over conventional solutions. For example, one knows that when temperature rises, relative humidity of the air decreases.

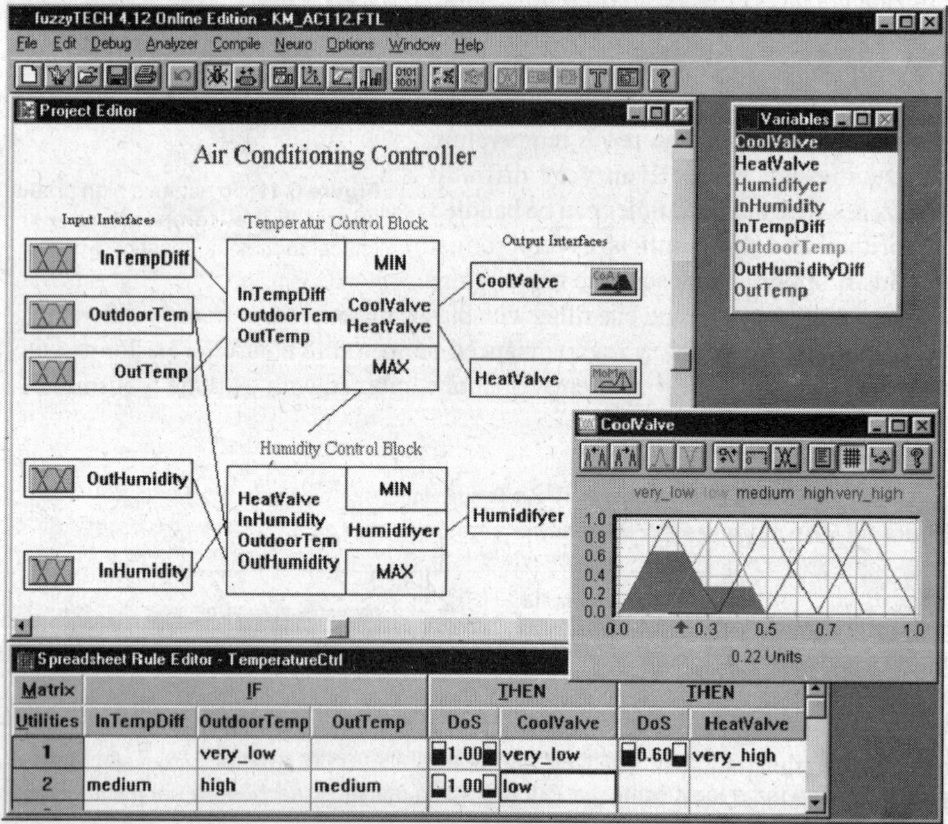

Figure 6.14: Fuzzy Logic allows to increase the energy efficiency of an A/C system by evaluating several process values.

This knowledge can be exploited by implementing a fuzzy logic control strategy that allows the temperature controller "to tell" the humidity controller that it is going to activate the heater valve. The humidity controller now can respond to this before it can detect it by its sensor. The result is an increase in control quality.

8. Wind Energy Converter Control: In recent years, technological advancements made the commercial use of wind energy feasible. A trend to larger plants further improved the cost/performance ratio. However, such large wind energy converters require advanced control systems both to ensure high efficiency and long life. The controller sets the angle of the rotor blades based on the wind situation (pitch control). However, wind is not a one-dimensional figure. Strength, gustiness, and fluctuation of the wind angle must be evaluated to determine the optimal rotor blade angle.

Figure 6.15: To maximize the efficiency of a wind energy converter, the pitch controller must consider many inputs

There is a trade-off between efficiency, safety and wear of the wind energy converter. If the blade angle is set to draw the maximum amount of energy from the wind, the risk of sudden wind gusts causing excessive mechanical stress on the converter increases. For these reasons, an Aerodyn wind energy converter was enhanced with a fuzzy system based on human experience to find the best compromise to this trade-off. The first implemented system is running in a field test and shows quite promising results. The quality of the controller is not only measured in constancy of the delivered power, but also in measures of mechanical stress on the tower, the nacelle and the rotor blades. The next step will be the application of the achieved results to the first 1.2 MW systems that are to be launched in the marketplace in 1996.

6.2.4 Conclusions

As a consequence of the high degree of awareness raised by a large number of publications over the past five years in Europe, a substantial number of successful applications have been generated. Of these, we have presented a selection of eight (8) recent applications in this paper. In all applications, the key to success lies in the clever combination of both conventional automation techniques and fuzzy logic. Fuzzy logic by no means replaces conventional control engineering. Rather, it compliments conventional techniques with a highly efficient methodology to implement multi-variable control strategies. Thus, the major potential for fuzzy logic lies in the implementation of supervisory control loops.

6.3 FUZZY LOGIC SUPERVISORY CONTROL FOR COAL POWER PLANT

The High Temperature Winkler Gasification (HTW) process that was developed by Rheinbraun AG has been used for many years in pilot and demonstration plants to generate synthesis gas and fuel gas out of brown coal. Conventional methods were used before to control the gas throughput. While the conventional control engineering implementation was able to run the process in a stable operating point, improvements were necessary to use the HTW process in a coal power station with integrated coal gasification:

- More precise control of gas throughput under fluctuations of the coal quality
- More robust control in cases of fast load changes
- Automation of supervisory control operation

On top on the existing base level automation, a supervisory fuzzy logic control strategy was implemented on the HTW plant in Berrenrath/Germany. Fuzzy Logic was used because the control problem was strongly non-linear and involves multiple measured and command variables. On the other hand, extensive operator knowledge about the process was available. The implemented fuzzy logic supervisory control strategy successfully improved throughput control quality as well as the adaptation to different coal parameters.

6.3.1 High Temperature Winkler Gasification

The process that is used to gasify the coal is called High Temperature Winkler method (HTW). The HTW Gasification method uses a high temperature fluid bed process to convert brown coal into synthesis gas, a mixture of carbon monoxide (CO) and hydrogen (H_2). This gas mix can be used to produce chemical base products like aldehydes or organic acids. Alternatively it can be used in a power plant gas turbine to generate electricity. The gas produced by the demonstration plant is used for chemical synthesizes. Later in the power plant application the gas will be used to run a gas turbine / steam turbine combination.

The HTW process has been used for the gasification of coal by the German coal company Rheinbraun since 1956. The demonstration plant started operation in 1985. It converts 720 t of coal per day into 900.000 m^3 (iN) synthesis gas. In 1996 Inform added a fuzzy logic supervisory control to enable the process for a power plant application. Figure 6.16 shows a photo of this plant.

Figure 6.16: HTW plant in berrenrath, germany

The main inputs for the HTW process are coal, oxygen and steam. The coal is first ground to small pieces and pre-dried before it is fed into the bottom part of the fluid bed reactor. The steam and the oxygen are fed into the reactor on four different levels, into and above the fluid bed. In the fluid bed the coal reacts with the oxygen and the steam. This reaction takes place at a temperature of around 800°C and at a pressure of 10 bar. After the reaction in the fluid bed the generated gas enters the hot zone above the fluid bed. At temperatures around 1000 °C additional oxygen and steam is added and left over coal particles react with the gases. This way additional gas is produced and by-products like methane and other hydrocarbons are converted to carbon monoxide and hydrogen. The produced gases leave the reactor at the top through the reactor head. At this point the gas is still mixed with a lot of particles. These are filtered out and fed back into the fluid bed with a zyklon filter and a feed back tube.

The coal ashes accumulate at the bottom of the fluid bed reactor. They are removed from there out of the reactor by two conveyor spirals. The hot raw gas is cooled down to 270°C. Its heat is used to generate pressure steam, some of which is recycled back into the process. Ceramic filters remove remaining dust particles out of the gas. The following gas washer removes NH_3, HCL and other gas components. The following CO conversion creates the correct carbon monoxide / hydrogen mix for the methanol synthesis. After a compression to 37 bar the gas is processed in a non-selective rectisol washer ($C0_2/H_2S$ washer). At temperatures below -40°C liquid methanol is used to wash out carbondioxide and sulfuric components. The methanol is used again after recycling it and the purified synthesis gas is used at a nearby chemical plant. Figure 6.17 shows the process diagram of the HTW plant.

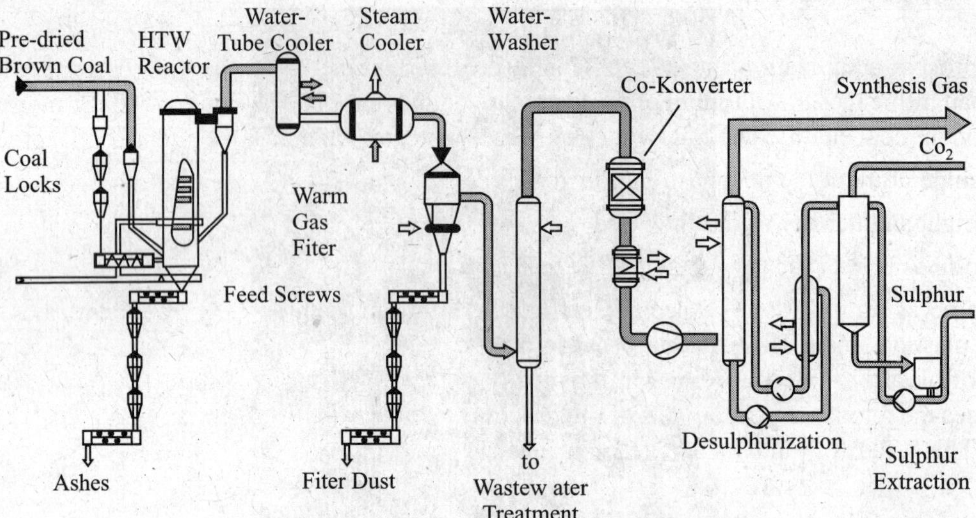

Figure 6.17: Process diagram of HTW plant

The coal input, the oxygen input, the distribution of the oxygen input over the eight different nozzles and the ash removal rate have to be controlled to use the coal efficiently and to generate the correct mixture of gases.

Instead of coal a mixture of coal and plastic refuse can be used in the HTW process. This way the coal consumption is reduced and the plastic refuse is recycled into synthesis gas.

6.3.2 Conventional Control

The HTW demonstration plant is controlled with an Eckhardt PLS-80E DCS system. This system controls over 6000 measurements and actuators. The main control room is equipped with 10 Unix based operator consoles and four real-time servers. So far nearly all the set points of the underlying control circuits are set and adjusted manually by the operators. They constantly monitor the process condition and adjust the set points of the underlying control circuits accordingly (i.e. coal input, oxygen input, ...) A few years ago it was tried to automatically generate some set points using a conventional PID controller But the results were not satisfying. This supervisory control only worked fine when the coal quality was very constant. Otherwise the process quality would deteriorate significantly and the operators had to intervene and switch back to manual operation.

6.3.3 Supervisory Fuzzy Logic Control

Two main tasks have been defin]ed for the supervisory fuzzy logic control: Regulation of the gas throughput and process stabilization.

The fuzzy logic must keep the gas throughput at the set point and it has to respond to set point changes with the correct dynamic speed. The set point can vary from 70% (partial load) to 100% (full load). The fluctuations of the gas throughput result mainly from variations of the coal quality (humidity, ash content and granularity). These effects have to be compensated by the fuzzy logic.

The process stabilization must keep several process parameters in the optimum range. The reactor load influences the optimum of these process parameters. The position of the optimum also depends on the coal quality. The following parameters were used to define the quality of the process:

- Temperature in the post gasification zone
- Height and density of the fluid bed
- Composition of the produced gas (CO, CH_4, H_2)

The process stabilization is especially difficult when the HTW process is fed with a mixture of coal and plastic refuse. This is done because plastic refuse is a very inexpensive fuel. But the addition of plastic to the coal results in drastically different process conditions. The fuzzy logic control uses the regular measurements of the process conditions to detect any addition of plastic to the coal. This will result into an adapted control strategy of the fuzzy logic control.

6.3.4 Fuzzy Logic Control Design

The specification of the control task resulted into a preliminary concept of the fuzzy logic controller. The operator knowledge was than used to specify the control strategy of the fuzzy logic system. Several structured audits took place to evaluate the operator knowledge systematically. The audits focused on the operators' manual control strategies and on the relationships between the inputs and the outputs of the process. This procedure is in accordance with the standardized fuzzy logic design method.

The audits resulted into the following concept for the fuzzy logic control: Deviations of the gas throughput from its set point immediately result into a correction of the oxygen input. The coal input is adjusted accordingly to keep the ratio between coal and oxygen at a constant level. Changes of the reactor pressure predict changes of gas throughput. Therefore the pressure gradient is used as an early warning indicator for changes of the gas throughput.

For process stabilization and for the adaptation to different coal qualities the fuzzy logic controller uses the following parameters to keep the process in a stable operating condition:

- Coal to oxygen ratio
- Distribution of the oxygen between the fluid bed zone and the gasification zone.
- Ash outtake
- Fluidification with steam and inert gas

Sometimes one and the same process input value has to be modified to keep several different critical measurements (temperature, fluid bed height, ...) in the optimum range. This can have conflicting results.

For example: A too low fluid bed is normally corrected with an increase of the coal input. A too low temperature is corrected with a reduction of the coal input and a too low dust output is also corrected with a reduction of the coal input. But a too low temperature can occur together with a too low fluid bed. The ability of the fuzzy controller to weight different conflicting indications based on their significance and to use a lot of inputs to determine the best reaction to each situation is very useful to control complex processes.

The fuzzy logic controller has a total number of 24 inputs and 8 outputs. A preprocessing reduces the 24 inputs to 10 characteristic descriptors. These are fed into the fuzzy logic system. The fuzzy outputs go through a post-processing step to generate the actual set points for the process inputs. Figure 6.18 shows the core structure of the fuzzy logic system.

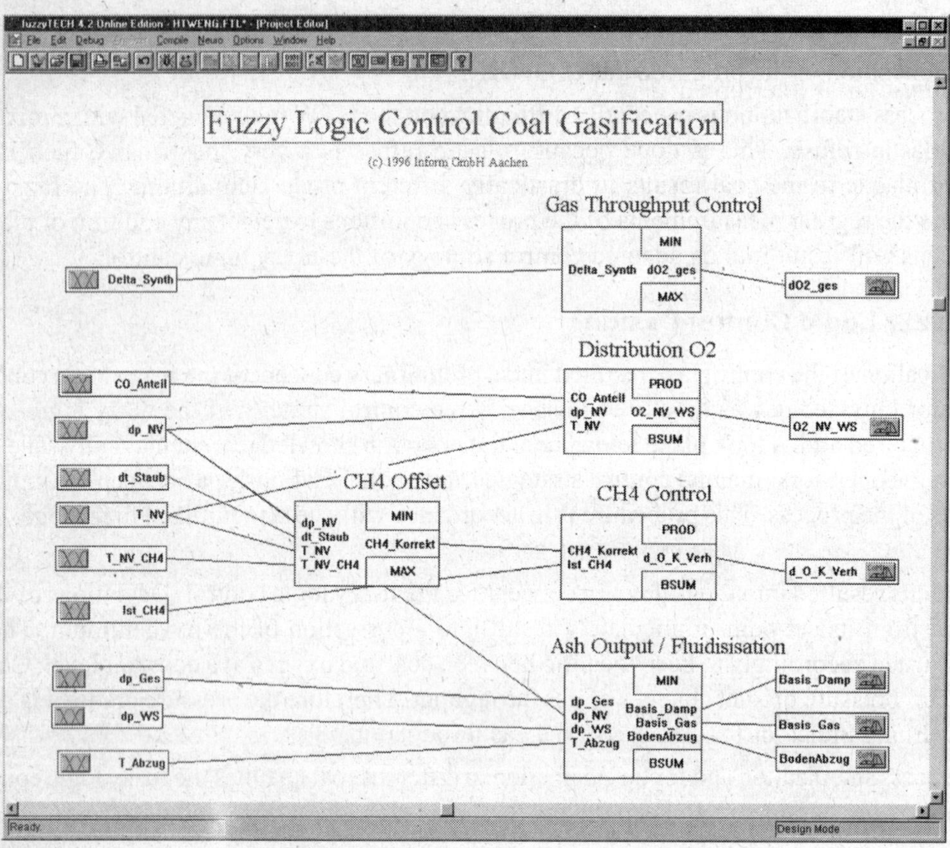

Figure 6.18: Fuzzy controller structure

6.3.5 Integration of Fuzzy Logic Into the DCS

The process measurements are coming to the fuzzy logic control through the Eckhardt DCS. The fuzzy logic system generates set point values for the underlying PID controllers. The fuzzy logic controller was implemented on an OS/2 PC. Therefore the set up of the communication between the DCS and the fuzzy logic controller was an important part of the whole project. The communication was implemented using Factory Link, a well-known SCADA program by US-Data. A factory link application is running on the same OS/2 PC together with the fuzzy logic controller. The fuzzy logic controller reads data out of the Factory Link Real Time DataBase and it also writes data back into it. Another Factory Link task is communicating with the DCS through the Eckhardt DCS bus. This way an image of the process measurements is created in the Factory Link RTDB and the fuzzy outputs are forwarded to the DCS.

Factory Link initiates a new fuzzy logic evaluation every 10 seconds. The DCS either uses the external set points generated by fuzzy logic or the internal set points entered by the operators. The operators can switch from the 'manual mode' to the 'fuzzy logic mode' and back. The 'fuzzy logic mode' can only be activated when all the critical system variables are in a predefined safe range. The DCS automatically switches back into 'manual mode' whenever a system variable exceeds the safe range. The fallback to 'manual mode' also takes place if the communication between the DCS and Factory Link is interrupted.

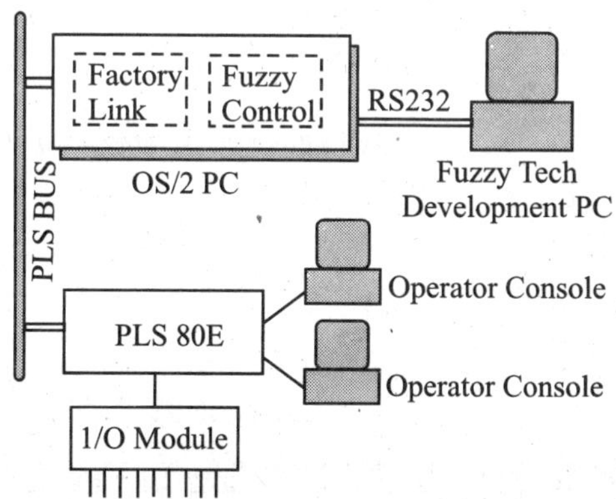

Figure 6.19: Integration of fuzzy logic into DCS

Figure 6.19 shows the integration of the fuzzy logic control into Factory Link and the Eckhardt DCS. The OS/2 PC is also connected with a serial cable to a WIN95 PC, on which the *fuzzy*TECH development system is installed. This program was used to develop the fuzzy logic control and to generate C-Code for the implementation on the OS/2 PC. The WIN95 PC is also used for On-line optimization and visualization of the fuzzy logic controller. The serial link to the OS/2 PC enables the user to modify the fuzzy system on the fly from the *fuzzy*TECH development system on the WIN95 PC while the system is running and controlling the process.

6.3.6 Setting the Fuzzy Logic Control Into Operation

The first design of the fuzzy logic control, the data preprocessing and post-processing were tested using the simulation tool VisSim. This way the concept was checked for any structural errors and an early prototype was presented to the customers. Figure 6.20 shows a test of the fuzzy logic system using simulated data as input.

After the successful completion of the simulations the fuzzy logic was tested off-line with real time data from the DCS. To do this the fuzzy logic control first was implemented on the OS/2 PC. The fuzzy controller than used real time DCS measurement values to generate set points values for the DCS. But during these off-line simulations the DCS was only using the internal manual set points and not the fuzzy logic set points. By comparing the external fuzzy logic set points with the internal operator set points deviations between manual and automatic operation could be detected and if necessary eliminated.

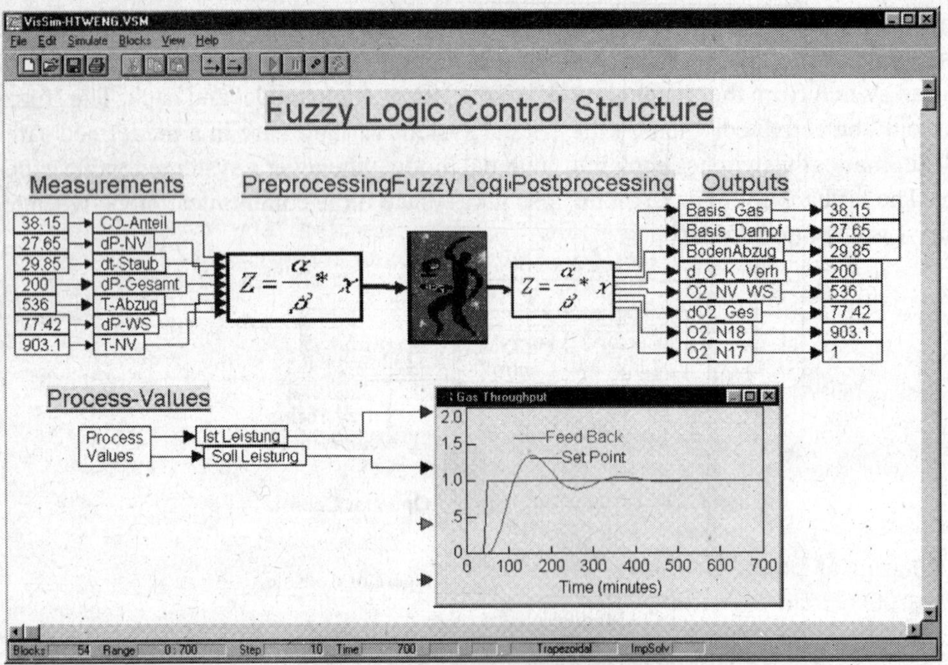

Figure 6.20: Simulation with VisSim

After the off-line testing was finished successfully the on-line testing started. For the on-line tests the DCS activated the external set points and so the closed loop performance of the fuzzy logic controller could be tested. The fuzzy logic controller was optimized while running in the closed loop mode from the *fuzzy*TECH development tool on the WIN 95 PC. To do this the OS/2 PC was connected with a serial cable to the WIN 95 PC. This way the fuzzyfication, inference and defuzzification were visualized in *fuzzy*TECH. Modifications of the rule base or term definitions were also entered in *fuzzy*TECH and than send to the fuzzy logic controller on the OS/2 PC.

6.3.7 Results

The fuzzy controller proved to be working very effectively during the first few on-line tests. After that a long series of evaluation tests started. During these tests the performance of the fuzzy controller was tested using a lot of different coal qualities and different loads (70% to 100%).

1. **Regulation of gas throughput:** The conventional control focussed on process stabilization not keeping the throughput at its set point. The following diagram shows the changes in the gas throughput when fuzzy controller is active. The fuzzy logic control clearly improves the throughput control. It compensates fluctuations in the granulation of the coal.

   Figure 6.21 Shows the fluctuations of the synthesis gas throughput with and without fuzzy logic.

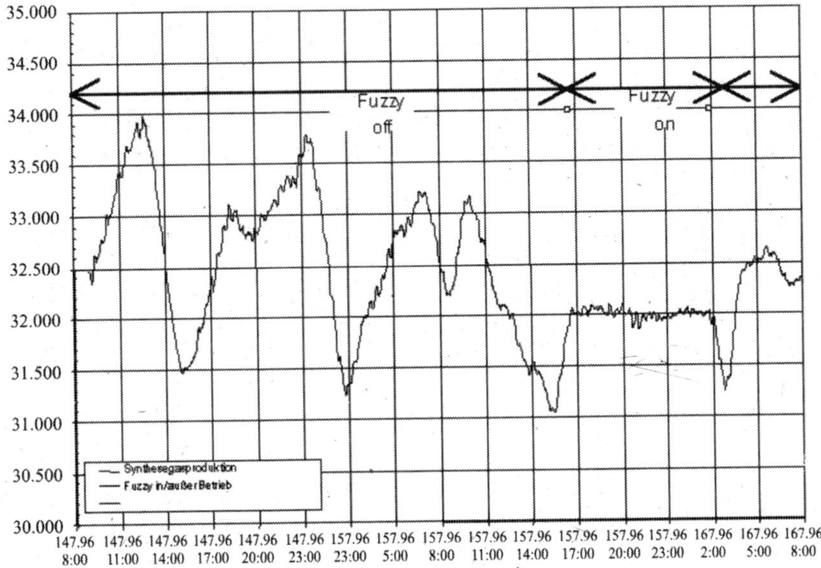

Figure 6.21: Throughput control with and without fuzzy control

2. **Change of Load:** The fuzzy controller has to regulate the gas throughput in the range 70 % to 100 % load with a maximum load gradient of 4% / min.

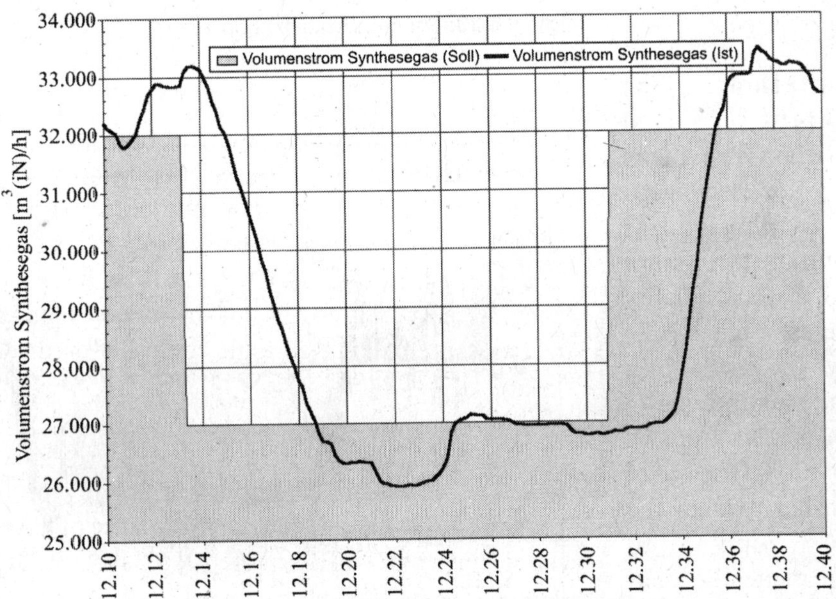

Figure 6.22: Change of load with fuzzy control

Figure 6.22 shows a load change from 94 % to 76 % and back to 94 %. The resulting load gradient was 3,2 % /min. Currently the load change behavior is being improved by using a modified pressure evaluation.

3. **Adaptation to coal add-ons:** Sometimes the HTW process is fed with a mixture of coal and plastic refuse. The resulting process parameters vary greatly from the standard operating conditions. For example the content of methane in the raw gas increases. The fuzzy controller recognizes the different operating conditions and generates a matching internal set point for methane. Figure 6.23 illustrates how this enables the fuzzy controller to stabilize the process.

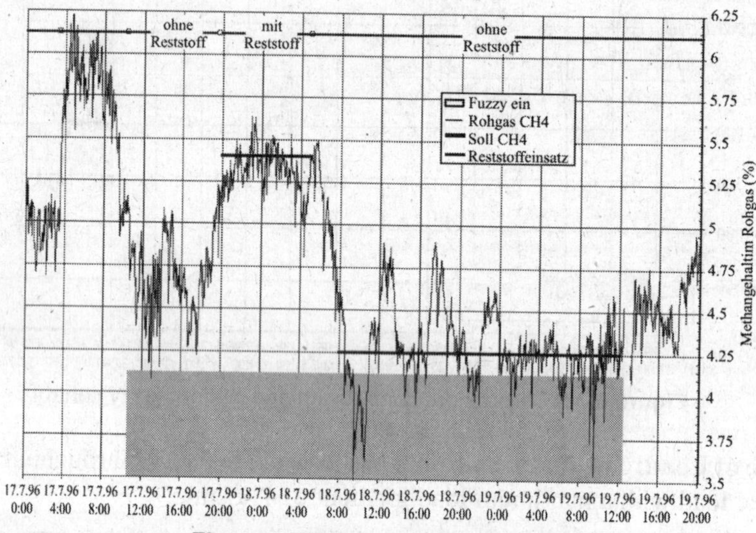

Figure 6.23: Process stabilization

4. **Adaptation to different coal qualities:** The fuzzy controller also keeps the synthesis gas throughput constant when the coal quality changes. Figure 6.24 shows the results of a change of the coal's water content from 18 % to 12 %. The fuzzy controller reduces the coal input to compensate the coal change. Later after switching back to moist coal the coal input is increased accordingly.

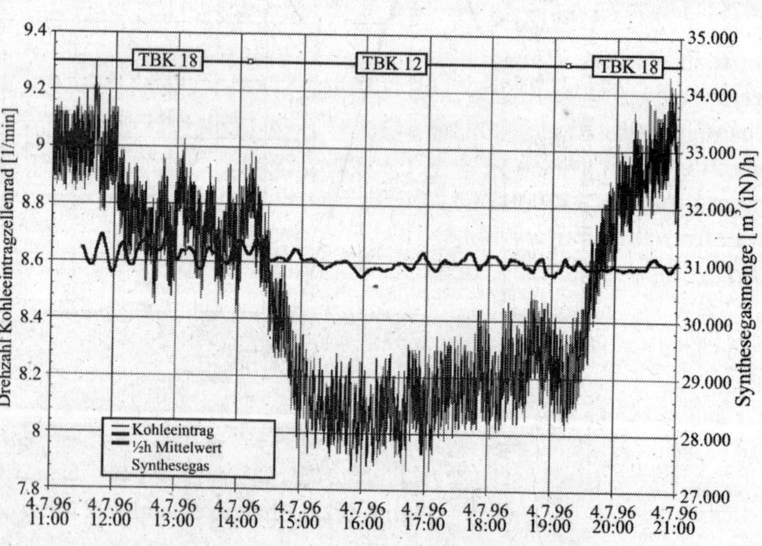

Figure 16.24: Constant Gas Throughput With Different Coal Qualities

6.3.8 Conclusion

The fuzzy controller was implemented very quickly. The transfer of the process know-how into the fuzzy controller and its realization took 15 days. So far over 1100 hours of operating time have been evaluated. In nearly all situations the performance of the fuzzy controller was much superior to the manual control. It was able to keep the process parameters in the optimum range whenever the coal quality changed. It was also able to adjust the gas throughput with the necessary change rate. The average gas throughput was kept at the set point. The operating personal has accepted the fuzzy controller as a helpful component because its transparent integration into the PLS makes it easy for them to use it.

6.4 OPTIMIZATION OF A WATER TREATMENT SYSTEM

This case study is about a fuzzy logic solution in biochemical production at the world's largest oral penicillin production facility in Austria. After extracting the penicillin from the microorganisms that generated it, a waste water treatment system further processes the remaining biomass. Fermentation sludge obtained in the course of this treatment contains microorganisms and remnants of nutrient salts. It is the basic material for a high quality fertilizer and sold as a by-product of the penicillin production. To render the fertilizer, the sludge is concentrated in a decanter and then cleared of the remaining water in a vaporizer. In order to reduce energy costs of the vaporizing process, the separation of water and dry substance in the decanter must be optimized. Before the implementation of the fuzzy logic solution, operators controlled the process manually.

6.4.1 Fuzzy Logic Replaces Manual Control

Due to its complexity, operators control the process of proportioning decanter precipitants manually. Drainage control in the decanter is very crucial. To save energy cost in the vaporizing process, the decanter must extract as much water as possible. However, to achieve optimal results requires an operating point close to the point where the decanter becomes blocked. If blockage occurs the process must be stopped and the decanter manually cleaned, thus operators run the process far away from this optimal point. Alas, this results in high operational energy costs. In this case study, a fuzzy logic system replaced the sub-optimal manual control of the operators.

Picture of a Decanter

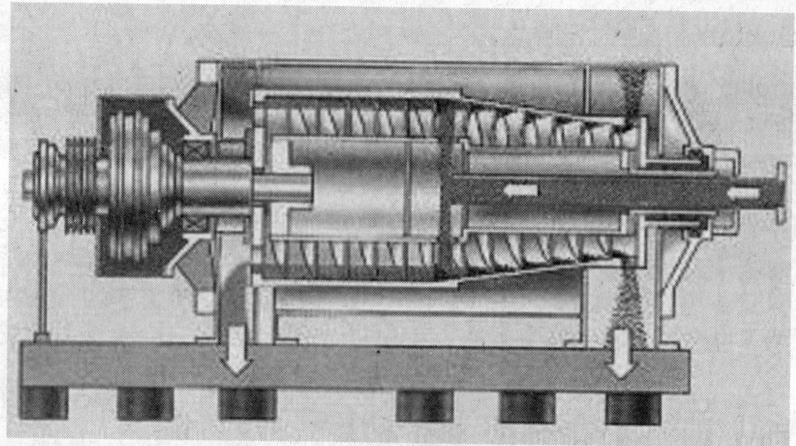

Schematic

6.4.2 Fuzzy Logic Applications in Chemical Industry

A number of conventional control techniques exist to automate continuous processes in chemical industry. To keep single variables of the process constant, PID controllers or the like are very common. Even though, most technical processes are non-linear and PID controllers are a linear model, this works fine. This is because within a continuous process, the behavior of the process can be well-approximated linearly near the operation point. In processes with simple time behavior (no dead times etc.), even P (proportional) controllers and bang-bang controllers often suffice.

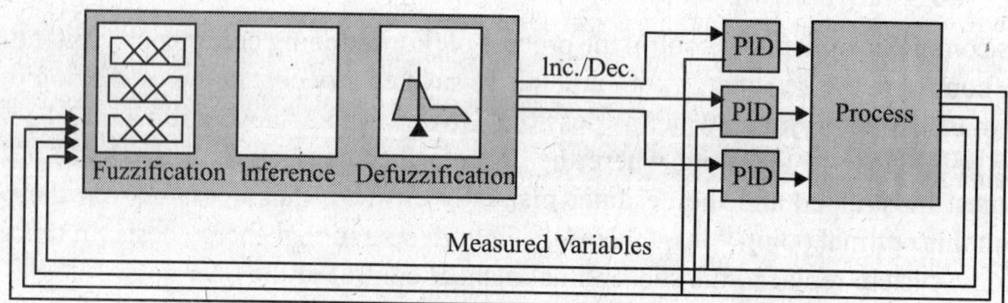

Figure 6.25: Using a fuzzy logic controller to determine the set values for underlying PID control loops

While keeping single process variables at their command values is rather simple, the determination of the optimal operation point as the combination of all set values of the variables is often a complex multi-variable problem. In most cases a solution based on a mathematical model of the process is far beyond acceptable complexity. In some cases, the derivation of a mathematical model of the plant consumes many man years of effort. Hence, in a large number of plants, operators prefer to control the operation point of the process manually.

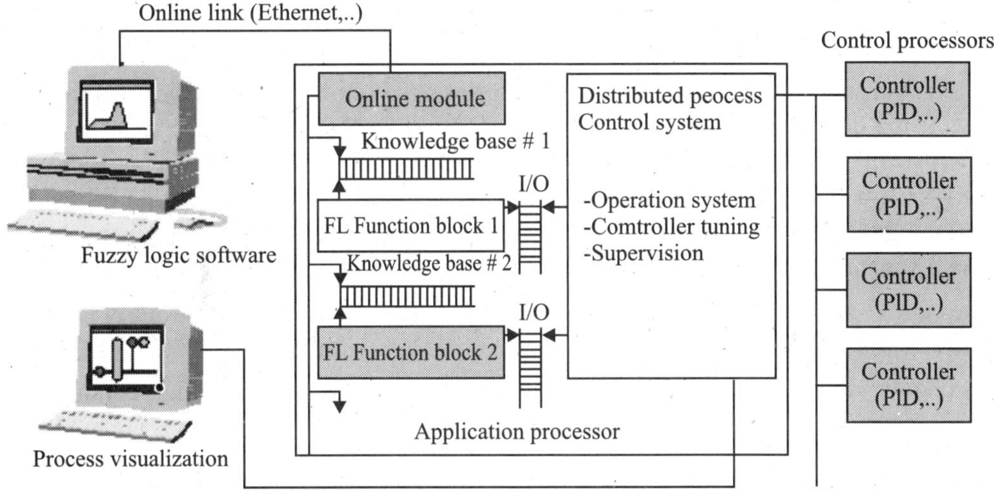

Figure 6.26: Integration of a fuzzy logic component in a distributed control system

In these cases, fuzzy logic provides an efficient technology for putting the operator control strategies into an automation solution with minimum effort. Figure 6.25 shows how to combine the fuzzy logic system with underlying PID controllers. In practical implementations, the PID controllers run on the same Distributed Process Control Systems (DCS) as the fuzzy logic controller. Figure 6.26 shows the technical integration of fuzzy logic into DCS.

6.4.3 Decanter Control

The sewage of the fermenters contains about 2% dry substance. In a first step, milk of lime neutralizes the sewage. Second, a fermenter biologically degrades the sewage. Third, bentonite is added in a large reactor. This results in a pre-coagulation of the sludge. Next, the slurry is enriched with cationic polymer before the water is separated in the decanter. The cationic polymer discharges the surface charge of the sludge particles and hence leads to coagulation.

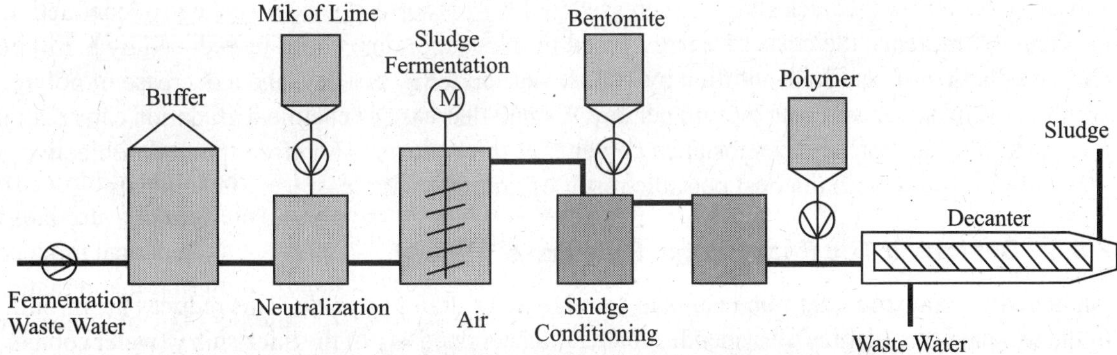

Figure 6.27: Process Diagram of Sludge Draining

Bentonite and polymer addition exert a fundamental influence on the drainage quality obtained in the decanter. In order to achieve a high drainage quality, the gradation of chemicals has to be optimized. A changed bentonite proportioning causes only a slow change in the precipitation process because of the dead time of the reactor of about 20 minutes (reactor capacity 30 m^3 at a volume flow of 90 m^3/h) and the dead time of the decanter of about 5 to 7 minutes. An increase in bentonite addition principally results in an improvement of coagulation. Implementation of just a polymer proportioning controller must only consider the dead time of the decanter. An increase in polymer addition first results in an improvement of coagulation, but with further addition coagulation impairs.

The control strategy of the operators uses two measured variables: A turbidity meter measures the purity of the water. High turbidity indicates a high remaining solids content of the water.

A conductivity meter measured the draining degree of the slurry. A high conductivity of the slurry indicates a high water content.

6.4.4 Control Strategy Objectives

The prime objective of the control strategy is to minimize the operational cost of the total drying process. In particular, the objectives are:

- Minimize amount of precipitants. The polymer used is very expensive.
- Minimize remaining water content. The vaporization of the remaining water consumes large amounts of energy.
- The biological mass content of the sewage water of the decanter should be 0.7 g/l. Exceeding a value of 1.5 g/l reduces the operability of the clarification plant and can even result in a breakdown of the next sewage stage because of its limited capacity to degrade biological mass.

The third objective has an absolute priority, above other objectives, to ensure safe operation. If the biological mass content reaches its upper limits, the control strategy reduces it regardless of economic considerations. Besides the critical biological mass content of the sewage water, only the first two objectives are relevant. A rough cost estimation shows that the most effective way to reduce the expenses of the process is to minimize the energy used in the evaporators. If the dry substance content of the thick slurry is increased by 1% (this corresponds to a change of conductivity of about 0.5 mS/cm), the costs of energy (used in the evaporator) could be reduced by $ 140 per day. A reduction of bentonite addition by 10% saves about $30 per day, and a decrease of polymer addition by 10% reduces costs by $ 40 per day. A small decrease of chemical gradation can result in a significant reduction of dry substance contents in thick slurry. Therefore the main objective of optimization is to obtain the best possible result of draining with least use of chemicals.

6.4.5 Designing The Fuzzy Logic Rule Base

An increase of polymer addition results in an increase of drainage grade. This reduces the turbidity of the sewage water (degree of suspended matter) and conductivity of the thick slurry (water content). Exceeding the optimum polymer gradation, further addition of polymer leads to a decline of the separation power in the decanter. The separation power on polymer gradation L=f(dmpolymer/dt) follows a parabolic curve (Figure 6.28). Conductivity of the slurry is used as an indicator for the separation power obtained. Hence, the control strategy is to find the minimum of conductivity by modifying the polymer addition.

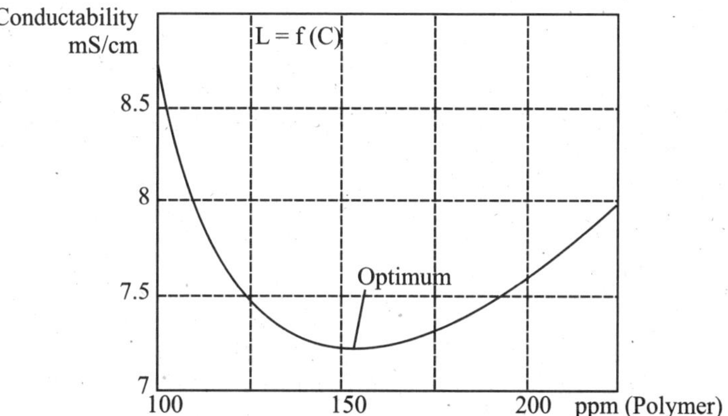

Figure 6.28: Thick slurry conductivity over polymer proportion

The problem with this is that the shape of the curve and hence also the level and position of the minimum may significantly vary over time. The only way to find out the direction to the minimum from the current operating point is to apply a change in the polymer gradation and evaluate its effects. If the draining of thick slurry improves, the conclusion is that this decision was correct and can be repeated. If the decision results in a decline, the fuzzy logic controller pursues the opposite strategy. The stronger the system's reaction to a change in polymer addition is, the greater is the current operation point's distance to the optimum.

Likewise, an increase in bentonite addition leads to an increase in separation power of the decanter until an optimum is reached. If more bentonite is added beyond this point, neither improvement nor decline occurs. Thus, an increase in bentonite addition beyond the optimal point is less critical than an increase in polymer addition. However, bentonite addition should be kept as low as possible to minimize operating cost.

6.4.6 Structure of the Decanter Controller

A change in bentonite addition has a greater long-term effect than a change in polymer addition, due to the larger dead time. As a correlation between bentonite and polymer addition exists, it is sensible to change the polymer addition independent of the separation quality in the short term and to let the bentonite controller run with delay.

Sewage quality is only restricted by an upper limit, whereas slurry quality is of great economical importance. For these reasons, polymer addition is controlled by a first set of rules in correlation to the slurry quality. An absolute point of reference does not exist because of the changing optimum of the polymer addition characteristics. Hence, no absolute input or output values are used. The controller determines its position in the objective function from a prior change in polymer addition and the resulting reaction of conductivity.

Difference in Conductability (d_conductab)

Previous Decision (pr_decision)	N	Z	P
N	N	Z	P
Z	Z	Z	P
P	P	N	N

Figure 6.29: Matrix Representing the Control Strategy of Polymer Proportion. N Represents "negative", Z represents "zero", and P represents "positive"

The first rule block of the fuzzy logic controller works on the targeting. Input values for this rule block are the increment of set point in the previous cycle (pr_decision) and the resulting change in conductivity (d_conductab). The output of the rule block is the increment (polymer1) on the set point of the polymer PID controller. Figure 6.29 shows the control strategy of this rule block as a matrix. The entries in the matrix represent the output variable polymer1 of the rule block.

A positive change in conductivity implies a decline of the plant's operating state. If the controller in the previous cycle (pr_decision) recommended "negative" (reduce polymer addition) and conductivity increased as a reaction to this, the controller must now operate in the opposite direction and increase polymer addition. If the controller recommended "positive", polymer addition must be reduced. Conductivity may increase although the controller has not given a recommendation in the previous cycle (pr_decision = 0). In this case, the optimum moved by external influence and action must be taken.

As the fuzzy logic controller does not know in which direction the optimum moved, it has to choose one direction. For this, it increases polymer addition to test the reaction of the process. It tests with a polymer increase rather then a decrease, as the curve in the figure rises more gently into the positive direction, and an increased use of polymer is cheaper than the raised energy costs that stem from the evaporation process.

If the test result is favorable, this will be confirmed in the next cycle. If it is negative, the controller will simply change the signs of the output in the subsequent cycle (see matrix in Figure 6.29). This only represents the basic principle of the rule block. The final implementation of the rule block contains additional rules that more finely differentiate the input value. As such, the fuzzy logic controller can differentiate between several cases and thus adapt the size of gradation change to the reaction of the process that is, to the proximity to the optimum.

The turbidity of the sewage water forms a restriction that in some cases forbids the reduction of the precipitant addition. Therefore, a second rule block evaluates the turbidity of the sewage water (turbidity) and the output of the first rule block (polymer1) to determine the final polymer addition increment (polymer2). Figure 6.30 shows the structure of the fuzzy logic system. As long as turbidity units are below 2500 TE/F, the second rule block transfers the first block's recommendation to the output. Starting at about 3000 TE/F, all recommendations of the first rule block are transferred, except recommendations to reduce polymer addition. If about 3500 TE/F are exceeded, the second rule block always recommends an increase of flocculent addition. Only the rate of increase of flocculent addition changes, depending on the recommendation of the first rule block.

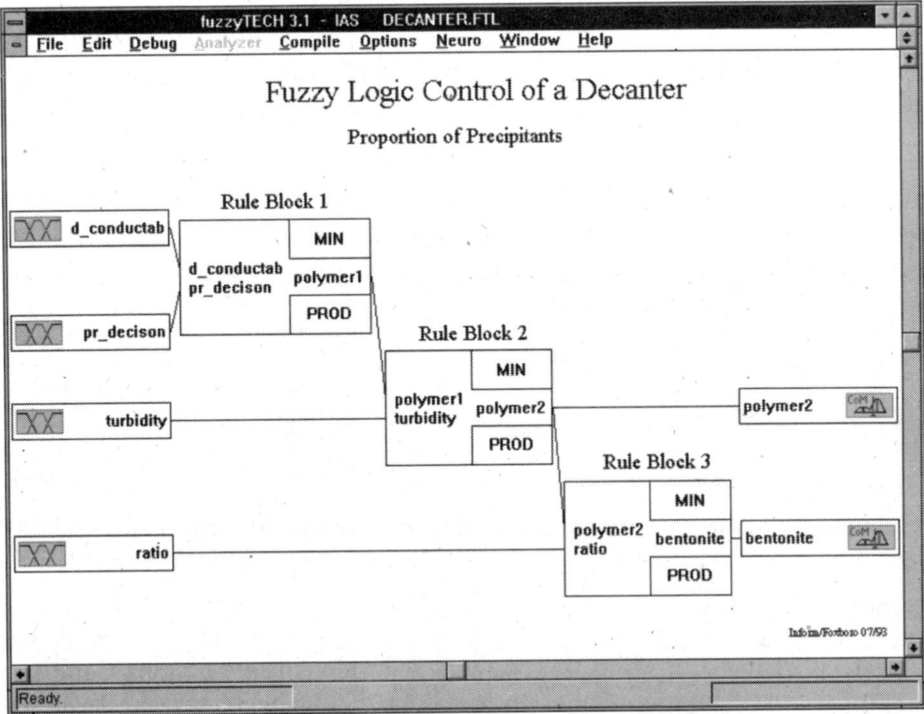

Figure 6.30: Structure of the Fuzzy Logic Controller

To determine the betonite addition, a third rule block uses the output of the second rule block and a fourth input variable, called ration. The ratio is calculated outside the fuzzy logic system.

6.4.7 Integrating the Fuzzy Logic Controller in the System

Figure 6.31 shows the total structure of the entire control system. In addition to the fuzzy logic system, function blocks (CALC, RATIO) provide preprocessing of the sensor signals, ramp generation, and ratio control. The entire control system is implemented using a standard distributed process control system (DCS).

The most important input variable of the controller is the change in the conductivity of the slurry. Alas, the conductivity measurement circuitry is subject to strong signal noise. Hence, a low pass filter is used that determines the average change in conductivity during the last ten minutes at one minute intervals. This forms the input variable d_conductab of the fuzzy logic system. Turbidity, the fuzzy system's second input, uses a similar filter.

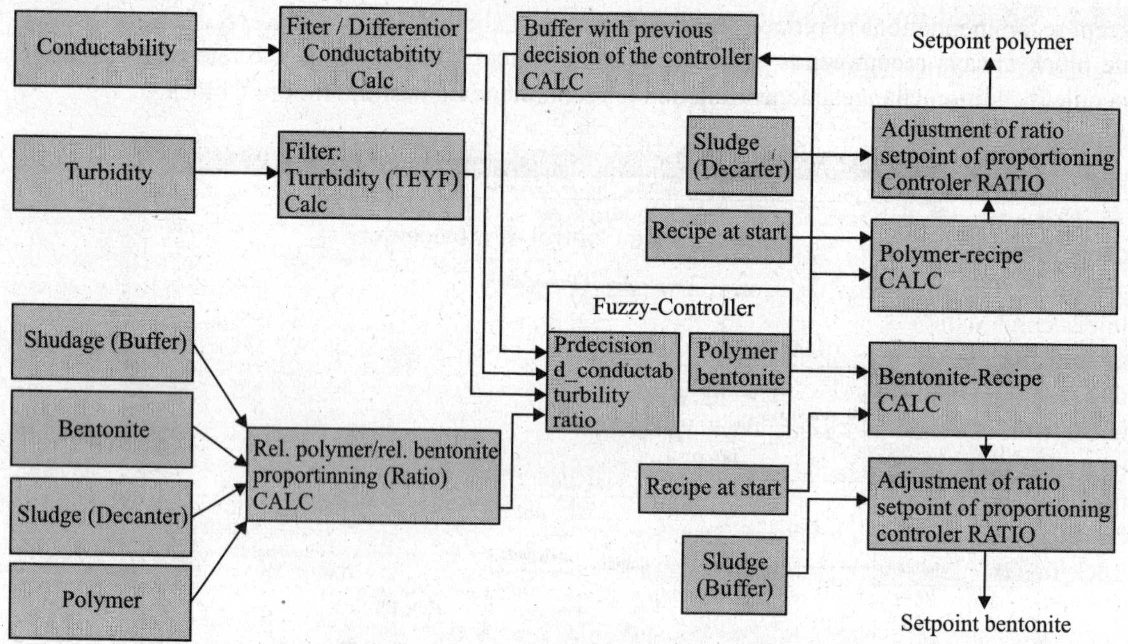

Figure 6.31: Total controller structure with preprocessing and postprocessing

6.4.8 Results

About two months of engineering effort was required to develop the application. Compared to the manual operation, the fuzzy logic controller saves about $70,000 in energy costs per year.

6.5 TRUCK SPEED LIMITER CONTROL BY FUZZY LOGIC

In Europe, commercial trucks in compliance with European legislation, which have a maximum load of more than 12 tons, are required to be equipped with a speed limiter that limits their maximum speed to 53.3 mph (86 km/h). This case study focuses on the electro-pneumatic design of such a speed limiter. In this design, a pneumatic cylinder mechanically limits the throttle opening angle of the fuel pump arm. The cylinder pressure is controlled by a pulse proportional electromechanical valve. This valve is connected to an electronic control unit that uses a microcontroller to drive the valve according to the actual speed of the truck. The design of an algorithm for this control problem proved to be difficult, since the same speed limiter device is used in a variety of different trucks which exhibit different behaviors. In addition to this, the dynamic behavior of a truck differs very much depending on whether it is fully loaded or empty. Conventional control algorithms, such as PID controls, assume a linear model of the process under control and can hence not be used for a solution. A solution using a mathematical model of the truck is first laborious to build and second of prohibitive computational effort for a low-cost 8-bit microcontroller. Hence, fuzzy logic control was used to design the control algorithm.

6.5.1 Speed Limiter Requirements and Conventional Control

Figure 6.32 exemplifies the function of a truck speed limiter. When the truck approaches the maximum velocity, the pneumatic valve reduces the throttle opening angle of the fuel pump arm so that the maximum velocity vs is not surpassed. If the driver pushes down the accelerator pedal even more, the speed limiter has to ensure a smooth ride at the maximum velocity.

However, due to the dead time and non-linearities involved with this control action, an actual overshoot and hunting occurs when using a proportional or on-off controller. Adding a differential and integral part yields a PID controller model. A PID controller generates the command value as a linear combination of the error (P), the derivative of the error with respect to time (D) and the integral of the error with respect to time (I). To tune a PID controller, the combined weights of these three (3) components must be chosen, so that they approximate the nonlinear behavior of the process under control at its operating point. While this works with most processes that are at only one operating point, it fails when the operating point moves. With a truck speed limiter, the operating point moves because of the different load situations, such as driving uphill or downhill, as well as driving empty or with a full load. Furthermore, the characteristic of the pneumatic valve and the truck fuel injection are highly non-linear and vary from one truck to another.

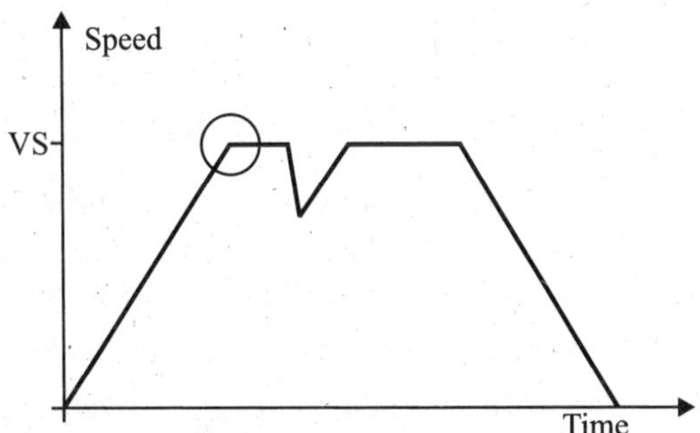

Figure 6.32: The function of as speed Limiter is to stop the truck from driving faster than the maximum allowed speed (vs)

Hence, if a PID control algorithm is used in a truck speed limiter, it can only be tuned well for one operation point and one type of truck. For other operation points and different truck types, overshoot and hunting occurs. The European legislation hence allows operation of the speed limiter within a certain tolerance. Figure 6.33 shows an example of this. When reaching the maximum speed, an initial overshoot of 5 km/h is tolerated. After this, the speed must be kept constant within an interval of ± 1.5 km/h. Even though this overshoot and hunting is tolerated by the European legislation, it causes annoying speed fluctuations when driving.

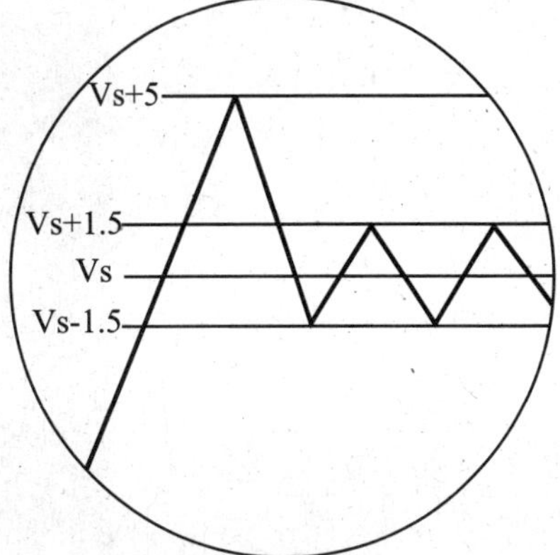

Figure 16.33: Tolerances for the operation of the speed limiter

6.5.2 Mechanical Design of the Speed Limiter

Figure 6.34 sketches the outline of the mechanical design of the speed limiter. An electronic control unit (ECU) compares the digital pulse signal from the speedometer with the maximum speed value pre-set in the device. Based on this, it computes the command value for the pulse proportional valve (PPV) that controls the air pressure in the cylinder. The air stems from the vehicle's pressured air system. In a non-linear but proportional ratio, the cylinder shortens the arm linking the accelerator pedal to the fuel pump so that the fuel pump is throttled.

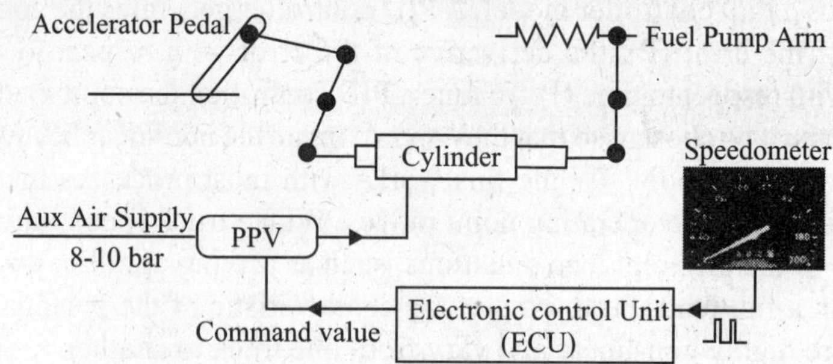

Figure 6.34: Mechanical design of the speed limiter

6.5.3 Design of the Speed Limiter Electronic Control Unit

The electronic control unit itself is designed as a mixed digital and analog circuit. Speedometer signal processing, the fuzzy logic control algorithm, and diagnosis functions are computed by a PIC 8-bit microcontroller (MCU). The MCU uses an external E²PROM to store parameters of the truck and speedometer, the maximum velocity, and diagnosis variables.

The MCU also generates a pulse-width modulated signal (PWM) that is amplified by a power stage to drive the PPV. The analog part is responsible for the preprocessing and filtering of the speedometer signal. Figure 6.35 shows a photo of the unit.

Figure 6.35: The electronic control unit of the speed limiter using a pic 8-bit microcontroller

6.5.4 The Fuzzy Logic Controller

Fuzzy logic is an innovative technology to design solutions for multi-parameter and non-linear control problems. It uses human experience and experimental results rather than a mathematical model for the definition of a control strategy. As a result, it often delivers solutions faster than conventional control design techniques. In addition, fuzzy logic implementations on microcontrollers are very code space and execution speed efficient.

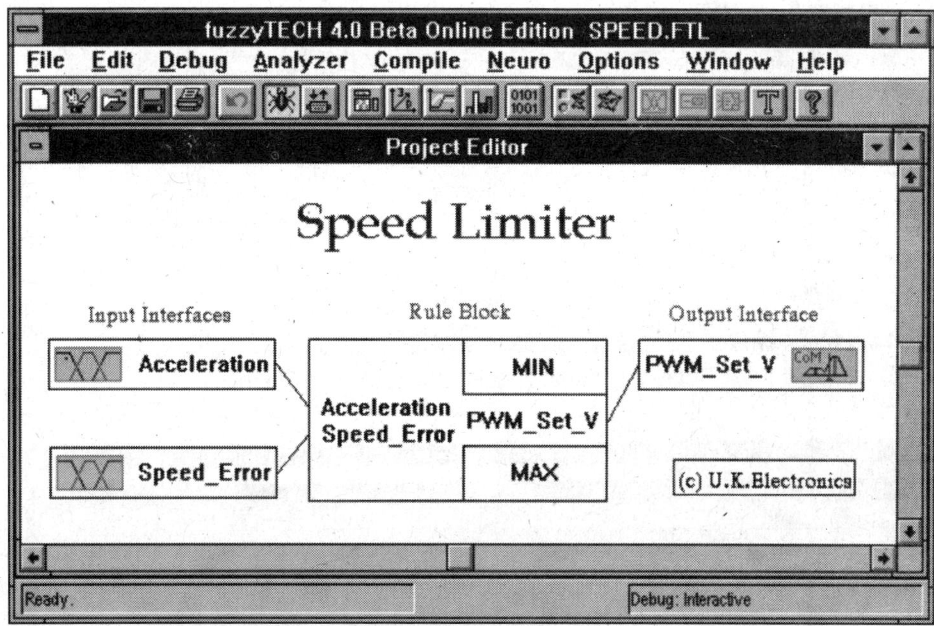

Figure 6.36: Structure of the fuzzy logic speed limiter controller

The entire fuzzy logic algorithm was developed, tested and optimized using the software tool *fuzzy*TECH®. This integrated design environment features automatic assembly code generation on all PIC microcontroller families. Figures 6.36 – 6.38 all show screen shots of the fuzzy logic speed limiter design in various editors and analyzers of *fuzzy*TECH. Figure 6.36 displays the Project Editor featuring the structure of the fuzzy logic system. On the left side, two input interfaces fuzzify the two input variables "Acceleration" and "Speed_Error". The rule block in the middle contains all the fuzzy logic rules that represent the control strategy of the system. On the right side, the output variable "PMV_Set_Value" is defuzzified in an output interface.

Figure 6.37 shows more details of the fuzzy logic system. Each linguistic variable is displayed in a variable editor window and the rules are displayed in the Spreadsheet Rule Editor window. Each linguistic variable contains five (5) terms and membership functions. They are connected by a total of 12 fuzzy logic rules. All membership functions are of Standard types. As a defuzzification method, the Center-of-Maximum (CoM) method is used.

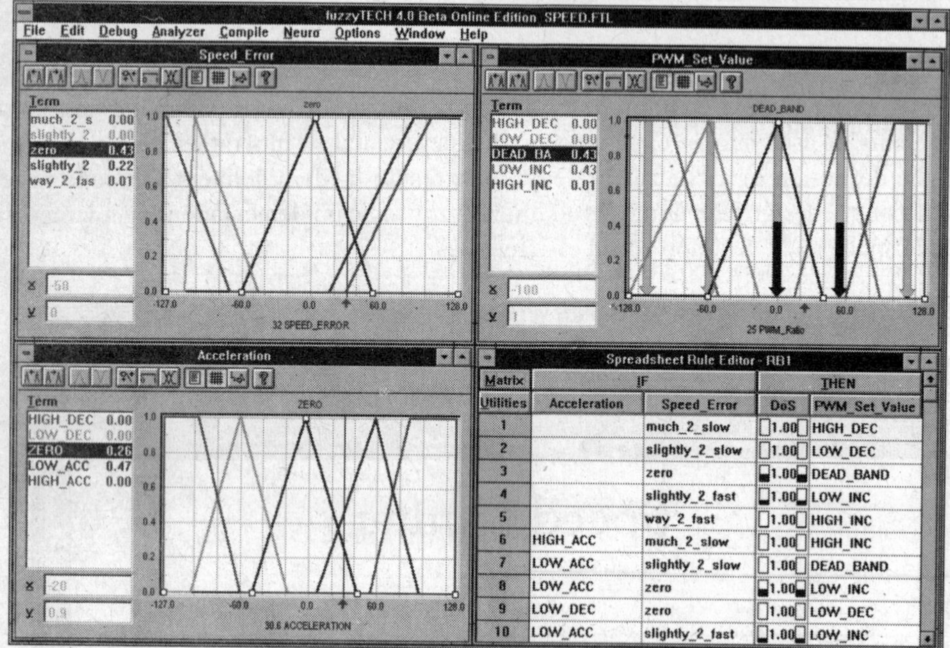

Figure 6.37: Definition of the Linguistic Variables and the Rule Table

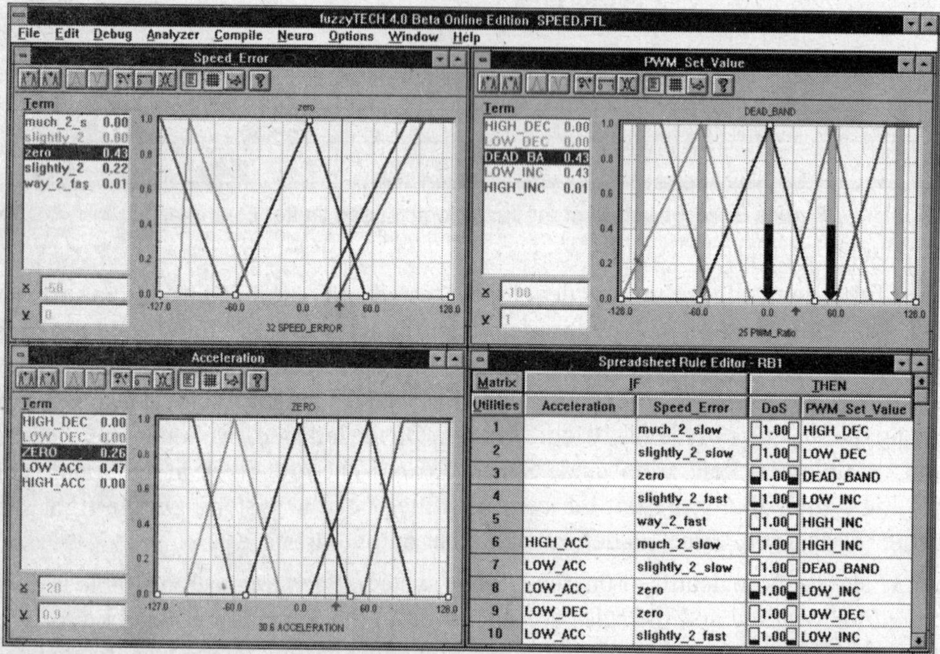

Figure 6.38: Debugging of the fuzzy logic system - transfer characteristics of the fuzzy logic controller under testing

All rules in the fuzzy logic system now let the designer define the best reaction (output variable value) for a given situation. The situation is described by the combination of the input variables. After such a control strategy has been defined by the designer, a number of different analyzer tools can be used to verify the system's performance. Figure 6.38 shows the 3D Plot as an example. In the 3D Plot, the two horizontal axes show the two input variables "Acceleration" and "Speed_Error". The vertical axis plots the output variable, "PWM_Set_Value", the set value for the PWM unit on the microcontroller. Rule 1, as shown in Figure 6.37, indicates:

IF Speed_Error = much_2_slow THEN PWM_Set_Value = HIGH_DEC

This rule represents the engineering knowledge that if the truck is way under the speed limit, no pressure should be applied to the cylinder. The membership function of the term "much_2_slow" is shown also in the respective variable editor in Figure 6.37. The 3D Plot in Figure 6.38 plots the transfer characteristic as a result of this. In the front part of the curve, the value of the output variable is very low (color of surface light). As you proceed to the left along the Acceleration axis, the output variable value gets higher. This is a result of Rule 6 that defines:

IF Acceleration = HIGH_ACC AND Speed_Error = much_2_slow THEN PWM_Set_Value = HIGH_INC

This rule represents the engineering knowledge that if in the same general case of the truck being way slower than the limit, the special case of a high acceleration should result in medium pressure on the cylinder. This ensures that the cylinder is already filled with some pressure if the truck reaches the limit quickly. If this rule would not have been formulated, a speed overshoot would occur as sketched in Figure 6.33.

6.5.5 Optimization and Implementation

A fair deal of optimization was accomplished off-line on the PC since *fuzzy*TECH can simulate the fuzzy logic system without the target hardware. However, final optimization and verification of the system was conducted on real trucks.

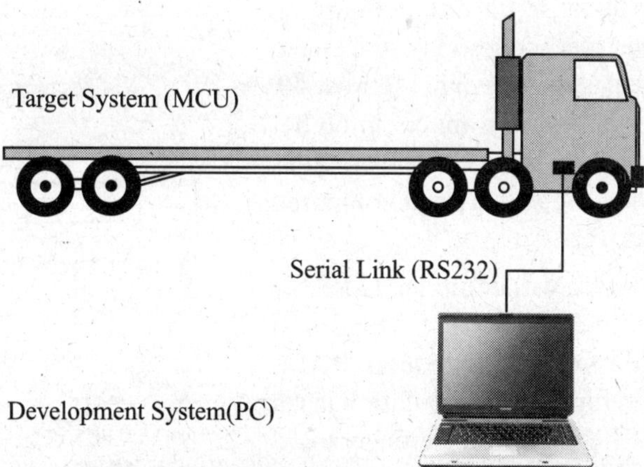

Figure 6.39: Cross optimization of the running fuzzy logic controller by a serial link

Figure 6.39 shows the test and optimization setup. The target system, the MCU of the electronic control unit, is mounted in the truck and connected to the development PC (notebook in the truck's cabin) by a serial cable. Such serial connection allows for modification of the running fuzzy logic controller "on-the-fly". This development technique is very efficient because it allows for the developer to analyze how a certain behavior of the fuzzy logic controller is caused by the membership function definition and the rules. Also, since modifications can be done in real time, the effects can be "felt" on the truck instantly.

One way to enable "on-the-fly" debugging is to link the *fuzzy*TECH RTRCD Module (real-time remote cross debugger) to the fuzzy logic controller that runs on the MCU and connect it to a serial driver. The RTRCD Module consumes about ½ Kbytes of ROM, a few Bytes of RAM, and some computing resources to serve the serial communication on the MCU.

Since the PIC16 MCU used in this application cannot provide such resources, the serial debug mode of *fuzzy*TECH was used rather than the RTRCD Module. In serial debug mode, the values of the input variables are sent from the MCU to *fuzzy*TECH running on the development PC via the serial cable and the results are sent back. *fuzzy*TECH shows the entire fuzzy logic computation in its editor and analyzer windows, and allows for "on-the-fly" modifications. To support serial communication, a piggyback board containing a MAX232 driver IC was mounted on the speed limiter board shown in Figure 6.35.

The advantage of using the serial debug mode of *fuzzy*TECH over the RTRCD Module is that code size and computation effort that previously was required for the fuzzy logic computation on the MCU are now saved and can thus be used for the serial communication. The disadvantage of the serial debug mode of *fuzzy*TECH is that it computes the systems' results on the PC where real-time response cannot be guaranteed. Also, any crash of MS-Windows, the PC, or the serial communication will halt computation in serial debug mode. The RTRCD Module, in contrast, is not affected by this.

6.5.6 Results

After optimization of the fuzzy logic rule strategy on different trucks and various load conditions, the speed limiter showed a response curve as shown in Figure 6.40. The fuzzy logic controller achieves a much smoother response, does not show overshoot behavior, and provides a higher accuracy of keeping the speed limit compared to a conventional controller.

The final fuzzy logic system was compiled to PIC16 assembly code by the *fuzzy*TECH MP-Edition and required 417 words of ROM space and 32 bytes of RAM. The RAM space can be used for other computation tasks such as preprocessing and filtering while the fuzzy logic system is not running. The entire fuzzy logic system needs less than 2 milliseconds to compute on the PIC16 MCU.

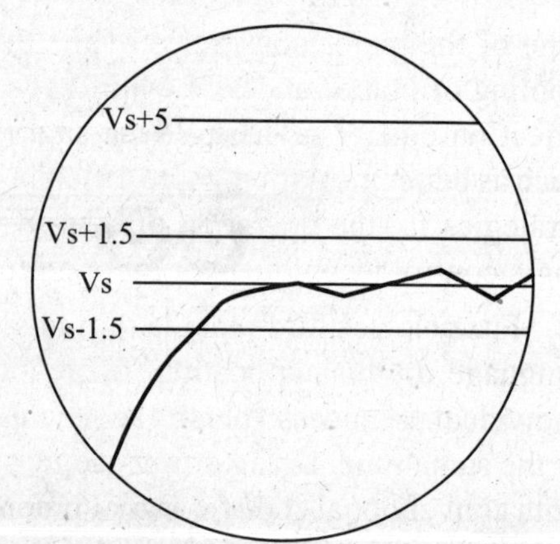

Figure 16.40: Speed limiter performance of the fuzzy logic controller

6.6 FUZZY LOGIC AND NEUROFUZZY IN APPLIANCES

Fuzzy Logic is an innovative technology that enables the implementation of 'intelligent' functions in embedded systems. One of its advantages is that even complicated functions and adaptive control loops can be implemented with the limited resources of low-cost 8 bit microcontrollers. Using three case studies in ABS, engine control, and automatic gearbox control, we will show how superior performance is achieved using fuzzy logic and neural-fuzzy design techniques. We will discuss development methodologies, tools used, and code speed/size requirements of three case studies.

The first case study shows how an existing product is enhanced with new, intelligent functions. In home air conditioners, the enhancement of the thermostat by fuzzy logic control techniques allows for a better adaptation to the requirements of the user. This results in a higher comfort level. Also, detection of low load situations yields energy savings.

The second case study covers the replacement of sensors with fuzzy logic state estimators. In the example of a central heating system control, a 35 outdoor temperature sensor and its installation were replaced. Comparisons show that the fuzzy logic solution better adapts to high and low heat demand periods, thus yielding higher comfort and energy savings at the same time. The presented system is now in production in Germany (350,000 units per year).

The third case study focuses on the automated generation of fuzzy logic systems or parts thereof. For laundry load detection in washing machines, neural-fuzzy technologies are employed that set up a fuzzy logic system using experimental data. The results of washing experiments, evaluated by experts, form this data base. The introduction of the resulting fuzzy logic laundry load detector saves an average of 20% on water and energy. The presented system is now in production in Germany (400,000 units per year).

The following discussion assumes the reader is familiar with basic fuzzy logic design principles.

6.6.1 Energy Saving AC Control

One of the major consumers of the total of all energy produced in the world is the heating and cooling of homes and office buildings. Hence, increasing efficiency of these systems has a great effect on energy savings. These savings can be realized either by constructional improvements, such as better insulation, more efficient heating/cooling systems or by using more intelligent control strategies for the operation of these devices. This case study focuses on the application of fuzzy logic control techniques for air conditioning systems.

Fuzzy logic allows for the formulation of a technical control strategy using elements of everyday language. In this application, fuzzy logic was used to design a control strategy that adapts to the individual user needs, thereby achieving both a higher comfort level and reduced energy consumption at the same time. Using a fuzzy logic software development system, the entire system, containing both conventional code for signal preprocessing and the fuzzy logic system, can be implemented on industry standard 8-bit microcontrollers. Using fuzzy logic on such a low-cost platform enables this solution to be implemented in most air conditioning systems.

1. Fuzzy Logic in AC Control

Quite a few air conditioning systems already use fuzzy logic control. In 1990, Mitsubishi introduced their first line of fuzzy logic controlled home air conditioners. Also, industrial air conditioning systems in Japan have been using fuzzy logic since 1990. Four years later, most Korean, Taiwanese, and European AC controllers also use fuzzy logic as a standard control technique.There are different incentives to use fuzzy logic:

- Industrial AC systems use fuzzy logic to minimize energy consumption. The implementation of complex control strategies optimizes that the set values for the heater, cooler, and humidifier shall be set in a certain load state.
- Car AC systems use fuzzy logic to estimate the temperatures at the head of the driver from multiple indirect sensors.
- Home AC systems are much simpler. They do not contain a humidifier and can only either cool or heat at one time. They use fuzzy logic for robust temperature control.

2. Air Condition Control Thermostats

The application discussed in this case study falls more into the second category. Each AC system has a thermostat that measures the room temperature and compares it with the set temperature that is set on a dial. Figure 6.41 shows the principle of such a thermostat.

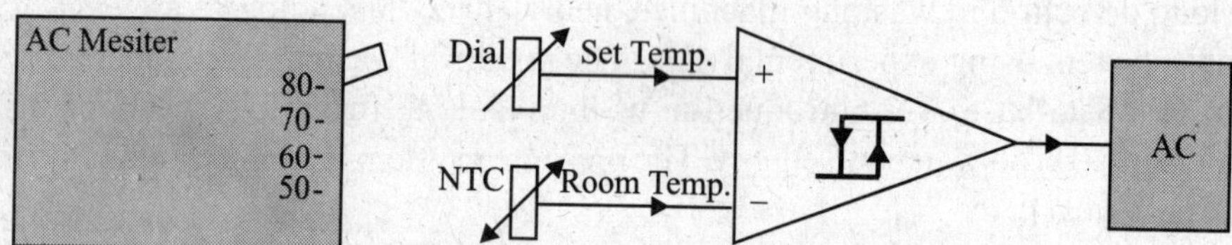

Figure 6.41: A conventional thermostat compares room temperature with the set temperature to turn ac on and off

The thermostat compares the set temperature that is selected on the dial by the user with the actual room temperature. To minimize the number of starts for the AC, a hysterisis is used. Both mechanical and electronic thermostats are used for this. Figure 6.41 shows the principle of an electronic analog AC controller.

3. Intelligent Fuzzy Logic Thermostat

This method works well to maintain a certain temperature level in a room. However, the actual room temperature does not always correspond to the subjective temperature feeling of the people in the room. A certain comfort level is reached with different room temperatures, depending on a number of conditions:

1. During the day, the temperature may be higher than during the night.
2. The same room temperature is perceived warmer if the sun shines.

Empirical analysis on how people adjust the temperature dial on their ACs has shown even more factors:

1. Someone who turns down the set temperature wants a large cooling effect. Due to this, most people tend to put the temperature dial lower than necessary. Usually, people forget to turn the temperature dial up again. Before this is corrected, the increased cooling wastes energy.
2. Someone who turns down the AC just a little bit is not interested in a quick response but rather in an accurate temperature. Reacting too much to this can cause an overshoot in the room temperature.
3. If someone changes the room temperature very often, the control should be sensible.
4. If room temperature varies strongly, the room is often used. Hence, control should be sensible.

The objective in this case study is to design an "intelligent" thermostat that "understands" both different environment conditions and the current needs of the user. For this, knowledge as contained in 6.41.-6.42. and A)-D) must be implemented in the thermostat. Since this kind of knowledge is hard to model mathematically, as well as hard to code in a conventional algorithm, fuzzy logic has been used for implementation.

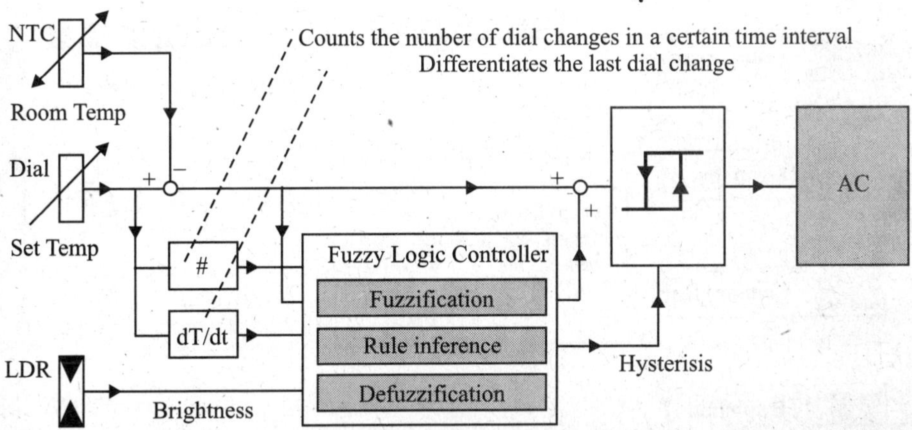

Figure 6.42: Fuzzy thermostat

Figure 6.42 shows the structure of the "intelligent" thermostat. To measure the brightness in the room, a LDR photo sensor is added. The fuzzy logic system corrects the signal before the threshold unit and sets its hysterisis. For that, the fuzzy logic system uses four input variables:

1. Difference between set and room temperature (Temp_Error)

   When the difference between set temperature and room temperature is very large, the fuzzy logic system increases the signal so the desired temperature is reached faster (Rule 5 and 6). At the same time, the hysteresis is set to large, so minor disturbances do not cause unnecessary on/off switches.
2. Time differentiated set temperature (dTemp_by_dt)

   The set temperature signal is differentiated with a time constant of 30 minutes. The fuzzy logic system uses this signal to understand when the user wants the AC to cool down a room quick (Rule 3). Also, the hysterisis is set large, so disturbances do not interrupt the cooling process. As this signal is a differentiated signal, it disappears if the user does not modify the dial.

3. Number of set temperature changes (Changes)

   This input signal is used to identify a user who tries to set the room temperature very precisely (Rule 4). To satisfy such a user, the hysterisis is set to small. This variable counts each time the user moves the dial. Every 6 hours, this variable is counted down until 0 is reached.

4. Brightness in the room (Brightness)

   If direct sunlight hits the room, the set temperature is automatically reduced (Rule 2). During the day or when lights are on in the room, the set temperature is slightly increased (Rule 1) and the hysterisis is set to small.

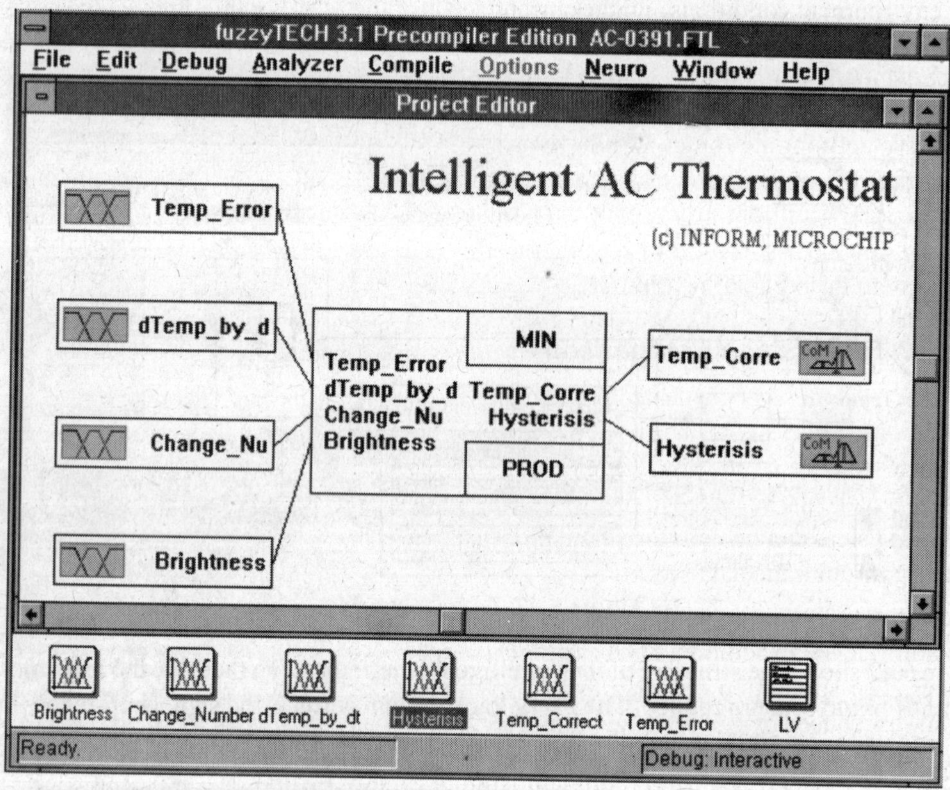

Figure 6.43: Structure of the fuzzy logic system in the thermostat

4. Implementation of a Fuzzy Logic Control Strategy

Figure 6.43 shows the structure of the fuzzy logic system as designed with the *fuzzy*TECH development system. All input variables have three (3) terms with standard membership functions. The output variable "Correction" has five (5) terms and uses Center-of-Maximum defuzzification. The output variable "Hysterisis" has three (3) terms and uses also Center-of-Maximum defuzzification.

Spreadsheet Rule Editor								
Matrix	IF				THEN		THEN	
Utilities	Temp_Error	dTemp_dt	Changes	Brightness	DoS	Correction	DoS	Hysterisis
1				medium	1.00	warmer	1.00	small
2				high	1.00	cooler		
3		negative			1.00	much_cool	1.00	large
4			frequent				1.00	small
5	too_cold				1.00	warmer	1.00	large
6	too_warm				1.00	cooler	1.00	large
7	OK	zero			1.00	zero	1.00	small
8								

Figure 6.44: The fuzzy logic rules represent the knowledge that the thermostat uses to correct the set temperature and the hysterisis

Figure 6.44 shows part of the rule base that defines the strategy of the system. This spread sheet representation is appropriate for small rule bases. Each row represents a rule. The left part of the screen under the [IF] button shows all input variables of the rule block; the right part under the [THEN] button shows all output variables. The column [DoS] that is displayed for each output variable allows for the association of a weight to this conclusion. This enables fine tuning of the fuzzy logic system during optimization.

5. Simulation Results and Comparison

The fuzzy logic system has been tested using data that has been recorded in various rooms under various conditions. This test data has been preprocessed using the spreadsheet software MS-Excel. To test the performance of the fuzzy logic solution, *fuzzy*TECH's Excel link has been used. It allows for MS-Excel cells be linked to fuzzy logic input and output variables. As this link is dynamic, the fuzzy logic system can be monitored and modified using the *fuzzy*TECH analyzers and editors while browsing through the data sets.

As a result, the room temperature as controlled by the fuzzy logic thermostat, results in an increased comfort level. In addition, the fuzzy logic thermostat detected situations where less cooling effort suffices. The simulation revealed that in an average residential house, the average energy consumption was reduced by 3.5%. At the same time, the comfort level was increased, since, depending on the situation, the fuzzy logic thermostat reduced the room temperature 5°F more than the conventional thermostat.

Picture of a Home Air Conditioner

The fuzzy logic thermostat does not require any modification of the AC itself. Hence, by replacing existing temperature controllers, even old ACs can be upgraded. By also controlling the ventilation, an even more improved performance could be reached.

6.6.2 Adaptive Heating System Control

To maximize both the economics and comfort of a private home heating system, fuzzy-logic control has been used by a German company in a new generation of furnace controllers. The fuzzy-logic controller ensures optimal adaptation to changing customer heating demands while using one sensor less than the former generation. Both the fuzzy-logic controller and the conventional control system were implemented on a standard 8-bit microcontroller. Design, optimization and implementation of the fuzzy controller were supported by the software development system *fuzzy*TECH.

1. European Heating Systems

Most European houses have a centralized heating system that uses a furnace for diesel-type fuel to heat the water supply (boiler). From the boiler, the hot water is distributed by a pipe system to individual radiators in the rooms of the house. To meet the different needs of customer heating habits, the temperature of the furnace-heated water must constantly be adjusted in relation to the outdoor temperature (heat characteristic). To measure the outdoor temperature, a sensor is installed on the outside of the house.

Viessmann Home Heating System

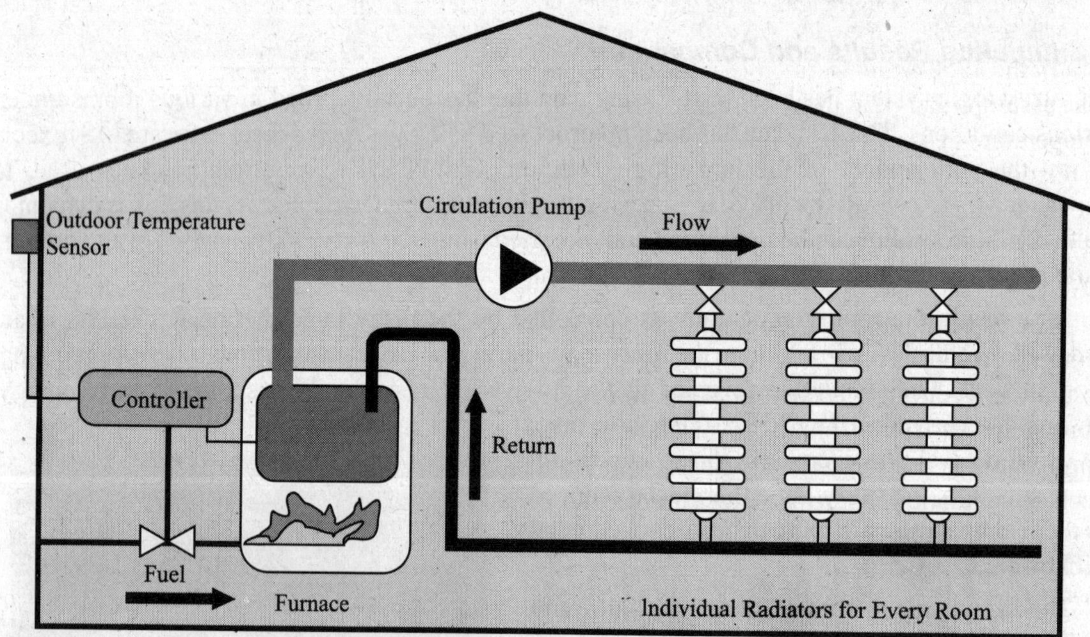

Figure 6.45: Schematic of a Centralized Heating System

The basic structure of a controller for this system is shown in Figure 6.46. The controller itself realizes an on-off characteristic. If the water temperature in the furnace drops to 2 Kelvin below the set temperature, the fuel valve opens and the ignition system starts the burning process. When the water temperature in the boiler itself rises to 2 Kelvin above the set temperature, the fuel valve closes. This on-off control strategy involving hysterisis minimizes the number of starts while assuring that the boiler temperature remains within the desired tolerance.

Although the structure of this control loop is quite simple, the task of determining the appropriate set boiler temperature is not. The maximum heat dissipation of the room radiators depends on the temperature of the incoming water (approximately the boiler temperature). For that, the set point for the water temperature in the boiler must never be set so low that it cannot warm the house when necessary. On the other hand, an excessively high setting of the boiler temperature would result in energy loss in both the furnace and the piping system. Thus the set boiler temperature needs to be carefully set to ensure both user comfort and energy efficiency.

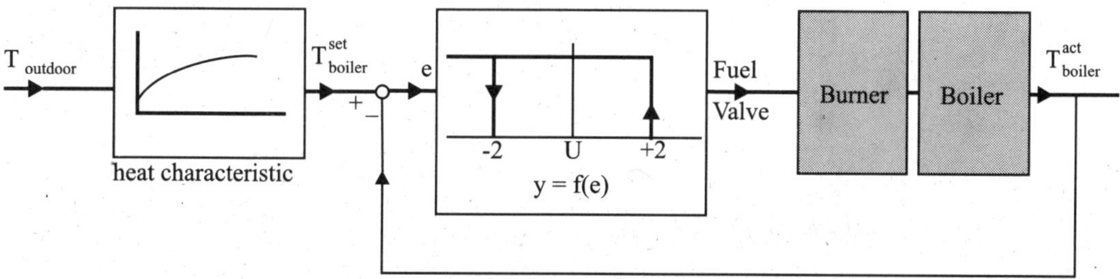

Figure 6.46: Block schematic of the conventional furnace controller

In the 1950's, the German Electrical Engineering Society (VDE) defined a procedure for this. The assumption is that the maximum amount of heat required by the house depends on the outdoor temperature ($T_{outdoor}$). A parametric function $T^{set}_{boiler} = f(T_{outdoor})$ adjusts the set boiler temperature in relation to the outside temperature. This function is also called the "heat characteristic". Parameters are the insulation coefficient of the house and a so-called "comfort parameter". The physical model of this is one in which the maximum amount of available heat equals the amount of heat disposed by the house plus some excess energy to compensate occasional door and window opening.

The assumption that the amount of energy a heating system has to deliver is largely outdoor-temperature dependent, was true back in those days when most houses only had poor thermal insulation. Today, this is obsolete. Due to rising energy costs and environmental concerns, modern houses are built with improved insulation. Therefore, to achieve high efficiency, the outdoor temperature is not the only parameter which reflects the required energy amount. Other factors, such as ventilation, door/window openings and personal lifestyle, have to be considered as well.

2. The Fuzzy Controller

Two approaches for determining the appropriate set boiler temperature for a well-insulated house exist:

- Extensive use of sensors (that is temperature sensors in every room) and use of a mathematical model.

- Definition of engineering heuristics to determine the set boiler temperature based on a knowledge-based evaluation of existing sensor data.

Since the use of extensive sensors is expensive and the construction of a comprising mathematical model is of overwhelming complexity, the second approach has been chosen for realizing the new generation of heating system controllers.

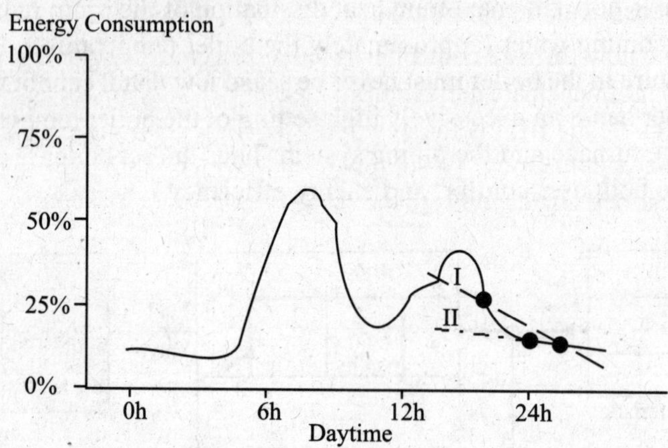

Figure 6.47: Actual energy consumption of the house (draft)

The most important criterion about individual customer heat demand patterns comes from the actual energy consumption curve of the house, which is measured by the on/off-ratio of the burner. An example of such a curve is given in Figure 6.47. From this curve, four descriptive parameters are derived:

- Current energy consumption, indicating current load. <
- Medium term tendency (I), indicating heating-up and heating-down phases.
- Short term tendency (II), indicating disturbances like door/window openings.
- Yesterday average energy consumption, indicating the general situation and house heating level..

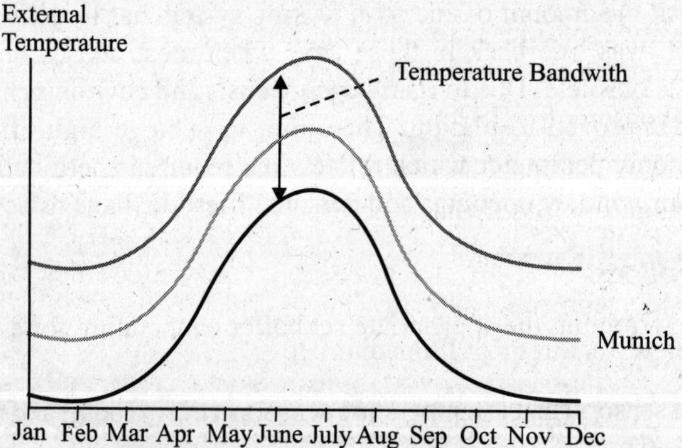

Figure 6.48: Average outside temperatures in munich

These parameters were used to heuristically form rules for the determination of the appropriate set boiler temperature. To allow for the formulation of plausibility rules (such as "temperatures below thirty degrees Fahrenheit are rare in August") the appropriate average outdoor temperature for that season is also a system input parameter. These curves are plotted in Figure 6.48. Since the average temperature curves are given, no outdoor temperature needs to be measured. Hence, the outdoor temperature sensor can be eliminated.

The structure of the new furnace controller is shown in Figure 6.49. The fuzzy controller uses a total of five inputs: four of which are derived from the energy consumption curve using conventional digital filtering techniques; the fifth is the average outdoor temperature. This input comes from a look-up table within the system clock. The output of the fuzzy system represents the estimated heat requirement of the house and corresponds to the $T_{outdoor}$ value in the conventional controller (Figure 6.46).

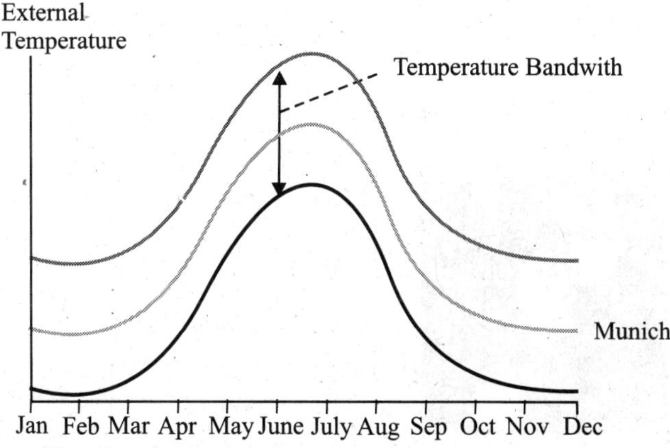

Figure 6.49: Schematic of the new furnace controller

3. Development of the System

The objective of the fuzzy controller is to estimate the actual heat requirement of the house. For this, if-then rules were defined to express the engineering heuristics of this parameter estimation:

IF current_energy_consumption IS low

AND medium_term_tendency IS increasing

AND short_term_tendency IS decreasing

AND yesterday_average IS medium

AND average_outside_temperature IS very_low

THEN estimated_heat_requirement IS medium_high

In total, 405 rules were defined for the parameter estimation. To develop and optimize such a large system efficiently, *fuzzy*TECH's matrix representation was used. This technique enables rule bases to be viewed and defined graphically rather than in text form. Figure 6.50 shows a screen shot of such a rule matrix. In this representation, all linguistic labels of two selected linguistic variables (established heating requirement and yesterday's average energy consumption) are displayed. All other variables (medium term tendency) are kept at a selected label. The matrix may be browsed to show the entire rule base by selecting other terms for these variables.

Within the matrix, a white square indicates rule plausibility whereas a black square indicates rule implausibility (not existent in the rule base). For instance, the highlighted rule in Figure 6.50 is valid. Its textual representation (in the lower part of the window) can be read as:

IF medium_term_tendency IS stable

AND yesterday_avg IS medium

THEN est._heat_req. IS medium.

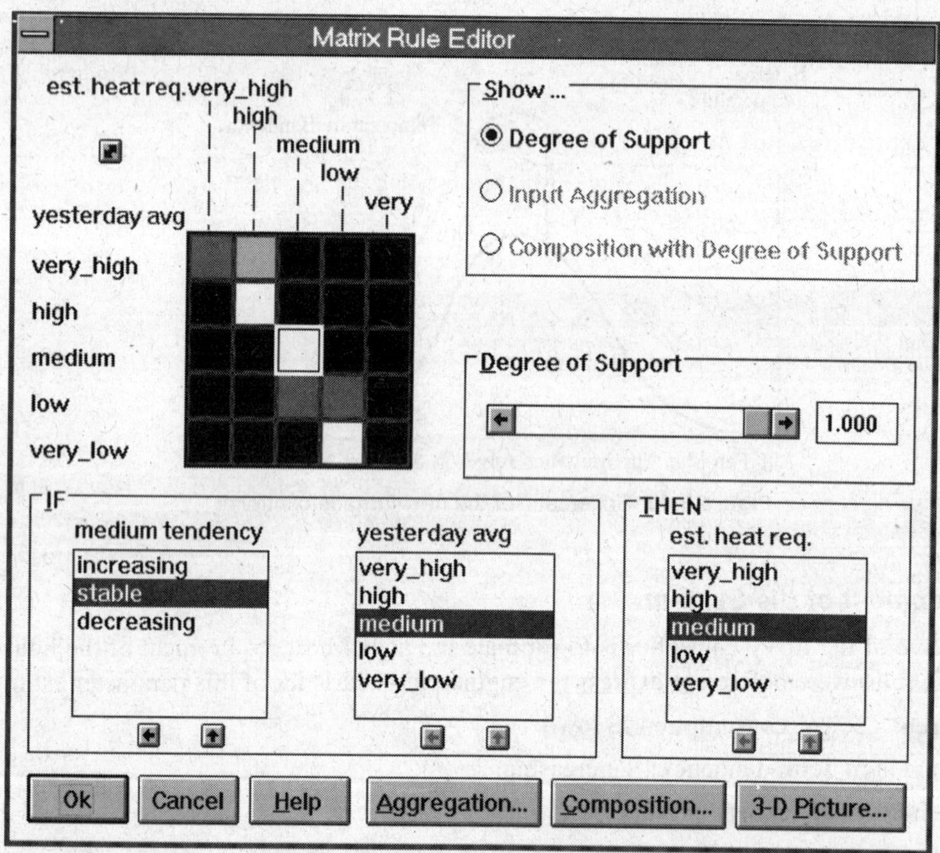

Figure 6.50: Screen shot of rule base as matrix representation

For the formulation of these IF-THEN rules, an initial systems prototype was built. During system optimization, however, it became apparent that some rules were more important than others and that mere rule addition/deletion was too inexact of a system-tuning method. Thus the inference strategy had to be extended to allow rules to be associated with a "degree of support". Such a degree of support is a number between 0 and 1 that expresses the individual importance of each rule with respect to all other rules. The degree of support for each rule is indicated in the matrix by a gray-shaded square. This allows for the expression of rules like:

IF medium_term_tendency IS stable

AND yesterday_avg IS very_high

THEN est_heat_req IS between high and very_high, rather more high.

The inference method used to represent individual degrees of support is based on approximate reasoning and Fuzzy Associative Map (FAM) techniques. After fuzzification, all rule premises are calculated using the minimum operator for the representation of the linguistic AND and the maximum operator for the representation of the linguistic OR. Next, the premise's degree of validity is weighted with the individual degree of support of the rule, resulting in the degree of truth for the conclusion. In the third step, all conclusions are combined using the maximum operator. The result of this is a fuzzy set. The Center-of-Maximum defuzzification method is used to arrive at a real value from a fuzzy output.

The entire structure of the fuzzy controller is shown in Figure 6.51. In this screen shot, the large block in the middle represents the previously described rule base while the small blocks represent input and output interfaces. The icons show the fuzzification/defuzzification methods used in the respective interfaces.

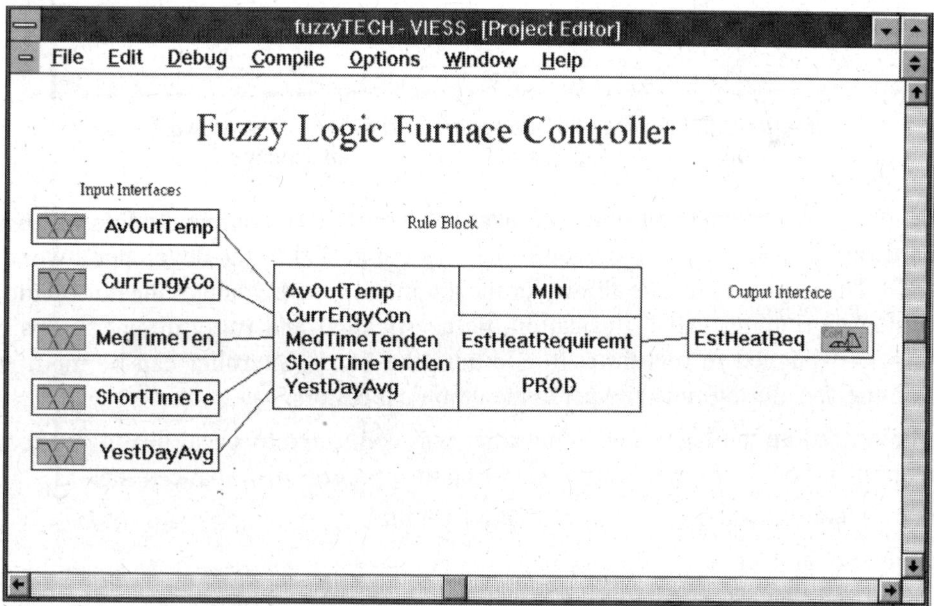

Figure 6.51: Structure of the fuzzy logic controller

4. Implementation and Optimization

After completion of the design of the fuzzy controller and the definition of linguistic variables, membership functions and rules, the system was compiled to the assembly language of the target microcontroller. With this technology, the fuzzy controller only uses 2 KB ROM on a standard 8-bit microcontroller. Once the fuzzy controller had been linked to the entire furnace controller code, the system was optimized.

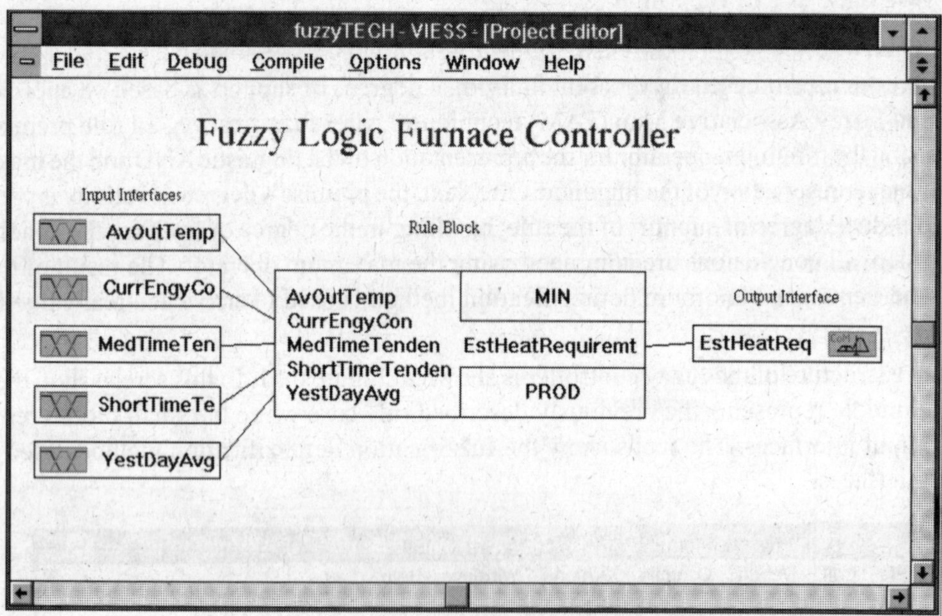

Figure 6.52: Optimization using the "online" technique allows for cross-debugging and "on-the-fly" modifications

To achieve the most efficient system optimization, *fuzzy*TECH's online module was used and the target hardware using an 8-bit microcontroller was connected to the developer's workstation (Windows-PC). The online technique allows for the graphical visualization of the information flow while the system is running. All fuzzification, defuzzification and rule inference steps can be graphically cross-debugged in real-time. In addition, the fuzzy controller can be modified and optimized "on-the-fly" during run-time using the graphical editors.

During optimization, the fuzzy logic controller was connected to a real heating system. This enabled the optimization of the system robustness against process disturbances such as:

- Preparation of hot water (for example for a bath tub)
- Opening of windows
- Extended departure, like for a vacation

5. Performance

To evaluate system performance, both the conventional controller and the fuzzy controller were connected to a test house. One such example is shown in Figure 6.53. Over a period of 48 hours, three graphs were plotted:

- Optimal boiler temperature (calculated from the external/internal house condition).
- Set boiler temperature, as derived from the conventional controller (considering outdoor temperature).
- Set boiler temperature, as derived from the fuzzy controller.

The result of the comparative performance tests showed that the fuzzy controller was highly responsive to the actual heat requirement of the house. It was very reactive to sudden heat demand changes like the return of house inhabitants from vacation. Besides this, the elimination of the outdoor temperature sensor saved about $30 in production costs and even more in installation costs that average about $120. By setting the set boiler temperature beneath the level typically used by a conventional controller in low load periods, the fuzzy controller saves energy. Long-term studies collecting statistical data for quantifying exactly how much energy per house could be saved annually are currently being investigated. In addition to this, the two knobs parameterizing the heat characteristic for the individual house (confer Figure 6.46) used by conventional heating systems, are no longer necessary with the fuzzy logic controller. This eases the use of the heating system, since setting the parameters of the heating curves requires an expertise most home owners do not have.

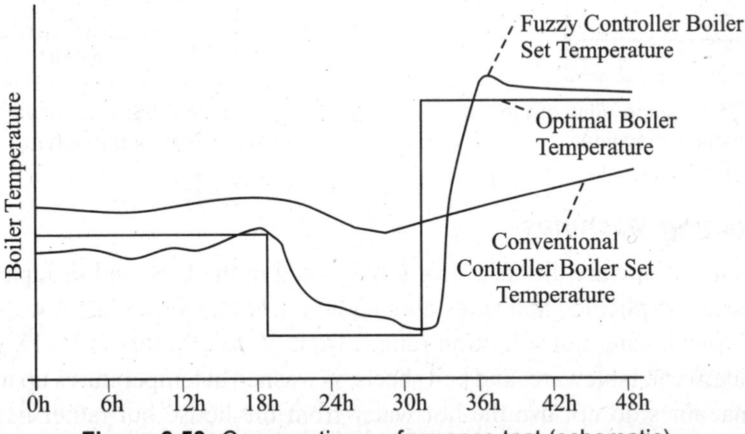

Figure 6.53: Comparative performance test (schematic)

With this new generation of fuzzy logic heating controller, we achieved:

- Improved energy efficiency, since the fuzzy controller reduces heat production at low heat demand periods.
- Improved comfort, due to the detection of sudden heat demand peaks.
- Easy setup, since the heat characteristic does not need to be parameterized manually.
- Savings both in production and installation cost.

Taking into account the benefits of introducing engineering heuristics, formulated using fuzzy logic technologies, the price was rather low. In the product, the fuzzy logic controller only requires 2 KB of ROM. Using matrix rule representation and online development technology, the optimization of a complex fuzzy logic system containing 405 rules was done efficiently. Click here to view the Fuzzy Logic Viessmann Heating System Controller.

6.6.3 Neurofuzzy Signal Analysis in Washing Machines

In some applications, the knowledge about the system solution is contained in sample data. In these cases, NeuroFuzzy is the method of choice. The following case study is a good example to show the potential of NeuroFuzzy technologies. The German home appliance manufacturer AEG used the *fuzzy*TECH NeuroFuzzy Module to design an environment-friendly washing machine. The NeuroFuzzy system analyzes the signal of an existing sensor to estimate the laundry volume and type. This information is used to optimize the washing program. In an average home, this technology saves about 20% on water and energy. Click here for a picture of the AEG NeuroFuzzy washing machine or its presentation at the INFORM Fuzzy Logic User's Conference.

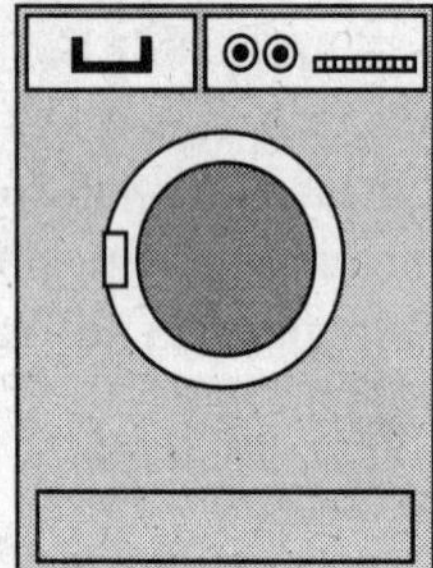

Figure 6.54: Outside View of the washing machine

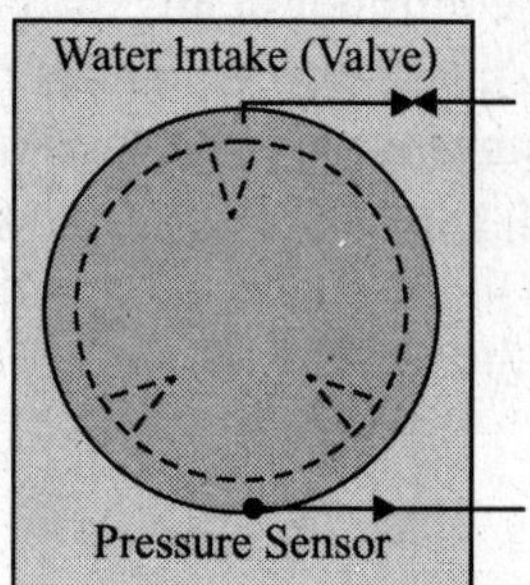

Figure 6.55: Cut view of the washing machine

1. European Washing Machines

Washing machines in Europe are different from those used in the U.S. and in Japan. The washing process is much more complicated and takes about 2 hours. On the other hand, water consumption is much lower. A typical water consumption ranges from 50 to 60 liters (13 - 18 gallons). White laundry, such as underwear, tableware, and bed sheets, is washed at temperatures up to 95°C (203°F). Hence, washing machines do not use the hot water from the house but rather heat up the water electrically.

The complex washing process consists of multiple wash, process, bleach, rinse and spin steps. To control this, today's washing machines use microcontroller hardware and multiple sensors:

- Tachometer for the drum spin.
- Analog pressure sensor for the water level (Figure 6.54, left).
- Digital sensor to detect strong unevenness during spinning.
- Digital sensor to detect excessive foam.

To determine the optimal washing program, actual laundry load (type and volume) of the washing machine must be known. Sensors that could measure these parameters directly are expensive and unreliable. Hence, the objective for AEG was to design a system that estimates the actual laundry load only from the existing sensors.

2. Water Absorption Curves

Figure 6.56 plots the pressure sensor curve over time. The plot starts when the water intake valve first opens.

- The water intake valve opens at T_0. At T_1, the water level reached set value. This duration does not depend much on the laundry load since the laundry in the non-rotating drum does not absorb much water.
- At T_1, the drum starts to rotate in a certain rhythm, causing the laundry to absorb water. Since the weight of the laundry is held by the drum, the water pressure measured by the sensor decreases. At a later time T_2, the new pressure is stored and the difference to the pressure at T_1 gives an indication of the absorption speed.
- At T_2, the current water pressure is stored again. It gives an indication of the absorption volume, as the laundry is mostly saturated at this time. At T_2, the water valve is opened again to fill up the water level to the set point.

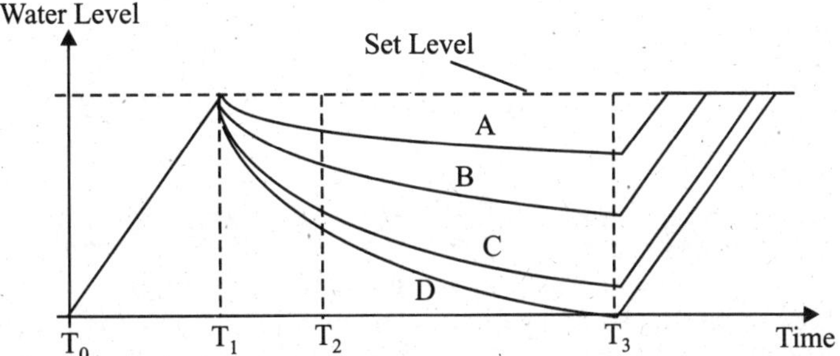

Figure 6.56: Water level in the drum of the washing machine during initial water intake. by interpreting the curves, an estimation of laundry type and volume is possible

As there is no mathematical model on the relation of the water absorption curves to the laundry load, AEG decided to use fuzzy logic to design a solution based on the knowledge of their washing experts. Figure 6.57 shows the structure of the fuzzy logic system that estimates the water requirement in washing and rinse steps. The input variables of the fuzzy logic system stem from the water absorption curve.

The upper fuzzy logic rule block estimates the water requirement during washing (WaterLev1) from absorption speed (AbsorbSp) and absorption volume (AbsorbVol). Both these input variables are calculated from T1 - T0 and T2 - T1. The two lower fuzzy logic rule blocks estimate the water requirement during rinse (WaterLev2). Inputs to the intermediate rule block are water requirement during washing, as determined by the upper rule block, and total absorption volume. These are combined to describe the total absorption characteristic (AbsorbChar). This variable is not an output of the fuzzy logic system, but only used as one input for the lower fuzzy logic rule block.

The lower rule block estimates the water requirement during the rinse step (WaterLev2). Other inputs are the ration of the bounded soap, the number of rinse steps given by the selected washing program, and the selected intensity of the spin step. All membership functions are of Standard type (Z, Lambda, S) and the defuzzification employs Center-of-Maximum (CoM) method.

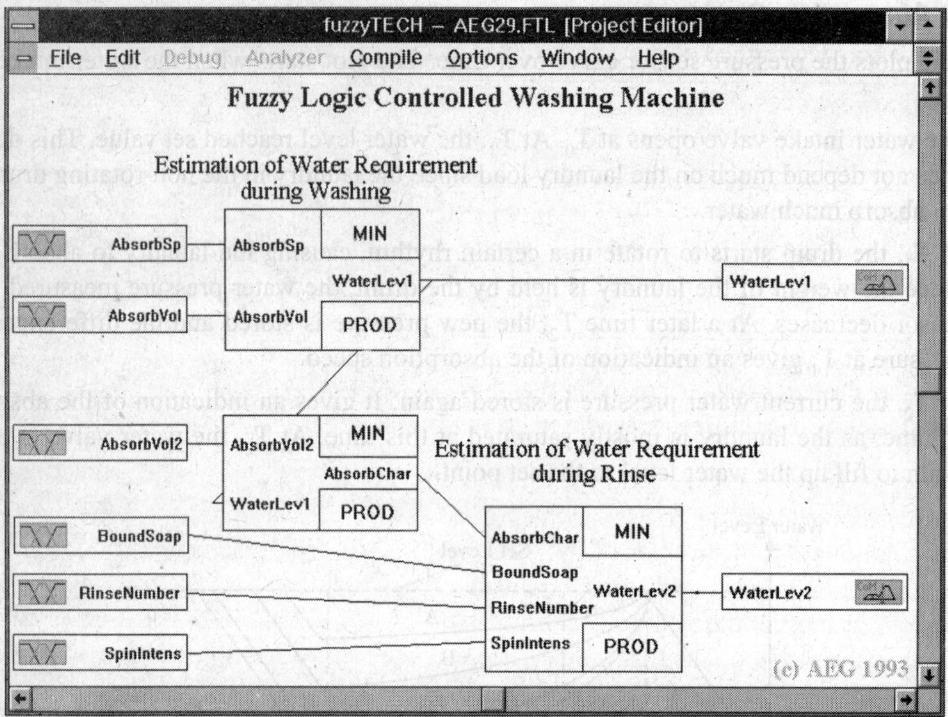

Figure 6.57: The Multi Level Fuzzy Logic System interprets the water intake function and determines the amount of water to be used in the subsequent washing steps. Also, the further washing program is optimized according to the load

3. Fuzzy Logic vs. NeuroFuzzy

The approach of interpreting the water absorption curve to estimate the laundry load is innovative, and hence, not much engineering "know-how" on the interpretation of the curves exists. As engineering "know-how" on the application is essential to building a solution with fuzzy logic, the first try of AEG to find a satisfying set of fuzzy logic rules failed.

On the other hand, AEG already recorded water absorption curves for various known laundry loads. The optimal water requirement for these laundry loads can easily be determined by the washing experts. Using these experimental results as training examples, AEG's next try was to use NeuroFuzzy techniques. Figure 6.58 shows some of these training examples. The left column (Laundry load) lists the materials used for this washing experiment, the next two columns (Water absorption speed and volume) give parameters from the water absorption curve. AEG showed the washing experts the first columns with the actual known load and asked them to recommend the optimum water requirement for this load.

The NeuroFuzzy training used the right column as the desired output and the middle two columns as the respective inputs. The training cannot use the left column as the actual load is not known to the washing machine during operation. The aim of this training is that after training, the fuzzy logic system, which the NeuroFuzzy Module trains, responds with the appropriate water level recommendation determined of the actual values of the input variables.

Laundry load	Water absorption speed	Water absorption volume	Water requirement in subsequent washing steps (from expert)
4 kg Wool / 1 kg Cotton	0.67	2.44	3.5
3 kg Wool / 1 kg Cotton	0.61	2.1	3.1
2 kg Wool / 2kg Cotton	0.62	1.99	2.8
...	...	...	...

Figure 6.58: The Sample Data for the NeuroFuzzy Training Has Been Gained Through Extensive Washing Experiments. In Each Experiment, Different Laundry Types and Volumes Were Used. For Each Experiment, the Washing Expert Gave His Recommendation for the Amount of Water to Be Used in Subsequent Washing Steps.

The NeuroFuzzy learning process created 159 rules in the fuzzy logic system shown in Figure 6.57. The solution was able to estimate the water requirement with a maximum difference from the optimum value of 0.35 liters (0.09 gallons). In an average home, this saves about 20% of the water consumption. As most of the electricity consumed by the washing machine is used to heat up water, 20% of energy is saved too. The fuzzy logic system that the NeuroFuzzy learning process generated, was implemented on a standard 8 bit microcontroller.

6.7 DATA ANALYSIS OF ENVIRONMENTAL DATA FOR TRAFFIC CONTROL

Traffic control is based on the analysis of traffic data and environmental conditions. Particularly bad environmental conditions may cause hazard to drivers. In this paper, we discuss the use of fuzzy logic for the analysis of environmental conditions such as road surface condition, visual range and weather conditions detected by local sensor stations and road sensors. Because detection of environmental conditions involves a number of uncertainties, conventional approaches do not deliver satisfactory solutions. The fuzzy logic solution discussed in this paper in contrast:

- takes into account the different types and quality of equipment used at the different detection stations,
- uses a two-step plausibility check to determine the quality of sensor signals,
- computes substitute values for missing information using sensors from other detection stations,
- leads to more appropriate results for the evaluation of road surface conditions and visual range to indicate slippery road conditions or fog warning.

The discussed fuzzy logic solution was developed for an existing traffic control system of the B27 in Germany, a state highway between Stuttgart city, Stuttgart airport, and Tuebingen. The unit is part of a larger fuzzy logic traffic control system which will be implemented as an additional step in the B27 control system.

6.7.1 Traffic Management

The first traffic management systems used in Germany were implemented on roads with frequent accidents caused by fog or icy road conditions. Later, these system were extended to detect and control traffic to increase the traffic capacity. These traffic control systems use several detection stations along the road. These stations employ magnetic sensors for traffic detection, as well as weather stations transmitting environmental data from road surface and the air layer near the ground.

A central traffic control computer collects the data transmitted from the section stations. A control strategy derives an adequate speed limit for every section. The control objectives are:

- keep traffic flowing in case of peak traffic,
- slow down traffic at the inflow to congestion, and
- warn for bad weather conditions such as fog or ice.

Along the road of such an "intelligent" highway, alterable road signs posted on traffic sign gantries display speed limits for each lane and display non-regular events such as road work, warnings for traffic back-ups, breakdowns, an accident or dangerous weather conditions (Figure 6.59).

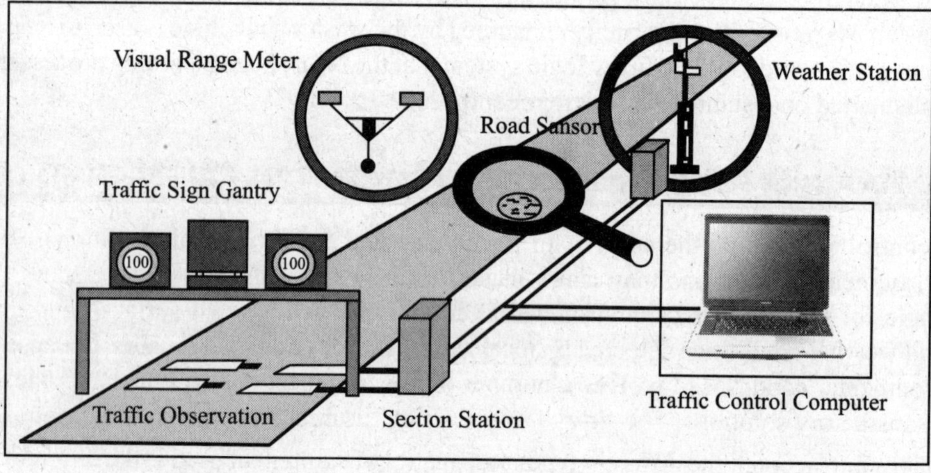

Figure 6.59: Environmental and traffic sensors in a traffic control system

6.7.2 Environmental Data Analysis

The traffic situations depend highly on environmental conditions. An intelligent highway thus should warn drivers of slippery road conditions and low visibility. Sensors are used to indicate and classify icy or wet road pavement and to indicate the visual range.

An ideal weather station uses road sensors measuring road surface temperature, road surface moisture, water film depth, and salt content of water film. Near the road, the ideal weather station detects air and ground temperature, amount of precipitation, type of precipitation, wind velocity and direction, sun beam intensity and illumination.

However, most existing weather stations are not equipped with this full range of sensor equipment. In addition, some sensors do not work reliably under all conditions. For example, a standard salinometer needs a wet road surface to measure the remaining salt content on the road. Besides measurement problems, sensors frequently fail because of "biological attacks" such as spiders or butterflies that cover the surface of visual based detectors. Conventional traffic control systems misinterpret this as high rain intensity or low visual range. This can cause completely wrong traffic warnings. Because sensors often stem from different vendors, conventional systems do not use interrelationships between the signals of different detection stations to identify such implausibilities.

6.7.3 Fuzzy Logic System Architecture

The fuzzy logic data analysis unit was designed as part of a larger traffic control system. As shown in earlier applications, fuzzy logic is well suited to create solutions for traffic control systems. Figure 6.60 shows the architecture of the analysis unit, separating a component to verify the sensor information from components to evaluate the road surface and visual range condition.

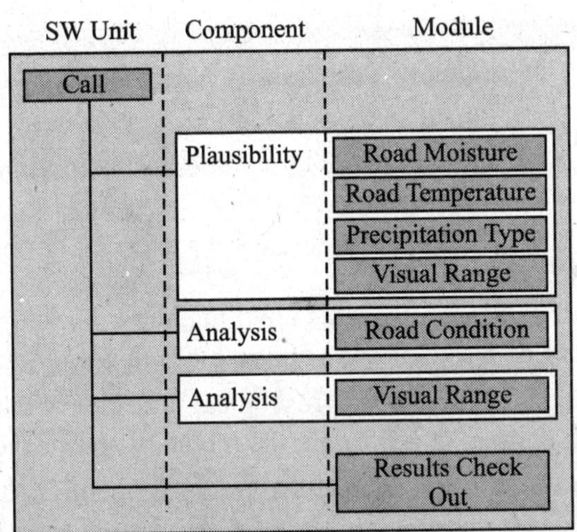

Figure 6.60: Architecture of environmental data analysis

6.7.4 Sensor Plausibility Analysis

A two-step approach was used to verify the sensor signals. The first step utilizes the fact that no weather signal remains constant. In particular, if the signal jumps abruptly or remains completely constant over time, the sensor signal is considered to be faulty.

In this case, the fuzzy logic system regenerates the information from other sensors. To design this fuzzy logic system, meteorological knowledge about the maximum gradients of all sensor signals, a time frame for a required movement of the signals, and maximum jumps of the gradients to identify discontinuity were acquired from experts.

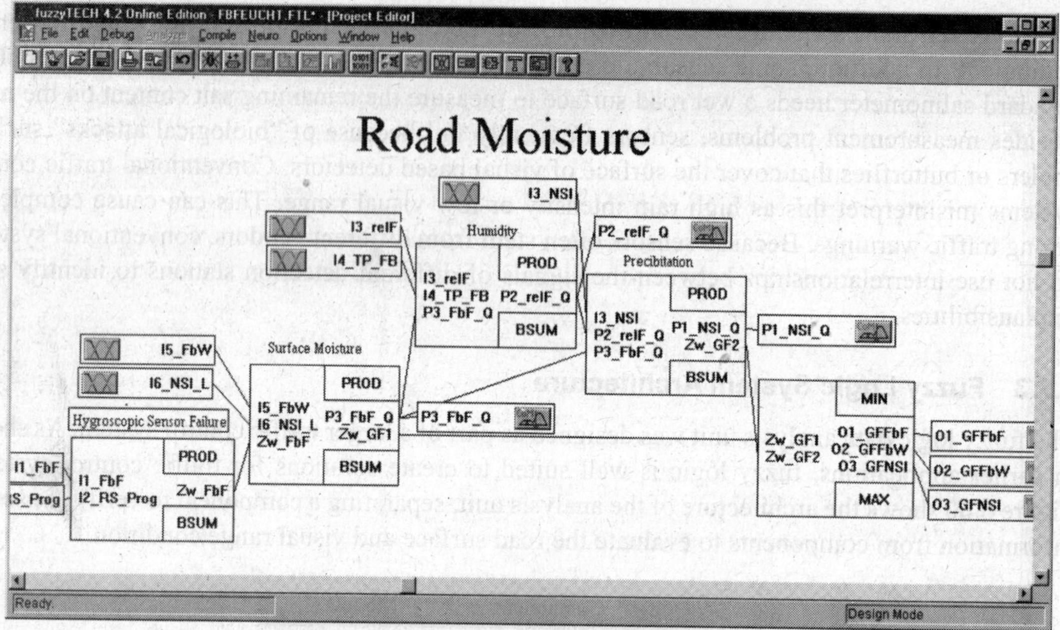

Figure 6.61: Road moisture fuzzy logic module

The second step uses four separate fuzzy logic modules to combine interrelated signals:

A. Road Moisture Module

This module, combines all data, that indicates anything about moisture or water on the road. The fuzzy logic module consists of 5 rule blocks (Figure 6.61) that implement:

1. A compensation rule block for the hygroscopical behavior of the road moisture sensors. For example, if the salt content is very high, the moisture sensor indicates higher values.
2. A cross check rule block between detected road surface moisture, the sensors that detect a water film on the road, and the amount of precipitation ions detected during the last 30 minutes. For example, if strong rain was detected over the past minutes, the road must be wet.
3. A cross check rule block of the humidity sensor using dew point, road temperature, and a moisture sensor. For example, if the dew point is lower than the road temperature and the verified moisture indicates a dry road, the humidity signal must be wrong.
4. A cross check rule block to the precipitation sensor.
5. A diagnosis rule block to derive an error message from the given signal situation.

As result, the module produces verified signals of road moisture, amount of precipitation, and humidity.

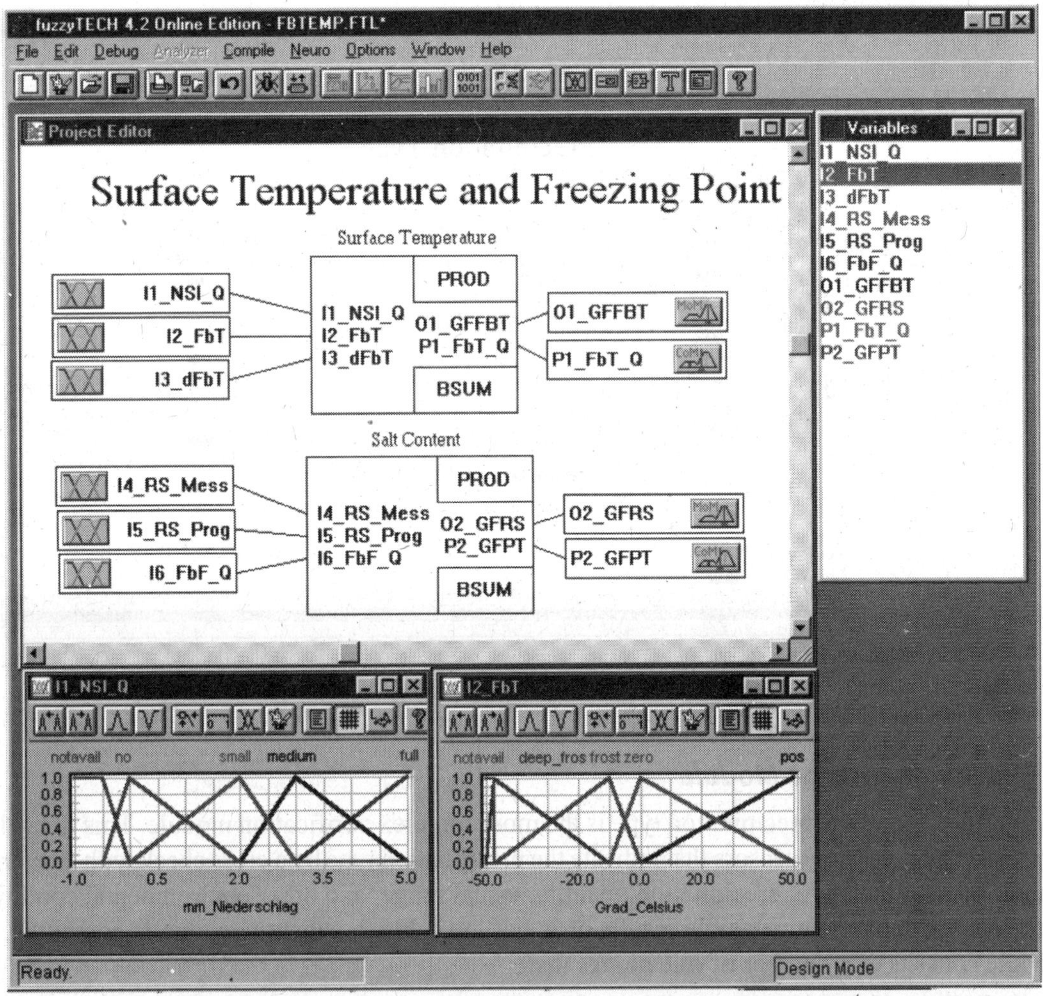

Figure 6.62: Road temperature fuzzy logic module

B. Road Temperature Module

This fuzzy logic module contains two rule blocks (Figure 6.62) to compute:

1. A verified value of the road surface temperature by cross check of the temperature signal, the gradient of this signal, and the precipitation. For example, the temperature signal can only decrease rapidly if a large amount of precipitation is detected.
2. A verified value of the freezing point, taking into account salt content and road surface moisture. Because the salt content sensor does not work with dry road conditions, a salt content forecast is used when the signal is not available.

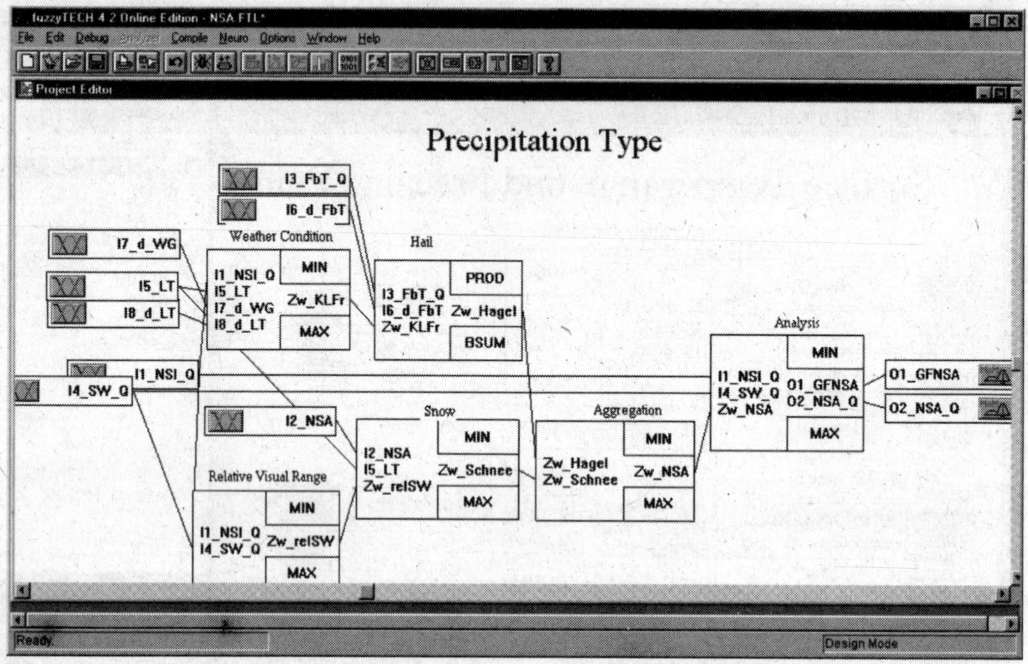

Figure 6.63: Precipitation type fuzzy logic module

C. Precipitation Type Module

The verification of the precipitation type is the most complex verification module. This fuzzy logic module verifies existing sensors that indicate the precipitation type by a cross check with the verified signals of road moisture, precipitation quantity, visual range, and other environmental conditions. If the sensor delivers implausible results or is not available, a substitute value is computed. The module consists of a number of rule blocks that:

1. Indicate if the weather conditions allow for hail or snow. For example, an air temperature level is defined at which snow is implausible.
2. Compare the visual range with the precipitation quantity.
3. Aggregate the information with the precipitation quantity and visual range.

D. Visual Range Module

The visual range fuzzy logic module computes a verified value of the visual range by using two rule blocks (Figure 6.64) that:

1. Cross check the visual range with the precipitation quantity. For example, there is no fog during heavy rain.
2. Cross check the visual range with air humidity. For example, fog only occurs during very high humidity.

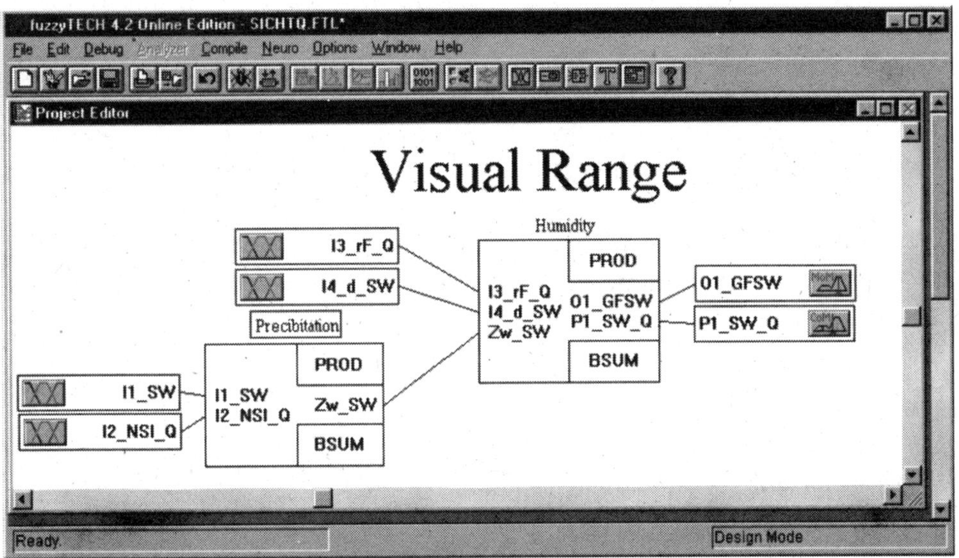

Figure 6.64: Visual Range Fuzzy Logic Module

Using these verified signals, the subsequent two components conclude road and fog conditions. The Road Condition component (Figure 6.65) uses the qualified values of precipitation type and quantity, as well as the road moisture to indicate a dangerously wet road. Precipitation type, freezing point, and road temperature indicate icy conditions. A final rule block aggregates the information to a standardized road condition classification code. An additional component aggregates the verified values of visual range and precipitation type to compute the standardized visual range classification code.

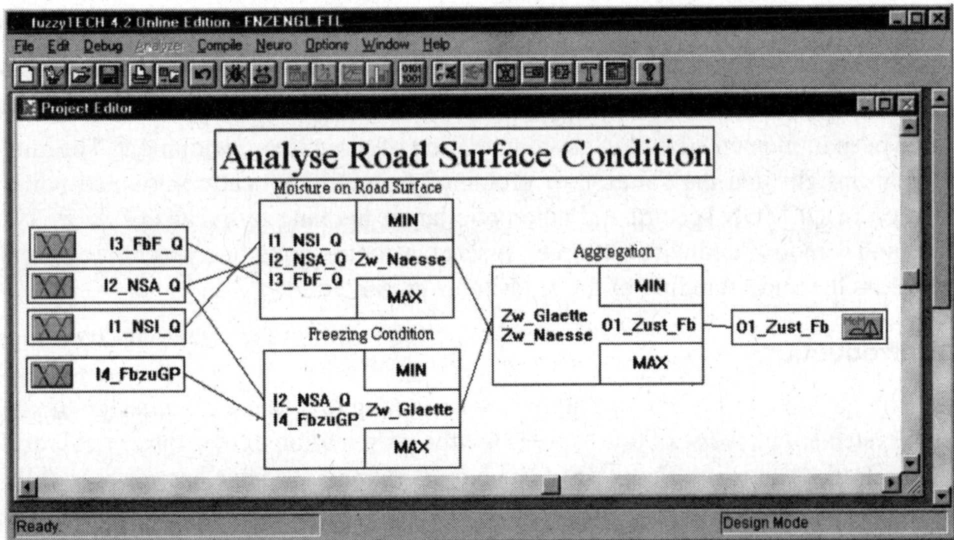

Figure 6.65: Analysis of road surface condition

6.7.5 Results

Conventional traffic systems are susceptible to faulty weather sensor signals. The fuzzy logic approach presented delivers more reliable results using meteorological expertise. The solution discussed was implemented using the fuzzy logic development software *fuzzy*TECH. The table in Figure 6.66 shows the number of variables, structures, rules and memberships of each component and the complete system used.

Module	Variable	Rule blocks	Rules	MBFs
Road Moisture	16	5	489	70
Road Temperature	10	2	130	39
Pricipitation Type	15	6	204	60
Visual Range	7	2	142	36
Analysis Road Condition	7	3	60	33
Analysis Visual Range	3	1	35	14
Complete Unit	**58**	**19**	**1060**	**255**

Figure 6.66: Size of Fuzzy Logic Unit and Its Modules

In day to day operation, the fuzzy logic solution has shown that it can prevent traffic control system malfunction in most sensor breakdown situations. In addition "biological attack" situations were detected and misleading rain or fog detection was avoided.

In a complete traffic control system, analysis of environmental conditions is only one component of its functionality. However, faulty weather detection can cause the entire traffic control system to malfunction. Thus, the enhancement of traffic control systems by fuzzy logic greatly improves the reliability of traffic control.

6.8 FUZZY TECHNOLOGY IMPLEMENTED IN SONAR SYSTEMS

In this section, applications of fuzzy algorithms in the domain of sonar systems are introduced which have been implemented in the latest generation of Atlas sonar equipment. The aim has been to provide an insight into the solution of problems from an application-oriented point of view. Classification of DEMON spectra and automatic target tracking by means of fuzzy systems are introduced and demonstrated with examples. A short introduction to fuzzy technology is also given which supports the understanding of the algorithms presented.

6.8.1 Introduction

Modern techniques such as fuzzy algorithms are beginning to influence the design of sonar signal processing systems. The scope of this paper is not the presentation of new theoretical results in this area but an introduction to problems where such modern methods have been successfully applied. In other words, the applications of fuzzy theory discussed in Sections 6.8.3 and 6.8.4 have been implemented in the latest sonar systems of Atlas Elektronik.

This paper is devoted to two sonar applications of fuzzy theory. The first is concerned with the automatic detection of the propeller shaft rate and number of propeller blades of ships and submarines by analysis of the DEMON spectrum. The second application is an automatic target traking system which incorporates two fuzzy modules. In particular, the main component of the so-called "traking filter" is itself a fuzzy system.

Fuzzy logic and the method of approximate reasoning led to new concepts in control theory and in the design of expert systems. These concepts imitate human thought processes better than do conventional methods. Besides the above-mentioned applications, important notions from fuzzy theory are explained which are needed for the understanding of the fuzzy algorithms considered. Rule-based fuzzy systems can be used if human expert knowledge is available which can be expressed in the form of if-then rules.

6.8.2 Basic Concepts of Fuzzy Theory

Before the applications of fuzzy theory in sonar systems introduced below can be discussed in detail, some basic concepts of this theory have to be considered. Those readers who are familiar with fuzzy systems can skip this section.

The efficiency of knowledge-based expert systems depends on the degree to which human knowledge can be reproduced. Classical mathematical logic, which is the basis of conventional inference machines, can formalise human knowledge and make it computable via algorithms to a very restricted degree only. To overcome the problems of binary logic, the theory of fuzzy logic was developed by Lotfi A. Zadeh. He introduced fuzzy sets in order to describe and process inexact and incomplete data, which is often encountered in real situations. Since fuzzy logic is capable of dealing with linguistic information, it is ideal for serving as a basis for knowledge-based systems.

In contrast to classical logic, which knows only two crisp truth values, yes or no, true or false, 0 or 1, the concept of fuzzy logic is based on so-called "membership functions", which can take arbitrary values from the interval [0, 1]. The membership function describes the degree to which an object belongs to a certain set. Moreover, further important notions from the field of fuzzy systems which are beyond the scope of this paper are discussed in these publications.

Let A, for example, be the set of all possible numbers of spots on a die; we can then define the set "high number of spots" by means of a membership function. In the case of classical logic, the corresponding membership function is depicted in Figure 6.67 where only the two crisp values 0 and 1 are admissible. In contrast to this, the fuzzy set "high number of spots", shown in Figure 6.68, coincides much better with the human concept of "high", since smooth transitions between membership and non-membership are possible.

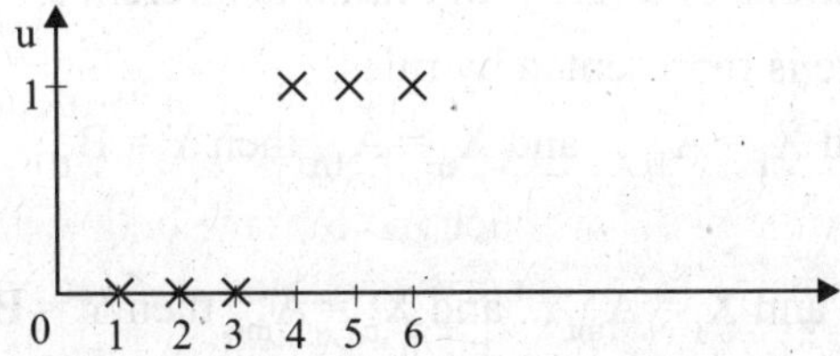

Figure 6.67: Crisp set "high number of spots"

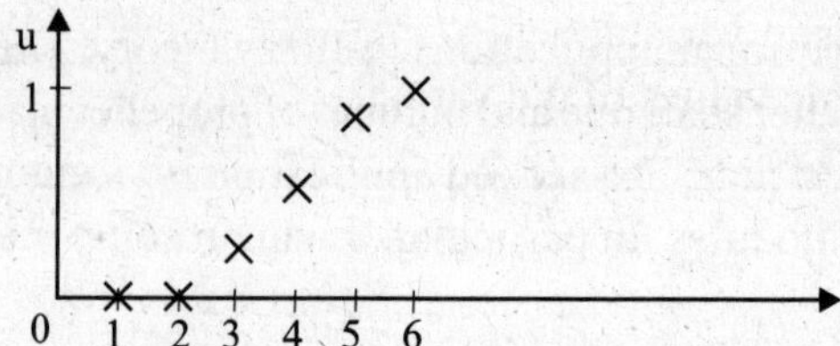

Figure 6.68: Fuzzy set "high number of spots"

The membership function is the essential component of a fuzzy set. Thus, the operations "intersection", "union" and "complement" of fuzzy sets are defined via the membership functions of the sets involved. The number of operators proposed in the literature is large. The reason for the variety of definitions for the operations "AND" (intersection) and "OR" (union) is the context-dependent way in which these operations are performed in human thinking. The choice of the appropriate operator is not trivial in practical situations and needs much experience and a proper analysis of the underlying problem.

Fuzzy inference is the most important operation in fuzzy expert systems and fuzzy controllers. In order to clarify this type of operation we first have to introduce the notion of "linguistic variable". A linguistic variable is a variable whose values are sentences in a natural language. The meaning attached to the values of a linguistic variable are fuzzy sets. This abstract explanation can be illustrated by the following example. We define a linguistic variable "distance". As the domain of interest (universe of discourse) we consider distances between 0 and 100 km. The linguistic variable "distance" can take as values the expressions {very near, near, medium, far, very far}. These expressions are the names of fuzzy sets whose membership functions are depicted in Figure 6.69.

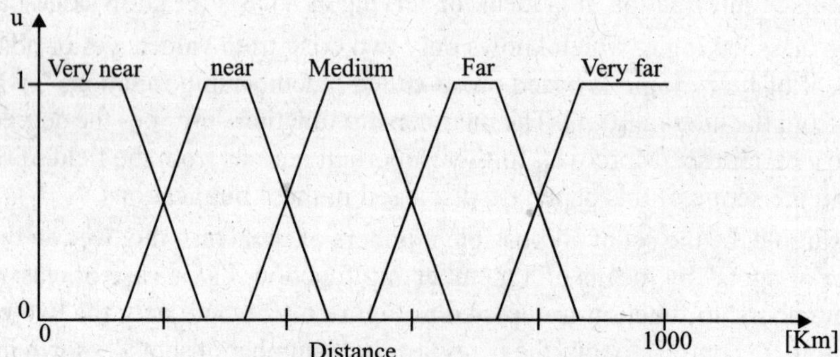

Figure 6.69: Linguistic variable "distance"

One of the essential operations of a fuzzy algorithm is inference.

The underlying knowledge is represented by rules:

Rule 1: If $X_1 = A_{11}$ ... and $X_i = A_{1i}$ ... and $X_n = A_{1n}$ then $Y = B_1$

⋮

Rule m: If $X_1 = A_{m1}$ ... and $X_i = A_{mi}$ ... and $X_n = A_{mn}$ then $Y = B_m$

$X_1,...,X_n$ and Y are linguistic variables, $A_{1i},...,A_{mi}$ are possible values of the variable X_i, i = 1,...,n, and $B_1,...,B_m$ are possible values of the variable Y.

There exist different types of fuzzy inference which can be divided into the following categories:

- MAX-MIN inference
- approximate reasoning
- plausible reasoning.

The terms approximate and plausible reasoning describe techniques which should not be confused with those used in probabilistic concepts. If the MAX-MIN inference is used, then the rules are supposed to be absolutely true, i. e., the consequent term is true to that degree to which the antecedent term is fulfilled. In contrast to this, if approximate reasoning is applied, then not every rule is supposed to be absolutely true. For every rule there is a corresponding number from the interval [0, 1] which represents the degree of confidence in this rule (0 = no confidence, 1 = full confidence). If we operate a fuzzy system, this rule weight is taken into account. If we consider plausible reasoning, then we try, on the basis of additional information, to deduce implications which are not given explicitly.

The mechanism of approximate reasoning will be explained in the following. General fuzzy systems can be described by Figure 6.70. Essentially, they consist of blocks of the types "fuzzification", "rule base", and "defuzzification", which are interconnected. The interfaces with the environment are the fuzzification and defuzzification blocks. The expression "fuzzification" describes the conversion of a crisp value s into a fuzzy set with the special membership function depicted in Figure 6.71. The expression "defuzzification" describes the conversion of a fuzzy set into a crisp value. The latter is often defined as the abscissa of the center of gravity of the area under the membership function of the fuzzy set considered (see Figure 6.72).

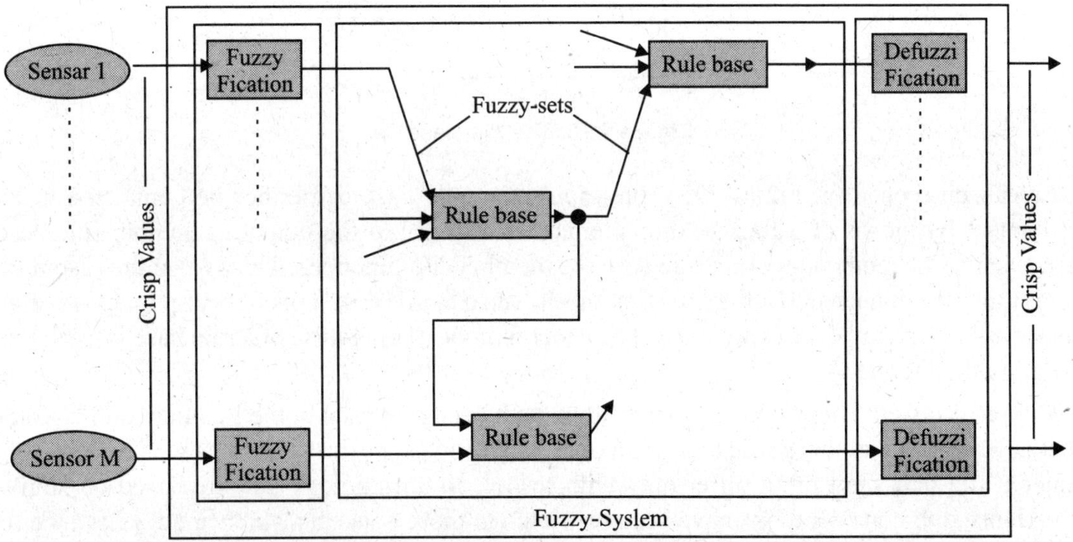

Figure 6.70: General form of a fuzzy system

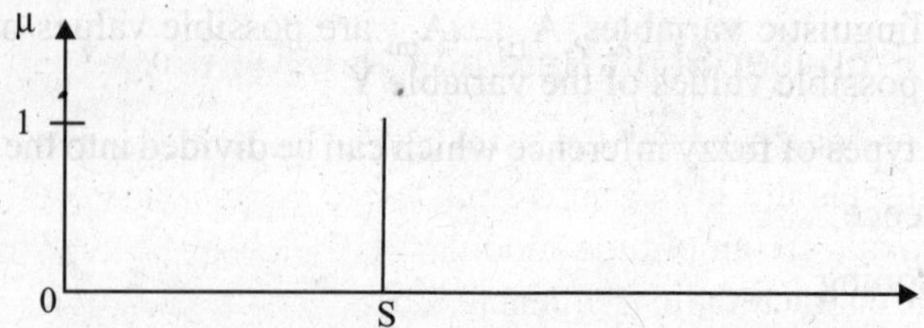

Figure 6.71: Membership function of acrisp value

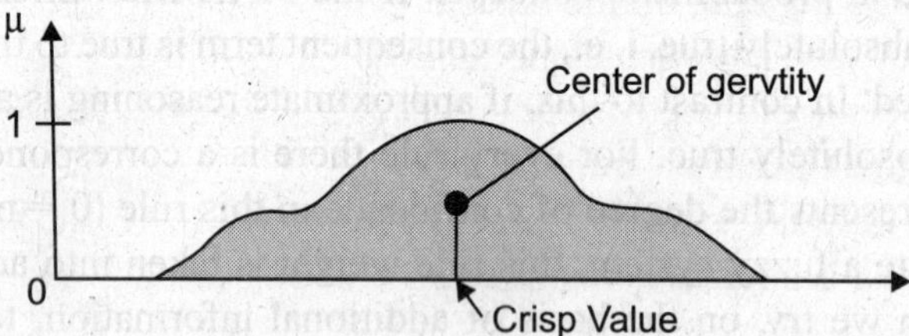

Figure 6.72: Defuzzification

The third element, the rule base, is depicted in Figure 6.73, which comprises the so-called "production rules". The output value and the input values of a rule base are membership functions of fuzzy sets. To the output and to each input of a rule base we assign a linguistic variable (designated here as 0 and I_1,..., I_N). The elements of a rule base, the production rules, have already been introduced. The computational method with which such a rule base is processed is called "fuzzy inference".

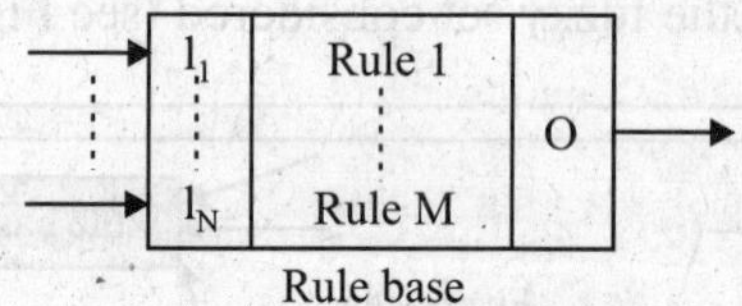

Figure 6.73: The rule base

As can be seen from Figure 6.70, the input of a rule base can either be connected to the environment by means of a fuzzification element or directly to the output of another rule base. Consequently, the input values of a rule base are membership functions. This is also the case if the input is directly connected to a fuzzification block, since in this case a membership function of the type depicted in Figure 6.71 is involved. The general mode of operation of a rule base is explained in detail in the literature.

Naturally, different types of fuzzy algorithm have been proposed in the literature and it would be beyond the scope of this paper to give an overview. However, fuzzy concepts which seem to be distinct at the first sight often differ only with respect to terminology and are based on similar ideas. Hence, our considerations have been restricted to those concepts which are of relevance for the applications introduced in this paper.

6.8.3 Detection of Propeller Shaft Rate and Number of Blades

Passive sonar systems are designed for the reception of underwater sound emitted by unknown vessels. These sound signals are either active pulses or engine noise superimposed on ambient noise. Some of these signals are amplitude-modulated, such as the sound caused by the cavitation of a ship's propeller. The characteristic frequencies of the modulating signal will be the topic of our further considerations.

The sound signals received by a passive sonar system are, on the one hand, used for the determination of target bearing and, on the other hand, for the classification of the sound emitter. One of the components of such a system demodulates the broadband noise signal for the detection of low frequency components of the envelope signal. In this context, the spectrum of the envelope signal (demodulated signal) plays an important role. This component of the signal processing algorithms of a passive sonar system is called DEMON analysis (detection of envelope modulation on noise). In this section, we examine how fuzzy technology has been applied to DEMON processing.

DEMON analysis requires the demodulation of the broadband receiver signal, and is often performed by processing the magnitude of the signal with a low-pass filter, and normalising the resulting spectrum to obtain a constant spectral noise background. The steps for the computation of the DEMON spectrum are summarized in Figure 6.74.

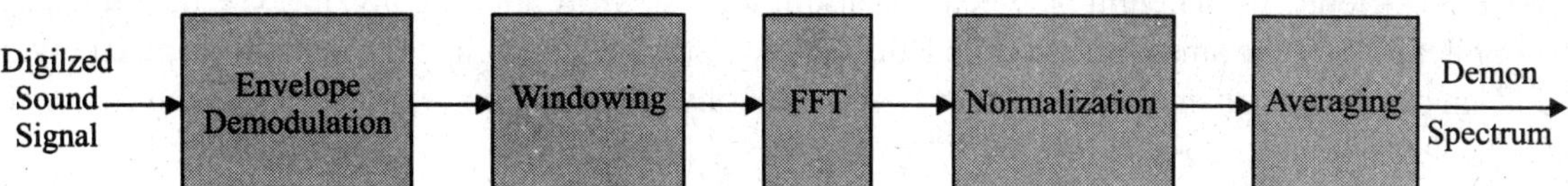

Figure 6.74: Computation of the DEMON spectrum

Human experts usually are able to determine the propeller shaft rate and the number of propeller blades of a detected vessel by analysing the waterfall representation of the DEMON spectrum (see Figure 6.75). Our aim was to replace the human expert with a fuzzy system in order to automate this classification task.

Before the corresponding fuzzy algorithm is introduced, we shall examine the features of the DEMON spectrum which enable the classification task defined above to be accomplished. As already mentioned, cavitation caused by the ship's propeller produces intensity-modulated sound signals. Mathematically, such a signal can be described by

$$\boxed{s(t) = \left(1 + \sum_{i=1}^{I} A_i \sin(i2\pi f_s t + |\phi_i) \, n(t)\right)} \qquad (1)$$

where the quantities $i * f_s$ are modulation frequencies and n(t) is a broadband noise signal. In other words, the amplitude of the noise signal n(t) is modulated by a set of harmonics. Usually, the amplitudes A_i of these sine signals are much smaller than 1. The determination of the basic frequency f_s from the time signal s(t) is one of the tasks of the DEMON analysis.

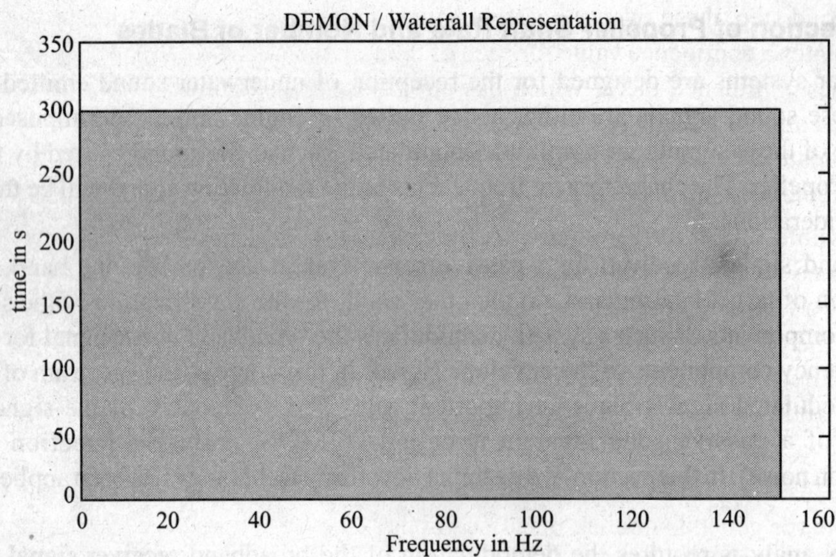

Figure 6.75: Example of the waterfall representation of a DEMON spectrum

The basic frequency f_s in Hz corresponds to the propeller shaft rate expressed in revolutions per second. Hence, f_s has to be determined. Furthermore, the number of propeller blades can be determined from the differences in height between the amplitudes A_i. More specifically, let B be the number of propeller blades; the amplitude of each Bth characteristic frequency line is then dominant. In Figure 6.76 an example is given which implies B = 3. For convenience of notation we define the frequency

$$f_B = B\, f_s. \tag{2}$$

We have developed a fuzzy algorithm that determines the two parameters f_s (propeller shaft rate) and B (number of propeller blades). DEMON spectra can become arbitrarily poor in practice so that even human experts would not be able to classify them correctly. Hence, it is desirable that the quality of the underlying DEMON spectra be indicated by the sonar system. A factor is provided by the fuzzy algorithm which makes it possible to judge the degree of confidence in the displayed values for f_s and B. Such a feature is of great importance for an operator, since nonsensical values can be suppressed by looking at the associated confidence factor.

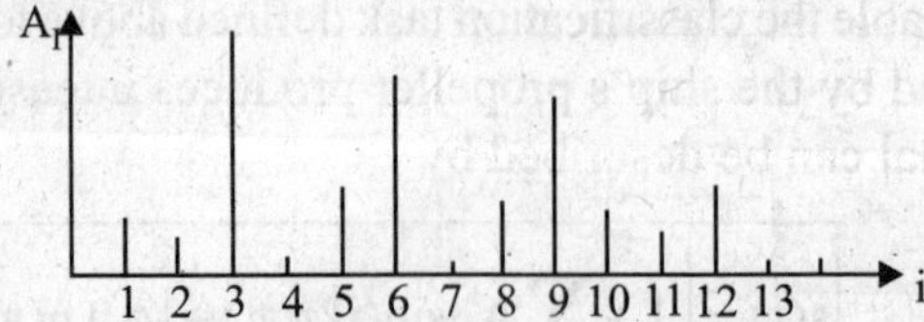

Figure 6.76: Possible distribution of the A_i for B = 3

The algorithm itself is composed of conventional procedures (such as searching for maxima, computing distances between frequency lines, or determining the median of a set of numbers) and fuzzy modules. By using conventional techniques, approximately twenty candidates for f_s are determined. The details of this procedure are of no interest within the context of the topic of this paper.

In a second step, these twenty possible values for the shaft rate are tested by a fuzzy module which calculates a confidence value for each of them. Each of these confidence values is combined with a further confidence factor which has already been determined in the first step. The latter depends on a comparison between the frequency spacing of the largest lines of the DEMON spectrum and the candidate value for f_s. The propeller shaft rate candidate with the greatest resulting confidence factor is accepted and displayed.

The possible values for the number of propeller blades 3, 4, ..., 9 are multiplied by the value just determined for f_s, which provides seven candidates for f_B (see eq. (2)). These seven candidates are tested by a fuzzy module which calculates a confidence value for each of them. The candidate for f_B with the greatest confidence factor is accepted. Finally, the global confidence factor already mentioned is derived from the two confidence factors which have been associated with the accepted values for f_s and B. The number of propeller blades results from the relation $B = f_B/f_s$, where f_B and f_s are the two accepted values.

The two fuzzy systems mentioned above are depicted in Figures 6.77 and 6.78. Obviously, they correspond to the general structure discussed in the last subsection. Both systems are connected to the environment via three input ports and one output port.

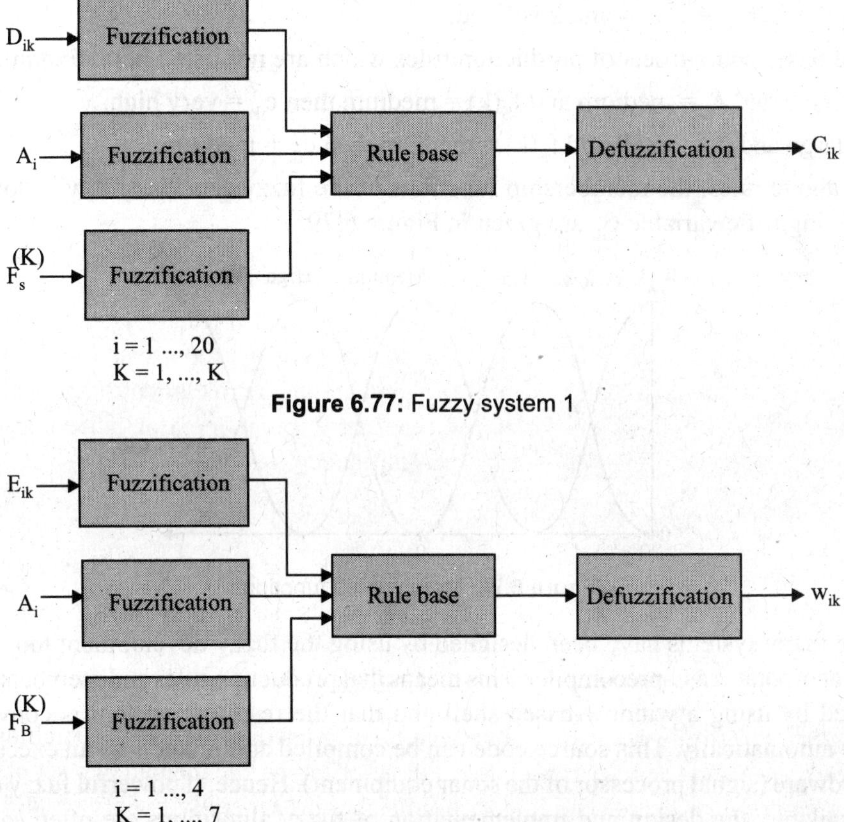

Figure 6.77: Fuzzy system 1

Figure 6.78: Fuzzy system 2

Let $f_s^{(k)}$, k = 1,...,K, be the candidates for f_s, f_i, i = 1,...,20, the frequency locations of the twenty strongest frequency lines of the DEMON spectrum, and A_i, i = 1,...,20, the corresponding amplitudes; we then define

$$\boxed{d_{ik} = \min_{q \ni N} |f_i - q\, f_s(k)|} \tag{3}$$

In other words, d_{ik} is a measure that indicates whether f_i can be interpreted as a harmonic of $f_s^{(k)}$. For each candidate $f_s^{(k)}$, the corresponding confidence factor is the mean of the output values c_{ik} of the fuzzy module, where i = 1,...,20 and k is fixed.

Similarly, $f_B^{(k)}$, k = 1,...,7, are the candidates for f_B, f_i, i = 1,...,4, the frequency locations of the four strongest frequency lines of the DEMON spectrum, and A_i, i = 1,...,4, the corresponding amplitudes.

$$\boxed{e_{ik} = \min_{q \ni N} |f_i - q\, f_B(k)|}$$

The distance is a measure that indicates whether f_i can be interpreted as a harmonic of $f_B^{(k)}$. For each candidate $f_B^{(k)}$, the corresponding confidence factor is the mean of the output values w_{ik} of the fuzzy module, where i = 1,...., 4 and k is fixed.

The rule bases contain sets of production rules which are not listed here. Examples are:

If d_{ik} = small and A_i = medium and $f_S(k)$ = medium then c_{ik} = very high.

If d_{ik} = large and A_i = small and $f_S(k)$ = medium then c_{ik} = medium.

For the above rules, the membership functions of the fuzzy sets "very low", "low", ..., "very high" of the linguistic variable c_{ik} are given in Figure 6.79.

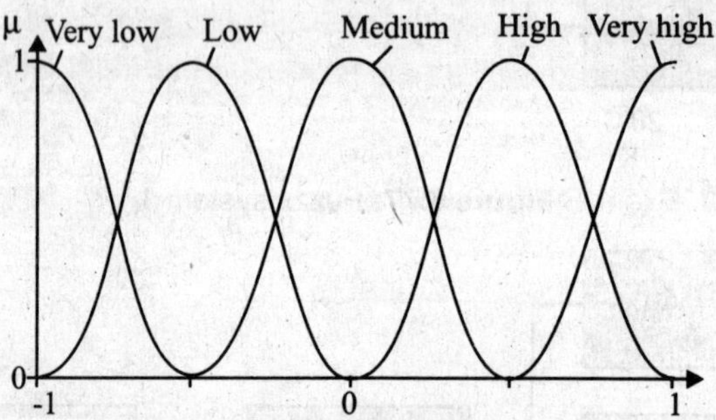

Figure 6.79: Membership functions

The two fuzzy systems have been designed by using the fuzzy development tool "*fuzzy*TECH 2.0" which incorporates a C-precompiler. This means that production rules and membership functions can be edited by using a window-based shell and that the resulting system is converted into C source code automatically. This source code can be compiled and linked into an executable file on the final hardware (signal processor of the sonar equipment). Hence, if powerful fuzzy development tools are available, the design and implementation of fuzzy algorithms are often easier than the implementation of conventional algorithms.

An example of the performance of the algorithm described above for the detection of fs and B from DEMON spectra is given in Figures 6.80 - 6.83. In Figure 6.80 an example of the waterfall representation of DEMON spectra is given where the intensity of the tracks obviously decreases with time. Note that, in contrast to the usual waterfall representations, the time and frequency axes have been interchanged to make the comparison with Figures 6.81 – 6.82 easier.

The corresponding curve of the global confidence factor, which has been determined by the fuzzy algorithm, is shown in Figure 6.81. And indeed, the decrease of the quality of the DEMON spectra with time is indicated by this curve. The propeller shaft rate in revolutions per minute and the number of propeller blades detected by the fuzzy systems are depicted versus time in Figure 6.82 and Figure 6.83, respectively. The correct values are 900 - 920 RPM and 3 blades, respectively. This performance is much better than that which has been achieved by the non-fuzzy algorithm yet used in Atlas sonar systems.

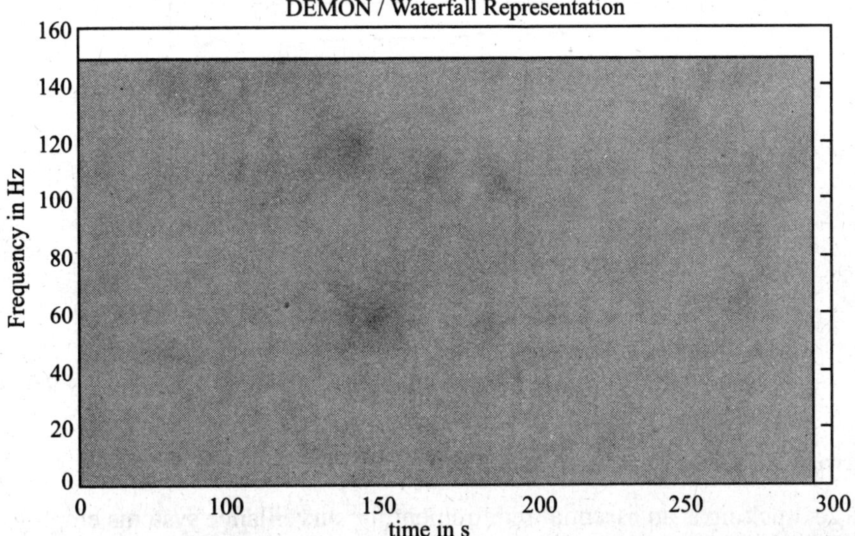

Figure 6.80: Example of the waterfall representation of DEMON spectra

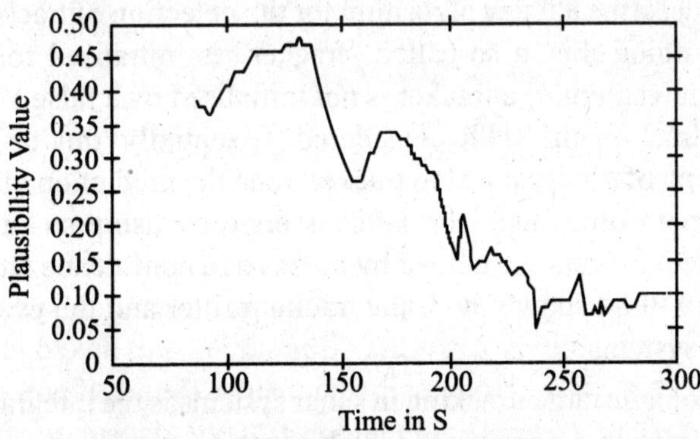

Figure 6.81: Curve of the quality factor

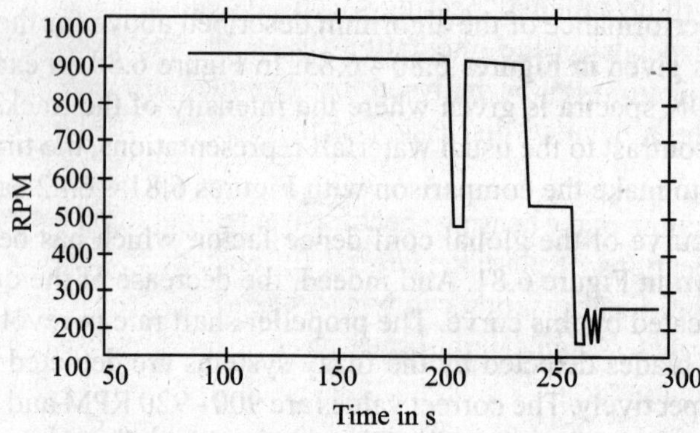

Figure 6.82: Detected propeller shaft rate / correct value » 600 RPM

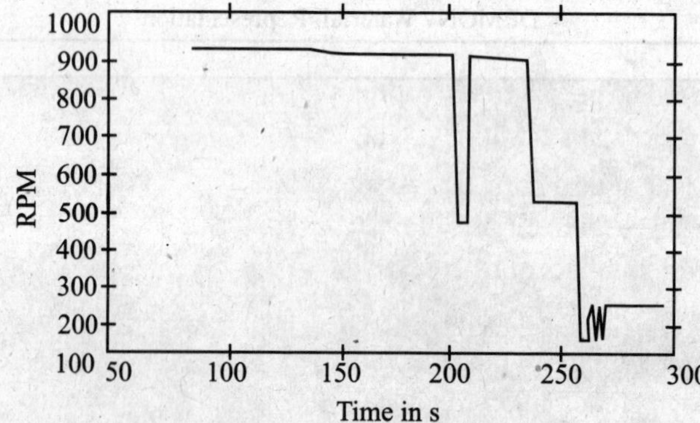

Figure 6.83: Detected number of propeller blades / correct value = 3 blades

6.8.4 Automatic Target Tracking (ATT)

Automatic target tracking is an essential requirement for surveillance systems employing multiple sensors, together with computer subsystems, to interpret an environment that includes both true targets and false alarms.

In the following, we describe a fuzzy algorithm for the detection of tracks (targets) in a bearing/time record (BTR). For doing this, a so-called "tracker" is initialised for each observed target which tries to follow its movement. If a tracker is not initialised by a false alarm, then its trajectory should correspond to a track in the BTR considered. Essentially, this task is composed of two central features. The pairing of observations to trackers, and the prediction of the bearing of already-detected targets for the next time step. The latter is done by using so-called "tracking filters". Furthermore, the initialised trackers are judged by means of a confidence factor, which is also used for their termination. As will be shown, both the tracking filter and the evaluation of the trackers can be realized by fuzzy systems.

The basic data for automatic target tracking in sonar systems is the integrated magnitude-squared response of a scanning beam in a noise field which contains moving targets. This energy versus bearing representation will be called a "bearing spectrum" and is computed for consecutive time frames of length T (T depends on the integration time). In other words, after time T (e.g. one second) a new bearing spectrum can be analysed. The computation of bearing spectra can be done in several ways; however, a detailed discussion of these various methods would be beyond the scope of this paper.

Usually, the local maxima of the bearing spectra are determined and the corresponding bearings are interpreted as the locations of possible targets. In most cases, preprocessing of the bearing spectra is necessary before local maxima can be searched for. Otherwise, too many false alarms would be accepted. Nevertheless, some of the observations are due to noise and have to be suppressed during the actual tracking phase.

The detection of tracks in the waterfall representation of the bearing spectra can be made more difficult by gaps in the tracks, local maxima of the bearing spectrum which have been caused by noise, and tracks which are not smooth curves but fluctuate randomly around the ideal curve.

The tracking of detected targets is made more difficult by the crossing of tracks. The following situations can occur:

1. The crossing of tracks, i.e., both targets maintain their courses. This does not necessarily lead to collision since two targets having the same bearing can have different ranges. Range is not taken into account by the computation of the waterfall representation of bearing spectra.
2. The touching of tracks, i.e., two tracks converge to the same point and afterwards diverge again without crossing each other. At least one of the two targets undergoes a course change at the point of touching.
3. The merging of tracks. After the tracks have merged, the two targets proceed either close together or one behind the other.

In practice, it is difficult to decide whether case 1 or case 2 is present since the corresponding patterns in the waterfall representation are very similar in both cases. Hence, further features have to be taken into account in order to make these two scenarios distinguishable. An example is given in Figure 6.84 where on the left-hand side the touching of two tracks is shown and in the middle the crossing of two tracks. However, these differences are not visible in Figure 6.84. The white areas next to the tracks are due to the fact that only local maxima have been displayed.

The automation of the target detection and tracking process is the task of the fuzzy system introduced below. It is able to distinguish between the two cases "crossing of tracks" and "touching of tracks". Short gaps in tracks are bridged automatically and the end of a track is recognised within a short time. Naturally, in the case of a poor signal-to-noise ratio, tracks are often blurred and false alarms can consequently occur. Hence, a confidence factor is assigned to each initialised tracker in order to improve the meaningfulness of the displayed results.

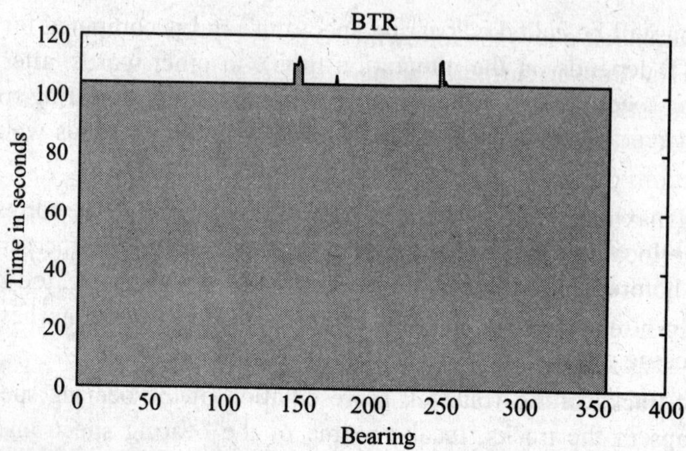

Figure 6.84: Example of the waterfall representation of bearing spectra

In general, batch or sequential approaches for automatic track detection could be considered. In the first case, the bearing spectra could be stored for a certain time interval and afterwards analysed in one step. In other words, the available three-dimensional data record (amplitude versus bearing versus time) could be processed with known pattern recognition algorithms. However, a considerable lag between signal reception and signal analysis would be the result since a time record of approximately 5-10 minutes should be available. In order to be able to respond to the current situation instantaneously, such an approach cannot even be considered. Hence, the sequential approach has been adopted which is outlined in the following. After an initialization procedure has been executed, several possible tracks have been localised, i.e., trackers have been initialised. Their current bearing is stored. By taking into account the latest history of the trackers, the respective bearing for the next time step is predicted by means of tracking filters. Usually, the latter are realised by Kalman or filters. In our approach, however, a fuzzy tracking filter has been realised. As soon as observed data is available for the new time step an observation to tracks assignment has to be performed (data association). If observations occur which cannot be assigned to one of the trackers already initiated, they are considered as the beginning of possible new tracks.

Conversely, if no observation can be associated with a tracker already in existence, then penalty points are added to a score. Two different confidence measures are assigned to each tracker. The local confidence factor describes the short term behaviour and the global confidence factor takes into account the history of the tracker. More precisely, the data association is not performed exclusively, i.e., one observation can be assigned to several trackers in the case of crossings. However, different trackers are not treated equivalently with respect to the assignment of observations. The order in which trackers are processed depends on their current ranks. The latter are newly computed after every 16th time step and depend on the counts of the local confidence factors. These local confidence factors are also newly computed after every 16th time step and additionally increase or decrease the global confidence factors. The global confidence factor of each tracker influences the size of the corresponding gate for data association and terminates the tracker if it drops below a given boundary value. In other words, it represents a measure of the quality of the respective tracker. The computation of the local confidence factors is done by a fuzzy module.

The data association itself obeys thc following rules. All existing trackers are processed in the order of their ranks. The tracker currently being considered is associated with that observation from the interior of a gate around its location which has the greatest amplitude. The assigned observation is marked. Observations which cannot be assigned to a tracker already in existence are considered as the locations of new tracks. The tracking filter predicts the bearing of each tracker for the next time step. The main component of the tracking filter is a fuzzy system. The further details of the tracking algorithm are of no interest within the context of this paper. Only the two fuzzy systems should be examined in more detail.

The fuzzy tracking filter estimates the momentary bearing rate of each of the targets already detected and predicts the corresponding bearing for the next time step (see Figure 6.85). In other words, the predicted bearing results from

$$x_p(k+1) = x_p(k) + T\, v(k), \tag{4}$$

where T is the sampling period. The bearing rate v(k) is non-linearly computed from e(k), the difference between predicted, $x_p(k)$, and observed bearing, $x_o(k)$, for the time instant k.

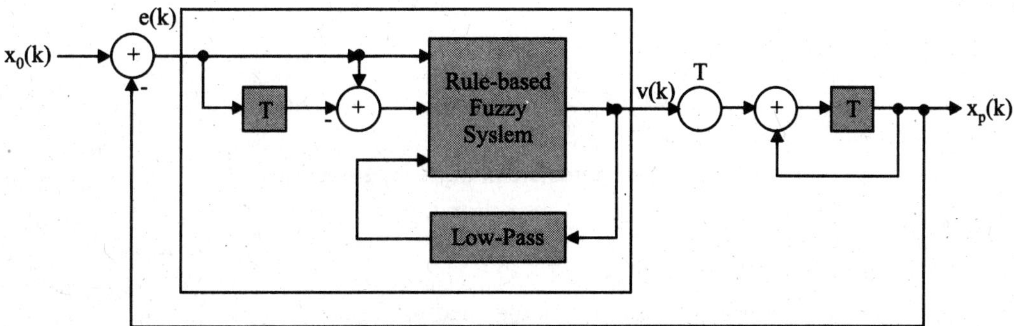

Figure 6.85: The tracking filter

The main component of the tracking filter is the rule-based fuzzy system which has the following input signals:

- prediction error e(k)
- change of e(k)
- low-pass filtered bearing rate v(k).

The use of fuzzy systems for tracking problems has been proposed.

The second fuzzy module computes the increase or decrease of the local certainty factor for each active tracker to which an observation has been assigned. It consists of two rule bases and has the following input signals:

- prediction error e(k) (difference between predicted and observed bearing),
- rank of the assigned observation (position in a list of all observations sorted with respect to the corresponding amplitude of the bearing spectrum),
- magnitude of the difference between the rank of the assigned observation and the rank of the observation assigned in the previous time step,

– magnitude of the difference between the numbers of the frequency bands in which, respectively the present and the previous observation have been localised (the bearing spectrum is computed for different frequency bands of the array signals).

The first input signal is a measure for the likelihood that the assigned observation is indeed the continuation of the track. A low rank of an observation indicates that it might be a false alarm. The third and fourth input signals are measures relating to the continuity of the observations.

Rule base 1 (cf. Figure 6.86) combines input signals 3 and 4 to an intermediate quality variable q which is fed to rule base 2. The latter computes from input signals 1 and 2 and the intermediate variable q a number v ∈ [–1, 1], which is added to the local confidence factor. Naturally, the whole set of production rules contained in the rule bases cannot be listed here. Examples are:

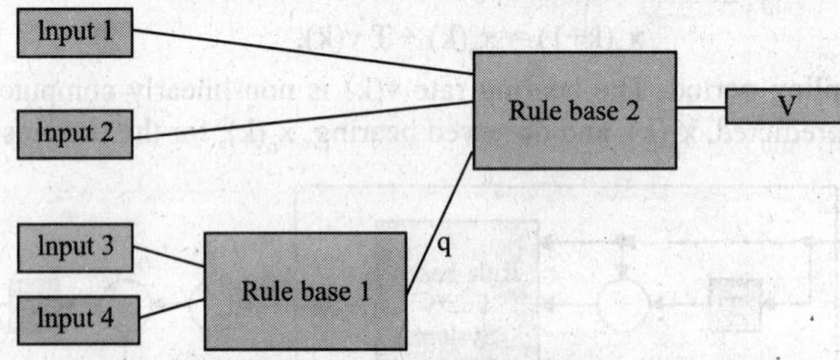

Figure 6.86: Structure of the fuzzy system

Rule base 1:

If input 3 = high and input 4 = high then q = low.

If input 3 = low and input 4 = medium then q = medium.

⋮

Rule base 2:

If input 1 = high and input 2 = high and q = low then v = very low.

If input 1 = high and input 2 = low and q = medium then v = medium.

⋮

Many trackers (usually started by false alarms caused by noise) will be terminated shortly after initialization. Hence, only those trackers whose respective global confidence factor has crossed a certain boundary value will be considered as true targets and the corresponding bearing versus time curves (tracks) will be displayed. All other trackers are suppressed.

In Figure 6.87, a simulated bearing versus time scenario (randomly fluctuating tracks with superimposed noise) is shown which contains (from left to right) the following situations:

– a track which originates at the right-hand side of the scenario,

– the touching of two tracks,

– the crossing of two tracks,

– a track with gaps,

– the touching of two tracks with a long common path,

– the origin of the first track.

The corresponding tracks detected by the automatic tracking algorithm described above are shown in Figure 6.88. Connected branches of a track are marked with the same number which distinguishes between the situations "crossing" and "touching". Obviously, the different situations have been recognised correctly by the algorithm. Only the fifth situation (touching of two tracks with long common path) produced problems in the upper part. Due to the long common path, one of the two trackers had terminated before the bifurcation had been reached. Therefore, a new traker was initialized for the left branch of the bifurcation.

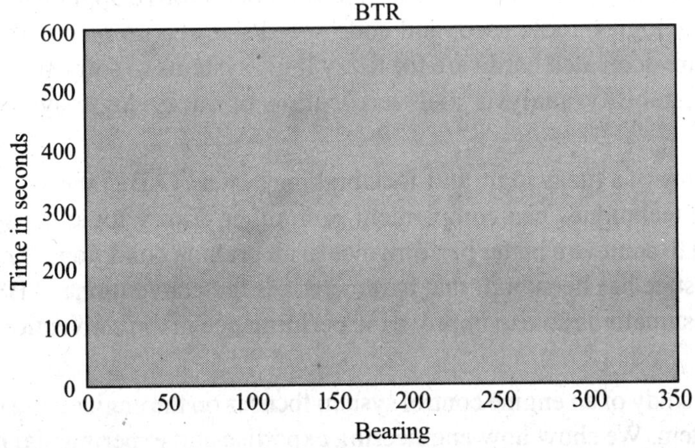

Figure 6.87: Example of the waterfall representation of bearing spectra

Fuzzy algorithm / fuzzy filter

Time in Seconds

Bearing

Figure 6.88: Detected tracks

6.8.5 Concluding Remarks

In this paper, rule-based fuzzy systems for classification problems and automatic target tracking have been discussed. Furthermore, a short introduction to fuzzy theory has been given. It should be noted that the above-mentioned applications of fuzzy logic have been already implemented in the latest generation of Atlas sonar equipment.

6.9 FUZZY LOGIC IN AUTOMOTIVE ENGINEERING

Fuzzy Logic is a powerful technology which allows designers to quickly incorporate engineering expertise into products. In this presentation, we focus on automotive applications. We will discuss development methodologies, tools used, and code speed/size requirements of three case studies. Also, we will compare dedicated hardware for fuzzy logic systems to software implementations. A final discussion of stability analysis and verification of fuzzy logic systems concludes the presentation.

The first case study of a fuzzy logic anti-lock braking system (ABS) shows how fuzzy logic and conventional design techniques can complement each other. Fuzzy logic is used to optimize the existing ABS system to achieve a better performance in all braking conditions. An estimation system for the road surface state has been built that parameterizes the conventional ABS. Road tests show that the fuzzy logic estimator is able to improve the performance of the conventional ABS, especially on dry surfaces.

The second case study of an engine control system focuses on the engineering process of building up a fuzzy logic system. We show how engineering expertise and experimental results can be used together with model-based system design to reduce time-to-market. Also, we present design technologies and tools that expedite design and support verification of fuzzy logic systems.

The third case study of an automatic gearbox control gives an outlook into future user adaptive systems. Such a system automatically identifies the user's needs in any situation and adapts the control strategies to his specific requirements and preferences. The gearbox control example shows that fuzzy logic is an enabling technology for these applications.

A fourth case study concerning an anti-skid steering system exemplifies what further innovations can result from the use of fuzzy logic in automotive engineering.

6.9.1 Fuzzy Logic In Automotive Engineering

One of the areas where fuzzy logic is a common design technology is the automotive industry. In Japan, Germany and France, cars with fuzzy logic controlled components already sell very successfully.

The reasons are manifold: first, control systems in cars are complex and involve multiple parameters. Second, the optimization of most systems is based on engineering expertise rather than mathematical models. "Good handling", "Fahrvergnügen", and "riding comfort" are optimization goals that cannot be defined mathematically. Third, automotive engineering is very competitive on an international scale. A technology that provides a competitive advantage is soon commonly used.

The following discussion assumes the reader is familiar with basic fuzzy logic design principles.

6.9.2 Anti-lock Braking Systems with Fuzzy Logic

In 1947, Boeing Corporation developed the first anti-lock braking system for airplanes as a mechanical system. Today, anti-lock braking systems (ABS) are standard equipment with most cars. They use electronic sensors that measure the speed of every wheel and microcontrollers to control the fluid pressure for the brake cylinders. Mathematical models for the braking system of a car do exist, but the interaction of the braking system with the car and the road is by far too complex to model adequately. Hence, today's anti-lock braking systems contain the engineering knowledge of years of testing in different roads and climates.

1. Fuzzy Anti-lock Braking Systems in Production

Fuzzy logic is a very efficient technology for putting engineering knowledge directly into a technical solution. Hence, it is no surprise that already many applications with anti-lock braking systems are on the market. Currently Nissan and Mitsubishi ship cars with fuzzy ABS. Honda, Mazda, Hyundai, BMW, Mercedes-Benz, Bosch and Peugeot are working on solutions.

Another reason why anti-lock braking systems benefit from fuzzy logic is the high computational efficiency of its implementation. In an ABS, the control loop time is in the order of 5 milliseconds. Within this interval, the microcontrollers must fetch all sensor data, preprocess it, compute the ABS algorithm, drive the bypass valves, and conduct the test routines. Any additional functions must be very computationally efficient. Most ABS systems use 16 bit microcontrollers, which can compute a medium size fuzzy logic system in about ½ millisecond using only about 2 KB ROM space.

2. Adapting the ABS to the Road Surface

The implementations of fuzzy logic ABS are very different. The implementation of Nippondenso, which I am now presenting as a case study, also exhibits an intelligent combination of conventional techniques with fuzzy logic. First, some basics of the braking process.

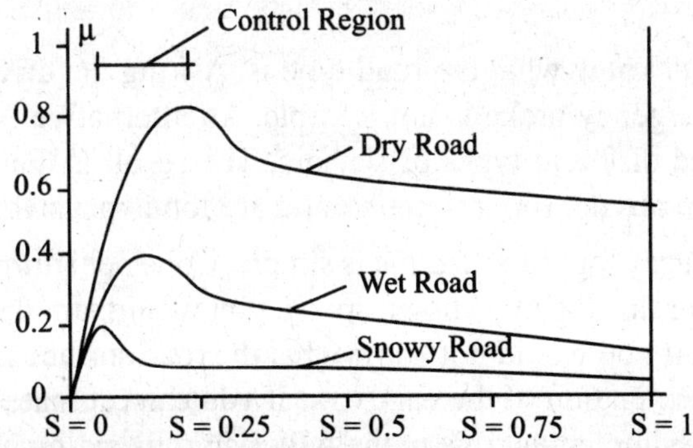

Figure 6.89: Plot of brake effect over the wheel slack s for dry, wet and snowy road surfaces (μ: friction coefficient, measure of brake effect)

If a wheel rotates exactly as fast as it corresponds to the speed of the car, the wheel is experiencing no braking effect at all. If a wheel does not rotate at all, it is blocked. This situation has two disadvantages. First, a car with blocked wheels is impossible to steer. Second, the brake effect is not optimal. The point of optimum brake effect is between these two extremes.

Road condition	Optimum slack
Dry road	0.2
Slippery or wet asphalt	0.12
Ice or Snow	0.05

Figure 6.90: The slack value for maximum brake effect depends on the type of road

The speed difference between the car and the wheel during braking is called "slack". Its definition is:

$$s = (V_{Car} - V_{Wheel}) / V_{Car}$$

where:

s : slack, always between 0 (no braking) and 1 (blocking)

V_{Car} : velocity of the car

V_{Wheel} : velocity of the wheel

Figure 6.89 plots the relation between brake effect and slack for different road surfaces. For $s = 0$, the speed of the wheel equals the speed of the car. In the case of $s = 1$, the wheel blocks completely. The curves show that the optimum brake effect lies between these two extremes. However, the point of maximum brake effect depends on the type of road. Figure 6.90 lists typical values.

3. Estimation of Road Surface using Fuzzy Logic

A conventional anti-lock braking system controls the bypass valves of the brake fluid so that the slack equals a set value. Most manufacturers program this set value to a slack of 0.1, because this is a good compromise value for all road conditions. As figures 6.89 and 6.90 show, this set value is not optimal for every road type. By knowing the road type, the braking effect could further be enhanced.

The problem is how to know what the road type is. Asking the driver to push a button on the dash board before an emergency brake is not feasible. An alternative is the use of sensors. Many companies have evaluated different types of sensors. The result is that sensors that deliver good road surface identification are not robust enough and are too expensive.

The idea of the cited fuzzy logic application is simple. Consider sitting in your own car equipped with a standard ABS. After driving at a known speed, you would jam the brake pedal such that the ABS starts to work. Even if you would not know what the road surface is like, you could now have a good guess just from the reaction of the car. Now, if you can estimate the road surface just from the car's reaction, why not implement this in the ABS using fuzzy logic?

This is just what Nippondenso did. When the ABS first detects blocking of a wheel, it starts to control the brake fluid valves so that each wheel rotates with a slack of 0.1. The fuzzy logic system then evaluates the reaction of the car to the braking and estimates the current road surface. Considering this estimation, the ABS then corrects the set value for the slack so that it achieves the best braking effect.

The fuzzy logic system only uses input data that stems from the existing sensors of the ABS. Such input variables are deceleration or speed of the car, deceleration or speed of the wheels and hydraulic pressure of the brake fluid. These input variables are an indirect indicator of the current operation point of the braking (Figure 6.89) and its behavior over time. Experiments showed that a first prototype with just six (6) fuzzy logic rules already improved performance significantly. One test track alternates from snowy to wet road. Here, the fuzzy logic ABS detected the change even during braking.

4. Other Applications of Fuzzy Logic in ABS

Due to the high competition in this area, most manufacturers are reluctant to publish any details about the technologies they use. The cited application only shows results from an experimental fuzzy logic system. The details about the final product are not published.

Also, some companies worry about the negative connotation of the word "fuzzy". As it implies "imprecision" and "inexact", manufacturers are afraid drivers could think of a "fuzzy ABS" as something inferior. Others feel threatened by the scenario in which a clever lawyer sues them by suggesting to a laymen's jury that fuzzy logic ABS is something hazardous. In Japan, where an appreciation for ambiguity lies in the culture, "fuzzy" does not have a negative connotation. In contrast, it is considered an advantage because it enables intelligent systems such as the cited application. Hence, companies are proud of its use and even use it in advertising

In Germany for example, the situation is different. Here, the concepts of fuzziness and engineering masterpiece do not fit in the public perception. Hence, most manufacturers that use fuzzy logic in ABS actually hide the fact. After all, a fuzzy logic system is only a segment of assembly code in a microcontroller once implemented. Who could actually tell that this code implements fuzzy logic? Some engineers already talk about "hidden fuzzy logic"

5. Stability of a Fuzzy ABS

Some engineers, especially those who went to a well-reputed university, argue the stability of fuzzy logic systems. In the case of the Fuzzy ABS shown, this is not an issue. The conventional ABS was considered to be stable for any slack value in the interval from 0.05 to 0.25. Hence, a fuzzy logic road surface estimator that only tunes this value to the optimum can principally not make this system unstable.

6.9.3 Engine Control with Fuzzy Logic

The control of car and truck engines becomes increasingly more complex due to higher emission standards and the constant push for higher fuel efficiency. Twenty years ago, control systems were mechanical (carburetor, distributor and breaker contact). Now, microcontroller based systems control fuel injection and ignition point. Since the control strategy for an engine depends strongly on the current operating point (revolutions, momentum,...), linear control models, such as PID, are not suitable. On the other hand, no mathematical model that describes the complete behavior of an engine exists. Because of this, most engine controllers use a look-up-table to represent the control strategy. The look-up-table is generated from the results of extensive testing and the engineer's experience.

The generation of such a look-up-table, however, is only suitable for three dimensions (2 inputs, 1 output). Also, the generation and interpretation of these look-up-tables is difficult and considered a "black art". Replacing these look-up-tables hence is a potential for fuzzy logic. Alas, most manufacturers are unwilling to publish any details on their fuzzy logic engine control solution. This is due to the fact that the rules of the fuzzy logic system contain the entire engine control knowledge of the company and are completely transparent. Hence, manufacturers are afraid that their competitors could learn too much about the solution by disassembling the fuzzy logic rules.

1. Identification of Driving Condition

The case study of an engine control system by NOK and Nissan illustrates the benefits of using fuzzy logic. Figure 6.91 sketches the components of the engine controller that contains three fuzzy logic modules. The basic idea of the system is that it first identifies the operational condition of the engine by the linguistic variable "Situation" that has the following linguistic terms:

linguistic variable Situation

{

Term 1: Start

Control strategy is that the cold engine runs smooth - ignition is timed early and the mix is fat;

Term 2: Idle

Control ignition timing and fuel injection depending on engine temperature to ensure that the engine runs smooth;

Term 3: Normal drive, low or medium load

Maximize fuel efficiency by meager mix, watch knocking;

Term 4: Normal drive, high load

Fat mix and early ignition to maximize performance - the only constraint is the permitted emission maximum;

Term 5: Coasting

fuel cut-off, depending on situation;

Term 6: Acceleration

Depending on the load, fattening of the mix

}

The determination of the linguistic variable "Situation" is a state estimation of the operation point. As "Situation" is a linguistic variable, more than one term can be valid at the same time. This allows for expressing combinations of the operational points defined by the terms. Hence, a possible value of "Situation" could be: {0.8; 0; 1; 0; 0; 0.3}. Linguistically, this value represents the driving condition *engine started just a short while ago, normal drive condition at medium or low load, slightly accelerating*. From this operation point identification, the individual fuzzy logic modules control injection, fuel cut-off, and ignition.

Similar to ABS systems described in the previous section, engine control requires a very short loop time. Some systems are as fast as 1 millisecond for an entire control loop. For this, some manufacturers design the system using fuzzy logic, but then translate it into a look-up-table for faster processing. Even though, a look-up-table is very fast to compute, the memory requirements may be prohibitive. For a look-up-table with 2 inputs and 1 output, all 8 bit resolution already requires 64 Kbytes of ROM. Restricting the resolution of the input variables to 6 bit each, the look-up-table still requires 4 Kbytes. A look-up-table with 3 inputs and 1 output, all inputs of 6 bit resolution would require ¼ Mbyte. Some engineers tried to implement a look-up-table with a very limited resolution and to use an interpolation algorithm. Comparison, however, shows that the interpolation requires about as much computing time as the fuzzy logic system itself.

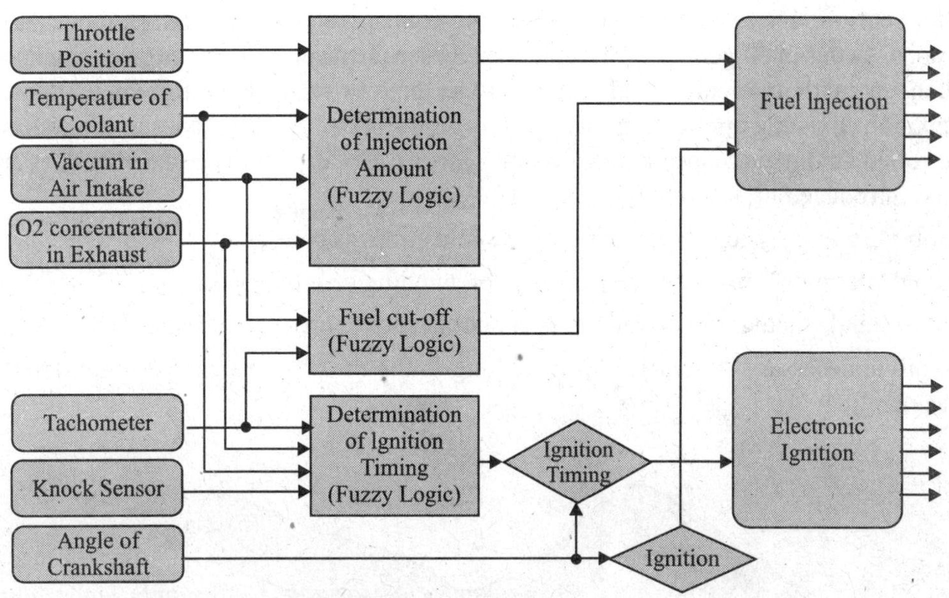

Figure 6.91: Modules of the fuzzy logic engine controller of nok

Another published application of fuzzy logic in engine control is an idle control unit by Ford Motor Corporation.

6.9.4 Adaptive 5-speed Automatic Transmission

When the first 3-speed automatic transmissions appeared on the market about 30 years ago, the engine power of most cars was just sufficient enough to keep the car in pace with traffic. The necessity of getting maximum momentum from the engine determined the shift points for the gears.

Now that most car engines can deliver much more power than necessary to keep the car in pace with traffic, automatic transmission systems have up to five (5) speeds and fuel efficiency is an important issue, plus the control is much more complex.

The higher engine power and five (5) speeds to chose from give the automatic transmission system a much higher degree of freedom. Driving at 35 mph (56 km/h), a 3-speed automatic transmission has no choice but selecting the second gear. A 5-speed automatic transmission with a powerful engine could select the second gear if maximum acceleration is required, the third gear in a normal driving condition, and the fourth gear if only a little acceleration is needed.

1. Acceleration vs. Fuel Efficiency

Unfortunately, the goal for the control strategy is in a dilemma. For maximum fuel efficiency, you must select the next higher gear as early as possible. For maximum performance, you switch to the next higher gear later. If you have a shift gear box, you can choose the strategy depending on the traffic conditions. An automatic gearbox has no understanding of the traffic conditions and the driver's wishes.

In this section, I will show how intelligent control techniques can enhance automatic transmissions. As this intelligent control technique is based on experience and engineering knowledge rather than on mathematical models, fuzzy logic proves to be an efficient technology for implementation. Existing applications are used as case studies. In 1991, Nissan introduced fuzzy logic controlled automatic 5-speed transmission systems. Honda followed one year later and GM/Saturn first introduced its solution in a car in 1993.

The job for the fuzzy logic system in these applications is similar:

- Avoid "nervous" shifting back and forth on winding or hilly roads.
- Understand whether the driver wants economical or sporty performance.
- Avoid unnecessary "overdrive" if switching to the next lower gear does not deliver more acceleration.

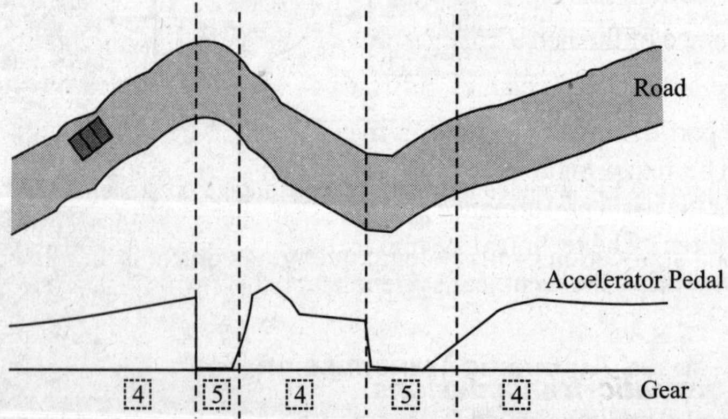

Figure 6.92: A 5-speed automatic transmission with fixed shift points always switches between 4th and 5th gear on a winding road. A driver with a shift gear box would stay in the 4th gear.

Figure 6.92 shows a typical situation on a winding road. While a driver with a shift gear box would stay in the 4th gear, a 5-speed automatic transmission switches between the 4th and the 5th gear.

The fuzzy logic controller in the automatic transmission evaluates more than just the current speed of the car. It also analyzes how the driver accelerates and brakes. To detect the condition of a winding road for instance, the fuzzy logic controller looks at the number of accelerator pedal changes within a certain period. Figure 6.93 shows the definition of the linguistic variable "Accelerator pedal changes". Also, the variance of the accelerator pedal changes is an input to the fuzzy logic controller.

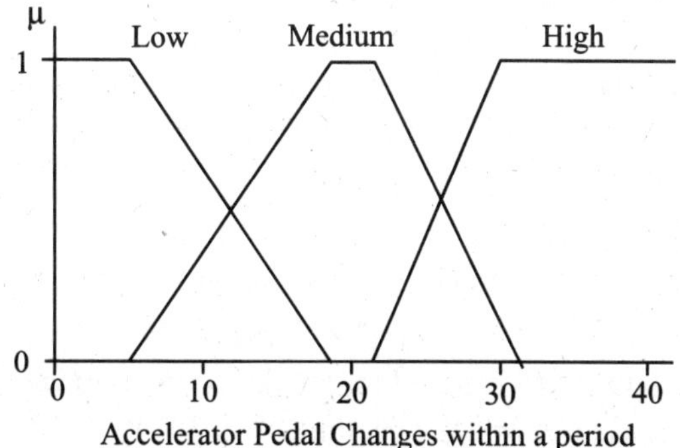

Figure 6.93: Classification of driving condition using a linguistic variable. The variable linguistically interprets the amplitude of accelerator pedal changes within a certain period

Some of the rules that estimate the driving conditions from these input variables are:

- Many pedal changes within a period indicate a fast and winding road
- Few pedal changes within a period indicate a freeway
- Many pedal changes within a period and a very high variance of the pedal changes indicate a slow and winding road
- Medium variance of the pedal changes indicates a fast and winding road
- Low variance of the pedal changes indicates a freeway

The interesting part of this application is that it uses the driver as the actual sensor for the driving condition. The fuzzy logic controller only interprets the driver's reaction to the driving condition and adapts the car's performance accordingly. This could be used as the definition of an intelligent control system. The technical system tries to understand whether the human is satisfied with its performance. If not, the technical system adapts itself to suit the needs of the human that uses it.

2. "Intelligent" Automatic Transmissions

Another example of an automatic transmission system, currently under development in Germany, shows this even better. The following situation is typical, if the driver is not satisfied with the acceleration of a car. The driver pushes down the accelerator pedal and within 1 to 1.5 seconds, he pushes the pedal down even a little bit more. This is the subconscious reaction to a non-satisfying acceleration. Most drivers do not even consciously realize that they like the car to accelerate faster. If the automatic transmission system is capable of detecting this, it could move the shift points higher to achieve more acceleration. The opposite case is similar. If the automatic transmission detects that the driver accelerates very carefully and takes the foot off from the accelerator long before red lights, chances are that the driver wants high fuel efficiency.

3. Why Fuzzy Logic?

The question remains, why do you need fuzzy logic to implement these intelligent functions? The answer is, certainly you can use other techniques to implement these control strategies. But fuzzy logic may be the most efficient one:

- Intelligent control strategies stem from experience and experiments rather than from mathematical models. Hence, a linguistic formulation is more efficient.
- Intelligent control strategies mostly involve a large number of inputs. Most of the inputs are only relevant for some specific condition. Using fuzzy logic, this input is only considered in the relevant rule. This keeps even complex systems transparent.
- Intelligent control strategies implemented in mass-market products have to be very cost efficient to be implemented. Compared to conventional solutions, fuzzy logic is often much more computational and code space efficient.

6.9.5 Anti-skid Steering Systems

Active stability control systems in cars have a long history. First, anti-locking brakes (ABS) improved braking performance by reducing the amount of brake force to what the road conditions can handle. This avoids sliding and results in shorter braking distances. Second, traction control systems that do essentially the same thing improved acceleration. Reducing engine power applied to the wheels to what the road can handle, it maximizes acceleration and minimizes tire wear. The next logical step, after skid-controlled braking and skid-controlled acceleration, is skid-controlled steering. Such an anti-skid steering system (ASS) reduces the steering angle to the amount the road can take. As such, it optimizes the steering action and avoids sliding. A sliding car is very hard to stabilize, especially for drivers not used to it.

Figure 6.94: Model car for high-speed driving experiments

Though an anti-skid steering system (ASS) makes a lot of sense from a technical point of view, such a system is hard to market. For an ABS, one can prove that it never performs worse than a traditional brake system. For an ASS, this is very hard to prove. Also, it may be difficult to sell cars that "take over the steering" in emergency situations. Even ABS faced a long period of rejection by customers, because they felt uneasy about a system inhibiting their brake action. For these reasons, it may take a long time before an ASS system is implemented in a production car. All results shown in this section stem from a research project of a German car manufacturer. As this system is one of the most complex fuzzy logic embedded systems, it shows well the potential of the technology.

1. The Test Vehicle

Real experiments were made on a modified Audi sedan and on a 20" model car (Figure 6.94). In the following, I will only present the results derived from the model car experiments. A one-horsepower electric motor powers the car, rendering the power-to-weight-ratio of a race car. This allows it to perform skidding and sliding experiments in extreme situations at high speeds. On a dry surface, the car reaches a velocity of 20 mph in 3.5 seconds with top speed up to 50 mph. The speed for most experiments ranges from 20 to 30 mph. Each wheel features individual suspension and has a separate shock absorber. The car has disk brakes and a lockable differential.

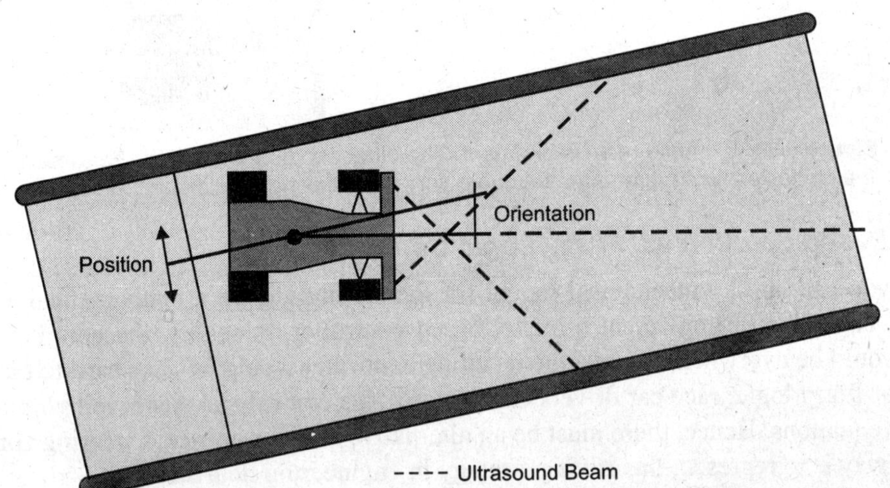

Figure 6.95: Three ultrasound sensors guide the car on the track

The controller of the car uses the motherboard of a 12 MHz notebook 286-PC connected to an interface board that drives actors and sensors. Actors are power steering servo, disk brake servo, and pulse width modulated motor control. Sensors are three ultrasound distance sensors for track guidance and infrared reflex sensors in every wheel for speed. The control loop time, from reading in sensor signals to setting the values for the actors, is 10 milliseconds.

To measure the dynamic state of the car, such as skidding and sliding, infrared sensors measure the individual speed of all four wheels. Evaluating wheel speed differences, the fuzzy logic system interprets the current situation. Three fixed mounted ultrasound sensors measure the distance to the next obstacle to the front, the left and the right. This allows for an autonomous operation of the car. Intentionally, low-cost sensors have been used in this study rather than CCD cameras and picture recognition techniques, to prove that expensive sensors can be replaced by a fuzzy logic control strategy.

Figure 6.96 shows the example of an experiment involving the model car. The obstacle (block) is placed right after the curve, so that the ultrasound sensors of the car will "see" the obstacle too late. To not hit the obstacle, the car has to decide for a very rapid turn. To optimize the steering effect, the anti-skid controller has to reduce the desired steering angle to the maximum the road can take, avoiding both sliding and hitting the obstacle.

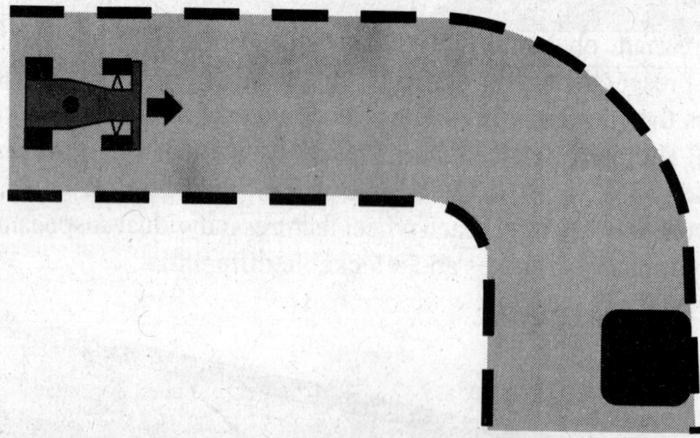

Figure 6.96: Example of an experiment. The ultrasound sensors of the car detect the obstacle placed right after the curve very late, making a quick turn necessary

2. Model Based Solution vs. Fuzzy Logic Control

In theory, you can build a mechanical model for the car and derive a mathematical model with differential equations to implement a model based controller. In reality, the complexity of this approach would be overwhelming and the resulting controller would be very hard to tune. Here is the point for fuzzy logic: race car drivers can perform this control task very well without solving differential equations. Hence, there must be an alternative way for anti-skid steering control. This alternative way is to represent the driving strategy in engineering heuristics.

Though there are multiple ways of expressing engineering heuristics, fuzzy logic has proven to be very effective, due to the following reasons:

- You can often formulate engineering heuristics in "if-then" causalities. The "if" part usually represents a certain state of a process while the "then" part represents the action to be taken in this case.
- In contrast to other methods of expressing "if-then" causalities, such as expert systems, the computation in a fuzzy logic system is quantitative rather than symbolic. In a fuzzy logic system, you use a few rules to express general situations, then the fuzzy logic algorithm deduces decisions for the real occurring situations. A conventional expert system would need a rule for each possible situation.

- In a fuzzy logic system, every element is self-explanatory. Linguistic variables are very close to the human representation of continuous concepts. Fuzzy inference and fuzzy operators combine these concepts very much the way humans do.
- Fuzzy logic is non-linear and multi-parametric by nature. So it can better cope with complex control problems that are also non-linear and involve multiple parameters.
- Fuzzy logic can efficiently be implemented in embedded control applications. Even on a standard microcontroller, a fuzzy logic system can outperform a comparable conventional solution both by code size and computing speed.

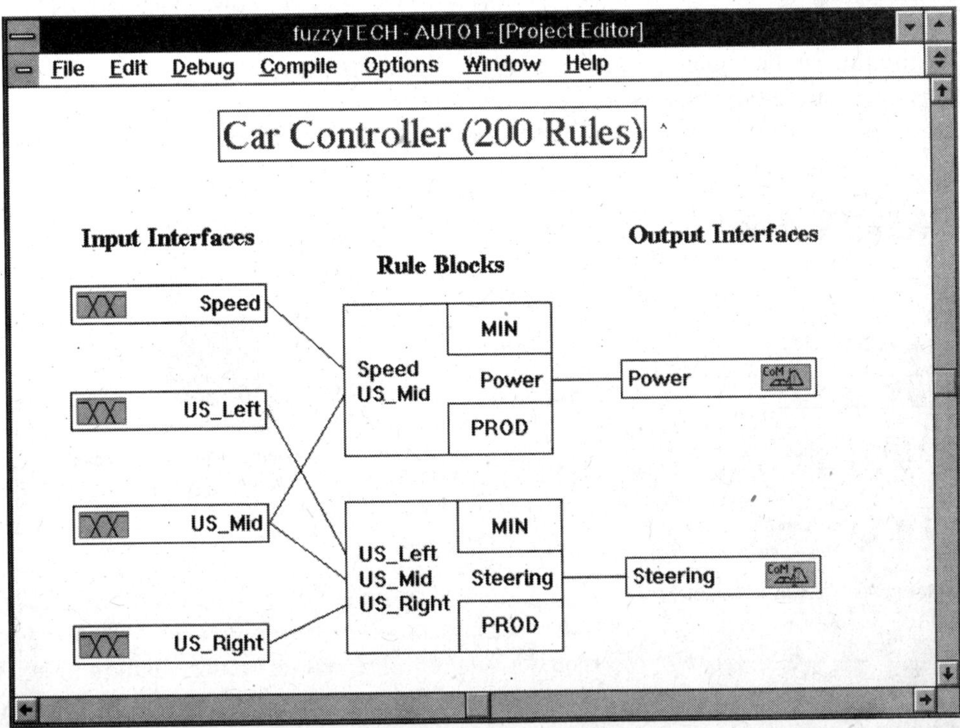

Figure 6.97: First version with 200 rules in two rule blocks. The four left boxes indicate input interfaces for sensors; the two right boxes indicate output interfaces for the actors and the two large boxes in the middle represent fuzzy logic rule blocks

3. Design and Implementation of a Fuzzy Logic Controller

Figure 6.97 shows the first version of a fuzzy logic controller for the car. The objective for this controller was autonomous guidance of the car in the track at slow speed, where no skidding and sliding occurs. In Figure 6.98, the lower rule block uses the distances measured by the three ultrasound sensors to determine the steering angle. The upper rule block implements a simple speed control by using the distance to the next obstacle measured by the front ultrasound sensor and the speed of one front wheel only. Due to the slow speeds, no skidding or sliding occurs. Hence, all wheel speeds are the same. The first version contains about 200 rules and took only a few hours to implement.

The second version of a fuzzy logic controller implements a more complex fuzzy logic system for dynamic stability control. It includes anti-locking brakes, traction and anti-skid steering control (Figure 6.99). This 600 rule fuzzy logic controller has two stages of fuzzy inference. The first stage, represented by the three left rule blocks, estimates the state variables of the dynamic situation of the car out of sensor data. The two lower rule blocks estimate skidding and sliding states out of speed sensor signals, while the upper rule block estimates position and orientation of the car in the test track. Note, the output of the left three rule blocks is linguistic rather than numerical. An estimated state of the car therefore could be: "the position is rather left, while the orientation is strongly to the right, and the car skids over the left front wheel".

The second stage, represented by the three right rule blocks, uses these estimations as inputs to determine the best control action for this situation. The upper rule block determines the steering angle, the middle one the engine power to be applied, and the lower one controls the brake. Such a two-stage control strategy is similar to the human behavior, which first analyzes the situation and then determines the action. Also, this allows for efficient optimization, since the total of 600 rule structures into 6 rule blocks that can be designed and optimized independently.

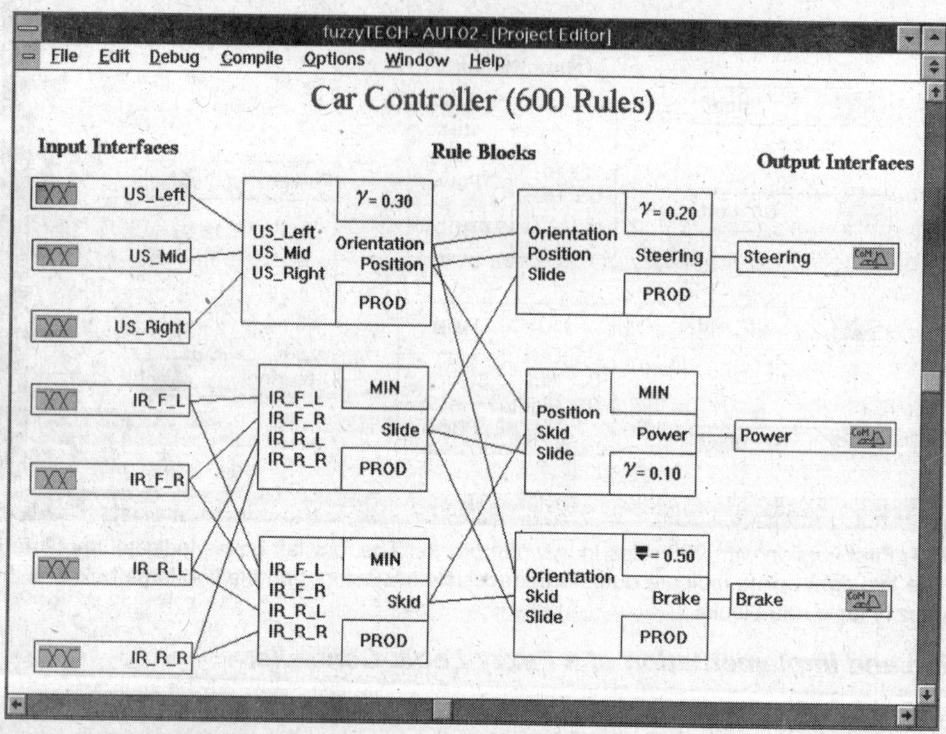

Figure 6.98: Second version of the fuzzy logic controller. the controller uses advanced fuzzy logic design technologies and contains a total of 600 rules

The first version of the controller was only able to guide the car for autonomous cruising (Figure 6.97). The second version also succeeded to dynamically stabilize the car's cruising with anti-locking brakes, traction control, and anti-skid steering. However, this version required a lot longer design time before the results were completely satisfactory. The second version also uses advanced fuzzy logic technologies, such as FAM inference and the Gamma aggregational operator.

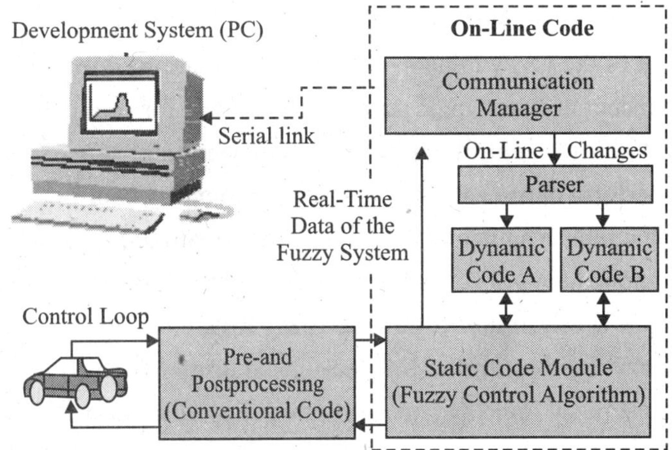

Figure 6.99: The fuzzyTECH Online Edition features both visualization of the running system and modifications "on-the-fly"

4. Online Development

The development of the fuzzy logic system involved the *fuzzy*TECH Online Edition. After the graphical definition of the system structure (Figure 6.97 and 6.98), the linguistic variables and the rule bases, then the compiler of *fuzzy*TECH generated the system as C code. This code was compiled and implemented on the PC mounted in the car. Figure 6.99 shows how the running fuzzy logic system was modified "on-the-fly" for optimization. The fuzzy logic code is separated into two segments. One contains all "static" code, which is code that does not need to be modified for system modifications. The other one contains all "dynamic" code, which is the code containing the membership functions of the linguistic variables, the inference structure, and the rules. The "dynamic" segment is doubled with only one of the segments active at a time. As such, the parser, linked to the development PC via a communications manager, can modify the inactive code segment. This allows for modifications of the running system without halting or compiling. At the same time, the entire inference flow inside the fuzzy logic controller is graphically visualized on the PC, since the communications manager also transfers all real-time data.

On the example of a anti-skid steering system, we have shown the applicability of fuzzy logic technologies for a complex control problem found in the automotive industry. The design of the fuzzy logic system has been done straightforward and without a mathematical model of the process. Existing engineering heuristics were implemented in fuzzy logic rules and linguistic variables. During optimization, we found the control strategy easy to optimize due to the linguistic representation in the fuzzy logic system. Tests and verification were expedited due to the transparency of the controller. The poor computational performance of early fuzzy logic software solutions has been overcome with the new generation of software implementation tools.

EXERCISES

1. What is the various application of fuzzy logic?
2. Explain the use of the fuzzy logic in industrial automation?
3. Explain the concept of fuzzy logic supervisory control for coal power plant?
4. Explain the fuzzy logic control design for coal power plant?
5. How we can perform optimization of a water treatment system?
6. How fuzzy logic replaces manual control in water treatment system?
7. What are the applications of fuzzy logic in chemical industry?
8. Explain the truck speed limiter control by fuzzy logic?
9. Explain the fuzzy logic controller for truck speed limiter control?
10. How we can use fuzzy logic and neuro-fuzzy in appliances?
11. Explain the use of fuzzy logic in adaptive heating system control?
12. Explain the neuro-fuzzy analysis in machines?
13. Explain the use of fuzzy logic in data analysis of environmental data for traffic control?
14. Explain the architecture of environmental data analysis?
15. Explain the use of fuzzy technology in sonar system?
16. Explain the use of fuzzy logic in automotive engineering?

CHAPTER 7

Neuro-fuzzy Systems

7.1 INTRODUCTION

Soft computing includes fuzzy logic, neural networks, probabilistic reasoning, and genetic algorithms. Today, techniques or a combination of techniques from all these areas are used to design an intelligence system. Neural networks provide algorithms for learning, classification, and optimization, whereas fuzzy logic deals with issues such as forming impressions and reasoning on a semantic or linguistic level. Probabilistic reasoning deals with uncertainty. Although there are substantial areas of overlap between neural networks, FL, and probabilistic reasoning, in general they are complementary rather than competitive. Recently, many intelligent systems called neuro fuzzy systems have been used. There are many ways to combine neural networks and FL techniques.

Neuro-fuzzy refers to combinations of artificial neural networks and fuzzy logic. Neuro-fuzzy hybridization results in a hybrid intelligent system that synergizes these two techniques by combining the human-like reasoning style of fuzzy systems with the learning and connectionist structure of neural networks. Neuro-fuzzy hybridization is widely termed as Fuzzy Neural Network (FNN) or Neuro-Fuzzy System (NFS) in the literature. Neuro-fuzzy system (the more popular term is used henceforth) incorporates the human-like reasoning style of fuzzy systems through the use of fuzzy sets and a linguistic model consisting of a set of IF-THEN fuzzy rules. The main strength of neuro-fuzzy systems is that they are universal approximators with the ability to solicit interpretable IF-THEN rules.

7.2 BASICS OF NEURAL NETWORKS

Neural networks are computing systems modeled after the brain's mesh-like network of interconnected processing elements, called *neurons*. Like the brain, the interconnected processors in a neural network operate in parallel and interact dynamically with each other. This enables the network to "learn" from the data it processes. That is, it learns to recognize patterns and relationships in the data it processes. The more data examples it receives as input, the better it can learn to duplicate the results of the examples it processes. Thus, the neural networks will change the strengths of the interconnections between the processing elements in response to changing patterns in the data it receives and the results that occur.

Thus, a neural network can be defined as a network of many simple processors (called units) each possibly having a small amount of local memory. The units are connected by communication channels (called connections), that usually carry numeric (as opposed to symbolic) data, encoded by any of various means. The units operate only on their local data and on the inputs they receive via the connections. The restriction to local operations is often relaxed during training. Most neural networks have training rules whereby the weights of connections are adjusted on the basis of data. In other words, neural networks learn from examples to recognize dogs and exhibit some capability for generalization beyond the training data.

In principle, neural networks can compute any computable function; i.e. they can do everything that a normal digital computer can do or even more. In practice, neural networks are especially useful for classification and function approximation or mapping problems that are tolerant of some imprecision and have a lot of training data available.

Neural networks can be implemented on microcomputers and other traditional computer systems by using software packages that simulate the activity of a neural network. In addition, special-purpose neural net microprocessor chips are being used in specific application areas such as military weapons systems, image processing, and voice recognition. Other areas of application include signature verification, investment forecasting, data mining, and manufacturing quality control.

7.3 ARTIFICIAL NEURAL NETWORK (ANN)

An artificial neural network is a system based on the operation of biological neural networks, in other words, is an emulation of biological neural system. Why would be necessary the implementation of artificial neural networks? Although computing these days is truly advanced, there are certain tasks that a program made for a common microprocessor is unable to perform; even so a software implementation of a neural network can be made with their advantages and disadvantages.

7.3.1 Advantages

Following are the advantages of ANN:

1. A neural network can perform tasks that a linear program can not.
2. When an element of the neural network fails, it can continue without any problem by their parallel nature.
3. A neural network learns and does not need to be reprogrammed.
4. It can be implemented in any application.
5. It can be implemented without any problem.

7.3.2 Disadvantages

Following are the disadvantages of ANN:

1. The neural network needs training to operate.
2. The architecture of a neural network is different from the architecture of microprocessors therefore needs to be emulated.
3. Requires high processing time for large neural networks.
4. Another aspect of the artificial neural networks is that there are different architectures, which consequently requires different types of algorithms, but despite to be an apparently complex system, a neural network is relatively simple.

Artificial neural networks (ANN) are among the newest signal-processing technologies in the engineer's toolbox. The field is highly interdisciplinary, but our approach will restrict the view to the engineering perspective. In engineering, neural networks serve two important functions: as pattern classifiers and as nonlinear adaptive filters. We will provide a brief overview of the theory, learning rules, and applications of the most important neural network models. Definitions and Style of Computation An Artificial Neural Network is an adaptive, most often nonlinear system that learns to perform a function (an input/output map) from data. Adaptive means that the system parameters are changed during operation, normally called the training phase. After the training phase the Artificial Neural Network parameters are fixed and the system is deployed to solve the problem at hand (the testing phase).

The Artificial Neural Network is built with a systematic step-by-step procedure to optimize a performance criterion or to follow some implicit internal constraint, which is commonly referred to as the learning rule. The input/output training data are fundamental in neural network technology, because they convey the necessary information to "discover" the optimal operating point. The nonlinear nature of the neural network processing elements (PEs) provides the system with lots of flexibility to achieve practically any desired input/output map, i.e., some Artificial Neural Networks are universal mappers . There is a style in neural computation that is worth describing.

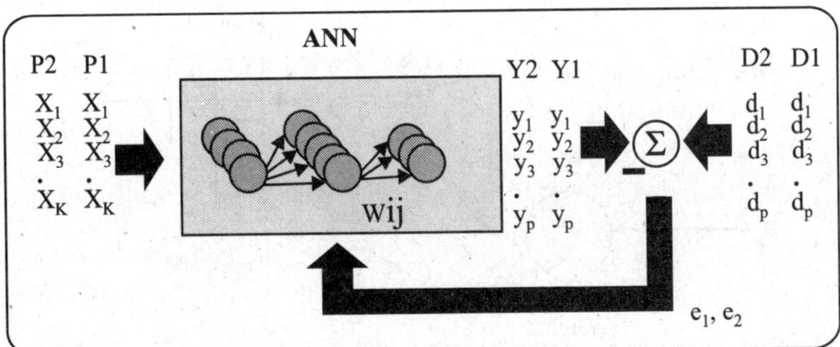

Figure 7.1: Working of artificial neuron

An input is presented to the neural network and a corresponding desired or target response set at the output (when this is the case the training is called supervised). An error is composed from the difference between the desired response and the system output. This error information is fed back to the system and adjusts the system parameters in a systematic fashion (the learning rule). The process is repeated until the performance is acceptable. It is clear from this description that the performance hinges heavily on the data. If one does not have data that cover a significant portion of the operating conditions or if they are noisy, then neural network technology is probably not the right solution. On the other hand, if there is plenty of data and the problem is poorly understood to derive an approximate model, then neural network technology is a good choice. This operating procedure should be contrasted with the traditional engineering design, made of exhaustive subsystem specifications and intercommunication protocols.

In artificial neural networks, the designer chooses the network topology, the performance function, the learning rule, and the criterion to stop the training phase, but the system automatically adjusts the parameters. So, it is difficult to bring a priori information into the design, and when the system does not work properly it is also hard to incrementally refine the solution. But ANN-based solutions are extremely efficient in terms of development time and resources, and in many difficult problems artificial neural networks provide performance that is difficult to match with other technologies. Denker 10 years ago said that "artificial neural networks are the second best way to implement a solution" motivated by the simplicity of their design and because of their universality, only shadowed by the traditional design obtained by studying the physics of the problem. At present, artificial neural networks are emerging as the technology of choice for many applications, such as pattern recognition, prediction, system identification, and control.

7.4 ELEMENTS OF ARTIFICIAL NEURAL NETWORKS

An artificial neuron as shown in Figure 7.2, is the basic element of a neural network. It consists of three basic components that include weights, thresholds, and a single activation function.

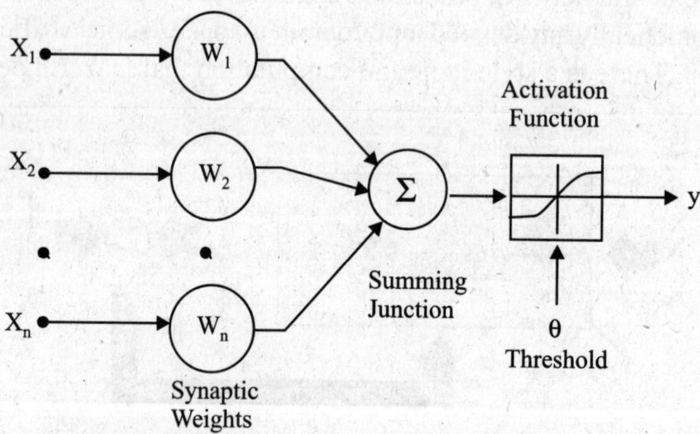

Figure 7.2: Basic elements of an artificial neuron

7.4.1 Weighting Factors

The values W_1, W_2, W_3,......,W_n are weight factors associated with each node to determine the strength of input row vector $X = [x_1, x_2, x_3, \ldots, x_n]^T$. Each input is multiplied by the associated weight of the neuron connection X^TW. Depending upon the activation function, if the weight is positive, X^TW commonly excites the node output; whereas, for negative weights, X^TW tends to inhibit the node output.

7.4.2 Threshold

The node's internal threshold è is the magnitude offset that affects the activation of the node output y as follows:

$$y = \sum_{i=1}^{n} (X_i W_i) - \theta \qquad (7.1)$$

7.4.3 Activation Function

In this subsection, five of the most common activation functions are presented. An activation function performs a mathematical operation on the signal output. More sophisticated activation functions can also be utilized depending upon the type of problem to be solved by the network.

7.5 NETWORK ARCHITECTURES

Two or more of the neurons shown earlier can be combined in a layer, and a particular network could contain one or more such layers. First consider a single layer of neurons.

7.5.1 A Layer of Neurons

A one-layer network with *R* input elements and S neuron follows. Inputs Layer of Neurons

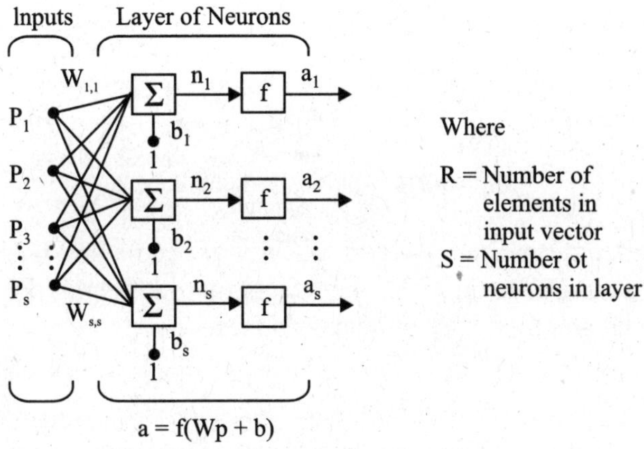

Figure 7.3: Input-layer neural network

In this network, each element of the input vector p is connected to each neuron input through the weight matrix W. The ith neuron has a summer that gathers its weighted inputs and bias to form its own scalar output n(i). The various n(i) taken together form an S-element net input vector n.

Finally, the neuron layer outputs form a column vector a. The expression for a is shown at the bottom of the figure.

Note that it is common for the number of inputs to a layer to be different from the number of neurons (i.e., R is not necessarily equal to S). A layer is not constrained to have the number of its inputs equal to the number of its neurons.

You can create a single (composite) layer of neurons having different transfer functions simply by putting two of the networks shown earlier in parallel. Both networks would have the same inputs, and each network would create some of the outputs.

The input vector elements enter the network through the weight matrix **W**.

$$w = \begin{bmatrix} W_{1,1} & W_{1,2} & \cdots & W_{1,R} \\ W_{2,1} & W_{2,2} & \cdots & W_{2,R} \\ & & & \\ W_{S,1} & W_{S,2} & \cdots & W_{S,R} \end{bmatrix}$$

Note that the row indices on the elements of matrix **W** indicate the destination neuron of the weight, and the column indices indicate which source is the input for that weight. Thus, the indices in $w_{1,2}$ say that the strength of the signal from the second input element to the first (and only) neuron is w1, 2.

The S neuron R input one-layer network also can be drawn in abbreviated notation.

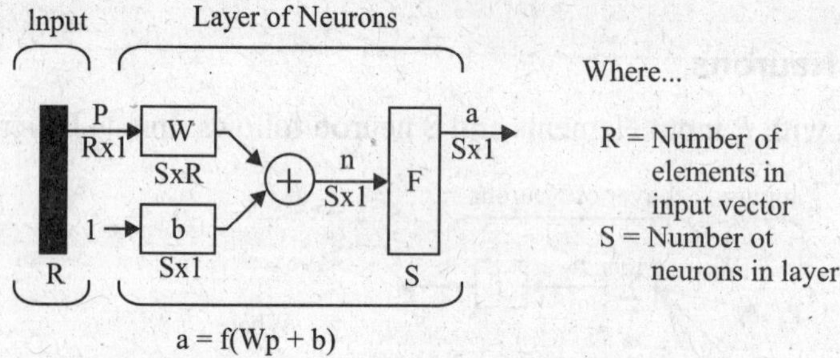

Figure 7.4: Abbreviated notation

Here **p** is an *R* length input vector, **W** is an *SxR* matrix, and **a** and **b** are *S* length vectors. As defined previously, the neuron layer includes the weight matrix, the multiplication operations, the bias vector **b**, the summer, and the transfer function boxes.

7.5.2 Inputsand Layers

To describe networks having multiple layers, the notation must be extended. Specifically, it needs to make a distinction between weight matrices that are connected to inputs and weight matrices that are connected between layers. It also needs to identify the source and destination for the weight matrices.

We will call weight matrices connected to inputs *input weights;* we will call weight matrices coming from layer outputs *layer weights.* Further, superscripts are used to identify the source (second index) and the destination (first index) for the various weights and other elements of the network. To illustrate, the one-layer multiple input network shown earlier is redrawn in abbreviated form below.

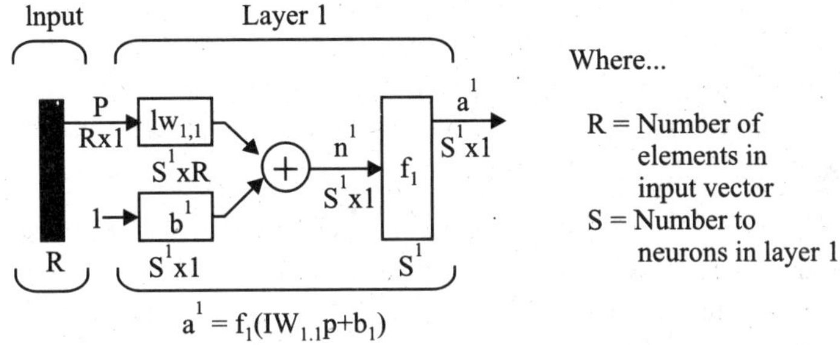

Figure 7.5: Inputs and layers

As you can see, the weight matrix connected to the input vector **p** is labeled as an input weight matrix (**IW**^{1,1}) having a source 1 (second index) and a destination 1 (first index). Elements of layer 1, such as its bias, net input, and output have a superscript 1 to say that they are associated with the first layer. "Multiple Layers of Neurons" uses layer weight (**LW**) matrices as well as input weight (**IW**) matrices.

7.5.3 Multiple Layers of Neurons

A network can have several layers. Each layer has a weight matrix W, a bias vector b, and an output vector a. To distinguish between the weight matrices, output vectors, etc., for each of these layers in the figures, the number of the layer is appended as a superscript to the variable of interest. You can see the use of this layer notation in the three-layer network shown below, and in the equations at the bottom of the figure.

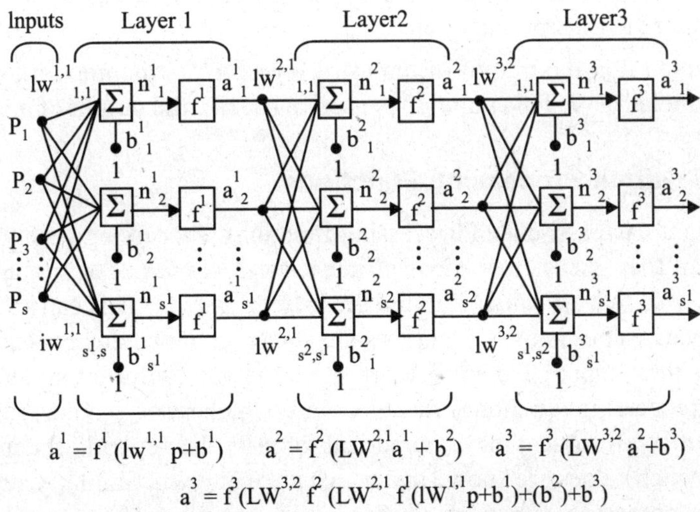

Figure 7.6: Multiple layers of neurons

The network shown above has R^1 inputs, S^1 neurons in the first layer, S^2 neurons in the second layer, etc. It is common for different layers to have different numbers of neurons. A constant input 1 is fed to the bias for each neuron. Note that the outputs of each intermediate layer are the inputs to the following layer. Thus layer 2 can be analyzed as a one-layer network with S^1 inputs, S^2 neurons, and an S^2xS^1 weight matrix W^2. The input to layer 2 is a^1; the output is a^2. Now that all the vectors and matrices of layer 2 have been identified, it can be treated as a single-layer network on its own. This approach can be taken with any layer of the network.

The layers of a multilayer network play different roles. A layer that produces the network output is called an *output layer*. All other layers are called *hidden layers*. The three-layer network shown earlier has one output layer (layer 3) and two hidden layers (layer 1 and layer 2). Some authors refer to the inputs as a fourth layer. This toolbox does not use that designation. The same three-layer network can also be drawn using abbreviated notation.

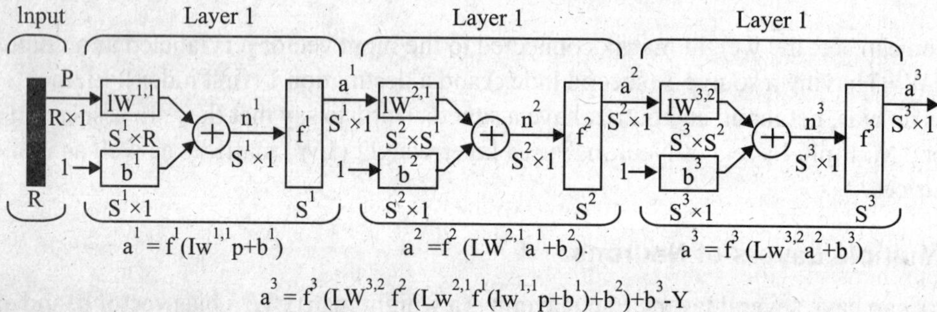

Figure 7.7: Abbreviated notation of multiple layers neural network

Multiple-layer networks are quite powerful. For instance, a network of two layers, where the first layer is sigmoid and the second layer is linear, can be trained to approximate any function (with a finite number of discontinuities) arbitrarily well. This kind of two-layer network is used extensively in Chapter 3, "Backpropagation."

Here it is assumed that the output of the third layer, $\mathbf{a}^3$, is the network output of interest, and this output is labeled as $\mathbf{y}$. This notation is used to specify the output of multilayer networks.

7.5.4 Input and Output Processing Functions

Network inputs might have associated processing functions. Processing functions transform user input data to a form that is easier or more efficient for a network.For instance, map min max transforms input data so that all values fall into the interval [–1, 1]. This can speed up learning for many networks. Remove constant rows removes the values for input elements that always have the same value because these input elements are not providing any useful information to the network. The third common processing function is fix unknowns, which recodes unknown data (represented in the user's data with Null values) into a numerical form for the network. fix unknowns preserves information about which values are known and which are unknown. Similarly, network outputs can also have associated processing functions. Output processing functions are used to transform user-provided target vectors for network use. Then, network outputs are reverse-processed using the same functions to produce output data with the same characteristics as the original user-provided targets.

7.6 NEURO FUZZY SYSTEM

Fuzzy neural network or **neuro-fuzzy system** is a learning machine that finds the parameters of a fuzzy system (i.e., fuzzy sets, fuzzy rules) by exploiting approximation techniques from neural networks.

7.7 COMBINING FUZZY SYSTEMS WITH NEURAL NETWORKS

Both neural networks and fuzzy systems have some things in common. They can be used for solving a problem (e.g. pattern recognition, regression or density estimation) if there does not exist any mathematical model of the given problem. They solely do have certain disadvantages and advantages which almost completely disappear by combining both concepts.

Neural networks can only come into play if the problem is expressed by a sufficient amount of observed examples. These observations are used to train the *black box*. On the one hand no prior knowledge about the problem needs to be given. On the other hand, however, it is not straightforward to extract comprehensible rules from the neural network's structure.

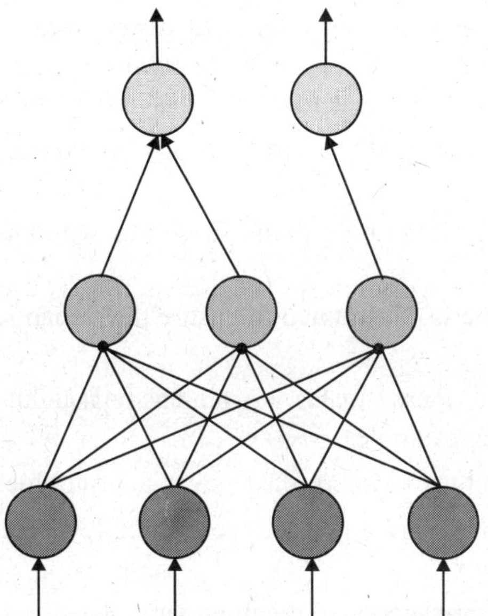

Figure 7.8: The architecture of a neuro-fuzzy system

On the contrary, a fuzzy system demands linguistic rules instead of learning examples as prior knowledge. Furthermore the input and output variables have to be described linguistically. If the knowledge is incomplete, wrong or contradictory, then the fuzzy system must be tuned. Since there is not any formal approach for it, the tuning is performed in a heuristic way. This is usually very time consuming and error-prone.

Table 7.1: Comparison of neural control and fuzzy control

Neural Networks	Fuzzy Systems
no mathematical model necessary	no mathematical model necessary
learning from scratch	apriori knowledge essential
several learning algorithms	not capable to learn
black-box behavior	simple interpretation and implementation

It is desirable for fuzzy systems to have an automatic adaption procedure which is comparable to neural networks. As it can be seen in Table 7.1, combining both approaches should unite advantages and exclude disadvantages.

7.7.1 Characteristics

Compared to a common neural network, connection weights and propagation and activation functions of fuzzy neural networks differ a lot. Although there are many different approaches to model a fuzzy neural network (Buckley and Hayashi, 1994, 1995; Nauck and Kruse, 1996), most of them agree on certain characteristics such as the following:

- A neuro-fuzzy system based on an underlying fuzzy system is trained by means of a data-driven learning method derived from neural network theory. This heuristic only takes into account local information to cause local changes in the fundamental fuzzy system.
- It can be represented as a set of fuzzy rules at any time of the learning process, i.e., before, during and after.
  - Thus the system might be initialized with or without prior knowledge in terms of fuzzy rules.
- The learning procedure is constrained to ensure the semantic properties of the underlying fuzzy system.
- A neuro-fuzzy system approximates a n-dimensional unknown function which is partly represented by training examples.
  - Fuzzy rules can thus be interpreted as vague prototypes of the training data.
- A neuro-fuzzy system is represented as special three-layer feedforward neural network as it is shown in Figure 7.8.
  - The first layer corresponds to the input variables.
  - The second layer symbolizes the fuzzy rules.
  - The third layer represents the output variables.
  - The fuzzy sets are converted as (fuzzy) connection weights.

– Some approaches also use five layers where the fuzzy sets are encoded in the units of the second and fourth layer, respectively. However, these models can be transformed into a three-layer architecture.

One can basically distinguish between three different kinds of fuzzy neural networks, i.e., cooperative, concurrent and hybrid FNNs.

7.8 COOPERATIVE FUZZY NEURAL NETWORK

In the case of cooperative neural fuzzy systems, both artificial neural network and fuzzy system work independently from each other. The ANN tries to learn the parameters from the fuzzy system. This can be either performed offline or online while the fuzzy system is applied. Figure 7.9 depicts four different kinds of cooperative fuzzy neural networks.

The upper left fuzzy neural network learns fuzzy set from given training data. This is usually performed by fitting membership functions with a neural network. The fuzzy sets are then determined offline. They are then utilized to form the fuzzy system by fuzzy rules that are given (not learned) as well.

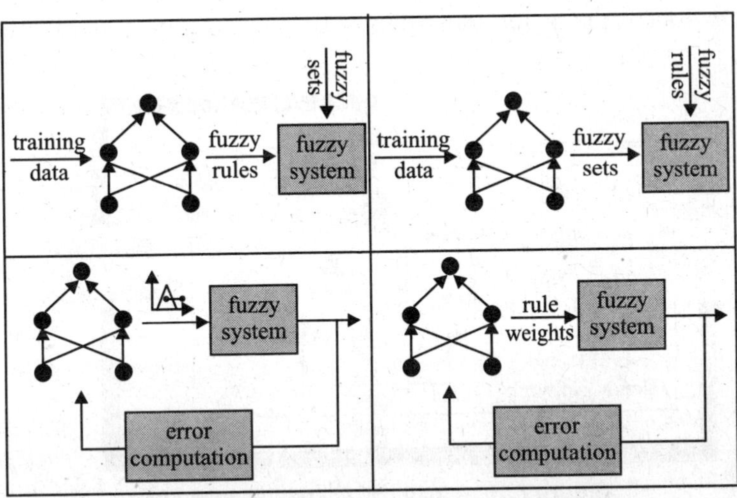

Figure 7.9: Different cooperative fuzzy neural networks

The upper right neuro-fuzzy system determines fuzzy rules from training data by a neural network. Here as well, the neural networks learns offline before the fuzzy system is initialized. The rule learning usually done by clustering on self-organizing feature maps (Bezdek et al., 1992; Vuorimaa, 1994). It is also possible to apply fuzzy clustering methods to obtain rules.

In the lower left neuro-fuzzy model, the system learns all membership function parameters online, i.e., while the fuzzy system is applied. Thus initially fuzzy rules and membership functions must be defined beforehand. Moreover, the error has to be measured in order to improve and guide the learning step.

The lower right one determines rule weights for all fuzzy rules by a neural network. This can be done online and offline. A rule weight is interpreted as the influence of a rule (Kosko, 1992). They are multiplied with the rule output. In (Nauck et al., 1997) the authors argue that the semantics of rule weights are not clearly defined. They could be replaced by modified membership functions. However, this could destroy the interpretation of fuzzy sets. Moreover, identical linguistic values might be represented differently in dissimilar rules.

7.9 HYBRID FUZZY NEURAL NETWORK

Hybrid neuro-fuzzy systems are homogeneous and usually resemble neural networks. Here, the fuzzy system is interpreted as special kind of neural network. The advantage of such hybrid NFS is its architecture since both fuzzy system and neural network do not have to communicate any more with each other. They are one fully fused entity. These systems can learn online and offline. Figure 7.10 shows such a hybrid FNN.

The rule base of a fuzzy system is interpreted as a neural network. Fuzzy sets can be regarded as weights whereas the input and output variables and the rules are modeled as neurons. Neurons can be included or deleted in the learning step. Finally, the neurons of the network represent the fuzzy knowledge base. Obviously, the major drawbacks of both underlying systems are thus overcome.

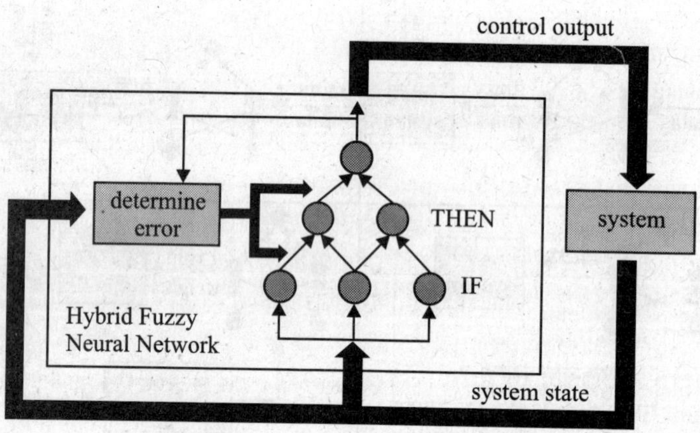

Figure 7.10: A hybrid fuzzy neural network

In order to build a fuzzy controller, membership functions which express the linguistic terms of the inference rules have to be defined. In fuzzy set theory, there does not exist any formal approach to define these functions. Any shape (e.g., triangular, Gaussian) can be considered as membership function with an arbitrary set of parameters. Thus the optimization of these functions in terms of generalizing the data is very important for fuzzy systems. Neural networks can be used to solve this problem.

By fixing a distinct shape of the membership functions, say triangular, the neural network must optimize their parameters by gradient descent (Nomura et al., 1992). Thus, aside information about the shape of the membership functions, training data must be available as well.

Another approach (Hayashi et al., 1992) is to group the training data $\{(x_i, y_i)| x_i \in X, y_i \in Y, i = 1, 2,\ldots, l\}$ into M clusters. Every cluster represents a rule R_m where m= 1,2,..., M. Hence these rules are not defined linguistically but rather by crisp data points $x = (x_1, x_2,\ldots, x_n)$. Thus a neural network with n input units, hidden layers and m output units might be applied to train on the pre-defined clusters. For testing, an arbitrary pattern x is presented to the trained neural network. Every output unit m will return a degree to which extend x may fit to the antecedent of rule R_m.

To guarantee the characteristics of a fuzzy system, the learning algorithm must enforce the following mandatory constraints:

- Fuzzy sets must stay normal and convex.
- Fuzzy sets must not exchange their relative positions (they must not *pass* each other).
- Fuzzy sets must always overlap.

Additionally there do exist some optional constraints like the following:

- Fuzzy sets must stay symmetric.
- The membership degrees must sum up to 1.

An important hybrid fuzzy neural network has been introduced in (Berenji, 1992). The ARIC (approximate reasoning-based intelligent control) is presented as a neural network where a prior defined rule base is tuned by updating the network's prediction. Thus the advantages of fuzzy systems and neural networks are easily combined as presented in Table 7.1.

7.10 PROPERTIES OF NEURO FUZZY SYSTEMS

Modern neuro-fuzzy systems are usually represented as special multilayer feedforward neural networks (see for example models like ANFIS, NEFCON). However, fuzzifications of other neural network architectures are also considered, for example self—organizing feature maps. In those neuro—fuzzy networks, connection weights and propagation and activation functions differ from common neural networks.

Although there are a lot of different approaches, we usually use the term *neuro—fuzzy system* for approaches which display the following properties:

1. A neuro-fuzzy system is based on a fuzzy system which is trained by a learning algorithm derived from neural network theory. The (heuristical) learning procedure operates on local information, and causes only local modifications in the underlying fuzzy system.
2. A neuro-fuzzy system can be viewed as a 3-layer feedforward neural network. The first layer represents input variables, the middle (hidden) layer represents fuzzy rules and the third layer represents output variables. Fuzzy sets are encoded as (fuzzy) connection weights. It is not necessary to represent a fuzzy system like this to apply a learning algorithm to it. However, it can be convenient, because it represents the data flow of input processing and learning within the model.

   Remark: Sometimes a 5-layer architecture is used, where the fuzzy sets are represented in the units of the second and fourth layer.

3. A neuro-fuzzy system can be always (i.e.\ before, during and after learning) interpreted as a system of fuzzy rules. It is also possible to create the system out of training data from scratch, as it is possible to initialize it by prior knowledge in form of fuzzy rules. ***Remark:*** Not all neuro-fuzzy models specifiy learning procedures for fuzzy rule creation.
4. The learning procedure of a neuro-fuzzy system takes the semantical properties of the underlying fuzzy system into account. This results in constraints on the possible modifications applicable to the system parameters.

   Remark: Not all neuro-fuzzy approaches have this property.
5. A neuro-fuzzy system approximates an n-dimensional (unknown) function that is partially defined by the training data. The fuzzy rules encoded within the system represent vague samples, and can be viewed as prototypes of the training data. A neuro-fuzzy system should not be seen as a kind of (fuzzy) expert system, and it has nothing to do with fuzzy logic in the narrow sense.

7.11 NEURAL NETWORKS AND FUZZY LOGIC

Neuro Fuzzy (NF) computing is a popular framework for solving complex problems. If we have knowledge expressed in linguistic rules, we can build a FIS (Fuzzy inference system), and if we have data, or can learn from a simulation (training) then we can use ANNs. For building a FIS, we have to specify the fuzzy sets, fuzzy operators and the knowledge base. Similarly for constructing an ANN for an application the user needs to specify the architecture and learning algorithm. An analysis reveals that the drawbacks pertaining to these approaches seem complementary and therefore it is natural to consider building an integrated system combining the concepts. While the learning capability is an advantage from the viewpoint of FIS, the formation of linguistic rule base will be advantage from the viewpoint of ANN.

Neural networks and fuzzy logic are two complimentary technologies. Neural networks can learn from data and feedback; however, understanding the knowledge or the pattern learned by the neural networks has been difficult. More specifically, it is difficult to develop an insight about the meaning associated with each neuron and each weight. Hence, neural networks are often viewed as a "black box" approach – we can understand what the box does, but not how it is done conceptually.

In contrast, fuzzy rule-based models are easy to comprehend because it used linguistic terms (linguistic expressions in general) and the structure of if-then rules. Unlike neural networks, however, fuzzy logic does not come with a learning algorithm. The learning and identification of fuzzy models need to adopt techniques from other areas (e.g. statistics, linear system identification, etc.) as we have seen in Chapter 14. Since neural networks can learn, it is natural to marry the two technologies. This marriage has created a new term – neuro-fuzzy system. A neuro-fuzzy system can be loosely defined as a system that uses a combination of fuzzy logic and neural networks.

Neuro-fuzzy systems can be classified into three categories:

1. A fuzzy rule-based model constructed using a supervised NN learning technique.

2. A fuzzy rule-based model constructed using reinforcement-based learning.
3. A fuzzy rule-based model using NN to construct its fuzzy partition of the input space.

7.12 NEURO-FUZZY ARCHITECTURES

A neuro-fuzzy system describes a fuzzy rule-based model using an NN-like structure (i.e., involving nodes and links). A neuro-fuzzy system differs from an NN in four major ways. First, the nodes and links in a neuro-fuzzy system usually are comprehensible because they each correspond to a specific component in a fuzzy system. For example, the first layer of a neuro-fuzzy architecture shown in Figure 7.11 describes the antecedent membership functions of input variables. Second, a node in a neuro-fuzzy system is usually not fully connected to nodes in an adjacent layer. In fact, the connections between nodes in a neuro-fuzzy system reflect the rule structure of the system.

For instance, the second-layer nodes in Figure 7.11 are connected to only two nodes from the first layer, each one of which describes a condition about an input variable. The nodes in the second layer thus perform the "AND" (conjunction) operator in fuzzy rules. Hence, the number of links connected to a node in the second layer equals the number of input variables. Third, the nodes in different layers of a neuro-fuzzy system typically perform different operations. We will elaborate on this point below. Finally, a neuro-fuzzy system typically has more layers than neural networks.

Typically, a neuro-fuzzy architecture has five to six layers of node. The functionalities associated with different layers usually include the following:

1. Compute the matching degree to a fuzzy condition involving one variable
2. Compute the matching degree of a conjunctive fuzzy condition involving multiple variables.
3. Compute the normalized matching degree.
4. Compute the conclusion inferred by a fuzzy rule.
5. Combine the conclusion of all fuzzy rules in a model.

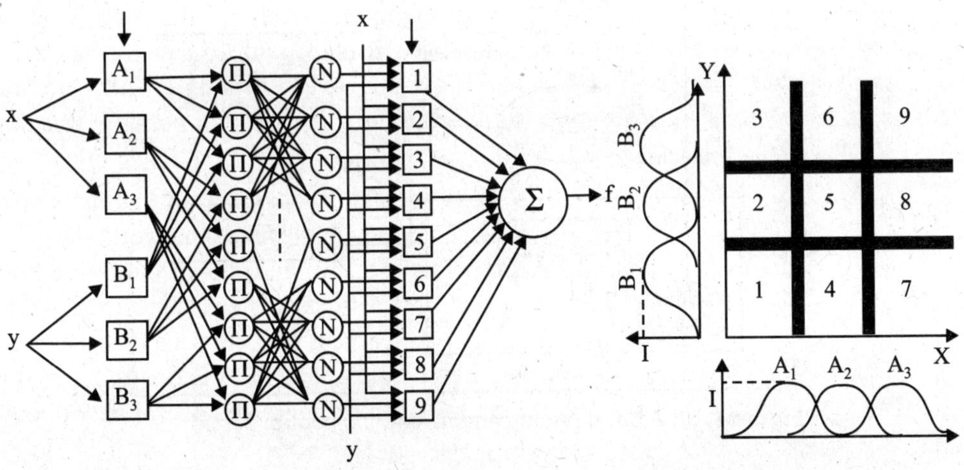

Figure 7.11: (a) ANFIS Architecture for a two-input sugeno fuzzy model with nine rules; (b) the input space that are partitioned into nine fuzzy regions.

7.13 REINFORCEMENT-BASED LEARNING OF FUZZY MODELS

Reinforcement learning used external reinforcement signals (rewards or punishments) to adjust parameters in a system (typically a rule-based system). Reinforcement learning was motivated by leaning theory in behavioral science that states people and animals can learn to change their behavior from positive reinforcements (rewards) and negative reinforcements (punishments).

The basic principles of reinforcement learning can be summarized as follows.

1. External reinforcement signals are generates based on the performance of the system being trained. For example, a system for balancing a pole will receive a negative reinforcement signal whenever the pole falls.
2. The external reinforcement signal is used to learn the desirability of recent states of the system being trained. A positive reinforcement will increase the desirability, while a negative reinforcement will decrease the desirability.
3. Because external reinforcements are generated infrequently and can be all negative or all positive, the learning algorithm generates a frequent internal reinforcement signal from both the external reinforcement and the change of state desirability. For example, changing from a less desirable state to a more desirable state without external reinforcement generates a positive internal reinforcement.

Reinforcement learning used two neuron-like units to carry out the ideas summarized above. It uses an Adaptive Critic Element (ACE) to generate internal reinforcement, and an Associative Search Element (ASE) to adjust the parameters of the system being trained. Figure 7.12 shows the basic architecture of a reinforcement learning system for training a rule-based controller.

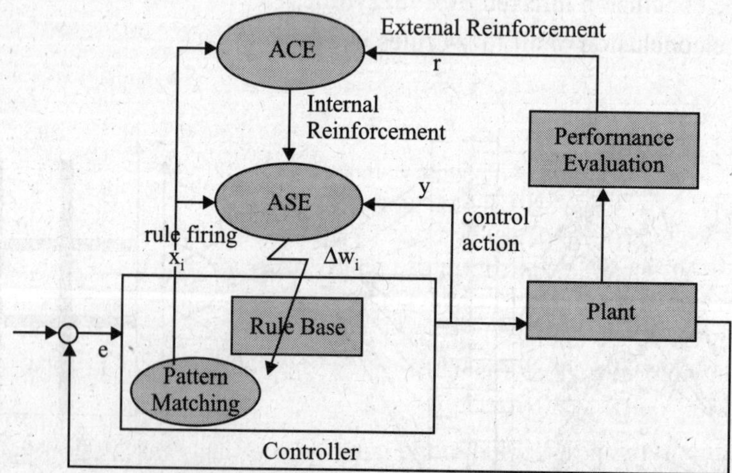

Figure 7.12: A basic reinforcement learning control system

7.14 USING NEURAL NETWORKS TO PARTITION THE INPUT SPACE

An important element of fuzzy rule-based modeling is the fuzzy partition of the input space. We have also discussed three major approaches to fuzzy partition: grid-based partition, tree-based partition, and scattered partition. However, the fuzzy subregions we have used to form these partition are all described in the form of "x_1 is A_{1i} and x_2 is A_{2i} ... and x_k is A_{ki-}" where x_1, x_2, ... x_k are linguistic variables and A_{1i}, A_{2i}, ...A_{ki} are linguistic labels of these variables. Such a fuzzy subregion forms a fuzzy hypercubes in the k-dimensional input space. Even though these fuzzy hypercubes are easy to comprehend, they do not offer the flexibility of partitioning using arbitrary nonlinear hypersurfaces. Since the latter can be achieved using NN, it offers an alternative way for constructing a fuzzy partition.

The basic idea of using a NN to construct a fuzzy partition is simple. We only need to construct a NN that takes input variables of a fuzzy model as input and generates the degrees the input data belong to a predetermined number of fuzzy regions. Figure 7.13 depicts a NN that partitions a two-dimensional input space into three fuzzy subregions. If the NN's output (i.e., A_1, $A\text{-}_{2\text{-}}$, A_3) were either 0 or 1, the NN performs a hard (nonfuzzy) partition. To perform a fuzzy partition, the NN's output needs to be a real number in the interval [0, 1]. Figure 7.13 (b) depicts the fuzzy partition generated by the NN. As shown in the figure, the boundary of each fuzzy region is a fuzzy hypersurface. Due to the flexibility of these fuzzy hypersurface, an NN can reduce the number of rules in a fuzzy model. We will leave this as an exercise.

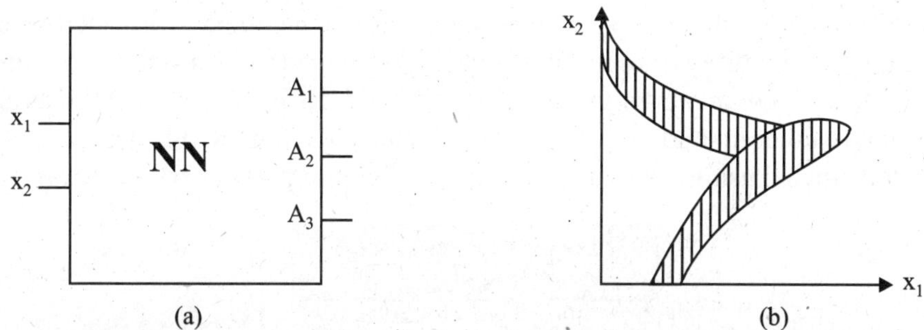

Figure 7.13: (a) An nn that partitions a two-dimensional input space (b) the corresponding fuzzy partition

In order to train the NN to partition the input space, we first need to have training data. The training data can be obtained in two ways: (1) by asking an expert of the problem domain to assign membership degrees to a sample set of input data, (2) by clustering a sample set of training data using a clustering algorithm (e.g., fuzzy e-means). The former approach is feasible only if such an expert is available.

Notice that the training data used in the latter approach contain desired input-output pairs for the fuzzy model being constructed. However, this training data cannot be used directly to train the NN for fuzzy partition because the target outputs of a fuzzy partition are the desired membership degrees in the partition's fuzzy subregions, which are different from the fuzzy model's outputs.

Hence, the data need to be first partitioned using a clustering algorithm. The classified dataset can then be used to train the NN for partitioning the input space.

7.15 NEURO-FUZZY MODELING EXAMPLES

In this section we provide two examples to show how the BP algorithm is used to estimate the parameters of a fuzzy model. For simplicity, we assume that the fuzzy model has a constant consequent constituents. That is,

R_i: If x_1 is A_{i1} and x_2 is A_{i2} and … and x_m is A_{im}

Then y is C_i, i = 1, 2, …, M. (7.2)

where c_i are the constant constituents. The antecedent membership functions are assumed to be Gaussian functions, as defined by

$$A_{ij} = \exp \frac{(x_i - m_{ij})^2}{2\sigma^2_{ij}} \tag{7.3}$$

In order to determine the structure (mainly the number of fuzzy rules constituting the underlying model) and the parameters of the model in an integrated manner, the BP algorithm is combined with the SVD-QR with column pivoting algorithm. The main steps of the process are shown in Figure 7.14. First, a candidate fuzzy model is considered, which may exhaustive and oversized (i.e., have a large rule base) but not undersized. The parameters of the model are trained using the BP algorithm. Second, the number of important fuzzy rules in the rule base is specified using SVD. Third, the position of these fuzzy rules in the rule base is identified using a subset selection algorithm known as SVD-QR with column pivoting algorithm. Finally, the important fuzzy rules are retained, while the less important or redundant fuzzy rules are removed from the rule base. A compact fuzzy model is then constructed using the retained fuzzy rules whose parameters are retrained using BP.

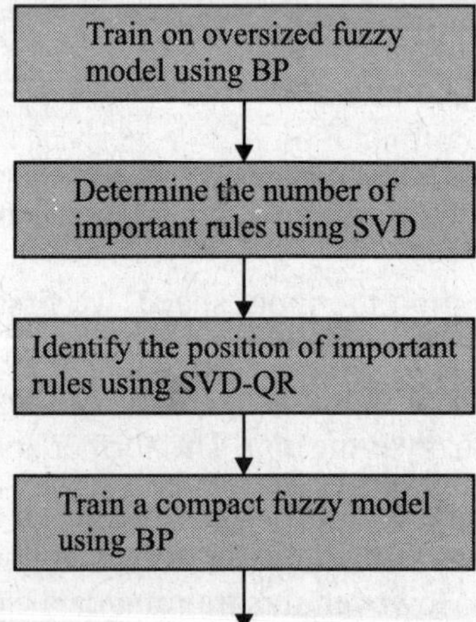

Figure 7.14: Fuzzy model identification using a BP-SVD combination.

Consider the nonlinear function

$$Y = \frac{\sin x}{x}$$

We want to approximate this function using the fuzzy model described in Equation 7.2 For this purpose, we generated 100 training data points using equally spaced x values in the interval [–10, 10].

We first built a fuzzy model with 30 rules whose antecedent and consequent parameters were trained using the BP algorithm with the initial parameter values $c_i(0)$ ε [–1, 1], $m_{ij}(0)$ ε[–10, 10] and $\sigma_{ij}(0)$ ε[1, 2]. These fuzzy rules were labeled as 1, 2, ..., 30 to indicate their position in the rule base. For each of the 100 input data points x(k), k = 1, 2, ..., 100 to the model, we computed the normalized firing strength of the 30 rules. A 100-by30 firing strength matrix P was then formed.

Applying SVD to P, the resulting singular values are shown in Figure 7.15. Based on the distribution of the singular values, we retained 12 rules that were used to construct a reduced fuzzy model. The position of these retained rules in the rule base was identified using the SVD-QR with column pivoting algorithm as 3, 5, 30, 16, 1, 13, 8, 24, 19, 29, 23, 14. The order of the position also indicated the importance of the associated fuzzy rules in the rule model.

The antecedent and consequent parameters of the reduced 12-rule fuzzy model were re-trained using the BP algorithm with the initial parameter values determined in the 30-rules fuzzy model.

Figure 7.16 shows the log-MSE (Mean Squared Error) curves of the 30-rule fuzzy model and the 12-rule fuzzy model over 1000 epochs of BP training. As a comparison, Figure 7.16 also shown a 12-rule fuzzy model trained using the BP algorithm with random initial parameter values $c_i(0)$ ε[–1, 2], $m_{ij}(0)$ ε[-10, 10], and $s_{ij}(0)$ ε[1, 2]. Table 7.2 gives the MSEs of the three fuzzy models after 1000 epochs. From Figure 7.15 and Table 7.2 we know that the reduced 12-rules model with predetermined initial parameter values has achieved its feasible parameter sets much faster than the one with random initial parameter values. This is because the BP algorithm is a nonlinear optimization algorithm and its convergence depends to a great extent on the choice of initial parameter values. The original 30-rule fuzzy model gives a small MSE compared with the two reduced 12-rule fuzzy models. This is not surprising because the former contains a larger number of fuzzy rules. However, good fit on training data points does not always assure good performance on untrained data points. A fuzzy model with a large number of rules may have a high risk of overfitting: capable of fitting training data points completely, but incapale of generalizing to untrained data points satisfactorily. We will see this point in the following example. Figure 7.17. shows the real output of the nonlinear function and the outputs of 30-rule fuzzy model and 12-rules fuzzy model with predetermined initial parameter values. Figure 7.18 shows the membership functions of the input variable x in the 30-rule fuzzy model and in the 12-rule fuzzy model with predetermined initial parameter values.

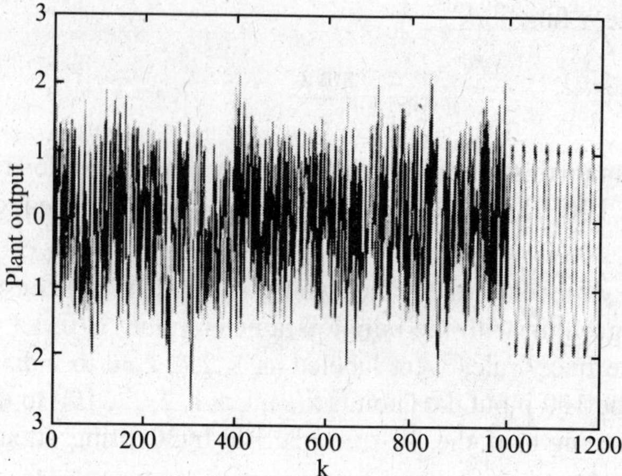

Figure 7.15: Distribution of singular values of the 100-by-30 firing strength matrix

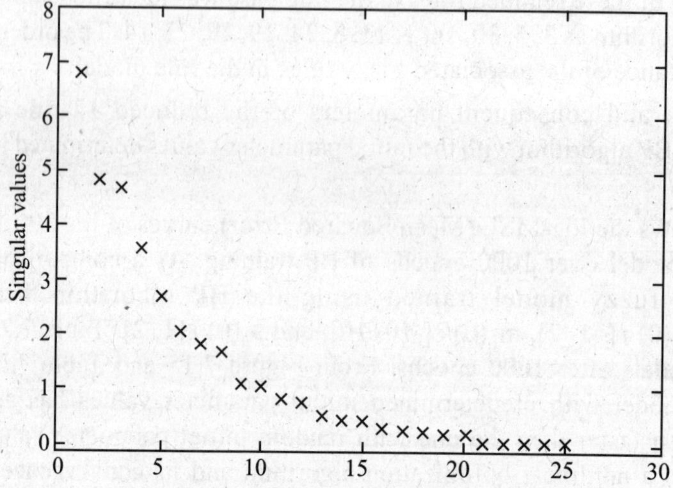

Figure 7.16 Log-MSE curves for three fuzzy models trained using the bp algorithm

Table 7.2: MSEs of three fuzzy models after 1000 epochs of BP training

Fuzzy Model	MSE
Original Model (30 rules)	2.7902e-6
Reduced model (12 rules, with predetermined intial values	2.8342e-6
Reduced model (12 rules, with random initial values)	6.8712e-6

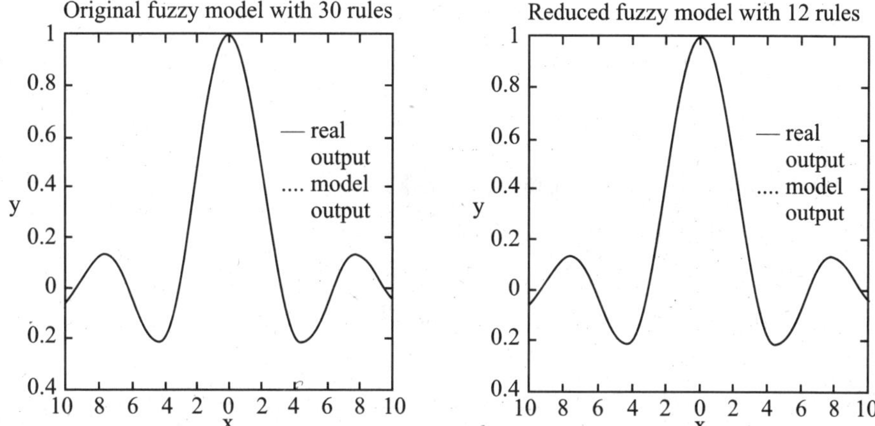

Figure 7.17: Comparison of outputs of real system and identified fuzzy models.

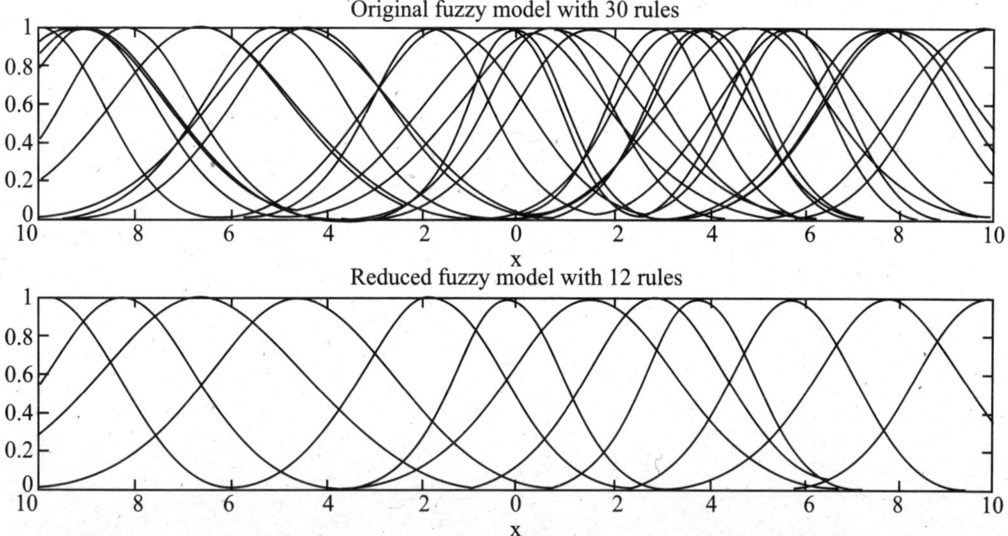

Figure 7.18: Membership functions of input x in the original and reduced models.

EXERCISES

1. What do you mean by neural networks?
2. What do you mean by artificial neural network?
3. What are the various advantages and disadvantages of neural network?
4. Explain the working of ANN?
5. What are the various element of ANN?

6. Explain the network architectures of ANN?
7. What do you mean by neuro-fuzzy systems?
8. How we can combine fuzzy systems and neural networks?
9. Explain the characteristic neuro-fuzzy systems?
10. Explain the cooperative fuzzy neural network?
11. Explain the hybrid fuzzy neural network?
12. Explain the properties of neuro-fuzzy system?
13. What do you mean by neuro-fuzzy computing?
14. What are the various architectures of neuro-fuzzy systems?
15. Explain the ANFIS architecture for a two input sugeno fuzzy model with nine rules?
16. Explain the reinforcement based learning of fuzzy models?
17. How we can use neural networks to partition the input space?
18. Explain the examples of neuro-fuzzy modeling?

CHAPTER 8

Genetic Algorithm

8.1 INTRODUCTION

Genetic Algorithms (GAs) are adaptive heuristic search algorithm premised on the evolutionary ideas of natural selection and genetic. The basic concept of GAs is designed to simulate processes in natural system necessary for evolution, specifically those that follow the principles first laid down by Charles Darwin of survival of the fittest. As such they represent an intelligent exploitation of a random search within a defined search space to solve a problem.

First pioneered by John Holland in the 60s, Genetic Algorithms has been widely studied, experimented and applied in many fields in engineering worlds. Not only does GAs provide an alternative method to solving problem, it consistently outperforms other traditional methods in most of the problems link. Many of the real world problems involved finding optimal parameters, which might prove difficult for traditional methods but ideal for GAs. However, because of its outstanding performance in optimisation, GAs have been wrongly regarded as a function optimiser. In fact, there are many ways to view genetic algorithms. Perhaps most users come to GAs looking for a problem solver, but this is a restrictive view [De Jong ,1993] .

Herein, we will examine GAs as a number of different things:

1. GAs as problem solvers
2. GAs as challenging technical puzzle
3. GAs as basis for competent machine learning
4. GAs as computational model of innovation and creativity
5. GAs as computational model of other innovating systems
6. GAs as guiding philosophy

However, due to various constraints, we would only be looking at GAs as problem solvers and competent machine learning here. We would also examine how GAs is applied to completely different fields.

Many scientists have tried to create living programs. These programs do not merely simulate life but try to exhibit the behaviours and characteristics of a real organism in an attempt to exist as a form of life. Suggestions have been made that a life would eventually evolve into real life. Such suggestion may sound absurd at the moment but certainly not implausible if technology continues to progress at present rates. Therefore it is worth, in our opinion, taking a paragraph out to discuss how a life is connected with GAs and see if such a prediction is far fetched and groundless.

8.2 GENETIC ALGORITHM

A **genetic algorithm (GA)** is a search technique used in computing to find exact or approximate solutions to optimization and search problems. Genetic algorithms are categorized as global search heuristics. Genetic algorithms are a particular class of evolutionary algorithms (EA) that use techniques inspired by evolutionary biology such as inheritance, mutation, selection, and crossover.

8.2.1 Methodology

Genetic algorithms are implemented in a computer simulation in which a population of abstract representations (called chromosomes or the genotype of the genome) of candidate solutions (called individuals, creatures, or phenotypes) to an optimization problem evolves toward better solutions. Traditionally, solutions are represented in binary as strings of 0s and 1s, but other encodings are also possible. The evolution usually starts from a population of randomly generated individuals and happens in generations.

In each generation, the fitness of every individual in the population is evaluated, multiple individuals are stochastically selected from the current population (based on their fitness), and modified (recombined and possibly randomly mutated) to form a new population. The new population is then used in the next iteration of the algorithm. Commonly, the algorithm terminates when either a maximum number of generations has been produced, or a satisfactory fitness level has been reached for the population. If the algorithm has terminated due to a maximum number of generations, a satisfactory solution may or may not have been reached.

Genetic algorithms find application in bioinformatics, phylogenetics, computational science, engineering, economics, chemistry, manufacturing, mathematics, physics and other fields.

A typical genetic algorithm requires:

1. a genetic representation of the solution domain,
2. a fitness function to evaluate the solution domain.

A standard representation of the solution is as an array of bits. Arrays of other types and structures can be used in essentially the same way. The main property that makes these genetic representations convenient is that their parts are easily aligned due to their fixed size, which facilitates simple crossover operations. Variable length representations may also be used, but crossover implementation is more complex in this case. Tree-like representations are explored in genetic programming and graph-form representations are explored in evolutionary programming. The fitness function is defined over the genetic representation and measures the *quality* of the represented solution. The fitness function is always problem dependent.

For instance, in the knapsack problem one wants to maximize the total value of objects that can be put in a knapsack of some fixed capacity. A representation of a solution might be an array of bits, where each bit represents a different object, and the value of the bit (0 or 1) represents whether or not the object is in the knapsack. Not every such representation is valid, as the size of objects may exceed the capacity of the knapsack. The *fitness* of the solution is the sum of values of all objects in the knapsack if the representation is valid, or 0 otherwise. In some problems, it is hard or even impossible to define the fitness expression; in these cases, interactive genetic algorithms are used.

Once we have the genetic representation and the fitness function defined, GA proceeds to initialize a population of solutions randomly, then improve it through repetitive application of mutation, crossover, inversion and selection operators.

8.2.2 Initialization

Initially many individual solutions are randomly generated to form an initial population. The population size depends on the nature of the problem, but typically contains several hundreds or thousands of possible solutions. Traditionally, the population is generated randomly, covering the entire range of possible solutions (the *search space*). Occasionally, the solutions may be "seeded" in areas where optimal solutions are likely to be found.

8.2.3 Encoding of a Chromosome

The chromosome should in some way contain information about solution which it represents. The most used way of encoding is a binary string. The chromosome then could look like this:

Chromosome 1	1101100100110110
Chromosome 2	1101111000011110

Each chromosome has one binary string. Each bit in this string can represent some characteristic of the solution. Or the whole string can represent a number.

Of course, there are many other ways of encoding. This depends mainly on the solved problem. For example, one can encode directly integer or real numbers, sometimes it is useful to encode some permutations and so on.

8.2.4 Selection

During each successive generation, a proportion of the existing population is selected to breed a new generation. Individual solutions are selected through a *fitness-based* process, where fitter solutions (as measured by a fitness function) are typically more likely to be selected. Certain selection methods rate the fitness of each solution and preferentially select the best solutions. Other methods rate only a random sample of the population, as this process may be very time-consuming.

Most functions are stochastic and designed so that a small proportion of less fit solutions are selected. This helps keep the diversity of the population large, preventing premature convergence on poor solutions. Popular and well-studied selection methods include roulette wheel selection and tournament selection.

8.2.5 Reproduction

The next step is to generate a second generation population of solutions from those selected through genetic operators: crossover (also called recombination), and/or mutation.

For each new solution to be produced, a pair of "parent" solutions is selected for breeding from the pool selected previously. By producing a "child" solution using the above methods of crossover and mutation, a new solution is created which typically shares many of the characteristics of its "parents". New parents are selected for each new child, and the process continues until a new population of solutions of appropriate size is generated. Although reproduction methods that are based on the use of two parents are more "biology inspired", some research suggests more than two "parents" are better to be used to reproduce a good quality chromosome.

These processes ultimately result in the next generation population of chromosomes that is different from the initial generation. Generally the average fitness will have increased by this procedure for the population, since only the best organisms from the first generation are selected for breeding, along with a small proportion of less fit solutions, for reasons already mentioned above.

1. Crossover

After we have decided what encoding we will use, we can make a step to crossover. Crossover selects genes from parent chromosomes and creates a new offspring. The simplest way how to do this is to choose randomly some crossover point and everything before this point copy from a first parent and then everything after a crossover point copy from the second parent.

Crossover can then look like this (| is the crossover point):

Chromosome 1	11011 | 00100110110
Chromosome 2	11011 | 11000011110
Offspring 1	11011 | 11000011110
Offspring 2	11011 | 00100110110

There are other ways how to make crossover, for example we can choose more crossover points. Crossover can be rather complicated and very depends on encoding of the encoding of chromosome. Specific crossover made for a specific problem can improve performance of the genetic algorithm.

2. Mutation

After a crossover is performed, mutation takes place. This is to prevent falling all solutions in population into a local optimum of solved problem. Mutation changes randomly the new offspring. For binary encoding we can switch a few randomly chosen bits from 1 to 0 or from 0 to 1.

Mutation can then be following:

Original offspring 1	1101111000011110
Original offspring 2	1101100100110110
Mutated offspring 1	1100111000011110
Mutated offspring 2	1101101100110110

The mutation depends on the encoding as well as the crossover. For example when we are encoding permutations, mutation could be exchanging two genes.

8.2.6 Crossover and Mutation Probability

There are two basic parameters of GA - crossover probability and mutation probability.

1. **Crossover probability** says how often will be crossover performed. If there is no crossover, offspring is exact copy of parents. If there is a crossover, offspring is made from parts of parents' chromosome. If crossover probability is **100%**, then all offspring is made by crossover. If it is **0%**, whole new generation is made from exact copies of chromosomes from old population (but this does not mean that the new generation is the same!). Crossover is made in hope that new chromosomes will have good parts of old chromosomes and maybe the new chromosomes will be better. However it is good to leave some part of population survive to next generation.
2. **Mutation probability** says how often will be parts of chromosome mutated. If there is no mutation, offspring is taken after crossover (or copy) without any change. If mutation is performed, part of chromosome is changed. If mutation probability is **100%**, whole chromosome is changed, if it is **0%**, nothing is changed. Mutation is made to prevent falling GA into local extreme, but it should not occur very often, because then GA will in fact change to **random search**.

8.2.7 Termination

This generational process is repeated until a termination condition has been reached. Common terminating conditions are:

- A solution is found that satisfies minimum criteria
- Fixed number of generations reached
- Allocated budget (computation time/money) reached
- The highest ranking solution's fitness is reaching or has reached a plateau such that successive iterations no longer produce better results
- Manual inspection
- Combinations of the above

Simple generational genetic algorithm pseudocode:

1. Choose the initial population of individuals
2. Evaluate the fitness of each individual in that population
3. Repeat on this generation until termination: (time limit, sufficient fitness achieved, etc.)
   (a) Select the best-fit individuals for reproduction
   (b) Breed new individuals through crossover and mutation operations to give birth to offspring
   (c) Evaluate the individual fitness of new individuals
   (d) Replace least-fit population with new individuals

8.3 BASIC GENETIC ALGORITHM

Following are the steps of the genetic algorithm:

1. **[Start]** Generate random population of *n* chromosomes (suitable solutions for the problem)
2. **[Fitness]** Evaluate the fitness f(x) of each chromosome x in the population
3. **[New population]** Create a new population by repeating following steps until the new population is complete
   (a) [Selection] Select two parent chromosomes from a population according to their fitness (the better fitness, the bigger chance to be selected)
   (b) [Crossover] With a crossover probability cross over the parents to form a new offspring (children). If no crossover was performed, offspring is an exact copy of parents.
   (c) [Mutation] With a mutation probability mutate new offspring at each locus (position in chromosome).
   (d) [Accepting] Place new offspring in a new population
4. **[Replace]** Use new generated population for a further run of algorithm
5. **[Test]** If the end condition is satisfied, **stop**, and return the best solution in current population
6. **[Loop]** Go to step **2**

8.4 WORKING OF GENETIC ALGORITHMS

Genetic Algorithms (GA) are global search and optimization techniques modeled from natural genetics, exploring search space by incorporating a set of candidate solutions in parallel. A Genetic Algorithm (GA) maintains a population of candidate solutions where each candidate solution is usually coded as a binary string called a chromosome. A chromosome, also referred to as a genotype, encodes a parameter set (i.e. a candidate solution) for a set of variables being optimized. Each encoded parameter in a chromosome is called a gene. A decoded parameter set is called a phenotype. A set of chromosomes forms a population, which is evaluated and ranked by a fitness evaluation function. The fitness evaluation function plays a critical role in GA because it provides information about how good each candidate solution is. This information guides the search of a genetic algorithm. More accurately, the fitness evaluation results determine the likelihood that a candidate solution is selected to produce candidate solutions in the next generation. The initial population is usually generated at random.

The evolution from one generation to the next one involves mainly three steps: (1) fitness evaluation (2) selection, and (3) reproduction as shown in **Figure 8.1.** First, the current population is evaluated using the fitness evaluation function and then ranked based on their fitness values. Second GA stochastically select "parents" from the current population with a bias that better chromosomes are more likely to be selected. This is accomplished using a selection probability that is determined by the fitness value or the ranking of a chromosome, as shown in Figure 8.2. Third, the GA reproduces "children" from selected "parents" using two genetic operations: crossover and mutation. This cycle of evaluation, selection and reproduction terminates when an acceptable solution is found, when a convergence criterion is met, or when a predetermined limit on the number of iterations is reached.

The crossover operation produces offspring by exchanging information between two parent chromosomes. An example of crossover operation for binary GA is shown in Figure 8.3. The mutation operation produces an offspring from a parent through a random modification of the parent. The chances that these two operations apply to a chromosome are controlled by two probabilities: the crossover probability and the mutation probability. Typically, the mutation operation has a low probability of reducing its potential interference with a legitimately progressing search.

The genetic algorithm differs from the conventional optimization techniques in that it is inherently parallel. All individuals in a population evolve simultaneously without central coordination. They operate on a set of solutions rather than on one solution, hence multiple frontiers are searched simultaneously. The only feedback used by the genetic algorithm is the fitness evaluation. The GA has been shown to be an effective search technique on a wide range of difficult optimization problems.

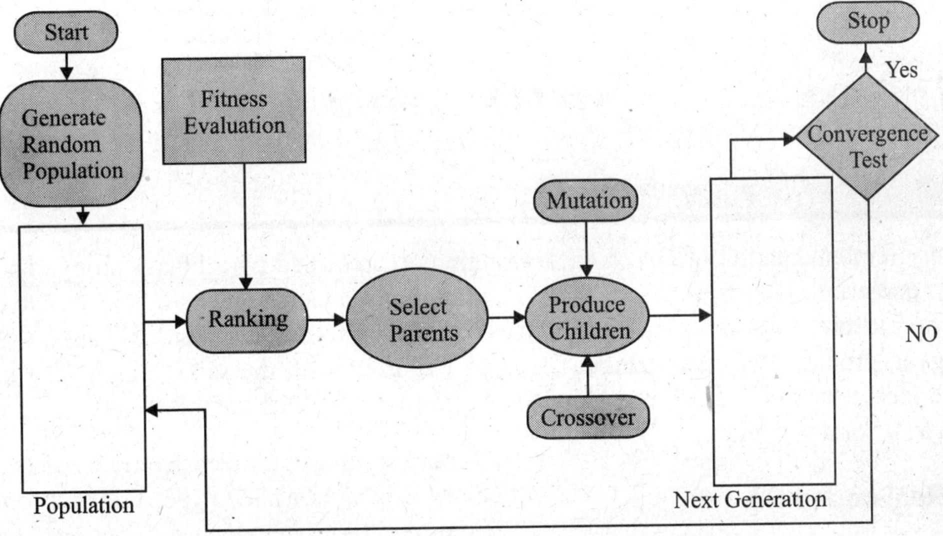

Figure 8.1: Architecture of the genetic algorithm

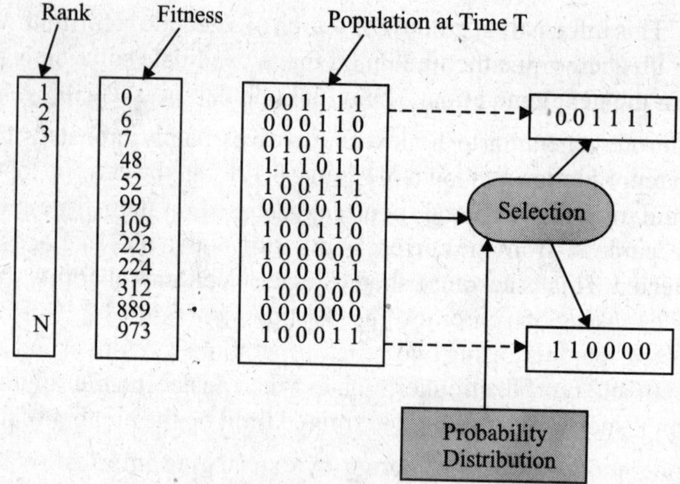

Figure 8.2 : Selection of parents

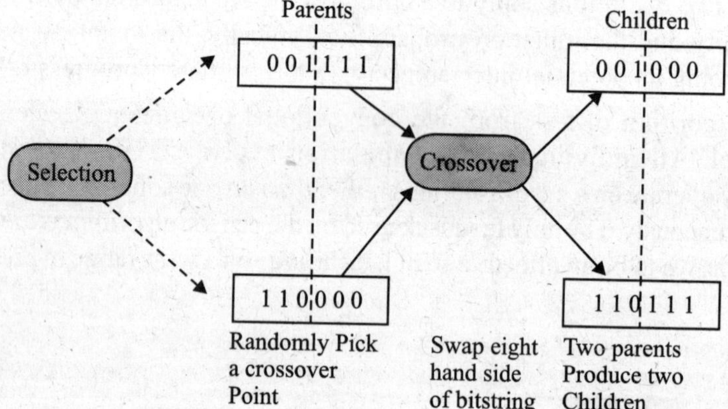

Figure 8.3: Binary crossover

8.5 BINARY GA IMPLEMENTATION

In a binary implementation of GA, a chromosome is represented by a binary string. The binary crossover operation consists of two steps. First, a randomly selected bit position is used to cut each parent chromosome (i.e. bitstring) into two substrings. The parents then exchange their right substrings to produce two new strings (i.e., their children) with the same length. The mutation operation replaces a randomly chosen bit of a chromosome with its complement (i.e., changing a "1" with a "0" or a "0" with a "1").

8.5.1 Real-coded GA

A real-coded GA is a genetic algorithm representation that uses a floating point. A chromosome in real-coded GA becomes a vector of floating-point numbers. With some modifications of genetic operators, real-coded GAs have resulted in better performance than binary-coded GA for certain problem. We briefly describe below some modified genetic operators recommended for real-coded GA.

The crossover operator of a real-coded GA is analogous to that of binary-coded GA except that its crossover points fall between genes (i.e., encoded parameters). Two mutation operators have been proposed for real-coded GA. A random mutation changes a gene with a random number in the feature's domain. A dynamic mutation stochastically changes a gene within an interval that narrows over time.

8.5.2 Dynamic Mutation of Real GA

The basic idea is to gradually reduce the range of the mutation operator over time such that the GA gradually changes from "explorative" search to focused search. The dynamic mutation operator is defined as

$$v'_k = \begin{cases} v_k + \Delta(t,\ UB - v_k) & \text{if a Random digit is } 0 \\ v_k + \Delta(t,\ v_k - LB) & \text{if a Random digit is } 1 \end{cases} \tag{8.1}$$

$$\Delta(t, y) = y \cdot \left[1 - r^{\left(1 - \frac{1}{t}\right)^b}\right] \tag{8.2}$$

where r is a uniform random number from [0, 1], T is the maximal generation number, a and b are system parameters determining the degree of dependency on an iteration number (a typical choice is b = 5).

8.6 DESIGN ISSUES IN GA

8.6.1 Choice of Encoding

For binary GA, the choice of an encoding scheme is one of the important design decisions. Because binary GA encodes each parameter value using a binary string (i.e., a fixed length of binary numbers), we need to find a scaling function that maps the real parameter alue into an integer in the interval $[0, 2^n - 1]$ where n is the length of the binary string. Such a scaling function can be easily constructed from (1) the range of the parameter values we wish GA to search, and (2) the length of the binary string. The role of the scaling function and its inverse in encoding and decoding a parameter set is shown in Figure 8.4.

In designing GA, we usually first decide the range of each parameter value based on background knowledge of the problem being optimized. Based on the range and the desired precision of the optimal value for each parameter, we can then calculate the length of the binary string required.

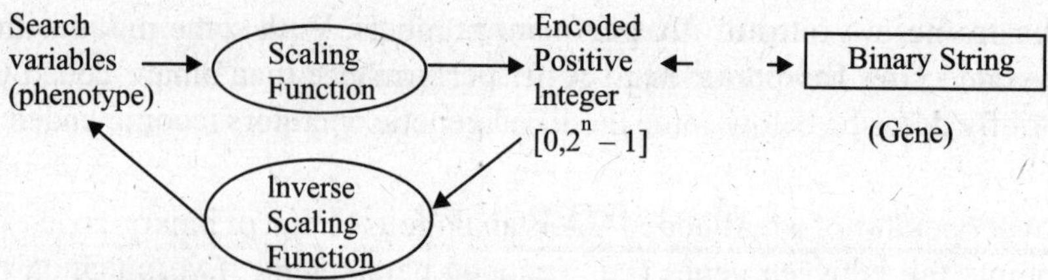

Figure 8.4: Encoding and decoding of search variables

8.6.2 Selection Probability

The probability that a chromosome is selected is selected to be a parent for reproduction can be based on (1) its fitness value or (2) its ranking. Most GA experiments reported in the literature recommend ranking-based selection probability, because using fitness-based selection probability often results in premature convergence. This is because the fitness of chromosomes in generation often varies widely, especially during the early stage of the search. Hence, a fitness-based selection probability may biase the selection process to such an extent that medium-ranked chromosomes are rarely selected if their fitness values are rarely selected if their fitness value are much lower then the fitness of those ranked on the top.

8.6.3 Mutation and Crossover Probability

The design of mutation and crossover probability differs significantly for binary GA and real – coded GA. This is because their roles are different in the two GA schemes. A binary GA mainly relies on the crossover operation to produce new point in the search space. The mutation operations plays a secondary role in binary GA by introducing "Stochastis randomness" into the reproduction process. In contrast, a real coded GA primarily uses its mutation operator to generate new point in search space. The crossover operation plays a secondary role of "Exchanging parameters". Because of these differences, the crossover probability of a binary GA is usually much higher then the mutation probability. IN contrast, the mutation probability of a real coded GA is usually much larger then the crossover probability.

8.6.4 Fitness Evaluation Function

A good design of fitness evaluation function is probably the most important factor in a successful application of GA. However, its importance can be easily overlooked. When a GA does perform well in solving an optimization problem, a natural temptation is to change a GA design parameter (e.g. population size, the crossover probability, or the mutation probability). Even though changing these parameter does effect the performance of GA, Tuning GA parameter will be in vain if the fitness evaluation function does not correctly reflected the desired optimization criteria.

There are atleast two type of fitness evaluation function: fitness-based and performance-based. A fitness-based function calculate how well a model using a parameter set in a chromosome fit a set of input output training data. In other words, the function computes the error between the target's output and the module's output. A performance-based evaluation function determines how well a system using the parameter set in a chromosome achieves a set of performance objectives.

EXERCISES

1. What do you mean by genetic algorithms?
2. Explain the methodology of genetic algorithms?
3. How we can encode a chromosome?
4. Explain the various genetic operators?
5. What do you mean by crossover reproduction?
6. What do you mean by mutation reproduction?
7. What are the two basic parameters of GA?
8. Explain the termination process of GA?
9. Write down the basic steps of the genetic algorithm?
10. Explain the working of genetic algorithm?
11. Explain the binary GA implementation?
12. What are the various design issues in GA?

CHAPTER 9

Fuzzy Logic and Probability Theory

9.1 INTRODUCTION

Most of the applications chapters in this book deal with the quantification of various forms of uncertainty, both numeric and nonnurneric. Uncertainty in numerical quantities can be random in nature, where probability theory is very useful, or it earl be the result of bias or an unknown error, in which case fuzzy set theory, evidence theory, or possibility theory might prove useful. Probability theory also has been used almost exclusively to deal with the form of uncertainty due to chance (randomness), sometimes called variability, and with uncer-tainties arising from eliciting and analyzing expert information. Three other prevalent forms of uncertainty are those arising from ambiguity, vagueness, and imprecision. While vague-ness and ambiguity can arise from linguistic uncertainly, they also can be associated with some numerical quantities. Such as "approximately 5." Imprecision is generally associated with numerical quantities, although applications may exist where this type of uncertainty is nonnumeric (i.e., qualitative), for example, "the missile was close to the target." How do variability, ambiguity, vagueness, and imprecision differ as forms of uncertainty?

In the sections that follow, we detail the most popular methods used to address these various forms of uncertainly whether they arc quantitative or qualitative. While fuzzy set theory and probability theory have been used for all these forms of uncertainty, this chapter will extend this scope somewhat by commenting on the use of possibility theory in the characterization of ambiguity.

Fuzzy logic and probability theory are two different tools, lime screw drivers and hammers. They were designed for different tasks. One could conceivably use a hammer to hammer a screw, yet it is much more effective to use a screw driver for the job. Only after we fully understand the tasks these tools are designed for can we use them properly. Too often, unfortunately, we have a tendency to avoid learning how to use a new tool, simply because we are using to use an old tool that we are familiar with. Professor Zadeh once said, "if the only tool you know is a hammer, everything looks like a nail".

9.2 VAGUENESS, IMPRECISION, AND CHANCE: FUZZINESS VERSUS PROBABILITY

Often vagueness and imprecision arc used synonymously, but they can also differ in the following sense. Vagueness can be used to describe certain kinds of uncertainty associated with linguistic information or intuitive information. Examples of vague information are that the data quality is "good" or that the transparency of an optical element is "acceptable."

Moreover, in terms of semantics, even the terms vague and fuzzy cannot be generally con-sidered synonyms, as explained by Zadeh (1995). For example, "I shall return sornetime" is vague and "I shall return in a few minutes" is fuzzy, The former is not known to be associated with any unit of (seconds, hours, clays), whereas the latter is associated with an uncertainty that is at least known to be on the order of minutes. However, notwithstand-ing this distinction, the terms vague and fuzzy used herein will represent the same kind of uncertainly; i.e.. They will be used interchangeably in our discussions of this general form of uncertainty. As explained by Zadeh (1995), "Usually a vague proposition is fuzzy, but the converse is not generally true."

9.2.1 A Historical Perspective on Vagueness

Black (1935) defines a vague proposition as a proposition where the possible states (of the proposition) are not clearly defined with regard to inclusion. For example, consider the proposition that a person is young. Since the term "young" has different interpretations to different individuals, we cannot decisively determine the age(s) at which an individual is young versus the age(s) at which an individual is not considered to be young. Thus the propo-sition is vaguely defined. Classical (binary) logic does not hold under these circumstances; therefore, we must establish a different method of interpretation.

Black introduced a consistency profile as a graphical representation of the membership of a preposition in a set of states where 1 denotes absolute membership and 0 denotes absolute complementary membership. These profiles are established to represent a precise (crisp) or vague proposition: a precisely defined proposition has a consistency profile that is a step function (Figure 9.1), while a vague proposition has a consistency profile that gradually ranges between the two extremes (Figure 9.2).

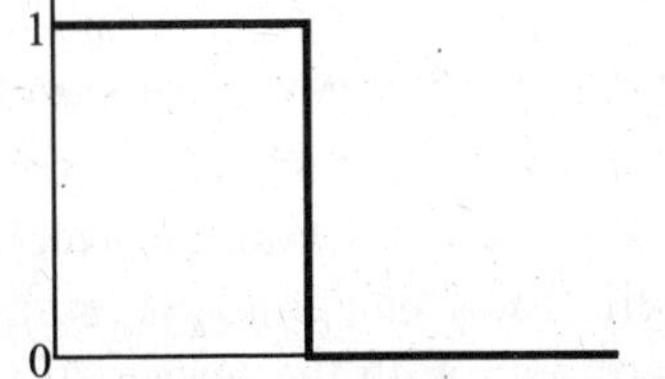

Figure 9.1: Precise consistency profile.

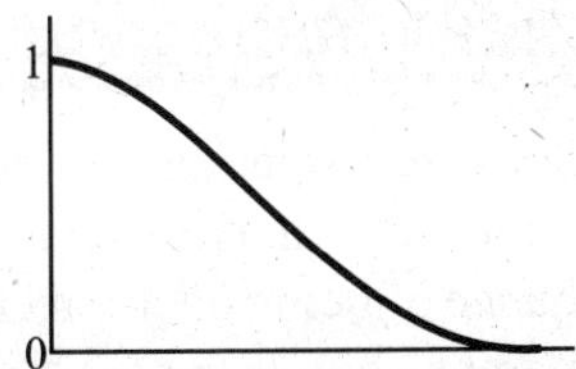

Figure 9.2: Vague consistency profile.

9.2.2 Imprecision

Imprecision can be associated with quantitative, or countable, data as well as noncountable data. An example of the latter might be, "the length of a flaw in an integrated circuit is long." An example of countable imprecision would be to report the length of such a flaw as 30 microns. If we use a microscope and measure the length of the flaw 100 times we will likely come up with 100 different values; the differences in the numbers will no doubt be on the order of the precision of the resolution limitations of the microscope and other measurement factors. Measurements using a light microscope (which has accuracy on the order of microns) will be less precise than those developed from an electron microscope (which has resolution on the order of nanometers). If we plot the flaw lengths on some sort of probit paper and develop a Gaussian distribution to describe the length of this flaw, we could state the imprecision in probabilistic terms. In this case, the length of the flaw is uncertain to some degree of precision that is quantified in the language of probability. Since we are not able to make this measurement an infinite number of times, there is also uncertainty in the statistics describing the flaw length. Hence, imprecision can be used to quantify random variability in the quantitative uncertainty, and it also can be used to describe a lack of knowledge for descriptive entities acceptable transparency, good data quality), Vagueness is usually related to non-measurable issues.

Many practitioners suggest that the uncertainty arising from vagueness makes use of fuzzy set theory, since this theory was developed to handle the vagueness inherent in natural language. Klir and Folger (1988) have shown that the relationships among Fuzzy set theory, probability theory, evidence theory, and possibility theory stem from a common framework of fuzzy measures in that they all have been used to characterize and model various forms of uncertainty. That they all are related mathematically (as fuzzy measures) is an especially crucial advantage in their use in quantifying the uncertainty spectrum. As more information about a problem becomes available, the mathematical description of uncertainty easily can transform from one theory to the next in the characterization of the uncertainty as the uncertainty diminishes or, alternatively, as the information granularity increases and becomes specific. There are various forms of fuzzy measures such as belief, plausibility, possibility, and probability, Yager (1993) has discussed the relationship between a possibility distribution and a fuzzy set. Ongoing research continues to provide theoretically based methods for translating uncertainties established in one of these measures into uncertainties in another without violating the fundamental axioms of either.

9.3 CHANCE VERSUS VAGUENESS

Suppose that you arc a basketball recruiter and are looking for a "very tall" player for the center position on a men's team. One of your information sources tells you that a hot prospect in Oregon has a 95% chance of being over 7 feet tall. Another source tells you that a good player in Louisiana has a high membership in the set "very tall" people. The problem with the information from the first source is that it is a quantity constrained by the law of the excluded-middle. There is a 5% chance that the Oregon player is not over 7 feet tall; this person could conceivably he of extremely short stature. The second source of information in this case, contain less uncertainty for the recruiter because if the player turned out to be less than 7 feet tail, then there is a high likelihood that this player would still he quite tall.

Suppose that we are allowed to measure the basketball players‘ heights. The prior probability of 0.95 becomes a posterior probability of 1.0 or 0.0; i.e., the player either is or is not over 7 feet tall. However, the membership value of 0.95 that measures the extent to which the player's height is over 7 feet remains 0.95 after measuring. This example illustrates very clearly the difference in the information content between chance and vague events.

This brings us to the clearest distinction between fuzziness and randomness: Fuzzi-ness describes the vagueness of an event, whereas chance describes the uncertainty in the occurrence of the event. The event will or will not occur; but is the description of the event clear and specific enough to measure its occurrence or nonoccurrence?

9.4 MANY-VALUED LOGIC

Binary logic pertains to propositions that are either true or false. However, Lukasiewicz (1930) recognized the existence of propositions that are simultaneously true and false at various levels. For example, a degraded yet functioning system cannot be classified as being in state 1(perfect Functioning), nor can it be classified as being in state 0 (total failure). For such propositions, their membership is neither 1 nor 0. Therefore, Lukasiewiez assigned a third number, $\frac{1}{2}$ as its associated truth value (ie., membership value) to account for any deviation from states 0 or 1. For example, a degraded component (system) would be considered in state $\frac{1}{2}$, This concept defines a three-valued logic.

Lukasicwicz (1930) defined the truth table corresponding to the implication X → Y for two propositions X and Y("if X, then Y") and negation X` (propositions complementary to X); see tables 9.1 and 9.2.

Table 9.1: Three-valued truth Table for X→ Y

X→ Y		**Values of proposition Y**		
		0	$\frac{1}{2}$	**1**
Values of proposition Y	0	1	1	1
	$\frac{1}{2}$	$\frac{1}{2}$	1	1
	1	0	$\frac{1}{2}$	1

Table 9.2: Three-valued truth table for X'.

Values of proposition X	Values of proposition X'
0	1
$\frac{1}{2}$	$\frac{1}{2}$
1	0

From the logical equivalencies for conjunction ("AND," denoted $\wedge$) and disjunction ("OR," denoted), we have

$$X \wedge Y = (X \rightarrow Y) \rightarrow Y$$

and

$$X \vee Y = (X' \rightarrow Y')'$$

Truth tables can be found in Malinowski (1993); also see Tables 9.3 and 9.4. As a result,

Table 9.3: Three-valued truth Table for $X \wedge Y$

$X \wedge Y$		Values of proposition Y		
		0	$\frac{1}{2}$	**1**
Values of proposition Y	0	0	0	0
	$\frac{1}{2}$	0	$\frac{1}{2}$	$\frac{1}{2}$
	1	0	$\frac{1}{2}$	1

Table 9.4: Three-valued truth Table for $X \vee Y$

$X \vee Y$		Values of proposition Y		
		0	$\frac{1}{2}$	**1**
Values of proposition Y	0	0	$\frac{1}{2}$	1
	$\frac{1}{2}$	$\frac{1}{2}$	$\frac{1}{2}$	1
	1	1	1	1

$$X \wedge Y = \min(X, Y)$$

and

$$X \vee Y = \max(X, Y).$$

These ideas can be generalized to define an n-valued logic in that propositions are true and false simultaneously but with varying degrees of truth (or falsity). Furthermore, extensions of the n-valued logic to the continuum lead to the notions of vagueness and fuzzy logic.

9.5 AXIOMATIC STRUCTURE OF PROBABILITY AND FUZZY LOGICS

To attempt to bring some relevance to the historical confusion between the logics associated with probability theory and fuzzy set theory, a paper by Gaines. (1978) does an eloquent job of addressing this issue. Historically, probability and fuzzy sets have been presented as distinct theoretical foundations for reasoning and decision-making in situations involving uncertainty. Yet when one examines the underlying axioms of both probability and fuzzy set theories, the two theories differ only by one axiom in a total of 16 axioms needed for a complete foundation! The material that follows is a brief summary of Gaines' paper which established a common basis for both forms of logic of uncertainty in which basic uncertainty logic is defined in terms of truth valuation on a lattice of propositions. Addition of the axiom of the excluded-middle to the basic logic defines standard probability logic. Alternatively, addition of a requirement for strong truth functionality yields a fuzzy logic.

In this discussion, fuzzy logic is taken to be a many-valued extension of Boolean logic based on fuzzy set theory in which truth values are a continuous function between the endpoints of the interval [0, 1]. This is seen to be an extension of the idea proposed by Lukasiewicz (1930) discussed in the previous section. The normal logical operations of both probability theory and fuzzy logic are defined in terms of arithmetic operations on values $x \in [0, 1]$: the vales are regarded as degrees of membership to truth. The logic operations and associated arithmetic operations arc those of conjunction, disjunction, and negation. Gaines (1978) points out that the use of the max and min operators in fuzzy logic is not sufficient to distinguish it from probability theory—both operators arise naturally in the calculation of the conjunction and disjunction of probabilistic events. Our association of addition and multiplication as natural operations upon probabilities comes from our frequent interest in statistically independent events, not from the logic of probability itself.

In developing a basic uncertainty logic (one that embraces both a fuzzy set theory and a probability theory), we begin first by defining a lattice consisting of a universe of discourse X, a maximal element T, a minimal element F, a conjunction $\wedge$, and a disjunction $\vee$. This lattice will he denoted L (X, T, F, $\wedge$, $\vee$), For the axioms (or postulates) to follow, the lower-case letters x, y, and z denote specific elements of the universe X within the lattice. The following 15 axioms completely specify a basic uncertainty logic. The basic uncertainty logic begins with the lattice L satisfying the following axioms:

1. Idempotency: for all $x \in L$, $x \vee x = x \wedge x = x$;
2. Commutativity: for all $x, y \in L$, $x \vee y = y \vee x$; $x \wedge y = y \wedge x$;
3. Associativity: for all $x, y, z \in L$, $x \vee (y \vee z) = (x \vee y) \vee z$;
4. Absorption: for all $x, y \in L$, $x \vee (x \wedge y) = x$ and $x \wedge (x \vee y) = x$;
5. Definition of maximal and minimal elements: $x \in L$, $x \vee T = T$, $x \wedge T = x$.

9.6 POSSIBILITY VERSUS PROBABILITY

Among all concepts and techniques in fuzzy logic, possibility theory is the one that is most often confused with probability theory. For this reason, we will first clarify the differences between them. Possibility and probability measure two different kinds of uncertainty. As we have mentioned in Chapter 2, the best way to introduce possibility theory is to start with the notion of interval values.

Imagine that you were a witness of a bank robbery. When the police asked you about the height of a male suspect, your answer may be one of the following:

- He is betweent 5 feet and 6 feet.
- He is somewhat tall.

Both of these answers impose a constraint (based on your impression) on the possible heights of the suspect. The first answer imposes a crisp constraint. That is, the suspect cant possibly be shorter than 5 feet, nor can he be taller than 6 feet. The second answer on the other hand, typically imposes an imprecise constraint on the suspect's height. Unlike the interval-value answer, the second response does not have a well-defined short boundary between the possible heights and the impossible ones. Rather, it suggests that a certain height is more possible than another one.

In general when we assign a fuzzy set, a variable whose value we don't know exactly, the assignment introduces an imprecise constraint on the variable's value. We call such a constraint a possibility distribution, because it specifies the degree of possibility for the variable to take a certain value. The constraint imposed by an internal-value assignment is a special kind of possibility distribution. In other words, the notion of possibility distribution generalizes the notion of intervalue to smooth the boundary between the possible values and the impossible values so that possibility becomes a matter of degree. We use $\prod(x)$ to denote the possibility distribution of a variable x.

Possibility measures the degree of ease for a variable to take a value, while probability measures the likelihood for a variable to take a value. Therefore, they deal with two different types of uncertainty. Possibility theory handles imprecision, and probability theory matical properties of their distributions. Being a measure of occurrence, the probability distribution of a variable must add up to exactly 1. The possibility Distribution, however, is not subject to this restriction since a variable can have multiple possible values. Returning to our example about the robbery suspect, we may use the following normal distributions with $\mu = 5$ ft, $\sigma = 0.2$ ft to describe the probabilities of the suspect's height:

$$P(h) = \frac{1}{0.2\sqrt{2\pi}} e^{-\frac{1}{2}\left(\frac{h-5}{0.2}\right)^2} \tag{9.1}$$

It is well known that the area under a normal distribution is 1.

9.7 PROBABILITY OF A FUZZY EVENT

An event is a subset of the sample space that shares a common characteristic that we are interested in. a day in Houston with a temperature between 70ºF and 80ºF is an event. The relevant sample space is all possible temperatures in Houston. Having more heads than tails in 20 tossing's of a coin, is a classical event in statistics textbooks.. the relevant sample space included all 21 possible outcomes (ranging from no head to 20 heads). There are situations when the event we are interested in does not have well-defined sharp boundaries. We call them fuzzy events. Formally, a fuzzy event is a fuzzy subset of the sampling space. For instance, "a day with a warm temperature" is a fuzzy event. Another example of a fuzzy event is "in 20 tosses of a coin, there are several more heads than tails."

The formula for calculating the probability of a fuzzy event A is generalization of the probability theory:

$$P(A) = \int mA(x) \times Px(x)\, dx \tag{9.2}$$

If X is continuous, or

$$P(A) = \sum_{i} \mu A(x_i) \times P_x(x_i) \tag{9.3}$$

If X is discrete where P_x denotes the probability distribution function of X.

9.7.1 Properties About Probability of Fuzzy Events

For any two events A and B of a sample space, we know from probability theory that

$$P(A \cup B) = P(A) + P(B) - P(A \cap B) \tag{9.4}$$

Does this relationship hold for fuzzy events? The answer to this question depends on the choice of the fuzzy union (i.e., fuzzy disjunction) and fuzzy intersection (i.e., fuzzy conjunction) operators. In fact, it is straightforward to show that Equation 9.4 holds for the following two choices:

1. Union: max, intersection: min
2. Union: algebraic sum, intersection: algebraic product (i.e. multiplication).

9.7.2 Conditional Probability of Fuzzy Events

Suppose A and B are two events of a sample space the conditional probability of A given B is defined in probability theory as

$$P(A/B) = \frac{P(A \cup B)}{P(B)} \tag{9.5}$$

It is easy to show that the conditional probability of A given B and the conditional probability of A's complement given B adds to 1, i.e.,

$$P(A/B) + P(A^C/B) = 1 \tag{9.6}$$

The conditional probability of fuzzy events can be defined in a similar way using Equation 9.5 However, Equation 9.6 holds only if we choose multiplication as the fuzzy intersection operator.

9.7.3 Independent Fuzzy Events

In probability theory, two events A and B are independent if the occurrence or non-occurrence of either one does not affect the occurrence of the other one, i.e., P (A/B) = P(A) and P(B/A) = P(B).

If we substitute P(A) for P(A/B) into Equation $P(A \cap B) = P(A/B) \times P(B)$, we have $P(A \cap B) = P(A) \times P(B)$, which we will use to formally define the independence of fuzzy events.

Two fuzzy events A and B are independent if and only if $P(A \cap B) = P(A) \times P(B)$.

9.7.4 Bayes' Theorem for Fuzzy Events

Bayes' theorem is the basis for many probabilistic inferences schemes (e.g., Bayes' networks, influence diagrams, etc.) used in intelligent systems. If $A_1, A_2, ..., A_k$ forms a partition of the sample space S (i.e., they are mutually exclusive and exhaustive and $P(A_i) \neq 0$ for i = 1, 2, …, k, then any event B is 5 such that $P(B) \neq 0$, Bayes' theorem enables us to infer $P(A_j/B)$ from and P(B/A):

$$P(A_j/B) = \frac{P(A_j) \times P(B/A_j)}{\sum_{i=1}^{k} P(A_i) \times P(B/A_i)} \tag{9.7}$$

for j = 1, 2, …., k.

If A_i and B are fuzzy events, we need to generalize the condition in Bayes' theorem to allow fuzzy events $A_1, ... A_k$ to form a fuzzy partition of S such that

$$\sum_{i=1}^{k} \mu_{Ai}(x) = 1 \text{ for } x \hat{I} S$$

We formally state the theorem below

If $A_1, A_2, ..., A_k$ are fuzzy events of S, such that

$$\sum_{i=1}^{k} \mu_{Ai}(x) = 1 \text{ for } x \in S \tag{9.8}$$

$P(A_i) \neq 0$ for i = 1, 2, …, k, and B is a fuzzy event of S such that $P(B) \neq 0$,

$$P(A_j/B) = \frac{P(B/A_j) \times P(A_j)}{\sum_{i=1}^{k} P(B/A_i) \times P(A_i)} \tag{9.9}$$

for j = 1, 2, …., k.

Proof: Form the definition of conditional probability for fuzzy events, we have

$$P(A_j/B) = \frac{P(A_i \cap B)}{P(B)} \tag{9.10}$$

In order to show that the right-hand side of Equation 9.9 equals the ratio above, we expand the denominator of Equation 9.9:

$$= \sum_{i=1}^{k} P(B/A_i) \times P(A_i)$$

$$= \sum_{i=1}^{k} P(A_i \cap B)$$

$$= \sum_{i=1}^{k} \sum_{x_k} \mu_{Ai}(x_k) \times \mu_B(x_k) \times P(x_k)$$

$$= \sum_{x_k} \mu_B(x_k) \times P(x_k) \times \left(\sum_{i=1}^{k} \mu_{Ai}(x_k) \right)$$

$$= \sum_{x_k} \mu_B(x_k) \times P(x_k)$$

$$= P(B)$$

Since, $P(B/A_j) \times P(A_j) = P(A_j \cap B)$, we can substitute the numerator and denominator of Equation 9.9 to get Equation 9.10 The theorem is thus proved.

9.8 FUZZY PROBABILITY

In classical probability theory, a probability measure is a number between 0 and 1. There are cases, however, when such a precise probability measure is difficult to obtain. This motivated the development of interval probability theories, which can represent and reason about the lower bound and the upper bound of the probability measure. The interval formed by these two bounds contains the true probability value, which we do not know precisely. In other words, interval probabilities allow us to describe the imprecision of our probability estimates. The width of the interval reflects the degree of imprecision. The wider the interval, the less precise our probability estimates. In the literature of interval probability theory, this interval is sometimes referred to as the degree of ignorance.

9.9 FUZZY MEASURE

Finally, it may be worthwhile to point out that both possibility measure and probability measure belong to a more general class of measures called fuzzy measure.

A probability P over a set of events S is a function from 2^S to [0, 1] such that

1. $P(\phi) = 0$
2. $P(S) = 1$
3. If $A \cap B = 0$

then $$P(A \cup B = P(A) + P(B)$$

where A, B are subsets of S.

4. $P(B|A) = \dfrac{P(A \cap B)}{P(A)}$ if $P(A) \neq 0$

It is easy to show we get the following properties about probabilities from these axioms:

- $P(A) + P(A^c) = 1$
- If A Ì B, then P (B) ³ P(A)

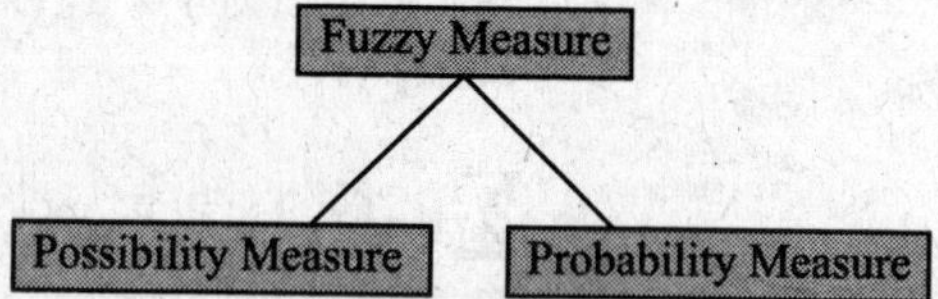

Figure 9.3: Relationships between fuzzy measure, probability, and possibility

A possibility measure Π over a set of events S is a function from 2^s to [0, 1] such that

1. $\Pi(\phi) = 0$
2. $\pi(S) = 1$
3. If $A \subset B$ then, $\pi((A) \leq \pi(B))$
4. $\pi(A \cup B) = \max \{\pi(A), \pi(B)\}$

A fuzzy measure g over a set of events S is a function from s to [0, 1] such that

1. $g(\phi) = 0$
2. $g(S) = 1$
3. if $A \subset B$, then $P(B) \geq P(A)$

Since the set of axioms for fuzzy measure is a subset of the axioms of probability and possibility measure above, it is more general than both of them.

EXERCISES

1. What do you mean by vagueness?
2. What do you mean by imprecision?
3. What do you mean by chance?
4. Explain the difference between fuzziness and probability?
5. Explain the historical perspective of vagueness?
6. Difference between chance and vagueness.
7. What do you mean by many valued logic?
8. Explain the axiomatic structure of probability and fuzzy logic?

9. Difference between possibility and probability.
10. What do you mean by probability of a fuzzy event?
11. Explain the following:
    (i) Properties about probability of fuzzy events
    (ii) Conditional probability of fuzzy events
    (iii) Independence fuzzy events
    (iv) Baye's theorem for fuzzy events
12. What do you mean by fuzzy probability?
13. Explain the concept of fuzzy measure?

CHAPTER 10

Fuzzy Implications and Approximate Reasoning

10.1 INTRODUCTION

In this chapter, we will discuss topics related to "fuzzy logic" in the narrow sense. Classical logic offers a formal framework for reasoning. A logic system has two major components: (1) a formal language for constructing statements about the world, and (2) a set of inference mechanisms for inferring additional statements about the world from those already given. Two of the most commonly used logic systems are (1) propositional logic, and (2) first order predicate logic.

Logic started as the study of language in arguments and persuasion, and it can be used to judge the correctness of a chain of reasoning—in a mathematical proof for instance. The goal of the theory is to reduce principles of reasoning to a code. The 'truth' or 'falsity' assigned to a proposition is its truth-value. In fuzzy logic a proposition may be true or false, or an intermediate truth-value such as maybe true. The sentence 'John is a tall man' is an example of a fuzzy proposition. For convenience we shall here restrict the possible truth-values to a discrete domain {0, 0.5, 1} for false, maybe true, and true. In doing so we are in effect restricting the theory to multi-valued logic, or rather three-valued logic to be specific. In practice one would subdivide the unit interval into finer divisions, or work with a continuous truth-domain. Nevertheless, much of what follows is valid even in a continuous domain as we shall see.

After a brief review of these two bivalent logic systems, we introduce fuzzy logic with an emphasis on fuzzy implications and approximate reasoning. We chose to focus on fuzzy implications for two reasons. First, it is the most commonly used reasoning scheme in applications of fuzzy logic (narrow sense). An important application of fuzzy implications is fuzzy expert systems, which we will discuss in next chapter.

The second reason we elaborate on fuzzy implications is the subject is complicated by the fact that there isn't unique definition of fuzzy implications. In fact, there are three major ways to define fuzzy implication, which lead to three families of fuzzy implications.

10.2 PROPOSITIONAL LOGIC

In daily conversation and mathematics, sentences are connected with the words and, or, if-then (or implies), and if and only if. These are called connectives. A sentence which is modified by the word 'not' is called the negation of the original sentence. The word 'and' is used to join two sentences to form the conjunction of the two sentences. The word 'or' is used to join two sentences to form the disjunction of the two sentences. From two sentences we may construct one, of the form 'If ... then ...'; this is called an implication. The sentence following 'If' is the antecedent, and the sentence following 'then' is the consequent. Other idioms which we shall regard as having the same meaning are 'p implies q', 'p only if q', 'q if p', etc. Letters and special symbols make the connective structure stand out. In propositional logic, a statement about the world is constructed by (1) representing simple sentences as basic units called propositions, and (2) connecting propositions with the following connectors to form complex sentences:

$\neg$ For 'not'

$\wedge$ For 'and'

$\vee$ for 'or'

$\Rightarrow$ for 'if then' (implication)

$\Leftrightarrow$ for 'if and only if' (equivalence)

For example, a statement such as

$\vee$

If today is a weekday and the current time is rush hour, then the traffic is congested.

Can be represented by first defining the following three propositions:

P: today is a weekday

Q: the current time is during rush hour

R: the traffic is congested

then connecting them using "and" and "implication" we have:

$$(P \wedge Q) \Rightarrow R \tag{10.1}$$

A classical logic statement can have two possible truth values: true or false. Since a logic connective is applied to a subformula or a pair of subformula, its meaning can be defined by listing the truth value of the resulted (compound) formula for all possible truth value combinations of the subformula. A table that provides such a listing is called a truth table. The truth table of logic connectives mentioned above are shown in Table below.

α	β	$\neg\alpha$	$\alpha \wedge \beta$	$\alpha \quad \beta$	$\alpha \Rightarrow \beta$
False	False	True	False	False	True
False	True	True	False	True	True
True	False	False	False	True	False
True	True	False	True	True	True

The implication connective is especially important, because it is the basis of fuzzy implication rules. An implication has two parts: a premise (the "if-part" preceding the implication connective) and a conclusion (the "then-part" following the implication connective). In the previous example (Equation 10.1) for instance $P \wedge Q$ is the premise and R is the conclusion.

An implication $\alpha \Rightarrow \beta$ is logically equivalent to $\neg\alpha \vee \beta$. That is an implication is true if either its premise is false or its conclusion is true. The rationale of this definition is that the implication should not tell us anything regarding whether $\alpha\beta$ is true when the premise is false. This can easily be verified using the truth table above. To find out the truth value of β when α is false and $\alpha \Rightarrow \beta$ is true, we identify those rows in the truth table that have the correct truth value assignments under the columns of α and $\alpha \Rightarrow \beta$ (i.e. the first and second rows). The truth table value β in these two rows are "False" and "True" respectively. Therefore, nothing can be inferred about the truth value of β (i.e. it is unknown).

One of the most important inference schemes in propositional logic is modus ponens. Given that an implication and its premise are true, modus ponens enables us to deduce that the consequent s true.

$$\alpha \Rightarrow \beta$$

For instance, assuming that we know today is a weekday and the time is during rush hour, we can deduce that the traffic is congested using the implication in Equation 10.1:

$$(P \wedge Q) \Rightarrow R \qquad \frac{\alpha}{\beta}$$

$$P$$

$$\frac{Q}{R}$$

Another inference scheme involving implication is modus tolens. From an implication and the negation of its conclusion, we can deduce the negation of its premise:

$$\alpha \Rightarrow \beta$$

$$\frac{\neg\beta}{\neg\alpha}$$

One of the main limitations of propositional logic is that is cannot easily describe knowledge that applies to a class of objects. To do this, we need first-order predicate calculus.

The next example illustrates how the symbolic forms expose the underlying logical structure.

Example 10.1: Baseball betting.

Consider the assertion about four baseball teams: If either the Pirates or the Cubs loose and the Giants win, then the Dodgers will be out of first place, and I will loose a bet. Since it is an implication, it may be symbolized in the form $r \Rightarrow s$. The antecedent is composed from the three sentences p (The Pirates lose), c (The Cubs lose), and g (The Giants win). The consequent is the conjunction of d (The Dodgers will be out of first place) and b (I will lose a bet). The original sentence may thus be represented by $(p \vee c) \wedge g) \Rightarrow (d \wedge b)$. An assertion which contains at least one propositional variable is called a propositional form. The main difference between proposition and propositional form is that every proposition has a truth-value, whereas a propositional form is an assertion whose truth-value cannot be determined until propositions are substituted for its propositional variables. But when no confusion results, we will refer to propositional forms as propositions. A truth-table summarizes the possible truth-values of an assertion. Take for example the truth-table for the two-valued propositional form $p \vee q$. The truth-table (below, left) lists all possible combinations of truth-values — the Cartesian product — of the arguments p and q in the two leftmost columns. The rightmost column holds the truth-values of the proposition. Alternatively, the truth-table can be rearranged into a two-dimensional array, a so-called Cayley table (below, right).

p	q	$p \vee q$
0	0	0
0	1	1
1	0	1
1	1	1

is equivalent to

Or

$p \vee q \;\rightarrow q$

$\downarrow p$	0	1
0	0	1
1	1	1

Along the vertical axis in the Cayley table, symbolized by arrow ↓ are the possible values 0 and 1 of the first argument p. Along the horizontal axis, symbolized by arrow →, are the possible values 0 and 1 of the second argument q. Above the table, the proposition $p \vee q$ reminds us that the table concerns disjunction. At the intersection of row i and column j (only counting the inside of the box) is the truth-value of the expression $p_i \vee q_j$. By inspection, one entry renders $p \vee q$ false, while three entries render $p \vee q$ true. Truth-tables for binary connectives are thus given by two-by-two matrices. A total of 16 such tables can be constructed, and each has been associated with a connective. We can derive the truth-table for 'nand' ('not and') from 'or'. By the definition $(\neg p) \vee (\neg q)$ we negate each variable of the previous truth-table, which is equivalent to reversing the axes and permuting the entries back in the usual ascending order on the axes,

Nand

$(\neg p) \vee (\neg q)$

$\downarrow p$	0	1 $\rightarrow q$
0	1	1
1	1	0

From 'nand' ('not and') we derive 'and' by negating the entries of the table ('not not and' = 'and'),

And

$\neg((\neg p) \vee (\neg q))$

p \ q	0	1
0	0	0
1	0	1

Notice that it was possible to define 'and' by means of 'or' and 'not', rather than assume its definition given as an axiom. By means of 'or' and 'not' we can proceed to define 'implication'. Classical logic defines implication $\neg p \vee q$, which is called material implication. We negate the p-axis of the 'or' table, which is equivalent to reversing the axis and permuting the entries back in the usual ascending order, thus

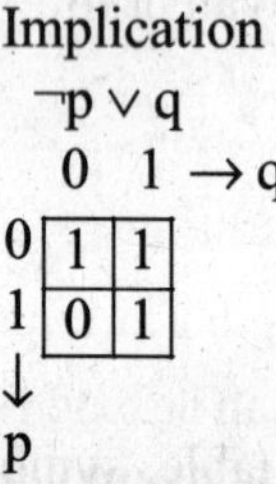
Implication

$\neg p \vee q$

p \ q	0	1
0	1	1
1	0	1

Equivalence is taken to mean $(p \Rightarrow q) \wedge (q \Rightarrow p)$, which is equivalent to the conjunction of each entry of the implication table with the elements of the transposed table, element by element, or

Equivalence

$(p \Rightarrow q) \wedge (q \Rightarrow p)$

p \ q	0	1
0	1	0
1	0	1

It is possible to evaluate, in principle at least, a logical proposition by an exhaustive test of all combinations of truth-values of the variables, and this is the idea behind array based logic. The next example illustrates an application of array based logic.

10.3 FIRST-ORDER PREDICATE CALCULUS

First-Order Predicate Calculus (FOPC) offers a formal language that is more powerful than that of propositional logic. More specifically, it allows the use of variables in a logic statement. A variable FOPC is associated with one of the two quantifiers: the universal quantifier $\forall$ (read "for all") and the existential quantifier ∃ (read "there exists"). The former is used to describe a statement that is true for all possible objects, while the latter is used to describe a statement that is true for at least one object.

Unlike propositional logic, FOPC uses predicates to describe simple sentences. A predicate represents a set of objects (e.g. the predicate Aggies represents the set of Aggies) or a relation (e.g. the predicate friend represents a friendship relation between two persons). A predicate has a number of arguments, which can be variables or constants.

The following are some examples of predicates with constant arguments:

Aggies(John) John is an Aggie.

RushHour(5pm): Five o'clock in the afternoon is during rush hour.

Friend(Jack, Jill): Jack and Jill are friends.

Like propositional logic, FOPC combines simple logic expressions into complex ones using logic connectives. For instance, a statement such as "all Aggies like Aggie traditions" can be described in a logic system called first-order predicate logic as follows:

$$\forall x, y \text{ Aggies}(x) \wedge \text{AggieTraditions}(y) \Rightarrow \text{Like}(x, y) \tag{10.2}$$

where x and y are variables; Aggies, Aggie Tradition and Like are predicates.

All inference rules in propositional logic can be extended to FOPC by finding proper substitutions of variables using a unification algorithm. For example, given the following facts

Aggie(John)

AggieTradition(Bonfire)

modus ponens can be applied to Equation 10.2 by substituting variable x and y with John and Bonfire respectively, denoted as {John/x, Bonfire/y}.

$\forall$ x,y Aggies(x) $\wedge$ AggieTradition(y) $\Rightarrow$ Like(x, y)

Aggie(John)

Aggie Tradition(Bonfire)

Like(John, Bonfire) ϕ = {John/x, Bonfire/y}

where ϕ denotes a variable substitution. Such variable substitutions are called unifiers. The algorithms for finding these variable substitutions are called unification algorithms.

Example 10.2: Array based logic

In the baseball example, we had the relation $((p \vee c) \wedge g) \Rightarrow (d \wedge b)$. The proposition contains five variables, and each variable can take two truth-values. There are therefore $2^5 = 32$ possible combinations. Only 23 are legal, in the sense that the proposition is true for these combinations, and $32 - 23 = 9$ cases are illegal, in the sense that the proposition is false for those combinations. If we are interested only in the legal combinations for which I win the bet' (b = 0), then the following table results

p	c	g	d	b
0	0	0	0	0
0	0	0	1	0
0	0	1	0	0
0	0	1	1	0
0	1	0	0	0
0	1	0	1	0
1	0	0	0	0
1	0	0	1	0
1	1	0	0	0
1	1	0	1	0

There are thus 10 winning outcomes out of 32 possible.

By analogy we can define similar truth-tables for fuzzy logic connectives. If we start again by defining negation and disjunction, we can derive the truth-tables of other connectives from that point of departure. Let us define disjunction as set union, that is,

$$p \vee q \equiv \max(p, q) \tag{10.3}$$

We can then build the truth-table for the fuzzy connective 'or',

Or

$p \vee q$

p ↓ \ q →	0	0.5	1
0	0	0.5	1
0.5	0.5	0.5	1
1	1	1	1

Like before, the p-axis is vertical and the q-axis horizontal. At the intersection of row i and column j (only regarding the inside of the box) is the value of the expression max(pi, qj) in accordance with (10.3). When looking for definitions of fuzzy connectives, we will require that such connectives should agree with their classical counterparts for the truth-domain {0, 1}.

In terms of truth-tables, the values in the four corners of the fuzzy Cayley table, should agree with the Cayley table for the classical connective. Let us define negation as set complement, that is,

$$\neg p \equiv 1 - p.$$

The truth-table for 'nand' is derived from 'or' by the definition $(\neg p) \vee (\neg q)$ by negating the variables. That is equivalent to reversing the axes in the Cayley table. And moving further, 'and' is the negation of the entries in the truth-table for 'nand', thus

Nand

$(\neg p) \vee (\neg q)$

p ↓ \ q →	0	0.5	1
0	1	1	1
0.5	1	0.5	0.5
1	1	0.5	0

And

$\neg((\neg p) \vee (\neg q))$

p ↓ \ q →	0	0.5	1
0	0	0	0
0.5	0	0.5	0.5
1	0	0.5	1

It is reassuring to observe that even though the truth-table for 'and' is derived from the truth-table for 'or', the truth-table for 'and' is identical to one generated using the min operation, set intersection. The implication, however, has always troubled fuzzy logicians. If we define it as material implication, $\neg p \vee q$, then we get a fuzzy truth-table which is unsuitable, as it causes several useful logical laws to break down. It is important to realise, that we must make a design choice at this point, in order to proceed with the definition of implication and equivalence. The choice is which logical laws we wish to apply. Not all laws known from two-valued logic can be valid in fuzzy logic. Take for instance the propositional form

$$p \vee \neg p \Leftrightarrow 1 \tag{10.4}$$

which is equivalent to the law of the excluded middle. Testing with the truth-value p = 0.5 (fuzzy logic) the left hand side yields $0.5 \vee \neg 0.5 = \max(0.5, 1 - 0.5) = 0.5$. This is different from the right hand side, and thus the law of the excluded middle is invalid in fuzzy logic. If a proposition is true with a truth-value of 1, for any combination of truth-values assigned to the variables, we shall say it is valid. Such a proposition is a tautology. If the proposition is true for some, but not all combinations, we shall say it is satisfiable. Thus (10.4) is satisfiable, since it is true in two-valued logic, but not in three-valued logic.

One tautology that we definitely wish to apply in fuzzy logic applications is

Tautology 1:
$$[p \wedge (p \Rightarrow q)] \Rightarrow q \tag{10.5}$$

Or in words: If p, and p implies q, then q. We have labelled it tautology 1, because we need it later in connection with the modus ponens rule of inference. Another tautology that we definitely wish to apply in fuzzy logic applications is the transitive relationship

Tautology 2:
$$[(p \Rightarrow q) \wedge (q \Rightarrow r)] \Rightarrow (p \Rightarrow r) \tag{10.6}$$

Or in words from left to right: if p implies q which in turn implies r, then p implies r. Whether these propositions are valid in fuzzy logic depends on how we define the connectives. Or rather, we must define the connectives, implication in particular, such that those propositions become valid (Jantzen, 1995[5]). One candidate, not necessarily the best, is the so-called sharp implication. It can be defined

$$p \Rightarrow q \equiv p \leq q \tag{10.11}$$

This choice is motivated by the following argument. When the crisp set X is included in the crisp set Y, then X is said to imply Y. The fuzzy set A is included in the fuzzy set B, iff $\mu_A(x) \leq \mu_B(x)$, therefore we define implication by (10.11). Once it is agreed that $p \Leftrightarrow q$ is the same as $(p \Rightarrow q) \wedge (q \Rightarrow p)$, the truth-table for equivalence ($\Leftrightarrow$) is determined from implication and conjunction,

Example 10.3: Fuzzy baseball

The baseball example illustrates what difference three-valued logic makes. The proposition

$$((p \vee c) \wedge g) \Rightarrow (d \wedge b)$$

contains five variables, and now each can take three truth-values. This implies $3^5 = 243$ possible combinations; 148 of these are legal in the sense that the proposition is true (truthvalue 1). If we are interested again in the legal combinations for which 'I win the bet' (b = 0), then there are 33 winning outcomes out of 148. Instead of listing all, we show one for illustration,

$$(p, c, g, d, b) = (0.5, 0.5, 0, 1, 0).$$

With two-valued logic we found 10 winning outcomes out of 32 possible. The example indicates that fuzzy logic provides more solutions, compared to two-valued logic, and it requires more computational effort. It is straight forward to test whether tautologies 1 and 2 are valid, because it is possible to perform an exhaustive test of all combinations of truth-values of the variables, provided the domain of truth-values is discrete and limited.

Example 10.4: Testing tautology 1

Tautology 1 is,

$$[p \wedge (p \Rightarrow q)] \Rightarrow q$$

Since the proposition contains two variables p and q, and each variable can take three truth-values, there will be $3^2 = 9$ possible combinations to test. The truth-table has 9 rows,

p	q	$p \Rightarrow q$	$[p \wedge (p \Rightarrow q)]$	$[p \wedge (p \Rightarrow q)] \Rightarrow q$
0	0	1	0	1
0	0.5	1	0	1
0	1	1	0	1
0.5	0	0	0	1
0.5	0.5	1	0.5	1
0.5	1	1	0.5	1
1	0	0	0	1
1	0.5	0	0	1
1	1	1	1	1

Columns 1 and 2 are the input combinations of p and q. Column 3 is the result of sharp implication, and column 4 is the left hand side of tautology 1. Since the rightmost column is all 1's, the proposition is a tautology, even in three-valued logic.

Example 10.5: Suggests a new tautology, in fact. If we study closely the truth-values for $[p \wedge (p \Rightarrow q)]$ (column 4 in the example), and compare them with the truth-table for conjunction, we discover they are identical. We can thus postulate,

Tautology 3: $$[p \wedge (p \Rightarrow q)] \Leftrightarrow p \wedge q$$

We shall use this result later in connection with fuzzy inference. The main objective of the approach taken here, is not to show that one implication is better than another, but to reduce the proof of any tautology to a test that can be programmed on a computer. The scope is so far limited to the chosen truth domain {0, 0.5, 1}; this could be extended with intermediate values, however, and the test performed again in case a higher resolution is required. Nevertheless, it suffices to check for all possible combinations of {0, 0.5, 1} if we wish to check the equality of two propositions involving variables connected with ∧, ∨, and ¬. For propositions involving sharp implication, which cannot be transcribed into a definition involving the said three connectives only, we have to conjecture the results for fuzzy logic. Since implication can be defined in many possible ways, one has to determine a design criterion first, namely the tautologies, before choosing a proper definition for the implication connective.

Originally, Zadeh interpreted a truth-value in fuzzy logic as a fuzzy set, for instance Very true. Thus Zadeh based fuzzy (linguistic) logic on treating Truth as a linguistic variable that takes words or sentences as values rather than numbers. Please be aware that our approach differs, as it is built on scalar truth-values rather than vectors.

Example 10.6: Mamdani implication

The so-called Mamdani implication, is often used in fuzzy control. Let A and B be fuzzy sets defined on X and Y respectively, then the Mamdani implication is a fuzzy set in X × Y with the membership function

$$\{\langle\langle x, y\rangle, \mu_{A' \Rightarrow' B}(x, y)\rangle \mid x \in X, y \in Y, \mu_{A' \Rightarrow' B}(x, y) = \min \mu_A(x), \mu_B(y))\}$$

Notice the definition is similar to the definition of the fuzzy cartesian product. Its Cayley table, using the minimum operation, is

Mamdani' Implication'

(p, q)

p ↓ \ q →	0	0.5	1
0	0	0	0
0.5	0	0.5	0.5
1	0	0.5	1

One discovers by inspection that only one out of the four corner-values matches the truthtable for two-valued implication. Therefore, it is not an implication, and Mamdani 'inference' would be a more appropriate name, as we shall see later.

10.4 INFERENCE

Logic provides principles of reasoning, by means of inference, the drawing of conclusions from assertions. The verb 'to infer' means to conclude from evidence, deduce, or to have as a logical consequence (do not confuse 'inference' with 'interference'). Rules of inference specify conclusions drawn from assertions known or assumed to be true. One such rule of inference is modus ponens. It is often presented in the form of an argument:

$$\frac{\begin{array}{c} P \\ P \Rightarrow Q \end{array}}{Q}$$

In words: If 1) P is known to be true, and 2) we assume that $P \Rightarrow Q$ is true, then 3) Q must be true. Restricting for a moment to two-valued logic, we see from the truth-table for implication,

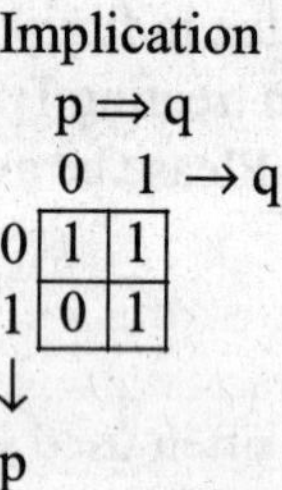

whenever $P \Rightarrow Q$ and P are true then so is Q; by P true we consider only the second row, leaving Q true as the only possibility. In such an argument the assertions above the line are the premises, and the assertion below the line the conclusion. Notice the premises are assumed to be true, we are not considering all possible truth combinations as we did when proving tautologies.

On the other hand, underlying modus ponens is tautology 1, which expresses the same, but is valid for all truth-values. Therefore modus ponens is valid in fuzzy logic, if tautology 1 is valid in fuzzy logic.

Example 10.7: Four useful rules of inference

There are several useful rules of inference, which can be represented by tautological forms. Four are presented here by examples from medicine.

(a) Modus ponens: Its tautological form is

$$[p \wedge (p \Rightarrow q)] \Rightarrow q.$$

Let p stand for 'altitude sickness,' and let $p \Rightarrow q$ stand for 'altitude sickness causes a headache'. If it is known that John suffers from altitude sickness, p is true, and $p \Rightarrow q$ is assumed to be true for the case of illustration, then the conclusion q is true, that is, John has a headache.

(b) Modus tollens: Its tautological form is

$$[\neg q \wedge (p \Rightarrow q)] \Rightarrow \neg p.$$

Let p and q be as in (a). Thus, if John does not have a headache, then we may infer that John does not suffer from altitude sickness.

(c) Disjunctive syllogism: Its tautological form is

$$[(p \vee q) \wedge \neg p] \Rightarrow q.$$

Let p stand for 'altitude sickness' as previously, but let q stand for 'dehydration'. Thus, if it is known for a fact that John's headache is due to either altitude sickness or dehydration, and it is not altitude sickness, then we may infer that John suffers from dehydration.

(d) Hypothetical syllogism: Its tautological form is tautology 2:

$$[(p \Rightarrow q) \wedge (q \Rightarrow r)] \Rightarrow (p \Rightarrow r).$$

Let p stand for 'high altitude and fast ascent', let q stand for 'altitude sickness', and let r stand for 'a headache'. Further assume that high altitude and fast ascent together cause altitude sickness, and in turn that altitude sickness causes a headache. Thus, we may infer that John will get a headache in high altitude if John ascends fast. Provided the tautological forms are valid in fuzzy logic, the inference rules may be applied in fuzzy logic as well. The inference mechanism in modus ponens can be generalised. The pattern is: given a relation R connecting logical variables p and q, we infer the possible values of q given a particular instance of p. Switching to vector-matrix representation, to emphasize the computer implementation, with p a (column) vector and R a two-dimensional truth-table, with the p-axis vertical, the inference is defined

$$q^t = p^t \circ R$$

The operation $\circ$ is an inner $\vee - \wedge$ product. The $\wedge$ operation is the same as in $p \wedge (p \Rightarrow q)$ and the $\vee$ operation along the columns yields what can possibly be implied about q, confer the rightmost implication in $[p \wedge (p \Rightarrow q)] \Rightarrow p$. Assuming p is true corresponds to setting

$$P = \begin{pmatrix} 0 \\ 1 \end{pmatrix}$$

But the scheme is more general, because we could also assume p is false, compose with R and study what can be inferred about q. Take for instance modus ponens, thus

$$R = \begin{pmatrix} 1 & 1 \\ 0 & 1 \end{pmatrix}$$

which is the truth-table for $p \Rightarrow q$. Assigning p as above;

$$q^t = p^t \circ R = (0 \quad 1) \circ \begin{pmatrix} 1 & 1 \\ 0 & 1 \end{pmatrix} = (0 \quad 1)$$

The outcome q^t is a truth-vector pointing at q true as the only possible conclusion, as expected. Testing for instance with $p = (10)^t$ yields

$$q^t = p^t \circ R = (1 \;\; 0) \circ \begin{pmatrix} 1 & 1 \\ 0 & 1 \end{pmatrix} = (1 \;\; 1)$$

Thus q could be anything, true or false, as expected. The inference could even proceed in the reverse direction, from q to p, but then we must compose from the right side of R to match the axes. Assume for instance q is true, or $q = (10)^t$, then

$$P = R \circ q = \begin{pmatrix} 1 & 1 \\ 0 & 1 \end{pmatrix} \circ \begin{pmatrix} 1 \\ 0 \end{pmatrix} = \begin{pmatrix} 1 \\ 0 \end{pmatrix}$$

To interpret: if q is false and $p \Rightarrow q$, then p is false (modus tollens).

The array based inference mechanism is even more general, because R can be any dimension n ($n > 0$ and integer). Given values of $n - 1$ variables, the possible outcomes of the remaining variable can be inferred by an n-dimensional inner product. Furthermore, given values of $n - d$ variables (d integer and $0 < d < n$), then the truth-array connecting the remaining d variables can be inferred.

Generalising to three-valued logic p and q are vectors of three elements, R a 3-by-3 matrix, and the inner $\vee - \wedge$ product interpreted as the inner max-min product. Assuming p is true, corresponds to assigning

$$P = \begin{pmatrix} 0 \\ 0.5 \\ 1 \end{pmatrix}$$

In modus ponens

$$R = \begin{pmatrix} 1 & 1 & 1 \\ 0 & 1 & 1 \\ 0 & 0 & 1 \end{pmatrix},$$

which is the truth-table for sharp implication. With p as above,

$$q^t = p^t \circ R = (0.5 \;\; 1) \circ \begin{pmatrix} 1 & 1 & 1 \\ 0 & 1 & 1 \\ 0 & 0 & 1 \end{pmatrix}, = (0 \;\; .5 \;\; 1)$$

To interpret, p true and $p \Rightarrow q$ true, implies q true, as expected because tautology 1 is valid in three valued logic.

The inner product $p^t \circ R$ can be decomposed into three operations.

1. A Cartesian product

$$R^1 = P \times 1^t = \begin{pmatrix} 0 \\ 0.5 \\ 1 \end{pmatrix} \times (1 \;\; 1 \;\; 1) = \begin{pmatrix} 0 & 0 & 0 \\ 0.5 & 0.5 & 0.5 \\ 1 & 1 & 1 \end{pmatrix}$$

called the cylindrical extension. The result is a matrix whose columns are the vector p repeated as many times as necessary to fit the size of R.

2. An element-wise intersection

$$R^2 = R^1 \wedge R = \begin{pmatrix} 0 & 0 & 0 \\ 0.5 & 0.5 & 0.5 \\ 1 & 1 & 1 \end{pmatrix} \wedge \begin{pmatrix} 1 & 1 & 1 \\ 0 & 1 & 1 \\ 0 & 0 & 1 \end{pmatrix} = \begin{pmatrix} 0 & 0 & 0 \\ 0 & 0.5 & 0.5 \\ 0 & 0 & 1 \end{pmatrix}$$

This operation does not have a name in the literature.

3. A V-operation along the columns of R^2,

$$q^t = \bigvee_p r^2_{pq} = (0 \quad 0.5 \quad 1)$$

which is the projection of R on the q-axis.

In general, the max-min composition

$$b^t = a^t \circ R$$

consists of three operations: 1) the cylindrical extension $R^1 = a^t \times 1_b$, 2) the element wise intersection

$$R^2 = r^1_{ab} \wedge r_{ab},$$

and the projection onto the b-axis

$$b^t = \bigvee_b r^2_{ab}.$$

This constitutes the compositional rule of inference, where b is inferred from a by means of R.

10.5 THE MATERIAL IMPLICATION

Let p = "x is in A" and q = "y is in B" are crisp propositions, where A and B are crisp sets for the moment. The implication $p \to q$ is interpreted as $\neg(p \wedge \neg q)$. "p entails q" means that it can never happen that p is true and q is not true. It is easy to see that

$$p \to q = \neg p \vee q$$

The full interpretation of the material implication $p \to q$ is that the degree of truth of $p \to q$ quantifies to what extend q is at least as true as p, i.e.

$$p \to q \text{ is true} \Leftrightarrow \tau(p) \le \tau(q)$$

$$p \to q = \begin{cases} 1 & \text{if } \tau(p) \le \tau(q) \\ 0 & \text{otherwise} \end{cases}$$

p	q	p→q
1	1	1
0	1	1
0	0	1
1	0	0

The truth table for the material implication.

Example 10.8: Let p = "x is bigger than 10" and let q = "x is bigger than 9". It is easy to see that p $\rightarrow$ q is true, because it can never happen that x is bigger than 10 and x is not bigger than 9.

This property of material implication can be interpreted as:

if $X \subset Y$ then $X \rightarrow Y$

Other interpretation of the implication operator is

$$X \rightarrow Y = \sup\{Z | X \cap Z \subset Y\}.$$

10.6 FUZZY IMPLICATIONS

Consider the implication statement if pressure is high then volume is small. The membership function of the fuzzy set A, big pressure, illustrated in the figure

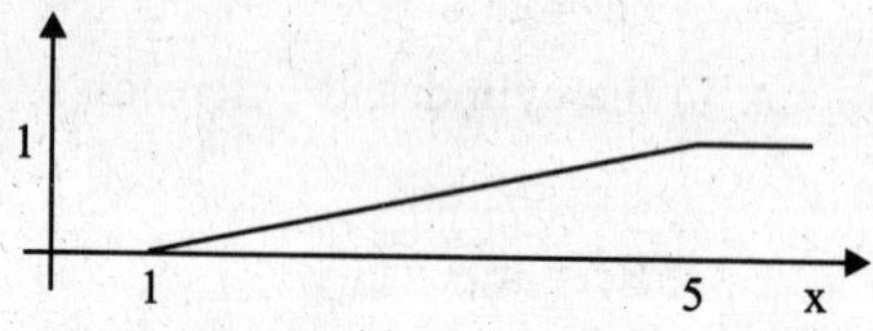

Membership function for 'big pressure'.

can be interpreted as

- 1 is in the fuzzy set big pressure with grade of membership 0
- 2 is in the fuzzy set big pressure with grade of membership 0.25
- 4 is in the fuzzy set big pressure with grade of membership 0.75
- x is in the fuzzy set big pressure with grade of membership 1, for all $x \geq 5$

$$A(u) = \begin{cases} 1 & \text{if } u \geq 5 \\ 1 - \dfrac{5-u}{4} & \text{if } 1 \leq u \leq 5 \\ 0 & \text{otherwise} \end{cases}$$

The membership function of the fuzzy set B, small volume, can be interpreted as (see figure)

- 5 is in the fuzzy set small volume with grade of membership 0
- 4 is in the fuzzy set small volume with grade of membership 0.25
- 2 is in the fuzzy set small volume with grade of membership 0.75
- x is in the fuzzy set small volume with grade of membership 1, for all $x \leq 1$

$$B(\upsilon) = \begin{cases} 1 & \text{if } \upsilon \leq 1 \\ 1 - \dfrac{\upsilon-1}{4} & \text{if } 1 \leq \upsilon \leq 5 \\ 0 & \text{otherwise} \end{cases}$$

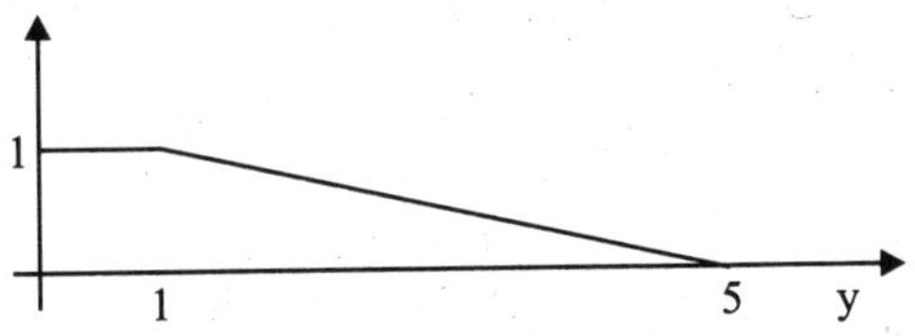

Membership function for 'small volume'.

If p is a proposition of the form x is A

where A is a fuzzy set, for example, big pressure and q is a proposition of the form y is B. For example, small volume then we defines the fuzzy implication $A \to B$ as a fuzzy relation.

It is clear that $(A \to B)(u, v)$ should be defined pointwise and likewise, i.e. $(A \to B)(u, v)$ depends only on A(u) and B(v).

That is $(A \to B)(u, v) = I(A(u), B(v)) = A(u) \to B(v)$

In our interpretation A(u) is considered as the truth value of the proposition "u is big pressure", and B(v) is considered as the truth value of the proposition "v is small volume.

that is u is big pressure $\to$ v is small volume $\equiv A(u) \to B(v)$ Remembering the full interpretation of the material Implication

$$p \to q = \begin{cases} 1 \text{ if } \tau(p) \le \tau(q) \\ 0 \text{ otherwise} \end{cases}$$

One possible extension of material implication to implications with intermediate truth values can be

$$A(u) \to B(\upsilon) = \begin{cases} 1 \text{ if } A(u) \le B(\upsilon) \\ 0 \text{ otherwise} \end{cases}$$

"4 is big pressure" $\to$"1 is small volume" $= A(4) \to B(1) = 0.75 \to 1 = 1$

However, it is easy to see that this fuzzy implication operator (called Standard Strict) sometimes is not appropriate for real-life applications.

Namely, let

$$A(u) = 0.8 \text{ and } B(v) = 0.8.$$

Then we have

$$A(u) \to B(v) = 0.8 \to 0.8 = 1$$

Suppose there is a small error of measurement in B(v), and instead of 0.8 we have 0.7999. Then

$$A(u) \to B(v) = 0.8 \to 0.7999 = 0$$

This example shows that small changes in the input can cause a big deviation in the output, i.e. our system is very sensitive to rounding errors of digital computation and small errors of measurement.

A smoother extension of material implication operator can be derived from the equation

$$X \to Y = \sup\{Z | X \cap Z \subset Y\}$$

That is

$$A(u) \to B(v) = \sup\{z | \min\{A(u), z\} \leq B(v)\}$$

so,

$$A(u) \to B(\upsilon) = \begin{cases} 1 \text{ if } A(u) \leq B(\upsilon) \\ B(\upsilon) \text{ otherwise} \end{cases}$$

This operator is called Godel implication. Other possibility is to extend the original definition,

$$p \to q = \neg p \vee q$$

using the definition of negation and union

$$A(u) \to B(v) = \max\{1 - A(u), B(v)\}$$

This operator is called Kleene-Dienes implication. In many practical applications they use Mamdani's implication operator to model causal relationship between fuzzy variables.

This operator simply takes the minimum of truth values of fuzzy predicates

$$A(u) \to B(v) = \min\{A(u), B(v)\}$$

It is easy to see this is not a correct extension of material implications, because $0 \to 0$ yields zero. However, in knowledge-based systems, we are usually not interested in rules, where the antecedent part is false.

Major fuzzy implication functions:

Larsen	$x \to y = xy$
Lukasiewicz	$x \to y = \min\{1, 1 - x + y\}$
Mamdani	$x \to y = \min\{x, y\}$
Standard Strict	$x \to y = \begin{cases} 1 \text{ if } x, \leq y \\ 0 \text{ otherwise} \end{cases}$
Godal	$x \to y = \begin{cases} 1 \text{ if } x, \leq y \\ y \text{ otherwise} \end{cases}$
Gaines	$x \to y = \begin{cases} 1 \text{ if } x, \leq y \\ y/x \text{ otherwise} \end{cases}$
Kleene-Dienes	$x \to y = \max\{1 - x, y\}$
Lleene-Dienes-LUK	$x \to y = 1 - x + xy$

10.7 FUZZY RULES

A fuzzy rule has the form

If x is A then y is B,

in which A and B are fuzzy sets, defined on universes X and Y, respectively. This is an implication, where the antecedent is 'x is A', and the consequent is 'y is B'. Examples of such rules in everyday conversation are

1. If it is dark, then drive slowly
2. If the tomato is red, then it is ripe
3. If it is early, then John can study
4. If the room is cold, then increase the heat
5. If the washing machine is half full, then wash shorter time

Other forms can be transcribed into the if-then form, for example 'when in Rome, do like the Romans' becomes 'if in Rome, then do like the Romans'. Examples 4 and 5 could appear in a computer embedded in a heating unit or a washing machine. To understand how a computer can infer a conclusion, take rule 3,

If it is early, then John can study

Assume that 'early' is a fuzzy set defined on the universe

$$\mu = (4, 8, 12, 16, 20, 24).$$

These are times t of the day, in steps of four hours, in 24 hour format to distinguish night from day numerically. Define 'early' as a fuzzy set on U,

early = {(4, 0) , (8, 1) , (12, 0.9) , (16, 0.7) , (20, 0.5) , (24, 0.2)}

For simplicity define 'can study' as a singleton fuzzy set μstudy = 1. If the hour is truly early, for instance 8 o'clock in the morning, then $\mu_{early}(8) = 1$, and thus John can study to the fullest degree, that is $\mu_{study} = 1$. However, at 20 (8 pm) then $\mu_{early}{}^{(20)} = 0.5$, and accordingly John can study to the degree 0.5. The degree of fulfillment of the antecedent (the if -side) weights the degree of fulfillment of the conclusion—a useful mechanism, that enables one rule to cover a range of hours. The procedure is: given a particular time instant t0, the resulting truth-value is computed as $\min(\mu_{early}(t_0), \mu_{study})$.

10.8 LINGUISTIC VARIABLES

Whereas an algebraic variable takes numbers as values, a linguistic variable takes words or sentences as values (Zadeh in Zimmermann, 1993[16]). The name of such a linguistic variable is its label. The set of values that it can take is called its term set. Each value in the term set is a linguistic value or term defined over the unive'rse. In summary: A linguistic variable takes a linguistic value, which is a fuzzy set defined on the universe.

Example 10.9: Term set Age

Let x be a linguistic variable labelled 'Age'. Its term set T could be defined as

T (age) = {young, very young, not very young, old, more or less old}

Each term is defined on the universe, for example the integers from 0 to 100 years.

A hedge is a word that acts on a term and modifies its meaning. For example, in the sentence 'very near zero', the word 'very' modifies the term 'near zero'. Examples of other hedges are 'a little', 'more or less', 'possibly', and 'definitely'. In fuzzy reasoning a hedge operates on a membership function, and the result is a membership function. Even though it is difficult precisely to say what effect the hedge 'very' has, it does have an intensifying effect. The hedge 'more or less' (or 'morl' for short) has the opposite effect. Given a fuzzy term with the label A and membership function $\mu_A(x)$ defined on the universe

X, the hedges 'very' and 'morl' are defined

$$\text{very A} \equiv \left\{\langle x, \mu_{\text{very A}}(x)\rangle \mu_{\text{very A}}(x) = \mu_A^2(x), x \in X\right\}$$

$$\text{morl A} \equiv \left\{\langle x, \mu_{\text{morl A}}(x)\rangle \mu_{\text{morl A}}(x) = \mu_A^{\frac{1}{2}}(x), x \in X\right\}$$

We have applied squaring and square root, but a whole family of hedges is generated by μ_A^k or $\mu_A^{\frac{1}{k}}$ (with integer k).

For example

$$\text{Extremely A} \equiv \left\{\langle x, \mu_{\text{very A}}(x)\rangle \mu_{\text{very A}}(x) = \mu_A^3(x), x \in X\right\}$$

$$\text{Slightly A} \equiv \left\{\langle x, \mu_{\text{very A}}(x)\rangle \mu_{\text{very A}}(x) = \mu_A^{\frac{1}{3}}(x), x \in X\right\}$$

A derived hedge is for example somewhat A defined as morl A and not slightly A. For the special case where $k = 2$, the operation μ^2 is concentration and $\mu^{\frac{1}{2}}$ is dilation. With $k = \infty$ the hedge μ_A^k could be named exactly, because it would suppress all memberships lower than 1.

Example 10.10: Very on a discrete membership function

Assume a discrete universe U = (0, 20, 40, 60, 80) of ages. In Matlab we can assign u = [0 20 40 60 80] and young = [1 .6 .1 0 0]

The discrete membership function for the set 'very young' is young. ∧ 2,

1 0.36 0.01 0 0

The notation '∧' is Matlab notation for the power operator. The set 'very very young' is, by repeated application, young. ∧ 4,

1 0.13 0 0 0

The derived sets inherit the universe of the primary set.

A primary term is a term that must be defined a priori, for example Young and Old in Fig. 4, whereas the sets Very young and Not very young are modified sets. The primary terms can be modified by negation ('not') or hedges ('very', 'more or less'), and the resulting sets can be connected using connectives ('and', 'or', 'implies', 'equals'). Long sentences can be built using this vocabulary, and the result is still a membership function.

10.9 MODUS PONENS INFERENCE

Modus ponens generalised to fuzzy logic is the core of fuzzy reasoning. Consider the Argument

$$\frac{\begin{array}{c}A' \\ A \Rightarrow B\end{array}}{B'}$$

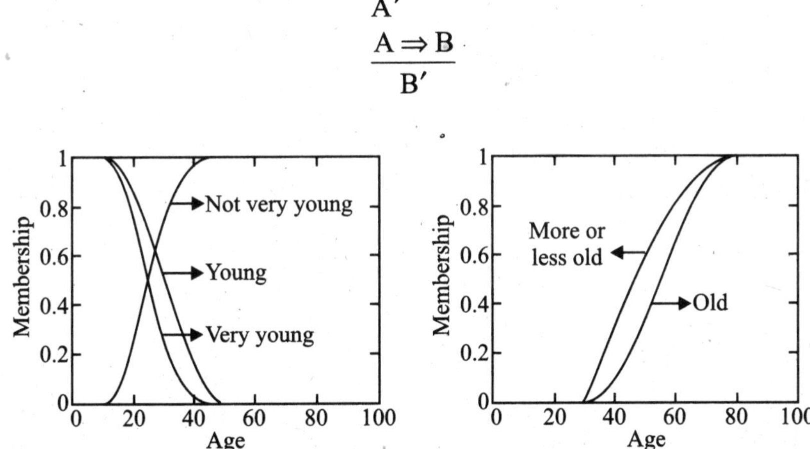

Figure 10.1: The membership functions for very young and not very young are derived from young (left), and the membership function for more or less old from old (right).

It is based on modus ponens, but the premise A is slightly different from A and thus the conclusion B' is slightly different from B. For instance, given the rule 'if x is High, then y is Low'; if x in fact is 'very high', we would like to conclude that y is 'very low'. Let A and A' be fuzzy sets defined on X, and B a fuzzy set defined on Y. Then the fuzzy set B′, induced by 'x is A' from the fuzzy rule

if x is A then y is B,

is given by

$$B' = A' \circ (A \Rightarrow B).$$

The operation $\circ$ is composition, the inner $\vee - \wedge$ product.

Example 10.11: Generalized modus ponens

Given the rule 'if altitude is High, then oxygen is Low'. Let the fuzzy set High be defined on a set of altitude ranges from 0 to 4000 metres (about 12 000 feet),

High = {(0, 0) , (1000, 0.25) , (2000, 0.5) , (3000, 0.75) , (4000, 1)}

and Low be defined on a set of percentages of normal oxygen content,

Low = {(0, 1), (25, 0.75), (50, 0.5) , (75, 0.25) , (100, 1)}

As a shorthand notation we write the rule as a logical proposition High ⇒ Low, where it is understood that the proposition concerns altitude and oxygen. We construct the relation R connecting High and Low using sharp implication, or $x \le y$,

	1	.75	.5	.25	0
0	1	1	1	1	1
.25	1	1	1	1	0
.5	1	1	1	0	0
.75	1	1	0	0	0
1	1	0	0	0	0

R =

The matrix is displayed with boxes and axis annotations to make the construction of the table clear: each element r_{xy} is the evaluation of $\mu_{High}(x) \le \mu_{Low}(y)$. The numbers on the vertical axis correspond to μ_{High} and the numbers on the horizontal axis correspond to μ_{Low}. Assuming altitude is High, we find by modus ponens

$$\mu^t = \mu^t_{High} \circ R$$

$$= (0\ \ .25\ \ .5\ \ .75\ \ 1) \circ \begin{pmatrix} 1 & 1 & 1 & 1 & 1 \\ 1 & 1 & 1 & 1 & 0 \\ 1 & 1 & 1 & 0 & 0 \\ 1 & 1 & 0 & 0 & 0 \\ 1 & 0 & 0 & 0 & 0 \end{pmatrix}$$

$$= (1\ \ .75\ \ .5\ \ .25\ \ 0)$$

The result is identical to Low, thus modus ponens returns a result as expected in that case. Assume instead altitude is Very High,

$$\mu^t_{very\ High} = (0\ \ .06\ \ .25\ \ .56\ \ 1),$$

the square of μ^t_{High}. Modus ponens yields

$$\mu^t = \mu^t_{very\ High} \circ R$$

$$= (0\ \ .06\ \ .25\ \ .56\ \ 1) \begin{pmatrix} 1 & 1 & 1 & 1 & 1 \\ 1 & 1 & 1 & 1 & 0 \\ 1 & 1 & 1 & 0 & 0 \\ 1 & 1 & 0 & 0 & 0 \\ 1 & 0 & 0 & 0 & 0 \end{pmatrix}$$

$$= (1\ \ .56\ \ .25\ \ .06\ \ 0)$$

The result is identical to the square of μ_{Low}. Written as an argument, we have

$$\frac{\begin{array}{c}\text{Very High} \\ \text{High} \Rightarrow \text{Low}\end{array}}{\text{Very Low}}$$

This is not always the case, though. With a slightly different definition of Low, say,

$$\text{Low} = \{(0, 1), (25, 0.8), (50, 0.5), (75, 0.3), (100, 0)\}$$

the resulting vector μ^t would be the same as previously, but only approximately equal to Very Low.

10.10 FUZZY LOGIC

Fuzzy logic generalizes the notion of truth values in classical logic (i.e., true or false) into a matter of degree. A statement in fuzzy logic, thus, can be partially true. A truth value is a number between 0 (false) and 1 (true). For example, the fact that one of the authors is only somewhat bald, but not entirely bald, yet, can be represented by assigning a small truth value (say 0.4) to the predicate Bald(John Yen).

An important goal of fuzzy logic is to be able to make reasonable inference even when the condition of an implication rule is partially satisfied. This capabilities of sumtimes referred to as approximate reasoning. As we have mentioned before, this is achieved in fuzzy logic by two related techniques: (1) representing the meaning of a fuzzy implication rule using a fuzzy relation, and (2) obtaining an inferred conclusion by applying the compositional rule of inference to the fuzzy implication relation.

10.10.1 Truth Values and Tables in Fuzzy Logic

Fuzzy logic uses linguistic variables. The values of a linguistic variable are words or sentences in a natural or artificial language. For example, height is a linguistic variable provided approximate characterization of a complex problem. The name of the variable, the universe of discourse and a fuzzy subset of universe of discourse characterize a fuzzy variable. A linguistic variable is a variable of a higher order than a fuzzy variable and its values are taken to be fuzzy variables. A linguistic variable is characterized by

1. name of the variable (x);
2. term set of the variable, t(x);
3. syntactic rule for generating the values of x;
4. semantic rule for associating each value of x with its meaning.

Apart from the linguistic variables, there exists what are called as linguistic hedges (linguistic modifiers). For example, in the fuzzy set "very tall" the word "very" is a linguistic hedge. A few popular linguistic hedges include: very highly, slightly, moderately, plus, minus, fairly, rather.

Reasoning has logic as its basis, whereas propositions are text sentence expressed in any language and are generally expressed in an canonical form as

$$z \text{ is } P,$$

where

z = symbol of the subject,

P = predicate designing the characteristics of the subject.

For example, "London is in United Kingdom" is a proposition in which "London" is the subject and "in United Kingdom" is the predicate, which specifies a property of "London", i.e. its geographical location United Kingdom. Every proposition has its opposite called negation. For assuming opposite truth values, a proposition and its negation are required.

Truth tables define logic functions of two propositions. Let X and Y be two proposition either of which can be true or false. The basic logic operations performed over the propositions are the following.

1. **Conjunction (∧):** X AND Y
2. **Disjunction (∨):** X OR Y
3. **Implication or conditional (⇒):** IF X THEN Y
4. **Bidirectional or equivalence (⇔):** X IF AND ONLY IF Y.

On the basis of these operations on propositions, inference rules can be formulated. Few inference rules are as follows

$$[X \wedge (X \Rightarrow)] \Rightarrow Y$$

$$[\overline{Y} \wedge (X \Rightarrow Y)] \Rightarrow \overline{X}$$

$$[(X \Rightarrow Y) \wedge *Y \Rightarrow Z) \Rightarrow (X \Rightarrow Z)$$

The above rules produce certain propositions that are always the irrespective of the truth values of propositions X and Y. Such propositions are called tautologies. An extension of set-theoretic bivalence logic is the fuzzy logic where the truth values are terms of the linguistic variable "truth".

The truth values of propositions in fuzzy logic are allowed to range over the unit interval [0, 1]. A truth value in fuzzy logic "very true" may be interpreted as a fuzzy set in [0, 1]. The truth value of the proposition "Z is A" or simply the truth value of A, denoted by w(A) is defined by a point in [0, 1] (called the numerical truth value) or a fuzzy set in [0, 1] (called the linguistic truth value).

The truth value of a proposition can be obtained from the logic operations of other propositions whose truth values are known. If tv(X) and tv(Y) are numerical truth values of propositions X and Y, respectively then

$$tv(X \text{ AND } Y) = tv(X) \wedge tv(Y) = \min [tv(X), tv(Y)\}$$

$$tv(X \text{ OR } Y) = tv(X) \vee tv(Y) = \max [tv(X), tv(Y)\}$$

$$tv(\text{NOT } X) = 1 - tv(X)$$

$$tv(X \Rightarrow Y) = tv(X) \Rightarrow tv(B)$$

$$= \max \{1 - tv(X), \min [tv(X), tv(Y)]\}$$

10.11 FUZZY PROPOSITIONS

For extending the reasoning capability fuzzy logic uses fuzzy predicates, fuzzy-predicate modifiers, fuzzy quantifiers and fuzzy qualifiers in the fuzzy propositions. The fuzzy propositions make the fuzzy logic differ from classical logic.

The fuzzy propositions are as follows:

1. **Fuzzy predicates:** In fuzzy logic the predicates can be fuzzy, for example, tall, short, quick. Hence, we have proposition like "Peter is tall". It is obvious that most of the predicates in natural language are fuzzy rather than crisp.

2. **Fuzzy-predicate modifiers:** In fuzzy logic, there exists a wide range of predicate modifiers that act as hedges, for example, very, fairly, modifiers are necessary for generating the values of a linguistic variable. An example can be the proposition "Climate is moderately cool".
3. **Fuzzy quantifiers:** The fuzzy quantifiers such as most, several, many, frequently are used in fuzzy logic. Employing these, we can have proposition like "Many people are educated". A fuzzy quantifier can be interpreted as a fuzzy number or a fuzzy proportion, which provides an imprecise characterization of the cardinality of one or more fuzzy or nonfuzzy sets. Fuzzy quantifiers can be used to represent the meaning of propositions containing probabilities; as a result they can be used to manipulate probabilities within fuzzy logic.
4. **Fuzzy qualifiers:** There are four modes of qualification in fuzzy logic, which are as follows:
   - **Fuzzy truth qualification:** It is expressed as "x is r", in which r is a fuzzy truth value. A fuzzy truth value claims the degree of truth of a fuzzy proposition. Consider the example, (Paul is Young) is NOT VERY True. Here the qualified proposition is (Paul is Young) and the qualifying fuzzy truth value is "NOT Very True."
   - **Fuzzy probability qualification:** It is denoted as "x is λ," where λ is fuzzy probability. In conventions logic, probability is either numerical or an interval. In fuzzy logic, fuzzy probability is expressed by terms such as likely, very likely, unlikely, around so on. Consider the example, (Paul is Young) is Likely, Here the qualifying fuzzy probability is "Likely". These probabilities may be interpreted as fuzzy numbers, which may be manipulated using fuzzy arithmetic.
   - **Fuzzy possibility qualification:** It is expressed "x is π," where π is a fuzzy possibility and can be of the following forms: possible, quite possible, almost impossible. These values can be interpreted as labels of fuzzy subsets of the real line. Consider the example. (Paul is Young) is Almost Impossible. Here the qualifying fuzzy possibility is "Almost Impossible"
   - **Fuzzy usuality qualification:** It is expressed as "usually (X) = usually (X is F), in which the subject X is a variable taking values in a universe of discourse U and the predicate F is a fuzzy subset of U and interpreted as a usual value of 'X' denoted by U (X) = F. The propositions that are usually true or the events that have high probability of occurrence are related by the concept of usuality qualification.

10.12 FORMATION OF RULES

The general weay of representing human knowledge is by forming natural language expressions given by

IF antecedent THEN consequent

The above expression is referred to as the IF-THEN rule-based form. There are three general forms that exist for any linguistic variable. They are:

1. Assignment statements;
2. Conditional statements;
3. Unconditional statements

1. **Assignment statements:** They are of the form

y = small

Orange color = orange

a = s

Paul is not tall and not very short

Climate = autumn

Outside temperature = normal

2. **Conditional statements:** The following are some examples.

IF y is very cool THEN stop.

IF A is high THEN B is low ELSE B is not low.

IF temperature is high THEN climate is hot.

Table 10.1: The canonical form of fuzzy rule based system

Rule 1:	If condition $\underset{\sim}{C}_1$ THEN restriction $\underset{\sim}{R}_1$
Rule 2:	If condition $\underset{\sim}{C}_2$, THEN restriction $\underset{\sim}{R}_2$
⋮	
Rule n:	If condition $\underset{\sim}{C}_3$, THEN restriction $\underset{\sim}{R}_3$

3. **Unconditional statements:** They can be of the form

Goto sum.

Stop.

Divide by a

Turn the pressure low,

The assignment statements limit the value of a variable to a specific quantity. The canonical rule formation for a fuzzy rule-based system is given in Table 10.1.

Generally both unconditional as well as conditional statements place some restriction on the consequent of the rule-based process. Fuzzy sets and relations generally model the restrictions. The restriction statements, irrespective of conditional or unconditional statements, are usually connected by linguistic connectives such as "and" "or" or "else". The restrictions denoted as $R_1, R_2, \ldots, R_n$ apply to the consequent of the rules.

10.13 DECOMPOSITION OF RULES (COMPOUND RULES)

A compound rule is a collection of many simple rules combined together. Any compound rule structure may be decomposed and reduced to a number of simple canonical rule forms. The rules are generally based on natural language representations. The following are the methods used for decomposition of compound linguistic rules into simple canonical rules.

1. **Multiple conjunctive antecedents**

   IF x is $\underset{\sim}{A}_1, \underset{\sim}{A}_2, \ldots, \underset{\sim}{A}_n$ THEN y is B_m.

   Assume a new fuzzy subset $\underset{\sim}{A}_m = \underset{\sim}{A}_1 \cap \underset{\sim}{A}_2 \cap \underset{\sim}{A}_n$

   and expressed by means of membership function

   $$\mu\underset{\sim}{A}_n(x) = \min[\mu\underset{\sim}{A}_1(x), \mu\underset{\sim}{A}_2(x), \ldots, \mu\underset{\sim}{A}_n(x)].$$

   In view of the fuzzy intersection operation, the compound rule may be rewritten as

   IF $\underset{\sim}{A}_m$ THEN $\underset{\sim}{B}_m$

2. **Multiple disjunctive antecedents**

   IF x is $\underset{\sim}{A}_1$, OR x is $\underset{\sim}{A}_2$,..., OR x is $\underset{\sim}{A}_n$ THEN y is $\underset{\sim}{B}_m$.

   This can be written as

   IF x is $\underset{\sim}{A}_n$ THEN y is $\underset{\sim}{B}_m$

   where the fuzzy set $\underset{\sim}{A}_m$ is defined as

   $$\underset{\sim}{A}_m = \underset{\sim}{A}_1 \cup \underset{\sim}{A}_2 \cup \underset{\sim}{A}_3 \cup \ldots \cup \underset{\sim}{A}_n$$

   The membership function is given by

   $$\mu\underset{\sim}{A}_m(x) = \max[\mu\underset{\sim}{A}_1(x), \mu\underset{\sim}{A}_2(x), \ldots, \mu\underset{\sim}{A}_n(x)].$$

   which is based on fuzzy union operation.

3. **Conditional statements (with ELSE and UNLESS):**

   Statements of the kind

   If $\underset{\sim}{A}_1$ THEN ($\underset{\sim}{B}_1$ ELSE $\underset{\sim}{B}_2$)

   can be decomposed into two simple canonical rule forms, connected by "OR":

   If $\underset{\sim}{A}_1$ THEN ($\underset{\sim}{B}_1$ ELSE $\underset{\sim}{A}_2$)

   Can be decomposed as

   IF $\underset{\sim}{A}_1$ THEN $\underset{\sim}{B}_1$

   OR

   If $\underset{\sim}{A}_2$ THEN NOT $\underset{\sim}{B}_1$

   IF $\underset{\sim}{A}_1$ THEN ($\underset{\sim}{B}_1$) ELSE IF THEN ($\underset{\sim}{B}_2$)

   can be decomposed into the form

IF $\underset{\sim}{A}_1$ THEN $\underset{\sim}{B}_1$

OR

IF NOT $\underset{\sim}{A}_1$ AND IF $\underset{\sim}{A}_2$ THEN $\underset{\sim}{B}_2$

4. Nested-IF-THEN rules:

The rule "IF $\underset{\sim}{A}_1$ THEN [IF $\underset{\sim}{A}_2$ THEN (B_1)]" can be of the form

IF $\underset{\sim}{A}_1$ AND $\underset{\sim}{A}_2$ THEN B_1

Thus based on all the above-mentioned methods compound rules can be decomposed into series of canonical simple rules.

10.14 AGGREGATION OF FUZZY RULES

The rule-based system involves more than one rule. Aggregation of rules is the process of obtaining the overall consequents from the individual consequents provided by each rule. The following two methods exist that aid in determining the aggregation of fuzzy rules:

1. **Conjunctive system of rules:** For a system of rules to be jointly satisfied, the rules are connected by "and" connectives. Here, the aggregated output, y, is determined by the fuzzy intersection of all individual rule consequents, y_i, where i = 1 to n, as

$$y = y_1 \text{ and } y_2 \text{ and } \ldots \text{ and } y_n$$

or

$$y = y_1 \cap y_2 \cap y_3 \cap \ldots \cap y_n$$

This aggregated output can be defined by the membership function

$$\mu_y(y) = \min[\mu_y 1_{(y)}, \mu_{y2}(y), \ldots, \mu_y n_{(y)}] \text{ for } y \in Y.$$

2. **Disjunctive system of rules:** In this case, the satisfaction of at least one rule is required. The rules are connected by "or" connectives. Here, the fuzzy union of all individual rule contributions determines the aggregated output, as

$$y = y_1 \text{ or } y_2 \text{ or } \ldots \text{ or } y_n$$

or

$$y = y_1 \cup y_2 \cup y_3 \cup \ldots \cup y_n.$$

Again it can be defined by the membership function

$$\mu_y(y) = \max[\mu_y 1_{(y)}, \mu_{y2}(y), \ldots, \mu_y n_{(y)}] \text{ for } y \in Y.$$

10.15 FUZZY REASONING (APPROXIMATE REASONING)

In fuzzy logic both the antecedents and consequents are allowed to be fuzzy propositions. There exist four modes of fuzzy approximate reasoning, which include:

1. Categorical reasoning
2. Qualitative reasoning
3. Syllogistic reasoning
4. Dispositional reasoning

10.15.1 Categorical Reasoning

In this type of reasoning, the antecedents contain no fuzzy quantifiers and fuzzy probabilities. The antecedents are assumed to be in canonical form. For understanding the inference rules of categorical reasoning in fuzzy logic, one should take note of the following notations:

$$\underset{\sim}{L}, \underset{\sim}{M} \text{ and } \underset{\sim}{N} \ldots = \text{Fuzzy variables taking in the universes U, V, W;}$$

$$\underset{\sim}{A}, \underset{\sim}{B}, \underset{\sim}{C} = \text{fuzzy predicates.}$$

1. The projection rule of inference is defined by

$$\frac{\underset{\sim}{L}, \underset{\sim}{M}, \text{is } \underset{\sim}{R}}{\underset{\sim}{L} \text{ is } [\underset{\sim}{R} \downarrow \underset{\sim}{L}]}$$

   where $[\underset{\sim}{R} \downarrow \underset{\sim}{L}]$ denotes the projection of fuzzy relation $\underset{\sim}{R}$ on $\underset{\sim}{L}$

2. The conjunction rule of inference is given by

$$\underset{\sim}{L} \text{ is } \underset{\sim}{A}, \underset{\sim}{L} \text{ is } \underset{\sim}{B} \Rightarrow \underset{\sim}{L} \text{ is } \underset{\sim}{A} \cap \underset{\sim}{B}$$

$$(\underset{\sim}{L}\,\underset{\sim}{M}) \text{ is } \underset{\sim}{A}, \underset{\sim}{L} \text{ is } \underset{\sim}{B} \Rightarrow \underset{\sim}{L}\,\underset{\sim}{M} \text{ is } \underset{\sim}{A} \cap (\underset{\sim}{B} \times V)$$

$$(\underset{\sim}{L}\,\underset{\sim}{M}) \text{ is } \underset{\sim}{A}, (\underset{\sim}{M}\,\underset{\sim}{N})\,\underset{\sim}{B} \Rightarrow (\underset{\sim}{L}, \underset{\sim}{M}, \underset{\sim}{N}) = (\underset{\sim}{A} \times \underset{\sim}{W}) \cap (\underset{\sim}{U} \times \underset{\sim}{B})$$

3. The disjunction rule of inference is given by

$$\underset{\sim}{L} \text{ is } \underset{\sim}{A} \text{ OR } \underset{\sim}{L} \text{ is } \underset{\sim}{B} \Rightarrow \underset{\sim}{L} \text{ is } \underset{\sim}{A} \times \underset{\sim}{B}$$

$$\underset{\sim}{L} \text{ is } \underset{\sim}{A}, \underset{\sim}{M} \text{ is } \underset{\sim}{B} \Rightarrow (\underset{\sim}{L}, \underset{\sim}{M}) \text{ is } \underset{\sim}{A} \times \underset{\sim}{B}$$

4. The negative rule of inference is given by

$$\text{NOT}(\underset{\sim}{L}, \text{is } \underset{\sim}{A}) \Rightarrow \underset{\sim}{L} \text{ is } \bar{\underset{\sim}{A}}$$

5. The compositional rule of inference is given by

$$\underset{\sim}{L} \text{ is } \underset{\sim}{A}, (\underset{\sim}{L}, \underset{\sim}{M}) \text{ is R} \Rightarrow \underset{\sim}{M}, \text{is } \underset{\sim}{A} \cdot \underset{\sim}{R}$$

   where $\underset{\sim}{A} \cdot \underset{\sim}{R}$ denotes the max-min composition of a fuzzy set A and a fuzzy relation R given by

$$\mu\underset{\sim}{A} \cdot \underset{\sim}{R}(v) = \underset{\mu}{\max} \min[\mu\underset{\sim}{A}(u)\ \mu\underset{\sim}{R}(u, v)]$$

6. The extension principle is defined as

$$\underset{\sim}{L} \text{ is } \underset{\sim}{A} \Rightarrow f(\underset{\sim}{L}) \text{ is } f(\underset{\sim}{A})$$

where "f" is a mapping from m to v so that L is mapped into $(\underset{\sim}{L})$; and based on the extension principle, the membership function of $f(\underset{\sim}{A})$ is defined as

$$\mu_{f'(\underset{\sim}{A})}(v) = \underset{v=1f(u)}{\text{Sup}}\ \mu_{(\underset{\sim}{A})}(u)\ u\ \varepsilon\ U,\ v\ \varepsilon\ V.$$

10.15.2 Qualitative Reasoning

In qualitative reasoning the input-output relationship of a system is expressed as a collection of fuzzy IF THEN rules where the antecedents and consequents involve fuzzy linguistic variable. Qualitative reasoning is widely used in control system analysis. Let $\underset{\sim}{A}$ and $\underset{\sim}{B}$ be the fuzzy input variables and $\underset{\sim}{C}$ be the fuzzy output variable. The relation among $\underset{\sim}{A}$, $\underset{\sim}{B}$ and $\underset{\sim}{C}$ may be expressed as

If $\underset{\sim}{A}$ is x_1 AND $\underset{\sim}{B}$ is y_1, THEN $\underset{\sim}{C}$ is z_1

If $\underset{\sim}{A}$ is x_2 AND $\underset{\sim}{B}$ is y_2, THEN $\underset{\sim}{C}$ is z_2

⋮

If $\underset{\sim}{A}$ is x_n AND $\underset{\sim}{B}$ is y_n, THEN $\underset{\sim}{C}$ is z_n

where x_i, y_i and z_i i = 1 to n, are fuzzy subsets of their universe of discourse. This is similar to the canonical rule formation shown in Table 10.1.

10.15.3 Syllogistic Reasoning

In syllogistic reasoning, antecedents with fuzzy quantifiers are related to inference rules. A fuzzy syllogism can be expressed as follows

$$x = k_1 \text{ A's are B's}$$
$$y = k_2 \text{ C's are D's}$$
$$z = k_3 \text{ E's are F's}$$

In the above A, B, C, D, E and F are fuzzy predicates, k_1 and k_2 are the given fuzzy quantifiers and k_3 is the fuzzy quantifier which has to be decided. All the fuzzy predicates provide a collection of fuzzy syllogisms. These syllogisms create a set of inference rules, which combines evidence through conjunction and disjunction.

Given below are some important fuzzy syllogisms:

1. Produce syllogism: $C . A \wedge B, F = C \wedge D$
2. Chaining syllogism: $C = B, F = D, E = A$
3. Consequent conjunction syllogism : $F = B \wedge D, A = C = E$
4. Consequent disjunction syllogism: $F = B \vee D, A = C = E$

5. Precondition conjunction syllogism: $E = A \wedge C, B = D = F$
6. Precondition disjunction syllogism: $E = A \vee C, B = D = f$

10.15.4 Dispositional Reasoning

In this kind of reasoning, the antecedents are dispositions that may contain, implicitly or explicitly, the fuzzy quantifier "usually". Usuality plays major role in dispositional reasoning and it links together the dispositional and syllogistic modes of reasoning.

The important inference rules of dispositional reasoning are the following:

1. **Dispositional projection rule of inference:**

$$\text{usually } ((L, M) \text{ is } R) \Rightarrow \text{usually } (L \text{ is } [R \downarrow L]).$$

where $[R \downarrow L]$ is the projection of fuzzy relation R on L.

2. **Dispositional chaining hypersyllogism:**

k_1 A's are B's, k_2B's are C's, usually ($B \subset A$)

usually ($\rightarrow$(Q_1 (.) (Q_2) A's are C's).

3. **Dispositional consequence conjunction syllogism:**

usually (A's are B's) usually (A's are C's) $\Rightarrow$ (2 usually (-) 1 (A's are (B and C)'s)

is a specific case of dispositional reasoning.

4. **Dispositional entailment rule of inference:**

$$\text{usually } (x \text{ is } A), A \subset B \Rightarrow \text{usually } (x \text{ is } B)$$

$$x \text{ is } A, \text{usually } (A \subset B) \Rightarrow \text{usually } (x \text{ is } B)$$

$$\text{usually } (x \text{ is } A), \text{usually } (A \subset B) \Rightarrow \text{usually } (x \text{ is } B)$$

is the dispositional entailment rule of inference. Here "usually" is less specific than "usually".

EXERCISES

1. What is propositional logic?
2. Explain the concept of first order predicate calculus?
3. Explain the concept of fuzzy implications?
4. What do you mean by fuzzy inference?
5. Explain four useful rules of inference?
6. What do you mean by material implication?
7. Write down the major fuzzy implication functions?
8. What is linguistic variable?
9. Explain the concept of various fuzzy prepositions?
10. Explain the concept of fuzzy reasoning (approximate reasoning) in detail?

CHAPTER 11

Fuzzy Model Identification

11.1 INTRODUCTION

Fuzzy model identification is an effective tool for the approximation of uncertain nonlinear systems on the basis of measured data. The identification of a fuzzy model using input-output data can be divided into two tasks: structure identification, which determines the type and number of the rules and membership functions, and parameter identification. For both structural and parametric adjustment, prior knowledge plays an important role. Hence, in this book the rules of the fuzzy system are designed based on the available a priori knowledge and the parameters of the membership, and the consequent functions are adapted in a learning process based on the available input-output data.

A fuzzy model is a nonlinear model that consists of a set of fuzzy if-then mapping rules, which we discussed in previous Chapter (Fuzzy if then rules). It has a transparent and interpretable model structure and is capable of representing a highly nonlinear functional relation using a reasonable number of fuzzy rules.

The problem of fuzzy model identification of fuzzy modeling is generally referred to as the determination of a fuzzy model for a system or a process by making use of one or both of two kinds of information:

- Linguistic information obtained from human expert
- Numerical information obtained from measuring apparatus.

As we discussed in previous chapters, one of the most important issues about fuzzy rule-based modeling is the construction of their membership functions. The design of early fuzzy models involved a manual tuning of their membership functions based on the performance of the model. Even though such a design procedure has led to a large number of successful applications, it was time consuming and difficult to deal with high-dimensional problems.

Furthermore, it is subject to criticism for its lack of principles and systematic methodologies. In fact, the construction of suitable membership functions for a model identification, which includes the following issues:

- Establishing the criteria for evaluating fuzzy models
- Selecting input variables relevant to the model
- Selecting the type of fuzzy models
- Choosing the structure of membership functions.
- Determining the number of fuzzy rules.
- Identifying the parameters of antecedent membership functions
- Identifying the consequent parameters of rules.

These issues can be grouped into three categories: model validation, structure estimation, and parameter estimation.

Hence, this chapter is devoted mainly to the parameter identification of the proposed fuzzy models, but certain structure identification tools are also discussed.

11.2 FUZZY RULE-BASED MODELS

The concept of a mathematical model is fundamental to systems analysis and design which require the representation of systems phenomena as a functional dependence between interacting input and output variables. For example, mathematical models are essential for prediction and control purposes. An early mathematical model for a system is constructed by analyzing input-output measurements from the system. These numerical measurements are important because they represent the behavior of the system in a quantitative fashion.

Very often, there exists another important information source for many engineering systems: knowledge from human experts. This knowledge, known as linguistic information, provides qualitative instructions and descriptions about the system and is especially useful when the input-output measurements are difficult to obtain.

Fuzzy models are capable of incorporating this kind of information naturally and conveniently, with conventional mathematical models usually fail to do so. Moreover, it is interesting to note that fuzzy models have the same ability to process numerical information as conventional models, if such information is available. In fact, most of this chapter will discuss how to identify fuzzy models from input-output measurements. Being able to deal with linguistic information and numerical information in a systematic and efficient manner is one of the most important advantages of fuzzy models.

The second important property of fuzzy models is their ability to handle nonlinearity. It is a well known fact that most engineering systems are nonlinear to some extent. Although it may be possible to represent such systems by a linear model over a restricted operating range (e.g., around the operating point). In general, nonlinear processes can only be adequately characterized by a nonlinear model. Since a mathematical description of a process is often a prerequisite to analysis and controller design, the study of system identification techniques has become an established branch of control theory. However, whereas system identification techniques for linear system are now well developed and have been widely applied, very few results exist for the identification of nonlinear systems. This may be attributed to the inherent complexity of nonlinear systems and the difficulty increasing need for nonlinear modeling. By ingeniously constructing fuzzy partitions, a fuzzy model is capable of approximation a highly nonlinear functional relation using a small number of fuzzy rules.

Interpretability is another salient feature of fuzzy models. A fuzzy model has a transparent model structure. Each rule in the model acts like a "local model" in the sense that it only covers a local region of the input-output space, and its contribution to the whole output of the model is easily understood. Neural networks are another powerful tool for modeling nonlinear systems, but they are essentially a "black box" model and difficult to interpret.

For notational simplicity, all fuzzy models discussed in this chapter are assumed to be multi-input single-output models. Extension to the multi-input multi-output models, however, is direct. In particular, we want to find a mapping f from an s-dimensional input space $U = U_1 \times U_2 \times \ldots\ U_s \subset R^s$ to a one-dimensional output space V, i.e. f. $U \subset R^s \rightarrow V \subset R$.

11.3 APPROXIMATION ABILITY OF FUZZY MODELS

One of the major applications of fuzzy models is its approximation ability to making a decision. Mathematically this amounts to finding a mapping from the input space to the output space. Hence, to a certain extent, the problem of constructing fuzzy models can be viewed as a function approximation problem. A natural question to ask, then, is how well a fuzzy model can approximate an unknown function. Several researchers have proved that fuzzy models generated by different inferential and defuzzification methods, as well as different membership functions, are universal approximators, which means that the models can uniformly approximate any real continuous function to an arbitrary degree of accuracy in a compact domain. These theoretical analyses not only confirm the approximation ability of fuzzy models, but also lay a mathematically sound foundation for fuzzy model identification. We should also point out that the universal approximation capability is not unique to fuzzy mode. Many other types of function approximators, such as feedforward neural networks, radial basis function networks, and nonparametric regressors also possess the same (or even better) universal approximation ability. The unique feature of a fuzzy model, which is not shared by other types of function approximators, is its facility for explicit knowledge representation in the form of fuzzy if-then rules, the mechanisms of reasoning in humanly understandable terms, and the capacity of taking linguistic information from human experts and combining it with numerical information.

11.4 FUZZY SYSTEM IDENTIFICATION

Fuzzy system identification consists of three basic problems:

1. Structure specification
2. Parameter estimation
3. Model validation

Figure 11.1 shown below describes these three problems. *Structure specification* involves finding the important input variables from all possible input variables, specifying membership functions, partitioning the input space, and determining the number of fuzzy rules comprising the underlying model. *Parameter estimation* involves the determination of unknown parameters in the model using some optimization method based on both linguistic information obtained from human experts and numerical data obtained from the actual system to be modeled. Structure specification and parameter estimation are interwoven, and neither of them can be independently identified without resort to the other. *Model validation* involves testing the model based on some performance criterion (e.g., accuracy). If the model cannot pass the test, we must modify the model structure and re-estimate the model parameter. It may be necessary to repeat this process many times before a satisfactory model is found. We will discuss these three problems, respectively, in detail in the following sections.

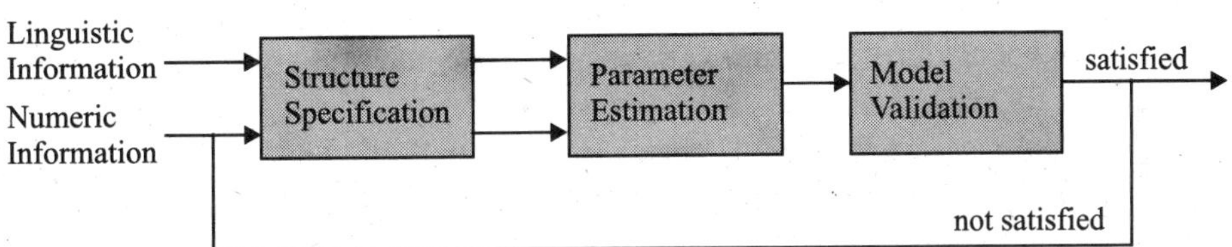

Figure 11.1: Fuzzy system identification diagram.

11.5 STRUCTURE SPECIFICATION

11.5.1 Input Selection

The selection of appropriate input variables is a major issue in constructing any model (including fuzzy models). This is because there are usually many factors that can potentially affect the output of the model. However, we only want to include the most relevant factors. Including an irrelevant factor not only complicates the task of the model identification but also may lead to misleading interpretations of the model. Therefore, there are varieties of practical and economical reasons for reducing the number of input variables in the final model.

In addition, variable deletion may be desirable in terms of the statistical properties of the parameter estimates and the construction of the final model. On the other hand, we do not wish to exclude any important relevant factor. Doing so will obviously limit the accuracy of the model being constructed. The decision as to which of these input variables should be included in the final model is not an easy one. Various input selection techniques have been proposed for linear regression modeling in the statistical community, but the criterion employed in each technique seems quite arbitrary and is known to provide different solutions for the same problem.

The input selection problem is even more difficult for fuzzy modeling as a fuzzy model is a nonlinear steps, and the addition or the deletion of an input variable will affect (also be affected by) other identification steps. For example, the number of input variables may affect the number of fuzzy partitions in the input space.

In following section we introduce several methods of selecting input variables for fuzzy models and discuss their merits and drawbacks. Like those used in linear regression modeling, these methods cannot guarantee that the selected input variables are the best. Instead, they only suggest an "acceptable" subset of input variables.

1. Forward Selection Procedure

This procedure starts with one input variable in the model and one variable at a time based on a specific performance criteria until the model is satisfactory.

A performance criterion for forward selection procedure is:

(i) Mean Squared Error (MSE)

(ii) Unbiasedness Criterion (UC)

The input variable considered for inclusion at any step is the one giving the best performance among those eligible for inclusion.

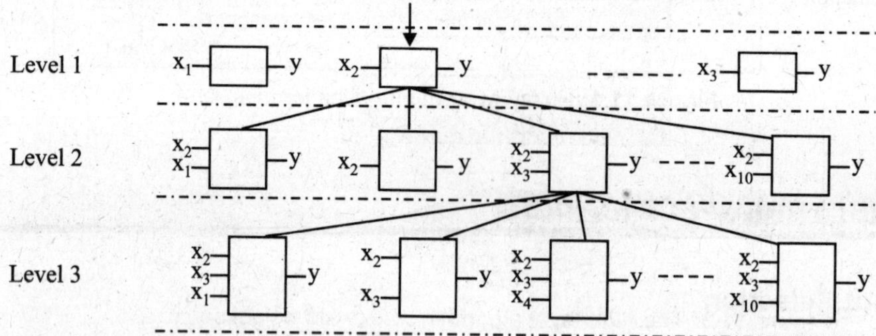

Figure 11.2: An example of forward selection procedure.

We illustrate the forward selection procedure using the example shown in Figure 11.2. Suppose we have identified ten potential input variables (x_1, x_2, x_3, x_4, … x_9, x_{10}) for a fuzzy modeling problem whose output variable is y. Applying the forward selection procedure to this problem, we first construct fuzzy models using only one input variable.

For case of discussion, we call these models level-one fuzzy models, as shown in the figure. A total of ten fuzzy models are constructed. These fuzzy models can be constructed using any techniques for identifying their fuzzy partitions and their consequent parameters, which we will discuss later. Once these level-one models have been constructed, they are evaluated based on a model validation criteria. Suppose the model with x_2 as input gives the best performance. It is used as baseline fuzzy models in the next level (i.e. level two). More specifically, we construct fuzzy models with x_2 and another input variable as inputs (i.e. x_2x_1, x_2x_3, x_2x_4, …, x_2x_{10}).

We also include a fuzzy model containing only the input variable from the previous level (i.e. x_2). This model, however, will have a finer fuzzy partition (i.e. more fuzzy rules). The rationale is that one way to improve the best fuzzy model from the previous level is instead of introducing new input variables, to partition the original input space into smaller subregions. We then construct all the level two fuzzy models, and evaluate them. The best level two fuzzy models (say the model with x_2x_3 as inputs) is chosen as the baseline for constructing level three fuzzy models.

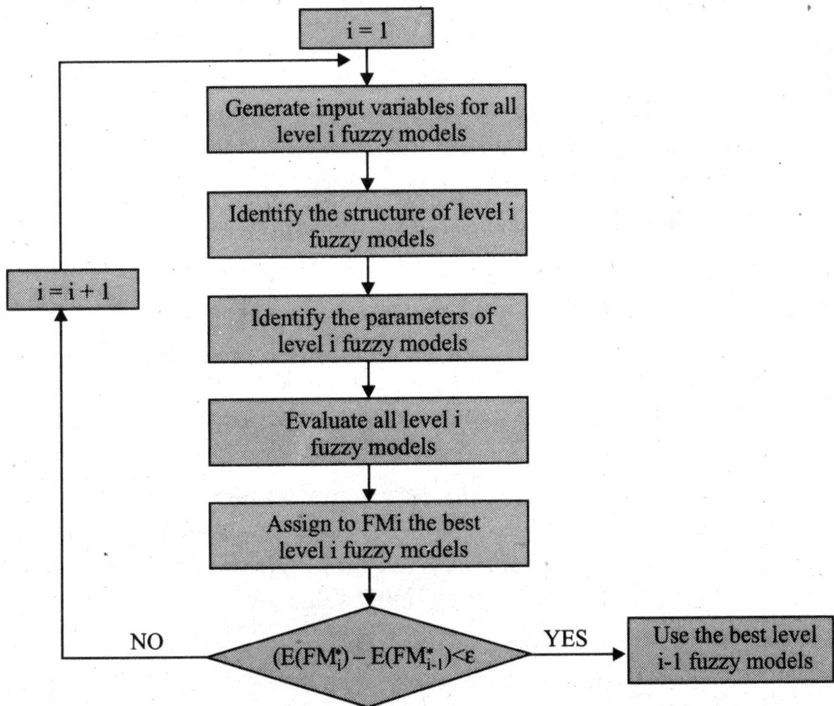

Figure 11.3: The high-level algorithm of forward selection procedure.

These steps iterate until the performance improvement from one level to the next level is less than a threshold. The high-level algorithm of forward selection procedure is shown in Figure 11.3, where $E(FM_i^*)$ and $E(FM^*_{i-1})$ denote the evaluation results of the best fuzzy model at level i and i -1, respectively.

Merits and Demerits of Forward Selection Procedure

This procedure is computationally efficient because it avoids considering all possible combinations of input variables by focusing on improving the best model obtained at every state. It is one of the most commonly used procedures for input selection in linear regression analysis and also applied by T. Takagi and M. Sugeno to fuzzy modeling. However, a criticism of this procedure is that there is no reason why the subset of k variables which gives the best performance should contain the subset of (k-1) variables that gives the best performance for (k-1) variables. A. Miller provide data input selection example in linear regression modeling in which the best-fitting subsets of three and two variables selected using this procedure have no variables in common. The same problem can appear in fuzzy modeling. Hence there is no guarantee that forward selection will find the best-fitting subsets of any size except for k = 1 and k = m. Nevertheless, it suggests an "acceptable" subset of input variables.

2. Backward Elimination Procedure

The forward selection procedure begins with one variable at a time, and subsequently increases the number of variables in the model until a decision is reached on the model to use. The backward elimination procedure is an attempt to achieve a similar conclusion working from the other direction. That is, it removes variables in turn until the model is satisfactory. The order of removal is determined by using the same performance criterion as that used in the forward selection procedure such as MSE or UC. This basic procedure is as follows.

First we build a model using all m input variables, and let MSE_m and UC_m be the corresponding values of mean squared error and regularity criterion of the model. Then we build models using m – 1 variables of the m variables and totally get $C^m_{m-1} = m - 1$ such models. We check the MSE_{m-1} or UC_{m-1} of these models and choose the model with the smallest MSE_{m-1} or UC_{m-1} as the best model of this stage. This mean-while determines the variable that should be removed. Similarly, at the following stage, the variable from the remaining m – 1 variable which yields the smallest MSE_{m-2} or UC_{m-2} is deleted. The process continues until there is only one variable left, or until some stopping criterion is satisfied.

This is a satisfactory procedure, especially for users who like to see all the variables in the model in order "not to miss anything". Like forward selection, backward elimination is widely used by statisticians for selecting input variables for linear regression models. K. Tanaka, M. Sano and H. Watanabe also used this procedure for the input selection of fuzzy models.

Backward elimination usually requires more computation than forward selection. If for instance we have 20 variables available and expect to select a subset of less than 5 of them, in forward selection we would only proceed until about 5 or so variables have been included. In backward elimination we start with 20 variables, then 19, 18 until eventually we reach the size of interest.

One computationally efficient backward elimination procedure was recently proposed by S. Chiu. This procedure only needs to build a model which consists of all m input variables and does not reestimate the parameters of the model when a variable is removed, and thus it can find a subset of input variables with acceptable accuracy based on a specific performance (say MSE or UC) very quickly. However, one possible criticism of this procedure is that the coefficients of the remaining variables in the model will change when one variable is removed from the model. Nevertheless, this procedure provides a simple and practically feasible alternative for selecting input variables in building very high dimensional fuzzy models.

Similar to forward selection, backward elimination cannot guarantee the selected subset of input variables to be the best; rather, it only suggests an acceptable subset of input variables. Moreover, we must recognize that once a variable has been eliminated in this procedure it is gone forever. Thus all alternative models using eliminated variables are not available for possible examination.

3. "Best Subset" Procedure

This procedure tries to build a model using a "best subset" of r variables from the m variables available, where r is known a priori. The "best subset" here means the subset will lead to a model that has a highest accuracy in terms of a specific performance criterion such as MSE or UC. This is an exhaustive search procedure, and the best subset of input variables can always be found with the given number r. For instance, if we have a modeling problem with 10 candidate input variables and we want to find the most important 3 variables as the input of model, we need to construct C_3^{10} = 120 models (each with different combination of 3 input variables) and compute their MSEs or UCs. The model that has the smallest MSE or UC is selected as the best model, and correspondingly the subset of 3 variables comprising the model is taken as the best subset.

Obviously, such a procedure is computationally costly. J. Jang improved the method by changing the procedure of computing MSE or UC. In particular, J. Jang computed the MSEs or UCs of the models just after one epoch of training rather than when the training process is completed, which may take a great number of epochs of training. He then chosen the model with the best performance and proceeded for further training to get the final parameters of the model. The improved procedure is based on the assumption that the model with the smallest MSE or UC after one epoch of training has a greater potential of achieving a lower MSE or UC when given more epochs of training. This assumption is not absolutely true, but it is a reasonable heuristic.

The limitation of this procedure is that is needs to know in advance the exact number of variables that are needed to construct increases exponentially as the number of candidate input variables increases. The main benefit of this procedure is that it is the only one that can find the "best subset" of input variables, as its name implies.

4. Other Procedures

An alternative procedure used in selecting input variables for fuzzy models is to fold the input selection problem into the fuzzy partitioning problem. In this case, fuzzy models with increasingly complex partition patterns are generated based on some performance criterion such as UC; input variables that required no partitioning are the ones that can be removed from the model. This approach is novel conceptually, but it is computationally expensive. The search for the optimal partition pattern in the procedure must start by considering all input variables and still requires generating different models to test each partition pattern.

There exist other procedure for input selection, most of which appear in the statistical literature. In principle, all these procedures can be applied to the selection of input variables for fuzzy models, but there always exist practical difficulties in applying these procedures and much work needs to be done before they can become a valuable addition to the fuzzy modeling workers' tool kit.

11.5.2 Membership Function Specification

The choice of membership functions affects how well a fuzzy model behaves. We have introduced major types of membership functions in Chapter 3. From the viewpoint of fuzzy model identification, the Gaussian membership functions have some interesting properties.

A unique property of Gaussian membership functions is that they are factorizable. To demonstrate this important property, consider the simple case of a Gaussian membership function with unit width in two dimensions:

$$\begin{aligned}\text{Gaussian }(\vec{x}-\vec{m}) &= \text{Gaussian }(\|\vec{X}-\vec{m}\|^2)\\ &= \exp(-\|\vec{x}-\vec{m}\|^2)\\ &= \exp(-(x_1-m_1)^2-(x_2-m_2)^2)\\ &= \exp(-(x_1-m_1)^2)\exp(-(x_2-m_2)^2)\\ &= \text{Gaussian }(x_1;m_1)\text{ gaussian }(x_2;m_2)\end{aligned} \tag{11.1}$$

Equation 11.1 shows that a two-dimensional Gaussian membership function Gaussian $(\vec{X}-\vec{m})$ with a center $\vec{m} = [m_1, m_2]^T$ is equivalent to the product of a pair of one-dimensional Gaussian membership functions Gaussian $(x_1; m_1)$ and Gaussian $(x_2; m_2)$ where x_1 and x_2 are the elements of the vector x, and $m\text{-}_1$ and m_2 are the elements of the center $\vec{m}$.

The result of Equation 11.1 may be readily generalized for the case of a multivariate Gaussian membership function that computed the weighted norm, assuming that weighting matrix A is a diagonal matrix. To be specific suppose that we have

$$\wedge = \text{diag}[\sigma_1, \sigma_2, \ldots, \sigma_s] \tag{11.2}$$

We may then factorize Gaussian $(\vec{x}-\vec{m}, \wedge)$ = gaussian $(\|x-m\|_{\wedge}^2)$

$$\begin{aligned} &= \prod_{k=1}^{s} \exp\left(-\frac{(x_k-m_k)^2}{\sigma_k^2}\right) \\ &= \text{gaussian }(x_1; m_1, \sigma_1,)\ldots \text{ gaussian}(x_s; m_s, \sigma_s)\end{aligned} \tag{11.3}$$

where m_k denotes the kth element of the center $\vec{m}$.

Given such a property, we may synthesize a multidimensional membership function as the product of one-dimensional membership functions. Also, we may obtain the parameters of one dimensional membership functions by first determining the parameters of the multidimensional membership function. More importantly, since the model can be expressed in a compact form (in multidimensional membership function), the "curse of dimensionality" caused by the exponential increase in the number of rules resulting from the exhaustive combination of membership function of separable variables can be dealt with. Whereas it is believed that the choice of membership functions does affect the performance of the resultant models, there exist no sound principles yet for guiding the choice of membership functions.

11.5.3 Fuzzy Partitioning of Input Space

A fuzzy partition of the input space defines the antecedents of a fuzzy model. The number of fuzzy subregions in a fuzzy partition corresponds to the number of fuzzy rules in the model. Fuzzy partition techniques can be classified into three categories:

1. grid partition,
2. tree partition, and
3. scatter partition.

We will discuss each one of these techniques below.

One of the most commonly used fuzzy partitioning methods in practice (particularly in control applications) is the grid partition. A grid partition, as shown in Figure 11.4(a), is formed by "fuzzy cuts" that divide the input space into several fuzzy slices along each dimension. Each fuzzy slice is specified by a membership function. The intersection of these fuzzy slices from "fuzzy cells" is a grid partition. For instance, each fuzzy cell in the grid partition of a two-input modeling problem is described in the form of "x_1 is A_i and x_2 is B_j." Figure 11.4(a) shows a grid partition of a two-dimensional input space formed by three membership functions (i.e. three "slices") in each dimension.

Obviously, a grid partition can be uniform or nonuniform. The former, illustrated in Figure 11.4(a) is formed by uniformly spaced symmetric membership functions. The latter, illustrated in Figure 11.4(b), is formed by nonuniformly spaced asymmetric membership functions. While a uniform grid partition is easier to construct, a nonuniform partition is more flexible in adapting to the specific nonlinear characteristics of the function being approximated.

An adaptive fuzzy grid partition can be obtained if we use learning techniques to construct the partition. Specifically, we may take the uniformly partitioned grids as an initial partition and then use the learning procedure to optimize the parameters of the antecedent membership functions. As the parameters in the antecedent membership functions are adjusted, the grid evolves. Two typical learning procedures used in practice are the gradient descent method suggested by J. Jang and genetic algorithms suggested by C. Karr.

Grid partition is convenient to use, but it may encounter serious "rule explosion" problems when the number of input variables is large. This problem is closely related to the so-called "curse of dimensionality" the well-known problem of exponentially increasing model complexity as the number of input variables increases. For instance, a fuzzy model with 10 inputs and 2 membership functions on each input would result in $2^{10} = 1024$ fuzzy if-then rules, which is prohibitively large. Thus, the grid partition method is usually applied to fuzzy model with few input variables. Most fuzzy models used in control applications fall into this category.

Tree partition is the second method used in partitioning an input space. Figure 11.4(c) gives an example of a tree partition in a two-dimensional input space. A tree partition results from a series of guillotine cuts. By a guillotine cut, we mean a cut that is made across the subspace to be partitioned; each of the regions so produced can then be subjected to further independent guillotine cutting. At the beginning of the its iteration step, the input space is partitioned into i regions. Then another guillotine cut is applied to one of the regions to further partition the entire space into (i + 1) regions. There are various strategies to decide which dimension to cut and where cut it at each step. Some are based merely on the distribution of training examples; others take the parameter identification methods into consideration.

Tree partition relives the problem of rule explosion to a great degree, but it is not easy to use in practice. A number of heuristics are usually needed to find a proper tree structure, and there may be difficulties in designing an optimal tree partition. Due to the variety and arbitrariness of partition strategies, different users may design quite different tree structures, and thus get fuzzy models with quite different performance. Also, errors may accumulate from level to level in a large tree.

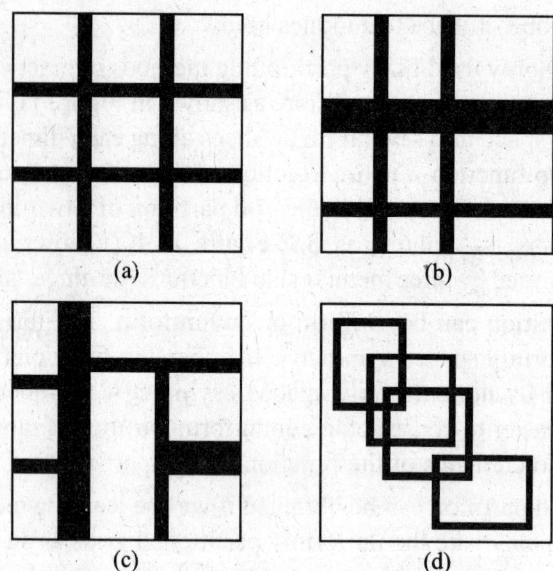

Figure 11.4: Various methods for partitioning the input space: (a) Grid partition (uniform); (b) Grid partition (nonuniform); (c) Tree partition: (d) Scatter partition

The third type of fuzzy partition is the scatter partition. An example of such a partition is shown in Figure 11.4(d). Instead of covering the whole input space, this method tries to find a subset of the input space that characterizes the fuzzy regions of possible occurrence of training examples. Each fuzzy region is associated with one (multidimensional) membership function or a combination of several (one-dimensional) membership functions. It is usually difficult to find such a partition intuitively or manually. Hence, learning techniques have to be adopted to automate the construction of scatter partition.

11.5.4 Determining the Number of Fuzzy Rules

When deciding the number of fuzzy rules for a fuzzy model, there are two contradictory concerns. On one hand it is desired that the model include as many rules as possible so that it minimize errors from training data with sufficient "patches." On the other hand, it is also desired that the model includes as few rules as possible because the generalization capability of the model decreases as the number of fuzzy rules increases. By generalization capability, we are referring to the model's ability in approximating testing data, which are not used in training the model.

Theoretically, the fuzzy rules, the better the approximate ability of the model. In practice, however, good fit on training data does not always assure good performance on future data, especially if the data have noise and the number of adjustable parameters in the model is large compared to the available training data. A fuzzy model with a large number of rules is liable to encounter the risk of "overfitting" capable of fitting training data completely but incapable of generalizing to untrained data satisfactorily. Figure 11.5 shows an example of model overfitting.

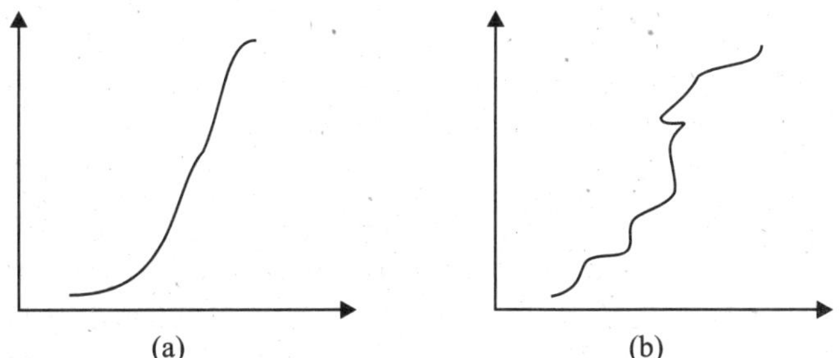

Figure 11.5: An example of model overfitting: (a) A good model (b) An overfitted model

The trade-off between goodness of fit and simplicity is a fundamental principle underlying various general theories of statistical modeling and inductive inference. Several research efforts have been made in the fuzzy logic community to strike a balance between reducing the fitting error and reducing the model complexity. In particular, orthogonal transformation methods have been used for selecting important fuzzy rules from a given rule base. Unlike conventional methods where multiple iterations are usually required to find the "optimal" number of fuzzy rules, orthogonal transformation methods are a noniterative procedure. They start with an oversized rule base and then remove redundant or less important fuzzy rules through a "one-pass" operation. Therefore, orthogonal transformation methods are computationally less expensive compared to the conventional methods, especially when the number of input variables is large. Moreover, they are extremely robust numerically and can be implemented using some well-established numerical computation packages. In this section we introduce how to use Singular Value Decomposition (SVD) to select the most important fuzzy rules from a given rule base and construct compact fuzzy models with better generalization ability. In this section we will introduce several methods that determine the number of fuzzy rules by finding a good trade-off between fitting training data and high generalizing ability.

11.6 PARAMETER ESTIMATION

In this section we will introduce several commonly used methods for estimating fuzzy model parameters. The parameter estimation and the structure identification of a fuzzy model are two interwoven issues and neither of them can be performed independently of the other. However, as far as most parameter estimation techniques are concerned, the structure of the fuzzy model is given.

The goal of parameter estimation is to find the best values for a set of model parameters. The optimality of parameter values is determined by (1) how well the model fits the training data, and (2) how well, the model performs for a given task. The first approach is often used for modeling a plant, a process, or a set of time series data. The second approach is often used for designing a controller. The two approaches also imply different modeling requirements. The former requires training data, while the latter requires clearly specified performance objectives. Finally, the techniques used by the two approaches are often different. Techniques for parameter estimation using training data include backpropagation learning, recursive least square algorithm, the least mean square algorithm, Kalman filters, Singular Value Decomposition (SVD), and the genetic algorithm. Techniques for parameter estimation based on performance include reinforcement learning and genetic algorithms. Even though genetic algorithms can be applied to both types of parameter estimation, is it more commonly used for the latter type.

There are two types of parameters in a fuzzy model: (1) parameters of the antecedent membership functions, and (2) parameters in the consequent part of rules. Antecedent parameters are often identified using clustering techniques. Consequent parameters can be estimated using most of the techniques mentioned earlier. We will focus on three of these techniques: SVD-based techniques, the Recursive Least Square (RLS) algorithm, and the Least Mean Square (LMS) algorithm.

11.6.1 Estimation of Antecedent Parameters

Antecedent parameters of a fuzzy model can be estimated independent of consequent parameters using various clustering techniques. The rationale is to find "groupings" of input training data and use the clustering results to determine the parameters of a fuzzy partition (i.e. parameters of antecedent membership functions).

Clustering can be applied either to the input training data or to the input-output training data. All clustering techniques, whether they find hard clustering or soft computing, can be applied. Examples include fuzzy c-means and fuzzy k-nearest neighborhood, which we introduced in Chapter 13. Another clustering technique proposed for finding a fuzzy partition is the mountain method proposed by R. Yager.

Clustering usually produces a scattered fuzzy partition of the input space. The parameters of the antecedent membership functions, are usually constructed from the mean and the variance of each cluster. For instance, we may use multidimensional Gaussian membership functions

$$\mu_{A_i}(x) = \exp\left[\frac{-(-m_i)^T(x-m_i)}{\sigma_i^2}\right] \tag{11.4}$$

whose mean m are cluster centers.

Once the centers are established, the width σ_i of each cluster can be determined. The goal in setting the width is to achieve a certain amount of response overlap between each cluster and its neighbors so that they form a smooth and contiguous interpolation over those regions of the input space which they represent. An appropriate width can be determined from the K-nearest neighbor heuristic:

$$\sigma_i = \frac{1}{k}\sum_{l=1}^{k} \| \vec{x} - \vec{m} \|_2^2 \tag{11.5}$$

where $\vec{m}_l$ are the K-nearest neighbors of $\vec{m}_i$. In J. Moody and C. Darken k = 2 was suggested. The K-nearest neighbor heuristic is one of the simplest methods for determining the width σ_i. Several more complicated methods which tend to provide improved performance were discussed in M. Musavi et al. and S. Roberts and L. Tarassenko.

As compared with the basic Backpropagation (BP) algorithm (to be discussed in Chapter 16), this approach can converge very quickly. However, a drawback of the algorithm is that it may not provide an "optimal" parameter estimate. The reason is obvious: the K-means clustering and the K-nearest neighbor heuristic determine the antecedent parameters based only on input data and do not take into account any information in the output data. Thus, the performance of the model identified using this clustering approach is usually inferior to that of the model identified using the BP algorithm.

11.6.2 Estimation of Consequent Parameters

The parameter estimation algorithm introduced in this section can be applied to all additive fuzzy models. In our discussion, however, we will use the zero-order TSK model to illustrate these techniques, which is rewritten as follows:

R_i: If x_1 is A_{i1} and x_2 is A_{i2} and … and x_s is A_{is}

$$\text{Then } y \text{ is } c_i,\ i = 1, 2, \ldots, M. \tag{11.6}$$

The membership functions in rule antecedents are assumed to be of the Gaussian type:

$$\mu_{A_i}(x) = \exp\left(\frac{(x_j - m_{ij})^2}{\sigma_{ij}^2}\right) \tag{11.7}$$

Algorithm for other types of additive fuzzy models with various membership functions can be derived in a similar manner and are left to the reader as an exercise.

As shown, the total output of the zero-order TSK model using product as the fuzzy conjunction operator is computed by

$$y = \frac{\sum_{i=1}^{M} w_i c_i}{\sum_{i=1}^{M} w_i} \equiv \frac{\sum_{i=1}^{M} \prod_{j=1}^{s} \mu_{A_{ij}}(x_j) c_i}{\sum_{i=1}^{M} \prod_{j=1}^{s} \mu_{A_{ij}}(x_j)} \tag{11.8}$$

Note that the "product" operator instead of the "min" operator has been used in calculating w_i in Equation 11.8. The parameters to be estimated in the model are m_{ij} and σ_{ij} in the antecedent membership functions and the constant constituents c_i in the consequents.

We can analyze Equation 11.8 from two points of view. First, if we view all the parameters m_{ij}, σ_{ij} and c_i in the model as free design parameters, then the estimation problem is nonlinear-in-the-parameters. In order to compute these parameters, we must use some nonlinear optimization technique such as the gradient descent algorithm. On the other hand, we can fix the parameters m_{ij}, σ_{ij} in the antecedent membership functions at the beginning of the estimation procedure so that the only free design parameters are the constant constituents c_i in the consequents. This is the approach adopted by S. L. Chiu and L. Wang and R. Langari where the parameters of antecedent membership functions were predetermined using different clustering algorithms. Note that the problem becomes linear in the parameters in this situation, and thus a wide range of linear optimization techniques would be at our disposal for solving c_i. Below we will describe three algorithms based on the two different points of view: (1) SVD-based estimation algorithm, (2) recursive least square (RLS) estimation algorithm, and (3) least mean square (LMS) estimation algorithm.

11.6.3 Simultaneous Estimation of Antecedent and Consequent Parameters

1. Backpropagation (BP) Algorithm

There is a rapidly growing interest in the fusion of neural networks and fuzzy systems to obtain the advantages of both paradigms while avoiding their individual drawbacks. Ion the one hand, the theory of fuzzy logic provides a formal framework to abstract the approximate-reasoning characteristic of human decision making and, furthermore, conveys an excellent mode of knowledge representation in the form of if-them rules. However, a common bottleneck in fuzzy logic systems is their dependence on the specification of good rules by human experts. Neural networks, on the other hand, attempt to replicate the learning capabilities possessed by biological species, but it is not always possible to extract and interpret the learned knowledge contained within them. The possibility of the integration of these two paradigms has given rise to a rapidly emerging field of fuzzy neural systems that are intended to capture the capabilities and advantages of both neural and fuzzy logic systems. Fuzzy neural systems have become an area of much activity in practice and many interesting problems have been successful addressed.

We should remember that a fuzzy model has its own unique structure that should be taken into consideration in developing the training algorithms. In particular, a fuzzy model comprises an antecedent component and a consequent component. If the parameters in the antecedent component are fixed (temporally!), the estimation problem is linear with respect to the parameters in the consequent are fixed (temporally!), the estimation problem is linear with respect to the parameters in the consequent component; if, on the other hand, the parameters in the consequent component (of course, the estimation problem is always a nonlinear are fixed or not). Thus, it is possible to estimate the parameters in the two components using different types of optimization algorithms (linear or nonlinear). This is exactly the idea proposed J. Jang where an LMS algorithm is used to train the antecedent parameters while an RLS algorithm is used to train the consequent parameters. Jang shows that the combination of RLS with LMS could in general cut down the convergence time substantially. This algorithm may be viewed as the hybrid algorithm in the sense that a linear algorithm (RLS) and a nonlinear algorithm (LMS) are incorporated into a single procedure for estimating the parameters. In the following section we will introduce another hybrid type algorithm in which, as in Jang's algorithm, the consequent parameters are computed using the RLS, but the antecedent parameters are computed using a cluster nearest neighbor method.

2. Evolutionary Computations

Evolutionary Computation (EC) is a class of computation techniques that are based on Darwin's models of biological evolution. EC includes genetic algorithms, Evolutionary Strategies, and evolutionary programming. These techniques can perform search and optimization in the large and complex space. Since parameter identification can be viewed as a global optimization problem, it is natural to use EC for parameter identification, whether is for identifying the antecedent parameters and the consequent parameters simultaneously.

11.7 MODEL VALIDATION

Once a model structure has been chosen, the parameter estimation procedure provides us with a particular model this structure. This model may be the best available one, but the crucial question is whether it is good enough for the intended purpose. Testing whether a given model is appropriate is known as model validation.

This section discusses three techniques for model validation:

1. cross-validation
2. residual analysis, and
3. information-theoretic criteria

11.7.1 Cross-validation

Is it not so surprising that a model will perform well when evaluated by its performance for the data set to which it was adjusted. The real test is whether it will be capable of also describing fresh data sets from the process. A suggestive way of comparing two different models is to evaluate their performance when applied to a dataset (known as validation or testing a dataset) to which neither of them was adjusted. We would then favor that model that shows the better performance. Such a procedure, known as cross-validation, is a standard tool for parameter estimation and model validation in statistics.

An attractive feature of cross-validation is its pragmatic character. The comparison among candidate models needs neither any probabilistic arguments nor any assumptions about the real process. Its disadvantage is that a fresh data set has to be saved for the validation and therefore we cannot use all our information to build the models. In the situations where only limited training samples are available, this procedure can not be used.

The basic idea of the cross-validation method is as follows: divided the available training data an estimation subnet (denoted as N_E) and a validation subnet (denoted as N_V). The estimation subnet N_E is used of the model (i.e. training the model which consists of a certain number of fuzzy rules) and the validation subnet N_V is used for evaluation of the performance of the model. The motivation here is to validate the model on a dataset different from the one used for parameter estimation. In this way, we may use the training set to assess the performance of various candidate model structures that contain different number of fuzzy rules, and thereby choose the "best" one. The particular model with the best-performing number of fizzy rules in then trained on the full training set.

Cross validation does not necessarily use one subset exclusively for one purpose (Estimation and validation); it allows all the training data to be used for both purposes. For instance, we can partition the full training set into P subset; compute and estimate from all the subset but one; and validate estimate from the left-out subset. Then, we perform the estimation- validation with the different left-out. We can repeat this P times.

There are various formulas for expressing cross-validation. The most commonly used performance measure for model validation is mean squared error (MSE), as defined by

$$MSE = \frac{1}{n_v}\sum_{k=1}^{n_v}[y(k) - y(k)]^2 \tag{11.9}$$

where y(k) and $\hat{y}(k)$ are the desire (target) and the actual output of the model at time k, respectively, and n_v is the number of samples in the validation data set.

Another performance measure, which is used by T. Takagi and M. sugeno in their pioneer work in fuzzy model identification, is the unbiasedness criterion (UC). As shown in Figure 11.6, this model validation scheme divides the data set into two subset: dataset A and dataset B. each dataset is used to construct a fuzzy model. We call these two fuzzy model FM_A and FM_B respectively. We then compute the difference between the output of two fuzzy models for dataset A.

$$\sum_{i=1}^{n_A}(FM_A(YA_i) - FM_B(YA_i))^2 \tag{11.10}$$

where n_A is the size of data set A, and YA_i denote the input of the ith data in dataset A. similarly, we compute the difference between the output of the two fuzzy model for dataset B.

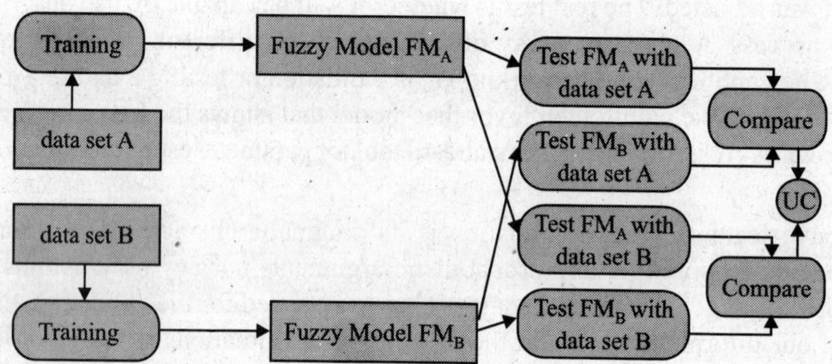

Figure 11.6: Calculating the unbiased criteria.

$$UC = \sqrt{\sum_{i=1}^{n_A}(FM_A(YA_i) - FM_B(YA_i))^2 + \sum^{n_B}(FM_A(YB_i) - FM_B(YB_i))^2} \tag{11.11}$$

The rationale of criterion is that a good model should not be a sensitive to the choice of training data. Hence, it should have low UC value.

Cross-validation essentially tries to find the model structure by checking two subset of training data and does not take into account the complexity of the resulting model if enough different model structure are considered, cross –validation may often find a model that has a low error on the two subsets of training data but will not generalize well to new untrained data. The information-theoretic criteria introduced below will take into account the structure complexity explicitly when building a fuzzy model and thus avoid the problem encountered in applying cross-validation.

11.7.2 Residual Analysis

This method is based on the analysis of the residuals $e(k) \equiv y(k) - \hat{y}(k)$ of the identified model. In general, if the identified model is not adequate (for example, some needed variables are left out), then the residuals will be correlated and hence will not behave the way the random error component is supposed to. In other words, the model will not capture all of the pattern component in the data set, and part of the pattern component will remain in the residuals.

The traditional residual analysis method used in linear systems identification is to test whether the autocorrelation function of the residuals is an impulse and whether the cross-correlation function between the residuals and the input is zero. The generalization of this method to the nonlinear case is considered by S. Billings and W. Voon where several higher-order correlation functions are introduced to detect the presence of unmodeled linear and nonlinear terms in the residuals.

Alternatively, I. Leontaristis and S. Billings propose using a chi-squared statistical test method in the validation of nonlinear models. This method is a generalization of the same test method used in the validation of linear models and has been successfully applied to the validation of nonlinear autoregressive moving average models, radial basis function networks, and fuzzy basis function models. Here we introduce the basic principle of this method.

This method starts by defining a d-dimensional vector-valued function

$$\Omega(k) = [w(k), w(k-1), \ldots., w(k-d+1)]^T \tag{11.12}$$

where w(k) is some chosen function of the residuals and the past observations. Let

$$\Gamma^T\Gamma = \frac{1}{N}\sum_{k=1}^{N}\Omega(k)\Omega^T(k) \tag{11.13}$$

The chi-squared statistic is then calculated according to

$$\zeta = Nv^T(\Gamma^T\Gamma)^{-1}v$$

where

$$v = \frac{1}{N}\sum_{k=1}^{N}\Omega(k)e(k)/\sigma_e \tag{11.15}$$

and σ_e^2 is the variance of the residual e(k). Under the null hypothesis that the data are generated by the model, the statistic ζ is asymptotically chi-squared distributed with d degrees of freedom. If the values of ζ for several different choice of w(k) are withing the 95% acceptance region, that is

$$\zeta < \chi_d^2(\alpha) \tag{11.16}$$

the model is regarded as adequate, where $\kappa_d^2(\alpha)$ is the critical value of the chi-squared distribution with d degree of freedom for the given significance a (0.05). The choices of w(k) should generally include some nonlinear functions, say $w(k) = e^2(k-1)\, y^2(k-1)$.

Note that the statistic ζ has been formed based on the dataset used to identify the model. When there are sufficient training samples, a fresh dataset should be saved and then used to construct the static ζ. This is exactly the idea used in cross-validation.

11.7.3 Information-theoretic Criteria

Various information-theoretic criteria for model-complexity selection have been proposed in the statistical community. For a more detailed discussions of these criteria, we refer the reader to A. Grasa. Although these criteria do indeed differ from each other in their exact details, they share a common form of composition, as described in M. Priestley and S. Haykin:

$$\begin{pmatrix}\text{Model} - \text{complexity} \\ \text{criterion}\end{pmatrix} = \begin{pmatrix}\text{mod el} \\ \text{accuracy}\end{pmatrix} + \begin{pmatrix}\text{mod el} - \text{compleixty} \\ \text{penalty}\end{pmatrix} \tag{11.17}$$

The basic philosophy of these information-theoretic criteria is best described by advice from Professor Lennart Ljung: "If I am going to accept a more complex model (according to my own complexity measure) it has to prove to be significantly better !".

The difference between the various criteria lies in the definition of the model-complexity penalty. The structure of these criteria reflects a balance between the ideas of goodness of fit and complexity; that is, the selected model yields a balance between two information sources; the sum of squares of the residuals and the number of parameters of the model.

In principle, all these criteria can be applied to the structure identification of fuzzy models. However, unlike statistical modeling where a single model is used to describe the global behavior of a system, fuzzy modeling is essentially a multimodel approach in which individual rules (where each rule acts like a "local model") are combined to describe the global behavior of the system. The complexity of a fuzzy model is determined not only by the number of parameters in the antecedents and consequents of the rules but also by the number of fuzzy rules in the model. Thus, we need to revise these criteria in determining the structure of a fuzzy model. In particular, the penalty given for model complexity should be no longer only limited to the number of parameters in the model, it should take into account the number of fuzzy rules in the model as well. Based on these considerations, several modified information-theoretic criteria are suggested in J.Yen and L. Wang. One typical criterion, known as Schwarz-Rissanen Information Criterion (SRIC), which is based on the one derived independently by Schwarz andssanen is given below [526, 504]:

$$\text{SRIC}(m_a, m_c, m_r) = \log\left(\hat{\sigma}_\varepsilon^2\right) + \frac{\log(N)c(m_a, m_c, m_r)}{N} \tag{11.18}$$

Where $\hat{\sigma}_\varepsilon^2$ is the estimated variance of model residuals, N is the number of training data, m_a is the number of antecedent parameters, m_c is the number of consequent parameters, m, is the number of fuzzy rules constituting the model, and c(.) is a complexity function defined by

$$s(m_a, m_c, m_r) = m_a + m_c + \eta m_r \tag{11.19}$$

The number of antecedent parameters m_a depends on the dimensionality of the antecedent membership functions. Most fuzzy models combine one-dimensional membership functions using fuzzy conjunction (i.e. the AND operator) in the rule antecedents. For these models, the number of parameters associated with an antecedent variable x_i is the produce of the number of membership functions for variable (denoted as k_i) and the number of parameters for each membership function of x_i (denoted by α_i). The total number of antecedent parameters is thus

$$m_a = \sum_{i=1}^{p} (k_1 \times \alpha_i) \tag{11.20}$$

where p is the number of antecedent (input) variables. Some fuzzy models use p-dimensional membership functions in the antecedents of rules, where p, as before, denoted the number of antecedent variables. For fuzzy models of this kind, each antecedent membership function corresponds to a fuzzy rule. Suppose that all membership functions have the same number of parameters (denoted as α). Then we have

$$m_a = m_r \times \alpha \tag{11.21}$$

Depending on the type of fuzzy models, the consequent parameter count m_c may or may not be related to the rule number m_r. For TSK type models, the number of consequent parameters is proportional to the number of rules. More precisely, if the consequent part of a rule in the model consists of a linear regression equation, then we have

$$m_c = q \times m_r \times (p + 1) \tag{11.22}$$

where q is the number of consequent (output) variables. For Mamdani type models, the number of consequent parameters is not directly related to the number of fuzzy rules; rather it depends on the number of membership functions for each membership function of y_i (denoted as β_i)and the total number of consequent variables (i.e. q). More precisely, we have

$$m_c = \sum_{i=1}^{q} (l_i \times \beta_i) \tag{11.23}$$

The parameter in η Equation 11.19 represent the relative cost for each fuzzy rule. A large value of η will lead to fewer rules being used and thereby a more "parsimonious" model. There exists no simple rule for choosing η, however. The best value for η in a practical modeling problem may depend on the number of available training data N, and even the type of fuzzy model being used. Although it is theoretically possible to regard η as a parameter of the procedure and solve it using some optimization algorithm, it is computationally too costly to be useful in practice. It was shown that the resulting fuzzy model and its accuracy were fairly insensitive to the value chosen for η in a particular range and choosing a value for η in the interval 2 to 5 often resulted in a good parsimonious model.

SRIC (also other criterion) may be used in two ways. First, it can be used to compare fuzzy models with a different number of fuzzy rules and pick the model with the minimum SRIC value as the best one. Second, it can be used to find the most important rules in a given rule base. Several recent researches have shown that if the less important fuzzy rules are removed from the rule base, the performance of the model constructed using the retaining rules can be high.

11.7.4 Model Interpretability

An important feature of a fuzzy model is its interpretability: Each rule in the model acts like a "local model" in the sense it only covers a local region of the input-output space, and its contribution to the total output of the model is easily understood. However, this advantage may get lost for some fuzzy models (typically the TSK model) if they are not adequately identified. The problem appears mainly in the parameter estimation stage where the parameters of the model are obtained by minimizing an objective function defined based on the errors between the desired (global) output and the actual (global) output of the model. If we are lucky enough to catch the "optimal" parameters of the model, then the resulting fuzzy rules can describe not only the correct global behavior but also the correct local behavior. Unfortunately, the nonlinearity of the parameter estimation problem may often make us trap a "suboptimal" solution. In this situation the fuzzy rules may show a very erratic local behavior, while they together generate a correct global behavior.

This important issue has not been addressed until recently (Yen and Gilliespie and Babuska et al. and much work remains to be done.

EXERCISES

1. What do you mean by fuzzy rule based models?
2. What is the approximation ability of fuzzy models?
3. Explain the three sub problems of fuzzy system identification?
4. What do you mean by structure specification? Explain with the help of example?
5. Explain the forward selection procedure backward elimination procedure?
6. Explain the best subset procedure?
7. Explain the techniques that can be used for fuzzy partition?
8. Explain the concept of parameter estimation in detail?
9. Explain the concept of model validation?
10. Explain with the help of example the technique of fuzzy model identification?

CHAPTER 12

Fuzzy Logic in Database and Information Systems

12.1 INTRODUCTION

Unlike the previous generation of database systems, the relational model did not rely on embedded pointers, links, and other internal structural edifices to maintain relationships between data elements. Instead of links andteb pointers, a relational database creates its relationships through a shared set of common data elements (that is, the data itself) carefully structured (in a process called normalization) throughout the database. Once fuzzy relations are defined, it is possible to develop fuzzy relational databases. The first fuzzy relational database, FRDB, appeared in Maria Zemankova's dissertation. Nearly all model development (as well as data mining) projects begin with an exploration of the underlying data space. With the exception of statistical analysis, the most common tool for data exploration is the Structured Query Language (SQL) facilities associated with nearly all modern relational databases. In this chapter, we examine ways of improving SQL requests using fuzzy forms of the where and having statements. By applying fuzzy logic and approximate reasoning to the evaluation of record selection and clustering, we significantly improve the robustness and utility of database query operations. In this chapter, we will be primarily concerned with the where statement and its various forms. We will also be examining the way database columns are decomposed into fuzzy sets.

In the rush to apply advanced computational intelligence, clustering, and factoring techniques to large databases, knowledge and data mining engineers often bypass an important analytical tool: the SQL processor associated with the database. SQL gives business analysts, knowledge engineers, and others a powerful method for seeking out and exploiting patterns in data. Although SQL does not necessarily discover patterns in the same sense as rule induction or multidimensional clustering, as a tool to augment the analyst's exploration of data it has the ability to see through database noise and expose relationships that are not readily visible. With general ideas in hand about how the data should be organized and what information or patterns are expected in the data, analysts can manipulate data to verify that the data has these patterns and structure. The ability to connect tables, filter records, and combine columns enables the exploration of probable patterns in data. Thus, SQL is a tool for combining a cognitive model with the actual data model. In a data mining, knowledge discovery, and even ordinary business process, modeling this is a very important capability and lies at the heart of any knowledge acquisition project. Some fuzzy querying languages have been defined, highlighting the SQLf by P. Bosc et al. and the FSQL by J. Galindo et al. These languages define some structures in order to include fuzzy aspects in the SQL statements, like fuzzy conditions, fuzzy comparators, fuzzy constants, fuzzy constraints, fuzzy thresholds, linguistic labels and so on.

12.2 VOCABULARY OF RELATIONAL DATABASES AND QUERIES

A complete discussion of relational database systems and the calculus of relational queries is beyond the scope or intent of this chapter. Modern relational databases are, in principal, simply a collection of rectangular tables connected by the data they share. In that the fuzzy SQL approach is designed to access and retrieve data from these tables, a basic understanding of the principal nomenclatures used in relational databases is important. This preview of the vocabulary will make reading and understanding the material in this chapter much easier. It is not always possible, while maintaining an uncluttered and coherent discussion of both the ideas associated with database organization and queries against that organization, to ensure that every term is introduced before it is used. Many of these terms are, of course, redefined or defined in more detail later in this chapter.

12.2.1 Column

Each row in a table consists of one or more columns of data. A column represents a unique class or category of data and has a unique name within the table. A column also has a date type (numeric, string, Boolean, and so on) and a domain (a restriction on the allowable value for the column, which, in many but not all cases is implicit in the data type). In the same way that rows are more or less the same as records in a file system, columns are similar to fields in a record.

12.2.2 Composite Key

Every column in a relation is identified by its primary identifier. This can be a single value or a set of values. When the primary key consists of multiple values it is called a composite key. Table 12.1, for example, illustrates the composite key for a project precedence relationship table. Each precedence relationship is defined by two values: a base (From) project identifier and a successor (To) project identifier. The table also contains the type of relationship (in this case, a finish-to-start connection) and any lead or lag value that offsets the precedence relationship. Figure 12.1 shows the critical path precedence network defined by the composite keys in this table.

Table 12.1: Project precedence table

From-Project	To-Project	Type	Lead-Log
A	B	FS	0
A	C	FS	0
B	D	FS	0
C	D	FS	0
D	E	FS	0

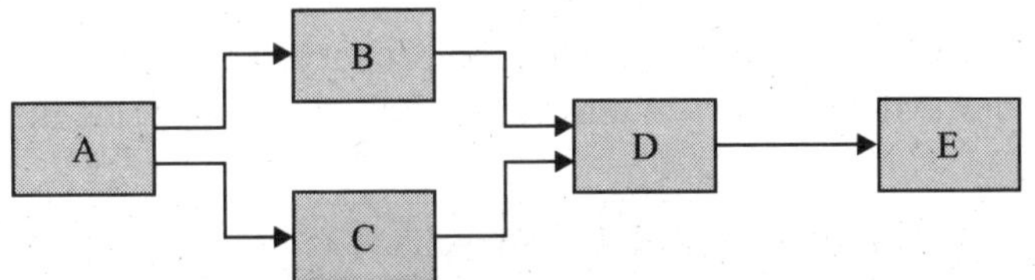

Figure 12.1: The precedence network from the composite keys.

A composite key uniquely identifies a single row in the table. Composite keys can consist of any number of columns, but the complete set of columns must be specified to access the corresponding row.

12.2.3 Crisp Number

A crisp number is an ordinary number that has a single value (see the fuzzy logic vocabulary in Chapter 4 for a discussion of crispness and expectancy).

12.2.4 Domain

A column's domain is its universe of allowable values. Unless otherwise specified, it is usually associated with the column's underlying data type numeric columns are limited to numbers, string columns can contain text, Boolean columns contain true or false values, and so forth). A column can also have an extended domain. When used in this sense, a domain is an explicit constraint on a column's value and takes the form of a lookup table, an if-then-else rule, or an arithmetic or logical expression.

12.2.5 Weighted Tuples

A tuple with a partial membership in a relation is often referred to as a "weighted tuple". A weighted tuple t in a relation R is a tuple associated with its membership degree in R, denoted $\mu_R(t)$.

12.2.6 Foreign Key

A column in one table that contains data values from the primary key of another table is a foreign key. Table 12.2, for example, shows a projects table. The table has a primary key (the project identifier) and two foreign keys.

Table 12.2: Project table

Project Id	Status	Duration	Department	Project Mgr
P_1	Active	190	MKTG	1077
P_2	Active	30	IT	1633
P_3	Pending	65	IT	1601
P_3	Complete	205	ENGR	5809
Primary key			**Foreign Key**	**Foreign Key**

The Department column contains values from the primary identifier of the departments table (see Table 12.3). The ProjectMgr column contains values from the primary identifier of the employees table (see Table 12.4).

Table 12.3: Departments table

Department	Dept Mgr	Site
ENGR	8932	East
IT	7734	East
MKTG	3077	West
Primary Key	**Foreign Key**	

Table 12.4: Employees table

Employed Id	Last Name	Salary
1077	Jones	32000
1633	Miller	43000
1601	Smith	25400
893 2	Sommers	67050
Primary Key		

The DeptMgr column in the departments table is also a foreign key because it contains employee ID values from the Employees table. The connections made through foreign keys are one of the principal ways relationships are established through the database. Foreign keys are also important domain management mechanisms in the database (so that, as an example, you cannot enter a department name in the projects table that does not also exist in the departments table).

12.2.7 Fuzzy Number

A number whose value is "smeared" out over an underlying range of values is called a fuzzy number. Fuzzy numbers are generally bell curves, but can be triangles and trapezoids. A fuzzy number can be part of the variable's term set or it can be created by the application of an approximation hedge.

12.2.8 Index

Columns containing non-key data can be indexed for high-performance retrieval and joins. An index is a multi-way tree that organizes the column's data in a manner that allows individual data items or collections of rows with the same data item to be found and retrieved very quickly. In many database systems, foreign keys are automatically indexed. For example, consider the Status column in the projects table (see Table 12.2). If there are thousands of projects in the table, finding all active projects would require searching the entire table, comparing the content of the Status column with the string Complete? An index extracts each unique value from the column, as well the set of all rows that have that value. Thus, finding all complete projects by indexing the Status column is extremely fast.

12.2.9 Join

The process of connecting two (or more) tables based on common data is called a join. Joins are the primary mechanism in a relational database for realizing structure in the data. This structure can be quite deep. A simple example of a join, using the projects and departments tables (see Tables 12.2 and 12.3), would be to answer a query such as "What projects are being run out of the East site?" In this case, the projects and departments tables are joined using the Department column in the projects table and the Department column in the departments table. The conventional SQL query to perform the join and then select those projects in the East site looks as follows.

```
Select ProjectId, Site
From Projects, Departments
Where Projects. department = Departments. Department
And Departments.Site = "East";
```

There are many types of joins. A join on the same data is called an equi-join

(an equal join). Relational query languages also support more advanced types of joins, such as unions, outer joins, and inner joins—used to connect and then create new tables based on the presence or absence of data values.

12.2.10 Normal Form

The process of organizing data in a relation to remove redundancies and eliminate update or deletion anomalies is called normalization. There are three principal levels of normalization.1 The first level is concerned with the basics of how rows and columns appear in a relation. The last two are basically concerned with eliminating redundancies and ensuring that all columns are dependent on the primary key set. In first normal form (1NF), every row contains the same columns and every row and column intersection contains a single value (that is, a column cannot be an array or some other multivalued form). In second normal form (2NF) and third normal form (3NF), all columns that are not fully dependent on the primary key are removed and placed in their own relation.

12.2.11 Predicate

A predicate is a fuzzy or crisp expression in the where (or having) statement that is evaluated to produce a truth value. Predicates determine which rows in a table participate in a query. A query often contains many predicates, as the following is an example.

```
Select projects
    Where project_length is Long
    And project_budget is High
    And project_priority is Low;
```

This is a query with three predicates in the where statement. The predicates evaluate fuzzy relationships involving the project length (duration), budget, and priority.

12.2.12 Primary Identifier (or primary key)

Each row in a table must be identified by a unique key. This is the primary identifier. The identifier can consist of one or more contiguous columns (if it consists of more than one column, it is a composite key). In the projects table (Table 12.2), the project ID is the primary identifier. No other row in the table can have the same value in this column. Note that although usually considered a poor design it is possible for a table to have more than one unique key (a project might also have a unique budget reference number, for example), in which case the other unique identifiers are called candidate keys.

12.2.13 Query Compatibility Index (Qcix)

The degree of compatibility with the semantic intent of a fuzzy SQL query is called the query compatibility index (QCIX). Each returned row from a query is assigned its own QCIX value. The fuzzy SQL query manager automatically ranks the returned row set in descending order by the QCIX. The QCIX reflects, in essence, the distance between the complete realization of the query and the degree of semantic membership in the returned row.

12.2.14 Relation (Table)

Data in the relational database is maintained in tabular form. When organized according to a set of precise rules, the tabular data is called a relation (or relation table). In general use, however, the relations are simply called tables. Each table consists of a fixed number of columns and a varying number of rows. Tables are connected through the join process, and these connections establish the rich variety of relationships in the relational model.

12.2.15 Row

Each table consists of one or more rows of data. A row consists of one or more columns, and each row contains the same number of columns. A row is more or less equivalent to a record in a file system.

12.2.16 Secondary Identifier (or key)

Any indexed column is known as a secondary identifier. Secondary identifiers play an important role in data modeling, query, and organization.

12.3 FUZZY INFORMATION

Fuzzy information can appear for different reasons. First, it may be due to the imprecision of real data values. For instance, a sensor data may be a distribution, rather than a precise value. Second, fuzzy information can arise from subjective judgments. For example a database containing information about real estate for family housing may need to describe the quality of public schools, the safety of the neighborhood, the estimated appreciation of housing prices, and so on. Representing this information using precise values would often fail to capture the soft boundaries between qualitative descriptions such as poor, fail, good, excellent, etc. Thus, it is important to find a data model that can represent and manipulate fuzzy information. Third, the information that a user is interested in may not be precise. For example, a college senior may be increased in finding a university that has a good graduate engineering program and low living costs. The meaning of "good" and "low" in the previous sentence is imprecise. Formulating this query using thresholds such as "annual living cost is less than n dollars" will exclude those universities whose annual living cost is slightly above n, but whose graduate engineering school is excellent. In other words, representing an imprecise query using a precise formalism is likely to miss information that the user wishes to obtain. Traditional databases were designed primarily for the efficient storage and convenient retrieval of large amounts of precise data.

However, the rapid advancement of telecommunication and information technology in the 1989 has introduced a new "cyberspace" in which a user can have direct access to a tremendous amount of information on the World Wide Web. As information services providers, software companies, and related industries (e.g. financial industry, entertainment, media, etc) explore a wide range of exciting opportunities that were not possible a decade ago, one thing is for sure – the nature of information of interest to a user has become far more imprecise than what was conceived by the designers of traditional databases and information systems.

12.4 FUZZY LOGIC IN DATABASE SYSTEMS

Fuzzy logic plays very important role in database systems. Fuzzy logic has used to extend database systems in two areas:

1. **Imprecise Information:** For storing and updating information that is imprecise by nature.
2. **Imprecise Queries:** For processing queries that are imprecise.

In this section, we give an overview of the major roles that fuzzy logic plays in extending conventional database systems in these two areas.

12.4.1 Imprecise Information

Information that is incomplete or having no logical value is called imprecise information. Imprecise information in a database system can be classified in two types:

1. Imprecise attribute values in a tuple.
2. Partial membership of a tuple in a relation.

1. Imprecise attribute values in a tuple

An attribute value in a tuple (also referred to as a domain value in the database literature may be imprecise due to the subjective nature of the attribute (e.g. the rating of movies) or a lack of precise information (e.g. the height of the suspect for a robbery case is around six feet).in the latter case the attribute itself (i.e. the height of a person) is not always subjective. Hence, its value can be precise if it is measured objectively (e.g. in a hospital). In the former case, however, the value of an attribute is intrinsically imprecise due to its subjectiveness. These two different causes of imprecise attribute value in database systems motivated two approaches for representing fuzzy data:

(i) Similarly-based approaches

(ii) Possibility-based approaches

(i) Similarly-based approaches: A similarity-based approach use linguistic terms (e.g. poor, fair, god, excellent) to describe attribute values. The impreciseness of these terms is characterized by a similarity matrix, which records the degree of similarity between pairs of linguistic terms in a domain. For example, let us consider a database that stores information about job openings and applicants. Suppose the speciality areas of an applicant may include robotics, AI, expert systems and statistics. A similarity-based fuzzy database system can use a similarity matrix such as the one shown in Table 12.2 to determine the matching degree between a job opening an and applicant.

(ii) Possibility-based approaches: An alternative approach for representing imprecise data is to use a possibility distribution as the value of an attribute. We call such approaches possibility-based approaches. For instance, the height of a bank robbery suspect, who has been described by a witness as around six feet tall, can be represented by a possibility distribution associated with the linguistic description "around 6 feet." If the police later want to find all case that may be linked to another murder case whose suspect is known to be 5 feet 22 inches, a possibilistic representation of the suspect's height information would enable the police to retrieve the bank robbery suspect, because the possibility distribution partially matches the height description of the murder suspect. Based on possibility theory, there are two kinds of matching degrees can be calculated for possibilistic-based approaches: the possibility measure and the necessity measure. These two measures represent the minimal degree and the maximal degree that possibilitic data satisfy a fuzzy condition in a query.

2. Partial Membership in a Relation

The second type of imprecise information in a database is the partial membership of a tuple in a relation. Membership in a relation is a black-and-white matter in a conventional database. For instance, a person is either an employee or not an employee of a company. However, there are relations whose membership has a gray area. For example, the relation Endangerd_species may include wild animals whose quantity has been significantly decreasing over the years but have not been officially declared as "endangered_species". These animals can thus be considered as somewhat endangered, and hence a partial member of an Endangered_species relation. Even though membership degree in a relation can be represented internally as an attribute of the relation, its meaning is fundamentally different from other attributes. In a fuzzy object-oriented database, for instance, partial membership of an object in a class directly affects the way the object inherits its properties from its classes. We will discuss this in the next section fuzzy object oriented database.

12.4.2 Imprecise Queries

In addition to representing imprecise information, fuzzy logic can also be used to retrieve imprecise information from a database or an information repository such as the World Wide Web.

The imprecision of information retrieved can be due to two reasons:

1. The information stored in the system is imprecise
2. The query (i.e. question) posted by the user is imprecise in nature.

We call the latter an imprecise query. A query is imprecise if it includes at least one of the following components:

- Imprecise conditions
- Imprecise operators
- Imprecise quantifiers

We will give an example of each of these below. Consider the following query to a database of the International Revenue Service (the U.S. government agency for collecting processing and auditing federal income tax returns):

Find all tax payers who have been audited in 1997 and whose annual family income is less than 30K.

The condition "annual family income is less than 30K" may be more naturally represented by an imprecise condition for describing a low-income family:

Find all tax payers who have been audited in 1997 and whose annual family income is LOW.

Where the meaning of LOW is characterized by a membership function.

A query often involves comparison operators such as "equal to," "greater than" "less that,". For instance, the following query uses the equality operator:

Find all countries whose top three imported goods are identical to the top three imported goods of the US.

Sometimes users are interested in information that is best described through imprecise operations such as "about equal to" "somewhat greater than," "significantly less than," An example of such a case is given below:

Find all countries whose top three imported goods are about the same as the top three exported goods.

Where "about the same" is an imprecise operator. An imprecise operator "about the same" an be represented as a fuzzy relation characterized by the following membership function.

$$\mu_{\text{About-the-same}}(I_3(c), I_3(US)) = \frac{\| I_3(c) \cap I_3(US) \|}{3} \tag{12.1}$$

where $I_3(c)$ denotes the set of the top three imported goods.

A query often involves quantifiers such as "for all" or "there exist". For instance, the former is used in the query below:

Find companies whose customers are ALL from government agencies.

An imprecise quantifier allows us to weaken or strengthen a classical quantifier so that the query can reflect the user's intent more closely. For instance, the query below uses the quantifier "MOSTLY" which is not as rigorous as "ALL".

Find companies whose customers whose customers are Al from government agencies.

The quantifier "Mostly" in the example above can be expressed by a fuzzy set hose universe of discourse is the ratio

$$r = \frac{\|\text{The company's customers from government agencies}\|}{\|\text{All customers of a company}\|} \quad (12.2)$$

and whose membership function is shown in Figure 12.2.

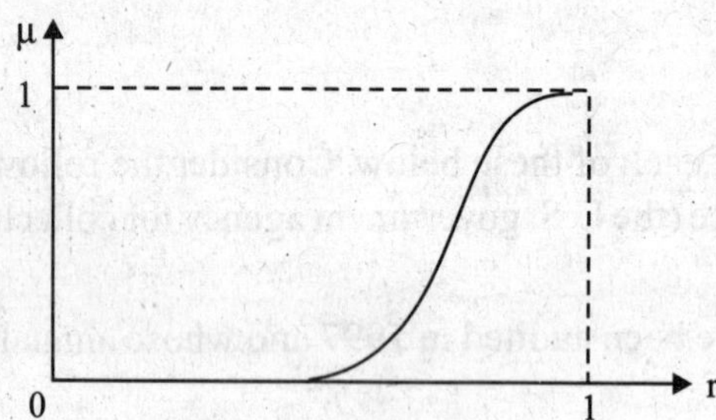

Figure 12.2: Membership Function of the quantifier MOSTLY.

12.5 REDUNDANCY AND FUNCTIONAL DEPENDENCY

Incorporating imprecise information into conventional database does introduce new issues that need to be resolved. Redundancy and functional dependency are two of the important ones.

A tuple in a relation is redundant if its content is identical to another tuple in the relations. A database management system needs to remove redundant tuples so that it not only avoids wasting storage space but also avoids anomalies (e.g. inconsistency) due to redundancy. The issue of redundancy removal becomes more complicated if a database system allows imprecise information. This is because the "identity" relationship between two fuzzy tuples is no longer black and white. Two fuzzy tuples can be partially identical, and yet partially different at the same time. The notion of redundancy thus needs to be extended to deal with this problem.

The concept of functional dependency is important in designing a relational database. More specifically, it plays a critical role in determining the keys of a relation (i.e. attributes that are unique for each tuple in the relation). We illustrate the basic idea of functional dependency using a relation R that has five attributes: A, B, C, D, E. If any two tuples in R with identical values for A and B also have identical values for C, D, and E, we say C, D and E are functionally dependent of A and B. Under such circumstances, A and B can be used as the primary key of the relation. If these attributes can have imprecise values, the fact that these attribute values can be partially identical complicates the issue of functional dependency. Both issues mentioned above are due to a common fundamental question regarding fuzzy databases:

How similar do two fuzzy tuples need to be for them to be considered identical?

We will discuss the techniques for addressing these issues in the next sections.

12.6 BASIC RELATIONAL DATABASE CONCEPTS

In the 1970s the concept of a relational database emerged as the standard way of representing large quantities of complex information. Unlike the previous generation of database systems, the relational model did not rely on embedded pointers, links, and other internal structural edifices to maintain relationships between data elements. Instead of links and pointers, a relational database creates its relationships through a shared set of common data elements (that is, the data itself) carefully structured (in a process called normalization) throughout the database. The basic building block of a relational database is the table: a fixed set of columns and a varying number of rows. Each row and column intersection contains a single data element. Figure 12.3 shows how these tables are organized in a database.

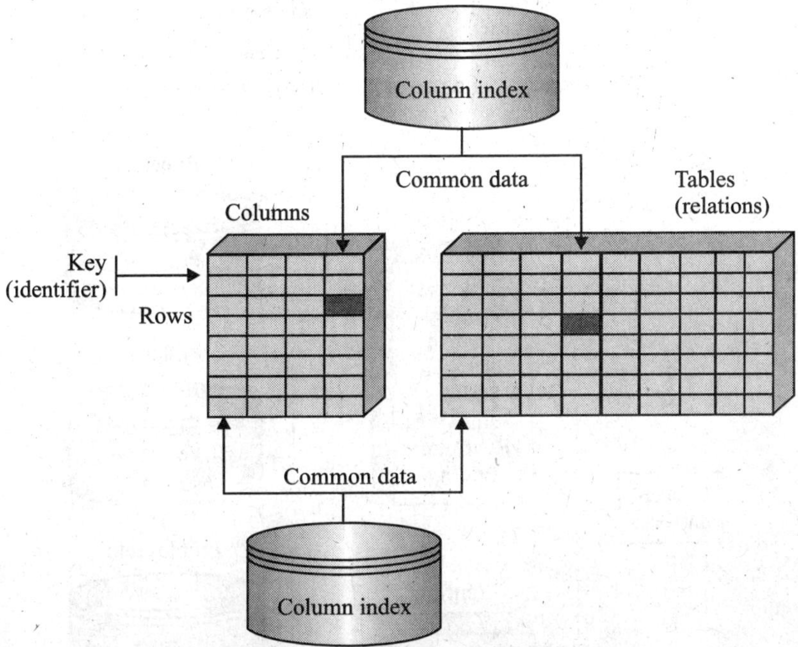

Figure 12.3: Relational database tables.

Tables are connected through a process is called a join. Rows are selected based on the content of their columns. To provide high-speed joins, primary and secondary keys are indexed. This allows sets of records containing a specific value to be retrieved without reading the entire table. We can see how a relational database is organized by examining a corporate information technology division's projects database. Figure 12.4 shows the schematic representation of the various tables in the database.

Focusing on a small segment of the database gives us some insight into the fine-grain details of the database organization at the table level. The project table contains information about each active project. The staffing table contains information about each employee. Figure 12.5 shows the structure of the database.

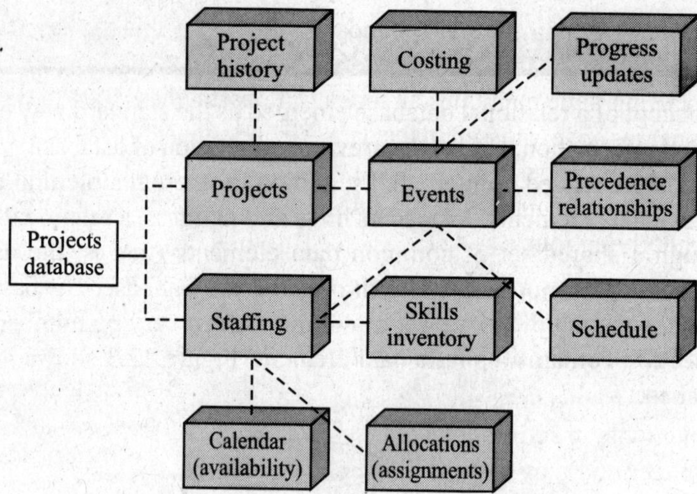

Figure 12.4: The projects database structure.

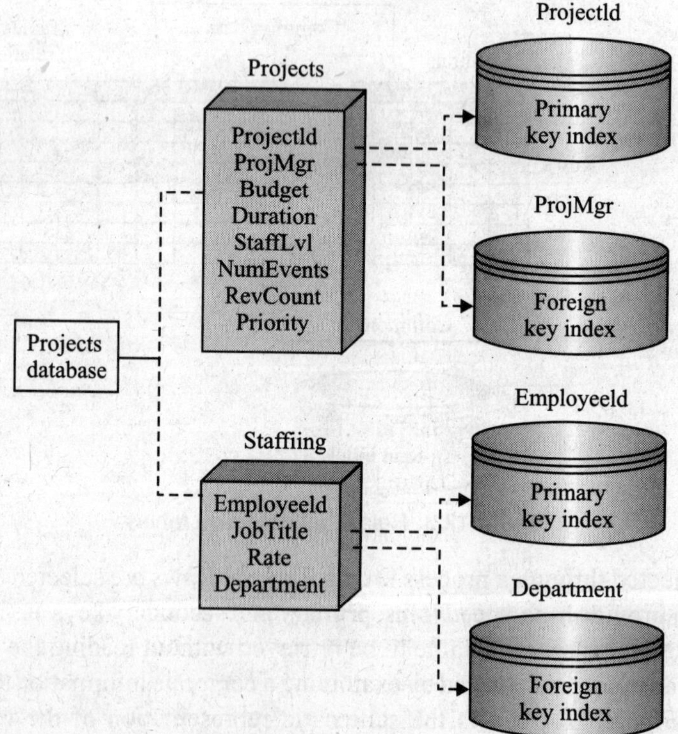

Figure 12.5: The projects and staffing table structure.

Each table is uniquely indexed on a primary key, ProjectId and EmployeeId, respectively. This unique index ensures that no duplicate records are entered in the table. In addition to the table's primary key, a table can contain several secondary keys. A secondary key (which refers to the primary key of another table) is called a foreign key. The project table maintains an index of project managers, and the staffing table maintains an index of departments associated with each resource. The database relationships are expressed in the data. The relationships are actually realized through the join operation. For example, suppose we want to find projects with budgets in excess of $80,000 that are managed by project managers in the Engineering department. Figure 12.6 illustrates the schematics of the underlying join.

A join between the projects and the staffing tables connects the proper staffing record with each project manager, ensuring that we have the ability to find only those project managers in the Engineering department. The result of a join is a new, physical table (using a temporary relation).

Forming a new table from a join, a process known as closure, ensures that these new tables can be used like any other table in additional joins (some of which are performed automatically by the database query manager and may be invisible to the client). In fact, it is the task of a relational database's query language to manage the implicit relationships among database tables.

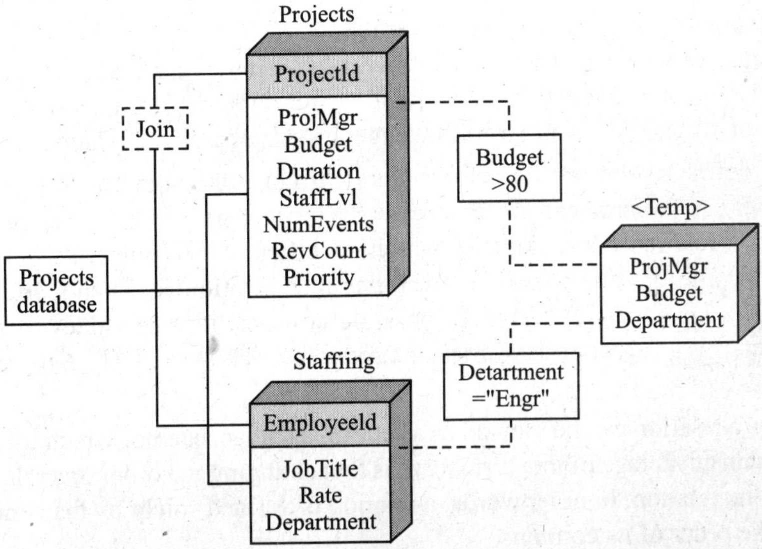

Figure 12.6: Explicit joins between project and staffing.

12.7 FUZZY RELATIONAL DATA MODELS

A data model is an abstract model of the data stored in a Database Management System (DBMS). This abstraction allows the user of a DBMS to focus on the context of the information, rather than the details of its physical data storage (i.e. file systems).

To provide such an abstraction, a data model has two components:

1. A notation for describing data and
2. A set of operations for manipulating the data.

Major data models include relational models, entity-relationship models, and object-oriented models.

In this section and the following section, we will introduce fuzzy relational models and fuzzy object-oriented models. We skip fuzzy network models because they are not as significant as the other two.

Table 12.5: Professor relation

Fname	Lname	JobType	Expertise
Gurpreet	Singh	Academic	AI
Mandeep	Mann	Industry	Expert System
Nancy	Kaur	Government	Robotics

12.8 RELATIONAL DATA MODELS

A relational model organizes data into relations, which can be viewed as tables with meaningful names. The columns of this table are called attributes of the relation, while the rows are called tuples. For example Table 12.5 shows a relation whose attributes are Fname (First Name), Lname (Last name), JobType, and Expertise. Conceptually, the relation describes the preferred carriers and the expertise of job candidates in a job search agency's database. The relation is named Professor.

To formally define a relation, we need to first introduce the notation of domains. A domain is a set of values. A domain can be discrete (e.g.,, the real numbers between 0 and 100). Each attribute in a relation has a domain, which specifies all possible values for the attribute. Let D_1, D_{2-}, ..., D_k be the domains of k attributes in a relation R. Then Cartesian product of these domains $D_1 \times D_2 \times \ldots \times D_4$ forms all possible combinations of values of the k attributes. The relation R hence is a subset of the Cartesian product $D_1 \times D_2 \times \ldots \times D_4$. A tuple is a member in a relation.

Alternatively, a relation can be viewed as a set of mappings, each of which maps each domain to a value. The main advantage of this formalism is that changing the order of a relation's attributes does not change the relation. In other words, a relation is defined solely by the content of its table, independent of the order of its columns.

In the original model, the domains for each attribute have a set of predefined values. Using the similarity matrix approach, the imprecision is implicitly in the similarity matrix and so the representation is still the same. Thus, this approach is very close to the conventional relational model. The possibility approach requiring changing the data representation to a representation of fuzzy attribute values. For example, if we have an age attribute in a given database, then originally this attribute will have numeric values. Using possibility distributions, we will introduce terms like Young, Old, Middle-aged that are characterized by corresponding possibility distributions. In the next tow subsections, a more detailed description of the two approaches will be presented. Furthermore, these two approaches will be discussed through example to enable the reader to grasp how the fuzzy query operations are handled.

Table 12.6: A Similarity Matrix for Expertise Areas				
	Robotics	**Expert Systems**	**AI**	**Statistics**
Robotics	1.0	0.6	0.6	0.2
Expert systems	0.6	1.0	0.9	0.2
AI	0.6	0.9	1.0	0.2
Statistics	0.2	0.2	0.2	1.0

12.8.1 Similarity-based Fuzzy Relations

In a similarity-based fuzzy relation, the impreciseness of attribute value is primarily in their meaning. For example, the values of the attributes EXPERTISE in the relation shown in Table 12.5 often partially overlap. The overlapping degrees of these areas of expertise are specified by a similarity matrix such as the one shown in Table 12.6. In addition to imprecision due to semantics, a similarity-based fuzzy relation could also describe that that age of a suspect is 19 or 20. To do this, an tribute in a tuple is allowed to have a set of values, which describe all possible values for the attribute in the tuple. A similarity-based fuzzy relation involving domains D_1, D_2,...., D_k is thus a subset of the Cartesian produce $2^{D}{}_1 \times 2^{D}{}_2 \times \ldots \times 2^{D}{}_k$. Furthermore, as we discussed earlier, the values in domains D_1, D_2,..., D_k are related by a similarity relations S_1, S_2,...,S_k that map each pair of values in a domain to the interval [0, 1]. A similarity measure of 1 means that the pair is identical, whereas a similarity measures of 0 means the pair is entirely different.

A similarity relation S for a domain D is a fuzzy relation that maps pairs of domain values in D to the unit interval, i.e. S: $D \times D \rightarrow [0, 1]$, with the following three properties for all x, y, z in D:

1. **Reflexive:** $S_D(x, x) = 1$
2. **Symmetric:** $S_D(x, y) = S_D(y, x)$
3. **Transitive:** $S_D(x, z) \geq \max_{y \varepsilon D} (\min (S_{D-}(x, y), S_D(y, z))$

The first two properties are intuitive. The usefulness of the third property will become clear when we discuss the issue of redundancy in a fuzzy database.

An example of the similarity relation is given in Table 12.6 in a matrix form. The matrix describes the similarity within domain values of a given attribute. In our example, for the attribute Expertise, the domain values are Robotics, Expert Systems, AI, and Statistics. For each pair of expertise areas, the similarity matrix describes one degree to which each expertise area is similar to the others.

A similarity relation cannot be freely constructed. It has to satisfy the three properties listed above. In fact, whenever we specify two different similarity measure s(x, y) and S(y, z), the similarity measure between x and z must be the smaller of S(x, y) and S(y, z).

12.8.2 Possibility-based Fuzzy Relations

The possibility-based approach is, as the name implies, based on the possibility distribution theory.

The possibility/necessity approach is more general than the similarity approach in the sense that it handles all types of information. As described above, the similarity based approach uses domains with discrete values. Even though an extension was added to it to handle the fuzzy number, the similarity approach still heavily depends on discrete values.

A possibility-based fuzzy relation generalizes a relation by allowing the value of an attribute A to be a possibility distribution $\Pi_{A(t)}$ of the attribute's domain. Let $D_1, D_2, \ldots, D_k$ be the attributes of a fuzzy relation R. A tuple in a possibility-based fuzzy relation is denoted $(v_1, v_2, \ldots, v_k)$ where $v_1, v_2, \ldots, v_k$ are fuzzy subsets of $D_1, D_2, \ldots, D_k$. The interest of such an approach is its ability to represent, in a unified manner, precise values (singletons), NULL values, as well as fuzzy values. This is further illustrated in Figure 12.7.

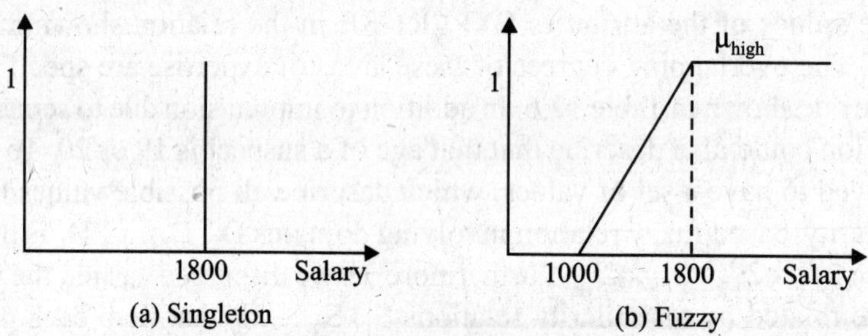

Figure 12.7: Possibility-based representations.

It should be noted that since the data are imprecise, then the result of the query will also be imprecise. In theory, both possibility measure and necessity measures can be used for processing queries in fuzzy databases. In practice, however, the necessity measures are rarely used.

To characterize the impression the response to a query, we use possibility measure and necessity measure introduced in Chapter 4.

For example, if we are given a possibility distribution of a suspect's age, and we want to find all young suspects, we can calculate the possibility degree and necessity degree is as follows:

$$\text{Poss (Young} \mid \Pi_x) = \sup_x \left[\min, \Pi_X \, \mu_{young}(x)) \right] \tag{12.3}$$

$$\text{Nec (Young} \mid \Pi_x) = \inf_x \left[\max \Pi_x, 1 - \mu_{young}(x)) \right] \tag{12.4}$$

Example 12.1: Let the universe of discourse of a person's age be {10, 15, 20, 25, 30, 35, 40, 45, 50}, and the age possibility distribution of a suspect (denoted J) be:

$$\Pi_{Age}(J) = 0.2/15 + 0.5/20 + 1/25 + 0.8/30$$

Suppose that the membership function for the linguistic term Young is defined as a discrete fuzzy set as follows:

$$\text{Young} = 1/10 + 1/15 + 1/20 + 0.8/25 + 0.4/30 + 0.2/35$$

Using Equation 12.3, we calculate the possibility degree for suspect J to satisfy the condition "young suspect":

$$\text{Poss (Young } \Pi_{\text{Age}} \text{ J)} = \max \{0.2 \wedge 1, 0.5 \wedge 1, 1 \wedge 0.8, 0.8 \wedge 0.4\}$$
$$= \max \{0.2, 0.5, 0.8, 0.4\}$$
$$= 0.8$$

To calculate the necessity measure, we first calculate the complement of the possibility distribution of a suspect J's are:

$$1 - \Pi_{\text{Age}} \text{(J)} = 1/10 + 0.8/15 + 0.5/20 + 0/25 + 0.2/30 + 1/35 + 1/40 + 1/45 + 1/50$$

The necessity measure is obtained using Equation 12.4

$$\text{Nec (Young}|\Pi_{\text{Age}} \text{(J))} = \min \{1 \vee 1, 1 \vee 0.8, 1 \vee 0.5, 0.8 \vee 0, 0.4 \vee 0.2, 0.2 \vee 1, 0 \vee 1, 0 \vee 1, 0 \vee 1)$$
$$= \min \{1, 1, 1, 0.8, 0.4, 1, 1, 1, 1\}$$
$$= 0.4$$

Therefore, the possibility that suspect J is young is 0.8, while the necessity that he/she is young is 0.4.

12.9 OPERATIONS IN FUZZY RELATIONAL DATA MODELS

Operations in the relational data model are often expressed in algebraic notation, called relational algebra, where queries are expressed by applying specialized operators to relations. Here we describes basic operations in relational algebra and their generalizations for handling fuzzy relations. We need to address at least two issues regarding the operations in fuzzy relational algebra. First, we need to determine the membership of a tuple in the new relation produced by an operation. Some of these generalizations (e.g. for union, difference and Cartesian product) are based on fuzzy set theory introduced in Chapters 4, while others (e.g. selection, projection and join) are defined specially for managing fuzzy relational databases. Second, we need to remove redundant tuples in the new relation generated by an operation. To do this, a uniqueness criterion needs to be established first to determine how dissimilar two tuples need to be in order for them to be considered "not identical". Using a uniqueness criterion, tuples that are "identical" in a fuzzy relation are collected and the tuple with the highest membership degree in the relation is kept. Others are discarded. We discuss these two issues regarding operations in fuzzy relational models below.

12.9.1 Fuzzy Relational Algebra

Following are the operations apply on relational algebra:

1. **Union:** The union of two relations R and S, denoted $R \cup S$, is the set of tuples that are in at least one of the relations. R and S should have the same number of attributes. The union of two fuzzy relations is defined as

$$\mu_{R \cup S}(t) = \mu_R(t) \oplus \mu_S(t) \tag{12.5}$$

where $\oplus$ denotes a fuzzy disjunction operator (e.g., max), and t denotes tuples.

2. **Set difference:** The difference of relations R and S, denotes R-S, is the set of tuples in R but not in S. Like the union operation, R and S need to have the same arity. The difference of two fuzzy relations is defined based on intersection are compliment of fuzzy relations:

$$\mu_{R-S}(t) = \mu_R(t) \oplus (1 - \mu_S(t)) \tag{12.6}$$

where $\oplus$ denotes a fuzzy conjunction operator (e.g. min).

3. **Cartesian product:** Let R and S be relations of arity k_1 and k_2, respectively. The Cartesian product of R and S, denoted R × S is the set of all possible $(k_1 + k_2)$ tuples formed by concatenating a tuple from R with a tuple from S. The membership in the Cartesian produce of fuzzy relations R and S is defined as

$$\mu_{R\times S}(t_{12}) = \mu_R(t_1) \oplus (1 - \mu_R(t_2)) \tag{12.7}$$

where t_{12} is a tuple formed by concatenating t_1 and t_2.

4. **Projection:** The projection of a relation R selects a subset of R's attributes (i.e. columns) that the user is interested in. Let $a_1, a_2, \ldots, a_k, a_{k+1}, \ldots, a_n$ be attributes of relation R, a projection of R on a_2, a_k and a_1 denoted as $\pi_{a_2, a_k, a_1}(R)$. For example, if we form a projection of the Professor relation, given in Table 12.5, on JobType, we will generate the relation shown in Table 12.7.

Table 12.7: The projection of professor relation on jobtype

JobType
Academic
Industry
Government

The projection of a fuzzy relation is typically followed by the redundancy removal step to be discussed in the next section.

5. **Selection:** The selection of a relation R based on condition C, denoted $\sigma_C(R)$ is the set of tuples in R that satisfy the condition C. The condition C can be described by comparing one or more attribute values of R with constants or other attributes using =, ≤, ≥, <, >. Multiple simple conditions can be combined using logical operators ∧ (and), ∨ (or), and ¬ (not).

Example 12.2: Returning to our job search example, suppose we want to find the profile information of applicants whose last name is Singh. We can retrieve the information using selection on Lname = Singh followed by a projection on all attributes of the Professor relation. This query can be expressed using relational algebra as follows:

$$R_1 = \sigma_{\text{Lname} = \text{Singh}}(\text{Professor}) \tag{12.8}$$

The result is shown in Table 12.8.

Table 12.8

Fname	Lname	JobType	Expertise
Gurpreet	Singh	Academic	AI

6. **Join:** The q-join of relations R and S on attributes a_i and b_j, written as R ∞ $a_i\theta b_j$ S, is the shorthand of $\sigma_{R\cdot ai\theta S\cdot bj}(R \times S)$, where θ is an arithmetic comparison operator (=, <, and so on). That is the q-join R and S is the set of tuples in the Cartesian produce $R \times S$ such that the relation θ holds between the attribute a_i in R and the attribute b_j in S. If θ is the equality relation =, the join operation is often called an equi-join.

   The natural join of R and S, written R ∞ S, is formed by (a) finding the equi-join on all attributes common (i.e. having identical name) to both relations, and (b) removing the redundant attributes in the resulted join. We illustrate the join operation using the Job relation in Table 12.9. The Job relation contains the following information about job openings: employer name, jobtype, expertise required, and location of the opening.

Table 12.9: Job relation

Employer	JobType	Expertise	Location
IBM	Academic	AI	Texas
SUN Microsystems	Industry	Expert Systems	California
Microsoft	Government	Statistics	DC
NASA Ames	Government	Robotics	California

Example 12.3: Suppose we wish to find all job applicants in the Professor relation whose preferred job type matches the type of the openings in the Job relation? This can be achieve by performing a join of the Professor relation and the Job relation on the condition P.JobType = j.JobType. Therefore, the join can be expressed as

$$R_1 = \sigma_{\text{P.JobType} = \text{J.JobType}}(P \times S) \quad (12.9)$$

$$P \infty J = \Pi_{\text{Name, Fname, Lname, P.JobType, Expertise, Location}} R1 \quad (12.10)$$

where P and J are the shorthand notations for the Professor Relation Job relation (defined in Tables 12.5, 12.9), respectively. The result of the join is shown in Table 12.10.

Table 12.10 Join operation

Fname	Lname	JobType	Expertise	Location
Gurpreet	Singh	Academic	AI	Texas
Mandeep	Mann	Industry	Expert Systems	California
Nancy	Kaur	Government	Statistics	DC
John	Hunt	Government	Robotics	California

12.10 STRUCTURED QUERY LANGUAGE FUNDAMENTALS

SQL evolved from the work of Edgar Codd and Chris Date as a standard and uniform method of creating, accessing, and manipulating relational databases. In SQL, the user tells the computer what columns they want, which tables are involved, how the tables should be joined, and which rows from the tables will participate in the query. The query language also provides a clear method of performing joins among all specified tables. SQL is a relational calculus approach to database access and information management: it selects and organizes sets of records through a high-level language that tells the system what records to select, not how to select records. In this way it becomes a tool for expressing the desired result of database retrieval instead of the mechanics necessary to achieve this result. Expressing the mechanics of a query is a relational algebra process. For example, the following is an example of a relational algebra query against project and staffing tables.

```
define TotalCost as double;
define ThisResCost as double;
open table projects, table staffing;
TotalCost=0;
for each project find projects.dept = "ENGR";
connect staffing via projects.projmgr=staffing.employeeid;
If connect.status=0 do;
If projects,budget > 40 then
compute ThisResCost=projects.duration*staffing.rate;
TotalCost=TotalCost+ThisResCost;
end if;
end if;
end for;
```

Most of the older database query languages took this approach. They required their client to open tables, set up working variables, and explicitly navigate through the database (such as following links between hierarchical relationships). SQL, the outgrowth of the initial SEQUEL language of IBM's System R database project, removed the client from the mechanical view. This freed the user to focus on data management and data analysis issues. As Figure 12.8 schematically illustrates, SQL incorporates a variety of data management features

12.10.1 Where Clause

The where statement performs a dual role of specifying how tables should be joined and which rows from a table should be selected. Thus, it filters and connects multiple tables in the database. For example, the following SQL request shows a join and a filter.

```
select projectid,projects.duration*staffing.rate
from projects,staffimg
where projects.projmgr = staffing.employee
And projects.budget > 4000.00;
```

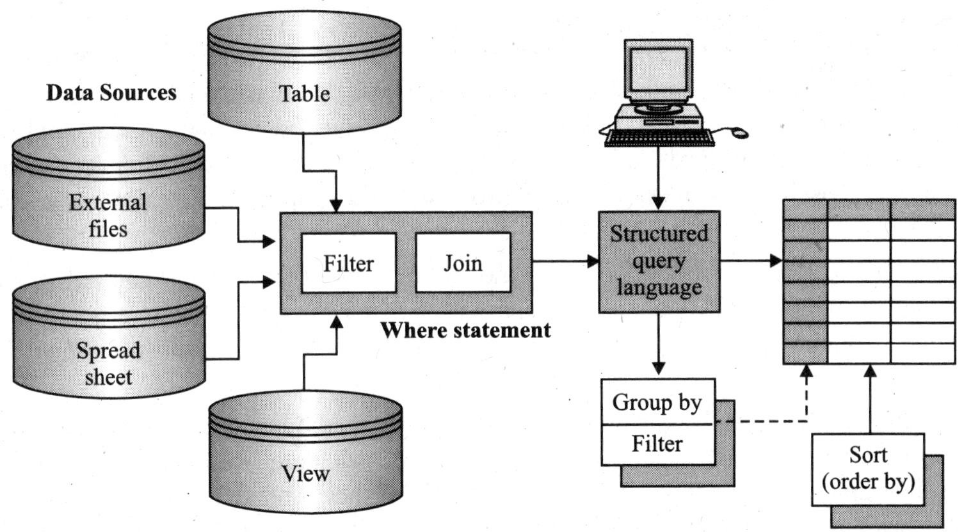

Figure 12.8: SQL data management features.

This request connects each project manager to his or her staffing (personnel) table entry so that the total management costs for each project with a budget in excess of $4000 can be calculated (compare this to the previous relational algebra request, which does the same thing). On the other hand, the group by statement collects sets of records according to one or more related columns. The associated having statement functions like a filter on the group, indicating which records should participate in the group. The following example illustrates the use of a group by and having statement.

```
select projmgr from projects
group by projectid Having count(*) > 1
```

This query selects all project managers who manage more than one project. The having statement provides a way of applying a filter to an entire collection of records.

An important characteristic of a relational query language is the idea of closure. This means that the result of a query is a new table, not simply a collection of rows. Using SQL we can connect any number of database tables to produce a result. How the tables are connected and which rows are selected are determined by the arithmetic, logical, and string comparisons found in the where statement. As criteria become more and more complex, the set of records selected by the where statement becomes more and more brittle. Thus, as a component of any data mining engineer's toolkit SQL has several significant limitations. In this chapter, we address one of its principal analytical shortcomings: its lack of discrimination among database records. The precise nature of an SQL request's selection and grouping of predicates, as we will see, lies at the heart of this shortcoming.

12.11 PRECISION AND ACCURACY

We live in a world obsessed and infused with precision. We wear wrist watches accurate to a hundredth of a second a year (often automatically coupled to the atomic clock at the National Institute of Standards and Technology (NIST). Ultra-high-density computer chips are made possible by nearly nanometer-level placement of circuits on a silicate substrate.

Hunters, hikers, drivers, and, of course, the military use the Global Positioning System (GPS), which can locate individuals and troops within a meter or so anywhere on earth. As a demonstration of manipulating nanometer objects, IBM wrote its name with individual Xenon atoms.

Intelligent missiles speed near ground level across a thousand miles of mountainous terrain to strike a single target in a crowded city. We can calculate irrational numbers, such as pi, to over a billion decimal places. Our space craft slingshot around the sun and rendezvous a year later with a distant planet on a time schedule that is exact to a few hundredths of a second. And changes in the economy are measured, and reported, down to a tenth of a percent.

These are our models of precision—models that provide the gauge for measuring other physical phenomena. We judge our weather forecasts, for example, as highly imprecise (and consequently less accurate) because they cannot predict the exact weather for this weekend. We believe statistical analysis is less precise than calculus. And we believe, above all other things, that numbers are more precise than words. In our modern analytical world, tempered by the rise of the scientific method, fields of study that cannot reduce their axiomatic truths to sets of equations are viewed with skepticism and placed outside the scope of the "hard" sciences.

And this type of drive for precision has been carried forward to our tools for data analysis and knowledge discovery. It is, in fact, the often unstated assumption that precision is a necessary requirement of truth and rigor that has impeded the use of such technologies as fuzzy logic.

12.12 WHY WE SEARCH DATABASES

It seems like a trivial question to ask why we search databases, yet it lies to the heart of our need for precision and accuracy (as well as how we measure both of these properties). The simple answer is: To retrieve data we need to make a decision. The "we" can be either a person sitting at a computer terminal or an application running on some computer. And this simple answer is important. It links the process of data retrieval with the cognitive process of decision making. In making a decision we want to have all the facts. And we want the facts to be as accurate as possible. In a perfect world, with perfect tools, we might expect complete access to the supporting facts. In fact, however, due to the ambiguous and imprecise nature of information actual "facts" are difficult to discover.

Table 12.11: The project table (subset)			
Project Id	Budget (x00)	Duration	StaffLvl
P01	55	108	29
P02	48	115	33
P03	57	90	10
P04	81	87	40
P05	78	92	16
P06	63	102	25
P07	91	125	41
P08	90	88	27
P09	65	117	37
P10	73	102	30
P11	93	93	45
P12	60	110	31
P13	59	121	37
P14	89	92	18
P15	51	101	23

Before we jump into the middle of how this dilemma can be resolved, we should examine a relatively simple example to understand how and why the problem exists in real databases and other information repositories. Let us consider a few of the columns in the projects table, as shown in Table 12.11. Suppose we need to find all projects with a high budget and a short duration. In a conventional query, we must decide on a clear set of boundaries defining what set of budgets are considered "high" and what set of durations are considered "short." In this case, we decide a budget over \$80,000 is high and duration less than 90 days is short. The SQL query is cast as follows.

Select ProjectNo, Budget, Duration

From Projects

Where Budget > 80 and Duration < 90;

The query selects the projects that have both a budget greater than

\$80,000 and a duration less than 90 days. Table 12.12 shows the result of this query.

The query meets the precise requirements of the selection criteria expressed in the where statement. As Figure 12.9 shows, the query delimits a decision space in the data.

Table 12.12: Selected rows			
Project Id	Budget (x00)	Duration	StaffLvl
P01	55	108	29
P02	48	115	33
P03	57	90	10
P04	**81**	**87**	**40**

P05	78	92	16
P06	63	102	25
P07	91	125	41
P08	**90**	**88**	**27**
P09	65	117	37
P10	73	102	30
P11	93	93	45
P12	60	110	31
P13	59	121	37
P14	89	92	18
P15	51	101	23

Table 12.13: Row matching intent of query

Project Id	Budget (×00)	Duration	StaffLvl	
P01	55	108	29	
P02	48	115	33	
P03	57	90	10	
P04	**81**	**87**	**40**	←
P05	**78**	**92**	**16**	←
P06	63	102	25	
P07	91	125	41	
P08	**90**	**88**	**27**	←
P09	65	117	37	
P10	73	102	30	
P11	**93**	**93**	**45**	←
P12	60	110	31	
P13	59	121	37	
P14	**89**	**92**	**18**	←
P15	51	101	23	

However, the query is not very accurate in terms of our intended objective. There are projects with budget and duration values that are conceptually close to our ideas of high and short but are not selected by the query. Table 12.13 illustrates some of these candidate rows.

In a small database, such as our example, this is not a problem because we can visually see other candidate records. But in large production databases such visual pattern recognition is not possible. Thus, how can we improve our ability to find the needed data? There are two ways: by expanding the scope of our selection criteria or by changing the way we perform our query against the database. We will look at each in turn.

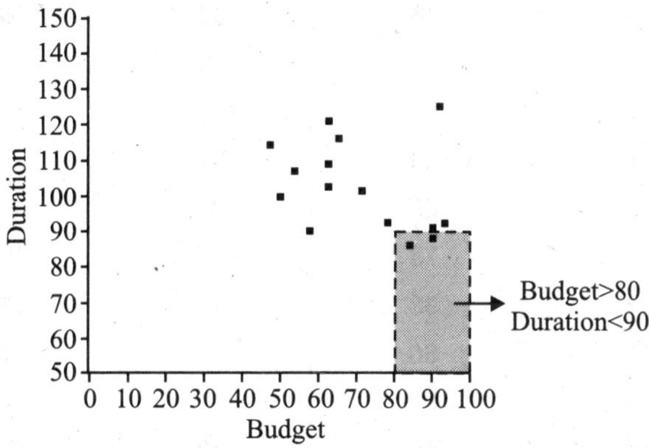

Figure 12.9: The boolean high budget and short duration space.

12.13 EXPANDING THE QUERY SCOPE

One intuitively obvious way of enriching the amount of data retrieved from the database is by expanding the scope of our query. This means changing the selection criteria so that they encompass more data. As an example, in our previous query we might extend the selection criteria as follows.

Select ProjectNo, Budget, Duration

From Projects

Where Budget > 75 and Duration < 100

This moves the budget limit down to projects with a budget greater than $75,000 and moves the duration threshold up to durations less than 100 days. Indeed, as Table 12.14 shows, we now pick up the rows shown in Table 12.13. This seems to solve the problem. We simply have to broaden the search criteria. As Figure 12.10 shows, this expansion neatly encloses several of the neighboring data points.

But extending the search space introduces several additional problems. First, we have diluted the meaning of the query in order to capture these adjacent records. Second, we have no way of telling which additional records are closely associated with the intent of our query and which are, essentially, "satellite" records. And third, of course, we now miss records that are near our new boundaries. Table 12.15 shows some candidate neighboring records (P07 and P10) that might be included in the new selection space.

Table 12.14: Rows selected by expanding selection criteria scope

Project Id	Budget (x00)	Duration	StaffLvl
P01	55	108	29
P02	48	115	33
P03	57	90	10
P04	**81**	**87**	**40**

P05	**78**	**92**	**16**
P06	63	102	25
P07	91	125	41
P08	**90**	**88**	**27**
P09	65	117	37
P10	73	102	30
P11	**93**	**93**	**45**
P12	60	110	31
P13	59	121	37
P14	**89**	**92**	**18**
P15	51	101	23

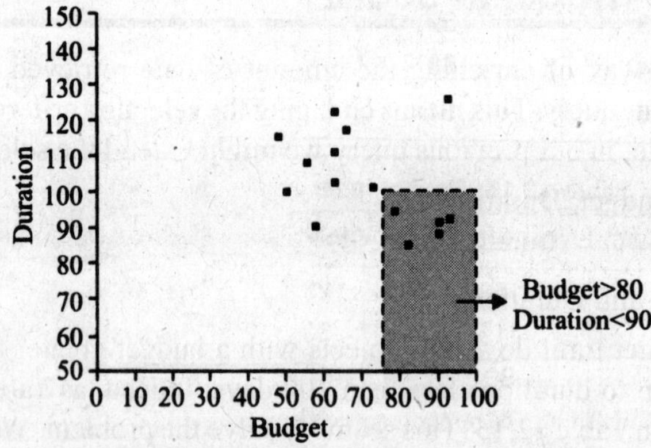

Figure 12.10: The extended boolean decision space.

We now begin to see the futility of extending the scope of the selection criteria. More records from the database are selected, but we have completely lost the accuracy of our query. The pool of returned records includes both those that meet our criteria of high budget and short duration and many others selected simply to catch information along the "edge" of the decision space. In a simple two-predicate query against a small table of data, the intrinsic brittleness of Boolean selection criteria is not often apparent (in that we can visually see adjacent records and discern patterns). But against a large complex database, we lose this ability to see which records out of several hundred belong to the core set of desired records. For example, Table 12.16 outlines a projects table with some additional columns.

In assessing project risk or anticipating project bottlenecks, we want to find projects with "a high budget, short duration, moderate to large staffing, fair complexity (at least 45 events or tasks), previous revisions to the project plan, and high to moderate priority." Such a query might look as follows.

Project Id	Budget (x00)	Duration	StaffLvl	
P01	55	108	29	
P02	48	115	33	
P03	57	90	10	
P04	**81**	**87**	**40**	
P05	**78**	**92**	**16**	
P06	63	102	25	
P07	**91**	**125**	**41**	←
P08	**90**	**88**	**27**	
P09	65	117	37	
P10	**73**	**102**	**30**	←
P11	**93**	**93**	**45**	
P12	60	110	31	
P13	59	121	37	
P14	**89**	**92**	**18**	
P15	51	101	23	

Table 12.15: Neighboring records in the extended scope

Table 12.16: Project table with additional columns

Project	Budget (x00)	Duration	StaffLvl	Num Events	Rev Count	Priority
P01	55	108	29	14	0	3
P02	48	115	33	77	3	1
P03	57	90	10	22	0	1
P04	81	87	40	31	1	5
P05	78	92	16	49	5	0

```
Select * From Projects
Where Budget > 80
and Duration < 90
and Staff > 30
and NumEvents > 45
and RevCount > 2
and Priority < 5
```

Applied against the project operational data store or (in a data mining exercise) against a database of historical projects, this query may retrieve many hundreds of records. Along each dimension of the where statement, there will be values that are close to the cutoff threshold. To ensure that we capture a robust set of records we might relax our selection criteria somewhat to capture a portion of these nearby records. However, given the set of selected records there is no effective way to tell which records are strongly compatible with the meaning of our query and which are only weakly compatible.

The question is, how do we go about making a database query that improves the accuracy of our results? The problem lies in how we express our query. Instead of simply changing the boundary conditions in the where statement, we need to change the way in which the where statement is evaluated. More to the point, the Boolean or crisp predicates are replaced with fuzzy predicates. Making this change has some far-reaching and important consequences. We now turn our attention to some fundamental principles of the relational database before addressing the issues associated with fusing fuzzy logic and the relational query language.

12.14 FUZZY QUERY FUNDAMENTALS

A fuzzy SQL request introduces a new way of retrieving information from a relational database. Using this query facility, you tell the computer what you want based on concepts rather than numbers and text strings. These concepts are sometimes vague and often imprecise. For example, you can look for risky projects in the corporate project database using a query such as the following.

select * from projects
where projects.budget is **High**
and projects.duration is **Short**

With fuzzy SQL, terms such as High replace the more conventional (and restrictive) method of specifying a range of budget values, such as the following.

project.budget >= 40 and project.budget =< 80

The same type of conceptually based query is used across a wide spectrum of public, corporate, governmental, and military databases. For example, a military query against division-level resources might take the following form.

select battalionid from imemilorg.divmrrpt
where toe_staffing is **complete**
and mr_availability is **near toe.staffing**
and transport_redline is **low**

This query accesses the materiel readiness report to find battalions within a division for which TO&E (table of organization and equipment) staffing is complete, the morning report availability is close to the staffing level (nearly everyone is present), and the number of vehicles on redline (in for repair) is low.

The idea behind a fuzzy query process is simply this: you tell the computer what you want in terms that mean something to you. These terms, expressed as the names of fuzzy sets, define the semantics of a query rather than the mechanics of a query. By expressing your thoughts through semantics rather than arithmetic, Boolean, and comparison operators, you can find information that expresses the intent of your query. In a while we will see why this new way of qualifying records from a database is not only more natural but much more powerful and comprehensive. But first, we briefly review the idea of fuzzy sets in the context of query requests (the building blocks of fuzzy SQL) and see how they work and how they are used in a basic query process.

12.14.1 Understanding Fuzzy Query Predicates

Most of us are familiar with conventional logic. This is often called Boolean logic after George Boole, the nineteenth-century cleric and mathematician who formalized its rules of logic. The core of both Boolean and fuzzy logic is the idea of a set. A set is a collection of things, both real and imaginary. The big difference between the two is simply this: in Boolean logic a thing is either a member of a set or it is not a member of the set. In fuzzy logic, things can have a partial membership in a set. As we will shortly see, such partial memberships have far-reaching implications. A rather easy way to see the difference between Boolean sets (which we often call crisp sets) and fuzzy sets is by examining the concept of Tall. In conventional set membership, we must specify a boundary point: individuals with heights above the boundary are Tall and those below the boundary are not Tall.

Suppose we select 6 feet as the boundary. Equation 12.11 shows how the set is defined.

$$\mu_{Tall} = \{\text{height e} \geq 6\} \tag{12.11}$$

As a reminder, throughout the chapter we continue to use the Greek μ (mu) to indicate a set membership. Figure 12.11 shows what this set looks like in crisp form.

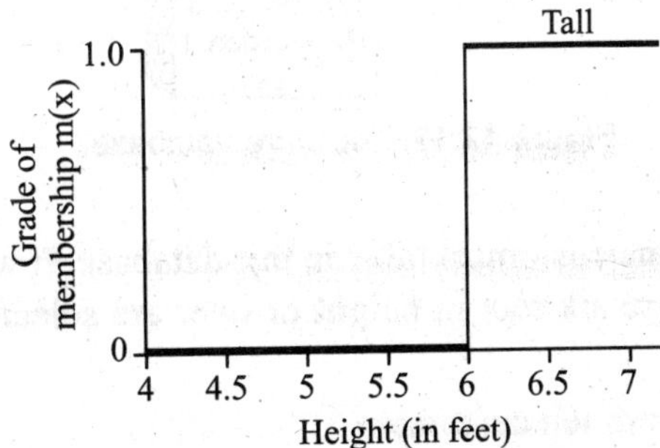

Figure 12.11: The crisp tall definition.

We can see that the most obvious characteristic of the Boolean set is the sharp boundary between the items not in the set and those that are members of the set. Thus, someone five and one-half feet in height is not Tall, whereas someone six feet three inches is a member of Tall. This sharp boundary also introduces some artificial classification constraints on the logic that uses the set. These constraints are most pronounced in real-world applications in which the boundaries between states of some value are continuous. In the case of Tall, this means that someone five feet eleven and seven-eighths inches is not Tall. However, by adding one-eighth of an inch the set membership immediately shifts into the Tall set.

From a database selection viewpoint, this can lead to some significant problems. Consider a (hypothetical) retailer's store database. Figure 12.12: schematically illustrates how this database might be organized. The marketing department is using the information to find prospects for a sale of special items. They want to find Tall, Heavy, and Middle-aged men who have bought expensive suits in the past few months (for a sale of large suits in a conservative cut).

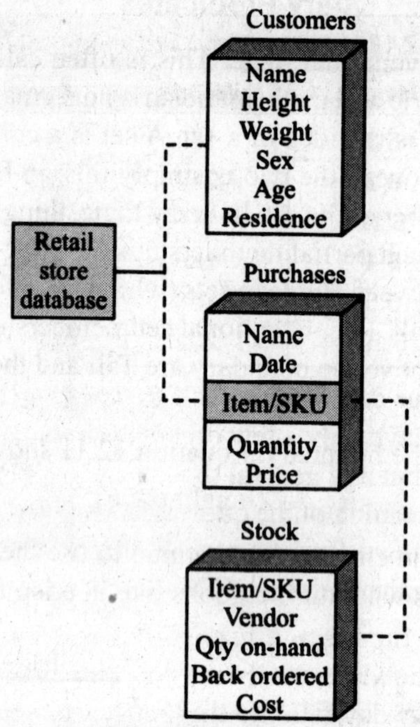

Figure 12.12: The store database.

Table 12.17 shows part of the customers table in this database. If we use the Boolean definition of Tall, only individuals that are six feet in height or over are selected. The corresponding SQL query would look as follows.

```
select name from ieh.customers
where customer.height >= 6;
```

Only two individuals are selected from the customers table. Table 12.18 shows these two individuals. A quick review of the Height column shows, nevertheless, that some of these customers (such as Miller and Freeman) are very close to being categorized as Tall. But this is the penalty we pay for using crisp logic in our selection criteria.

Table 12.17 The customers table (partial)

Name	Height	Weight	Age
Jackson	5′3″	170	38
Sanders	6′2″	215	52
Miller	5′11″	157	25
Cassey	6′1″	188	40
O' Malley	5′5″	163	48
Freeman	5′10″	202	443

Table 12.18: Tall customers (boolean criteria)

Name	Height	Weight	Age	Tall
Jackson	5′3″	170	38	
Sanders	**6′2″**	**215**	**52**	←
Miller	5′11″	157	25	
Cassey	**6′1″**	**188**	**40**	←
O′ Malley	5′5″	163	48	
Freeman	5′10″	202	44	

Naturally, we could change our definition of Tall by lowering the boundary between Tall and not Tall. In the case in which we have only a few outlier records (as in the previous example), this might be an acceptable approach, but as a general solution it will not work. Changing the boundary points on our query changes the meaning of the query and introduces records whose relationship to the idea behind our query is unknown (see the section "Expanding the Query Scope"). What we need is a better way of expressing the concept of Tall.

This brings us to the idea of a fuzzy set. A fuzzy set does not represent fuzzy data; it is simply a method of encoding and using knowledge that does not have clearly defined boundaries. Many of the phenomena we encounter every day fall into this class. Tall is one example. Other concepts—such as heavy, high, low, fast, slow, full, empty, many, few, light, and dark—are often associated with variables that have ill-defined boundaries. A fuzzy set maps a value in the data to its degree of membership in a set of ill-defined elements. To see this, let's look at a fuzzy set that might define the idea of Tall. Figure 12.13 shows this fuzzy set definition.

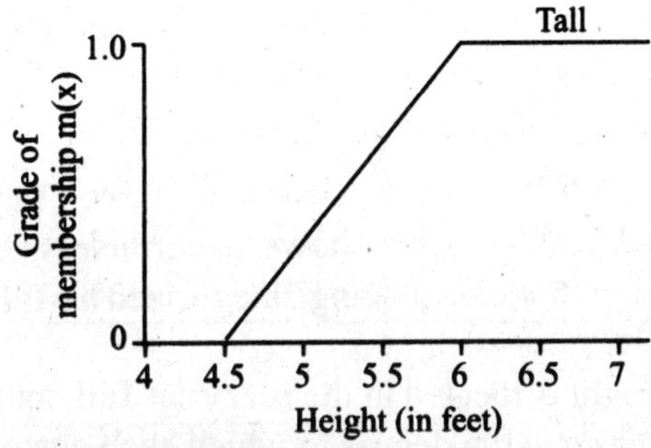

Figure 12.13: The fuzzy tall definition.

Here we have a completely different type of representation for Tall. The line moving diagonally up and across the height values is the membership function for the fuzzy set. It associates a height value with a degree of membership. Figure 12.14 shows how the value of five feet has a membership of [0.43] in the fuzzy set Tall.

What does a number such as [0.43] mean? It means that a height of five feet is a moderate member of the fuzzy set Tall. We can look at membership values as a measure of compatibility or a measure of representation. They answer questions such as the following.

- How compatible is five feet with the concept Tall?
- To what degree is five feet representative of the concept Tall?

Thus, a fuzzy set takes a concept, such as Tall, and expresses it through a mapping of data to membership functions. The magnitude of the number reflects how well an item matches the semantics (or meaning) of the fuzzy set. Using this new tool, we can now find Tall customers with a slight change in our query statement.

select name from ieh.customers
where customers.height is Tall;

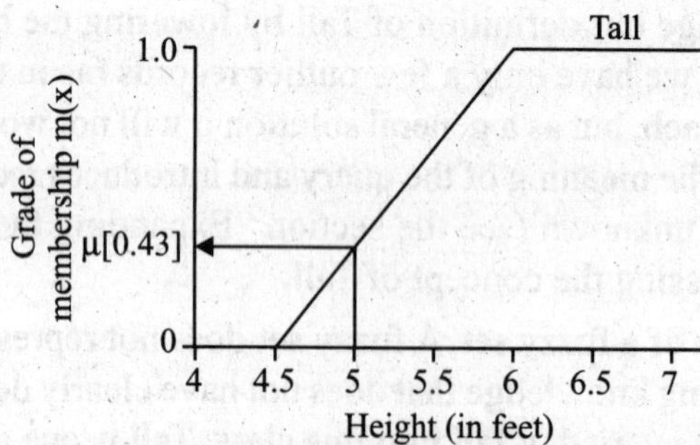

Figure 12.14: Fuzzy memberships.

Table 12.19: Tall customers per QCIX

Name	Height	Weight	Age	μ(Tall)
Sanders	6′2″	215	52	**.91**
Cassey	6′1″	188	40	**.90**
Miller	5′11″	157	25	**.87**
Freeman	5′10″	202	34	**.83**
O′ Malley	5′5″	163	48	**.62**
Jackson	5′3″	170	38	**.53**

Each value of customers.height is located in the fuzzy set Tall, and its degree of membership is returned. This type of query measures the degree to which each customer's height is a member of the Tall fuzzy set. This degree of membership, called the QCIX, is used to rank the selected records according to how well they agree with our request (we discuss this in more detail in the section "Measuring Query Compatibility"). Table 12.19 shows the result of this query. The resulting table is sorted in descending order by the compatibility index, which in this case is the membership of Height in the fuzzy set Tall. Because our definition of Tall covers the entire possible domain of interested heights and is linear (a straight line), each record will be graded according to its membership. You can fine-tune the definition of Tall by changing its range of values or the shape of its membership function.

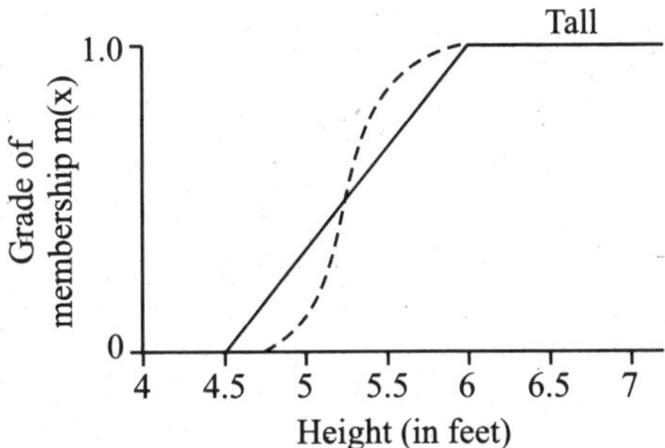

Figure 12.15: Redefining the Tall fuzzy set.

Figure 12.15 illustrates a possible reorganization of the set using an S-curve rather than a linear curve (the underlying linear curve is shown in the background).

In this example of Tall we have moved the curve to the right and changed it into an S-curve (also known as a growth curve). Membership values fall off rapidly below the "inflexion" point. Table 12.20 shows the result of the same fuzzy SQL query using the new fuzzy set. Note the change in membership values.

This new set of membership functions brings us to an important fact about fuzzy sets. They are not universal descriptors. They are dependent on your data and on your own, sometimes subjective, judgment about the way a concept is expressed in the data. The shape of a fuzzy set reflects the meaning of the concept. This is an important notion: fuzzy sets couple the semantics of your request to the actual mechanics of the request.

Table 12.20: Tall customers per new fuzzy set

Name	Height	Weight	Age	μ(Tall)
Sanders	6′2″	215	52	**.91**
Cassey	6′1″	188	40	**.88**
Miller	5′11″	157	25	**.79**
Freeman	5′10″	202	34	**.67**
O′ Malley	5′5″	163	48	**.13**
Jackson	5′3″	170	38	**.00**

As a consequence, we are able to state our queries in a form that means something to both us and the computer. But first we have to tell the computer what we mean by such terms as Tall. This meaning is expressed in terms of the fuzzy set membership functions. Changing the membership function changes what we mean when we issue a query. Figure 12.16 illustrates this by showing four different but plausible versions of the Tall fuzzy set.

When you design a fuzzy set in the fuzzy SQL system you must ask yourself how data values in the table (or spreadsheet) are related to your semantic concept. However, it is important to realize that this mapping need not be extremely exact. As the membership functions in Figure 12.13 illustrate, the general shape of the curve is sufficient to make the connection. The final fuzzy sets, naturally, may need to "tune" your function after selecting and examining sets of data.

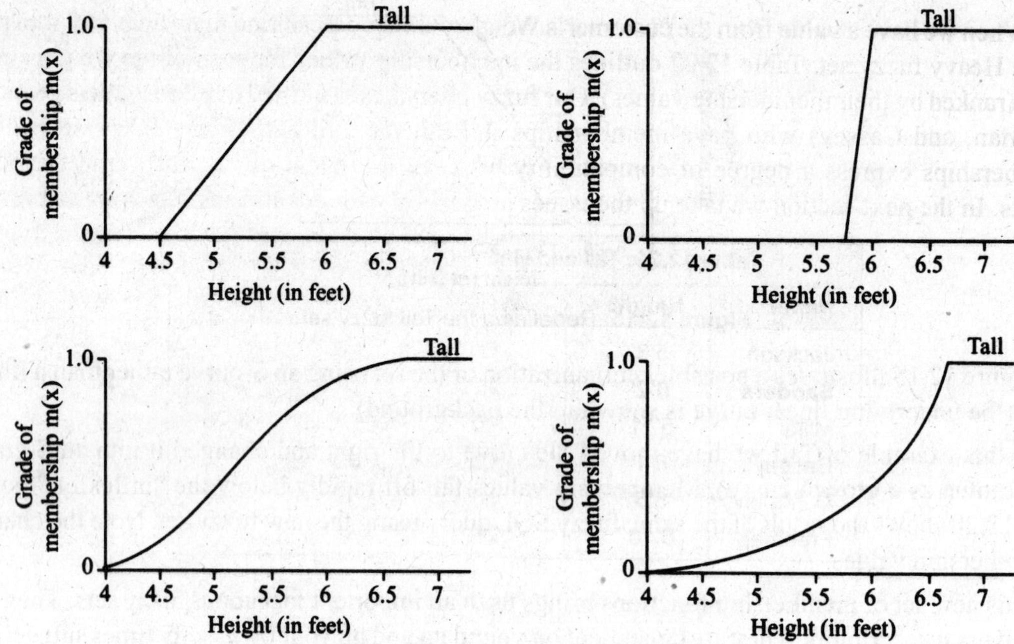

Figure 12.16: Different forms of the Tall fuzzy set.

12.14.2 Combining Fuzzy Sets

The real potential of fuzzy queries becomes apparent when we move from one fuzzy set to queries that combine many fuzzy sets. With multiple fuzzy sets we want to find candidates in the data that have, to some degree, characteristics of our combined concepts. Let's look at the query for Tall and Heavy men. In our crisp query we need to establish a boundary point for the definition of Heavy. Suppose we select 195 pounds. Then the SQL query is as follows.

```
select name from ieh.customers
where customers.height >= 6
and customers.weight >= 195;
```

The result of this query is reflected in Table 12.21. Only a single customer is both Tall and Heavy. But if we glance down the table, it appears that several of the customers might be potential candidates. They are excluded simply because of the sharp boundary points imposed by the crisp SQL query. We can do better by replacing the query with its corresponding fuzzy version, as follows.

```
select name from ieh.customers
where customers.height is Tall and customers.weight is Heavy;
```

The intent of this query is obvious: we want customers that are both Tall and Heavy. To resolve the query we need to tell the computer what constitutes a Heavy person. Figure 12.17 shows one possible way to represent this concept.

When we have a value from the customer's Weight column we can find that value's membership in the Heavy fuzzy set. Table 12.22 outlines the membership values for each of the weights in the table (ranked by their membership values). Our fuzzy query has identified three customers (Sanders, Freeman, and Cassey) who have memberships in both the Tall and Heavy fuzzy sets. These memberships express a degree of compatibility between the intent of the query and the actual results. In the next section we take up the issues associated with quantifying this compatibility.

Table 12.21: Tall and Heavy Customer (Crisp)

Name	Height	Weight	Age	(Tall)
Jackson	5′3″	170	38	
Sanders	**6′2″**	**215**	**52**	←
Miller	5′11″	157	25	
Cassey	6′1″	188	40	
O′ Malley	5′5″	163	48	
Freeman	5′10″	202	34	

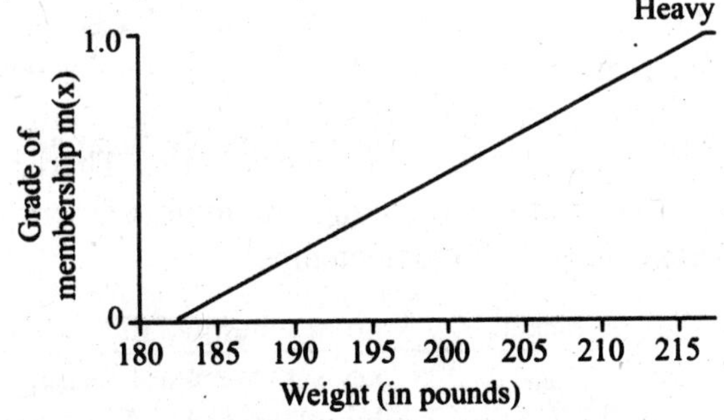

Figure 12.17: The heavy fuzzy set.

Table 12.22: Tall and heavy customers

Name	Height	Weight	Age	μ(Heavy)	μ(Tall)
Sanders	6′2″	215	52	.9	.91
Freeman	5′10″	202	34	.55	.83
Cassey	6′1″	188	40	.25	.90
Miller	5′11″	157	25	.00	.87
O′ Malley	5′5″	163	48	.00	.62
Jackson	5′3″	170	38	.00	.53

12.15 MEASURING QUERY COMPATIBILITY

We now need some way to combine the membership functions so that the total effect of the query can be expressed and ranked. The final result of evaluating a fuzzy where statement is the aggregation of each predicate's truth value. As we have seen, a typical SQL request specifies a set of columns from tables that meet a set of filtering and connection requirements.

select column1, column2, ..., column from table

where predicate1 AND predicate2 ... AND predicaten

Each predicate (qualifier) in the form defined by Equation 12.12,

$$\text{x is [not]} \quad , \tag{12.12}$$

involves a mapping of a value in the column (x) into one of the fuzzy sets defined for that column. This mapping returns a value in the interval [0,1], which is the degree of membership for that value in the fuzzy set. This degree of membership, as we discussed previously, indicates a degree of compatibility between the data value and the semantics imposed by the fuzzy set. Figure 12.18 shows the underlying truth-functional nature of a query predicate.

When a fuzzy query where statement contains multiple predicates, the aggregation or fusion of the predicates' truth values indicates a measurement of how well the query matched the intent of our query. This is called the CQIX, a major departure from the way conventional SQL queries treat retrieved data. Each record (or row) retrieved from a relational database with a fuzzy SQL query has an associated compatibility index. Records are returned in a descending-order ranking of the compatibility value (most compatible record first). This compatibility index is stored in a new column and can be used just like any of the other table columns. There are three broad methods of combining results to produce a compatibility ranking: minimum of memberships, weighted average of memberships, and weighted product of memberships.

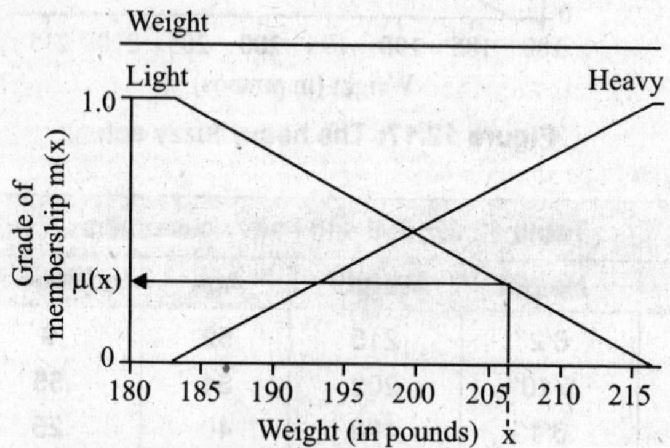

Figure 12.18: The truth-functional nature of a predicate.

12.15.1 Minimum-of-memberships Compatibility

The simplest method of calculating the overall compatibility index for a query X_i takes the minimum of the predicate truth memberships (this assumes, of course, that the predicates are connected with an And operator). Equation 12.13 shows how this QCIX is computed for the complete query.

$$X_{qcix} = \overset{n}{\underset{i=1}{\forall}} \min(\mu_i(p_i)) \tag{12.13}$$

Here,

X_{qcix} is the query compatibility index for query X

n is the number of evaluated predicates in the query

$\mu_i()$ is a function that returns the minimum membership value

p_i is the i-th predicate in the query

The minimum approach functions like the traditional And operator. Each query predicate is treated as an expression that is dependent on the complete set of predicates. Table 12.23 illustrates how the minimum-of-memberships value works.

Table 12.23: Minimum of tall and heavy customers

Name	Height	Weight	Age	μ(Heavy)	μ(Tall)	Minimum μ(Heavy, Tall)
Sanders	6′2″	215	52	.95	.91	.91
Freeman	5′10″	202	34	.55	.83	.55
Cassey	6′1″	188	40	.25	.90	.25
Miller	5′11″	157	25	.00	.87	.00
O′ Malley	5′5″	163	48	.00	.62	.00
Jackson	5′3″	170	38	.00	.53	.00

As you can see, the minimum of the membership values constrains the solution to the weakest element in the data. This means that all where statement and conditions must be true (or have some degree of truth) before the entire SQL statement is true. Thus, minimum compatibility measurements are highly sensitive to a single zero membership predicate (this includes predicate memberships that are zero because the original membership value fell below the query's alpha cut threshold).

12.15.2 Weighted-average-of-memberships Compatibility

A more robust method of viewing the compatibility measurement for query X_i takes the weighted average of the predicate truth values. In this approach, each column is given a bias weight in the interval [1,n], where n is a large number relative to all weights greater than 1. Equation 12.14 shows how the weighted average compatibility index is computed.

$$X_{qcix} = \frac{\sum_{i=1}^{n} (\mu_i(p_i)) x \ w_i}{\sum_{i=1}^{n} w_i} \tag{12.14}$$

Here,

X_{qcix} is the query compatibility index for query X

n is the number of evaluated predicates in the query

$\mu_i()$ is a function that returns the minimum membership value

p_i is the i-th predicate in the query

w_i is the contribution weight associated with the i-th predicate

When the weights for columns are ignored (each column weight is one [1]), Equation 12.14 shows that the QCIX is computed as the ordinary average for the complete query. The average membership approach computes the mean of the entire membership's values. This is reflected in Table 12.24.

Table 12.24: Average of tall and heavy customers

Name	Height	Weight	Age	μ(Heavy)	μ(Tall)	Average μ(Heavy, Tall)
Sanders	6′2″	215	52	.95	.91	.930
Freeman	5′10″	202	34	.55	.83	.960
Cassey	6′1″	188	40	.25	.90	.575
Miller	5′11″	157	25	.00	.87	.435
O′ Malley	5′5″	163	48	.00	.62	.310
Jackson	5′3″	170	38	.00	.53	.265

The averaging method balances the truth membership functions across each of the where statement predicates. Because it is an average, a low and high membership will produce a moderate truth value. However, as the last three rows in Table 12.24 illustrate, the average method often produces a significant truth result even when one of the selection criteria has a zero truth membership.

12.15.3 Weighted-product-of-membership Compatibility

A method that naturally biases the overall compatibility for query X_i toward the weakest truth memberships, but does not automatically settle on the single predicate with the minimum truth, takes the weighted product of the predicate truth values. In this approach, like the weighted average, each column is given a bias weight in the interval [1,n], where n is a large number relative to all weights greater than 1. Equation 12.15 shows how the weighted average compatibility index is computed.

$$X_{qcix} = \prod_{i=1}^{n} \min(\mu_i(p_i)) \times w_i \tag{12.15}$$

Here,

X_{qcix} is the query compatibility index for query X

n is the number of evaluated predicates in the query

$\mu_i()$ is a function that returns the minimum membership value

p_i is the i-th predicate in the query

w_i is the contribution weight associated with the i-th predicate

Table 12.25: Product of tall and heavy customers

Name	Height	Weight	Age	μ(Heavy)	μ(Tall)	Product μ(Heavy, Tall)
Sanders	6′2″	215	52	**.95**	**.91**	**.86**
Freeman	5′10″	202	34	**.55**	**.83**	**.46**
Cassey	6′1″	188	40	**.25**	**.90**	**.23**
Miller	5′11″	157	25	**.00**	**.87**	**.00**
O′ Malley	5′5″	163	48	**.00**	**.62**	**.00**
Jackson	5′3″	170	38	**.00**	**.53**	**.00**

When the weights for columns are ignored (each column weight is one [1]), Equation 12.14 shows that the QCIX is computed as the ordinary product for the complete query. The product membership approach computes the chained product of the entire membership values. This is reflected in Table 12.25.

The product, like the minimum method is sensitive to a predicate with zero truth membership. However, unlike the minimum method, which is totally biased toward the query predicate with the smallest degree of truth, the product method tends to move more slowly in the direction of the overall minimum (the interpretation of the membership products, of course, is a percentage of each other; thus, **prod**(.25,.90) is either 25% of 90 or 90% of 25).

12.16 COMPLEX QUERY COMPATIBILITY METRICS

Understanding the dynamics of a fuzzy query is fairly easy once you see how the query manipulates the set of incoming truth memberships. Let's complete our example by extending the fuzzy query to include Age. In this case, the marketing group is looking for Tall, Heavy, and Middleaged customers. Once more, the conventional SQL statement requires us to define what we mean by Middle-aged. Suppose we say that people between 35 and 45 are Middle-aged. The SQL query is then as follows.

```
select name
from ieh.customer
where customer.height >= 6
and customer.weight >= 195
and (customer.age >=35 and customer.age =< 45);
```

Table 12.26: Tall, heavy, and middle-aged customer (crisp)

Name	Height	Weight	Age	Tall, Heavy and Middle-aged
Jackson	5′3″	170	38	
Sanders	**6′2″**	**215**	**52**	←
Miller	5′11″	157	25	
Cassey	6′1″	188	40	
O′ Malley	5′5″	163	48	
Freeman	5′10″	202	34	

However, as Table 12.26 indicates, this criterion does not change the records retrieved from the database (because we only had one from the previous criterion). Thus, only Sanders is Tall, Heavy, and Middle-aged. Once more, examining the table we can see that there are customers who might be candidates if we can relax the crisp boundaries on our query. We can do better by replacing the query with its corresponding fuzzy version, as follows.

```
select name
from ieh.customer
where customer.height is Tall
and customer.weight is Heavy
and customer.age is MiddleAged;
```

The intent of this query is also obvious: we want customers that are Tall, Heavy, and Middle-aged. To resolve the query we need to tell the application what constitutes a Middle-aged person. Unlike the Tall and Heavy fuzzy sets, Middle-aged represents a fuzzy number. Fuzzy numbers are bell- or triangular-shaped fuzzy sets. The Middle-aged fuzzy set is centered around 40, the essential point of middle age. Figure 12.19 shows one possible way to represent this concept.

Now when we have a value from the customer's age column we can find its membership in the Middle-aged fuzzy set. Table 12.27 shows the membership values for each of the weights in the table (ranked by their membership values). With this extension to our fuzzy query, we have found that all of our customers have some small degree of membership in the Middle-aged fuzzy set, although two of these (Sanders and Miller) have very small degrees of membership. We note that in this final slice through the table (see Table 12.28) Sanders has moved from its top position toward the bottom of the list (for selected records with minimum method compatibility indexes greater than zero).

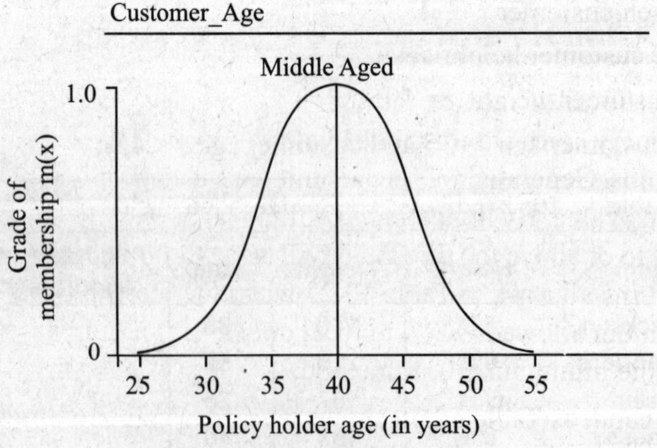

Figure 12.19: Middle-aged fuzzy set.

Table 12.27: Tall, heavy and middle-aged customers

Name	Height	Weight	Age	μ(MA)	μ(Heavy)	μ(Tall)
Cassey	6′1″	188	40	**1.0**	**.25**	**.90**
Jackson	5′3″	170	38	**.97**	**.00**	**.53**
Freeman	5′10″	202	34	**.90**	**.55**	**.83**
O′ Malley	5′5″	163	48	**.70**	**.00**	**.62**
Sanders	6′2″	215	52	**.12**	**.95**	**.91**
Miller	5′11″	157	25	**.10**	**.00**	**.87**

Table 12.28: Tall, heavy and middle-aged customers

Name	Height	Weight	Age	μ(MA)	μ(Heavy)	μ(Tall)	Min	Avg
Freeman	5′10″	202	34	**.90**	**.55**	**.83**	**.55**	**.760**
Cassey	6′1″	188	40	**1.0**	**.25**	**.90**	**.25**	**.716**
Sanders	6′2″	215	52	**.12**	**.95**	**.91**	**.12**	**.660**
Jackson	5′3″	170	38	**.97**	**.00**	**.53**	**.00**	**.500**
O′ Malley	5′5″	163	48	**.70**	**.00**	**.62**	**.00**	**.440**
Miller	5′11″	157	25	**.10**	**.00**	**.87**	**.00**	**.323**

Thus, using a fuzzy query approach instead of a conventional SQL query we have found three customer candidates instead of one. Indeed, the fuzzy query selected customers that matched the intent of our query rather than the strict algebraic rules of the query. As we can see, as the number of column attributes increases the brittleness of conventional SQL queries also rapidly increases. The fuzzy query approach strikes a balance in the process by including records that to some degree meet the intent of our query. Selecting the minimum or average result analysis then allows us to choose records that have some truth in each of the selection criteria (minimum) or some overall truth in the complete query (average).

12.17 COMPATIBILITY THRESHOLD MANAGEMENT

In practice, the retrieval of records through a fuzzy query can produce extensive lists ranked by ever-decreasing query compatibility index values. An analyst needs some mechanism for selecting just the first n records. Generally, we set the limit for n records by specifying the minimum acceptable compatibility index value. By indicating a QCIX threshold, only those records with a compatibility index value equal to or above the threshold will be actually returned by the query. For example, the query process returns all rows in Table 12.23 when the threshold is zero [0]. On the other hand, if we raise the minimum allowed QCIX to [0.2] only a subset of rows is returned. Table 12.29 shows the records from the minimum QCIX method.

On the other hand, as Table 12.30 shows, the same compatibility threshold returns all records when the average method is used.

The query threshold is a form of alpha cut threshold applied to the aggregate truth membership.

A QCIX value below the threshold is treated as though its value were zero. By adjusting the QCIX threshold, an analyst can enforce either a weak or strong degree of compatibility between the selected data rows and the underlying query concept. If the QCIX threshold is low, compatibility is weakly enforced, whereas a high QCIX threshold enforces a strong degree of compatibility.

Table 12.29: Minimum qcix method qcix method threshold screening with qcix threshold 0.2

Name	Height	Weight	Age	μ(MA)	m(Heavy)	m(Tall)	Min
Freeman	5¢10¢¢	202	34	.90	.55	.83	.55
Cassey	6′1″	188	40	1.0	.25	.90	.25

Table 12.30: Average qcix method threshold screening with qcix

Name	Height	Weight	Age	μ(MA)	μ(Heavy)	μ(Tall)	Avg
Freeman	5′10″	202	34	.90	.55	.83	.760
Cassey	6′1″	188	40	1.0	.25	.90	.716
Sanders	6′2″	215	52	.12	.95	.91	.660
Jackson	5′3″	170	38	.97	.00	.53	.500
O′ Malley	5′5″	163	48	.70	.00	.62	440
Miller	5′11″	157	25	.10	.00	.87	.323

12.18 FUZZY SQL PROCESS FLOW

Having examined the way where predicates control which records participate in the query, this section summarizes the flow of control and action in the fuzzy SQL environment. From this we lead into an example of a query from the Fuzzy Data Explorer. The basic fuzzy query paradigm is amazingly simple, thus providing a powerful data exploration tool available to both information technology (IT) users and knowledge engineers. Figure 12.20 shows a flow schematic for the query process. The fuzzy SQL process is essentially a protracted do ... while loop. Each record is read from the data date (or spreadsheet or flat file). The values for the variable specified in the where statement are extracted (x_1, x_2, x_3, ... x_n) and their memberships in the associated fuzzy sets determined.

As shown in Equation 12.16, this generates a vector, V^m, of memberships.

$$V^m = (\mu_1(x_1), \mu_2(x_2), \ldots \mu_n(x_n)) \qquad (12.6)$$

The QCIX processor also creates a default weight vector, as shown in Equation 12.17, containing the bias weights for each field.

$$V^w = (w_1(x_1), w_2(x_2), \ldots w_n(x_n)) \qquad (12.17)$$

Thus, as Equation 12.18 illustrates, the effective compatibility index is found by multiplying the actual membership vector by the weight vector.

$$V^c = V^m \times V^w \qquad (12.18)$$

Naturally, if column or field weights have not been specified the vector defaults to a series of ones [1] so that the result is simply the base membership values.

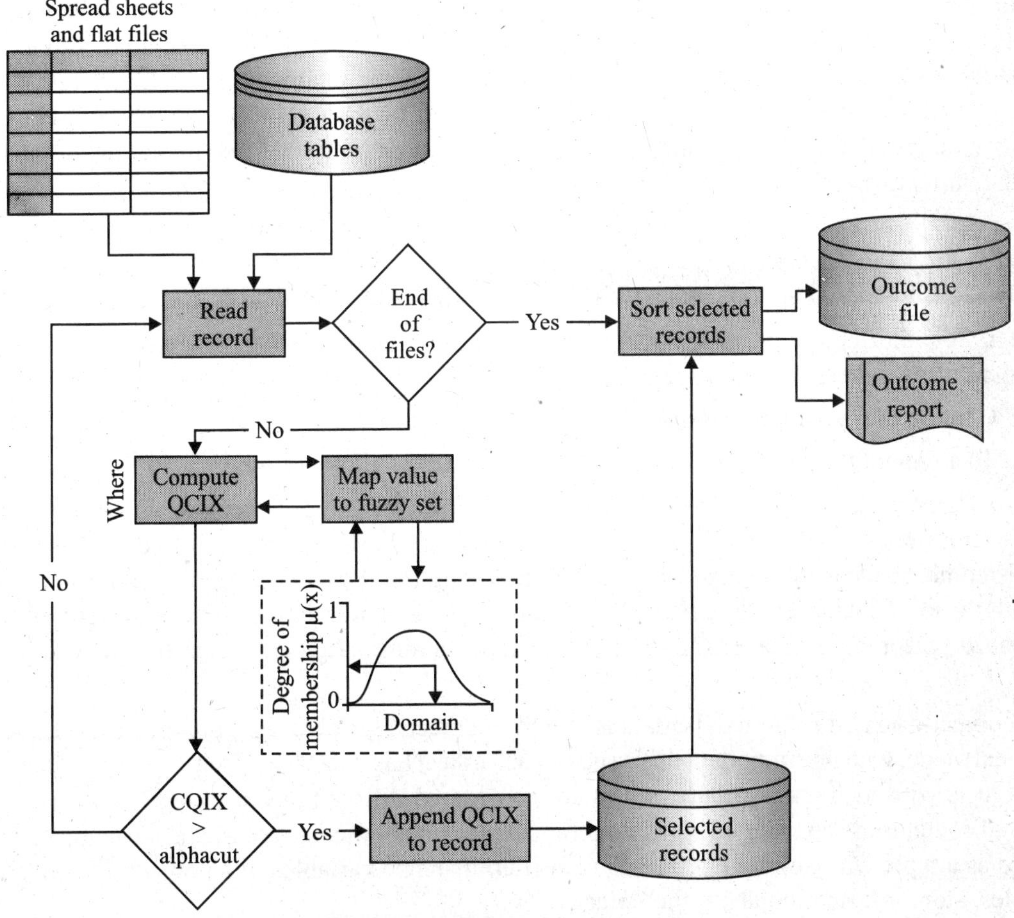

Figure 12.20: The fuzzy SQL flow schematic.

These vectors constitute the basic building blocks for the weighted average compatibility index. Equation 12.19 shows Equation 12.14 cast in terms of these vectors.

$$QCIX = \frac{\sum_{i=1}^{N} V_i^C}{\sum_{i=1}^{N} V_i^W} \tag{12.19}$$

Here,

QCIX is the query compatibility index for query

N is the number of evaluated predicate vectors

V^c is the effective compatibility index (see Equation 12.18)

V^w is vector of weights

Once the QCIX is computed, it is compared against the minimum QCIX threshold. Only records with a QCIX equal to or greater than this minimum value are selected. The selected record's QCIX is added as a new column, and the record is written to the query-retained records file. When the end of the file is encountered, the retained records are sorted by their QCIX (for rows with the same QCIX value, the sort uses the primary identifier or the first column specified in the select statement as a discriminator).

12.19 FUZZY OBJECT-ORIENTED DATABASE

In the 1980s, the rapid advancement in AI technology affected the database community in two important ways – there was a growing interest to

1. Capture the "meaning" of data
2. To augment the functionality of a DBMS with automatic reasoning capabilities

The former interest led to the development of object-oriented databases, whereas the latter interest contributed to the development of deductive database. Obviously, object-oriented data models combine ideas in Object-Oriented Programming (OOP) and knowledge representation in AI with those in database; while deductive databases incorporate into database the techniques of rule-based reasoning and/or PROLOG (an AI programming language based on horn clauses in logic).

In object-oriented data models, data is stored in objects. An object is analogous to a tuple in a relational model with one important difference – each object has its own implicitly identity. Therefore, two objects with identical attribute values are considered different, even though two tuples with identical contents are considered equivalent (and hence one of them is redundant). An object can be viewed as a tuple with an implicit unique identifier. Instance variables in an object, like attributes of tuples, store information about the object.

Objects belong to one or more classes. A class plays a role similar to that of a relation in a relation model – both of them group sets of lower-level information units (i.e. tuples or objects) into more abstract units. The main difference between relations and classes is that classes themselves can be further grouped into more abstract classes or specialized into more specific classes, but relations can't. The generalizations (i.e. more specific classes) are called subclasses. Hence, classes and their links to superclass/subclass form a hierarchical structure. This hierarchical structure enables an object-oriented data model to offer an important reasoning capability – to inherit the attribute values of an object from its classes. This capability, which originates in frame-based representation in AI, is called inheritance.

In addition to inheriting data, object-oriented data models also inherit procedures for manipulating data. This is achieved by using an important idea in object-oriented programming – separating the desired functionality of a procedure from its various specific implementations (depending on the classes of its argument). A desired functionality is referred to as a message, whereas the implementation of the message for objects in a class is specified as a method of the class.

Unlike relational data models, object-oriented data models do not have standard operations for retrieving information. They need to be coded in methods. Typical methods include those for retrieving and updating the value of an object's instance variables, for changing the class of an object, for finding all objects in a given class, and for selecting objects in a class that satisfy a given condition.

Imprecise information in an object-oriented database can be classified into three categories:

1. Imprecision of the data encapsulated in the object
2. Partial class membership
3. Fuzzy superclass/subclass relationship.

The first category, where the data encapsulated within an object is imprecise, is quite similar to the approaches discussed in the relational database section. Approaches like similarity measures or possibility distributions can be taken to capture this kind of imprecision.

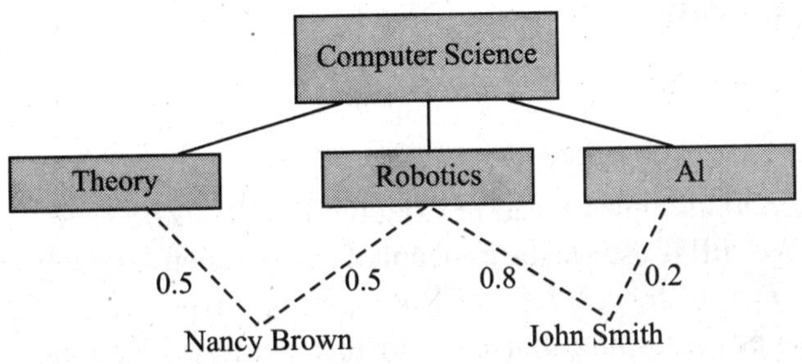

Figure 12.21: Partial class membership.

In previous sections, we have mentioned the need to represent partial membership in relational databases. For object-oriented databases, this need corresponds to representing partial membership of an object in a class. Suppose we want to use object-oriented databases to store the areas of faculty in a computer science department. Suppose Professor John Smith conducts research in robotics and AI areas, with more emphasis on robotics, and Professor Nancy Brown conducts research in theory and robotics with an equal emphasis. Suppose that this database is used by the department head to calculate the total number of faculty members in each area. Professors Smith and Brown with to be counted as a partial member in each of the two areas in which they are involved. A possible representation of this imprecise information is shown in Figure 12.21. Classes are depicted as rectangles in the figure, solid lines indicate superclass/subclass relationships, and dotted lines indicate class membership of objects.

Introducing partial membership, however, does affect the inheritance scheme. A common strategy is to use the membership degree of an object in a class as the priority of the class in searching for a source (i.e. a parent class) for inheriting the object's data and methods. In the example above, the object John Smith inherits information and methods first from the Robotics Class (e.g. having a physical robot lab). The object inherits information and methods from the AI class only if they cannot be found in the Robotics class. Obviously, the object inherits from Computer Science class if neither AI nor Robotics has the data or method needed by the object.

The third type is imprecise information – fuzzy superclass/subclass relationship is possible only for object-oriented databases. Once we allow a class to have partial members, a class becomes a fuzzy set of objects. A class C_1 is a superclass of another class C_2, also called C_1 subsume C_2 (denoted $C_1 > C_2$), if and only if all objects in C_2 are also in C_1. This can be formally written as

$$C_1 > C_2 \leftrightarrow \forall\ x\, C_2(x) \rightarrow C_2\,(x) \qquad (12.20)$$

Alternatively, we can define class subsumption in terms of the relationship of their extensions (i.e. the entire set of other objects):

$$C_1 > C_2 \leftrightarrow \varepsilon(C_1) \supset \varepsilon(C_2) \qquad (12.21)$$

where ε(C) denotes the extension of class C. If C_1 and C_2 becomes fuzzy sets, the formula can be extended using a fuzzy inclusion operator. Conceptually, this means that the degree C_1 is a superclass of C_2 is the degree C_2 is the degree C_1's extension includes C_2's extension.

Let C_1 and C_2 be two fuzzy classes. The degree that C_1 is a superclass of C_2, denoted by subsume (C_1, C_2) is defined as

$$\text{Subsume}\ (C_1, C_2) = \text{Subset}\ (\varepsilon\ (C_2, \varepsilon\ (C_1)) \qquad (12.22)$$

where Subset denotes a fuzzy subsethood measure.

Fuzzy subsethood operators introduced in Chapter 3 can thus be used to formalize superclass/subclass relationships. We will illustrate the concept of fuzzy superclass/subclass using our previous example. Suppose the Dean of the College of Engineering wished to establish a new program in computer engineering. Let us assume that most of the faculty in Robotics are considered in the computer engineering area, while some faculty in AI are in computer engineering, and almost none in Theory (except Professor Nancy Brown) is in computer engineering. We may represent these imprecision using fuzzy superclass/subclass relationships, as shown in Figure 12.22.

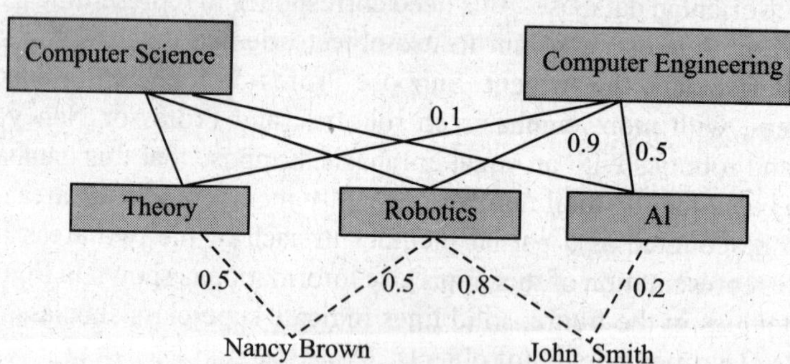

Figure 12.22: Fuzzy inheritance

Once we introduce fuzzy subsumption relationships, we need to be able to calculate the degree an object belongs to any class that can be reached by traversing one or more superclass links. For instance, we should be able to answer questions such as "To what degree does Prof. Nancy Brown belong to computer engineering faculty?" One solution is to multiply the weights of all the links on a path that reaches the "ancestor" class. If there are multiple paths, use the highest membership calculated among all paths. For instance, we can calculate the membership degree that Nancy Brown is a Computer Engineering faculty member as follows:

$$\mu_{\text{Computer Engineering}}(\text{Nancy Brown}) = \max\{0.5 \times 0.9, 0.5 \times 0.1\} = 0.45$$

Alternatively, we can replace the produce with the min operator or other fuzzy conjunction operators. Similarly, max can be replaced by other fuzzy disjunction operators.

The issue of multiple inheritance is very complicated in the original object-oriented methodologies, because it introduces some ambiguities such as which function of which class should it be called if there happens to be some overriding functions. These issues are moreover reinforced by having partial inheritance. Which superclass should we use? Should we take the super class with the highest membership degree?

EXERCISES

1. What do you mean by fuzzy information?
2. Explain the use of fuzzy logic in database systems?
3. What are imprecise information?
4. What do you mean by imprecise queries?
5. Explain the concept of partial membership in a relation?
6. Explain two approaches for representing in precise attribute values?
7. What do you mean by fuzzy relational data model?
8. Explain the following:
   (i) Redundancy in fuzzy logic
   (ii) Functional dependency in fuzzy logic
9. Explain the concept of similarity based fuzzy relation?
10. Explain the concept of possibility based fuzzy relation?
11. Explain the various operations performed in fuzzy relational data model?
12. What do you mean by fuzzy object oriented database?
13. What do you mean by fuzzy inheritance?
14. What do you mean by fuzzy SQL and intelligent queries?
15. What type of vocabulary used in relational database and queries?
16. What do you mean by fuzzy numbers?
17. Explain the basic concept of relational database?
18. Explain the fundamentals of SQL?
19. Why we search databases? Explain in detail.
20. What do you mean by procedure and accuracy?

21. How we can expand the query scope?
22. Explain the fundamental of fuzzy query?
23. How we can combine fuzzy sets?
24. How we can measure query compatibility?
25. Explain the flow of fuzzy SQL process?

CHAPTER 13

Fuzzy Logic and Artificial Intelligence

13.1 INTRODUCTION

Early AI research focused on various techniques for addressing important issues raised by efforts in developing various kinds of intelligent programs. Attempts to develop programs that can understand natural languages uncovered the problem of representing meaning of words, sentences, and contexts. This motivated the development of various knowledge representation and reasoning schemes such as frame-based representation (also known as semantic nets), which are the precursor of object-oriented paradigm.

Efforts to develop intelligent programs for playing chess and other types of games uncovered the combinatorial explosion problem – the number of possible situations that need to be analyzed by these programs increases exponentially as the "think-ahead" steps of the program increase. This led to various search strategies that aim to focus and analysis on more interesting situations. One of these search techniques, $\alpha - \beta$ pruning, has been implemented in special-purpose VLSI chip, which was used to build the famous chess machine – IBM's Deep Blue (a successor of a chess machine called Deep Thought developed at Carnegie Mellon University). In a 1997 "man versus machine chess match" that caught the attention of the entire world, Deep Blue challenged and beat the world chess champion Garry Kasparov in a six-games chess match (won 2, lost 1, tied 3). However the AI community and the public in general, realized that this result does not suggest that computers are more intelligent than human beings. Human intelligence is still far superior to machine intelligence. We just cannot do what God does.

An important idea adopted early by Ai is that an intelligent system for performing a specific task (e.g. diagnosis) in a problem domain (e.g. lung diseases) can often benefit from knowledge about the problem domain. This idea led to the development of a many expert systems, which are systems that are capable of performing a specific task that required human expertise. Real-world examples of these systems include Microsoft's WordWizard, which offers intelligent recommendations regarding desktop publishing to users of Microsoft Word, and Digital Equipment Corporations XCON which configures computer systems based on customer orders. One of the main challenges in developing expert systems is the fact that human experts often rely on judgmental knowledge (e.g. rules of thumb) that they learned from their experience. Even though the experts know that judgmental knowledge is not as certain as first principles, physical laws, or provable theories, they find if useful in drawing plausible conclusions. The principle of expert system technology is to capture human expert knowledge in a way such that of the human experts. A key element in this reasoning process is a scheme for representing uncertainty in the knowledge, for making inferences using uncertain knowledge, and for combining multiple inference results. Such a scheme is often referred to as a scheme for "reasoning under uncertainty" or for "uncertain management". Fuzzy logic offers one of the foundations for developing schemes for reasoning under uncertainty in expert systems.

Approaches for dealing with uncertainty in AI fall into four categories:

1. Bayesian probabilistic approach
2. Approaches based on the Dempster-Shafer (DS) theory
3. Fuzzy logic approach
4. Heuristic approaches

Baysian probabilistic approaches use probability to represent the degree of certainty and develop their probabilistic inference scheme based on Bayes' theorem. The D-S approaches use an interval probability to represent the degree of certainty. Instead of using Bayes' theorem, the DS approaches use the Dempster rule of combination to aggregate information collected from independent sources. The fuzzy logic approaches usually use fuzzy rules to describe knowledge that is uncertain. The degree of certainty is represented by a possibility measure. The most well-known heuristic approach for the management of uncertainty is the Certainty Factor of MYCIN, which is one of the pioneer expert systems.

Our discussion in this chapter will focus on fuzzy logic-based approaches for uncertainty management in AI.

13.2 MEANING OF AI

The phrase AI, which was coined by John McCarthy three decades ago, evades a concise and formal definition to date. One representative definition is pivoted around the comparison of intelligence of computing machines with human beings. Another definition is concerned with the performance of machines which "historically have been judged to lie within the domain of intelligence". None of these definitions or the like has been universally accepted, perhaps because of their references to the word "intelligence", which at present is an abstract and immeasurable quantity.

A better definition of AI, therefore, calls for formalization of the term "intelligence". Psychologist and Cognitive theorists are of the opinion that intelligence helps in identifying the right piece of knowledge at the appropriate instances of decision making.

The phrase "AI" thus can be defined as the simulation of human intelligence on a machine, so as to make the machine efficient to identify and use the right piece of "Knowledge" at a given step of solving a problem. A system capable of planning and executing the right task at the right time is generally called rational. Thus, AI alternatively may be stated as a subject dealing with computational models that can think and act rationally.

A common question then naturally arises: Does rational thinking and acting include all possible characteristics of an intelligent system? If so, how does it represent behavioral intelligence such as machine learning, perception and planning? A little thinking, however, reveals that a system that can reason well must be a successful planner, as planning in many circumstances is part of a reasoning process.

Further, a system can act rationally only after acquiring adequate knowledge from the real world. So, perception that stands for building up of knowledge from real world information is a prerequisite feature for rational actions. One step further thinking envisages that a machine without learning capability cannot possess perception. The rational action of an agent (actor), thus, calls for possession of all the elementary characteristics of intelligence. Relating AI with the computational models capable of thinking and acting rationally, therefore, has a pragmatic significance.

13.3 ARTIFICIAL INTELLIGENCE

Artificial intelligence (AI) is the study of how to make computers do things that; at the moment, people do better. This definition is; of course, somewhat ephemeral because of its reference to the current state of computer science but the fact remains that most attempt to define complex and widely used terms precisely are exercises in futility. To do this, we propose the above by no means universally accepted definition. It as well fails to include some areas of potentially very large impact, namely problems that cannot now be solved well by either computers or people. But it provides a good outline of what constitutes artificial intelligence, and it avoids the philosophical issues that dominate attempts to define the meaning of artificial or intelligence. Interestingly, though, it suggests a similarity with philosophy at the same timc it is avoiding it.

AI has embraced the larger scientific goal of constructing an information-processing theory of intelligence. If such a science of intelligence could be developed, it could guide the design of intelligent machines as well as explicate intelligent behaviour as it occurs in humans and other animals.

13.4 THE DISCIPLINES OF AI

The subject of AI spans a wide horizon. It deals with the various kinds of knowledge representation schemes, different techniques of intelligent search, various methods for resolving uncertainty of data and knowledge, different schemes for automated machine learning and many others. Among the application areas of AI, we have Expert systems, Game-playing, and Theorem-proving, Natural language processing, Image recognition, Robotics and many others. The subject of AI has been enriched with a wide discipline of knowledge from Philosophy, Psychology, Cognitive Science, Computer Science, Mathematics and Engineering. Thus in figure 13.1, they have been referred to as the parent disciplines of AI. An at-a-glance look at figure 13.1 also reveals the subject area of AI and its application areas.

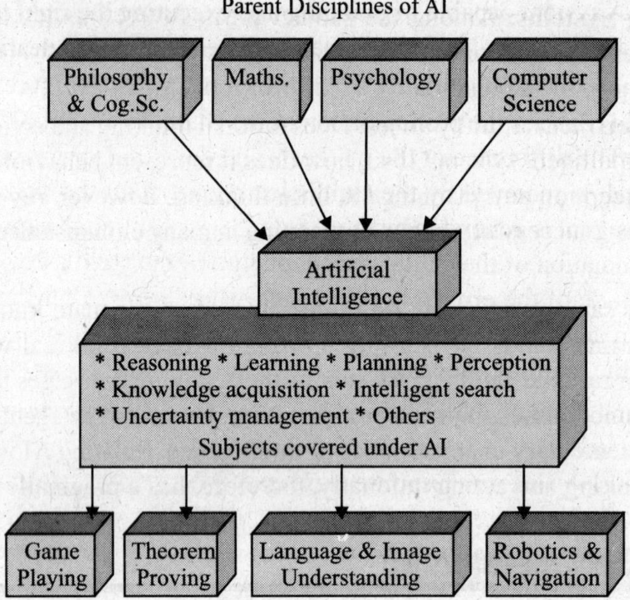

Figure 13.1: AI, its parent disciplines and application areas.

13.4.1 The Subject of AI

The subject of AI was originated with game-playing and theorem-proving programs and was gradually enriched with theories from a number of parent disciplines. As a young discipline of science, the significance of the topics covered under the subject changes considerably with time. At present, the topics which we find significant and worthwhile to understand the subject are outlined below.

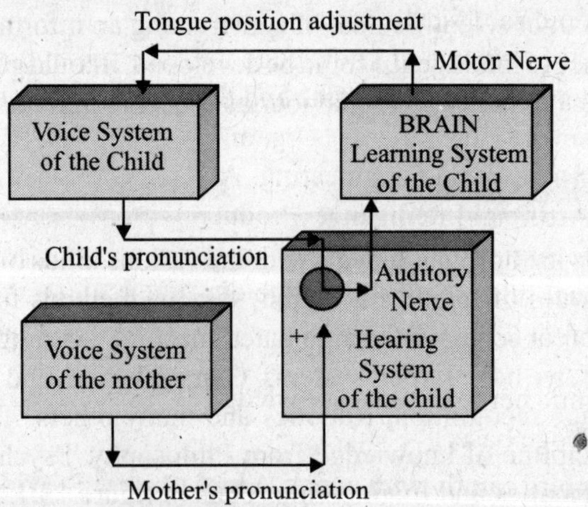

Figure 13.2: Pronunciation learning of a child from his mother.

1. **Learning Systems:** Among the subject areas covered under AI, learning systems needs special mention. The concept of learning is illustrated here with reference to a natural problem of learning of pronunciation by a child from his mother (Figure 13.2). The hearing system of the child receives the pronunciation of the character "A" and the voice system attempts to imitate it. The difference of the mother's and the child's pronunciation, hereafter called the error signal, is received by the child's learning system through the auditory nerve, and an actuation signal is generated by the learning system through a motor nerve for adjustment of the pronunciation of the child. The adaptation of the child's voice system is continued until the amplitude of the error signal is insignificantly low. Each time the voice system passes through an adaptation cycle, the resulting tongue position of the child for speaking "A" is saved by the learning process.

   The learning problem discussed above is an example of the well-known **parametric learning**, where the adaptive learning process adjusts the parameters of the child's voice system autonomously to keep its response close enough to the "sample training pattern". The artificial neural networks, which represent the electrical analogue of the biological nervous systems, are gaining importance for their increasing applications in supervised (parametric) learning problems. Besides this type, the other common learning methods, which we do unknowingly, are inductive and analogy-based learning. In inductive learning, the learner makes generalizations from examples. For instance, noting that "cuckoo flies", "parrot flies" and "sparrow flies", the learner generalizes that "birds fly". On the other hand, in analogy-based learning, the learner, for example, learns the motion of electrons in an atom analogously from his knowledge of planetary motion in solar systems.

2. **Knowledge Representation and Reasoning:** In a reasoning problem, one has to reach a pre-defined goal state from one or more given initial states. So, the lesser the number of transitions for reaching the goal state, the higher the efficiency of the reasoning system. Increasing the efficiency of a reasoning system thus requires minimization of intermediate states, which indirectly calls for an organized and complete knowledge base. A complete and organized storehouse of knowledge needs minimum search to identify the appropriate knowledge at a given problem state and thus yields the right next state on the leading edge of the problem-solving process. Organization of knowledge, therefore, is of paramount importance in knowledge engineering. A variety of knowledge representation techniques are in use in Artificial Intelligence. Production rules, semantic nets, frames, filler and slots, and predicate logic are only a few to mention. The selection of a particular type of representational scheme of knowledge depends both on the nature of applications and the choice of users.

Example 1: A semantic net represents knowledge by a structured approach. For instance, consider the following knowledge base:

Knowledge Base: A bird can fly with wings. A bird has wings. A bird has legs. A bird can walk with legs. The bird and its attributes here have been represented in Figure 13.3 using a graph, where the nodes denote the events and the arcs denote the relationship between the nodes.

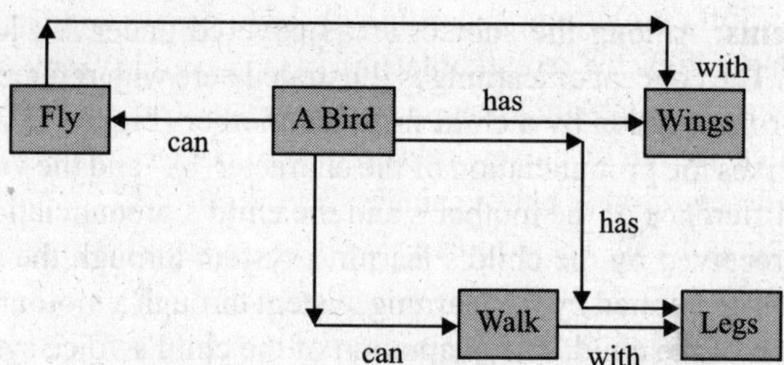

Fig. 13.3: A semantic net representation of "birds".

3. **Planning:** Another significant area of AI is planning. The problems of reasoning and planning share many common issues, but have a basic difference that originates from their definitions. The reasoning problem is mainly concerned with the testing of the satisfiability of a goal from a given set of data and knowledge. The planning problem, on the other hand, deals with the determination of the methodology by which a successful goal can be achieved from the known initial states. Automated planning finds extensive applications in robotics and navigational problems, some of which will be discussed shortly.
4. **Knowledge Acquisition:** Acquisition (Elicitation) of knowledge is equally hard for machines as it is for human beings. It includes generation of new pieces of knowledge from given knowledge base, setting dynamic data structures for existing knowledge, learning knowledge from the environment and refinement of knowledge. Automated acquisition of knowledge by machine learning approach is an active area of current research in Artificial Intelligence.
5. **Intelligent Search:** Search problems, which we generally encounter in Computer Science, are of a deterministic nature, i.e. the order of visiting the elements of the search space is known. For example, in depth first and breadth first search algorithms, one knows the sequence of visiting the nodes in a tree. However, search problems, which we will come across in AI, are **non-deterministic** and the order of visiting the elements in the search space is completely dependent on data sets. The diversity of the intelligent search algorithms will be discussed in detail later.
6. **Logic Programming:** For more than a century, mathematicians and logicians were used to designing various tools to represent logical statements by symbolic operators. One outgrowth of such attempts is **propositional logic,** which deals with a set of binary statements (propositions) connected by Boolean operators. The logic of propositions, which was gradually enriched to handle more complex situations of the real world, is called **predicate logic**. One classical variety of predicate logic-based programs is **Logic Program**. PROLOG, which is an abbreviation for **Pro**gramming in **Log**ic, is a typical language that supports logic programs. Logic Programming has recently been identified as one of the prime area of research in AI. The ultimate aim of this research is to extend the PROLOG compiler to handle spatio-temporal models and support a parallel programming environment. Building architecture for PROLOG machines was a hot topic of the last decade.

7. **Soft Computing:** Soft computing, according to Prof. Zadeh, is "an emerging approach to computing, which parallels the remarkable ability of the human mind to reason and learn in an environment of uncertainty and imprecision". It, in general, is a collection of computing tools and techniques, shared by closely related disciplines that include fuzzy logic, artificial neural nets, genetic algorithms, belief calculus, and some aspects of machine learning like inductive logic programming. These tools are used independently as well as jointly depending on the type of the domain of applications. The scope of the first three tools in the broad spectrum of AI is outlined below.
   - **Fuzzy Logic:** Fuzzy logic deals with fuzzy sets and logical connectives for modeling the human-like reasoning problems of the real world. A fuzzy set, unlike conventional sets, includes all elements of the universal set of the domain but with varying membership values in the interval [0,1]. It may be noted that a conventional set contains its members with a value of membership equal to one and disregards other elements of the universal set, for they have zero membership. The most common operators applied to fuzzy sets are AND (minimum), OR (maximum) and negation (complementation), where AND and OR have binary arguments, while negation has unary argument. The logic of fuzzy sets was proposed by Zadeh, who introduced the concept in systems theory, and later extended it for approximate reasoning in expert systems. Among the pioneering contributors on fuzzy logic, the work of Tanaka in stability analysis of control systems, Mamdani in cement kiln control, Kosko and Pedrycz in fuzzy neural nets, Bezdek in pattern classification, and Zimmerman and Yager in fuzzy tools and techniques needs special mention.
   - **Artificial Neural Nets:** Artificial neural nets (ANN) are electrical analogues of the biological neural nets. Biological nerve cells, called neurons, receive signals from neighboring neurons or receptors through dendrites, process the received electrical pulses at the cell body and transmit signals through a large and thick nerve fiber, called an axon. The electrical model of a typical biological neuron consists of a linear activator, followed by a non-linear inhibiting function. The linear activation function yields the sum of the weighted input excitation, while the non-linear inhibiting function attempts to arrest the signal levels of the sum. The resulting signal, produced by an electrical neuron, is thus bounded (amplitude limited). An artificial neural net is a collection of such electrical neurons connected in different topology. The most common application of an artificial neural net is in machine learning. In a learning problem, the weights and/or non-linearities in an artificial neural net undergo an adaptation cycle. The adaptation cycle is required for updating these parameters of the network, until a state of equilibrium is reached, following which the parameters no longer change further. The ANN support both supervised and unsupervised types of machine learning. The supervised learning algorithms realized with ANN have been successfully applied in control, automation, robotics and computer vision. The unsupervised learning algorithms built with ANN, on the other hand, have been applied in scheduling, knowledge acquisition, planning and analog to digital conversion of data.

- **Genetic Algorithms:** A genetic algorithm (GA) is a stochastic algorithm that mimics the natural process of biological evolution. It follows the principle of **Darwinism**, which rests on the fundamental belief of the "**survival of the fittest**" in the process of natural selection of species. GAs find extensive applications in intelligent search, machine learning and optimization problems. The problem states in a GA are denoted by chromosomes, which are usually represented by binary strings. The most common operators used in GA are crossover and mutation. The evolutionary cycle in a GA consists of the following three sequential steps.
  (a) Generation of population (problem states represented by chromosomes).
  (b) Genetic evolution through crossover followed by mutation.
  (c) Selection of better candidate states from the generated population.

  In step (a) of the above cycle, a few initial problem states are first identified. The step (b) evolves new chromosomes through the process of crossover and mutation. In step (c) a fixed number of better candidate states are selected from the generated population. The above steps are repeated a finite number of times for obtaining a solution for the given problem.

8. **Management of Imprecision and Uncertainty:** Data and knowledge- bases in many typical AI problems, such as reasoning and planning, are often contaminated with various forms of incompleteness. The incompleteness of data, hereafter called **imprecision**, generally appears in the database for
   (i) lack of appropriate data
   (ii) poor authenticity level of the sources.

   The incompleteness of knowledge, often referred to as **uncertainty**, originates in the knowledge base due to lack of certainty of the pieces of knowledge.

   Reasoning in the presence of imprecision of data and uncertainty of knowledge is a complex problem. Various tools and techniques have been devised for reasoning under incomplete data and knowledge.

Some of these techniques employ:

(i) Stochastic
(ii) Fuzzy
(iii) Belief network models

In a stochastic reasoning model, the system can have transition from one given state to a number of states, such that the sum of the probability of transition to the next states from the given state is strictly unity.

In a fuzzy reasoning system, on the other hand, the sum of the membership value of transition from the given state to the next state may be greater than or equal to one.

The belief network model updates the stochastic / fuzzy belief assigned to the facts embedded in the network until a condition of equilibrium is reached; following which there would be no more change in beliefs. Recently, fuzzy tools and techniques have been applied in a specialized belief network, called a **fuzzy Petri net,** for handling both imprecision of data and uncertainty of knowledge by a unified approach.

13.5 FUZZY LOGIC IN FRAME-BASED REPRESENTATION

A frame-based knowledge representation scheme uses a frame, sometimes referred to as a concept or a class to represent a collection of objects. The typical properties of a class are described using slots, which are also referred to as attributes. Typically, a slot has a name and a value. Even though frame-based representation has become one of the most useful knowledge representation techniques in AI, it can not represent and reason about imprecise attribute values. Suppose we wish to represent the concept of healthy family. Most of the properties of such a class are vague: having infrequent clinical visits, having low cholesterol meals, having regular exercise, etc.

Using fuzzy logic, a frame-based system can be extended to represent these vague properties of a class. To do this the slot of a frame can take a linguistic term as its value, and the meaning of the linguistic term is defined by a memberships function. For example, to represent "infrequent clinical visits" as a common property of healthy family we can sue a slot called clinical visits whose value can be in linguistic terms such as frequent, infrequent, very seldom, more or less seldom. The meanings of these linguistic terms are defined by their membership's functions. Therefore, such a fuzzy logic based extension to frame-based systems uses a dual representation to represent imprecise properties of a class: a symbolic representation using linguistic terms, and a quantitative representation using membership functions. In fact, a slot in such a system becomes a linguistic variable. It is obvious that the same kind of extension can also be made to object-oriented systems.

Since linguistic terms can be used to represent imprecise properties of a class, an instance can be partially in a class. Therefore, the class membership relationship between a class and an instance becomes a matter of degree. For example, a particular family may be partially a healthy family and partially a rich family. Partial class membership complicates an important issue in frame-based systems: the handling of multiple conflicting inheritance. In a conventional frame-based system, one way to deal with multiple conflicting inheritance is to establish a priority among superclasses of a class. These priorities determine the order in which the parent classes are searched for inheriting values to the instance. When the class-instance relationship becomes a matter of degree, these membership degrees should also affect the selection of the actual source of inheritance along multiple inheritance paths. Several research ideas for this problem have been proposed.

Generalizing frame-based systems using fuzzy logic also has significant impact on the reasoning about class subsumption and class membership. In early frame-based systems and object-oriented systems, the subsumption relationship between classes (i.e. IS-A links) and the membership relationship became and instance in these classes (i.e. instance of links) are all asserted by the developer of a knowledge base. Due to a problem about the meaning of IS-A links in these early frame-based systems, a family of more principled frame-based systems, called term subsumption systems, were later developed]8]. In a term subsumption system we can describe the defining characteristics of a class. Based on these class definitions, these systems can infer the subsumption relationship between classes. They can also infer the classes to which an instance should belong. Fuzzy logic can be used. Fuzzy logic has been used to generalize the syntax and the semantics of term subsumption languages so that (1) imprecise defining characteristics can be used to define a class (i.e.e.g., a fuzzy class), and (2) subsumption between fuzzy classes can be inferred from the semantics of their definitions.

13.6 EXPERT SYSTEMS

An expert system consists of a **knowledge base**, **database** and an **inference engine** for interpreting the database using the knowledge supplied in the knowledge base. The reasoning process of a typical illustrative expert system is described in next chapters.

The inference engine attempts to match the antecedent clauses (IF parts) of the rules with the data stored in the database. When all the antecedent clauses of a rule are available in the database, the rule is fired, resulting in new inferences. The resulting inferences are added to the database for activating subsequent firing of other rules. In order to keep limited data in the database, a few rules that contain an explicit consequent (THEN) clause to delete specific data from the databases are employed in the knowledge base. On firing of such rules, the unwanted data clauses as suggested by the rule are deleted from the database.

13.7 FUZZY LOGIC IN EXPERT SYSTEMS

The basic architecture of an expert system is shown in Figure 13.4. It consists of four major components:

1. A knowledge base
2. An inference engine
3. An explanation facility
4. A user interface module.

The knowledge base stores relevant knowledge obtained from human experts, which is often represented in the form of rules. The knowledge base also stores factual information about the system's specific problem domain. The inference engine uses rules and this factual information to infer additional information or to construct pieces of the solution. In either case, the execution of rulers modifies objects in the knowledge base. The knowledge base often contains description about goals/subgoals or tasks/subtasks that reflect the human expert's high-level problem solving strategy. The structure of goals and tasks can be used to organize rules into groups based on their functionality. An expert system not only needs to perform a task as competent as a human expert, it also needs to be able to explain the rationale of its conclusions. Hence, an expert system often has an explanation component, which generates explanations by tracing the rules fired by the inference engine.

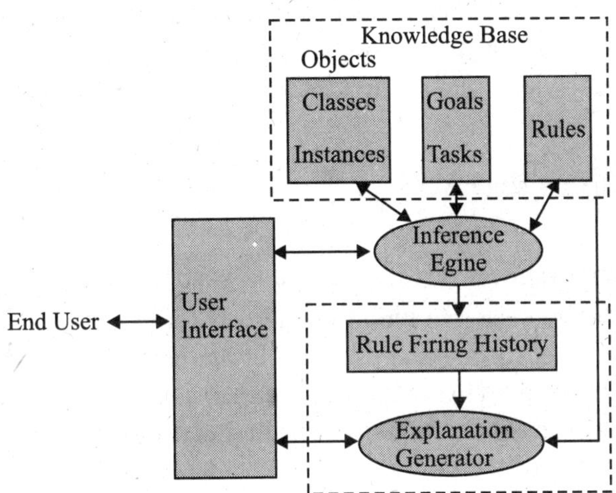

Figure 13.4: The basic architecture of expert systems.

The user interface component of an expert system interacts with the user to collect input data (e.g. symptoms of a patient for a medical diagnosis system), for displaying conclusions/solutions, and for providing explanations upon a user's request.

Expert systems often rely on human expert's judgmental knowledge (i.e. heuristics) to make decisions. This judgmental knowledge is usually uncertain. Hence, an expert system needs to be able to reason about how much certainty is associated with a particular conclusion drawn by a piece of heuristic knowledge within a particular context. Various fuzzy logic-based approaches have been developed for achieving this kind of reasoning under uncertainty. They differ in the types of uncertain knowledge they emphasize.

There are at least four kinds of uncertainty in expert systems. First, the situation for applying a piece of knowledge may not have a well-defined sharp boundary. For instance the symptom that "blood pressure is high" which is often used in medical diagnosis does not have a clear sharp boundary. Second, the knowledge that associates observations to hypotheses can be uncertain. Third, the nature of the conclusion can be imprecise. Typically, this occurs when the conclusion is about something that can be quantified (e.g. severity of a disease, a predicated stock market index etc.) Fourth, the data to which the knowledge is applied may be uncertain.

Even though many techniques have been developed for dealing with various types of uncertainties, fuzzy logic is uniquely suitable for handling the first and the third kind of uncertainty, because both of them are imprecise by nature. Most fuzzy logic-based expert systems use fuzzy if-then rules, discussed in Chapter 5, to associate vague conditions with a conclusion, which can be precise or imprecise. These rules are typically in the following form:

- IF (A_1 (o_1) is v_1) AND (A_2 (o_2) is v_2)... (A_k(o_k) is v_k) THEN it is likely (t) that A_{k+1} (o_{k+1}) is v_{k+1}

  where A_i, o_i and v_i denote attributes, objects, and values, respectively, while t denotes the truth value of the implication rule. The value v_i can be a fuzzy set. The truth value t can be a number [0, 1] or a fuzzy subset of [0, 1]. For example, a medical diagnostic system for checking liver function has the following rule [584]:

- IF GOT is Medium AND
  GPT is Medium AND
  Previous GOT is Very High AND
  GOT > GPT
  THEN it is somewhat likely that liver function is abnormal

GOT and GPT in the rule are two blood test results for checking liver function profiles. All attributes in this system refer to one identical object-the patient being diagnosed; therefore, the object is not explicitly represented in the rule. Terms such as Medium and Very High in the rule are fuzzy sets to describe imprecise conditions. The truth qualifier somewhat likely is a fuzzy set that characterizes the uncertainty of the rule.

The foundation of fuzzy rules in expert systems is fuzzy implication rules introduced in Chapter 9. Hence, the inference of these rules is based on approximation reasoning using fuzzy implication functions as described in Section 9.3.

In addition to fuzzy rules, fuzzy logic has also been used to develop other reasoning schemes for diagnostic expert systems. An important system in this category is a medical expert system called CADIAG developed by K.P. Adlassnig. CADIAG (Computer Assisted AIDGnosis) uses two measures to describe the relationships between symptoms and diseases: the frequency of occurrence and the strength of confirmation. These measures are derived from a large patient database. For instance, CADIAG's knowledge base for diagnosing rheumatic diseases was constructed from about 3500 patient records in a rheumatological hospital. The knowledge base includes 189 rheumatologicla diseases, 905 symptoms, findings, test results, and about 20,000 symptom-disease relationships (i.e. fuzzy rules).

CADIAG's inference scheme is based on composition of fuzzy relations. Let R_{SC} and R_{fc} denote fuzzy relations recording strength of confirmation and frequency of occurrences between a set of symptoms and a set of diseases. These relations are used to confirm, excuse, and rank diagnoses. For instance, a patient's confirmation degrees of diseases are computed from the composition of fuzzy relations as follows:

$$R_{CD} = R_s o R_{SC} \tag{13.1}$$

where R_S and R_{CD} denote one-dimensional fuzzy relations of the patient's symptoms and confirmed diagnoses respectively. The rational of the composition is that if the patient has a symptom s_i to a degree, and the symptom has a strength of confirmation β for disease d_j, then the patient is likely to have disease d_j to the degree min $\{\alpha, \beta\}$. Similarly if a symptom s_j always appear for a disease d_j but we do not obsereve the symptom in a patient, we can conclude that the patient does not have the disease d_j. This leads to the following composition for computing the degree that a disease should be exluded (i.e. rejected):

$$R_{ED} = (1 - R_S) \text{ o } R_{DC} \tag{13.2}$$

where R_{ED} denotes a one-dimensional fuzzy relation of excluded diagnoses for a given patient. CADIAG's inference scheme described above can also be justified using fuzzy implications and generalized modus ponens. We will leave this as an exercise.

CADIAG's inference scheme and generalized moduls tollen for ranking diagnoses is a weighted sum of R_{CD} and R_{ED}. Even though it involves an ad hoc assignment of weights, it is an effective heuristic approach for employing a large amount of complex diagnostic knowledge into an expert system.

An example of CADIAG's rule is given below:

IF the patient shows low back pain,

a limitation of motion of the lumbar spine,

a diminished chest expansion, and

the patient is male, and

is between 20 and 40 years old

THEN the diagnosis may be ankylosing spondylitis WITH the frequency of occurrence being very often (0.9) and the strength of confirmation being strong (0.8).

CADIAG has been extensively tested using more than 300 real patient cases. For instance, CADIAG-2/ RHEUMA, a second generation of CADIAG systems for diagnosing rheumatic diseases, was able to correctly diagnosis 81% of the test cases as either confirmed (68.2%) diseases or diagnostic hypotheses (12.8%).

OMRON uses fuzzy logic in a health management expert system that helps a large corporation by providing a personal health diagnosis and health management plan for its employees. The health management system uses 500 fuzzy if-then rules to capture medical knowledge of human experts regarding health diagnosis, life cycle evaluation, diet, physical fitness, and major diseases. The system provided personal health diagnoses and assists personal health management planning for employees in an organization. The use of fuzzy logic enables the system to process patients' inputs that are described using vague linguistic terms and to implement doctors linguistic and complex decision-making processes. In addition, it enables the expert system to represent medical knowledge in a smaller number of rules than conventional expert system. Fuzzy sets represent abstractions of clinical data (e.g. numerical data are low, normal, or high) as well as degree of severity of diseases. The system is able to support more than 10,000 individuals in an organization.

We have introduced the application of fuzzy logic in medical diagnostic expert systems. Medical diagnosis falls into a category of expert systems known as heuristic classification systems. A heuristic classification system classifies the description of a given problem into one of preenumerated categories using heuristic knowledge obtained from human experts. Other examples of heuristic classification expert systems include system for financial loan approval (i.e. classifying loan application data into classes such as approved, not-approved, insufficient data, etc.) systems for engine troubleshooting (classifying engine symptoms into one or multiple likely faults). Fuzzy rules can be used to develop these expert systems in a way similar to that of medical diagnostic systems.

13.8 INTELLIGENT AGENTS

A unified framework for AI systems called intelligent agents has been evolved in the 90s. Agent is a software system that interacts with an external environment by performing appropriate actions to the environment based on information received from the environment. An intelligent agent is an agent that demonstrates certain intelligent behaviors in its actions. S. Russel and P. Norvig classified agents into four classes:

1. Simple reflex agents
2. Agents that keep track of the world
3. Goal-based agents
4. Utility-based agents

We briefly summarize these four types of agents below.

A simple reflex agent uses condition-action rules to map sensor inputs directly to action. Agents that keep track of the world extend the simple reflex agent with an explicit description of the external environment, which is sometimes referred to as a state description or a world model.

The agent keeps track of changes in the environment by updating the internal state using three kinds of information:

1. Sensor input of the agent,
2. Information about how the world evolves independently of the agent,
3. Information about how the agent's own actions affect the world.

The motivation for this extension to the simple reflex agent is that the agents sensor input often does not provide complete information about the environment due to dynamic changes to the environment. Fuzzy logic and other schemes for reasoning under uncertainty (e.g. probabilistic reasoning) can contribute to this important issue in intelligent agents, as we will see later.

A goal-based agent is an agent that extends the second type of agents with an explicitly representation of its goals. The goals of the first two types of agents are implicitly incorporated in the condition-action rules. Explicitly representing these goals enables an agent to adapt to the environment by dynamically planning its course of action for accomplishing the goals. Even though these agents improve the adaptability of the first two types of agents, they are still limited in dealing with conflicting goals. That is due to the fact that the notion of achieving a goal in AI is typically a black-and-white matter. A goal-based agent that encounters conflicting goals has to either abandon some of its goals or to modify the goals. It cannot, however, explore an effective trade-off among these goals by considering the possibility of partially satisfying them.

In order to do this, we need the fourth type of agent-the utility-based agent. A utility-based agent extends the black-and-white notion of goal accomplishment into a continuum called the utility measure. Such an agent can then evaluate the utility of alternative actions or strategies. In the case that the outcome of an action is uncertain, the agent needs to consider the likelihood of possible outcomes as well as the utility (including cost) of these outcomes. An agent is said to be rational if it always chooses a decision/action that maximizes its overall expected utility. Figure

13.5 shows a basic architecture of a utility-based agent. The rectangles in the figure depict reasoning and information processing components of the agent.

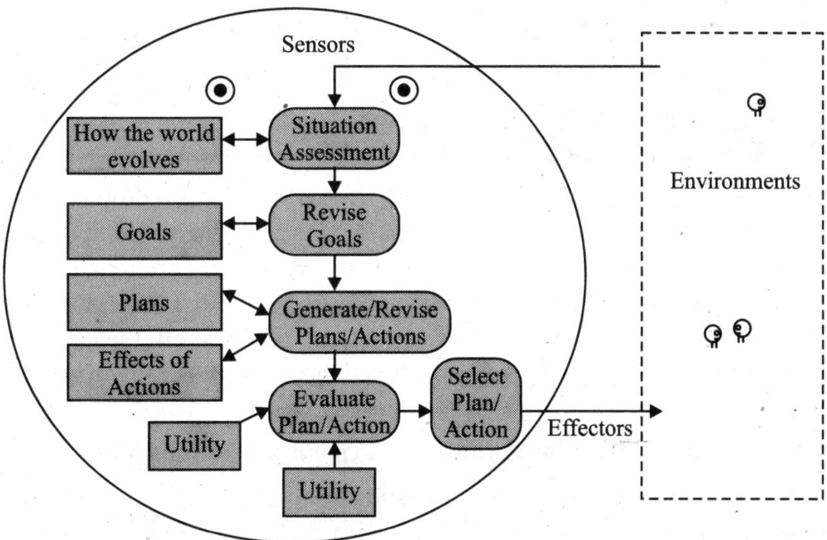

Figure 13.5: The architecture of a utility-based agent.

The environment may also include other agents, as shown in Figure 13.5. A set of agents that communicate with each other and collaborate in some capacity forms a multi-agent system.

Major techniques that support multi-agent systems include

- Standard languages for agents to communicate with each other. KIF is a standard knowledge representation language. KQML describes the syntax of messages and protocols of communication between agents.
- Organizational structure of agents can facilitate collaboration and reduce communication overhead (e.g. federation system with facilitators, broker agents)
- Problem solving architectures have been designed specifically for multiple agents to share information and to a collaborate in accomplishing common goals

13.8.1 Fuzzy Logic in Intelligent Agents

What roles can fuzzy logic play in intelligent agents? While the answer to this question is still evolving, we can identify at least four major areas that fuzzy logic can contribute to intelligent agents:

- Fuzzy rules can be used to implement simple reflex agents, especially if possible actions are in a continuous domain (e.g. turning direction of a mobile robot).
- Fuzzy logic can serve as a bridge between goal-based agents and utility-based agents. Fuzzy logic can be used to describe fuzzy goals that can be partially satisfied. This enables an agent to maximize the overall accomplishment by partially satisfying these goals that are conflicting.

- Fuzzy logic can be used to deal with a uncertainty about the environment especially if the uncertainty is imprecise in nature.
- Fuzzy logic can be used in an agent for situation assessment to combine information from multiple sources, especially if the information is quantitative in nature.
- Fuzzy logic can be used to model emotional intelligence in agents.

13.9 BUILDING A FUZZY EXPERT SYSTEM

To illustrate the design of a fuzzy expert system, we will consider a problem of operating a service centre of spare parts. A service centre keeps spare parts and repairs failed ones. A customer brings a failed item and receives a spare of the same type. Failed parts are repaired, placed on the shelf, and thus become spares. If the required spare is available on the shelf, the customer takes it and leaves the service centre. However, if there is no spare on the shelf, the customer has to wait until the needed item becomes available. The objective here is to advise a manager of the service centre on certain decision policies to keep the customers satisfied.

A typical process in developing the fuzzy expert system incorporates the following steps:

1. Specify the problem and define linguistic variables.
2. Determine fuzzy sets.
3. Elicit and construct fuzzy rules.
4. Encode the fuzzy sets, fuzzy rules and procedures to perform fuzzy inference into the expert system.
5. Evaluate and tune the system.

Step 1: Specify the problem and define linguistic variables

The first, and probably the most important, step in building any expert system is to specify the problem. We need to describe our problem in terms of knowledge engineering. In other words, we need to determine problem input and output variables and their ranges. For our problem, there are four main linguistic variables: average waiting time (mean delay) m, repair utilisation factor of the service centre ρ, number of servers s, and initial number of spare parts n.

The customer's average waiting time, m, is the most important criterion of the service centre's performance. The actual mean delay in service should not exceed the limits acceptable to customers. The repair utilisation factor of the service centre, ρ, is the ratio of the customer arrival rate, λ, to the customer departure rate, μ. Magnitudes of λ and μ indicate the rates of an item's failure (failures per unit time) and repair (repairs per unit time), respectively. Apparently, the repair rate is proportional to the number of servers, s. To increase the productivity of the service centre, its manager will try to keep the repair utilisation factor as high as possible.

The number of servers, s, and the initial number of spares, n, directly affect the customer's average waiting time, and thus has a major impact on the centre's performance. By increasing s and n, we achieve lower values of the mean delay, but, at the same time we increase the costs of employing new servers, building up the number of spares and expanding the inventory capacities of the service centre for additional spares.

Let us determine the initial number of spares n, given the customer's mean delay m, number of servers s, and repair utilisation factor, ρ. Thus, in the decision model considered here, we have three inputs – m, s and ρ, and one output – n. In other words, a manager of the service centre wants to determine the number of spares required to maintain the actual mean delay in customer service within an acceptable range. Now we need to specify the ranges of our linguistic variables. Suppose we obtain the results shown in Table 13.1 where the intervals for m, s and n are normalised to be within the range of [0,1] by dividing base numerical values by the corresponding maximum magnitudes.

Table 13.1: Linguistic variables and their ranges

Linguistic variable: Mean delay, m		
Linguisitic value	**Notation**	**Numerical range (normalised)**
Very short	VS	[0,0.3]
Short	S	[0.1, 0.5]
Medium	M	[0.4, 0.7]
Linguistic variable: Mean delay, s		
Linguisitic value	**Notation**	**Numerical range (normalised)**
Small	S	[0,0.35]
Medium	M	[0.30, 0.70]
Large	L	[0.60, 1]
Linguistic variable Mean delay, m		
Linguisitic value	**Notation**	**Numerical range (normalised)**
Low	L	[0,0.6]
Medium	M	[0.4, 0.8]
High	H	[0.6, 1]
Linguistic variable Mean delay, m		
Linguisitic value	**Notation**	**Numerical range (normalised)**
Very small	VS	[0,0.30]
Small	S	[0, 0.40]
Rather Small	RS	[0.25, 0.45]
Medium	M	[0.30, 0.70]
Rather Large	RL	[0.55, 0.75]
Large	L	[0,60, 1]
Very Large	VL	[0.70, 1]

Note, that for the customer mean delay m, we consider only three linguistic values – Very Short, Short and Medium because other values such as Long and Very Long are simply not practical. A manager of the service centre cannot afford to keep customers waiting longer than a medium time. In practice, all linguistic variables, linguistic values and their ranges are usually chosen by the domain expert.

Step 2: Determine fuzzy sets

Fuzzy sets can have a variety of shapes. However, a triangle or a trapezoid can often provide an adequate representation of the expert knowledge and at the same time significantly simplifies the process of computation. Figures 13.6 to 13.9 show the fuzzy sets for all linguistic variables used in our problem. As you may notice, one of the key points here is to maintain sufficient overlap in adjacent fuzzy sets for the fuzzy system to respond smoothly.

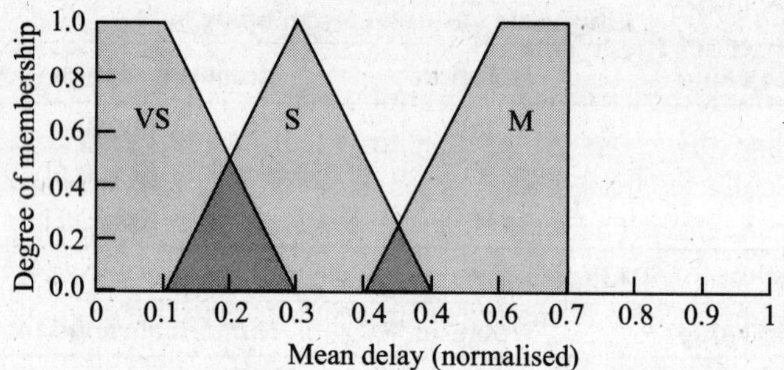

Figure 13.6: Fuzzy sets of mean delay m.

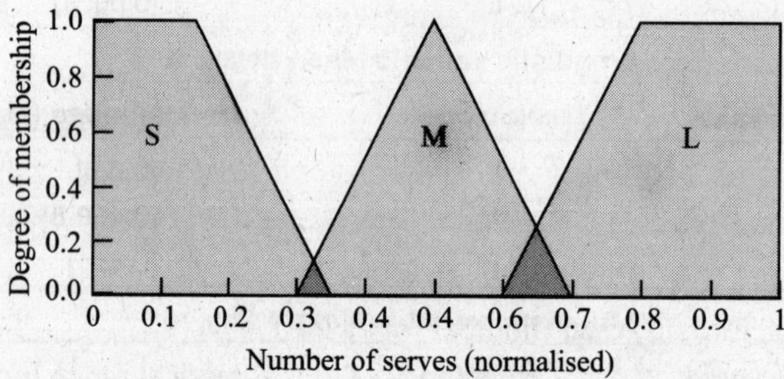

Figure 13.7: Fuzzy sets of number of servers s.

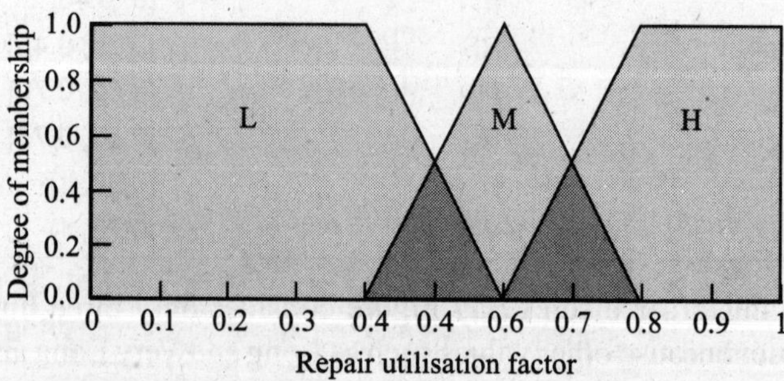

Figure 13.8: Fuzzy sets of repair utilisation factor ρ.

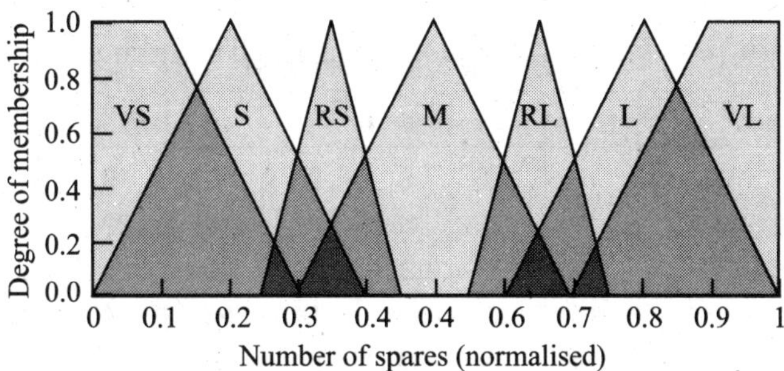

Figure 13.9: Fuzzy sets of number of spares n.

Step 3: Elicit and construct fuzzy rules

Next we need to obtain fuzzy rules. To accomplish this task, we might ask the expert to describe how the problem can be solved using the fuzzy linguistic variables defined previously. Required knowledge also can be collected from other sources such as books, computer databases, flow diagrams and observed human behaviour. There are three input and one output variables in our example. It is often convenient to represent fuzzy rules in a matrix form. A two-by-one system (two inputs and one output) is depicted as an M × N matrix of input variables. The linguistic values of one input variable form the horizontal axis and the linguistic values of the other input variable form the vertical axis. At the intersection of a row and a column lies the linguistic value of the output variable. For a three-by-one system (three inputs and one output), the representation takes the shape of an M × N × K cube. This form of representation is called a fuzzy associative memory (FAM).

Let us first make use of a very basic relation between the repair utilisation factor ρ, and the number of spares n, assuming that other input variables are fixed. This relation can be expressed in the following form: if ρ increases, then n will not decrease.

Thus we could write the following three rules:

1. If (utilisation_factor is L) then (number_of_spares is S)
2. If (utilisation_factor is M) then (number_of_spares is M)
3. If (utilisation_factor is H) then (number_of_spares is L)

Now we can develop the 33 FAM that will represent the rest of the rules in a matrix form. The results of this effort are shown in Figure 13.10.

Meanwhile, a detailed analysis of the service centre operation, together with an 'expert touch', may enable us to derive 27 rules that represent complex relationships between all variables used in the expert system. Table 13.2 contains these rules and Figure 13.11 shows the cube (333) FAM representation.

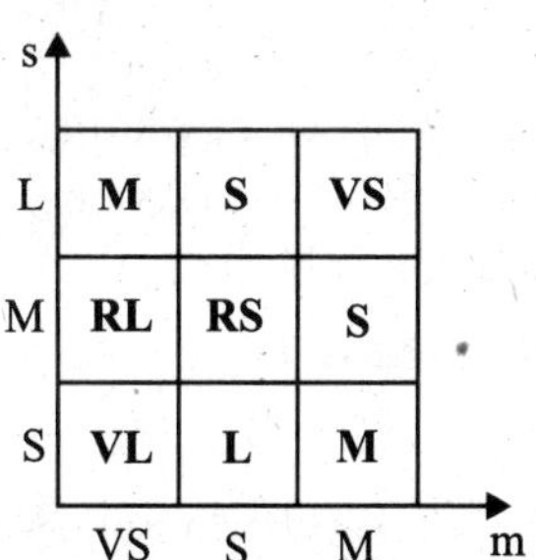

Figure 13.10: The square FAM representation.

Table 13.2: The rule table

Rule	m	s	ρ	n	Rule	m	s	ρ	n	Rule	m	s	ρ	n
1	VS	S	L	VS	10	VS	S	M	S	19	VS	S	H	VL
2	S	S	L	VS	11	S	S	M	VS	20	S	S	H	L
3	M	S	L	VS	12	M	S	M	VS	21	M	S	H	M
4	VS	M	L	VS	13	VS	M	M	RS	22	VS	M	H	M
5	S	M	L	VS	14	S	M	M	S	23	S	M	H	M
6	M	M	L	VS	15	M	M	M	VS	24	M	M	H	S
7	VS	L	L	S	16	VS	L	M	M	25	VS	L	H	RL
8	S	L	L	S	17	S	L	M	RS	26	S	L	H	M
9	M	L	L	VS	18	M	L	M	S	27	M	L	H	RS

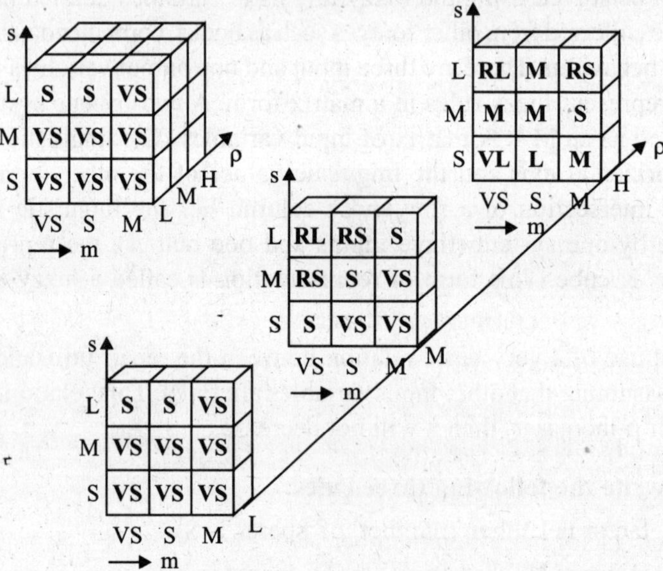

Figure 13.11: Cube FAM and sliced cube FAM representations.

First we developed 12 (3 + 3 × 3) rules, but then we obtained 27 (3 × 3 × 3) rules. If we implement both schemes, we can compare results; only the system's performance can tell us which scheme is better.

Rule Base 1

1. If (utilisation_factor is L) then (number_of_spares is S)
2. If (utilisation_factor is M) then (number_of_spares is M)
3. If (utilisation_factor is H) then (number_of_spares is L)
4. If (mean_delay is VS) and (number_of_servers is S)
   then (number_of_spares is VL)

5. If (mean_delay is S) and (number_of_servers is S) then (number_of_spares is L)
6. If (mean_delay is M) and (number_of_servers is S) then (number_of_spares is M)
7. If (mean_delay is VS) and (number_of_servers is M) then (number_of_spares is RL)
8. If (mean_delay is S) and (number_of_servers is M) then (number_of_spares is RS)
9. If (mean_delay is M) and (number_of_servers is M) then (number_of_spares is S)
10. If (mean_delay is VS) and (number_of_servers is L) then (number_of_spares is M)
11. If (mean_delay is S) and (number_of_servers is L) then (number_of_spares is S)
12. If (mean_delay is M) and (number_of_servers is L) then (number_of_spares is VS)

Rule Base 2

1. If (mean_delay is VS) and (number_of_servers is S) and (utilisation_factor is L) then (number_of_spares is VS)
2. If (mean_delay is S) and (number_of_servers is S) and (utilisation_factor is L) then (number_of_spares is VS)
3. If (mean_delay is M) and (number_of_servers is S) and (utilisation_factor is L) then (number_of_spares is VS)
4. If (mean_delay is VS) and (number_of_servers is M) and (utilisation_factor is L) then (number_of_spares is VS)
5. If (mean_delay is S) and (number_of_servers is M) and (utilisation_factor is L) then (number_of_spares is VS)
6. If (mean_delay is M) and (number_of_servers is M) and (utilisation_factor is L) then (number_of_spares is VS)
7. If (mean_delay is VS) and (number_of_servers is L) and (utilisation_factor is L) then (number_of_spares is S)
8. If (mean_delay is S) and (number_of_servers is L) and (utilisation_factor is L) then (number_of_spares is S)

9. If (mean_delay is M) and (number_of_servers is L) and (utilisation_factor is L) then (number_of_spares is VS)
10. If (mean_delay is VS) and (number_of_servers is S) and (utilisation_factor is M) then (number_of_spares is S)
11. If (mean_delay is S) and (number_of_servers is S) and (utilisation_factor is M) then (number_of_spares is VS)
12. If (mean_delay is M) and (number_of_servers is S) and (utilisation_factor is M) then (number_of_spares is VS)
13. If (mean_delay is VS) and (number_of_servers is M) and (utilisation_factor is M) then (number_of_spares is RS)
14. If (mean_delay is S) and (number_of_servers is M) and (utilisation_factor is M) then (number_of_spares is S)
15. If (mean_delay is M) and (number_of_servers is M) and (utilisation_factor is M) then (number_of_spares is VS)
16. If (mean_delay is VS) and (number_of_servers is L) and (utilisation_factor is M) then (number_of_spares is M)
17. If (mean_delay is S) and (number_of_servers is L) and (utilisation_factor is M) then (number_of_spares is RS)
18. If (mean_delay is M) and (number_of_servers is L) and (utilisation_factor is M) then (number_of_spares is S)
19. If (mean_delay is VS) and (number_of_servers is S) and (utilisation_factor is H) then (number_of_spares is VL)
20. If (mean_delay is S) and (number_of_servers is S) and (utilisation_factor is H) then (number_of_spares is L)
21. If (mean_delay is M) and (number_of_servers is S) and (utilisation_factor is H) then (number_of_spares is M)
22. If (mean_delay is VS) and (number_of_servers is M) and (utilisation_factor is H) then (number_of_spares is M)
23. If (mean_delay is S) and (number_of_servers is M) and (utilisation_factor is H) then (number_of_spares is M)
24. If (mean_delay is M) and (number_of_servers is M) and (utilisation_factor is H) then (number_of_spares is S)
25. If (mean_delay is VS) and (number_of_servers is L) and (utilisation_factor is H) then (number_of_spares is RL)

26. If (mean_delay is S) and (number_of_servers is L) and (utilisation_factor is H) then (number_of_spares is M)
27. If (mean_delay is M) and (number_of_servers is L) and (utilisation_factor is H) then (number_of_spares is RS)

Step 4: Encode the fuzzy sets, fuzzy rules and procedures to perform fuzzy inference into the expert system

The next task after defining fuzzy sets and fuzzy rules is to encode them, and thus actually build a fuzzy expert system. To accomplish this task, we may choose one of two options: to build our system using a programming language such as C or Pascal, or to apply a fuzzy logic development tool such as MATLAB Fuzzy Logic Toolbox1 from the MathWorks or Fuzzy Knowledge BuilderTM from Fuzzy Systems Engineering.

Most experienced fuzzy system builders often prefer the C/C++ programming language because it offers greater flexibility. However, for rapid developing and prototyping a fuzzy expert system, the best choice is a fuzzy logic development tool. Such a tool usually provides complete environments for building and testing fuzzy systems. For example, the MATLAB Fuzzy Logic Toolbox has five integrated graphical editors: the fuzzy inference system editor, the rule editor, the membership function editor, the fuzzy inference viewer, and the output surface viewer. All these features make designing fuzzy systems much easier. This option is also preferable for novices, who do not have sufficient experience in building fuzzy expert systems. When a fuzzy logic development tool is chosen, the knowledge engineer needs only to encode fuzzy rules in English like syntax, and define membership functions graphically. To build our fuzzy expert system, we will use one of the most popular tools, the MATLAB Fuzzy Logic Toolbox. It provides a systematic framework for computing with fuzzy rules and graphical user interfaces. It is easy to master and convenient to use, even for new fuzzy system builders.

Step 5: Evaluate and tune the system

The last, and the most laborious, task is to evaluate and tune the system. We want to see whether our fuzzy system meets the requirements

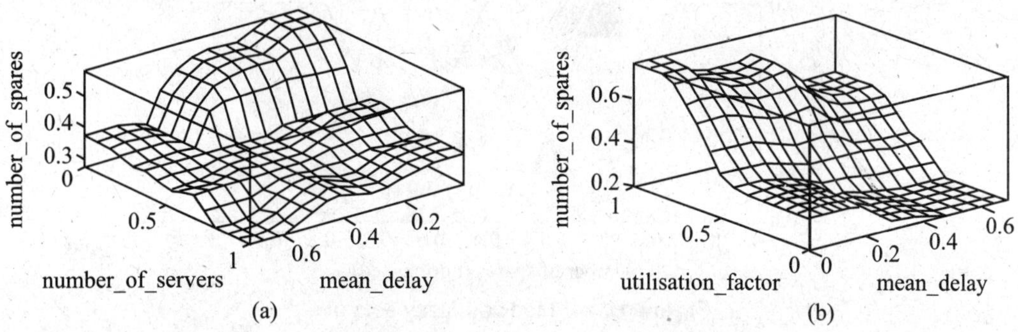

Figure 13.12: Three-dimensional plots for rule base 1.

Specified at the beginning. Several test situations depend on the mean delay, number of servers and repair utilisation factor. The Fuzzy Logic Toolbox can generate surface to help us analyse the system's performance. Figure 13.12 represents three-dimensional plots for the two-input one-output system. But our system has three inputs and one output. Can we move beyond three dimensions? When we move beyond three dimensions, we encounter difficulties in displaying the results. Luckily, the Fuzzy Logic Toolbox has a special capability: it can generate a three dimensional output surface by varying any two of the inputs and keeping other inputs constant. Thus we can observe the performance of our three-input one-output system on two three-dimensional plots. Although the fuzzy system works well, we may attempt to improve it by applying Rule Base 2. The results are shown in Figure 13.13. If we compare Figures 13.12 and 13.13, we will see the improvement. However, even now, the expert might not be satisfied with the system performance. To improve it, he or she may suggest additional sets – Rather Small and Rather Large – on the universe of discourse Number of servers (as shown in Figure 13.14), and to extend the rule base according to the FAM presented in Figure 13.15. The ease with which a fuzzy system can be modified and extended permits us to follow the expert suggestions and quickly obtain results shown in Figure 13.16.

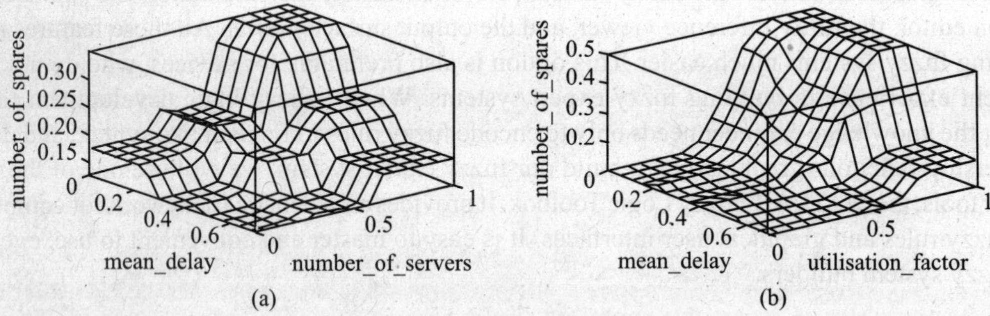

Figure 13.13: Three-dimensional plots for rule base 2.

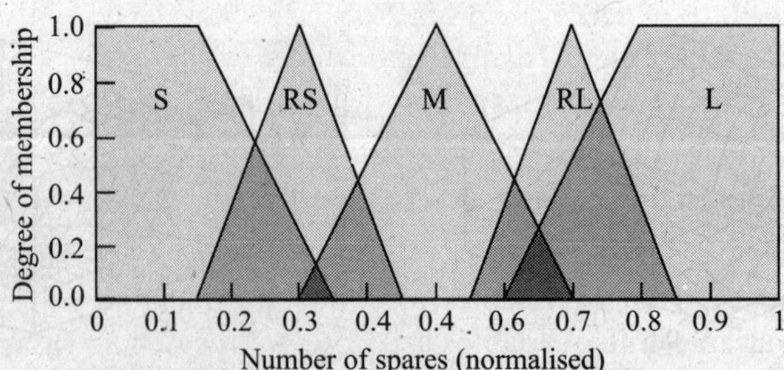

Figure 13.14: Modified fuzzy sets of number of servers s.

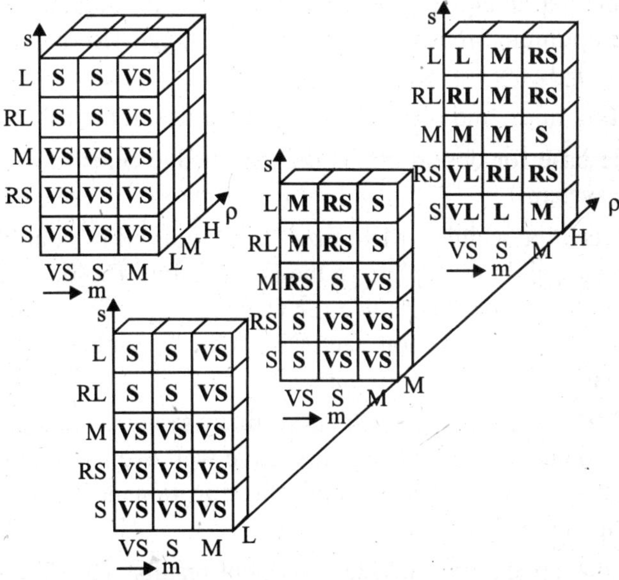

Figure 13.15: Cube FAM of rule base 3.

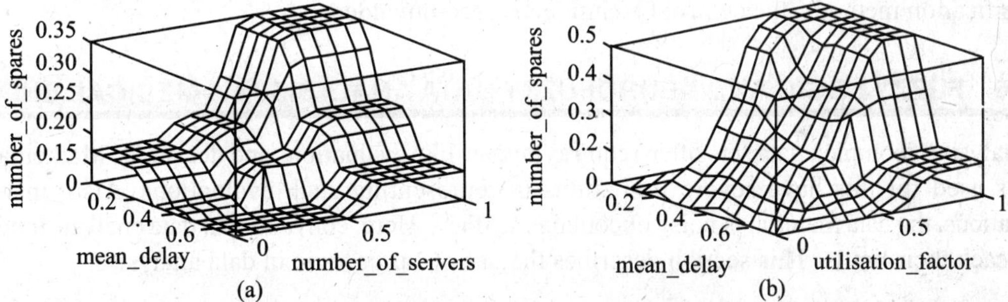

Figure 13.16: Three-dimensional plots for rule base 3.

In general, tuning a fuzzy expert system takes much more time and effort than determining fuzzy sets and constructing fuzzy rules. Usually a reasonable solution to the problem can be achieved from the first series of fuzzy sets and fuzzy rules. This is an acknowledged advantage of fuzzy logic; however, improving the system becomes rather an art than engineering.

Tuning fuzzy systems may involve executing a number of actions in the following order:

1. Review model input and output variables, and if required redefine their ranges. Pay particular attention to the variable units. Variables used in the same domain must be measured in the same units on the universe of discourse.
2. Review the fuzzy sets, and if required define additional sets on the universe of discourse. The use of wide fuzzy sets may cause the fuzzy system to perform roughly.

3. Provide sufficient overlap between neighbouring sets. Although there is no precise method to determine the optimum amount of overlap, it is suggested that triangle-to-triangle and trapezoid-to-triangle fuzzy sets should overlap between 25 and 50 per cent of their bases.
4. Review the existing rules, and if required add new rules to the rule base.
5. Examine the rule base for opportunities to write hedge rules to capture the pathological behaviour of the system.
6. Adjust the rule execution weights. Most fuzzy logic tools allow control of the importance of rules by changing a weight multiplier. In the Fuzzy Logic Toolbox, all rules have a default weight of (1.0), but the user can reduce the force of any rule by adjusting its weight. For example, if we specify If (utilisation_factor is H) then (number_of_spares is L) (0.6) then the rule's force will be reduced by 40 per cent.
7. Revise shapes of the fuzzy sets. In most cases, fuzzy systems are highly tolerant of a shape approximation, and thus a system can still behave well even when the shapes of the fuzzy sets are not precisely defined. But how about defuzzification methods? Should we try different techniques to tune our system?

The centroid technique appears to provide consistent results. This is a wellbalanced method sensitive to the height and width of the total fuzzy region as well as to sparse singletons. Therefore, unless you have a strong reason to believe that your fuzzy system will behave better under other defuzzification methods, the centroid technique is recommended.

13.10 FUZZY LOGIC AND NEUROFUZZY DATA ANALYSIS IN A MEDICAL SHOE

The analysis of complex data sets often requires human-like evaluations and decisions. Mathematical models used for this have severe limitations in representing such evaluations. Also, in many applications, the data material is noisy or contains artifacts. Here, conventional data analysis methods soon reach their limits. This section describes the use of fuzzy logic in data analysis.

13.10.1 Using Fuzzy Logic in Data Analysis

Most data analysis methods try to derive structural information out of given data sets. This structural information shall represent the system that produced the data sets. The goal is to identify internal parameters of the system that cannot directly be measured.

Today, many different methods and algorithms for data analysis exist. Most of these algorithms have difficulties coping with noisy data and data that contains artifacts. These applications have to use very robust data analysis techniques that can cope with errors and artifacts in the data material.

But how can fuzzy logic fix this? Here is a simple example: look at Figure 13.17. With the human eye as sensor, this looks like a non-sensical collection of gray squares. The human eye is already a very precise sensor that can distinguish about 100 different shades of gray, but even with better sensors Figure 13.17 remains a collection of gray squares. Only if you squeeze your lids so tight that the entire picture becomes "fuzzy", you see that the collection of gray squares is actually a picture of Abraham Lincoln. The lesson learned is that even the most precise method will not give you the information that is contained in the picture. Even if you would modify the grayness of some of the squares, the "fuzzy" look would still recognize Lincoln.

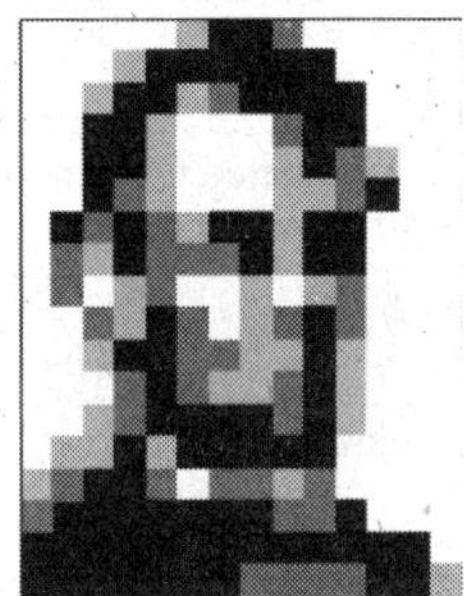

Figure 13.17: Only if you squeeze your lids so that the picture becomes "fuzzy", you recognize Abraham Lincoln.

To employ fuzzy logic in data analysis applications, many different combinations of fuzzy logic and conventional techniques exist. Which one is the best to use depends strongly on the application. The most common combinations of fuzzy logic and conventional techniques are:

(i) Fuzzy Cluster Analysis

Cluster analysis maps objects to pre-defined classes. For a quality control system, the classes could be *bad* and *good*. For this mapping, a vector of parameters describes each object. Each parameter denotes a certain property of the objects. For the classification of acoustic signals, these parameters could be the result of a Fourier transformation. Most cluster analysis algorithms use training algorithms to configure themselves from given sample data sets.

Using fuzzy logic in cluster analysis allows for the definition of "fuzzy" classes. The benefit of this is that even when a unique classification of some parameters is not possible, a good final solution can still be derived.

(ii) Fuzzy Rule Based Methods

Cluster analysis methods derive all necessary structural information by training from given sample data sets. This demands a very high quality of the sample data sets used. Also, there is no explicit modifications of the resulting system. This makes optimization and verification a difficult task.

Fuzzy rule based methods work differently. Here, "if-then" rules represent the entire classification. This is very similar to the application of fuzzy logic in intelligent control as described before. In contrast to fuzzy logic in control applications, fuzzy logic classification uses different inference and defuzzification methods.

The benefit of fuzzy rule based methods over fuzzy cluster analysis is that the information flow in the system is completely transparent. Since fuzzy logic systems are self-explanatory, explicit optimization and verification is easy. The disadvantage of fuzzy rule based methods is that the entire system has to be built up manually. In contrast to fuzzy cluster analysis, no automated training exist.

However, fuzzy rules based methods are the basis of many successful applications in data analysis and signal classifications.

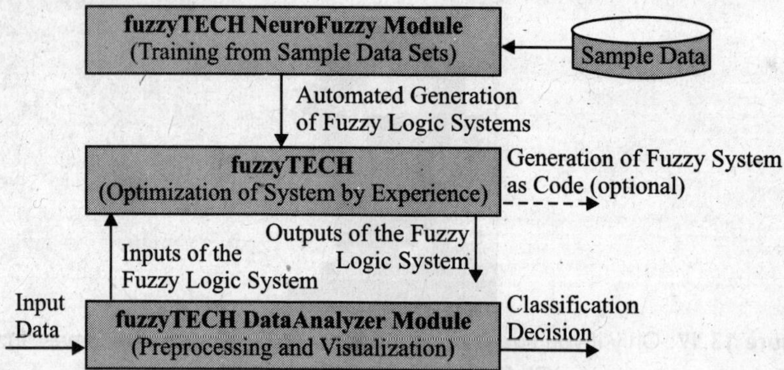

Figure 13.18: Linking the data analyzer module, the neurofuzzy module and fuzzyTECH creates an integrated development environment for fuzzy data analysis systems.

(iii) Adaptive Fuzzy Rule Based Methods

In summary, the advantage of fuzzy cluster analysis lies in its trainability while the advantage of fuzzy rule based methods lies in the inherent transparency of the system. However, some applications need trainability and transparency both at the same time. Here, the combination of a training algorithm with a fuzzy rule based method can make a successful solution. Because the training algorithm adapts the fuzzy rules and membership functions so that the behavior represents the sample data sets, this combination is called "adaptive fuzzy rule based method".

Although there are many ways to adapt a fuzzy logic system, the only approach that has been widely used in industrial applications is the NeuroFuzzy technique. Here, learning algorithms developed for neural nets are modified so that they can also train a fuzzy logic system.

The benefit of such a technology is that it can learn from given sample data sets and that the learned result can be further enhanced by hand. Especially for applications where only partial information for the solution stems from sample data, adaptive fuzzy rule based systems are the best choice. Another advantage is that the system developed is a 'pure' fuzzy logic system which can be implemented even on very inexpensive hardware platforms. Section 3 of this paper shows a good example of this.

13.10.2 Software Tools For Fuzzy Data Analysis

In most fuzzy data analysis systems, the input data needs extensive preprocessing before the fuzzy logic system. This preprocessing can include filtering, linearizations, or Fourier transformations. These functions are not part of most fuzzy logic applications in industrial control and, hence, are not part of most fuzzy logic software development tools.

For the *fuzzy*TECH development system, complete data analysis functionality is provided by an add-on tool, the DataAnalyzer Module. Figure 13.18 shows how *fuzzy*TECH, the DataAnalyzer

Module, and the NeuroFuzzy Module can be linked to form an integrated design environment. Linking all three components allows for the design of adaptive fuzzy rule based solution. If the NeuroFuzzy Module is left out, only fuzzy rule based solutions are possible.

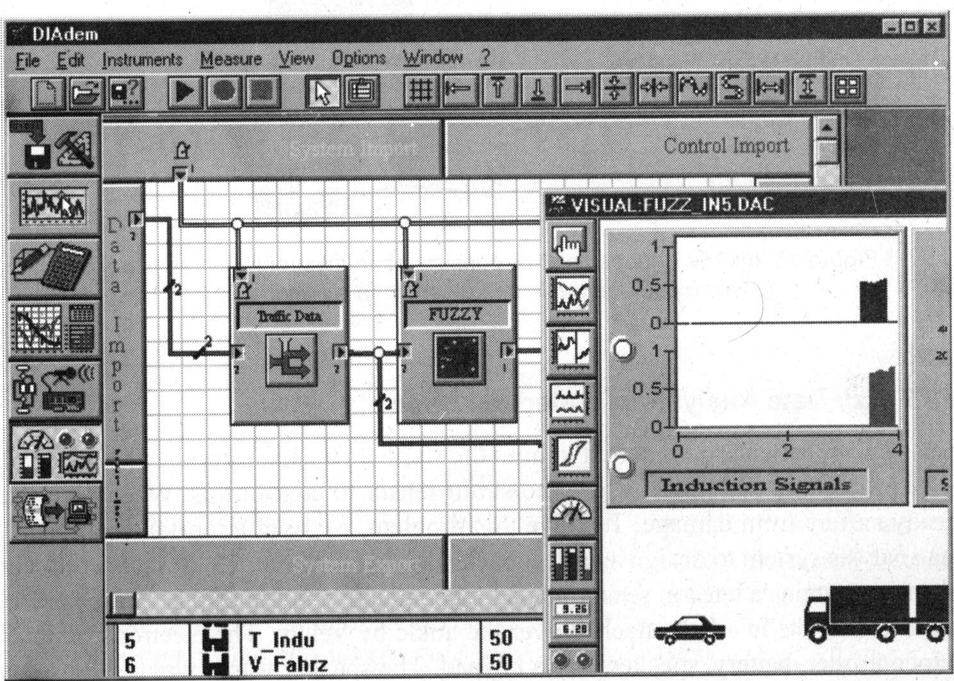

Figure 13.19: Development of a fuzzy data analyzer solution is completely graphical. Configuring pre-defined function blocks integrates conventional signal analysis techniques and fuzzy logic. Fuzzy Logic is also represented as a function block.

Figure 13.19 shows the visual design of a fuzzy data analyzer solution that supervises the wear of a machinery tool during operation. The two upper left function blocks drive A/D channels of a standard PC plug-in board. The upper channel links to a tension stripe sensor that acts as a microphone, the lower channel links to a temperature sensor mounted at the tool. The acoustic signal is pre-processed by a Spectrum block (fast fourier transformation) and inputted to the fuzzy logic function block. The second input to the fuzzy logic function is the temperature signal filtered by a low pass Filter. The third input to the fuzzy logic function block is the direct temperature signal after a Threshold function block. A fourth input comes from a visual inspection of the machine operator and is inputted by a slide in a separate window.

Both a Meter and a spectrum Scope visualize the outputs of the fuzzy logic function block. In case of an overload, a D/A channel outputs a speed overwrite signal to the machine to avoid destruction of the machinery tool. For documentation, a File function block writes the evaluation results to disk. The NeuroFuzzy Module resides on top of *fuzzy*TECH (Figure 13.18), hence, it is not displayed in Figure13.19.

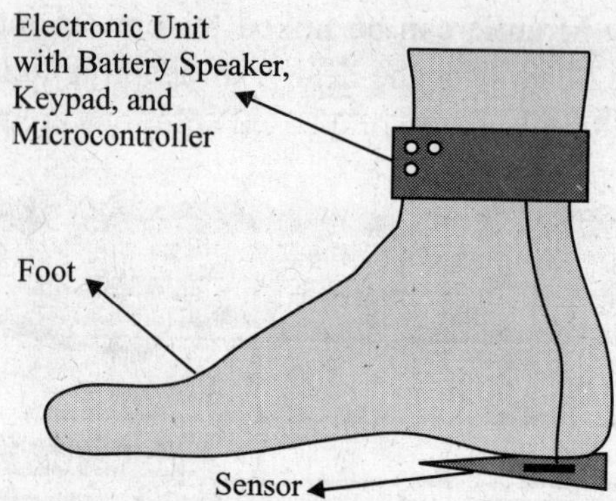

Figure 13.20: The orthopedic shoe consists of an electronic unit attached by velcro over the ankle and a sensor in a silicon inlay.

13.10.3 Fuzzy Data Analysis in a Medical Shoe

After knee surgery, patients are required to limit the strain on the knee during a long convalescence period. The problem is that humans have no strain sensor to control this. When pain occurs, the knee already suffers from damage. To solve this problem, we used a tension sensor and a fuzzy logic data analysis system to design a biofeedback shoe inlay. Figure 13.20 shows the schematics. A silicon inlay contains a tension sensor made of a conductive polymer. The sensor is wired to an electronic unit that sits in a belt attached over the ankle by Velcro. The electronic units contain a host microcontroller, battery, speaker, and a keypad. The speaker warns warns the user when the strain limit is reached. A/D conversion, signal pre-processing, and the fuzzy data analysis system all run on the 8-bit microcontroller.

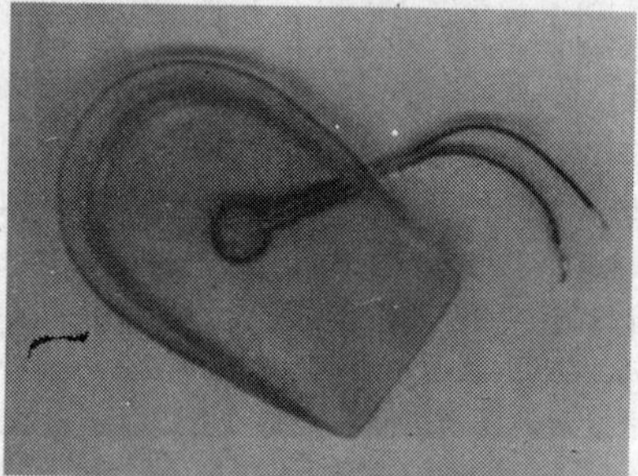

Figure 13.21: Silicon shoe inlay with pressure sensor.

The objective for the fuzzy data analysis system is to estimate the internal strain on the knee from the tension signal. If 80% of the maximum acceptable load is reached, a beep warns the user to take it easy from here. If 90% of the maximum acceptable load is reached, a repeating beep tells the user to not use the leg for a while and if the strain is over the maximum threshold that is set by the doctor, the beep sounds continuously.

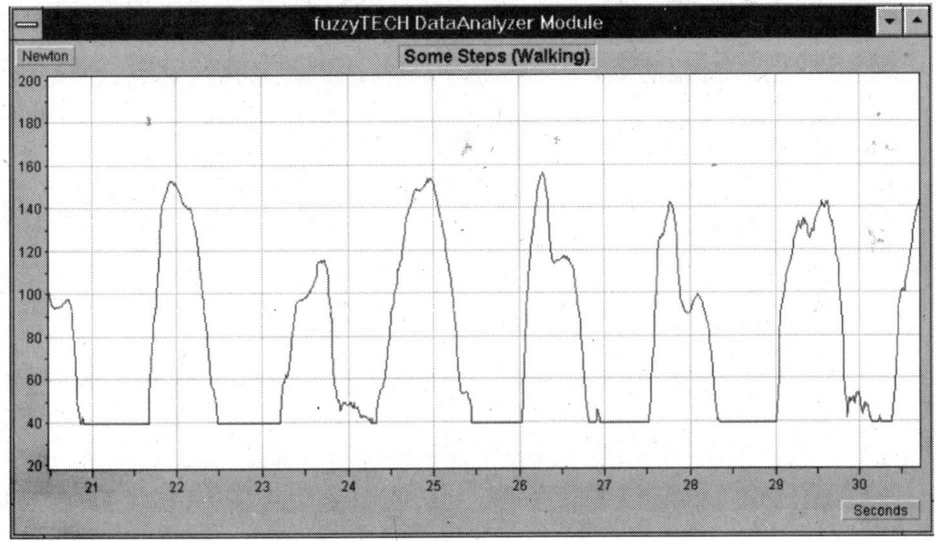

Figure 13.22: Typical tension sensor signal for step sequence.

The difficulty of this is to estimate the internal strain on the knee from just the tension signal. Figure 13.22 displays the tension sensor signal for a typical sequence of steps. To get more information from the tension sensor signal, pre-processing derives additional inputs to the fuzzy data analysis system. In total, this yields four inputs to the fuzzy logic function block:

- Act_Peak:

  Peak tension of the current step.
- Act_Slope:

  Slope of the tension signal of the current step.
- Hist_Short:

  Feedback of the average output signal of the fuzzy logic function block of the last five (5) minutes. This input is an indicator for the current strain situation in the knee.
- Hist_Long:

  Feedback of the average output signal of the fuzzy logic function block of the last 48 hours. This input is an indicator for the long-term strain situation in the knee.

Figure 13.23 shows a screen shot of the fuzzy logic system in the data analyzer. The upper window draws the structure of the system. The output variable “Alarm” stems from a rule block with the input variables “ActualLoad” and “TimeLoad”. Both these variables are outputs of other rule blocks. ActualLoad computes from the two input variables Act_Slope and Act_Peak, which are input variables of the fuzzy logic function block. The DataAnalyzer Module computes these variables from the tension sensor signal.

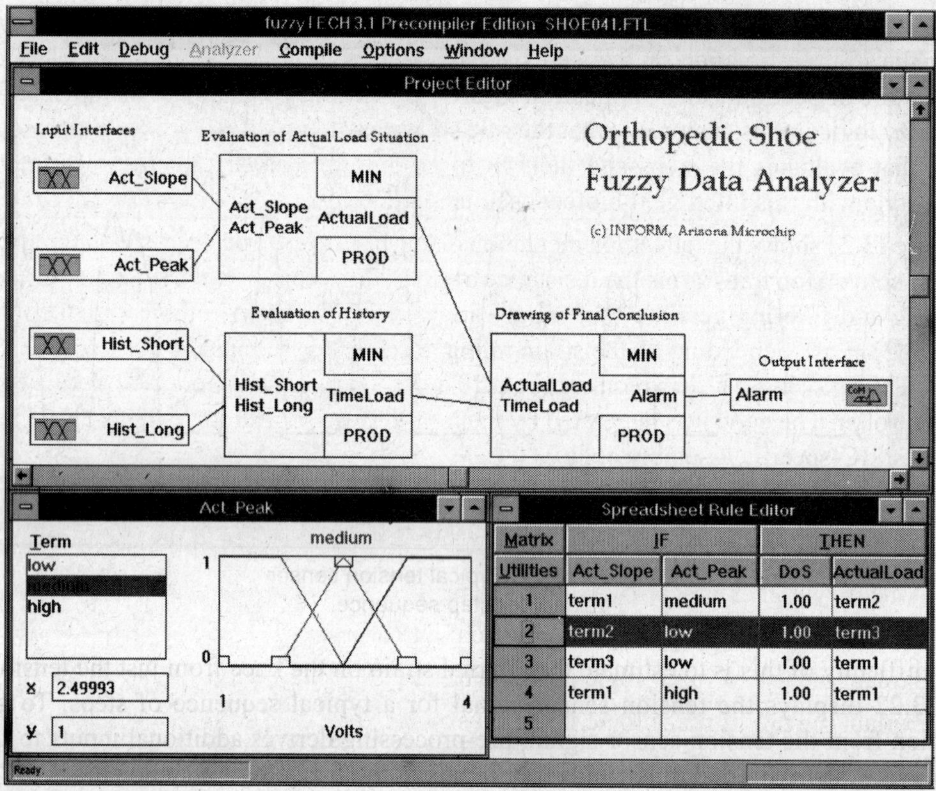

Figure 13.23: Structure of the fuzzy logic function block for the fuzzy data analysis system.

TimeLoad computes from the two input variables Hist_Short and Hist_Long that the DataAnalyzer Module computes out of the output signal from the fuzzy logic function block by averaging. The left lower window shows a typical membership function definition. Most linguistic variables use two (2) or three (3) membership functions of Standard MBF type. The lower right window shows four rules of the upper rule block. The total number of rules in the system is 39.

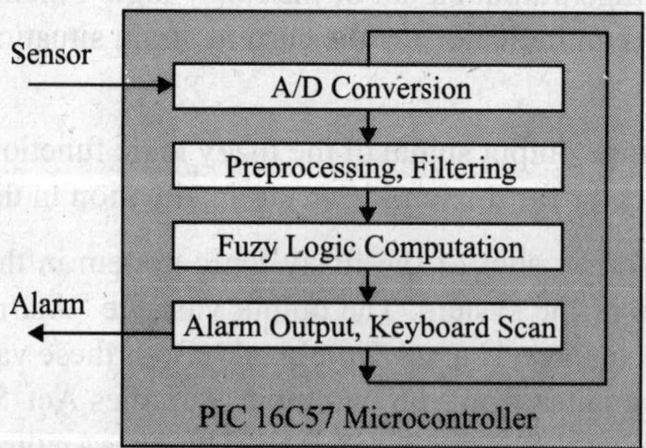

Figure 13.24: Implementation of the fuzzy data analyzer system on a microcontroller.

The rules were derived in close cooperation with orthopedic doctors. Since no good sample data for the strain estimation on a knee exists, the NeuroFuzzy Module was not used. Under the nomenclature of Section 1, this application uses "fuzzy rule based methods". Another advantage of using fuzzy logic in this example is that the rule set is easy to modify. For example, by designing a rule set that evaluates the steps and their fit to an optimal curve, runners could improve their running style with this intelligent biofeedback technique.

Figure 13.24 shows the total implementation on the PIC16C57 microcontroller. First, the analog-to-digital conversion transforms the resistance of the tension sensor into a digital 10-bit value. Pre-processing and filtering gets the four input variables for the fuzzy logic computation shown in Figure 13.23. Last, depending on the strain rating, the speaker outputs the alarm and the keypad is scanned. The fuzzy logic system requires about 20 bytes RAM and 590 words ROM on the PIC16C57 microcontroller. The code was generated by the *fuzzy*TECH MP Edition that generates fuzzy logic systems as PIC-specific assembly code.

EXERCISES

1. What do you mean by artificial intelligence?
2. Explain the use of fuzzy logic in artificial intelligence?
3. Explain the use of fuzzy logic in frame based representation?
4. Explain the use of fuzzy logic in expert system?
5. What do you mean by intelligent agents?
6. How we can implement fuzzy logic in intelligent agents?
7. Explain the building block of a fuzzy expert system?
8. Explain the applications of fuzzy logic and neuro fuzzy data analysis in a medical shoe?

CHAPTER 14

Fuzzy Logic and Pattern Recognition

14.1 INTRODUCTION

Pattern recognition is "the act of taking in raw data and taking an action based on the category of the pattern". Most research in pattern recognition is about methods for supervised learning and unsupervised learning.

Pattern recognition aims to classify data (patterns) based either on *a priori* knowledge or on statistical information extracted from the patterns. The patterns to be classified are usually groups of measurements or observations, defining points in an appropriate multidimensional space. This is in contrast to pattern matching, where the pattern is rigidly specified.

In this chapter we examine methods of analyzing data using fuzzy clustering techniques. Fuzzy clustering provides a robust and resilient method of classifying collections of data elements by allowing the same data point to reside in multiple clusters with different degrees of membership. By way of comparison, we also look at a crisp clustering method, the k-means algorithm. The algorithms we use in this chapter are the fuzzy c-means.

14.2 PATTERN RECOGNITION

A complete pattern recognition system consists of a sensor that gathers the observations to be classified or described, a feature extraction mechanism that computes numeric or symbolic information from the observations, and a classification or description scheme that does the actual job of classifying or describing observations, relying on the extracted features.

The classification or description scheme is usually based on the availability of a set of patterns that have already been classified or described. This set of patterns is termed the training set, and the resulting learning strategy is characterized as supervised learning. Learning can also be unsupervised, in the sense that the system is not given an *a priori* labeling of patterns, instead it itself establishes the classes based on the intrinsic regularities of the patterns.

The classification or description scheme usually uses one of the following approaches: statistical (or decision theoretic) or syntactic (or structural). Statistical pattern recognition is based on statistical characterizations of patterns, assuming that the patterns are generated by a probabilistic system. Syntactical (or structural) pattern recognition is based on the structural interrelationships of features. A wide range of algorithms can be applied for pattern recognition, from simple naive Bayes classifiers and neural networks to the powerful k-nearest neighbor algorithm decision rules.

Pattern recognition is more complex when templates are used to generate variants. For example, in English, sentences often follow the "N-VP" (noun - verb phrase) pattern, but some knowledge of the English language is required to detect the pattern. Pattern recognition is studied in many fields, including psychology, ethology, cognitive science and computer science.

Holographic associative memory is another type of pattern matching where a large set of learned patterns based on cognitive meta-weight is searched for a small set of target patterns.

14.2.1 Uses of Pattern Recognition

Within medical science, pattern recognition is the basis for computer-aided diagnosis (CAD) systems. CAD describes a procedure that supports the doctor's interpretations and findings.

Figure 14.1: The face was automatically detected by special software.

Typical applications are automatic speech recognition, classification of text into several categories (e.g. spam/non-spam email messages), the automatic recognition of handwritten postal codes on postal envelopes, or the automatic recognition of images of human faces. The last two examples form the subtopic image analysis of pattern recognition that deals with digital images as input to pattern recognition systems.

14.3 THE VOCABULARY OF FUZZY CLUSTERING

If you exclude mathematical equations, the vocabulary of fuzzy clustering is surprisingly sparse. In fact, much of the underlying terminology related to cluster configuration, membership, and overlap has already been covered in the chapters on fuzzy logic fundamentals. A review of some vocabulary terms used in fuzzy clustering, however, will make reading and understanding the material in this chapter somewhat easier. It is, however, not always possible, while maintaining an uncluttered and coherent discussion of the clustering process, to ensure that every term is introduced before it is used.

1. **Centroid:** The center of a cluster. A symmetric cluster can be visualized as an n-dimensional region balanced on its center of gravity. Hence, the center of a cluster is also called the centroid of the cluster.
2. **Cluster (Clustering):** A cluster is a group of observations ("things") that have similar properties. The process of clustering involves finding sets of groups (clusters), each containing all observations that share a collection of specified properties (or attributes). When the clusters or categories are not predefined, clustering provides a form of unsupervised knowledge discovery in which deeply buried or distributed patterns emerge, revealing a variety of behaviour patterns in the underlying data.
3. **Cluster Seeds:** Clustering often starts with an estimate of the cluster population (N clusters). These N cluster centers are then initially populated with random values drawn from the domain of each dimension in the cluster. The random values used to initialize the clusters are called the cluster seeds.
4. **Entropy (or Noise):** Large collections of data are often filled with noise (obvious outliers, and missing, improperly transcribed, erroneous, and duplicate data). The noise acts like background scattering and can obscure the actual patterns buried in the data. Entropy is a measure of disorder in a system. The higher the entropy the greater the degree of disorder. One of the goals of a clustering technique is to identify noise and reduce its impact on clustering.
5. **Euclidean Distance:** The most commonly used measure of the distance from the current cluster center to a data point, called the Euclidean distance, is based on the Pythagorean theorem. For two points, x and y, in N-dimensional space, Equation 14.1 is the Euclidean distance.

$$d = \sqrt{\sum_{i=1}^{N} (x_i - y_i)^2} \tag{14.1}$$

Here,

d is the distance

N is the number of dimensions in the data

x_i is the i-th value x

y_i is the i-th value y

This is generally considered the ordinary (or conventional) distance between two points—one that could, theoretically, be measured by a straight edge. There are many other methods for measuring the distance between points in multidimensional space, but the Euclidean distance is the most commonly used.
6. **Iteration:** The process of adding a new point to a cluster and then recomputing the center is called iteration. This is the core mechanism in compiling a cluster.
7. **Membership:** In conventional clustering, a data point is a member of one and only one cluster. In fuzzy clustering, a data point can have a membership in multiple clusters (each to a different degree). Membership is a measure of how strongly a data point is a member of a particular cluster. This measure is important in the rule-generation process.

8. **Stability** The idea of stability is a measure of the steady state of a cluster. As new data points are added to a cluster, the center is recalculated. The center moves as the weighted center of gravity changes. At some point, when enough points are added, the center no longer changes. At this point the cluster is stable.

14.4 CLUSTER ANALYSIS

Cluster analysis or **clustering** is the assignment of a set of observations into subsets (called clusters) so that observations in the same cluster are similar in some sense. Clustering is a method of unsupervised learning, and a common technique for statistical data analysis used in many fields, including machine learning, data mining, pattern recognition, image analysis and bioinformatics.

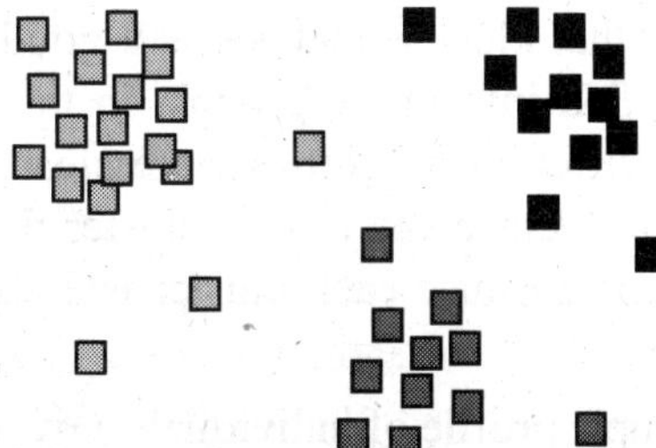

Figure 14.2: The result of a cluster analysis shown as the coloring of the squares into three clusters.

Clustering refers to identifying the number of subclasses of c clusters in a data universe X comprised of n data samples, and partitioning X into c clusters ($2 \leq c < n$). Note that $c = 1$ denotes rejection of the hypothesis that there are clusters in the data, whereas $c = n$ constitutes the trivial case where each sample is in a "cluster" by itself. There are two kinds of c-partitions of data: hard (or crisp) and soft (or fuzzy). For numerical data one assumes that the members of each cluster bear more mathematical similarity to each other than to members of other clusters. Two important issues to consider in this regard are how to measure the similarity between pairs of observations and how to evaluate the partitions once they are formed.

One of the simplest similarity measures is distance between pairs of feature vectors in the feature space. If one can determine a suitable distance measure and compute the distance between all pairs of observations, then one may expect that the distance between points in the same cluster will be considerably less than the distance between points in different clusters. Several circumstances, however, mitigate the general utility of this approach, such as the combination of values of incompatible features, as would be the case, for example, when different features have significantly different scales. The clustering method described in this chapter defines "optimum" partitions through a global criterion function that measures the extent to which candidate partitions optimize a weighted sum of squared errors between data points and cluster centers in feature space. Many other clustering algorithms have been proposed for distinguishing substructure in high-dimensional data. It is emphasized here that the method of clustering must be closely matched with the particular data under study for successful interpretation of substructure in the data.

Cluster Validity

In many cases, the number c of clusters in the data is known. In other cases, however, it may be reasonable to expect cluster substructure at more than one value of c. In this situation it is necessary to identify the value of c that gives the most plausible number of clusters in the data for the analysis at hand. This problem is known as cluster validity. If the data used are labelled, there is a unique and absolute measure of cluster validity: the c that is given. For unlabeled data, no absolute measure of clustering validity exists. Although the importance of these differences is not known, it is clear that the features nominated should be sensitive to the phenomena of interest and not to other variations that might not matter to the applications at hand.

14.4.1 Advantages of Cluster Analysis

Frisvad of BioCentrum-DTU said that cluster analysis is a good way for quick review of data, especially if the objects are classified into many groups. In the above example, 'Schools Like Mine', 23 clusters of school with different properties were clearly clustered. Cluster Analysis is easy for user to assign or nominate themselves in to a cluster they would most like to compare with in exist school cluster database because each cluster is clearly named with understandable terms.

Cluster Analysis provides a simple profile of individuals. Given a number of analysis units, for example school size, student ethnicity, region, size of civil jurisdiction and social economic status in this example, each of which is described by a set of characteristics and attributes. Cluster Analysis also suggests how groups of units are determined such that units within groups are similar in some respect and unlike those from other groups.

14.4.2 Disadvantages of Cluster Analysis

Object can be assigned in one cluster only. For example in 'Schools Like Mine', schools are automatically assigned into the first twenty-two clusters. However, if schools want to compare themselves with integrated schools, they will have to manually assign themselves into cluster twenty-three. Data-driven clustering may not represent the reality because once a school is assigned to a cluster; it cannot be assigned to another one. Some schools may have more than one significant property or fall on the edge of two clusters.

Clustering may have detrimental effects to teachers who work in low-decile schools, students who are educated in them, and parents who support them, by telling them the schools are classified as ineffective, when in fact many are doing well in some unique aspects that are not sufficiently illustrated by the clusters formed. In k-means clustering methods, it is often requires several analysis before the number of clusters can be determined. It can be very sensitive to the choice of initial cluster centres.

14.4.3 Applications of Clustering

Following are the various applications of clustering:

1. Biology

In biology **clustering** has many applications

- In imaging, data clustering may take different form based on the data dimensionality. For example, the SOCR EM Mixture model segmentation activity and applet shows how to obtain point, region or volume classification using the online SOCR computational libraries.
- In the fields of plant and animal ecology, clustering is used to describe and to make spatial and temporal comparisons of communities (assemblages) of organisms in heterogeneous environments; it is also used in plant systematic to generate artificial phylogenies or clusters of organisms (individuals) at the species, genus or higher level that share a number of attributes
- **In computational biology and bioinformatics:**
  - In transcriptomics, clustering is used to build groups of genes with related expression patterns (also known as coexpressed genes). Often such groups contain functionally related proteins, such as enzymes for a specific pathway, or genes that are co-regulated. High throughput experiments using expressed sequence tags (ESTs) or DNA microarrays can be a powerful tool for genome annotation, a general aspect of genomics.
  - In sequence analysis, clustering is used to group homologous sequences into gene families. This is a very important concept in bioinformatics, and evolutionary biology in general. See evolution by gene duplication.
  - In high-throughput genotyping platforms clustering algorithms are used to automatically assign genotypes.
- In QSAR and molecular modeling studies as also chemoinformatics.

2. Medicine

In medical imaging, such as PET scans, cluster analysis can be used to differentiate between different types of tissue and blood in a three dimensional image. In this application, actual position does not matter, but the voxel intensity is considered as a vector, with a dimension for each image that was taken over time. This technique allows, for example, accurate measurement of the rate a radioactive tracer is delivered to the area of interest, without a separate sampling of arterial blood, an intrusive technique that is most common today.

3. Market research

Cluster analysis is widely used in market research when working with multivariate data from surveys and test panels. Market researchers use cluster analysis to partition the general population of consumers into market segments and to better understand the relationships between different groups of consumers/potential customers.

- Segmenting the market and determining target markets
- Product positioning
- New product development
- Selecting test markets

4. Educational research

In educational research analysis, data for clustering can be students, parents, sex or test score. Clustering is an important method for understanding and utility of cluster in educational research. Cluster analysis in educational research can be used to find out data exploration, cluster confirmation and hypothesis testing. **Data exploration** is used when there is little information about which schools or students will be grouped together. It aims at discovering any meaningful clusters of units based on measures on a set of response variables. **Cluster confirmation** is used for confirming the previously reported cluster results. **Hypothesis testing** is used for arranging cluster structure.

Example of cluster analysis in educational research

In 2002, Hattie used cluster analysis in the project 'School like Mine' to compare students' achievement in literacy and numeracy by the type of school they attended. 2707 majority and minority students in New Zealand are classified into different clusters according to school size, student ethnicity, region, size of civil jurisdiction and socioeconomic status for comparison. The cluster in this research is calculated across five dimensions, decile, region, size, minority and rurality. All schools are placed into one of twenty clusters that are used in the asTTle software as a basis of student achievement comparison. The result shows that using the power of socioeconomic status to describe schools is analysed and found inadequate.

Euclidean distance was used as the clustering method in this research. Schools that are alike were clustered together. In addition, dendrogram. By clustering schools, Hattie suggested that school types had no significant relation with performance of schools.

Common cluster techniques in educational research

All cluster techniques have two basic concerns: firstly, the measurement of similarity between individual profiles; and secondly, the use of that measure to form the groups or clusters. Brennan described Iterative Relocation as the most important cluster technique in behavioral and educational research. It has been adopted at Lancaster to create typologies of pupils based on personality and behavioral items to identify types of students and to isolate the skills considered to be important for certain grades of technologist in industry. Other similarity coefficients are available and the one chosen will depend upon the type of data gained.

As described by Bennett, Iterative Relocation can better be understood in its procedures described below:

Number of groups should be decided. This is often an arbitrary decision and the groupings are random. The analysis then proceeds by computing the group profile (or group centroid) of each group, which is the cumulative frequencies of all variables measured. Each individual should be compared with each of the group centroids. A number of formulae are available for measuring this similarity. Among others, Wishart has found error sum of squares, a measure of dissimilarity, to be one of the most successful coefficients for continuous data. When relocate or alters the composition of groups and recalculate the group centroids are completed, a new iteration cycle commences. This sequence of comparison and relocation continues until all individuals are in the group whose central profile is most similar to their own. The solution is then said to be stable. The analysis is then continued by reducing the number of groups by one (N–1). This is achieved by a fushion process whereby a measure of dissimilarity (error sum of squares) between all pairs of group centroids is calculated again. The two most similar groups are then combined to reduce one group. Recalculate the group centroids and repeat steps 2 and 3 until the solution is stable for the N-1 group level. This process can continue until the two level group is reached, at which point the analysis is complete.

Solution to problems of Cluster Analysis in Educational Research

Hattie stated although Cluster analysis provides an easy way to make comparision between schools, no particular variable should be taken as the "short cut" for judging school quality. in order to overcome the unit reassignment issue, some researchers suggest a nonhierarchical cluster method which allows for reassignment of units from one cluster. This operates through an interative partitioning k- means algorithm, where k denotes the number of clusters. Nevertheless, to conduct a k-means analysis, the number of clusters needs to be specified at the start. This limits the exploratory power of cluster analysis.

Cluster Analysis t has to be very careful used in classifying schools into groups because results are heavily influenced by partial sampling, choice of clustering criteria and compositional variables, as well as cluster labeling. Like assigning schools into different bands, clustering may bring about unnecessary comparisons and inappropriate discriminations among schools, thereby adversely affecting students.

5. Other applications

Social network analysis

In the study of social networks, clustering may be used to recognize communities within large groups of people.

Software evolution

Clustering is useful in software evolution as it helps to reduce legacy properties in code by reforming functionality that has become dispersed. It is a form of restructuring and hence is a way of directly preventative maintenance.

Image segmentation

Clustering can be used to divide a digital image into distinct regions for border detection or object recognition.

Data mining

Many data mining applications involve partitioning data items into related subsets; the marketing applications discussed above represent some examples. Another common application is the division of documents, such as World Wide Web pages, into genres.

Search result grouping

In the process of intelligent grouping of the files and websites, clustering may be used to create a more relevant set of search results compared to normal search engines like Google. There are currently a number of web based clustering tools such as Clusty.

Slippy map optimization

Flickr's map of photos and other map sites use clustering to reduce the number of markers on a map. This makes it both faster and reduces the amount of visual clutter.

IMRT segmentation

Clustering can be used to divide a fluence map into distinct regions for conversion into deliverable fields in MLC-based Radiation Therapy.

Grouping of Shopping Items

Clustering can be used to group all the shopping items available on the web into a set of unique products. For example, all the items on eBay can be grouped into unique products. (eBay doesn't have the concept of a SKU)

Recommender systems

Recommender systems are designed to recommend new items based on a user's tastes. They sometimes use clustering algorithms to predict a user's preferences based on the preferences of other users in the user's cluster.

Mathematical chemistry

To find structural similarity, etc. for example, 3000 chemical compounds were clustered in the space of 90 topological indices.

Petroleum Geology

Cluster Analysis is used to reconstruct missing bottom hole core data or missing log curves in order to evaluate reservoir properties.

Physical Geography

The clustering of chemical properties in different sample locations.

Crime Analysis

Cluster analysis can be used to identify areas where there are greater incidences of particular types of crime. By identifying these distinct areas or "hot spots" where a similar crime has happened over a period of time, it is possible to manage law enforcement resources more effectively.

Evolutionary algorithms

Clustering may be used to identify different niches within the population of an evolutionary algorithm so that reproductive opportunity can be distributed more evenly amongst the evolving species or subspecies.

14.4.4 Comparisons Between Data Clusterings

There have been several suggestions for a measure of similarity between two clusterings. Such a measure can be used to compare how well different data clustering algorithms perform on a set of data. Many of these measures are derived from the matching matrix (aka confusion matrix), e.g. the Rand measure, Adjusted rand index and the Fowlkes-Mallows B_k measures. With small variations, such kinds of measures also include set matching based clustering criteria, e.g. the Mēila and Heckerman.

Several different clustering systems based on mutual information have been proposed. One is Marina Meila's 'Variation of Information' metric; another provides hierarchical clustering. The adjusted-for-chance version for the mutual information is the Adjusted Mutual Information (AMI), which corrects mutual information for agreement solely due to chance between clusterings.

Jia Li proposed a new Mallows Distance based method to take into account the distance between cluster representatives when assessing the similarity of clustering results.

14.5 PRINCIPLES OF CLUSTER DETECTION

Cluster analysis is a technique for breaking data down into related components in such a way that patterns and order become visible. In fact, cluster analysis has the virtue of strengthening the exposure of patterns and behaviours as more and more data becomes available. A cluster has a center of gravity, which is basically the weighted average of the cluster.

Data points arrayed around the center have, in the fuzzy clustering approach, a degree of membership in each of the centers. By evaluating the strength of membership in clusters for sets of records, we can often discover new and interesting relationships in the data. Clustering is an important approach to understanding business process models. By looking at the relationships between multiple attributes in the data (variables in the model) we expect to find indicators of the model performance. Isolating these indicators, such as market segmentation factors, provides valuable insights into the order hidden in the data. Figure 14.3, for example, shows a simplified retailing system and some of the common attributes associated with each component.

Our investigation of the retailing data might lead us to approach market segmentation by looking for discriminators among customers and purchases. We would like to know which customers are likely to purchase what quantities of products according to their pricing stratification. Figure 14.4 illustrates a hypothetical clustering of the data based on two attributes (income divided by age against amount spent and the price times quantity purchased).

In this example, two discrete and easily identifiable clusters emerge (such is of course not usually the case in the real world). Here, in examining the ratios two groups emerge. From this we might predict the purchasing habits of new clients, the product mix offered to current customers, or the profitability of potential clients. Clustering, then, is an attempt to gather points in the sample space that share similar attributes. This similarity can be explicit in the data or defined through some similarity or association function. In the end, we hope that clustering reveals hidden patterns and hidden order in the data so that new insights into our business processes are gained.

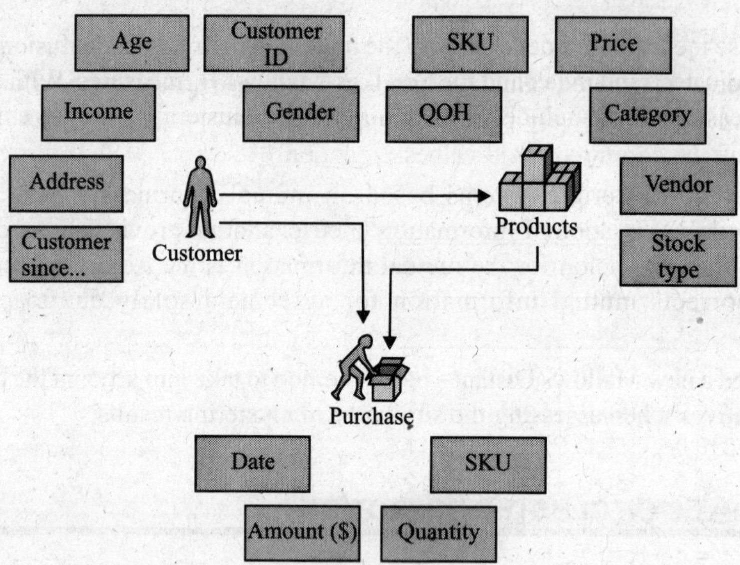

Figure 14.3: Patterns and relationships in a retailing system.

14.6 SOME GENERAL CLUSTERING CONCEPTS

As we will discuss shortly, clustering in actual data analysis often involves data with high dimensionality. In our example, we used two dimensional data groups (x_i , y_i), but normally our data contains many data elements (a_i , b_i , c_i , ..., z_i) so that cluster analysis penetrates deeply into our data's sample space. Before moving on to the process of crisp (hard) and fuzzy clustering methods, we need to understand some principles common to both approaches. These include the issues of what is clustered in the sample space and how we go about assigning a data point to a particular cluster. The first issue involves understanding the attributes of clustering, and the second centers on using these attributes to measure distances in a sample space of arbitrary dimensionality.

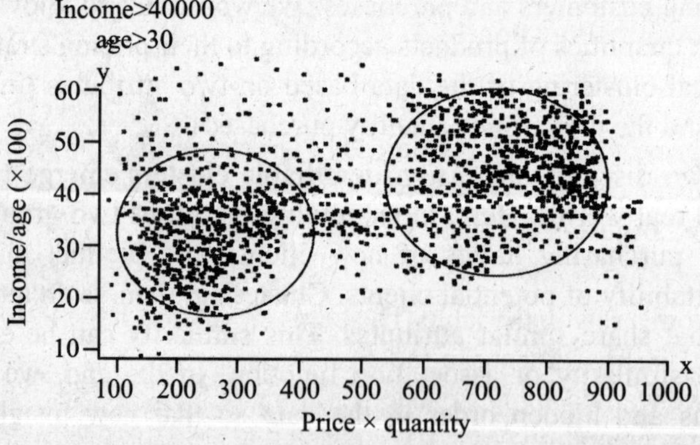

Figure 14.4: Clusters representing income versus spending habits.

14.6.1 Cluster Attributes

Clustering takes a vector of ordered values (columns in a database or spreadsheet, for example) and maps them into similar groups. Every point (x_i) in a cluster space consists of a multidimensional vector (X) containing the column or field values. Equation 14.2 shows how this is constructed.

$$X_i\ (x_{1i}, x_{2i}, x_{3i}, \ldots, x_{ni}) \tag{14.2}$$

	Attributes								
	MPG	CYL	DISP	HP	WGT	ACCL	YR	ORG	Model
Rows	18.0	8	307.0	130.0	3504.	12.0	70	1	"chevrolet chevelle malibu"
	15.0	8	350.0	165.0	3693.	11.5	70	1	"buick skylark 320"
	18.0	8	318.0	150.0	3436.	11.0	70	1	"plymouth satellite"
	16.0	8	304.0	150.0	3433.	12.0	70	1	"amc rebel sst"
	17.0	8	302.0	140.0	3449.	10.5	70	1	"ford torino"
	15.0	8	429.0	140.0	4341.	10.0	70	1	"ford galaxie 500"
	14.0	8	454.0	220.0	4354.	9.0	70	1	"chevrolet impala"
	14.0	8	440.0	215.0	4312.	8.5	70	1	"plymouth fury iii"
	14.0	8	455.0	225.0	4425.	10.0	70	1	"pontiac catalina"
	15.0	8	390.0	190.0	3850.	8.5	70	1	"amc ambassador dol"
	15.0	8	838.0	170.0	3563.	10.0	70	1	"dodge challenger se"
	14.0	8	340.0	160.0	3609.	8.0	70	1	"plymouth'cuda 340"
	15.0	8	400.0	150.0	3761.	9.5	70	1	"chevrolet monte carlo"
	14.0	8	455.0	225.0	3086.	10.0	70	1	"buick estate wagon(sw)"
	24.0	8	113.0	95.00	2372.	15.0	70	1	"toyota corona mark ii"

Vector

Figure 14.5: Components of cluster data attributes.

Correspondingly, every cluster center (C_k)—which is also a point in the cluster space—has the same organization, as shown by Equation 14.3.

$$C_k(x_{1k}, x_{2k}, x_{3k}, \ldots, x_{nk}) \tag{14.3}$$

In most cluster analyses, there may be hundreds or thousands (and sometimes millions) of points but only a few cluster centers. We can visualize the clustering operation as working on a relational database table. Figure 14.5 shows a table of automobile characteristics and their properties.

A vector is derived from a row in the table. The columns represent the vector attributes. Not all table columns, of course, will participate in the clustering operation. In the automobile database shown in Figure 14.5, if we want to apply a clustering algorithm to the cylinder (CYL), horsepower (HP), weight (WGT), and acceleration (ACCL) columns the input to the clustering process must be a set of vectors with just these attributes. It is these vectors that are used in the clustering algorithm.

14.6.2 Cluster Memberships

Membership in a cluster is determined by measuring the distance from a cluster center to a data point (see the previous section "Cluster Attributes"). Figure 14.6 shows the array of points around a cluster center with the distance metrics for several points.

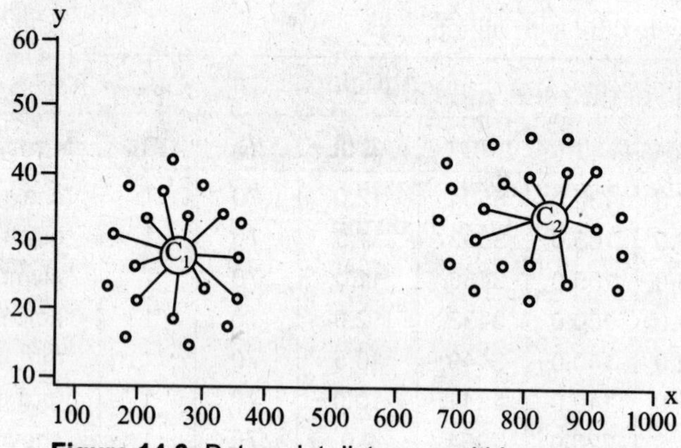

Figure 14.6: Data point distances within a cluster.

The overall process of clustering takes the distance between a point X_m and each of the clusters $C_{1...k}$ as the simple sum of the differences between X_m and C_i (any cluster center). If there are n attributes in each cluster vector, we can represent this process as Equation 14.4.

$$diff_{k \to C} = \sum_{i=1}^{n} (X(x_i) - C(x_i))^2 \tag{14.4}$$

Here,

diff is the difference (distance) between a data point and a cluster center

n is the number of attributes in a cluster

$X(x_i)$ is the i-th data point in vector X

$C(x_i)$ is the i-th data point in a cluster center (centroid)

Here, the Euclidean distance between the point and a center is calculated.

Other distance methods can be used, but the Euclidean calculation is fast and appears to work very well in a wide variety of real-world clustering applications.

More formally, perhaps, computing the distance between a point and the cluster center is done through a process called a sum of the squared difference. Equation 14.5 provides the mathematical summary of the approach.

$$d_k = \sum_{j=1}^{n} \| x_j^k - C_j^i \|^2 \tag{14.5}$$

Here,

d_k is distance of the k-th data point (where a "data point" is an individual vector of attributes, thus k will vary from 1 to M, the number of vectors being clustered)

n is the number of attributes in a cluster

X_j^k is the j-th value of the k-th data point

C_j^k is the j-th value of the i-th cluster center

A distance from X_k is calculated for each of the cluster centers ($C_1 \ldots C_i$) using the n attributes in each vector. To find the distance (dk) from point X_k to the center Ci we sum the squared difference between the j-th attribute of X_k and the j-th attribute of the i-th cluster center. From this we can see that if the X_k lies on or close to the cluster center the value will be at or near zero. On the other hand, as the distance between X_k and C_i increases the distance measure also increases rapidly. Listing 14.1 shows the code for computing a Euclidean distance between a cluster center and a data point.

```
double PE FCEucDist(
double dData[],double dCenters[],int iCentCnt,int
*ipStatus)
/*_____________________________________________________*
| Calculate the standard Euclidean distance from the |
| clusters to the data points. This is the sum of the |
| squared distances. |
*_____________________________________________________*/
{
int i;
double dSum;
*ipStatus=0;
dSum=0;
for(i=0;i<iCentCnt;i++)
dSum+=pow(dData[i]-dCenters[i],2);
return(dSum);
}
```

Listing 14.1: A Euclidean distance metric.

The distance represents the sum of the squared difference between each attribute of the data point vector (X_i) and the corresponding attributes of the cluster center (C_j).

We can now see that Figure 14.7 is a simplification. In actual clustering analysis, each point is measured from all cluster centers.

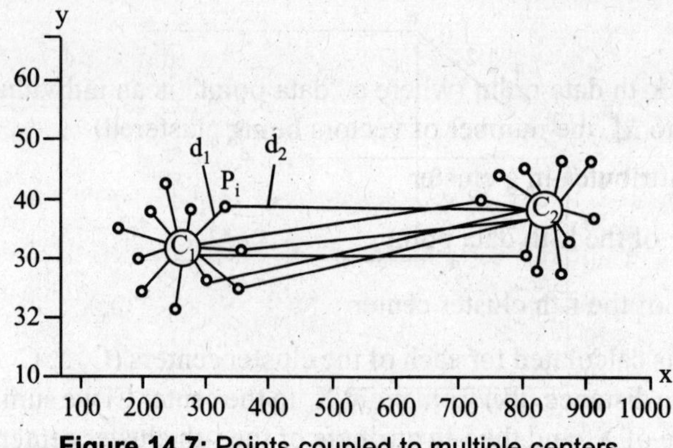

Figure 14.7: Points coupled to multiple centers.

The data points nearer one center than another move the point into that cluster. Figure 14.7 illustrates how a point (X_i indicated by point P_i) has a distance measurement to center C_1 (the d_1 distance) and center C_2 (the d_2 distance). Thus, the clustering technique computes a distance metric for each point to each cluster center. We then simply assign the point to the cluster center that has the smallest distance value (that is, of course, to the nearest cluster). This becomes the initial assignment of points to clusters. Figure 14.8 schematically illustrates how a cluster is identified by its center value.

Thus, in this example, the clusters are defined by two centers C_1 and C_2. Center C_1 is located at (30,250) and center C_2 is located at (38,875). Each point in the data is assigned a membership in one of these clusters. For crisp clustering, the membership is either [1] or [0] and a data point belongs unambiguously to one and only one cluster. For fuzzy clustering, the membership is in the interval [0,1] and a data point can belong to multiple clusters with varying degrees of membership.

14.6.3 Higher-dimensional Clustering

Although the majority of examples in this chapter deal with 2D clusters (for the sake of clarity and comprehension), real-world clusters are often spread out across many dimensions. Figure 14.9 illustrates a set of clusters arrayed in three dimensions.

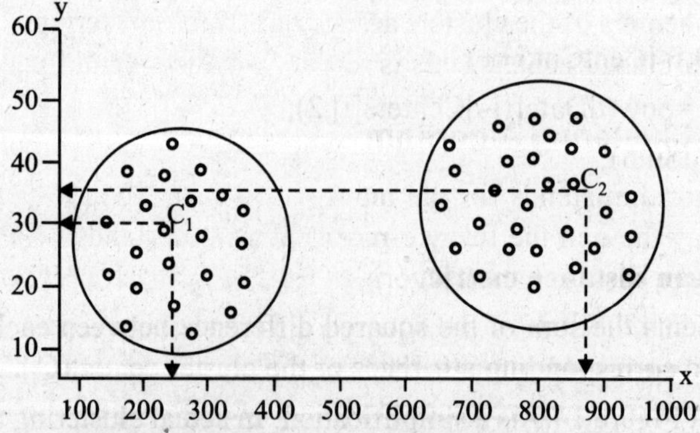

Figure 14.8: Clusters and cluster centers.

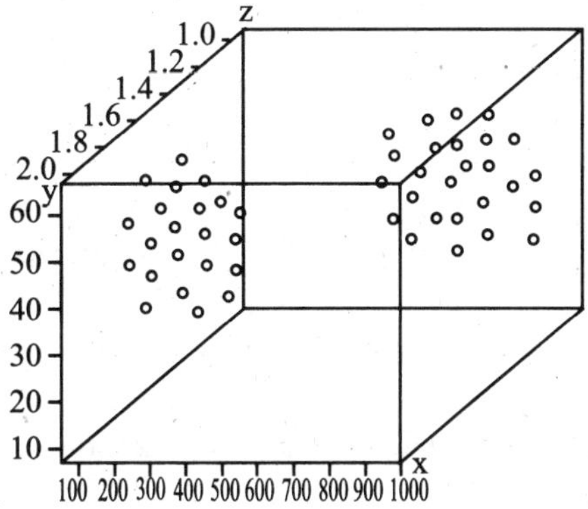

Figure 14.9: A 3D cluster space.

In the case of 3D clusters (as in Figure 14.9), each cluster center is defined by three values (the X, Y, and Z axes). Thus, for any n-dimensional cluster space the centers of the cluster (C_i) are defined by values along the axis of each dimension (d_k) as follows.

$$C_i(d_1, d_2, \ldots, d_n) \tag{14.6}$$

Both 2D and 3D clusters are generally easy to visualize, allowing us to check that our sense of an appropriate cluster center matches the center generated by the computer. Above three dimensions, however, this visualization is not usually possible. Although there are some mathematical techniques for evaluating the quality of a cluster set, we must quite often apply both a reductionist approach to cluster verification and some common sense. Reduction analysis simply consists of analyzing the clusters by slicing across two or three dimensions and evaluating the degree to which these clusters are reasonable.

14.7 CRISP CLUSTERING TECHNIQUES

Traditional clustering techniques attempt to segment data by grouping related attributes in uniquely defined clusters. Each data point in the sample space is assigned to only one cluster. And, as long as the data can be partitioned in this manner, crisp clustering approaches, such as the k-means algorithm, will perform satisfactorily. In partitioning the data, it is important to remember that none of the data points is moved. Only the centers of the clusters are moved. Thus, clustering is an iterative process of finding better and better cluster centers (this is true for both crisp and fuzzy clustering).

14.7.1 The K-means Clustering Algorithm

The k in the k-means algorithm stands for the number of cluster seeds initially provided to the algorithm (in the same way the c in the fuzzy c-means algorithm stands for the initial number of cluster centers). The crisp (or hard) k-means algorithm itself is fairly straightforward, involving the basic parameters outlined in Table 14.1.

The goal of the hard k-means algorithm is the assignment of each data point into one and only one cluster. The cluster centers are moved according to a nearness or similarity function defining the distance from a cluster center to the data point.

Table 14.1: Basic Parameters of the k-means algorithm	
x_i	A vector of training data where i = 1, 2 , ..., n. These are the cluster attributes selected form the source data element (such as columns in a database table).
k	The number of fuzzy clusters specified as part of the algorithm.
c_j	The center (or centroid) of a crisp cluster (j = 1, 2, ..., k). This value is repeatedly calculated by the algorithm.
s_j	A cluster in the sample space. This is a set of points associates with the cluster whose center is at c_j.
$\delta_{sj}(\ )$	The characteristic function of set s_j. Note that the characteristic function of a set A is as follows: $$\delta(\text{"}x_i\hat{I}\ A) = \begin{Bmatrix} 1 & x \in A \\ 0 & x \notin A \end{Bmatrix}$$ In other words, the function is one for all point of the set, but zero for points outside the set.

There are two fundamental equations used to manage the partitioning of data points. Equation 14.8 establishes the set membership for clusters.

$$S_j^{(t)} = \left\{ x_i \left\| x_i - c_j^{(t)} \right\| < \left\| x_i - c_k^{(t)} \right\|, j \neq k \right\} \tag{14.8}$$

Here,

$S_j^{(t)}$ is the set membership in the j-th cluster center under development. t is the current iteration cycle value. The value of t will vary from 1 to P, the maximum number of iterations used to define the final clusters.

x_i is the i-th data point.

c_j is the center of the j-th cluster.

c_k is the center of the k-th cluster.

That is, in iteration time (t) a point xi belongs to cluster S_j if its distance to the center of cluster S_j (indicated by c_j) is smaller than the distance to the k-th cluster center (for S_k). We skip over the current cluster center (we do not compare the distance to ourselves!). The distance ($\|\cdot\|$) is generally calculated using a Euclidean metric, but this could, of course,

be calculated via any standard distance method.

The cluster centers are initially seeded, usually with a random configuration drawn from the domains (ranges) of the attributes (for other approaches, see the section "Initial Clusters and Cluster Seeds").

The centers are then updated during each cycle (t) using Equation 14.9.

$$c_j^{(t+1)} = \frac{\sum_{i=1}^{n} x_i \delta_{S_j^t}(x_i)}{\sum_{i=1}^{n} \delta_{S_j^t}(x_i)} \tag{14.9}$$

Here,

$c_j^{(t+1)}$ is the set membership in the j-th cluster center under development. t is the current iteration cycle value. The value of t will vary from 1 to P, the maximum number of iterations used to define the final clusters.

x_i is the i-th data point.

$\delta(\ )$ is the characteristic or set membership determination function.

$S_j^{(t)}$ is the set membership function form (see Equation 14.8).

Note that a data point must belong to at least one cluster; otherwise, we will have a division by zero. From these expressions we formulate a somewhat formal definition of the k-means algorithm.

Initialize k=Number of Clusters,

Initialize c_j (cluster centers)

Set cycle variable t=1

Repeat:

For i = 1 to n: Distribute sample points (x_i) into the K clusters

For j = 1 to k: Resolve $S_j^{(t)}$ for x_i applying (14.8)

For j = 1 to k: Compute new cluster centers $c_j^{(t+1)}$ applying (14.9)

t = t+1

Until c_j estimates stabilize

The algorithm itself is fairly simple: cluster centers are randomly initialized and we assign data points (x_i) into clusters (S_j ; j = 1 to k) by resolving Equation 14.8. This beginning state is illustrated in Figure 14.10. The dashed line represents the initial assignment of points into cluster centers C_1 and C_2.

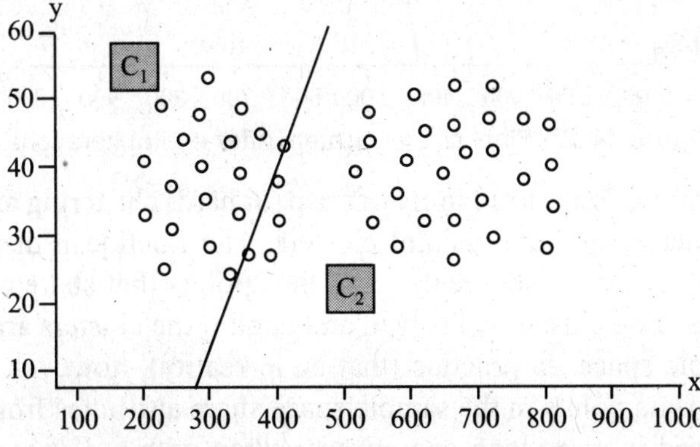

Figure 14.10: Initial k-means partitions.

When all data points have been assigned to clusters, new cluster centers (centroids) are calculated using Equation 14.10. As we can see in Figure 14.11, the cluster center calculation causes the previous centroid location to move toward the center of the cluster sets. This also changes the partitioning of the sample space.

The process of calculating cluster memberships and recalculating cluster centers continues until the cluster centers no longer change from one cycle to the next (or the change is so small that it falls below some threshold value). Thus, as Figure 14.12 illustrates, the shift in the cluster centers becomes smaller and smaller until it settles on the final value.

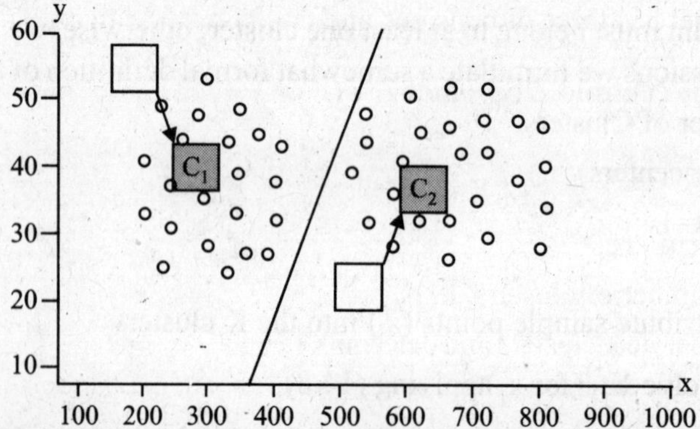

Figure 14.11: Cluster centers repositioned after iteration.

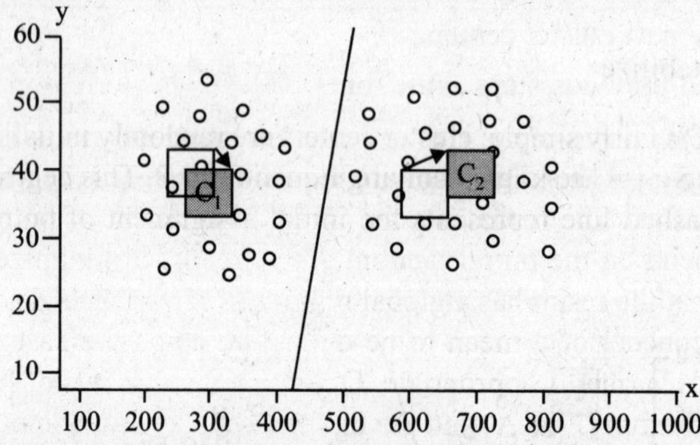

Figure 14.12: Final cluster centers after end of iterations.

The k-means algorithm belongs to a family of crisp (or hard) clustering techniques that uniquely partitions the sample data points into disjoint clusters. The Euclidean distance metric measures how far away a point is from a cluster center, and thus points that share common attributes will naturally cohere into the same cluster. All is well and good if the clusters are distinctly arranged in the n-dimensional sample space. In practice (that is, in reality), however, cluster perimeters are often quite ambiguous. Data points in the sample space share attributes from one or more clusters and should thus be placed in more than one cluster (albeit with a degree of membership in one cluster that is higher or lower than the degree of membership in another). This brings us to the focus of the chapter: fuzzy clustering and classification.

Concept Clustering

Another variation of the agglomerative clustering approach is conceptual clustering.

Partitional Clustering

K-means And Derivatives: K-means Clustering

The k-means algorithm assigns each point to the cluster whose center (also called centroid) is nearest. The center is the average of all the points in the cluster — that is, its coordinates are the arithmetic mean for each dimension separately over all the points in the cluster.

Example: The data set has three dimensions and the cluster has two points: $X = (x_1, x_2, x_3)$ and $Y = (y_1, y_2, y_3)$. Then the centroid Z becomes $Z = (z_1, z_2, z_3)$, where $z_1 = \frac{x_1 + y_1}{2}$, $z_2 = \frac{x_2 + y_2}{2}$ and $z_3 = \frac{x_3 + y_3}{2}$.

The algorithm steps are:

- Choose the number of clusters, k.
- Randomly generate k clusters and determine the cluster centers, or directly generate k random points as cluster centers.
- Assign each point to the nearest cluster center, where "nearest" is defined with respect to one of the distance measures discussed above.
- Recompute the new cluster centers.
- Repeat the two previous steps until some convergence criterion is met (usually that the assignment hasn't changed).

The main advantages of this algorithm are its simplicity and speed which allows it to run on large datasets. Its disadvantage is that it does not yield the same result with each run, since the resulting clusters depend on the initial random assignments. It minimizes intra-cluster variance, but does not ensure that the result has a global minimum of variance. Another disadvantage is the requirement for the concept of a mean to be definable which the case is not always. For such datasets the k-medoids variant is appropriate. Other popular variants of K-means include the Fast Genetic K-means Algorithm (FGKA) and the Incremental Genetic K-means Algorithm (IGKA).

14.8 FUZZY CLUSTERING CONCEPTS

A cluster brings together instances in the data that share a common set of attributes. For each of these clusters a central value representative of the cluster's principal value is calculated. This is the center of gravity (or centroid) of the cluster. An array of these centroids for a collection of data elements from a database provides the cluster centers, thus telling us which set of rows in the database are closely related.

In the simplest manifestation, clusters are groups of related data elements. These groups are defined through a set of attributes. For example, Figure 14.13 illustrates a clustering of data points for the attributes (X, Y). In this example, there are two well-defined clusters. We can visually pick out the clusters and there are no significant outliers (points well outside either cluster) or points that might belong ambiguously to one or more clusters. The goal of cluster analysis is the recognition and quantification of these groupings. This quantification involves two processes: identifying the membership of a data point in some group and locating the center of the cluster (the centroid). Establishing cluster centers is an iterative process (described in detail later in the chapter).

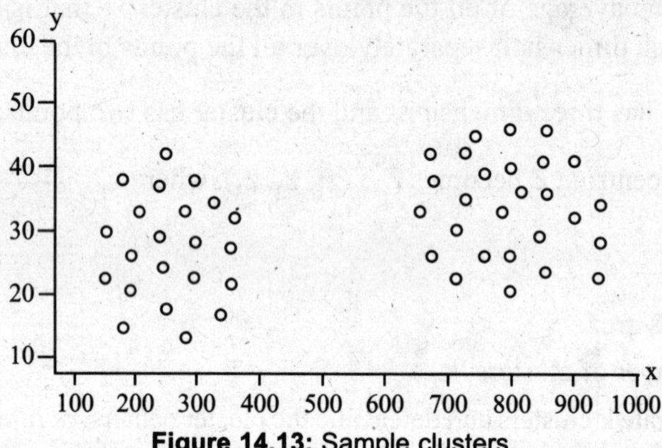

Figure 14.13: Sample clusters.

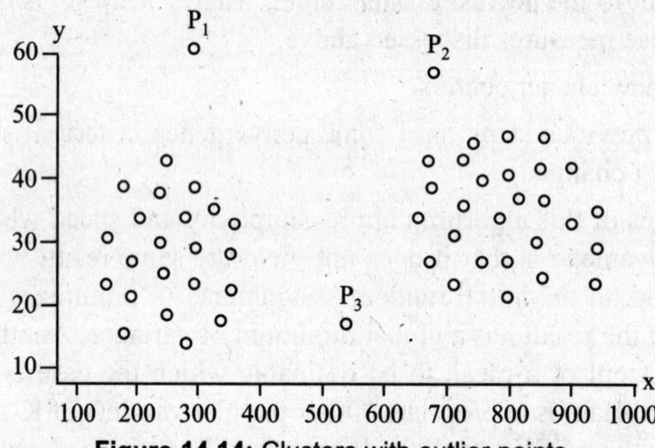

Figure 14.14: Clusters with outlier points.

Even in situations in which clearly defined clusters exist, the data is seldom neatly packaged in well-defined groups. As Figure 14.14 shows, there will often be points (such as P_1, P_2, and P_3) lying well outside the perimeter of any cluster.

These apparently extraneous data points, clearly belonging to neither of the clusters, are called outliers. Many crisp clustering techniques have difficulties handling extreme outliers, whereas fuzzy clustering algorithms tend to give them either very small or a higher than warranted membership degree in surrounding clusters (this latter effect is common in the fuzzy c-means algorithm, which we will discuss in some detail).

Real-world data is almost never arranged in such clear-cut groups as we see in Figure 14.13. Instead, clusters have ill-defined boundaries that smear into the data space, often overlapping the perimeters of surrounding groups. If we move our two clusters toward each other, Figure 14.15 illustrates this problem.

The grey area in Figure 14.14 shows the set of points that could conceivably belong to either of the two clusters. In conventional crisp techniques (such as the standard k-means clustering approach), the methodology is forced to make a difficult decision about which cluster "owns" a point.

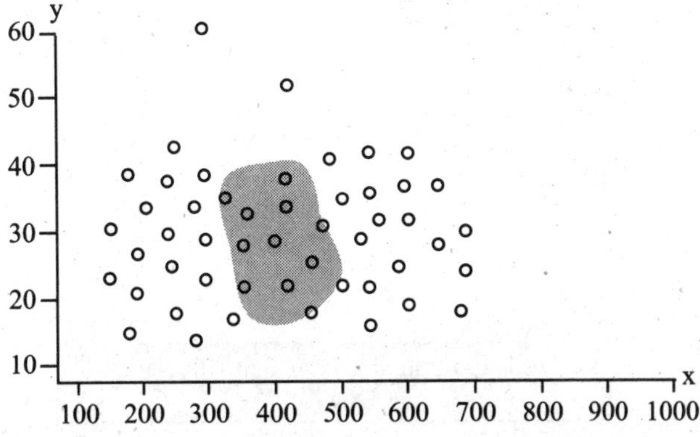

Figure 14.15: Ambiguous data points in two clusters.

In a fuzzy clustering approach, however, points are given partial degrees of membership in multiple nearby clusters. Figure 14.16 shows how a set of points, in the overlap area of the two cluster perimeters, 2 are partly in one set and partly in another.

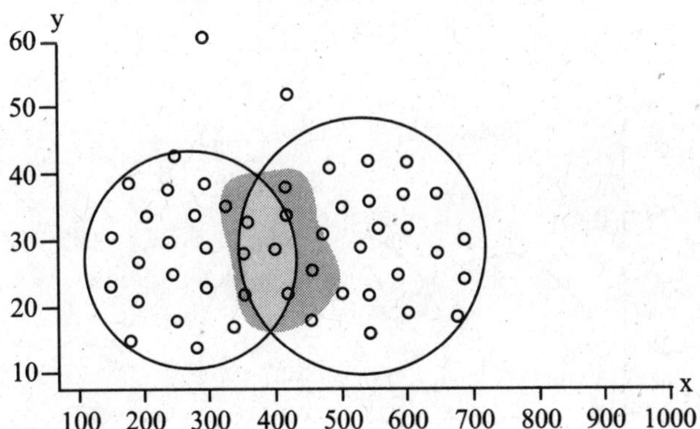

Figure 14.16: Common points in two neighbouring clusters.

Running a fuzzy clustering process on these data points using the fuzzy c-means algorithm, we can see the cluster centers as they are actually produced, as well as the membership values for each of the points. Figure 14.17 is a screen image from the Fuzzy Data Explorer showing the cluster centers and the points.

There are two cluster centers (C_1 and C_2) indicated by the squares in Figure 14.17. Table 14.2 outlines the calculated cluster centers at specific points.

A central theme in fuzzy clustering is the often nonunique partitioning of the data in a collection of clusters. Data points, specified as loci in the multidimensional decision space, are assigned membership values for each of the clusters. In some cases, this membership may be zero, but often the membership shows the degree to which the data point is considered representative of the cluster. Figure 14.18 shows the membership assignments for some data points in the overlap between two clusters (see also Figure 14.16).

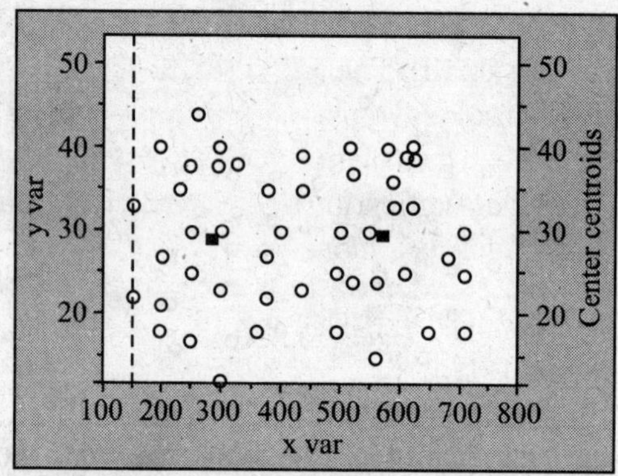

Figure 14.17: Output from fuzzy clustering.

Table 14.2: Fuzzy C-means cluster centres

Center	YVAR	XVAR
C_1	28.988	286.610
C_2	29.592	571.226

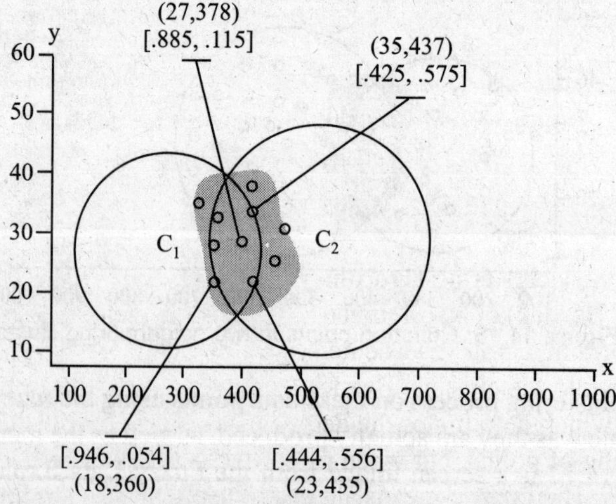

Figure 14.18: Points with partial degrees of membership.

As Figure 14.18: illustrates, a fuzzy clustering provides a flexible and robust method of assigning data points into clusters. Each data point will have an associated degree of membership for each cluster center in the range [0,1], indicating the strength of its placement in that cluster.

This becomes particularly important for those data points on the border between clusters. We can imagine the diameter of a cluster space as the base of a bell-shaped fuzzy set. The membership curve defines the degree to which a point is in the cluster. Figure 14.19 illustrates this relationship.

Thus, at the center of the cluster we are also at the apex of the member of-cluster fuzzy set, with data points in the region having a membership at or near [1.0]. As you move left or right away from the center, the degree of membership for data points drops toward zero (the tails of the curve never reach zero but become increasingly small). The tails of the fuzzy regions for neighbouring clusters overlap so that data points can be in several clusters simultaneously, affording us an opportunity to observe the actual relationship between data elements. Thus, unlike ordinary crisp cluster techniques we are not forced to make arbitrary classification decisions along cluster boundaries. The softness of the fuzzy clustering technique gives us a more realistic approach to data analysis.

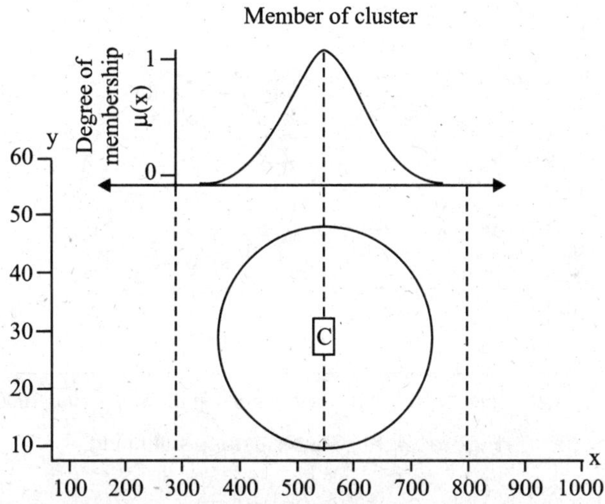

Figure 14.19: Fuzzy cluster membership mapping.

14.9 FUZZY C-MEANS CLUSTERING

The most well-known fuzzy clustering algorithm is fuzzy c-means, a modification by Jim Bezdek (see "Further Reading," Bezdek) of an original crisp clustering methodology. This initial approach, the hard ISODATA algorithm, employed a center of means technique, but provided a hard (or crisp) partitioning of elements into the clusters. Bezdek introduced the idea of a fuzzification parameter (m) in the range [1, n], which determines the degree of fuzziness in the clusters. When $m = 1$, the effect is a crisp clustering of points, but when $m > 1$ the degree of fuzziness among points in the decision space increases. The fuzzy c-means algorithm itself is fairly straightforward and involves the basic parameters outlined in Table 14.3. Essentially, the parameter m controls the permeability of the cluster horizon, which can be viewed as an n-dimensional cloud moving out from a cluster center. Figure 14.20 illustrates clustering when m = 1.

Table 14.3: Basic parameters of the fuzzy c-means algorithm	
x	A vector of training data where i = 1, 2 ,..., n. These are the cluster attributes selected form the source data element (such as columns in a database table).
d_{ij}	The distance of the i-th data point from; the j-th cluster center. Although we use the Euclidean distance, the choice of other distance metrics can ne easily incorporated into the fuzzy c-means algorithm.
p	The number of fuzzy clusters specified as part of the algorithm.
m	A fuzzification parameter in the range [>1, <w], including the width of the n-dimensional cluster parameter. The larger the number the more fuzzy the point assignmenty into each cluster. Normally m is the range [1.25, 2] inclusive.
q	The center (or centroid) of a fuzzy cluster (j = 1, 2, ..., p). This value is repeatedly calculated by the algorithm.
$\mu_j(x_i)$	A fuzzy membership qualification indicating the membership of sample x_j to the j-the cluster.

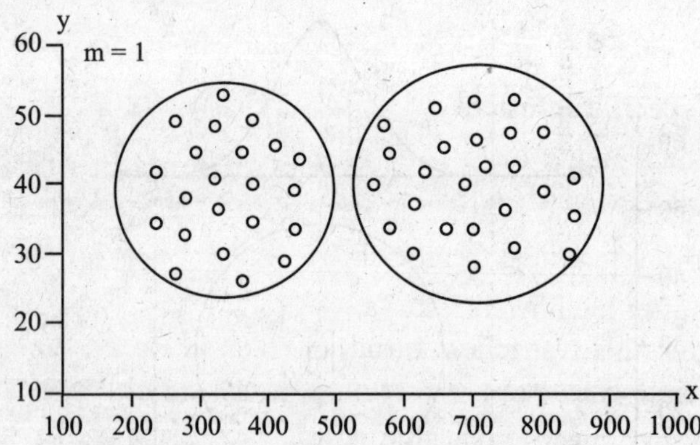

Figure 14.20: Crisp cluster partitioning.

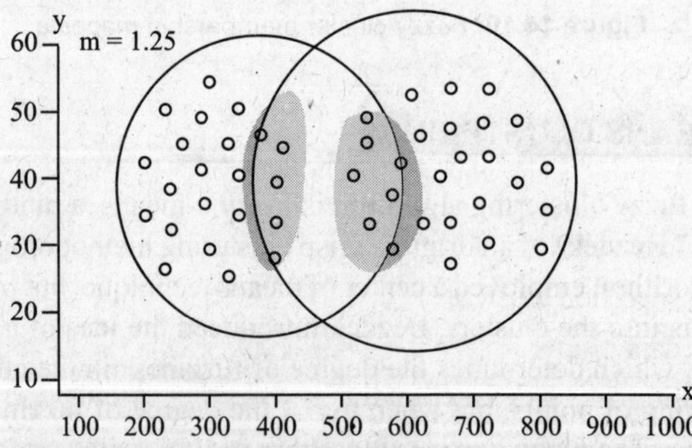

Figure 14.21 Overlapping clusters.

When m = 1, the clouds do not overlap, but as you increase the value of m (say, m = 1.25) the clouds begin to overlap and share many of the same points. Figure 14.21 illustrates a rough approximation of how two clusters overlap when the fuzzification parameter is increased. The fuzzy c-means algorithm uses a fixed number of cluster centers, indicated by the parameter (p). The algorithm, however, does not determine the number of clusters; this parameter (p), as well as the fuzzification parameter (m), must be supplied as an external constraint on the algorithm behavior. Before discussing the actual behavior of fuzzy c-means, we need to examine the algorithm itself and review some of its strengths and limitations.

14.9.1 The Fuzzy C-means Algorithm

Fuzzy C-means clustering involves two processes: the calculation of cluster centers and the assignment of points to these centers using a form of Euclidean distance. This process is repeated until the cluster centers have stabilized. Fuzzy c-means imposes a direct constraint on the fuzzy membership function associated with each point, as follows.

$$\sum_{j=1}^{P} \mu_j(x_i) = 1; \; i = 1, \; 2, \; 3, \ldots, k \tag{14.11}$$

Here,

p is the number of specified clusters

k is the number of data points

x_i is the i-th data point

$\mu_j()$ is a function that returns the membership of x_i in the j-th cluster

That is, the total cluster memberships for a point in the sample or decision space must add to [1]. As we will see later, this restriction introduces a major weakness into the algorithm when handling outliers or remote clusters.

The goal of the fuzzy c-means algorithm is the assignment of data points into clusters with varying degrees of membership. This membership reflects the degree to which the point is more representative of one cluster than another (or all the others). In effect, we are attempting to minimize a standard loss function, expressed simply as

$$1 = \sum_{k=1}^{P} \sum_{i=1}^{n} [\mu_k(x_i)]^m \|x_i - c_k\|^2, \tag{14.12}$$

where:

l is the minimized loss value

p is the number of specified clusters

n is the number of data points

$\mu_k()$ is (as in Equation 14.11) a function that returns the membership of x_i in the k-th cluster

x_i is the i-th data point m is the fuzzification parameter c_k is the center of the k-th cluster

From this we can derive the two fundamental equations necessary to implement the fuzzy c-means clustering algorithm. Equation 14.13 is used to calculate a new cluster center value.

$$C_j = \frac{\sum_i [\mu_j(x_i)]^m x_i}{\sum_i [\mu_j(x_i)]^m} \tag{14.13}$$

Here,

c_j is the center of the j-th cluster

$\mu_j()$ is (as in Equation 14.12) a function that returns the membership of xi in the j-th cluster

x_i is the i-th data point

m is the fuzzification parameter

You will note that this is simply a special form of weighted average. We modify the degree of fuzziness in x_i's current membership and multiply this by x_i. We then divide by the sum of the fuzzified membership.

14.9.2 The Behaviour of Fuzzy C-means

The fuzzy c-means approach to clustering suffers from several interrelated constraints that affect its overall performance. The chief behaviour shortcoming is the restriction that the sum of the cluster memberships

for a sample data point must equal. This is, in effect, a probabilistic approach to fuzzy clustering, relating the membership in each cluster as a fraction of the total possible membership in any of the clusters. One evident behavior from this approach is the assignment of membership values to outlier data points. The fuzzy c-means algorithm often assigns high degrees of membership to these atypical outlier points. Figure 14.22 illustrates this problem.

There are two cluster centers (C_1 and C_2) indicated by the squares in Figure 14.22. Table 14.4 outlines the calculated cluster centers at specific points.

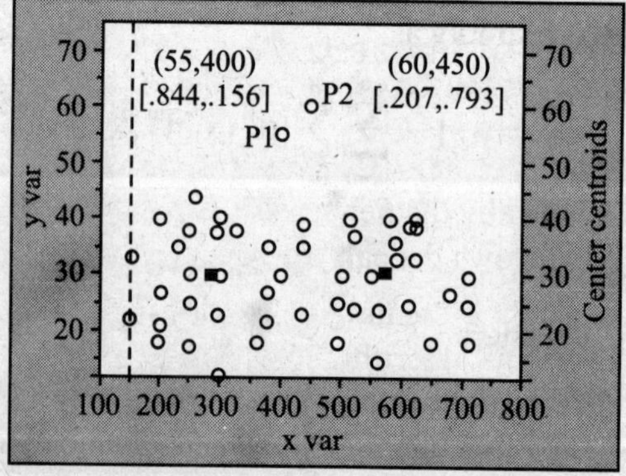

Figure 14.22: Outlier points with high membership values.

Table 14.4: Fuzzy C-means cluster centres

Center	YVAR	XVAR
C_1	29.589	276.723
C_2	31.137	561.048

Although the two outlier points (P_1 and P_2) are obviously outside either cluster, they have considerably high membership degrees in both clusters than is warranted by their locations in the sample space. Point P_1, for example, has $\mu[.844]$ in cluster center C_1 and point P_2 has $\mu[.793]$ in cluster center C_2. This results from the cluster optimization constraint in Equation 14.11.

A further related outcome behaviour is tied to the constraint imposed by Equation 14.11 – the membership of a data point in the sample space depends directly on the membership values associated with all other clusters. This means that the point assignment membership is transitively dependent on specifying the correct number of clusters. Figure 14.23 illustrates this problem by introducing a third cluster just above and between the two existing clusters.

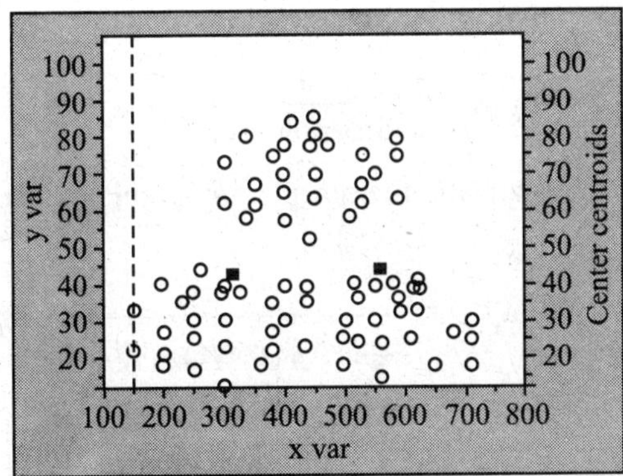

Figure 14.23: Clustering with inaccurate cluster count.

Table 14.5: Fuzzy C-means cluster centres

Center	YVAR	XVAR
C_1	42.884	314.147
C_2	43.780	557.391

Here we see that the two clusters centers (C_1 and C_2), indicated by the squares in Figure 14.22, have been pulled upward, influenced by the new cluster points (which have been assigned as part of clusters C_1 and C_2). Table 14.5 shows the calculated cluster centers at specific points.

Another behaviour problem, albeit common to most ordinary clustering techniques, is the spherical nature of the fuzzy c-means algorithm. The radius of the cluster sweeps out from the center at a constant distance. This approach means that the fuzzy c-means cannot directly model clusters that have ellipsoidal or arbitrarily irregular shapes. In general, this makes fuzzy c-means inappropriate for pattern recognition of images but does not generally impede its utility as a clustering mechanism for multidimensional data.

Fuzzy C-means clustering

In fuzzy clustering, each point has a degree of belonging to clusters, as in fuzzy logic, rather than belonging completely to just one cluster. Thus, points on the edge of a cluster, may be *in the cluster* to a lesser degree than points in the center of cluster. For each point x we have a coefficient giving the degree of being in the kth cluster $u_k(x)$. Usually, the sum of those coefficients for any given x is defined to be 1:

$$\forall x \left(\sum_{k=1}^{\text{num.clusters}} u_k(x) = 1 \right).$$

With fuzzy c-means, the centroid of a cluster is the mean of all points, weighted by their degree of belonging to the cluster:

$$\text{center}_k = \frac{\sum_x u_k(x)^m x}{\sum_x u_k(x)^m}$$

The degree of belonging is related to the inverse of the distance to the cluster center:

$$u_k(x) = \frac{1}{d(\text{center}_k, x)}$$

then the coefficients are normalized and fuzzyfied with a real parameter $m > 1$ so that their sum is 1. So

$$u_k(x) = \frac{1}{\sum_j \left(\frac{d(\text{center}_k, x)}{d(\text{center}_j, x)} \right)^{2/(m-1)}}$$

For m equal to 2, this is equivalent to normalising the coefficient linearly to make their sum 1. When m is close to 1, then cluster center closest to the point is given much more weight than the others, and the algorithm is similar to k-means.

The fuzzy c-means algorithm is very similar to the k-means algorithm:

- Choose a number of clusters.
- Assign randomly to each point coefficients for being in the clusters.
- Repeat until the algorithm has converged (that is, the coefficients' change between two iterations is no more than ε, the given sensitivity threshold):
  - Compute the centroid for each cluster, using the formula above.
  - For each point, compute its coefficients of being in the clusters, using the formula above.

The algorithm minimizes intra-cluster variance as well, but has the same problems as k-means; the minimum is a local minimum, and the results depend on the initial choice of weights. The expectation-maximization algorithm is a more statistically formalized method which includes some of these ideas: partial membership in classes. It has better convergence properties and is in general preferred to fuzzy-c-means.

QT clustering algorithm

QT (quality threshold) clustering is an alternative method of partitioning data, invented for gene clustering. It requires more computing power than k-means, but does not require specifying the number of clusters *a priori*, and always returns the same result when run several times.

The algorithm is:

- The user chooses a maximum diameter for clusters.
- Build a candidate cluster for each point by iteratively including the point that is closest to the group, until the diameter of the cluster surpasses the threshold.
- Save the candidate cluster with the most points as the first true cluster, and remove all points in the cluster from further consideration. Must clarify what happens if more than 1 cluster has the maximum number of points ?
- Recurse with the reduced set of points.

The distance between a point and a group of points is computed using complete linkage, i.e. as the maximum distance from the point to any member of the group (see the "Agglomerative hierarchical clustering" section about distance between clusters).

Locality-sensitive hashing

Locality-sensitive hashing can be used for clustering. Feature space vectors are sets, and the metric used is the Jaccard distance. The feature space can be considered high-dimensional. The *min-wise independent permutations* LSH scheme (sometimes MinHash) is then used to put similar items into buckets. With just one set of hashing methods, there are only clusters of very similar elements. By seeding the hash functions several times (e.g. 20), it is possible to get bigger clusters.

Graph-theoretic methods

Formal concept analysis is a technique for generating clusters(called formal concepts) of objects and attributes, given a bipartite graph representing the relation between the objects and attributes. This technique was introduced by Rudolf Wille in 1984. Other methods for generating *overlapping clusters* (a cover rather than a partition) are discussed by Jardine and Sibson (1968) and Cole and Wishart (1970).

Spectral clustering

Given a set of data points A, the similarity matrix may be defined as a matrix S where S_{ij} represents a measure of the similarity between points i, j ε A. Spectral clustering techniques make use of the spectrum of the similarity matrix of the data to perform dimensionality reduction for clustering in fewer dimensions.

One such technique is the *Normalized Cuts algorithm* by Shi-Malik, commonly used for image segmentation. It partitions points into two sets (S_1, S_2) based on the eigenvector v corresponding to the second-smallest eigenvalue of the Laplacian matrix

$$L = I - D^{-1/2} S D^{-1/2}$$

of S, where D is the diagonal matrix

$$D_{ii} = \sum_j S_{ij}.$$

This partitioning may be done in various ways, such as by taking the median m of the components in v, and placing all points whose component in v is greater than m in S_1, and the rest in S_2. The algorithm can be used for hierarchical clustering by repeatedly partitioning the subsets in this fashion.

A related algorithm is the *Meila-Shi algorithm*, which takes the eigenvectors corresponding to the k largest eigenvalues of the matrix $P = SD^{-1}$ for some k, and then invokes another (e.g. k-means) to cluster points by their respective k components in these eigenvectors.

14.10 TYPES OF CLUSTERING

Hierarchical algorithms find successive clusters using previously established clusters. These algorithms usually are either agglomerative ("bottom-up") or divisive ("top-down"). Agglomerative algorithms begin with each element as a separate cluster and merge them into successively larger clusters. Divisive algorithms begin with the whole set and proceed to divide it into successively smaller clusters.

Partitional algorithms typically determine all clusters at once, but can also be used as divisive algorithms in the hierarchical clustering.

Density-based clustering algorithms are devised to discover arbitrary-shaped clusters. In this approach, a cluster is regarded as a region in which the density of data objects exceeds a threshold. DBSCAN and OPTICS are two typical algorithms of this kind.

Subspace clustering methods look for clusters that can only be seen in a particular projection (subspace, manifold) of the data. These methods thus can ignore irrelevant attributes. The general problem is also known as Correlation clustering while the special case of axis-parallel subspaces is also known as *Two-way clustering*, *co-clustering* or biclustering: in these methods not only the objects are clustered but also the features of the objects, i.e. if the data is represented in a data matrix, the rows and columns are clustered simultaneously. They usually do not however work with arbitrary feature combinations as in general subspace methods. But this special case deserves attention due to its applications in bioinformatics.

Many clustering algorithms require the specification of the number of clusters to produce in the input data set, prior to execution of the algorithm. Barring knowledge of the proper value beforehand, the appropriate value must be determined, a problem on its own for which a number of techniques have been developed.

14.11 DISTANCE MEASURE

An important step in most clustering is to select a distance measure, which will determine how the *similarity* of two elements is calculated. This will intluence the shape of the clusters, as some elements may be close to one another according to one distance and farther away according to another. For example, in a 2-dimensional space, the distance between the point (x = 1, y = 0) and the origin (x = 0, y = 0) is always 1 according to the usual norms, but the distance between the point (x = 1, y = 1) and the origin can be 2, $\sqrt{2}$ or 1 if you take respectively the 1-norm, 2-norm or infinity-norm distance.

Common distance functions:

- The Euclidean distance (also called distance as the crow flies or 2-norm distance). A review of cluster analysis in health psychology research found that the most common distance measure in published studies in that research area is the Euclidean distance or the squared Euclidean distance.
- The Manhattan distance (aka taxicab norm or 1-norm)
- The maximum norm (aka infinity norm)
- The Mahalanobis distance corrects data for different scales and correlations in the variables
- The angle between two vectors can be used as a distance measure when clustering high dimensional data.
- The Hamming distance measures the minimum number of substitutions required to change one member into another.

Another important distinction is whether the clustering uses symmetric or asymmetric distances. Many of the distance functions listed above have the property that distances are symmetric (the distance from object A to B is the same as the distance from B to A). In other applications (e.g. sequence-alignment methods, see Prinzie & Van den Poel (2006)), this is not the case. (A true metric gives symmetric measures of distance.)

14.12 HIERARCHICAL CLUSTERING

Hierarchical clustering creates a hierarchy of clusters which may be represented in a tree structure called a *dendrogram*. The root of the tree consists of a single cluster containing all observations, and the leaves correspond to individual observations.

Algorithms for hierarchical clustering are generally either *agglomerative*, in which one starts at the leaves and successively merges clusters together; or *divisive*, in which one starts at the root and recursively splits the clusters.

Any valid metric may be used as a measure of similarity between pairs of observations. The choice of which clusters to merge or split is determined by a linkage criterion, which is a function of the pairwise distances between observations.

Cutting the tree at a given height will give a clustering at a selected precision. In the following example, cutting after the second row will yield clusters {a} {b c} {d e} {f}. Cutting after the third row will yield clusters {a} {b c} {d e f}, which is a coarser clustering, with a smaller number of larger clusters.

Agglomerative Hierarchical Clustering

For example, suppose this data is to be clustered, and the Euclidean distance is the distance metric.

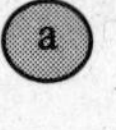

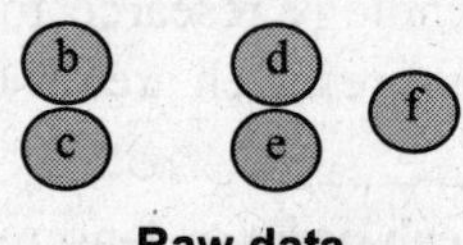

Raw data

The hierarchical clustering dendrogram would be as such:

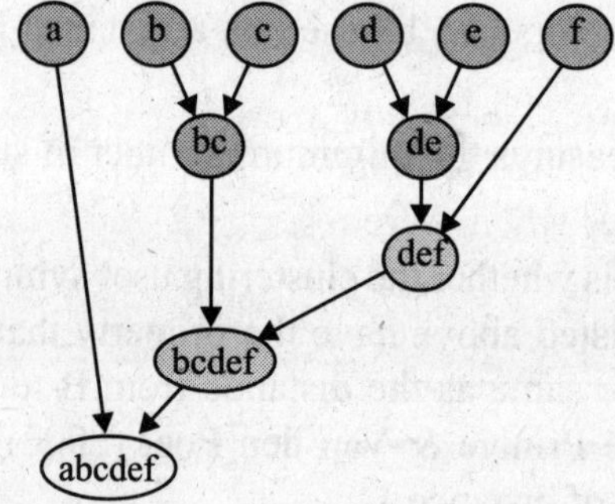

Traditional Representation

This method builds the hierarchy from the individual elements by progressively merging clusters. In our example, we have six elements {a} {b} {c} {d} {e} and {f}. The first step is to determine which elements to merge in a cluster. Usually, we want to take the two closest elements, according to the chosen distance.

Optionally, one can also construct a distance matrix at this stage, where the number in the i-th row j-th column is the distance between the i-th and j-th elements. Then, as clustering progresses, rows and columns are merged as the clusters are merged and the distances updated. This is a common way to implement this type of clustering, and has the benefit of caching distances between clusters. A simple agglomerative clustering algorithm is described in the single-linkage clustering page; it can easily be adapted to different types of linkage (see below).

Suppose we have merged the two closest elements b and c, we now have the following clusters {a}, {b, c}, {d}, {e} and {f}, and want to merge them further. To do that, we need to take the distance between {a} and {b c}, and therefore define the distance between two clusters. Usually the distance between two clusters A and B is one of the following:

- The maximum distance between elements of each cluster (also called complete linkage clustering):

$$\max\{d(x, y) : x \in A, y \in B\}.$$

- The minimum distance between elements of each cluster (also called single-linkage clustering):

$$\min\{d(x, y) : x \in A, y \in B\}.$$

- The mean distance between elements of each cluster (also called average linkage clustering, used e.g. in UPGMA):

$$\frac{1}{|A|\cdot|B|}\sum_{x \in A}\sum_{y \in B} d(x, y).$$

- The sum of all intra-cluster variance.
- The increase in variance for the cluster being merged (Ward's criterion).
- The probability that candidate clusters spawn from the same distribution function (V-linkage).

Each agglomeration occurs at a greater distance between clusters than the previous agglomeration, and one can decide to stop clustering either when the clusters are too far apart to be merged (distance criterion) or when there is a sufficiently small number of clusters (number criterion).

14.13 CLASSIFICATION

There is structure in nature. Much of this structure is known to us and is quite beautiful. Consider the natural sphericity of rain drops and bubbles; why do balloons take this shape? How about the elegant beauty of crystals, rhombic solids with rectangular, pentagonal, or hexagonal cross sections? Why do these naturally beautiful, geometric shapes exist? What causes the natural repetition of the mounds of sand dunes? Some phenomena we cannot see directly: for example, the elliptical shape of the magnetic field around the earth; or we can see only when certain atmospheric conditions exist, such as the beautiful and circular appearance of a rainbow or the repetitive patterns of the aurora borealis in the night sky near the North Pole. Some patterns, such as the helical appearance of DNA or the cylindrical shape of some bacteria, have only appeared to us since the advent of extremely powerful electron microscopes. Consider the geometry and colorful patterns of a butterfly's wings; why do these patterns exist in our physical world? The answers to some of these questions are still unknown; many others have been discovered through increased understanding of physics, chemistry, and biology.

Just as there is structure in nature, we believe there is an underlying structure in most of the phenomena we wish to understand. Examples abound in image recognition, molecular biology applications such as protein folding and 3D molecular structure, oil exploration, cancer detection, and many others. For fields dealing with diagnosis we often seek to find structure in the data obtained from observation. Our observations can be visual, audio, or any of a variety of sensor-based electronic or optical signals. Finding the structure in data is the essence of classification. As the quotation at the beginning of this chapter suggests, our experimental observations lead us to develop relationships between the inputs and outputs of an experiment. As we are able to conduct more experiments we see the relationships forming some recognizable, or classifiable, structure. By finding structure, we are classifying the data according to similar patterns, attributes, features, and other characteristics. The general area is known as classification.

In classification, also termed clustering, the most important issue is deciding what criteria to classify against. For example, suppose we want to classify people. In describing people we will look at their height, weight, gender, religion, education, appearance, and so on. Many of these features are numerical quantities such as height and weight; other features are simply linguistic descriptors and these can be quite non-numeric. We can easily classify people according to gender, or one feature. For this classification the criterion is simple: female or male. We might want to classify people into three size categories: small, medium, and large. For this classification we might only need two of the features describing people: height and weight. Here, the classification criterion might be some algebraic combination of height and weight. Suppose we want to classify people according to whether we would want them as neighbors. Here the number of features to be used in the classification is not at all clear, and we might also have trouble developing a criterion for this classification. Nevertheless, a criterion for classification must be prepared before we can segregate the data into definable classes. As is often the case in classification studies, the number and kind of features and the type of classification criteria are choices that are continually changed as the data are manipulated; and this iteration continues until we think we have a grouping of the data that seems plausible from a structural and physical perspective.

This chapter summarizes only two popular methods of classification. The first is classification using equivalent relations. This approach makes use of certain special properties of equivalent relations and the concept of defuzzification known as lambda-cuts on the relations. The second method of classification is a very popular method known as fuzzy c-means, so named because of its close analog in the crisp world, hard c-means. This method uses concepts in n-dimensional Euclidean space to determine the geometric closeness of data points by assigning them to various clusters or classes and then determining the distance between the clusters.

14.13.1 Statistical Cassification

Statistical classification is a supervised machine learning procedure in which individual items are placed into groups based on quantitative information on one or more characteristics inherent in the items (referred to as traits, variables, characters, etc) and based on a training set of previously labeled items.

Note: in community ecology, the term "classification" is synonymous with what is commonly known (in machine learning) as clustering. See that article for more information about purely unsupervised techniques.

14.14 CLASSIFICATION BY EQUIVALENCE RELATIONS

14.14.1 Crisp Relations

Define a set, $[x_i] = \{x_j \mid (x_i, x_j) \varepsilon R\}$, as the equivalent class of x_i on a universe of data points, X. This class is contained in a special relation, R, known as an equivalence relation (see Chapter 3). This class is a set of all elements related to x_i that have the following properties [Bezdek, 1974]:

1. $x_i \varepsilon [x_i]$ therefore $(x_i, x_i) \varepsilon R$
2. $[x_i \neq [x_j] \Rightarrow [x_i] \cap [x_j] = \theta$
3. $\cup_{x \varepsilon X} [x] = X$

The first property is that of reflexivity (see Chapter 3), the second property indicates that equivalent classes do not overlap, and the third property simply expresses that the union of all equivalent classes exhausts the universe. Hence, the equivalence relation R can divide the universe X into mutually exclusive equivalent classes, i.e.

$$X \mid R = \{[x] \mid x \varepsilon X\} \tag{14.14}$$

where X|R is called the quotient set. The quotient set of X relative to R, denoted X|R, is the set whose elements are the equivalence classes of X under the equivalence relation R. The cardinality of X|R (i.e. the number of distinct equivalence classes of X under R) is called the rank of the matrix R.

Example 14.1: Define a universe of integers X = {1, 2, 3, ... , 10} and define R as the crisp relation for "the identical remainder after dividing each element of the universe by 3." We have

$$R = \begin{array}{c} \\ 1 \\ 2 \\ 3 \\ 4 \\ 5 \\ 6 \\ 7 \\ 8 \\ 9 \\ 10 \end{array} \begin{array}{c} \begin{array}{cccccccccc} 1 & 2 & 3 & 4 & 5 & 6 & 7 & 8 & 9 & 10 \end{array} \\ \begin{bmatrix} 1 & 0 & 0 & 1 & 0 & 0 & 1 & 0 & 0 & 1 \\ 0 & 1 & 0 & 0 & 1 & 0 & 0 & 1 & 0 & 0 \\ 0 & 0 & 1 & 0 & 0 & 1 & 0 & 0 & 1 & 0 \\ 1 & 0 & 0 & 1 & 0 & 0 & 1 & 0 & 0 & 1 \\ 0 & 1 & 0 & 0 & 1 & 0 & 0 & 1 & 0 & 0 \\ 0 & 0 & 1 & 0 & 0 & 1 & 0 & 0 & 1 & 0 \\ 1 & 0 & 0 & 1 & 0 & 0 & 1 & 0 & 0 & 1 \\ 0 & 1 & 0 & 0 & 1 & 0 & 0 & 1 & 0 & 0 \\ 0 & 0 & 1 & 0 & 0 & 1 & 0 & 0 & 1 & 0 \\ 1 & 0 & 0 & 1 & 0 & 0 & 1 & 0 & 0 & 1 \end{bmatrix} \end{array}$$

We note that this relation is reflexive, it is symmetric, and, as can be determined by inspection (see Chapter 3), it is also transitive; hence the matrix is an equivalence relation. We can group the elements of the universe into classes as follows:

[1] = [4] = [7] = [10] = {1, 4, 7, 10} with remainder = 1

[2] = [5] = [8] = {2, 5, 8} with remainder = 2

[3] = [6] = [9] = {3, 6, 9} with remainder = 0

Then we can show that the classes do not overlap, i.e. they are mutually exclusive:

$[1] \cap [2] = \phi$ and $[2] \cap [3] = \phi$

and that the union of all the classes exhausts (comprises) the universe.

$$\cup [x] = X$$

The quotient set is then determined to have three classes,

$X \mid R = \{(1, 4, 7, 10), (2, 5, 8), (3, 6, 9)\}$

Not all relations are equivalent, but if a relation is at least a tolerance relation (i.e. it exhibits properties of reflexivity and symmetry) then it can be converted to an equivalent relation through max–min compositions with itself.

14.14.2 Fuzzy Relations

As already illustrated, crisp equivalent relations can be used to divide the universe X into mutually exclusive classes. In the case of fuzzy relations, for all fuzzy equivalent relations, their λ-cuts are equivalent ordinary relations. Hence, to classify data points in the universe using fuzzy relations, we need to find the associated fuzzy equivalent relation.

Example 14.2: Tolerance relation, say $\underset{\sim}{R}_t$, describing five data points, that was formed into a fuzzy equivalence relation, $\underset{\sim}{R}$, by composition; this process is repeated here for this classification example.

$$\underset{\sim}{R}_t = \begin{bmatrix} 1 & 0.8 & 0 & 0.1 & 0.2 \\ 0.8 & 1 & 0.4 & 0 & 0.9 \\ 0 & 0.4 & 1 & 0 & 0 \\ 0.1 & 0 & 0 & 1 & 0.5 \\ 0.2 & 0.9 & 0 & 0.5 & 1 \end{bmatrix} \rightarrow \underset{\sim}{R} \begin{bmatrix} 1 & 0.8 & 0.4 & 0.5 & 0.8 \\ 0.8 & 1 & 0.4 & 0.5 & 0.9 \\ 0.4 & 0.4 & 1 & 0.4 & 0.4 \\ 0.5 & 0.5 & 0.4 & 1 & 0.5 \\ 0.8 & 0.9 & 0.4 & 0.5 & 1 \end{bmatrix}$$

Table 14.6: Classification of five data points according to λ-cut level

λ-cut level	Classification
1.0	$[x_1][x_2][x_3][x_4][x_5]$
0.9	$[x_1]\{x_2 \cdot x_5\}[x_3][x_4]$
0.8	$\{x_1 \cdot x_2 \cdot x_5\}[x_3][x_4]$
0.5	$\{x_1 \cdot x_2 \cdot x_4 \cdot x_5\}[x_4]$
0.4	$\{x_1 \cdot x_2 \cdot x_3 \cdot x_4 \cdot x_5\}$

By taking λ-cuts of fuzzy equivalent relation R at values of λ = 1, 0.9, 0.8, 0.5, and 0.4, we get the following:

$$R_1 = \begin{bmatrix} 1 & & & & 0 \\ & 1 & & & \\ & & 1 & & \\ & & & 1 & \\ 0 & & & & 1 \end{bmatrix} \quad R_{0.9} = \begin{bmatrix} 1 & 0 & 0 & 0 & 0 \\ 0 & 1 & 0 & 0 & 1 \\ 0 & 0 & 1 & 0 & 0 \\ 0 & 0 & 0 & 1 & 0 \\ 0 & 1 & 0 & 0 & 1 \end{bmatrix} \quad R_{0.8} = \begin{bmatrix} 1 & 1 & 0 & 0 & 1 \\ 1 & 1 & 0 & 0 & 1 \\ 0 & 0 & 1 & 0 & 0 \\ 0 & 0 & 0 & 1 & 0 \\ 1 & 1 & 0 & 0 & 1 \end{bmatrix}$$

$$R_{0.5} = \begin{bmatrix} 1 & 1 & 0 & 1 & 1 \\ 1 & 1 & 0 & 1 & 1 \\ 0 & 0 & 1 & 0 & 0 \\ 1 & 1 & 0 & 1 & 1 \\ 1 & 1 & 0 & 1 & 1 \end{bmatrix} \qquad R_{0.4} = \begin{bmatrix} 1 & 1 & 1 & 1 & 1 \\ 1 & 1 & 1 & 1 & 1 \\ 1 & 1 & 1 & 1 & 1 \\ 1 & 1 & 1 & 1 & 1 \\ 1 & 1 & 1 & 1 & 1 \end{bmatrix}$$

where we can see that the clustering of the five data points according to the λ-cut level is as shown in Table 14.6.

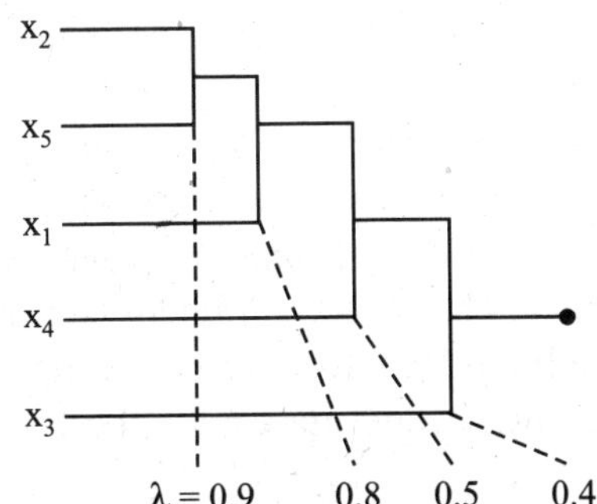

Figure 14.24: Classification diagram.

We can express the classification scenario described in Table 14.6 with a systematic classification diagram, as shown in Figure 14.24. In the figure you can see that the higher the value of λ, the finer is the classification. That is, as λ gets larger the tendency of classification tends to approach the trivial case where each data point is assigned to its own class.

14.15 C-MEANS CLUSTERING

Bezdek [1981] developed an extremely powerful classification method to accommodate fuzzy data. It is an extension of a method known as c-means, or hard c-means, when employed in a crisp classification sense. To introduce this method, we define a sample set of n data samples that we wish to classify:

$$X = \{x_1, x_2, x_3, \ldots, x_n\} \tag{14.15}$$

Each data sample, $\mathbf{x}_i$, is defined by m features, i.e.

$$X_i = \{x_{i1}, x_{i2}, x_{i3}, \ldots, x_{im}\} \tag{14.16}$$

where each $\mathbf{x}_i$ in the universe X is an m-dimensional vector of m elements or m features. Since the m features all can have different units, in general, we have to normalize each of the features to a unified scale before classification. In a geometric sense, each $\mathbf{x}_i$ is a point in m-dimensional feature space, and the universe of the data sample, X, is a point set with n elements in the sample space.

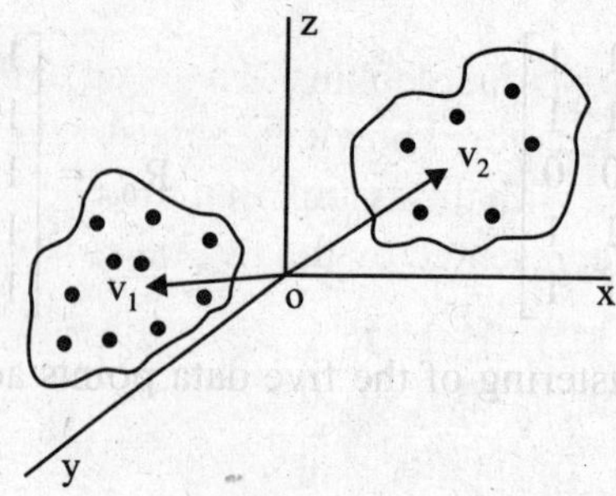

Figure 14.25: Cluster idea with hard c-means.

Bezdek [1981] suggested using an objective function approach for clustering the data into hyperspherical clusters. This idea for hard clustering is shown in three-dimensional feature space in Figure 14.25. In this figure, each cluster of data is shown as a hyperspherical shape with a hypothetical geometric cluster center. The objective function is developed so as to do two things simultaneously: first, minimize the Euclidean distance between each data point in a cluster and its cluster center (a calculated point), and second, maximize the Euclidean distance between cluster centers.

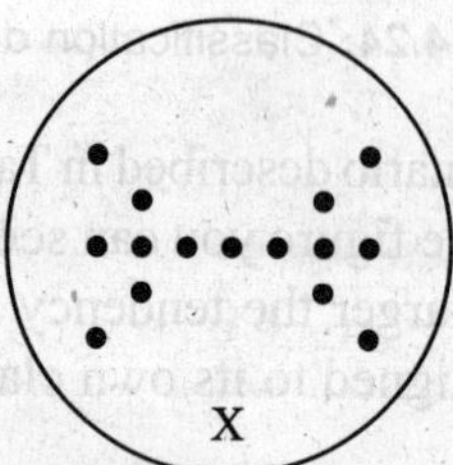

Figure 14.26: Butterfly classification problem [Bezdek, 1981].

Example 14.3: A good illustration of the iterative optimization method is rovided with the "butterfly problem" shown in Figure 14.26. In this problem we have 15 data points and one of them is on a vertical line of symmetry (the point in the middle of the data cluster). Suppose we want to cluster our data into two classes. We can see that the points to the left of the line of symmetry should be in one class and the points to the right of the line of symmetry should be in the other class. The problem lies in assigning the point on the line of symmetry to a class. To which class should this point belong? Whichever class the algorithm assigns this point to, there will be a good argument that it should be a member of the other class. Alternatively, the argument may revolve around the fact that the choice of two classes is a poor one for this problem. Three classes might be the best choice, but the physics underlying the data might be binary and two classes may be the only option.

In conducting the iterative optimization approach we have to assume an initial U matrix. This matrix will have two rows (two classes, c = 2) and 15 columns (15 data points, n = 15). It is important to understand that the classes may be unlabeled in this process. That is, we can look at the structure of the data without the need for the assignment of labels to the classes.

This is often the case when one is first looking at a group of data. After several iterations with the data, and as we become more and more knowledgeable about the data, we can then assign labels to the classes. We start the solution with the assumption that the point in the middle (i.e. the eighth column) is assigned to the class represented by the bottom row of the initial U matrix, $U^{(0)}$:

$$U^{(0)} = \begin{bmatrix} 1 & 1 & 1 & 1 & 1 & 1 & 1 & 0 & 0 & 0 & 0 & 0 & 0 & 0 & 0 \\ 0 & 0 & 0 & 0 & 0 & 0 & 0 & 1 & 1 & 1 & 1 & 1 & 1 & 1 & 1 \end{bmatrix}$$

After four iterations [Bezdek, 1981] this method converges to within a tolerance level of $\varepsilon = 0.01$, as

$$U^{(4)} = \begin{bmatrix} 1 & 1 & 1 & 1 & 1 & 1 & 1 & 0 & 0 & 0 & 0 & 0 & 0 & 0 & 0 \\ 0 & 0 & 0 & 0 & 0 & 0 & 0 & 1 & 1 & 1 & 1 & 1 & 1 & 1 & 1 \end{bmatrix}$$

We note that the point on the line of symmetry (i.e. the eighth column) is still assigned to the class represented by the second row of the U matrix. The elements in the U matrix indicate membership of that data point in the first or second class. For example, the point on the line of symmetry has full membership in the second class and no membership in the first class; yet it is plain to see from Figure 14.26 that physically it should probably share membership with each class. This is not possible with crisp classification; membership is binary – a point is either a member of a class or not.

14.16 FUZZY C-MEANS (FCM)

Let us consider whether the bubtterfly example in Figure 14.26 could be improved with the use of fuzzy set methods. To develop these methods in classification, we define a family of fuzzy sets $\{A_{\underset{\sim}{i}}\ i = 1, 2, \ldots, c\}$ as a fuzzy c-partition on a universe of data points, X. Because fuzzy sets allow for degrees of membership we can extend the crisp classification idea into a fuzzy classification notion. Then we can assign membership to the various data points in each fuzzy set (fuzzy class, fuzzy cluster). Hence, a single point can have partial membership in more than one class. It will be useful to describe the membership value that the kth data point has in the ith class with the following notation:

$$\mu_{ik} = \mu_{\underset{\sim}{A_i}}(x_k) \, \varepsilon \, [0,1]$$

with the restriction (as with crisp classification) that the sum of all membership values for a single data point in all of the classes has to be unity:

$$\sum_{i=1}^{c} \mu_{ik} = 1 \text{ for all } k = 1, 2, \ldots, n \tag{14.17}$$

As before in crisp classification, there can be no empty classes and there can be no class that contains all the data points. This qualification is manifested in the following expression:

$$0 < \sum_{k=1}^{n} \mu_{ik} < n \tag{14.18}$$

Because each data point can have partial membership in more than one class, the restriction is not present in the fuzzy classification case, i.e.

$$\mu_{ik} \wedge \mu_{jk} \neq 0$$

however,

$$\bigvee_{i=1}^{c} \mu_{A_i}(x_k) = 1 \text{ for all k}$$

$$0 < \sum_{k=1}^{n} \mu_{A_i}(x_k) < n \text{ for all i}$$

Before, in the case of c = 2, the classification problem reduced to that of the excluded middle axioms for crisp classification. Since we now allow partial membership, the case of c = 2 does not follow the restrictions of the excluded middle axioms, i.e. for two classes $\underset{\sim}{A}_i$ and $\underset{\sim}{A}_j$

$$\underset{\sim}{A} \cap A_j \neq \theta$$

$$\theta \subset \underset{\sim}{A}_i \subset X$$

We can now define a family of fuzzy partition matrices, M_{fc}, for the classification involving c classes and n data points,

$$M_{fc\text{-}} = \left\{ \underset{\sim}{U} \mid \mu_{ik} \,\varepsilon\, [0,1]; \sum_{i=1}^{c} \mu_{ik} = 1; 0 < \sum_{k=1}^{n} \mu_{ik} < n \right\}$$

where i = 1, 2, . . . , c and k = 1, 2, . . . , n.

Any $\underset{\sim}{U} \,\varepsilon\, M_{fc}$ is a fuzzy c-partition, and it follows from the overlapping character of the classes and the infinite number of membership values possible for describing class membership that the cardinality of M_{fc} is also infinity, i.e. $\eta_{M_{fc}} = \infty$.

14.17 PATTERN RECOGNITION

Pattern recognition can be defined as a process of identifying structure in data by comparisons to known structure; the known structure is developed through methods of classification as illustrated in Part I. In the statistical approach to numerical pattern recognition, which is treated thoroughly by Fukunaga, each input observation is represented as a multidimensional data vector (feature vector) where each component is called a feature. The purpose of the pattern recognition system is to assign each input to one of c possible pattern classes (or data clusters). Presumably, different input observations should be assigned to the same class if they have similar features and to different classes if they have dissimilar features. Statistical pattern recognition systems rest on mathematical models; it is crucial that the measure of mathematical similarity used to match feature vectors with classes assesses a property shared by physically similar components of the process generating the data. The data used to design a pattern recognition system are usually divided into two categories: design (or training) data and test data, much like the categorization used in neural networks. Design data are used to establish the algorithmic parameters of the pattern recognition system. The design samples may be labelled (the class to which each observation belongs is known) or unlabeled (the class to which each data sample belongs is unknown). Test data are labelled samples used to test the overall performance of the pattern recognition system.

In the descriptions that follow, the following notation is used:

$X = \{x_1, x_2, \ldots, x_n\}$ = the universe of data samples

n = number of data samples in universe

p = number of original (nominated) features

$x_k \in R^p$; kth data sample in X, in p-dimensional feature space

$x_{kj} \in R$; jth measured feature of x_k

s = number of selected or extracted features

c = number of clusters or classes

There are many similarities between classification and pattern recognition. The information provided in Figure 14.27 summarizes the distinction between the two made in this textbook. Basically, classification establishes (or seeks to determine) the structure in data, whereas pattern recognition attempts to take new data and assign them to one of the classes defined in the classification process. Simply stated, classification defines the patterns and pattern recognition assigns data to a class; hence, the processes of define and assign are a coupled pair in the process described in Figure 14.27. In both the classification process and the pattern recognition process there are necessary feedback loops: the first loop in classification is required when one is seeking a better segmentation of the data (i.e. better class distinctions), and the second loop is required when pattern matching fails (i.e. no useful assignment can be made).

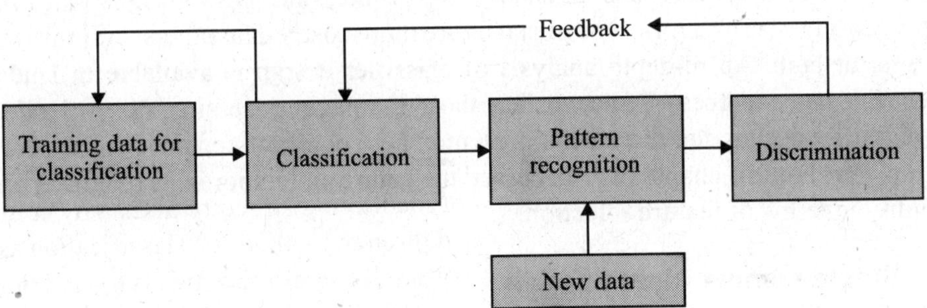

Figure 14.27: Difference between classification and pattern recognition.

14.18 FEATURE ANALYSIS

Feature analysis refers to methods for conditioning the raw data so that the information that is most relevant for classification and interpretation (recognition) is enhanced and represented by a minimal number of features. Feature analysis consists of three components: nomination, selection, and extraction. Feature nomination (FN) refers to the process of proposing the original p features; it is usually done by workers close to the physical process and may be heavily influenced by physical constraints, e.g. what can be measured by a particular sensor. For example, the nominated features can correspond to simple characteristics of various sensors that are represented by digitization of the sensor records. Feature selection (FS) refers to choosing the "best" subset of s features ($s < p$) from the original p features.

Feature extraction (FE) describes the process of transforming the original p-dimensional feature space into an s-dimensional space in some manner that "best" preserves or enhances the information available in the original p-space. This is usually accomplished mathematically by means of some linear combination of the initial measurements. Another method of feature extraction that lies closer to the expertise of the engineer is heuristic nomination and/or extraction. In other words, the process being examined may suggest choices for analytic features, e.g. in sensor records of measured pressures, the slopes (of rise and decay), areas (impulse or energy) during rise and decay, or even transformations (Fourier or Laplace) of the pressure waveform. Implicit in both FS and FE is a means for evaluating feature sets chosen by a particular procedure. The usual benchmark of feature quality is the empirical error rate achieved by a classifier on labelled test data. A second method of assessing feature quality is to refer algorithmic interpretations of the data to domain experts: do the computed results make sense? This latter test is less esoteric than the mathematical criteria, but very important.

14.18.1 Partitions of the Feature Space

Partitioning the feature space into c regions, one for each subclass in the data, is usually in the domain of classifier design. More specifically, crisp classifiers partition R^p (or R^s) into disjoint subsets, whereas fuzzy classifiers assign fuzzy label vectors to each vector in feature space. The ideal classifier never errs; since this is usually impossible, one seeks designs that minimize the expected probability of error or, if some mistakes are more costly than others, minimize the average cost of errors, or both. An in-depth analysis of classifier design is available in Duda and Hart [1973]. Because many sources of data, such as those in image processing, do not lend themselves readily to classifier design, the discussion presented here does not consider this aspect of pattern classification. Part I of this chapter has discussed the nature and importance of cluster analysis and cluster validity in terms of feature selection.

14.18.2 Single-sample Identification

A typical problem in pattern recognition is to collect data from a physical process and classify them into known patterns. The known patterns typically are represented as class structures, where each class structure is described by a number of features. For simplicity in presentation, the material that follows represents classes or patterns characterized by one feature; hence, the representation can be considered one-dimensional. Suppose we have several typical patterns stored in our knowledge base (i.e. the computer), and we are given a new data sample that has not yet been classified. We want to determine which pattern the sample most closely resembles. Express the typical patterns as fuzzy sets $\underset{\sim}{A}_1, \underset{\sim}{A}_2 .... \underset{\sim}{A}_m$. Now suppose we are given a new data sample, which is characterized by the crisp singleton, x_0. Using the simple criterion of maximum membership, the typical pattern that the data sample most closely resembles is found by the following expression:

$$\mu_{\underset{\sim}{A}_i}(x_0) = \max\{\mu_{\underset{\sim}{A}_1}(x_0), \mu_{\underset{\sim}{A}_2}(x_0), ..., \mu_{\underset{\sim}{A}_m}(x_0)\} \quad (14.19)$$

where x_0 belongs to the fuzzy set $\underset{\sim}{A}_i$, which is the set indication for the set with the highest membership at point x_0. Figure 14.28 shows the idea expressed by Eq. (14.19), where clearly the new data sample defined by the singleton expressed by x_0 most closely resembles the pattern described by fuzzy set $\underset{\sim}{A}_2$.

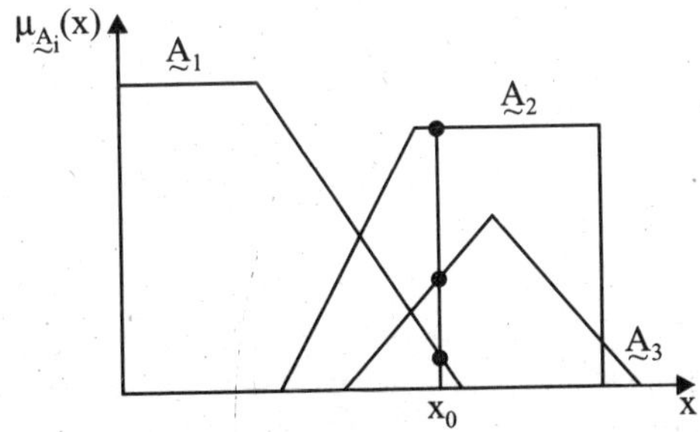

Figure 14.28: Single data sample using max member-ship criteria.

EXERCISES

1. What do you mean by fuzzy clustering?
2. Explain the vocabulary of fuzzy clustering?
3. Explain the various principles of cluster detection?
4. Explain some general clustering concepts?
5. Explain the crisp clustering techniques?
6. Write down the K means clustering algorithm?
7. Explain the concept of fuzzy clustering?
8. Explain the concept of fuzzy C means clustering and its algorithm?
9. What do you mean by fuzzy classification?
10. Explain the concept of classification by equivalence relation?
11. What do you mean by pattern recognition?
12. Difference between classification and pattern recognition?
13. Explain the concept of feature analysis?
14. Explain the applications of fuzzy logic used in pattern recognition?

Index

D

E

F

G

H

I

K

L

M

N